JOHANNES BRAHMS:

an annotated bibliography of the literature through 1982

by
THOMAS QUIGLEY

with a foreword by
MARGIT L. McCORKLE

The Scarecrow Press, Inc.
Metuchen, N.J., & London
1990

British Library Cataloguing-in-Publication data available

Library of Congress Cataloging-in-Publication Data

Quigley, Thomas, 1954-
 Johannes Brahms : an annotated bibliography of the literature
through 1982 / by Thomas Quigley ; with a foreword by Margit L.
McCorkle.
    p. cm.
 ISBN 0-8108-2196-6 (alk. paper)
 1. Brahms, Johannes, 1833-1897--Bibliography. I. Title.
ML134.B8Q5   1990
016.78'092--dc20   89-48412

CONTENTS

FOREWORD

A well-constructed bibliography--comprehensive, accurate, and up to date--is one of the most essential tools in research. In 1965 when the late Donald M. McCorkle began his documentary studies on the life and works of Johannes Brahms, he immediately noticed the lack of two fundamental bibliographical sources for this major composer, namely, a modern thematic catalogue of the works and an adequate bibliography of the literature. To be sure, several early efforts had been undertaken to address these lacunae, but the results were neither readily available nor adequate in scope and reliability to meet current research needs. The task initiated by McCorkle of preparing a definitive catalogue raisonné necessarily progressed hand in hand with the project of building a source collection of musical editions and relevant historical, bibliographical, and analytical literature. The present bibliography evolved from this source-collecting project.

Thomas Quigley worked as bibliographical research assistant on the Johannes Brahms Cataloguing Project under my direction at the University of British Columbia from 1978-1982. It was his responsibility to locate, collect, and catalogue the musical and literary sources required for the Johannes Brahms Thematisch-Bibliographisches Werkverzeichnis.[1] During the five years of his participation, he was able to cast a net worldwide for Brahms items, particularly through the agency of the Interlibrary Loan system, to build a core collection on which this bibliography is based. Since the Cataloguing Project was completed, he has amply augmented the original collected materials through an extended search, while concurrently reorienting the organization and evaluation of the accumulated information toward the development of a full-fledged and independent annotated bibliography.

The predecessors of this bibliography are principally three listings of the then existing Brahms literature. Earliest of these is the collaborative work of Otto Keller and Arthur Seidl, published in 1912 in two volumes of the journal Die Musik.[2] Otto Keller's "Johannes Brahms-Literatur" contained 466 entries; Arthur Seidl's supplement added 110 items. Thirty years later Lajos Koch published in Budapest his "Brahms-Bibliográfia" of some 1,544 entries.[3] "Das Schrifttum über Johannes Brahms in den Jahren 1933-1958," with 700 entries, was prepared by Ingrid Lübbe in 1960 as part of her studies at the

Hamburg Library School.[4] Each successive listing incorporated and
expanded the previous work in the field to bring the enumeration of
literature about Brahms more or less up to 1958. When Quigley began
his work, the Keller-Seidl bibliography had long since been superseded and hence was mainly of historical interest. It was the Koch
and Lübbe works dovetailed that provided a point of departure for
the initial stages of the collecting project; extensive use of the two
listings, however, revealed both gaps in specific items cited and in-
consistencies in the presentation of bibliographical information.[5]
Moreover, although the Cataloguing Project was able to obtain scarce
copies of these listings, neither was readily available in North America
for general use.

Since the inception of the present project, two additional listings
appeared, in 1983: "Zum Stand der Brahms-Forschung" was published
by Imogen Fellinger in Acta musicologica (with an update by the same
author in 1984)[6], and Siegfried Kross released his Brahms-
Bibliographie.[7] The former is, as the title indicates, a report on
the state of Brahms research, with a listing of 544 items. The latter
is an attempt to bring together finally in book form an up-to-date,
comprehensive bibliography of 2,736 entries. Though Kross's listing
might be expected to subsume all earlier efforts, it does not entirely
replace the Koch and Lübbe bibliographies, nor does it undertake to
verify antecedent information and correct or eliminate that which was
misleading or inaccurate in prior listings.[8]

Taken together, the existing bibliographies exhibit a host of
problems in the selection, presentation, and analysis of bibliographical
information, thus underscoring the urgent need for a definitive account
of the Brahms literature, to be organized systematically, annotated,
and indexed for maximum usefulness to both the scholar and less-
specialized user. The present bibliography aims to fill at long last
this persistent lacuna.

Covering approximately the same time span as the Kross bibliography (a sequel is planned by Quigley for literature published
after 1982), it is nonetheless expanded considerably, with 3,208
entries and references to a total of 4,715 items. Most importantly,
the presentation is no simple alphabetical listing; rather, the entries
are organized by subject matter. Each item is treated according to
modern standards for full bibliographical citation. Furthermore, the
entries are formatted in such a way as to reveal at a glance whenever
there is a derivative relationship among works by the same author--
a situation that happens often enough and that can be quite confusing.
Brief annotations help to describe the content of the items beyond
the information given in the titles. Finally, the citations are
thoroughly cross-referenced, and the bibliography as a whole is
elaborately indexed to provide wide-ranging access to the information
contained within.

Speaking from extensive personal experience with the Brahms
literature, I cannot overemphasize the significance of the contribution

this new bibliography will make in facilitating scholarly research, as well as whetting the appetite of all who appreciate the art of Brahms.

Margit L. McCorkle
Vancouver, January 1989

NOTES

1. Margit L. McCorkle, Johannes Brahms: Thematisch-Bibliographisches Werkverzeichnis. Herausgegeben nach gemeinsamen Vorarbeiten mit Donald M. McCorkle †. Munich: G. Henle Verlag, 1984.
2. Otto Keller, "Johannes Brahms-Literatur" Die Musik (Berlin) 12/2 (Bd.45) (10.1912), pp. 86-101; and Arthur Seidl, "Nachtrag (bis Ende Oktober 1912) zu Otto Kellers 'Johannes Brahms-Bibliographie,'" Die Musik (Berlin) 12/5 (Bd. 45) (12.1912), pp. 287-91.
3. Lajos [Louis] Koch, "Brahms-Bibliográfia," A Fővárosi könyvtar évkönye 12 (1942), pp. 65-149; Monograph "Sonderabdruck": Koch, Brahms-Bibliográfia/Brahms-Bibliographie. Budapest: Budapest Székesfőváros házinyomdája, 1943.
4. Ingrid Lübbe, "Das Schrifttum über Johannes Brahms in den Jahren 1933-1958" Prüfungsarbeit (examination paper), Hamburger Bibliotheksschule, 1960.
5. For a more detailed discussion of these three bibliographies, see Thomas Quigley, "Johannes Brahms and Bibliographic Control: Review and Assessment," Fontes artis musicae 30/4 (10.-12. 1983), pp. 207-14.
6. Imogen Fellinger, "Zum Stand der Brahms-Forschung," Acta musicologica 55/2 (7.-12.1983), pp. 131-201; idem, "Das Brahms-Jahr 1983: Forschungsbericht," Acta musicologica 56/2 (7.-12, 1984), pp. 145-210.
7. Siegfried Kross, Brahms-Bibliographie. Tutzing: Hans Schneider, 1983.
8. See Thomas Quigley [Review of the Kross Bibliographie], Fontes artis musicae 33/1 (1.-3.1986), pp. 123-24.

ACKNOWLEDGEMENTS

It is impossible to complete a work like this on one's own, and thanks are due to the many individuals who took the time to assist me. I hope that by mentioning them here, some of my appreciation can be expressed for all they did to help me.

It was Margit L. McCorkle who first broached the possibility that a bibliography like this would be a significant research tool for the musicological community. She provided assistance, encouragement, and graciously shared her knowledge and experience with me. The fruition of this work would have been impossible without her support. I am deeply indebted to her.

The groundwork for this bibliography was greatly facilitated by the information sources and documentation readily available in the Metropolitan Vancouver area. I would like to acknowledge the extensive resources of the University of British Columbia Library (Basil Stuart-Stubbs, former Director; Doug McInnis, current Director) and to salute Hans Burndorfer, Head of the UBC Music Library, for building the strongest music research collection in Western Canada. What could not be found locally was made available through the considerable efforts of the Interlibrary Loan staffs at both the University of British Columbia Library (Margaret Friesen, Head) and the Vancouver Public Library (Marlys Middleditch, Senior Clerk). Their sleuthing and expertise in slicing through bibliographic Gordian knots are much appreciated.

I am grateful to the librarians and staff at those North American institutions that I visited in search of Brahmsiana. Most particularly, Emma S. Davis, Head of Circulation at the Center for Research Libraries (Chicago), placed herself and her staff at my disposal during a brief but intense visit to the center; and the staff of the New York Public Library/Astor, Lenox, & Tilden Foundations were overwhelming in their provision of service to this visiting researcher. Closer to home, Monteria Hightower, Director, Downtown Library Services, Seattle Public Library, was of great assistance in the planning and execution of a research trip to that facility.

Many thanks are due those colleagues who heeded my far-reaching calls for information and responded with additional suggestions

for literature to be included in this work. The comprehensiveness
of the bibliography owes much to their efforts. I should also like
to acknowledge the many institutions and people who assisted me by
mail. In particular Malcolm Turner, Music Library, the British
Library; Seth Kasten, Union Theological Seminary Library (New
York); Dr. Karl Geiringer; Sarah Boslaugh, Music Department,
Boston Public Library; Ewa Barteczko, Biblioteka Narodowa (Warsaw);
Ingrid Zinnow, Johannes Brahms-Gesellschaft Internationale Vereinigung
e.V., and Dr. Bernhard Stockmann, Musiksammlung, Staats- und
Universitätsbibliothek Hamburg; Donald F. Wisdom (Serial and
Government Publications Division), William C. Parsons (Music Division),
and Margrit B. Krewson (European Division) at the Library of
Congress; Phil Lambert, Sibley Music Library, Eastman School of
Music at the University of Rochester; E. Schneider, and Hofrat Dr.
Guenter Brosche (Musiksammlung) at the Österreichische National-
bibliothek, Hofrat Dr. Ferdinand Baumgartner, Universitätsbibliothek
Wien, Dr. Otta Biba, Archiv of the Gesellschaft der Musikfreunde
in Vienna, and Hofrat Mag. Dr. Franz Patzer and Dr. Otto Brusatti
(Musiksammlung) at the Wiener Stadt- und Landesbibliothek.

The support of my family, friends, and coworkers over the
last eight years was a great encouragement to me. Dan Kravinchuk
should be recognized for his many frank and thoughtful comments
as the bibliography progressed from nebulous beginnings to this
final stage. Helio (Leo) Da Costa's suggestions were greatly appreciated throughout the drafting of the written materials. My brother
Michael and his family were most accommodating to my demands on
their home computer.

Lastly, I owe a great debt of gratitude to my life companion,
Ernest de Beaupré. He has stood by me throughout this project,
guiding me with his level-headedness and acumen. His unflagging
encouragement and respect for my single-minded determination have
been vital to the work's completion. I am honored to be using his
photograph of Brahms's grave for the frontispiece.

Thomas Quigley
Vancouver, British Columbia
Canada

INTRODUCTION

It is the objective of the present bibliography to provide a comprehensive, systematic guide to the literature written about Johannes Brahms and his music. The goal is not only to report more accurately and consistently basic bibliographic information on this literature than has hitherto been the case with previous bibliographies, but also to attempt for the first time to establish historical-bibliographical relationships among the different publications by the same author, dealing with topics in common. To give users full access to information throughout the work, extensive cross-references and indexes have been supplied. Included also is a checklist of bibliographic aids consulted, in order that users can ascertain the sources of cited references.

The publication date of December 1982 has been chosen as the termination date for literature contained in the bibliography. This date can be viewed as a natural break in the flow of writings about Brahms, preceding as it does the sesquicentenary of his birth in 1983, which stimulated a spate of new publications. To deal with the anniversary outpouring in print of renewed interest in the life and works of Brahms, a sequel to the bibliography is planned (to be published ca. 1997, in time for the centenary of his death).

The bibliography treats published and unpublished items appearing in a variety of formats, such as monographs, serials, dissertations, Congress proceedings, letters to the editor, etc. With few exceptions, the following types of materials are not cited here:

1. Audio-visual items--filmstrips, 8mm and 16mm films, videotapes, and phonorecordings. Users interested in information about resources in this format are advised to consult such bibliographic aids as the Library of Congress catalogs for music and film, The Video Source Book, and Videolog.[1]

2. Reviews of performances or phonorecordings. Users interested in this kind of information should consult McCorkle's Johannes Brahms: Thematisch-Bibliographisches Werkverzeichnis and Koch's Brahms-Bibliográfia for reference to reviews of performances occurring during Brahms's lifetime, and the Music Index for more recent performance or phonorecordings reviews.[2]

3. Reviews of music editions other than those for the original editions.

4. Book reviews or reports, unless they are critiques in another context, i.e., article format.

5. Concert program notes or record liner notes.

6. Public lectures and lecture-recitals given in partial fulfillment of degree requirements.

7. Lexical works, such as general and specialized encyclopedias or biographical dictionaries (relevant lexical works are cited as bibliographic aids in the "Checklist of Examined Indexes and Other Bibliographic Aids").

8. Abstracts of proceedings at society and chapter meetings.

9. Works in which reference to Brahms is diffuse or scant. Works in this category include general music histories, genre surveys, analytical overviews of the romantic period, etc.

Exceptions to the above exclusions occur when an item contributes significantly to the information available on its topic, or when the item is of historical-bibliographical interest in connection with material already cited in the bibliography.

The bibliography is divided by subject into seven main sections, reflecting the major topics of the literature, such as biographic studies, commentaries on the musical works, etc. Subsections within are devoted to more specific areas of interest. In instances where sections/subsections contain a large number of references, lists have been compiled that further group entries by theme. These lists are located at a section/subsection's beginning.

Material that addresses more than one topic is cited in the subject area it predominantly addresses. Cross-references are made from other appropriate subject areas to this entry. These cross-references are recorded by entry number and are listed at the end of a section/subsection. The use of an entry number in this bibliography refers to the entire entry, unless otherwise indicated.

Entries within each section/subsection are filed alphabetically word by word, with authored and anonymous items interfiled in one author/title sequence. There are two significant exceptions to this rule. Citations in which authorship is indicated only by initials are filed alphabetically by first letter, letter by letter; serial citations for which only a periodical name is known are filed alphabetically at the beginning of their section/subsection, word by word. Each entry in the bibliography consists of the following:

1. A principal bibliographic citation with an entry number.

Standardized formats for bibliographic citations are based on Turabian's A Manual for Writers of Term Papers, Theses, and Dissertations (4th ed.) and the University of Chicago Manual of Style.[3] The formats used in this work intentionally contain more detail than is normally found in academic bibliography because the author's experience with information verification indicates that the more information provided, the better for the users. Emphasis is on literal transcription of information following the Anglo-American Cataloguing Rules (2nd ed.).[4] Editorial commentary is used only to clarify information or to cast references in the standard formats used in such bibliographic aids as Union Lists of Serials and National Bibliographies. Editorial brackets within titles of citations are transcribed as double bracket sets: "[]" is transcribed as "[[]]."

Information is provided in the original language of the publication, following its rules of capitalization except when otherwise indicated in the source. Title translations are not generally provided. Romanization of titles in the Cyrillic alphabet follows the Library of Congress transliteration system.

The author has attempted to examine a broad base of material in order to describe the literature within its physical context; i.e., monographs within a larger edition, articles within the whole serial volume. Items seen only as offprints, isolated from their original context and lacking publication details of their original format, have been so indicated with a pound sign (#) before the entry number. Material not seen at all is indicated by an asterisk sign (*) before the entry number. Question marks (?) are used within entries to alert the user to either problems encountered in trying to locate the item from available citations, or to significant discrepancies that occur in the reporting of the citation in different bibliographic sources. A dagger (†) indicates that a person is dead.

Entries for material issued in multivolume sets, each volume having its own complex publication history, are constructed so that individual volumes are treated as entries within the main entry. Capital letters are added to the entry number--i.e., 39A, 39B, 39C, 39D--to flag this situation.

2. Collation information. This information is provided so that the user has some indication of the apparatus criticus and other features present in the publication. In entries where material on Brahms is only a portion of the entire reference, as for example, an article in a festschrift or Congress proceeding, the collation applies only to the Brahms section itself or to features that relate to the section, e.g., an index for the whole volume. The abbreviations used in the collation are:

a. Ill.--illustrations, including photographs or works of art.
b. Facsim.--facsimiles of Brahms's handwriting either in prose or music.

c. Mus.--musical examples taken from Brahms's compositions: these can range from a few bars to an entire work.
d. Fig.--figures, tables, graphs, charts, diagrams, schematics, plans.
e. Ind.--indexes.
f. Notes--documentation, footnote or endnote references, bibliography.
g. Discog.--discography.

   3. Publication history. The various editions and issues in which an item may have appeared in print are detailed here. This information may not be comprehensive, being based only on physical evidence or references from the bibliographic sources examined.

   4. Annotation. An annotation is provided when the title alone is not sufficiently explanatory or when it is necessary to describe the content, point of view, or intended audience. This can be a quotation from the item itself, a paraphrase, a quotation from other sources, or information obtained directly from the author. In the last two instances, the source is editorially indicated. Standardized vocabulary is used to prevent discrepancies in interpretation.

   Names of cities and geographic points in Germany and in states within the Habsburg Empire are not usually translated into English. German words that the author considers to be familiar terminology in Brahms studies are also not translated. RISM sigla are used, whenever possible, to indicate institutions referred to in the entry. Annotations only apply to the citation directly above the annotation.

   5. Bibliographic-historical remarks. The purpose of the information reported in this section of the entry is to make users aware of other sources of information with respect to citation content, and to flag bibliographic relationships between different references. Users thus have the fullest access to information from a variety of points of view and from different aspects of the literature. As many as five different kinds of remarks are possible:

a. Reprint. Exact duplication of text, though not necessarily in the same format as the original. Arrangement is chronological by date of publication.
b. Translation. The equivalent of the original text, but in a different language. Arrangement is alphabetical by language.
c. Excerpt. Portion of the text, in either its original language or in other languages.
d. Other. A literary relationship exists between the principal entry and another reference, though not in the sense of (a) or (b). Examples include ensuing discussion of a main entry's topic; articles that condense, elaborate, incorporate, or rework information from the principal entry; or letters to the editor.
e. Report/review. Articles summarizing or criticizing the content of a principal entry. Such materials are secondary literature once removed and as such, would not usually merit inclusion in a bibliography. However, they do provide information on material

and can be used to ascertain whether items not available locally are
relevant to one's research. They are included in this bibliography
in a subordinate position to their subject, the principal entry,
in order to avoid any confusion as to their bibliographic worth.

Lower-case Roman numerals are used to distinguish more than
one reference within each kind of remark. Each reference can, in
turn, become a principal entry, with its own publication history,
annotation, and bibliographic-historical remarks. To eliminate re-
dundancy, basic information is given subsequent to the principal
entry only when there is a change.

NOTES

1. U.S. Library of Congress, Library of Congress Catalog: Music
and Phonorecords. Washington, D.C.: Library of Congress,
1953- . [Subtitle varies: Music, Books on Music, and Sound
Recordings (1973-).] U.S. Library of Congress, Library of
Congress Catalog: Films. Washington, D.C.: Library of
Congress, 1953- . [Subtitle varies: Motion Pictures and Film-
strips (1954-72); Films and Other Materials for Projection (1973-
78); Audiovisual Materials (1979-).] The Video Source Book,
Professional volume, 8th ed. Syosset, N.Y.: National Video
Clearinghouse, 1986. Videolog. New York: Esselte Video,
1979- . [Place of publication and publisher varies.]
2. Margit L. McCorkle, Johannes Brahms: Thematisch-Bibliographisches Werkverzeichnis. Herausgegeben nach gemeinsamen Vorarbeiten mit Donald M. McCorkle †. Munich: G. Henle Verlag, 1984.
For Koch citation see "Foreword," note 3. The Music Index.
Detroit: Information Service, 1949- . [Name of publisher
varies.]
3. Kate L. Turabian, A Manual for Writers of Term Papers, Theses,
and Dissertations, 4th ed. Chicago and London: University of
Chicago Press, 1973. University of Chicago Press, The Chicago
Manual of Style, 13th ed., revised and expanded. Chicago and
London: University of Chicago Press, 1982.
4. Michael Gorman and Paul W. Winkler (eds.), Anglo-American
Cataloguing Rules, 2nd ed. Chicago: American Library Association;
Ottawa: Canadian Library Association, 1978.

CHECKLIST OF EXAMINED INDEXES AND OTHER BIBLIOGRAPHIC AIDS

This list includes sources examined for information on Brahms, and sources used to verify that information. It should be pointed out that a significant amount of the literature in this bibliography is a result of information noted and followed up from the materials themselves.

Items in this list are referred to by their siglum in the bibliography. Unless otherwise indicated in the annotation, all serial materials have been consulted up to December 1982.

ENCYCLOPEDIAS AND DICTIONARIES

S001   Das Grosse Lexikon der Musik.   Marc Honegger and Günther
        Massenkeil, eds. 8 Bde. Freiburg, Basel, Wien: Verlag
        Herder, 1978-82.

S002   Grove's Dictionary of Music and Musicians.   5th ed. Eric Blom,
        ed. 9 vols. London: Macmillan & Co. Ltd., 1954.

S003   Grove's Dictionary of Music and Musicians.   Supplementary
        Volume to the 5th ed.   Eric Blom, ed. London: Macmillan
        & Co. Ltd., 1961.

S004   Hugo Riemanns Musik-Lexikon.   10. Auflage. Alfred Einstein,
        ed. Berlin: Max Hesses Verlag, 1922.

S005   Die Musik in Geschichte und Gegenwart.   14 Bde. Kassel und
        Basel: Bärenreiter-Verlag, 1949-68.

S006   Die Musik in Geschichte und Gegenwart.   Supplement.   2 Bde.
        [=Die Musik in Geschichte und Gegenwart Bde. 15,16]
        Kassel et al: Bärenreiter-Verlag, 1973-79.

S007   The New Grove Dictionary of Music and Musicians.   Stanley
        Sadie, ed. 20 vols. London: Macmillan Publishers Limited,
        1980.

S008   Riemann, Hugo. Musik-Lexikon.   5. vollständig umgearbeitete
        Auflage. Leipzig: Max Hesse's Verlag, 1900.

S009 Riemann Musiklexikon. 12. völlig neubearbeitete Auflage. Wilibald Gurlitt, ed. 3 Bde. Mainz: B. Schott's Söhne, 1959-67. [Bde. 1,2=Personenteil; Bd. 3=Sachteil, begonnen von Wilibald Gurlitt fortgeführt und herausgegeben von Hans Heinrich Eggebrecht]

S010 Riemann Musiklexikon. Ergänzungsband. Personenteil. Carl Dahlhaus, ed. 2 Bde. Mainz: B. Schott's Söhne, 1972-75.

BIBLIOGRAPHIES

National and Trade

S011 Anuario del libro y de las artes gráficas. 1- . 1945- . Madrid: La Editorial católica s.a., 1945- . [title, publisher varies] Consulted 1945, 1947-57.

S012 Associazione italiano editori. Catalogo dei libri in commercio. Italian Books in Print. Milano: Editrice bibliografica.

S013 Biblio. Catalogue des ouvrages parus en langue française dans le monde entier. 1- . 1934- . Paris: Service bibliographique des messageries Hachette, 1935- . [title, publisher's name varies] Consulted 1934-1970.

S014 Bibliographische Berichte. Im Auftrag des Deutschen Bibliographischen Kuratoriums. 1- . 1959- . Frankfurt am Main: Vittorio Klostermann, 1959- . [title varies]

S015 Biblioteca centrala de stat a r.p.r. Bibliografia republicii populare romîne. Cărti, albume, hărţi, note muzicale. 1- . 1952- . Bucuresti: [Author]. [title varies] Consulted 1958- .

S016 Biblioteca nazionale centrale di Firenze. Bibliografia nazionale italiana. Catalogo alfabetico annuale. 1- . 1958- . Firenze: Author, 1961- . [publisher varies]

S017 Biblioteca nazionale centrale di Firenze. Catalogo cumulativo 1886-1957 del bollettino delle pubblicazione italiane. 39 vols. Nendeln: Kraus Reprint, 1969.

S018 Books in Print. Authors. New York: R. R. Bowker Company.

S019 Books in Print. Titles. New York: R. R. Bowker Company.

S020 Brinkman, Carel Leonhard. Brinkmans cumulative catalogus. 1846- . Leiden: A. W. Sijthoff's Uitgeversmaatschappij, 1846- . [title, publication information varies]

S021 British Library. Reference Division. General Catalogue of

Printed Books. 1976-82. [Microfiche Edition] 2 vols.
London: Author, 1982.

S022 British Museum. General Catalogue of Printed Books. Five-Year
Supplement. 1966-1970. Compact Edition. 3 vols. New
York: Readex Microprint Corporation, 1974.

S023 British Museum. General Catalogue of Printed Books. Ten-
Year Supplement. 1956-65. Compact Edition. 5 vols.
New York: Readex Microprint Corporation, 1969.

S024 British Museum. General Catalogue of Printed Books to 1955.
Compact Edition. 27 vols. New York: Readex Microprint
Corporation, 1967.

S025 The British National Bibliography 1950- . London: Council
of the British National Bibliography, Ltd., 1951- .
[publisher varies]

S026 Bulletin critique du livre français. 1- . 1946- . Paris:
L'Association pour la diffusion de la pensée française,
1946- . Consulted 1951- .

S027 Canadian Books in Print. Author and Title Index. Toronto:
University of Toronto Press.

S028 The Cumulative Book Index. 27th Annual Cumulation. [U.S.
Catalog. Supplement] July 1924- . New York: The H. W.
Wilson Company, 1925- . [title varies]

S029 Dansk bogfortegnelse. 1841- . Kjöbenhavn: G.E.C. Gad;
Gyldendalske Boghandling, C.C. Lose & Delbanco, 1861- .
[title, publication information varies]

S030 Deutsche Bibliographie. Herausgegeben und bearbeitet von
Deutschen Bibliothek. Frankfurt a.M. 1971- . Frankfurt
a.M.: Buchhändler-Vereinigung GmbH, 1971- .

S031 Forthcoming Books. New York: R. R. Bowker Co.

S032 Gesamtverzeichnis des deutschsprachigen Schrifttums (GV)
1700-1900. Bearbeitet unter der Leitung von Peter Geils
und Willi Gorzny. [Editors vary] 160 vols. München et al:
K.G. Saur, 1979-87.

S033 Gesamtverzeichnis des deutschsprachigen Schrifttums (GV)
1911-1965. Herausgegeben von Reinhard Oberschelp.
Bearbeitet unter der Leitung von Willi Gorzny. Mit einem
Geleitwort von Wilhelm Totok. 150 Bde. [Bde. 1-82:]
München: Verlag Dokumentation, 1976-78: [Bde. 83-150:]
München et al: K. G. Saur, 1979-81.

S034 Guide to Microforms in Print. Westport, Conn. and London: Meckler Publishing Corporation, 1977.

S035 Italy. Centro nazionale per il catalogo unico delle biblioteche italiane e per le informazioni bibliografiche. Primo catalogo collettivo delle biblioteche italiane. 1- . Roma: Author, 1962- . Consulted up to vol. 9.

S036 Library of Congress. The National Union Catalog. 1970- . Totowa, NJ: Rowman and Littlefield, 1970- . [publisher varies]

S037 Library of Congress. The National Union Catalog. Pre-1956 Imprints. 685 vols. London, Chicago: Mansell Information/ Publishing Limited, 1968-1980.

S038 Library of Congress. The National Union Catalog. Pre-1956 Imprints. Supplement. vol. 686- . London, Chicago: Mansell Information/Publishing Limited, 1980- . Consulted up to vol. 703.

S039 Library of Congress Catalog. Books: Subjects. 1950- Ann Arbor, MI: J. W. Edwards Publisher, 1955- . [title, publication information varies]

S040 La Librairie française. Catalogue général aes ouvrages parus. 1930-70. Paris: Au cercle de la librairie, 1931-70. Consulted 1930-45.

S041 La Librairie française. Tables décennales. 1966-1975. Répertoire cumulatif des livres de l'année-biblio. 6 vols. Paris: Cercle de la librairie, 1979.

S042 Libros españoles en venta. Spanish Books in Print. Madrid: Ministerio de cultura/Instituto nacional del libro español.

S043 Libros nuevos. Madrid: Instituto nacional del libro español. [publisher varies] Consulted 1964-78.

S044 Les Livres de l'année-biblio. 1971-79. Paris: Au Cercle de la librairie, 1971-79.

S045 Les Livres disponibles. Paris: Éditions du cercle de la librairie.

S046 Magyar könyvészet. 1921- . Budapest: Országos széchényi könyvtár. 1921- . Consulted 1921-60, 1963-76, 1978, 1980- .

S047 Magyar nemzeti bibliográfia. Bibliographia hungarica. 1946- .
     Budapest: Országos széchényi könyvtár, 1946- . Con-
     sulted 1977- .

S048 Ministere de l'instruction publique et des beaux-arts. Catalogue
     général des livres imprimés de la Bibliothèque National.
     Auteurs. 160 vols. Paris: Imprimerie nationale, 1897- .

S049 Norsk bokfortegnelse. 1911- . Kristiania: Norske bokhand-
     lerforenings forlag. 1923- . [place of publication varies]

S050 Paperbound Books in Print. New York: R. R. Bowker
     Company.

S051 Przewodnik bibliograficzny. 1- . 1945- . Warszawa:
     Biblioteka narodowa instytut bibliograficzny, 1946- .
     Consulted 1959- .

S052 Repertoires livres hebdo. 1981- . Paris: Editions profession-
     nelles du livre, 1982- .

S053 Subject Guide to Books in Print. New York: R. R. Bowker
     Company.

S054 Svensk bokförteckning. The Swedish National Bibliography.
     Stockholm: Tidningsaktiebolaget svensk bokhandel, 1953- .
     Consulted 1953, 1955- .

S055 Svensk bok-katalog. Stockholm: Samson & Wallin, 1866- .
     [publisher varies] Consulted 1866-1950.

S056 The United States Catalog. 3rd ed. Minneapolis and New
     York: The H. W. Wilson Company, 1912.

S057 The United States Catalog. Supplement. Books Published
     January 1918-June 1921. New York: The H. W. Wilson
     Company, 1921.

S058 The United States Catalog. Supplement. Books Published
     1912-17. New York: The H. W. Wilson Company, 1918.

S059 The United States Catalog. Supplement. July 1921-June
     1924. [Cumulative Book Index] New York: The H. W.
     Wilson Company, 1924.

S060 Verzeichnis lieferbarer Bücher. German Books in Print.
     Frankfurt a.M.: Verlag der Buchhändler-Vereinigung
     GmbH.

Union Lists and Guides to Periodicals and Newspapers

S061 British Union-Catalogue of Periodicals. James D. Stewart et al., eds. 4 vols. London: Butterworths Scientific Publications, 1955-58.

S062 British Union-Catalogue of Periodicals. Supplement to 1960. James D. Stewart et al., eds. London: Butterworths, 1962.

S063 Fellinger, Imogen. Verzeichnis der Musikzeitschriften des 19. Jahrhunderts. (Studien zur Musikgeschichte des 19. Jahrhunderts Bd. 10) Regensburg: Gustav Bosse Verlag, 1968.

S064 Hagelweide, Gert. Deutsche Zeitungsbestände in Bibliotheken und Archiven=German Newspapers in Libraries and Archives. Herausgegeben von der Kommission für Geschichte des Parlamentarismus und der politischen Parteien und dem Verein Deutscher Bibliothekare e.V. (Bibliographien zur Geschichte des Parlamentarismus und der politischen Parteien. Heft 6) Düsseldorf: Droste Verlag, 1974.

S065 Handbuch der Weltpresse. 5. Auflage. Herausgegeben vom Institut für Publizistik der Universität Münster unter Leitung von Henk Prakke, Winfried B. Lerg und Michael Schmolke. 2 Bde. Köln: Westdeutscher Verlag, 1970.

S066 Library of Congress. Library of Congress Catalogs: Newspapers in Microform. Foreign Countries. 1948-1972. Washington, D.C.: Author, 1973.

S067 Library of Congress. Library of Congress Catalogs: Newspapers in Microform. United States. 1948-1972. Washington, D.C.: Author, 1973.

S068 New Serial Titles. A Union List of Serials Commencing Publication after December 31, 1949. 1950- . Washington: Library of Congress, 1973- . [publication information varies]

S069 Union List of Serials in Libraries of the United States and Canada. 3rd ed. Edna Brown Titus, ed. 5 vols. New York: The H. W. Wilson Company, 1965.

Library Catalogs

S070 Boston Public Library. Dictionary Catalog of the Music Collection. 20 vols. Boston: G. K. Hall & Co., 1972.

S071 Boston Public Library. Dictionary Catalog of the Music Collection. First Supplement. 4 vols. Boston: G. K. Hall & Co., 1977.

S072 Center for Research Libraries. Catalogue: Newspapers. 2nd
     ed., cumulated. Chicago: Author, 1978.

S073 Center for Research Libraries. Catalogue: Serials. 2 vols.
     Chicago: Author, 1972.

S074 Center for Research Libraries. Catalogue: Serials. First
     Supplement. Chicago: Author, 1978.

S075 Detroit Public Library. Card Catalogue.

S076 New York Public Library. The Research Libraries. Dictionary
     Catalog of the Music Collection. 2nd ed. 45 vols. Boston:
     G. K. Hall, 1982.

S077 Seattle Public Library. Card Catalogue.

S078 University of British Columbia. Card Catalogue.

S079 University of California (Berkeley). Music Library. Card
     Catalogue.

S080 Washington Library Network. Subject Bibliographies.

Subject Bibliographies

S081 Abravenel, Clauae. "A Checklist of Music Manuscripts in
     Facsimile Edition" Notes 34/3 (3.1978) pp. 557-70.

S082 Adkins, Cecil, ed. Doctoral Dissertations in Musicology 5th
     ed. Philadelphia: American Musicological Society, 1971.

S083 Adkins, Cecil and Alis Dickinson, eds. International Index
     of Dissertations and Musicological Works in Progress. 1st
     ed. Philadelphia: American Musicological Society, Inter-
     national Musicological Society, 1977.

S084 Adkins, Cecil and Alis Dickinson, eds. International Index
     of Dissertations and Musicological Works in Progress.
     American-Canadian Supplement (1979). Philadelphia:
     American Musicological Society, 1979.

S085 Barth, Henrik, ed. Internationale Wagner-Bibliographie.
     International Wagner-Bibliography. Die Besetzung der
     Bayreuther Festspiele, 1876-1960. Bearbeitet von Käte
     Neupert. Bayreuth: Edition Musica, [1961].

S086 Barth, Henrik, ed. Internationale Wagner-Bibliographie, 1961-
     1966. International Wagner Bibliography. Bayreuth:
     Edition Musica, 1968.

S087 Beach, David. "A Schenker Bibliography" Journal of Music
     Theory 13/1 (1969) pp. 2-37.

S088 Bibliographic Guide to Music. 1975- . Boston, G. K. Hall &
      Co., 1975- .

S089 Brook, Barry S. Thematic Catalogues in Music: An Annotated
      Bibliography. (RILM Retrospectives no. 1) Hillsdale,
      N.Y.: Pendragon Press, 1972.

S090 Brown, A. Peter and James T. Berkenstock. In Collaboration
      with Carol Vanderbilt Brown. "Joseph Haydn in Literature:
      A Bibliography" Haydn-Studien Bd. 3/3/4 (7.1974) pp.
      173-352.

S091 Chicorel, Marietta, ed. Chicorel Bibliography to Books on
      Music and Musicians. (Chicorel Index Series vol. 10.
      1st ed.) New York: Chicorel Library Publishing Corp.,
      1974.

S092 Coover, James. "Music Manuscripts in Facsimile Edition:
      Supplement" Notes 37/3 (3.1981) pp. 533-56.

S093 de Lerma, Dominique-René, comp. A Selective List of Masters'
      Theses in Musicology. Bloomington: Denia Press, 1970.

S094 Fellinger, Imogen. "Zum Stand der Brahms-Forschung"
      Acta musicologica 55/2 (7.-12.1983) pp. 131-201.

S095 Gordon, Roderick D. Doctoral Dissertations in Music and
      Music Education, 1957-1963. Washington, D.C.: Music
      Educators National Conference, 1964. [=Journal of Research
      in Music Education 12/1 (Spring 1964)]

S096 Gray, Michael H. and Gerald D. Gibson. Bibliography of
      Discographies. Volume 1. Classical Music, 1925-1975.
      New York and London: R. R. Bowker Company, 1977.

S097 Gribenski, Jean. Theses de doctorat en langue française
      relatives à la musique: bibliographie commentée=French
      Language Dissertations in Music: An Annotated Bibliography.
      (Series I RILM Retrospectives no. 2) New York: Pen-
      dragon Press, 1979.

S098 Hartley, Kenneth R. Bibliography of Theses and Dissertations
      in Sacred Music. (Detroit Studies in Music Bibliography
      9) Detroit: Information Coordinators Inc., 1966.

S099 Internationale Hölderlin-Bibliographie. (IHB). Maria Kohler,
      bearbeiter. Stuttgart: frommann-holzboog, 1985.

S100 Kahl, Willi. Verzeichnis des Schrifttums über Franz Schubert
      1828-1928. (Kölner Beiträge zur Musikforschung Bd. 1)
      Regensburg: Gustav Bosse Verlag, 1938.

S101 Keller, Otto. "Johannes Brahms-Literatur" Die Musik (Berlin) 12/2 (Bd. 45) (10.1912) pp. 86-101.

S102 Kobylánska, Krystyna. Rekopisy utworów Chopina. Katalog. Manuscripts of Chopin's Works. Catalogue. vols. I, II. (Documenta Chopiniana 2) Krakow: Polskie wydawnictwo muzyczne, 1977.

S103 Koch, Lajos. Brahms-Bibliográfia. Brahms-Bibliographie. Budapest: Budapest Szekésfővares házinyomdája, 1943.

S104 Kross, Siegfried. Brahms-Bibliographie. Tutzing: Hans Schneider, 1983.

S105 Lübbe, Ingrid. "Das Schrifttum über Johannes Brahms in den Jahren 1933-1958" Prüfungsarbeit, Hamburger Bibliotheksschule, 1960.

S106 MacArdle, Donald W. Beethoven Abstracts. Detroit: Information Coordinators, Inc., 1973.

S107 McCorkle, Margit L. Johannes Brahms. Thematisch-Bibliographisches Werkverzeichnis. Herausgegeben nach gemeinsamen vorarbeiten mit Donald M. McCorkle †. München: G. Henle Verlag, 1984.

S108 Michałowski, Kornel. Bibliografia Chopinowska. Chopin Bibliography, 1849-1969. (Documenta Chopiniana 1) Krakow: Polskie wydawnictwo muzyczne, 1970.

S109 Munte, Frank. Verzeichnis des deutschsprachigen Schrifttums über Robert Schumann 1856-1970. Anhang: Schrifttum über Clara Schumann. Hamburg: Verlag der Musikalienhandlung Karl Dieter Wagner, 1972.

S110 Obermüller, Paul und Herbert Steiner, eds. Katalog der Rilke-Sammlung Richard von Mises. Unter Mitarbeit von Ernst Zinn. Frankfurt am Main: Insel-Verlag, 1966.

S111 Reichert, Herbert W. and Karl Schlechta, comps. and eds. International Nietzsche Bibliography. Revised and expanded. 2nd ed. (University of North Carolina. Studies in Comparative Literature no. 45) Chapel Hill: The University of North Carolina Press, 1968.

S112 Rösner, Helmut Max-Reger-Bibliographie. Das internationale Schrifttum über Max Reger 1893-1966. (Max-Reger-Institutes. Elsa-Reger-Stiftung. Veröffentlichungen. Heft 5) (Dümmlerbuch 8625) Bonn, Hannover, München: Ferdinand Dümmlers Verlag, 1968.

S113 Sandon, Nick, comp. "Register of Theses on Music in Britain and Ireland" RMA [Royal Musical Association] Research Chronicle 15 (1979) pp. 38-116.

S114 Sasse, Konrad. Händel Bibliographie. Unter Verwendung des im Händel-Jahrbuch 1933 von Kurt Taut veröffentlichten Verzeichnisses des Schrifttums über Georg Friedrich Händel. 2. verbesserte Auflage mit Nachtrag für die Jahre 1962-1965. Leipzig: VEB Deutscher Verlag für Musik, 1967.

S115 Sasse, Konrad. Händel Bibliographie. Unter Verwendung des im Händel-Jahrbuch 1933 von Kurt Taut veröffentlichten Verzeichnisses des Schrifttums über Georg Friedrich Händel. Abgeschlossen im Jahre 1961. Leipzig: VEB Deutscher Verlag für Musik, 1963.

S116 Schaal, Richard. Verzeichnis deutschsprachiger musikwissenschaftlicher Dissertationen 1861-1960. (Musikwissenschaftliche Arbeiten nr. 19) Kassel et al: Bärenreiter, 1963.

S117 Schaal, Richard. Verzeichnis deutschsprachiger musikwissenschaftlicher Dissertationen 1961-1970 mit Ergänzungen zum Verzeichnis 1861-1960. Kassel et al: Bärenreiter, 1974.

S118 Schneider, Otto and Anton Algatzy. Mozart-Handbuch. Chronik-Werk-Bibliographie. Wien: Verlag Brüder Hollinek, 1962.

S119 Seidl, Arthur. "Nachtrag (bis Ende Oktober 1912) zu Otto Kellers "Johannes Brahms-Bibliographie"" Die Musik (Berlin) 12/5 (Bd. 45) (12.1912) pp. 287-91.

S120 Shigihara, Susanne. Max-Reger-Bibliographie. Das internationale Schrifttum über Max Reger von 1967 bis 1981 nebst einem Nachtrag bis 1966 und Materialen des Max-Reger-Institutes. (Max-Reger-Institutes. Elsa-Reger-Stiftung. Veröffentlichungen. Heft 9) (Dümmlerbuch 8633) Bonn: Ferd. Dümmlers Verlag, 1983.

S121 Short, Michael. Gustav Holst (1874-1934). A Centenary Documentation. London et al: White Lion Publishers Limited, 1974.

S122 Strunk, W. Oliver. State and Resources of Musicology in the United States. A Survey. Washington, D.C.: American Council of Learned Societies, 1932. [=American Council of Learned Societies. Bulletin no. 19 (12.1932)]

S123 Sydow, Bronisław Edward. Bibliografia F. F. Chopina. Bibliographie de F. F. Chopin. (Towarzystwo naukowe warszawskie. Wydział II=Société des sciences et des lettres

de varsovie. Classe II.) Warszawa: Nakładaem towarzystwa
naukowego warszawskiego, 1949.

S124 Sydow, Bronisław E. Bibliografia F. F. Chopina. Bibliographie
de F. F. Chopin. Suplement. Supplément. Warszawa:
Pánstwowe wydawnictwo naukowe, 1954.

S125 Towarzystwo Imienia Fryderyka Chopina. Katalog Zbiorów.
Biblioteka. Ksiązki i czasopisma. Warszawa: Centralia
obslugi przedsiebiorstwo i instytucji artystycznych, 1969.

S126 Vinquist, Mary and Neal Zaslaw, eds. Performance Practice:
A Bibliography. New York: W. W. Norton & Company Inc.,
1971.

S127 Wenk, Arthur, comp. Analyses of Nineteenth-Century Music
1940-1980. Second Edition. (MLA Index and Bibliography
Series no. 15) Boston: Music Library Association, Inc.,
1984.

S128 Zippermann, Charles C. Gottfried Keller Bibliographie. 1844-
1934. Mit einem Geleitwort von William Guild Howard.
Einführung von Bayard Q. Morgan. Zürich et al: Rascher
& Cie. A.-G., Verlag, 1935.

INDEXING AND ABSTRACTING SERVICES
General

S129 A.L.A. Index to General Literature. Supplement 1900-1910.
Chicago: American Library Association Publishing Board,
1914.

S130 Bibliographie der deutschen Zeitschriften-Litteratur. 1896-
1964. 128 Bde. Osnabrück: Verlag Felix Dietrich, 1897-
1964. [series title, Internationale Bibliographie der
Zeitschriftenliteratur Abteilung A, added Bd. 30; place of
publication varies]

S131 Bibliographie der deutschen Zeitschriften-Literatur. Beilage-
Band. 1909-42. 29 Bde. Osnabrück: Verlag Felix
Dietrich, 1909-42. [Bde. 1-20 (1909-33)=Halbmonatliches
Verzeichnis von Aufsätzen aus deutschen Zeitungen. Bde.
21-29 (1934-42)=Monatliches Verzeichnis von Aufsätzen aus
deutschen Zeitungen]

S132 Bibliographie der deutschen Zeitschriften-Literatur. Ergänzungs-
Band. 20 Bde. Osnabrück: Verlag Felix Dietrich,
1908-[1912?]. [retrospective coverage, 1917 to 1861]

S133 Bibliographie der fremdsprachigen Zeitschriftenliteratur. 22 Bde.
[=1911-25]; Neue Folge. 51 Bde. [=1926-64] (Internationale
Bibliographie der Zeitschriftenliteratur. Abteilung B)

xxx / Checklist of Examined Indexes

Osnabrück: Verlag Felix Dietrich 1911-64. Consulted 1911-43, 1949-64.

S134 Canadian Periodical Index. 1938- Ottawa; Canadian Library Association=Association Canadienne des bibliothèques, 1962- [title varies]

S135 Comprehensive Dissertation Index. Five-Year Cumulation 1973-1977. Vol. 16. Language & Literature/[et al.]. Ann Arbor: Xerox University Microfilms, 1979.

S136 Comprehensive Dissertation Index. Supplement. 1978-82. Vol. 3. Social Sciences and Humanities. Parts 1 & 2. Ann Arbor, Mich.: Xerox University Microfilms, 1979-83.

S137 Comprehensive Dissertation Index 1861-1972. Vol. 31. Communications and the Arts. Ann Arbor: Xerox University Microfilms, 1973.

S138 Cumulated Magazine Subject Index 1907-1949. A Cumulation of the F. W. Faxon Company's Annual Magazine Subject Index. F. W. Faxon et al., eds. Cumulated by G. K. Hall & Co. 2 vols. Boston: G. K. Hall & Co., 1964.

S139 Deutsche Bibliothek. Frankfurt am Main. Deutsche Bibliographie. Hochschulschriften-Verzeichnis. 1972- . Frankfurt am Main: Buchhändler-Vereinigung GmbH, 1972- . Consulted 1972-81.

S140 Doctoral Dissertations Accepted by American Universities. no. 1- . 1933- . Compiled for the Association of Research Libraries. New York: The H. W. Wilson Company, 1934- . [title varies] Consulted no. 7- . 1939- .

S141 Fletcher, William I. The "A.L.A." Index. An Index to General Literature. 2nd ed. Boston: American Library Association Publishing Board, 1905.

S142 French Periodical Index. Compiled by Jean-Pierre Ponchie et al. vol. 1- . 1973- . (Useful Reference Series no. 106-) Westwood, Mass.: F. W. Faxon Company, Inc., 1976- . [title, publisher varies] Consulted 1973-80, 1982.

S143 Goode, Stephen H., comp. Index to American Little Magazines 1900-1919. To Which is Added a Selected List of British and Continental Titles for the Years, 1900-1950, together with Addenda and Corrigenda to Previous Indexes. 3 vols. Troy, N.Y.: The Whitston Publishing Company, 1974.

S144 Goode, Stephen H., comp. Index to American Little Magazines

1920-1939. Troy, N.Y.: Whitston Publishing Company
Incorporated, 1969.

S145 Goode, Stephen H., comp. Index to Little Magazines 1940-1942.
New York and London: Johnson Reprint Corporation, 1967.

S146 Goode, Stephen H., comp. Index to Little Magazines 1943-1947.
Denver: Alan Swallow, 1965.

S147 HAPI Hispanic American Periodicals Index. 1970- . Los
Angeles: UCLA [University of California (Los Angeles)]
Latin American Center Publications, 1984- .

S148 Index Analytique. 1-6. 1966-72. Quebec: Les Presses de
l'université Laval, 1966-72.

S149 Index to Little Magazines. 1948-1967. [1948-1965:] Denver:
Alan Swallow, 1949-1966; [1966-67:] Chicago: The Swallow
Press Inc., 1970.

S150 Index to Theses Accepted for Higher Degrees in the Universities
of Great Britain and Ireland. 1- . 1950- . London:
Aslib, 1953- . [title varies]

S151 International Index to Periodicals. 1- . 1907- New York:
The H. W. Wilson Company, 1907- . [title varies]

S152 Internationale Bibliographie der Zeitschriftenliteratur aus aller
Gebieten des Wissens=International Bibliography of Periodical
Literature covering all Fields of Knowledge=Bibliographie
internationale de la litterature periodique dans tous les
domaines de la connaissance. 1- . 1963- . Osnabrück:
Felix Dietrich Verlag, 1965- .

S153 Jahres-Verzeichnis der an den Deutschen Universitäten erschienenen Schriften. 1- . 1885- . Berlin: Königliche Bibliothek, 1887- . [title, publisher varies] Consulted 1885-
1978.

S154 Magazine Index. Belmont, Calif.: Information Access Co.

S155 Masters Abstracts. 1- . 1962- . Ann Arbor, Mich.:
University Microfilms, Inc., 1962- .

S156 Microfilm Abstracts. 1- . 1938- . Ann Arbor, Mich.:
University Microfilms, 1938- . [title varies]

S157 Nineteenth Century Readers Guide to Periodical Literature.
1890-1899. With Supplementary Indexing 1900-1922.
Helen Grant Cushing and Adah V. Morris, eds. 2 vols.
New York: H. W. Wilson Company, 1944.

S158 Organization of American States. Columbus Memorial Library.
Index to Latin American Periodical Literature. 1966-1970.
2 vols. Boston: G. K. Hall & Co., 1980.

S159 Pan American Union. Columbus Memorial Library. Index to
Latin American Periodical Literature. 1929-60. 8 vols.
Boston: G. K. Hall, 1962.

S160 Pan American Union. Columbus Memorial Library. Index to
Latin American Periodical Literature. 1961-1965. First
Supplement. 2 vols. Boston: G. K. Hall & Co., 1968.

S161 Périodex: index analytique de périodiques de langue française.
1- . 1972- . Montreal: La Centrale des bibliothèques,
1973- .

S162 Poole's Index to Periodical Literature. By William Frederick
Poole, with the assistance ... of William I. Fletcher ...
Revised ed. vol. 1. 1802-1881. [1 vol. in 2] Gloucester,
Mass.: Peter Smith, 1963. [reprint of 1882 issue]

S163 Poole's Index to Periodical Literature. The Fifth Supplement
from January 1, 1902 to January 1, 1907. By William I.
Fletcher and Mary Poole ... Gloucester, Mass.: Peter
Smith, 1963. [reprint of 1908 issue]

S164 Poole's Index to Periodical Literature. The First Supplement
from January 1, 1882 to January 1, 1887. By William
Frederick Poole and William I. Fletcher ... Gloucester,
Mass.: Peter Smith, 1963. [reprint of 1888 issue]

S165 Poole's Index to Periodical Literature. The Fourth Supplement
from January 1, 1897 to January 1, 1902. By William I.
Fletcher and Mary Poole ... Gloucester, Mass.: Peter
Smith, 1963. [reprint of 1903 issue]

S166 Poole's Index to Periodical Literature. The Second Supplement
January 1, 1887 to January 1, 1892. By William I. Fletcher
... Gloucester, Mass.: Peter Smith, 1963. [reprint of
1893 issue]

S167 People's Index to Periodical Literature. The Third Supplement
January 1, 1892 to December 31, 1896. By William I.
Fletcher and Franklin O. Poole ... Gloucester, Mass.:
Peter Smith, 1963. [reprint of 1897 issue]

S168 RADAR. Répertoire analytique d'articles de revues du Québec.
1- . 1973- . Montreal: Ministére des affaires culturelles,
1973- . [publisher varies]

S169 Readers' Guide to Periodical Literature. vol. 1- . 1900- .

Minneapolis: The H. W. Wilson Company, 1905- . [place
of publication varies]

S170 Sader, Marion, ed. Comprehensive Index to English-Language
Little Magazines 1890-1970. Series One. 8 vols. Millwood,
N.Y.: Kraus-Thomson Organization, Limited, 1976.

S171 Stad Johannesburg. Openbare Biblioteek. Index to South
African Periodicals. Repertorium van Suid-Afrikaanse
Tydskrifartikels. 1940- . Johannesburg: Author, 1940- .

S172 The Subject Index to Periodicals. 1915-61. London: The
Library Association, 1915-61. Consulted 1915-22, 1926-61.

S173 Wall, C. Edward, comp and ed. Cumulative Author Index for
Poole's Index to Periodical Literature 1802-1906. (Cumulative
Author Index Series no. 1) Ann Arbor: The Pierian Press,
1971.

Subject

S174 The American Humanities Index. Vol. 1- . 1975- . Troy,
N.Y.: The Whitston Publishing Company, 1976- .

S175 The Art Index. 1- . 1929- . New York: The H. W.
Wilson Company, 1933- .

S176 Bibliographia musicologica. A Bibliography of Musical Literature.
1968- . Utrecht: Joachimsthal, 1970- . Consulted
1968-76.

S177 Bibliographie des Musikschrifttums. 1936- . Leipzig: Verlag
von Friedrich Hofmeister, 1936- . [publication information
varies] Consulted 1936-39, 1950-77 [publication not issued
1940-1949]

S178 A Bibliography of Periodical Literature in Musicology and Allied
Fields and a Record of Graduate Theses Accepted. Assembled
by D. H. Daugherty. Nos. 1-2. Washington, D.C.:
American Council of Learned Societies, 1940-43. [coverage
is Oct. 1938-Sept. 1940]

S179 Blom, Eric. A General Index to Modern Musical Literature in
the English Language: Including Periodicals for the Years
1915-1926. (Curwen Edition 8323) London: J. Curwen &
Sons Ltd.; Philadelphia: Curwen Inc., n.d.

S180 British Humanities Index. 1962- . London: Library Association, 1962- .

S181 Business Index. Belmont, CA: Information Access Company.

S182 Degrada, Francesco. Indici de La Rassegna musicale (Annate
    XXIII-XXXII, 1953-1962) e dei quaderni della Rassegna
    musicale (N. 1,2,3, 1964-1965). (Società italiana di musi-
    cologia. Quaderni della rivista italiana di musicologia 2)
    Firenze: Leo S. Olschki Editore, 1968.

S183 Degrada, Francesco. Indice della Rivista musicale italiana.
    Annate XXXVI-LVII (1929-1955). (Società italiana di
    musicologia. Quaderni della rivista italiana di musicologia
    1) Firenze: Leo S. Olschki Editore, 1966.

S184 Guide to Indian Periodical Literature. (Social Sciences and
    Humanities). Vol. 1- . 1964- . Gurgaon: Indian
    Documentation Service, 1964- .

S185 Guide to the Musical Arts. An Analytical Index of Articles and
    Illustrations. 1953-56. S. Yancey Belknap, comp. New
    York: The Scarecrow Press, Inc., 1957. [title, place
    of publication varies]

S186 Guide to the Performing Arts. 1957-68. New York: Scarecrow
    Press, 1960-72. [place of publication varies]

S187 Harten-Flamm, Christa. Osterreichische Musikzeitschrift.
    Register 1946-1970. 1.-25. Jahrgang. Wien: [Agens-Werk
    Geyer & Co.,] 1975.

S188 Hofmeister, Adolph. Handbuch der musikalischen Literatur.
    1.-13. Ergänzungsband. Leipzig: Friedrich Hofmeister,
    1844-1923.

S189 Humanities Index. 1- . 1974- . New York: The H. W.
    Wilson Company, 1975- .

S190 Index to Religious Periodical Literature. An Author and Subject
    Index to Periodical Literature, including an Author Index
    of Book Reviews. 12 vols. 1949-76. [Chicago, Ill. :]
    American Theological Library Association, 1963-77. Con-
    sulted 1960-76.

S191 Indice general de publicaciones periodicas latinoamericanas.
    Humanidades y ciencias sociales=Index to Latin American
    Periodicals. Humanities and Social Sciences. 1- . 1961- .
    [publisher varies] Consulted 1961-June 1970.

S192 "Inhaltsverzeichniss" Allgemeine musikalische Zeitung.
    Neue folge. 1-3. (1863-65).

S193 "Inhaltsverzeichniss" Leipziger allgemeine musikalische Zeitung.
    1-17. (1866-82).

S194 Kahl, Willi and Wilhelm-Martin Luther. Repertorium der Musikwissenschaft. Musikschrifttum, Denkmäler und Gesamtaus-
gaben in Auswahl (1800-1950). Kassel und Basel: Bären-
reiter-Verlag, 1953.

S195 Krohn, Ernst Christopher. The History of Music: An Index
to the Literature available in a Selected Group of Musicological Publications. (Washington University Library Studies
no. 3) St. Louis: Washington University, 1952.

S196 Mecklenburg, Carl Gregor Herzog zu. Bibliographie einiger
Grenzgebiete der Musikwissenschaft. (Bibliotheca biblio-
graphica aureliana VI) Baden-Baden: Verlag Heitz GmbH,
1962.

S197 Music Article Guide. 1- . 1966- . Philadelphia: Author,
1966- . [publisher varies]

S198 The Music Index. 1- . 1949- . Detroit: Information
Service, Incorporated, 1949- . [publisher's name varies]

S199 Music Psychology Index. 2- . 1978- . Denton, TX: Institute for Therapeutics Research, 1978- .

S200 Music Therapy Index. 1. (1976). Lawrence, Kansas: National
Association for Music Therapy Inc., 1976.

S201 "Musikalische Zeitschriftenschau" Zeitschrift für Musikwissenschaft. 1-17. (1918-1935).

S202 Répertoire international de littérature musicale=International
Repertory of Music Literature=Internationales Repertorium
der Musikliteratur. RILM Abstracts of Music Literature.
1- . 1967- . [Flushing, N.Y.: n.p.] [place of
publication and publisher varies] Consulted 1967-1981.

S203 Social Sciences Index. 1- . 1974- . New York: The H. W.
Wilson Company, 1975- .

S204 Szczawińska, Elzbieta. Muzyka w polskich czasopismach liter-
ackich i spoŀeczynch 1864-1900. (Bibliografia muzyczna
polskich czasopism memuzycznych. Tom ᴵᴵᴵ) Kraków:
Polskie wydawnictwo muzyczne, n.d.

S205 Tudor, Dean and Nancy Tudor. Popular Music Perioaicals
Index. 1973-76. Metuchen: The Scarecrow Press, Inc.,
1974-77. [authors vary] Consulted 1973-74.

S206 The Times Literary Supplement Index 1902-1939. 2 vols. Reading,
England: Newspaper Archive Developments Limited, 1978.

S207   The Times Literary Supplement Index 1940-1980. 3 vols.
       Reading: Research Publications Ltd., 1982.

S208   The Times Literary Supplement Index 1981-1985. Reading,
       England; Woodbridge, Conn.: Research Publications,
       1986.

S209   "Verzeichniss der erschienenen Bücher und Schriften über
       Musik" Jahrbuch der Musikbibliothek Peters 1-45 (1894-
       1938).

S210   Wolf, Arthur S. Speculum. An Index of Musically Related
       Articles and Book Reviews. (MLA Index Series 9) Ann
       Arbor: Music Library Association, 1970.

S211   Zeitschriftendienst Musik. 1966- . Berlin: Deutscher
       Büchereiverband e.V., 1966- . [publisher varies]
       Consulted Jahresband for 1970-79: all issues for 1980-81.

S212   "Zeitschriftenschau" Zeitschrift der Internationalen Musikgesell-
       schaft 1-15 (1899-1914).

NEWSPAPER INDEXES

S213   The Canadian Newspaper Index. 1- . 1977- . Toronto:
       Information Access, 1977- . [title, publisher varies]

S214   Cumulated Index of the Christian Science Monitor. 1960-69.
       3 vols. [Corvallis, Or.:] Helen M. Cropsey, 1961-70.

S215   Current Abstracts of the Soviet Press. 1- . 1968- . New
       York: Joint Committee on Slavic Studies, 1968- . Con-
       sulted 1968-69, 1970.

S216   Current Digest of the Soviet Press. 1- . 1949- . New
       York: Joint Committee on Slavic Studies, 1949- . [pub-
       lisher varies] Consulted 1949-81.

S217   Christian Science Monitor. Index. 1970- . Compiled by
       Mrs. Helen M. Cropsey. [n.p.: Bell & Howell], 1971- .
       [title, publication information varies]

S218   Le Devoir. Index. 1- . 1966- . [Montreal: n.p., 1967-
       .] [title, publisher varies] Consulted 1967-73, 1976-
       82.

S219   Index to Pravda. 3 vols. 1975-77. Columbus, Ohio: American
       Association for the Advancement of Slavic Studies, 1976-
       78.

S220   Index to the Christian Science Monitor International Daily

Newspaper. 1950-59 [Boston:] Christian Science Publishing
Society, [1971-77?].

S221 The New York Times Index. The Master Key to the News.
1- . 1913- . New York: New York Times Company,
1913- .

S222 The New York Times Index. The Master Key to the News.
Prior Series. vols. 2-15. 1863-1912. New York: New
York Times Company, 1863-1912. [subtitle varies]

S223 Newspaper Index. Los Angeles Times. 1972- . Wooster,
Ohio: Bell & Howell Co., 1975- . [title varies] Consulted
1975-7.1981.

S224 Newspaper Index. The Washington Post. 1972-80. Wooster,
Ohio: Bell & Howell Co., 1975-81. [title varies] Consulted
1972-78, 1980.

S225 The Official Washington Post Index. 1979- . Woodbridge,
Conn.: Research Publications, Inc. 1983- .

S226 Palmer's Index to the Times Newspaper. [Primary sequence]
1830- . Shepperton-on-Thames: Samuel Palmer 1896- .
[title, publisher varies]

INDEXES TO MATERIAL IN COLLECTIONS

S227 Brewton, John E. and Sara W., comps. Index to Children's
Poetry. New York: The H. W. Wilson Company, 1942.

S228 Brewton, John E. and Sara W. comps. Index to Children's
Poetry. First Supplement. New York: The H. W. Wilson
Company, 1954.

S229 Brewton, John E. and Sara W., comps. Index to Children's
Poetry. Second Supplement. New York: The H. W. Wilson
Company, 1965.

S230 Bruncken, Herbert, comp. and ed. Subject Index to Poetry.
A Guide for Adult Readers. Chicago: American Library
Association, 1940.

S231 Canadian Essay and Literature Index. Compiled and edited
by Andrew D. Armitage and Nancy Tudor. Toronto and
Buffalo: University of Toronto Press, 1975-77. [Covers
1973-75]

S232 Canadian Essays and Collections Index. 1971-72. Ottawa:
Canadian Library Association, 1976.

S233 Chicorel, Marietta, ed. Chicorel Index to Poetry in Anthologies and Collections in Print. 4 vols. (Chicorel Index series vols. 5, 5A,5B,5C) New York: Chicorel Library Publishing Corp., 1974.

S234 Chicorel, Marietta, ed. Chicorel Index to Short Stories in Anthologies and Collections. 2 vols. (Chicorel Index Series vols. 12,12A) New York: Chicorel Library Publishing Corp., 1977. [Covers 1975-77]

S235 Essay and General Literature Index. 1900- . New York: The H. W. Wilson Company, 1934- .

S236 Gerboth, Walter. An Index to Musical Festschriften and Similar Publications. 1st ed. New York: W. W. Norton & Company, Inc., 1969.

S237 Granger, Edith, ed. An Index to Poetry and Recitations. Chicago: A. C. McClurg, 1904- . [editors, title, and publication information varies]

S238 Index to Poetry for Children and Young People. [various compilers] 1964- . New York: The H. W. Wilson Company, 1972- .

S239 Poetry Index Annual. 1982. Great Neck, New York: Granger Book Co., Inc., 1982.

S240 Short Story Index. New York: H. W. Wilson Company, 1953- . Consulted 1953-1983.

S241 Subject Index to Canadian Poetry in English for Children and Young People. 2nd ed. Kathleen M. Snow, Rickey Dabbs and Esther Gorosh, comps. [Ottawa:] Canadian Library Association, 1986.

S242 Subject Index to Poetry for Children and Young People. Violet Sell et al., comps. Chicago: American Library Association, 1957.

S243 Subject Index to Poetry for Children and Young People. 1957-1975. Dorothy B. Frizzell Smith and Eva L. Andrews, comps. Chicago: American Library Association, 1977.

S244 Voorhees, Anna Tipton. Index to Symphonic Program Notes in Books. (Keys to Music Bibliography No. 1) Kent, Ohio: Kent State University, School of Library Science, 1970.

MISCELLANEOUS

S245 Association for Recorded Sound Collections. Journal. 4- . (1972-).

S246 Berkovec, Jiří. Antonín Dvořák. (Hudebni profily) Praha: Editio Supraphon, 1969.

S247 Brahms, Johannes. Briefwechsel mit dem Mannheimer Bankprokuristen Wilhelm Lindeck 1872-1882. Michael Martin, bearbeiter. (Stadtarchivs Mannheim. Sonderveröffentlichung. Nr. 6) Heidelberg: Heidelberger Verlagsanstalt und Druckerei GmbH, 1983.

S248 Brahms-Studien. 1- . (1974-).

S249 Cum notis variorum. Newsletter of the Music Library, University of California (Berkeley) no. 1- . (1976-). Consulted 1982- .

S250 McCorkle, Donald M., "Research Papers".

S251 Riemann-Festschrift. Gesammelte Studien. Hugo Riemann zum sechzigsten Geburtstage überreicht von Freunden und Schülern. Tutzing: Hans Schneider, 1965. [reprint of 1909 edition]

S252 Rotterdam. Museum Boymans-van Beuningen. Max Klinger 1857-1920. Beeldhouwwerken. Schilderijen. Tekeningen. Grafiek. 30 September-12 November 1978. [Rotterdam: Author, 1978]

PART I. HISTORICAL AND RESEARCH INFORMATION

A. GENERAL STUDIES--LIFE AND WORKS

All material in this subsection discusses Brahms's life and music
in general. Annotations are provided only when this is not the
case, when additional types of information are included, or when
comment is necessary regarding material's presentation or significance.

1. Monographs and Dissertations

Juvenile literature: 28, 45, 51, 89.

1 #Antcliffe, Herbert. Brahms. (Bell's Miniature Series of Musicians)
      London: George Bell & Sons, 1905. viii, 56 pp. ill., facsim.,
      notes. Includes comments on Brahms the man and the composer.
      *issue: 1908.

2 *Appelbaum, Theodore. "Johannes Brahms." M.Mus. thesis,
      University of Rochester (Eastman School of Music), 1931. iii,
      105 pp. mus., notes. Biographical study, including analyses
      of Opp. 5, 19, 98, 102. [from Sibley Music Library, Eastman
      School of Music]

3 *Bayliss, Stanley A. Johannes Brahms, 1833-1897. [(Thumbnail
      Sketches of Great Composers)] London: W. Paxton & Co.,
      [1929]. 15 pp.
      (d) Bayliss. "Johannes Brahms. A Character Study in
      Miniature" Musical Mirror 10/3 (3.1930) Supplement
      [7 pp.] ill. Includes comments on Brahms the man
      and his musical style.

4 *Berger, Ludwig. [Ludwig Bamberger] Von Menschen Johannes
      Brahms. Hamburg: Christians [Stadtverwaltung(?)], 1958.
      42 pp. Speech given in Hamburg at the ceremony commemora-
      ting the 125th anniversary of Brahms's birth, 7.5.1958.
      [from 243]
      (d) expanded: Tübingen: Rainer Wunderlich Verlag Hermann

1

Leins, 1959. 75, [1] pp. Study of Brahms's life,
focuses on his character and its reflection in his
music.
(b) *Danish translation by Elisabeth Blohm: Om
mennesket Johannes Brahms. (Hasselbalchs
kulturbibliotek 262) [Copenhagen:] Hassel-
balch, 1967. 92 pp.

5 *Bergh, R[udolph]. S. Johannes Brahms. Et foredrag. Kjøbenhavn: Nordiske Forlag (Musikforlaget), 1897. 24 pp.
(d) reworked (biographical details only [from item]): Bergh.
"VIII. Ny-klassicismen. Johannes Brahms" in Bergh.
Musiken i det nittende aarhundrede. (Det nittende
aarhundrede XXVIII) Kjøbenhavn: Gyldendalske
Baghandel Nordisk Forlag, 1919. pp. 102-12. ill.
Brahms: pp. 102-09. Includes comments on Brahms
the composer, and his historical position.
(b) *Swedish translation by Axel Nihlen: Musiken
under det nittonde arhundradet. Stockholm:
P. A. Norstedt & Söner, [1920].

6 *Bruyr, José. Brahms. ([Collections microcosme.] Solfèges.
25) [Paris:] Editions du seuil, 1965. 192 pp. [185, [3](?) pp.]
ill., facsim., mus., notes., discog.

7 *Burkhart, Franz. Johannes Brahms. Kleines Brevier mit 49
Bildern. (Ewige Musik) Wien, Heidelberg, Zürich: Gerlach &
Wiedling, [1953]. 29, [32] pp. ill.

8 Chissell, Joan. Brahms. (The Great Composers) London:
Faber and Faber, 1977. 104 pp. ill., facsim., mus., ind.,
notes. Focuses on Brahms the man and his milieu.

9 #Crass, Eduard. Johannes Brahms. Sein Leben in Bildern.
Leipzig: VEB Bibliographisches Institut, 1957. 56, [24]
pp. ill., facsim., fig. Text to p. 56, followed by 128 illustrations.
(b) *Hungarian translation by László Passuth: Johannes
Brahms élete képekben. Budapest: Zeneműkiadó,
1960. 61, [24] pp.

10 Creuzburg, Eberhard. Johannes Brahms. Leben und Werk.
[(Breitkopf & Härtels kleine Musikerbiographien)] Leipzig:
Breitkopf & Härtel, [1939]. 83, [1] pp. ill., facsim., mus.,
notes.
*3. Auflage: Wiesbaden, 1947. 79 pp. adds ind.
*4. Auflage: 1954. 91 pp.

11 _____. Was weist du von Brahms? [Berlin: Breitkopf &
Härtel, 193-?] 23 pp. ill., facsim., mus. Cover has J.
Brahms' Leben on it [from S037]

12 #Culshaw, John. Brahms. An Outline of His Life and Music.
    With a Preface by Alex Robertson. [(Hinrichsen's Miniature
    Surveys no. 19)] London: Hinrichsen Edition Limited, [192-?].
    31 pp. mus., notes., discog.
    *issues: [1930's, 1948, 1949]

13 Dale, Kathleen. Brahms. A Biography with a Survey of Books,
    Editions and Recordings. [Recordings Survey compiled by
    Brian Redfern] (The Concertgoer's Companions) London:
    Clive Bingley, 1970. 118 pp. ind., notes., discog. Biography
    to p. 53.
    *also: [Hamden, Conn.:] Archon Books, [1970].
    *also: Hamden, Conn.: Shoe String Press, 1970.

14 Delvaille, Bernard. Johannes Brahms. L'Homme et son oeuvre.
    (Musiciens de tous les temps [15]) [Paris:] Edition Seghers,
    1965. 188, [3] pp. ill., facsim., mus., notes, discog. In-
    cludes section of other composers' comments on Brahms.
    *also: Lausanne: La Guilde du livre, [1965].

15 *Druskin, Mihail. Iogannes Brams. Moskva: Muzyka, 1970.
    111 pp. ill., mus.

16 Ehrmann, Alfred von. Johannes Brahms. Weg, Werk und Welt.
    Leipzig: Breitkopf & Härtel, 1933. xii, 534 pp. ill.,
    facsim., mus., ind., notes. Includes sections on the re-
    ception of Brahms's music internationally.
    (a) i) *reprint: Walluf-Nendeln: Sändig, 1974.
        ii) *reprint: Wiesbaden: Breitkopf & Härtel, 1980.
    (d) see: 313.
    (e) report: Abendroth, Walter. "Das neue Brahmsbuch"
        Allgemeine Musikzeitung 60/23 (9.6.1933) p. 312.

17 *Eppstein, Hans. Brahms. Stockholm: Lindfors, [1948].
    223 pp. ill., mus.

18 Erb, J[ohn]. Lawrence. Brahms. (Master Musicians) London:
    J. M. Dent & Co.; New York: E. P. Dutton & Co., 1905.
    xiii, [1], 178, [1] pp. ill., facsim., ind., notes. Includes
    comments on Brahms the man and musician.
    *issues: 1913, 1925.
    Revised Edition [Revised by Series Editor Eric Blom, with
    author's consent]: London: J. M. Dent & Sons Ltd.; New
    York: E. P. Dutton & Co., 1934. xi, [1], 187, [1] pp.
    (a) *reprint (of 1934 edition): Ann Arbor: Finch Press,
        n.d.
    (b) i) *Italian translation by Pietro Leoni (of 1934 edition?):
        Brahms. La Vita, le opere. (Storia della musica.
        Serie I, n. 6) Milano: Fratelli Bocca, 1946. 193 pp.
       ii) *Spanish translation by Eugenio Ingster (of 1934

edition?): Buenos Aires: n.p., 1952.
(d) superseded by: 41.

19 *Erhardt, Ludwik. Brahms. (Monografie popularne) [Wydanie
1.] [Kraków:] Polskie wydawnictwo muzyczne, [1969]. 403
pp. ill., facsim., mus., ind.
*Wydanie 2.: 1975. 325 pp.
*Wydanie 3.: 1984. 328 pp.
(b) *Hungarian translation by Judit Hary (of 1975 Wydanie):
[Bibliography by István Barna] Budapest: Zeneműkiadó Vállalat, 1978. 432 pp. omits ill., facsim.;
adds notes. Includes comments on Brahms and
Hungary. [from S202]

20 Ernest, Gustav. Johannes Brahms. Persönlichkeit, Leben und
Schaffen. Berlin: Deutsche Brahms-Gesellschaft m.b.H.,
1930. 416 pp. ill., facsim., mus., ind. 39 is the major
source of historical information. Includes comments on Brahms
the man and the composer, together with analysis of the
symphonies and some chamber and solo piano works.
(d) #Ernest. "Johannes Brahms" Medizinische Welt 5/51
(19.12.1931) Unterhaltung pp. 1841-44. Only has
notes. Describes characteristics of Brahms as seen
in his music; focuses on his childhood and the women
in his life. Includes comments on the qualities of
the music.
(e) i) report: see 61.e.i.
ii) report: Westermeyer, Karl. "Brahms, der
Niederdeutsche. Brahms-Biographien"
Berliner Tageblatt 62/211 (7.5.1933) Ausgabe
A [p. 9]. Includes reports on 55, 61.

21 *Fey, Hermann. Johannes Brahms. (Nedderdüütsche Welt. 6)
Hamburg: Hermes, [1919]. 16 pp.
(d) incorporated: Fey. "Johannes Brahms" in Fey.
Schleswig-Holsteinische Musiker von den altesten
Zeiten bis zur Gegenwart. Ein Heimatbuch. Hamburg:
Carl Holler Verlag, [1922]. pp. 6-15. Includes
genealogical background and works list from 73.
(c) #excerpt: Fey. Niedersachsen 27 (1922).
Omits the works list.

22 Friedrich, Julius. Johannes Brahms. (Musikalische Schriftenreihe der NS [National Sozialistische] Kulturgemeinde [Folge
1] [nr.] 4) Berlin-Schöneberg: Max Hesses Verlag, [1935].
15, [1] pp. ill., facsim., notes. Nazi propaganda using
Brahms as an example of a "good German"; focuses on life
before 1863, includes comments on Brahms's style.

23 *Fuller-Maitland, J[ohn]. A[lexander]. Brahms. (The New
Library of Music) London: Methuen, [1911]. xi, 263, [1]

pp. ill., facsim., ind., notes.
also: New York: John Lane Company, 1911.
  (a) *reprint (of London Edition): (Music and Musicians
     [original series omitted]) Port Washington, N.Y.:
     Kennikat Press, [1972].
  (b) German translation by A. W. Sturm (of London Edition):
     Berlin und Leipzig: Schuster & Loeffler, 1912. 186,
     89 pp. Only ill., facsim.
    *2.-4. Auflagen: 1912.
    (c) excerpt (of 1. Auflage): Fuller-Maitland.
     "Charakteristisches in Brahms' Kunstschaffen"
     Die Musik (Berlin) 12/2 (Bd. 45) (10.1912)
     pp. 67-76.
    (e) report (on 1. Auflage): see 2022.e.ii.
  (c) i) *excerpt (of London Edition): in 2915 pp. 283-84.
    ii) excerpt (of London Edition): Fuller-Maitland.
     "Brahms" in From Bach to Stravinsky. The History
     of Music by Its Foremost Critics. David Ewen, ed.
     New York: W. W. Norton & Company, Inc., 1933.
     pp. 227-50.
  (e) i) report (on New York Edition): [Henry T. Finck]
     Nation (New York) 92/2385 (16.3.1911) p. 276.
    ii) report (on London Edition): C. L. G. [Charles
    L. Graves] "Brahms and His Admirers"
    Spectator [106]/4317 (25.3.1911) pp. 443-44.
    Includes comments on the history of Brahms's
    reception.
    (a) *reprint: Graves, Charles L. "Two Books on
     Brahms" in Graves. Post-Victorian Music.
     With Other Studies and Sketches. London:
     Macmillan and Co., Limited, 1911. pp. 224-
     28 [total article paging: pp. 217-28]
     Includes report on 48.
     (a) reprint: Port Washington, N.Y.;
      London: Kennikat Press, 1970.
    iii) report (on London Edition): Sampson, George.
    "Brahms contra mundum" Bookman (London) 40/236
    (5.1911) pp. 85-86

24 Gal, Hans. Johannes Brahms. Werk und Persönlichkeit.
    Frankfurt a.M.: Fischer Bücherei KG, 1961. 161, [1] pp.
    ill., facsim., mus., ind., notes. Focuses on problem of
    personality and the creative process.
    (a) reprint: Gal. "Johannes Brahms. Werk und Persön-
     lichkeit" in Gal. Drei Meister--drei Welten. Brahms,
     Wagner, Verdi. Frankfurt a.M.: S. Fischer Verlag
     GmbH, 1975. pp. 11-182. omits ill.
    (b) English translation by Joseph Stein: Johannes Brahms.
     His Work and Personality [First American Edition]
     New York: Alfred A. Knopf, 1963. ix, [1], 245,
     [1], iv pp.

    *also: Westminster, Md.: Alfred A. Knopf, 1963.
    *also: London: Weidenfeld and Nicolson, 1963.
    *also: Toronto: Random House of Canada Limited, 1963.
    (a)   i) reprint (of London Edition): London: Severn
           House, 1975. vii, [3], 245, [1], iv pp.
           ii)*reprint (of New York Edition): Westport,
           Conn.: Greenwood Press, [1977], c1963.
    (c)   excerpt (of New York Edition): in 1380.

25 *Geiringer, Karl. Johannes Brahms. Leben und Schaffen eines
    deutschen Meisters. Brünn und Leipzig: Rohrer, 1934.
    also: Wien: Rudolf M. Rohrer, 1935. xi, 325 pp. ill., facsim.,
    mus., ind., notes.
    *2. erweiterte und verbesserte Auflage: Johannes Brahms.
    Sein Leben und Schaffen. Zürich, Stuttgart: Pan-Verlag,
    [1955]. 380, 8 pp.
    (a)   *reprint (of 1955 Auflage): Geiringer, Karl unter
           Mitarbeit von Irene Geiringer. (Bärenreiter-Taschen-
           bücher) Kassel: Bärenreiter, 1974.
    (b)   i) *English translation by H. B. Weiner and Bernard
           Miall (of 1935 Auflage): Brahms. His Life and Work.
           London: G. Allen & Unwin Ltd., [1936]. 352 pp.
           also: Boston and New York: Houghton Mifflin Company,
           1936. Includes comments on Brahms the man and
           composer. First use for documentation of Brahms
           correspondence preserved at the Gesellschaft der
           Musikfreunde (Wien).
           *issues (of London Edition):?
           *Second Edition, Revised and Enlarged, with a New
           Appendix of Brahms's Letters: New York: Oxford
           University Press, 1947. xv, 383 pp.
           *also: Fair Lawn, N.J.: Oxford University Press,
           1947.
           *also: London: G. Allen and Unwin, 1948.
           Discusses musical works that were discovered after
           the book was first published. Appendix contains
           29 letters 1853-90 [1853-96] previously unavailable
           in English translation: includes selections from 871,
           892, 954, 983, 1009, 1204, 1297, 1314.
           *issues (of London Edition): 1963-74.
           Anchor Edition [Pocketbook Edition of 2nd ed., New
           York]: (Anchor A248) Garden City, N.Y.: Anchor
           Books, Doubleday & Company, Inc., 1961. xi, [5],
           344 pp.
           Third Edition, Revised and Enlarged with a New Appendix:
           "Brahms as a Reader and Collector": Geiringer, Karl
           in collaboration with Irene Geiringer. (Da Capo
           Press Music Reprint Series) New York: Da Capo
           Press, 1982. xv, [1], 397 pp. Reprint of 2nd ed.,
           London, with appendix based on 672 and a supplemental,
           updated bibliography.

(b) i) *Hebrew translation (of 2nd ed., New York):
        Brahms. Tel Aviv: Ledori, 1955. 320 pp.
     ii) *Italian translation by Gianni Gae and Maffeo
        Zanon (of 2nd ed., New York): Brahms.
        Sua vita e sue opere. Milan, Rome?: G.
        Ricordi e C., 1952. xii, 318 pp.
    iii) *Japanese translation by Ginji Yamane (of
        2nd ed., New York): Brahms. Tokyo:
        Ongaku no tomo-sha, 1952. 466 pp.
        *also: [Paperback Edition] Tokyo: ?, 1958.
        reprints text from 1952 Edition with different
        ill. [from Geiringer]
        (b) *reprint (of Tokyo 1952 Edition): Tokyo:
            Geijutsu-gendai, 1975. v, 465 pp.
        (e) report (on 1st ed., London): H. B. [H. B.
            Weiner] "A Brahms Book" Musical Opinion
            and Music Trade Review 60/709 (10.1936) p.
            26.
     ii) *French translation by Marie-Anne Boehm-Trémeau
        (of 1955 Auflage?): Brahms. Sa vie et son oeuvre.
        (Collection musique) Paris: Editions Buchet Chastel,
        1982. 318, 320, or 400 pp.?
    iii) *Russian translation by G. Nasatyr' (of 1955 Auflage?):
        Iogannes Brams. Moskva: Muzyka, 1965. 432 pp.
(c) excerpt (of 1934 Auflage): "Johannes Brahms: schöp-
        ferische Entwicklung (Proben aus neuen Musikbio-
        graphien)" Anbruch 16/8 (10.1934) pp. 163-65.
(e) report (on 1934 Auflage): Reich, Willi. "Neue Brahms-
        Dokumente. I.II." Schweizerische Musikzeitung und
        Sängerblatt. Gazette musicale suisse 75/12,13 (15.6.
        and 1.7.;1935) pp. 441-44, 473-77. notes. Includes
        report on 819.
(d) Reich. "Neues von Brahms" Der Auftakt
        15/5-6 ([5.-6.] 1935) pp. 73-77. Includes
        reports on 32, 819, 1781.

26 Gerber, Rudolf. Johannes Brahms. (Unsterbliche Tonkunst.
    Lebens-und Schaffensbilder grosser Musiker) Potsdam   Aka-
    demische Verlagsgesellschaft Athanaion, 1938. 128 pp.
    ill., facsim., ind., notes. Includes comments on Brahms
    the man and composer.

27 *Goldron, Roman. [A. Louis Burkhalter] Johannes Brahms "le
    vagabond." Paris: Flammarion, [1956]. 349 pp.
    (b) *Italian translation by G. Ciocia: Johannes Brahms,
        il "vagabondo". (Biblioteca culturale S.A.I.E.
        Biografie) Torino: S.A.I.E., 1959. 477, [2] pp.
    (c) #excerpt: Goldron. "Johannes Brahms a Thoune"
        Feuilles musicales (Lausanne) 8 (1955) pp. 176-80.
        notes. 1886-1888: discusses works composed in
        Thun, Brahms's lodgings, daily activities and milieu.

(d) Goldron. Johannes Brahms. (Hommes et faits de l'histoire [38]) [Paris:] Club des éditeurs, [1960]. [2], 14, [4], 365, xv, [5] pp. ill., facsim., fig., ind., notes. Includes comments on Brahms and France, Brahms as a composer, and Brahms's historical position.

28 Goss, Madeleine and Robert Haven Schauffler. Brahms. The Master. Illustrated by Frederic Dorr Steele. New York: Henry Holt & Co., 1943. 351 pp. ill., mus., fig., ind. Juvenile literature: historical fiction. *issue: 1945.

29 *Grasberger, Franz. Johannes Brahms. Variationen um sein Wesen. Wien: P. Kaltschmid, [1952]. 464 pp. ill., facsim., fig., ind.

30 _____. Das kleine Brahmsbuch. Salzburg: Residenz Verlag, 1973. 119, [1] pp. ill., facsim., notes.

31 *Helm, Theodor. Johannes Brahms. Ein Festvortrag zur Feier des 50. Geburtstages des Meisters. Wien: Verlag der Horakschen Musikschulen, 1883.

32 Hernried, Robert. Johannes Brahms. (Musiker-Biographien. Bd. 27) Leipzig: Verlag von Philipp Reclam jun., 1934. 157, [1] pp. fig., ind., notes. also in monograph series: (Reclam Universal-Bibliothek nr. 7251/52) focuses on 1862-1897. (e) report: see 25.e.d.

33 Hill, Ralph. Brahms: A Study in Musical Biography. With a Preface by Evlyn Howard-Jones. London: Denis Archer, 1933. xv, 188 pp. ind., notes. Focuses on Brahms's character in relation to his works and milieu.
(d) *Hill. Brahms. (Great Lives [85]) London: Duckworth, [1941]. 143 pp. ill., notes.
#issue: 1947. Includes comments on Brahms the composer.
*also: (Great Musicians) New York: A. A. Wyn, [1948].
(a) *reprint (of 1941 Edition): Chester Springs, Penn.: Dufour Editions, 1968.

34 *Hillmann, Adolf. Johannes Brahms. Stockholm: Wahlström & Widstrand, 1918. 196 pp. ill.

35 *Hrabussay, Zoltán. Johannes Brahms. [1. vydání] (Hudobné profily, zv. 2) Bratislava: Státne hudobné vydavatel'stvo, 1963. 101 pp. ill., facsim., notes.

36 Hutschenruyter, Wouter. Brahms. (Beroemde musici. Deel
XII) 's-Gravenhage: J. Philip Kruseman, [1929]. 127 pp.
ill., facsim., fig., ind., notes. Includes comments on
Brahms the man, pianist, and conductor.

37 Imbert, Hugues. Johannès Brahms. Sa vie et son oeuvre.
Préface d'Edouard Schuré. Paris: Librairie Fischbacher,
1906. xix, [1], 170 pp. ill., notes. Includes comments on
Brahms's historical position, Brahms in France and Belgium,
and the French attitude towards Brahms and his music.
    (c) excerpt (German translation by Elisabet Mayer-Wolff):
        "Johannes Brahms. Aus H. Imberts Brahmsbiographie"
        Neue Zeitschrift für Musik 86/1/2-11/12, 13, 14/15,
        18/19 (16.1.-20.3.; 27.3.; 10.4.; 8.5.; 1919) pp.
        1-4, 15-17, 25-28, 37-40, 49-51, 61-64, 73-76, 82-85,
        106-08. Notes.
    (d) see: 147

38 James, Burnett. Brahms: A Critical Study. New York:
Praeger, 1972. xiii, 202 pp. ill., mus., ind., notes. An
attempt to view Brahms both from the perspectives of his
own time, and of the second half of the 20th century.
*also London: J. M. Dent & Sons Ltd., 1972.
    (e) report: Craft, Robert. "Oui, j'aime Brahms" World
        1/11 (21.11.1972) pp. 72-73. ill. Includes report
        on 1803.a.

39 Kalbeck, Max. [Johannes Brahms.]
    (a) reprint: 8 vols. in 4. Tutzing: Hans Schneider, 1976.
        Contains:
        Band I. Erster Halbband. 4. Auflage: 1921.
        Band I. Zweiter Halbband. 4. durchgesehene
            Auflage: 1921.
        Band II. Erster Halbband. 3. vermehrte und
            verbesserte Auflage: 1921.
        Band II. Zweiter Halbband. 3. vermehrte und
            verbesserte Auflage: 1921.
        Band III. Erster Halbband. 2. durchgesehene
            Auflage: 1912.
        Band III. Zweiter Halbband. 2. durchgesehene
            Auflage: 1913.
        Band IV. Erster Halbband. 2. verbesserte Auflage:
            1915.
        Band IV. Zweiter Halbband. 2. verbesserte Auflage:
            1915.
    (c) *excerpt (of ? Band, ? Auflage): see 1179.c.vi.
    (d) see also: 227, 358, 559.5, 2524.
    (e) i) report: see 708, 2328.
        ii) report: Söhle, Karl. "Zur Brahmsliteratur" Deutsches
            Volkstum 23/8 (8.1921) pp. 255-57. Includes report
            on 61; article interspersed with comments on Brahms
            and Wagner, and on Brahms's historical position.

39A Band I.
    *Kalbeck. Johannes Brahms. Sein Lebensgang vom Jahre 1833-
        1982. Wien: Wiener Verlag, [1903]. viii, 512 pp.
        also published as Johannes Brahms. I. 1833-1862. Wien und
        Leipzig: Wiener Verlag, 1904. mus., ind., notes.
        Erster Halbband.
        *2. durchgesehene Auflage: Johannes Brahms. I. Erster
            Halbband. 1833-1856. Berlin: Deutsche Brahms-Gesellschaft,
            1908.
        3. durchgesehene Auflage: 1912. xvi, 258 pp. ill., mus.,
            notes.
        4. Auflage: 1921.
        Zweiter Halbband.
        *[2. durchgesehene Auflage: Johannes Brahms. I. Zweiter
            Halbband. 1856-1862. Berlin: Deutsche Brahms-Gesellschaft,
            1908.]
        3. durchgesehene Auflage: 1912. 259-492 pp. mus., ind.,
            notes.
        4. durchgesehene Auflage: 1921.
            (a) reprints: see 39.a.
            (c) i) excerpt (of 1904 Auflage in English translation by
                    Piero Weiss): in 913. p. 266. 1 letter, Brahms to
                    Cossel, 1.1842.
                ii) excerpt (of Erster Halbband, ? Auflage): see 345.
                iii) excerpt (of Erster Halbband, 1908 Auflage): "Die
                    ersten Schritte des jungen Brahms in die Offent-
                    lichkeit (sic). Das zweite Kapitel der grossen
                    Brahmsbiographie von Max Kalbeck" in 3178 pp. 31-
                    51. ill., facsim., notes.
                iv) excerpt (of 1904 Auflage? in English translation by
                    Phoebe Rogoff Cave): Kalbeck: "How Brahms
                    Worked" in 758 pp. 336-40.
                v) excerpt (of 1903 Auflage): Kalbeck. "Schumann und
                    Brahms" Deutsche Rundschau 29/5 (Bd. 114) (2.1903)
                    pp. 231-58. notes. covers up to 1855,
                    (a) reprint: Kalbeck. Schumann und Brahms.
                        Berlin: Verlag von Gebrüder Paetel,
                        [1903].
                vi) excerpt (of Erster Halbband, ? Auflage): see 760.
                vii) excerpt (of Erster Halbband, ? Auflage): see 761.
            (d) i) incorporated (into 1903 Auflage): Kalbeck. "Aus
                    Brahms' Jugendzeit" Deutsche Rundschau 29/1 (Bd.
                    113) (10.1902) pp. 66-93. notes. Covers childhood
                    to the time that Brahms began to study with Marxsen.
                    Includes family genealogy and background on Marxsen.
                    (e) i) report: "Erinnerungen an Johannes
                            Brahms ... " Allgemeine Musikzeitung
                            29/41 (10.10.1902) p. 680.
                        ii) report: "Herinnerungen aan Johannes

Brahms" Weekblad voor muziek 11/32
(6.8.1904) pp. 311-12. Includes report on
617.
(e) i) *report (on 1904 Auflage): Zeitung für Literatur.
Beilage der Hamburger Correspondent. no. 23 (1904)
ii) report (on 1904 Auflage): A. J. J. "Johannes
Brahms" Musical Times 45/737, 738, 741 (1.;7.8.,
11.;1904) pp. 448-49, 516-17, 722-23. ill., mus.,
notes.
iii) report (on 1904 Auflage): Altman, Wilh[elm]. Die
Musik ₍Berlin) 3/24 (Bd. 12) (9.1904) pp. 458-60.
iv) report (on 1904 Auflage): Altmann, Wilhelm.
"Brahms' Jugendlieben" Die Zeit (Wien) Bd. 39/506
(11.6.1904) pp. 128-29. Discusses what Kalbeck
wrote on the topic.
v) *report (on Zweiter Halbband, 1908 Auflage): Kleffel,
Arno. "Joh[annes]. Brahms und Hermann Levi"
Berliner Tageblatt (1908?).
vi) report (on 1904 Auflage): Röttgers, B. "Der
Entwickelungsgang von Johannes Brahms. (Nach
der neuesten Darstellung seines Lebens.)" Neue
Musikzeitung 25/15,16(5.,19.;5.;1904) pp. 311-16,
332-38. ill., mus., notes.
vii) *report (on both Halbband, 1912 Auflagen): Zschorlich, P[aul]. "Zweimal Brahms" Die Hilfe [18 or
19]/50 (1912). [Includes report on 48.b?]

39B Band II.
Erster Halbband.

*Kalbeck. Johannes Brahms. II. Erster Halbband. 1862-1868.
Berlin: Deutsche Brahms-Gesellschaft, [1907?].
2. revidierte und vermehrte Auflage: 1908. xii, 282 pp.
ill., facsim., mus., notes.
3. vermehrte und verbesserte Auflage: 1921. xii, 286 pp.

Zweiter Halbband.

Kalbeck. Johannes Brahms. II. Zweiter Halbband. 1869-1873.
Berlin: Deutsche Brahms-Gesellschaft, 1909. vii, [1],
289-498 pp. facsim., mus., ind., notes.
2. vermehrte und verbesserte Auflage: 1910. vii, [1], 289-
500 pp.
3. vermehrte und verbesserte Auflage: 1921. vii, [1], 289-
499 pp.
(a) reprints: see 39.a.
(c) i) excerpt (of Erster Halbband, 1908 Auflage in English
translation by Piero Weiss): in 913. pp. 349-52.
4 letters, Brahms-Wagner, 6.1875.
ii) excerpt (of Zweiter Halbband, ? Auflage in English
translation by Margit L. McCorkle): see 1380 pp.
200-07. notes. Describes Op. 56a.

iii) #excerpt (of Zweiter Halbband, 1909 Auflage [forth-
coming]): Kalbeck. "Brahms, Levi und Stockhausen"
Berliner Tageblatt (16.11.1908) Der Zeitgeist no. 46
[2 pages, across the page tops]. notes.

iv) excerpt (of Erster Halbband, ? Auflage): Kalbeck.
"Brahms und Bülow" Signale für die musikalische
Welt 66/47 (18.11.1908) pp. 1470-72.

v) #excerpt (of Erster Halbband, 1907? Auflage): Kalbeck. "Brahms, Wagner, Cornelius. Aus einer
Brahms Biographie" Berliner Tageblatt (11.11.1907)
Der Zeitgeist no. 45 pp. [1-2] [across page tops].
notes.

(e) i) report (on Erster Halbband, 1908 Auflage): Altmann,
Wilh[elm]. Die Musik (Berlin) 7/18 (Bd. 27) (6.1908)
pp. 360-61.

ii) *report (on Zweiter Halbband, 1909 Auflage?): Karpath, Ludwig. "Neues von Brahms" Neues Wiener
Tagblatt (4.12.1909).

iii) *report (on Erster Halbband, 1907 Auflage?): R. H.
[Richard Heuberger] "Eine Brahms-Biographie"
[Wiener] Abendpost (5.1.1907).

iv) report (on Zweiter Halbband, 1909 Auflage):
Schmitz, Eugen. "Neues von Johannes Brahms"
Allgemeine Zeitung (München) 112/46 (13.11.1909)
pp. 1022-23. Focuses on the background of Opp.
45 and 56a.

v) report (on Erster Halbband, 1907? Auflage): "Der
zweite Band der Brahms-Biographie" Signale für die
musikalische Welt 65/60 (30.10.1907) pp. 1111-15.

39C Band III.

Erster Halbband.

Kalbeck. Johannes Brahms. III. Erster Halbband. 1874-1881.
Berlin: Deutsche Brahms-Gesellschaft, 1910. xiii, [1],
266 pp. ill., facsim., mus., notes.
2. durchgesehene Auflage: 1912.
*3. durchgesehene Auflage: 1922.

Zweiter Halbband.

Kalbeck. Johannes Brahms. III. Zweiter Halbband. 1881-1885.
Berlin: Deutsche Brahms-Gesellschaft, 1912. viii, 267-555
pp. facsim., mus., ind., notes.
2. durchgesehene Auflage: 1913.
(a) reprints: see 39.a.
(c) i) excerpt (of Erster Halbband, 1910 Auflage in English
translation by Piero Weiss): in 913. p. 368. 1
letter: Brahms to Weis, 12.1879.
ii) excerpt (of Zweiter Halbband, 1913 Auflage in English
translation by Piero Weiss): in 913. pp. 373-75.
1 letter: Brahms to Hanslick, 5.1884.

iii) excerpt (of Zweiter Halbband, 1912 Auflage in English translation): Kalbeck. "Brahms und Bruckner" New Music and Church Music Review 11/125 (4.1912) pp. 194-96.

iv) excerpt (of Zweiter Halbband, 1912 Auflage): Kalbeck. "Die dritte Symphonie (1883)." Der Merker (Wien) 3/2,3 (1.,2.;1912) pp. 47-56, 81-87. Historical background and analysis of work.

(e) *report (of Erster Halbband, 1910 Auflage): "Max Kalbeck's Brahms-Biographie" Der Bund (Bern) (28.12.1910).

39D Band IV.

Erster Halbband.

Kalbeck. Johannes Brahms. IV. Erster Halbband. 1886-1891. Berlin: Deutsche Brahms-Gesellschaft, 1914. xii, 258, [1] pp. ill., facsim., mus., notes.
2. verbesserte Auflage: 1915. xii, 258 pp.

Zweiter Halbband.

Kalbeck. Johannes Brahms. IV. Zweiter Halbband. 1891-1897. Berlin: Deutsche Brahms-Gesellschaft, 1914. x, 259-573 pp. ill., facsim., mus., ind., notes. Includes an Anhang containing memorabilia and lists of Hamburg/Wien residences, a poem on Op. 118, reprint of 1058, transcriptions of family letters, and a history of Deutsche Brahms-Gesellschaft.
2. verbesserte Auflage: 1915. x, 259-577 pp.
(a) reprints: see 39.a.
(d) incorporated (into Erster Halbband, 1914 Auflage): Kalbeck. "Brahms und Klinger" Sonntagsbeilage no. 44 to Vossische Zeitung (Berlin) no. 558 (2.11. 1913) pp. 345-47. notes. Discusses Klinger's Brahms-Phantasie.
(e) report (on Erster Halbband, 1914 Auflage): Paetow, W[alter]. "Zur Brahms-Literatur" Der Kunstwart 27/7 (1.1914) pp. 54-55.

40 Landormy, Paul. Brahms. (Les Maitres de la musique) Paris: Librairie Félix Alcan, 1920. 212, [1] pp. mus., notes. Includes comments on Brahms the man and composer.
Deuxième édition: 1921.
*Troisième-Dixième édition: 1921.
(a) *reprint? (of ? édition): (Leurs figures) [Paris:] Gallimard, [1948]. 185 pp. mus. only.
(b) Italian translation by Claudio Sartori (of ? édition): (Saggia di storia e letteratura musicale 3) [Milano:] Ed. Genio, [1946]. 125 pp.
(e) i) report (on 1920 édition): C. "A French View of Brahms" Musical Times 61/927 (1.5.1920) pp. 311-12.

notes. Focuses on Landormy's opinion of Brahms,
as an example of the French feelings in general.
ii) report (on 1920 édition): Nagel, W[illibald].
"Neue Brahms-Literatur" Neue Musikzeitung 41/22
(19.8.1920) pp. 346-48. Includes report on 61.
iii) report (on 1920 édition): Roquebrune, Fernand-
Georges. "Brahms et le goût français" Revue
critique des idées et des livres 28/162 (10.4.1920)
pp. 112-16. notes. Discusses the French reaction
to Brahms.

41 *Latham, Peter. Brahms. (The Master Musicians. New Series)
London: J. M. Dent, 1948. ix, 230 pp. ill., facsim.,
mus., fig., ind., notes. Replaces 18 (1934 Edition) in
series [from 1966 Edition].
*also New York: Pellegrini and Cudahy, 1949.
*issues (London Edition): 1951-1962.
[1962 Reprint Edition:] (The Master Musicians Series) London:
J. M. Dent & Sons Ltd.; New York: Farrar, Straus
and Cudahy, Inc., 1962. Focuses on the works; also discusses Brahms the man, and the English reaction to Brahms.
A few corrections and alteration of detail, but essentially
a reprint of the London 1948 Edition.
[1966 Edition:] 1966. Contains a few new facts, also some
corrections.
*issues: [1967?]-1970.
[1975 Edition:] London: J. M. Dent & Sons Ltd., 1975.
Contains a number of minor emendations and a revision of
the Brahms-Wagner account, bibliography is updated.
(a) *reprint (of 1949 Edition): New York: Octagon Books,
n.d.

42 Laufer, J. Brahms. [(Collection alternance)] Paris: Les
Editions du scorpion, 1963. 180, [8] pp. mus., notes.,
discog. Includes comments on Brahms's historical position
and musical style.

43 Laux, Karl. Der Einsame. Johannes Brahms. Leben und Werk.
Graz: Verlag Anton Pustet, 1944. 384 pp. mus., ind.
Includes comments on Brahms's historical position.

44 Lee, E[rnest]. Markham. Brahms. The Man and His Music.
London: Sampson Low, Marston & Co. Ltd., 1916. viii,
185 pp. ill., ind., notes. Includes comments on Brahms the
composer.
*also New York: C. Scribner's Sons, [1916].
(a) *reprint (of London 1916 Edition): New York: AMS
Press, 1978.

45 McLeish, Kenneth and Valerie. Brahms. (Composers and Their
World) London: Heinemann, 1979. [4], 90 pp. ill., facsim.,

mus., ind., notes. Juvenile literature; Brahms discussed
in relation to his milieu. Focuses on his works, with comments on Brahms the composer.

46 #Martens, Frederick H. Brahms. (Little Biographies.
Series I: Musicians) New York: Breitkopf Publications, Inc., [1925].
27 pp. ill., facsim., notes. Includes comments on Brahms
the man.

47 *Martinotti, Sergio. Brahms. Con contributi di Eduardo Rescigno,
Massimo Mila. 1. ed. (I Grandi della musica. Anno II, no.
6) Milano: Fabbri, 1980. 143 pp. ill., ind., notes, discog.

48 *May, Florence. The Life of Johannes Brahms. London: E.
Arnold, 1905. 2 vols. ill., facsim., mus., ind., notes.
Includes personal recollections of Brahms (incorporates 1086)
and contains appendices on Op. 33, the Hamburger Frauen-
chor, and a general discussion of programme music [from 2nd
Edition].
Second Edition revised by the Author, with Additional Matter and
Illustrations, and an Introduction by Ralph Hill. London:
William Reeves, [1948?]. Revisions made by May in 1910's,
taking into account newer literature for verification and cor-
rection. Includes new anecdotes and partially revised and
enlarged remarks on works. Omits program music appendix.
Enlarged and Illustrated Edition: Neptune City, N.J.: Pagani-
niana Publications, Inc., 1981. Reprint of 2nd Edition with
183 plates.
(a) *reprint (of 2nd Edition): St. Clair Shores, Mich.:
Scholarly Press, 1977.
(b) *German translation by Ludmille Kirschbaum (of 1905
Edition): Johannes Brahms. [2 parts in 1 volume]
Leipzig: Breitkopf & Härtel, 1911. xvi, 314, 362
pp.
*2. Auflage: 1925. xvii, 314, 362 pp.
(c) *excerpt (of 1911 Auflage): May. "Brahms als
Klavierlehrer" Rheinische Musik- und
Theaterzeitung (Köln) 13/32+ (1912).
(e) i) report (on 1911 Auflage): see 2022.e.ii.
ii) *report (on 1911 Auflage): Tucholsky,
B[erta]. "Erinnerungen an Johannes Brahms.
Nach englische Quellen" Hamburger Fremdenblatt (30.3.1911).
iii) report (on 1911 Auflage): see 39A.e.vii.
(c) #excerpt (of 1905 Edition): May. "Johannes Brahms
als Klavierlehrer" Autoriserte Ubersetzung von
Johanna Krause Hamburger Nachrichten. Beilage
nos. 4, 5 (27.1.; 3.2.; 1907) [6½ columns; 5 3/4
columns] notes. Describes being a piano student
of Brahms.

(e) i) *report (on 1905 Edition): Bertini, P. "Giovanni
Brahms secondo i biografi più recenti" Nuova
musica (Milan) 10/119 [(1905)].

ii) report (on 1905 Edition): C. L. G. [Charles L.
Graves] "Johannes Brahms" Spectator [95]/4035
(28.10.1905) pp. 652-53. Includes comments on
the English reception of Brahms's music.
(a) *reprint: in 23.e.ii.a. pp. 217-24.

49 *Michelmann, Emil. Johannes Brahms. Göttingen: Wurm, 1937.
4 pp. Speech given at Deutsche Brahms-Gesellschaft's 9th
Brahms Festival (Hamburg, 1937). [from 241]

50 #Mies, Paul. Johannes Brahms. Werk, Zeit, Mensch. (Wissenschaft und Bildung. Einzeldarstellungen aus allen Gebieten
des Wissens. 264) Leipzig: Verlag von Quelle & Meyer,
1930. 129 pp. mus., ind., notes., discog. Includes comments on Brahms the man and composer, and Brahms's historical position.

51 Mirsky, Reba Paeff. Brahms. Illustrated by W. T. Mars.
Chicago, New York: Follett Publishing Company, 1966.
160 pp. ill., mus. Juvenile literature.

52 *Misch, Ludwig. Johannes Brahms. Bielefeld: Velhagen &
Klasing, 1913. 34 pp. ill., mus.
[? Auflage:] [(Velhagen & Klasings Volksbücher nr. 79)]
Bielefeld und Leipzig: Verlag von Velhagen & Klasing, 1922.
86, [2] pp. Omits mus.; adds facsim., notes.

53 *Molnár, Antal. Johannes Brahms. (Kis zenei könyvtár 5)
Budapest: Gondolat, 1959. 258 pp. ill. Includes selections
from 1179. [from S046]

54 *Monma, Naomi. Brahms. (Dai-ongakuka: Hito to sakuhin 10)
Tokyo: Ongakunotomo, 1969. 201 pp. ill., notes., discog.

55 Müller-Blattau, Joseph. Johannes Brahms. Potsdam: Akademische
Verlagsgesellschaft Athenaion m.b.H., [1933]. 86, [2] pp.
ill., facsim., mus., notes. Includes comments on Brahms
the composer.
(c) excerpt: Müller-Blattau. "Das Deutsche Requiem von
Johannes Brahms" Athenaion-Blätter 2/1 (1934) pp.
3-6. ill. Discusses the work's history and tonalities.
(d) i) reworked: Müller-Blattau. Johannes Brahms. Leben
und Werk. [(Langewiesche Bücherei)] Königstein
im Taunus: Karl Robert Langewiesche Nachfolger
Hans Köster, [1960]. 63, [1] pp. ill., facsim.,
notes.
ii) #Müller-Blattau. "Der junge Brahms. (Ein Nach-
klang zum Brahms-Jubiläum)" Die Musik (Berlin)

26/3 (12.1933) pp. 168-76. mus. Details on childhood, showing Brahms's grasp of compositional
skills; describes meeting of Schumann and Brahms.
(a) reprint: Müller-Blattau. in 2732. pp. 37-45.
adds ill., notes.
(e) report: see 20.e.ii.

56 *Muller, H. J. M. Johannes Brahms. (Componisten-serie 6. boek)
Haarlem: J. H. Gottmer, [1948]. 271 pp. ill.

57 Murdoch, William [David]. Brahms, with an Analytical Study
of the Complete Pianoforte Works. London: Rich & Cowan,
1933. xii, [4], 17-394 pp. ill., ind., notes. Includes comment on Brahms the man, and his historical position. The
study includes works for piano solo, piano duet, and chamber
music for piano and other instruments.
*also: New York: Sears Pub. Co. Inc., [1933].
*issue (London Edition): 1938.
(a) *reprint (of London Edition): New York: AMS Press,
1978.

58 #Nagel, Willibald. Johannes Brahms. (Musikalische Volksbücher)
Stuttgart: J. Engelhorns Nachf[olger]., 1923. 164 pp.
ind., notes. Biography focuses on pre-1862 period. Includes comments on Brahms's historical position and musical
style.
(b) *Portuguese translation by Joaquim Clemente de Almeida:
Vida de Brahms. (Collecção cultura musical no. 9)
São Paulo: Edições cultura brasileira, 1935.
(d) incorporates: Nagel. "Johannes Brahms" Neue Musikzeitung 43/13 (6.4.1922) pp. 193-95. ill. Comments
on Brahms's historical position and Brahms the composer.
(e) report: see 1179.e.i.

59 Neunzig, Hans A[dolf]. Brahms. Der Komponist des deutschen
Bürgertums. Eine Biographie. Wien, München: Amalthea-
Verlag, 1976. 253, [1] pp. ill., facsim., mus., fig., ind., notes.

60. _____. Johannes Brahms in Selbstzeugnissen und Bilddo-
kumenten. (Rowohlts Monographien 197) Reinbek bei Hamburg:
Rowohlt Taschenbuch Verlag GmbH, 1973. 145, [2] pp.
ill., facsim., mus., notes, discog. Includes many quotations
from the Brahms literature; also examines Brahms in the context of his period, and discusses Brahms and the New German
School.
*[2. Auflage:] 1977.
(b) *Italian translation by Nino Muzzi and Angelika Storm:
(of ? Auflage): Johannes Brahms. (Contrappunti
12) Fiesole: Discanto, 1981. ix, 124 pp.

61 *Niemann, Walter. Brahms. 1. bis 10. Auflage. Berlin:
Schuster & Loeffler, [1920]. 437 pp. notes.
*11. bis 13. Auflage: (Klassiker der Musik) Stuttgart-Berlin:
Deutsche Verlags-Anstalt, 1922. 407 pp.
*14., neubearbeitete und erweiterte Auflage: Berlin: Max
Hesses Verlag, 1933. x, 420 pp.
(b) *English translation by Catherine Alison Phillips (of
1922 Auflage?): New York: A[lfred]. A. Knopf,
1929. xiii, [1], 492, [2] pp. mus., ind., notes.
*issues: 1930, 1935, 1941, 1946, 1947. First attempt
at a critical biography; includes comments on Brahms
the man. [from 1935 issue]
*New Edition: New York: Tudor Publishing Company,
1937. ill., mus.
*issue: 1945.
(a) i) reprint (of Knopf 1935 issue): New York:
Cooper Square Publishers, Inc., 1969.
ii) *reprint (of Tudor 1937 Edition): Totowa,
N.J.: Cooper Square Publishers, Inc.,
[1981].
(d) reworked (from 1920 Auflage?): Niemann. "Eine
Einführung in Brahms' Sinfonien. Zum Wiesbadener
Brahms-Fest 1921" Zeitschrift für Musik 88/11 (1.6.
1921) pp. 273-77. Descriptive analysis.
(e) i) report (on 1933 Auflage): "Literatur um Johannes
Brahms" Die Musik (Berlin) 25/8 (5.1933) pp. 605-07.
reports on 20, 61, 593.a, 959, 2624 by Max Fehling
and on Brahms's orchestral arrangements of Schubert
Songs [Hofmann nr. 171; McCorkle Anhang Ia, nos.
12, 13, 15] by H. Leichentritt.
(a) reprint: in 3186.c. pp. 45-47.
ii) report (on 1920 Auflage): see 40.e.ii.
iii) report (on 1920 Auflage): see 39.e.ii.
iv) report (on 1933 Auflage): see 20.e.ii.

62 #Orel, Alfred. Johannes Brahms. Ein Meister und sein Weg.
(Musikerreihe Bd. 3) Olten, Switzerland: Verlag Otto
Walter AG, 1948. 270 pp. fig., ind., notes. Includes comments on Brahms the man and an evaluation of Brahms on
the 50th anniversary of his death.

63 _____. Johannes Brahms. 1833-1897. Sein Leben in Bildern.
(Meyers Bild-Bändchen 32) Leipzig: Bibliographisches In-
stitut AG, 1937. 40, [38] pp. ill., facsim. Focuses on
Brahms's milieu, with 50 pictures.

64 *Ossovsky, A. [Aleksandr Viacheslavovich Ossovskiĭ] Johannes
Brahms. Biogr[aphische] Skizze. Petersburg: Verlag
der Akadem[ische]. Philharmonie, 1922.

65 *Oudemans, Christine. Uit het leven van Johannes Brahms.

Met een aanbevelend woord van Julius Röntgen. Haarlem:
De Erven F. Bohn, 1917. viii, 171 pp.
(d) *Oudemans. "Johannes Brahms en zijn tijdgenooten"
Caecilia (Utrecht) 73/?, 74/1,2 (15.10.1916; 15.,
1.-2.,1917) pp. 255+, 9-12, 80-91. notes. Discusses
Brahms and his milieu, focussing on von Bülow, the
Joachims and the Schumanns.

66 *Paladi, Marta. Brahms. Bucureşti: Editura muzicala, 1972.
163 pp. ill., notes.

67 Pauli, Walter. Brahms. (Moderne Geister nr. 2/3) Berlin:
Pan-Verlag, 1907. 136 pp. mus., notes. Focuses on the
works and Brahms's style; also comments on Brahms's historical position.

68 #Perger, Richard von. Brahms. (Musiker-Biographien. Bd.
27) Leipzig: Verlag von Philipp Reclam jun., [1908]. 85,
[2] pp. ill., notes. Includes personal recollections [see
1106]
(e) report: Conze, Joh[annes]. "Die verloren geglaubte
Messe von Joh[annes]. Brahms" Allgemeine Musikzeitung 35/36 (4.9.1908) p. 617. Discusses Perger's
comments on this work in his book, and his contact
with Marie Grimm and her holdings of her father's
manuscripts.

69 *Pfohl, Ferdinand. Johannes Brahms. Der Mensch und Künstler.
Hamburg: Hermann's Erben, 1933. 31 pp. Speech given
at the State Ceremony, 7.5.1933., as part of the
Reichs-Brahmsfest. [from 243]

70 Pulver, Jeffrey. Johannes Brahms. (Masters of Music) New
York and London: Harper & Brothers, 1926. xiii, [3],
345 pp. ill., ind., notes. Includes comment on Brahms
the man and composer.
*also: London: Kegan Paul, Trench, Trubner & Co., Ltd.,
1926. xiv, 376, [1] pp.
*also: London: Kegan Paul & Co.; J. Curwen & Sons, 1926.
*also: (Popular Edition) London: Kegan Paul, Trench, Trub-
ner & Co.; J. Curwen & Sons, 1933.

71 Rehberg, Walter and Paula. Johannes Brahms, sein Leben und
Werk. Zürich: Artemis-Verlag, 1947. 653 pp. ill., facsim.,
mus., ind., notes.
*2., von Paula Rehberg überarbeitete Auflage: Frankfurt a.M.,
Wien, Zürich: Büchergilde Gutenberg, 1963. 510 pp.
*also Zürich: Artemis Verlag, [1963].
*also Stuttgart: Deutscher Bücherbund, 1966.

72 Reich, Willi, ed. Johannes Brahms in Dokumenten zu Leben und

Werk. (Manesse Bibliothek der Weltliteratur) Zürich:
Manesse Verlag, 1975. 265, [1] pp. ill., facsim., notes.
Uses excerpts from the Brahms literature that describe
Brahms in his personal relationships or Brahms as musician.

73 Reimann, Heinrich. Johannes Brahms. (Berühmte Musiker.
Lebens- und Charakterbilder nebst Einführung in die Werke
der Meister. I) Berlin: Harmonie Verlagsgesellschaft für
Literatur und Kunst, [1897]. [5], 104, [3] pp. ill., facsim.,
mus., notes. Focuses on pre-1862 period; includes comments
on Brahms the man and composer. Also includes the Brahms
family tree and letters from Brahms to his mother (5) and
stepbrother (3) (1875-97). [letters in 837.d]
2. verbesserte und vermehrte Auflage: 1900. [3], 121 pp.
Uses new sources in biography; includes letters from Brahms
to Schumann (8) (1853-55). [letters in 1179]
*3. verbesserte und vermehrte Auflage: 1903. 127 pp.
*4. Auflage, revidert und ergänzt von Bruno Schrader: 1911.
[4], 130, [1] pp.
*5. Auflage durchgesehen und ergänzt von Bruno Schrader:
Schlesische Verlagsanstalt (vorm. Schottlaender), [1919].
136 pp.
*6. Auflage durchgesehen ... Schrader: [1922]. 124 pp.
(c) excerpt (of 1903 Auflage in English translation by
Piero Weiss): in 913. pp. 328-30, 396. 2 letters,
Brahms to his parents [1862] and 1897.
(e) i) report (on 1898 Auflage): see 618.a.e.ii.
ii) report (on 1898 Auflage): see 618.a.e.iii.
iii) report (on 1898 Auflage): Swayne, Egbert. "An
Interesting Book about Brahms" Music (Chicago)
14/[2] (6.1898) pp. 155-64. ill.

74 *Rémy, Ives Ada. Brahms. Paris: Librairie Hachette, n.d.
(b) *Spanish translation by Felipe Ximénez de Sandoval:
(Clásicos de la música) Madrid: Espasa-Calpe SA,
1977. 160 pp.
*2.ª ed.: 1981.

75 #Robertson, Alec. Brahms. ([Novello's] Biographies of Great
Musicians) London: Novello and Company Limited, [1939].
16 pp. notes. Includes comments on Brahms the man and
his historical position.

76 Rostand, Claude. Brahms. ([Collection] Amour de la musique)
Paris: Editions Le Bon Plaisir Librairie Plan, 1954-55. 2
vols. mus., ind., notes, discog. An introduction to Brahms
for the French reader; historical information based on 39
and 48.
(d) Rostand. Brahms. Préface de Brigitte et Jean Massin.
[Paris: Librairie Arthème] Fayard, 1978. 725,
[16] pp. Omits discog. Reprint of 1954-55 text with

new comments on Brahms and France, Brahms as
composer, his German personality, and his milieu.

77 *Ruiz Tarazona, Andrés. Johannes Brahms: un poeta solitario.
     (Colección músicos 4) Madrid: Real musical, 1974. 77,
     [2] pp. ill.

78 Schauffler, Robert Haven. The Unknown Brahms. His Life,
     Character and Works; Based on New Material. New York:
     Dodd, Mead and Company, 1933. xiv, 560 pp. ill., facsim.,
     mus., ind., notes. Discusses Brahms's historical position
     and incorporates previously unpublished information on
     Brahms's personality, including a psychological explanation
     of Brahms's attitude towards women. The author also gives
     details on his research methods.
     *issues: 1934, 1936
     *also: New York: Crown Publishers, 1940.
     (a) reprint (of 1933 Edition): Westport, Ct.: Greenwood
          Press Publishers, 1972.
     (b) *German translation (of ? Auflage): Schauffler, Robert
          H. Der unbekannte Brahms. Jörl: G. Ewald
          Schroeder, 1974.
     (c) i) excerpt (of 1933 Edition): Schauffler. "Brahms,
             Poet and Peasant" Musical Quarterly 18/4 (10.1932)
             pp. 547-48. ill., notes.
         ii) excerpt (of 1933 Edition): Schauffler. "Brahms
             the Selfless Musician" Etude 55/1 (1.1937) p. 62.
             Describes Brahms's flippant attitude towards his own
             work.
     (e) i) report (on 1933 Edition): "A New Work on Brahms"
             New York Times 80/26,888 (6.9.1931) Section 8, p.
             7. Describes Schauffler's research.
         ii) report (on 1933 Edition): Thompson, Oscar. "New
             Light on Signor Crescendo and Onkel Bähmsen"
             Musical America 54/13 (8.1934) pp. 3-18. "Brahms
             the Man": p. 18. ill.

79 Scherwatzky, Robert. Johannes Brahms. (Schöpferische
     Niederdeutsche Bd. 4) Osnabrück: Verlag A. Fromm,
     [1941]. 72 pp. ill., notes.

80 Sell, Sophie Charlotte von. Johannes Brahms. Ein deutscher
     Künstler. Stuttgart: J. F. Steinkopf, [1931]. 145, [1]
     pp. notes.

81 *Siegmund-Schultze, Walther. "Untersuchungen zum Brahmsstil
     und Brahmsbild" Phil.F. diss., Universität Halle, 1951. 182
     pp.
     (d) Siegmund-Schultze. Johannes Brahms. Eine Biographie.
          Leipzig: VEB Deutscher Verlag für Musik, 1966.
          281, [2] pp. ill., mus., ind., notes. Includes

comments on Brahms the composer. Anhang contains
excerpts from 983, 1179, 1215, 1280 and analyses of
Op. 59, no. 8, and Op. 117, no. 1.
*2. Auflage: 1974.
*[3. Auflage:] 1980.

82 *Specht, Richard. Johannes Brahms. Leben und Werk eines
deutschen Meisters. Hellerau: Avalun-Verlag, [1928].
397 pp. ill., facsim., mus. Includes reprint of 3013.
[from 82.b]
(b) English translation by Eric Blom: Johannes Brahms.
London and Toronto: J. M. Dent and Sons, Ltd.;
New York: E. P. Dutton & Co. Inc., 1930. viii,
[6], 371, [1] pp. Omits mus., adds notes. Includes
personal recollections of Brahms.
(e) i) report: Ehrlich, Leonard. "Brahms, Cre-
ator and Man" Saturday Review of Literature
7/11 (4.10.1930) pp. 174-75.
ii) report: Trend, J. B. "Brahms" Criterion
10/38 (10.1930) pp. 140-46. notes.
(c) #excerpt: Specht. "Späne zu einem Brahmsbuch" Die
Musikwelt (Hamburg) 9/4 (1.4.1929) pp. 2-5 (volume
pp. 154-57).

83 Stanford, Sir Charles V[illiers]. Brahms. (The Mayfair Biographies no. 2) London: Chappell & Co. Ltd., n.d. [26]
pp. ill., facsim., fig., notes. Biographical information
based on 39 and 48; includes comments on Brahms's historical
position.
also: London: Murdoch, [192-?]. 28 pp. Omits fig.
*issues (Chappell Edition): [1947].

84 *Stare, Ivar. Brahms. (Musikens mästare) Stockholm: Albert
Bonnier Förlag, 1955. 222, [1] pp. ind.
(b) i)*Danish translation by K. and H. Riis-Vestergaard:
København: Nyt Nordisk Forlag, 1956. 239 pp.
ii) *Finnish translation: Helsinki: Suomen Kaurinkoski,
1959.

85 Steiner, A. "Johannes Brahms. Teil 1,2" Neujahrsblatt der
allgemeinen Musikgesellschaft in Zürich nos. 86, 87 (1898,
1899) pp. 1-38, 1-47. ill., notes. Includes comments on
Brahms the composer.
(e) i) report: "Erinnerungen an Johannes Brahms" Neue
Musikzeitung 19/5 (24.2.1898) pp. 55-56.
ii) report: see 3102.
iii) report: see 618.a.e.iii.
iv) report: "Die Tonwerke von Johannes Brahms ..."
Neue Musikzeitung 20/9 (27.4.1899) pp. 111-12.
Discusses Steiner's comments on Brahms's works.

86   Thomas, Wolfgang A.   [Wolfgang Alexander Thomas-San-Galli]
     Johannes Brahms. Eine musikpsychologische Studie in fünf
     Variationen. Strassburg: J.H.Ed. Heitz (Heitz und Mündel),
     1905. 120 pp. ill., notes. Includes comments on Brahms
     the composer and excerpts on Brahms and composing from
     the Brahms literature.
     (c) excerpt: Thomas. "Johannes Brahms als Mensch und
          Künstler" Neue Zeitschrift für Musik 73/29/30 (Bd.
          102) (25.7.1906) pp. 621-24. notes. Includes Ab-
          schnitt II and IV.
     (d) *incorporates?: Thomas. Freiburger Tagblatt (1904).
          Includes Abschnitt II.[from 86]

87   Thomas-San-Galli, W[olfgang]. A[lexander]. Johannes Brahms.
     München: R. Piper & Co., 1912. xii, 278 pp. ill., facsim.,
     mus., ind. Popular biography; includes comments on Brahms
     the composer.
     *4. Auflage: 1919.
     *5. Auflage: 1922.
     (c) excerpt (of 1912 Auflage): Thomas-San-Galli. "Brahms:
          Die letzten Monologe" Der Merker (Wien) 3/21 (11.1912)
          pp. 800-04. Discusses Brahms's last years.

88   Tiénot, Yvonne. Brahms. Son vrai visage. [Preface by Claude
     Rostand?] (Pour mieux connaître [12]) Paris: Henry Lemoine
     et Cie, 1968. 447 pp. ill., facsim., mus., ind., notes.

89   *Uyldert, [Iman] Erik. Geen huis, geen vaderland. Het leven
     van Johannes Brahms (1833-1897). (Sonatinereeks. Levens
     van beroemde componisten verteld aan jonge mensen. no. 12)
     Tilburg: Nederlands boekhuis, 1953. 190 pp.

90   #Vogel, Bernhard. Johannes Brahms. Sein Lebensgang und
     eine Würdigung seiner Werke. (Musikheroen der Neuzeit IV)
     Leipzig: Max Hesse's Verlag, 1888. viii, 83, [1] pp. ill.,
     ind. Includes comments on Brahms the man and his historical
     position.

91   *Wallner, L[eopold]. Johannes Brahms. Notice biographique et
     critique. Bruxelles: Schott frères, 1909. 21 pp.

See also 111.d., 251, 649, 1179.c.ii, 1324.

See also "Brahms in Fiction" in VI.B.

     2. Serial and Section Materials

Juvenile literature: 102, 106, 112, 113, 143, 156, 201.

92 *Musical Herald (London) (1911).

93 *Bach, Beethoven, Brahms. Translated by E[gbert]. Schneider,
    H[artmut]. Albrecht, H[ans].-J[oachim]. Thier. (Bol'shaia
    sovetskaia entsiklopediia. Reihe Kunst und Literatur. 18)
    Berlin: Verlag der Nation, 1953. 33 pp. ill. [German
    translation of articles in Bol'shaia sovetskaia entsiklopediia
    2. izdája 51 Tomov ([Moskva:] Bol'shaia sovetskaia entsiklo-
    pediia, [1950]-58])
    *also: Berlin: Akademischer-Verlag, 1953.

94 *Bazaroff. "Brahms" Fővárosi lapok (Budapest) (10.12.1879).
    gives details on Brahms's life and comments on works per-
    formed at Budapest concerts, 12.1879 (Opp. 15, 60, 73).
    [from 241]

95 Bekker, Paul. "Johannes Brahms" Musik für Alle 7/3 (Nr. 75
    der Folge) [(1911)] pp. 37-40. ill. Includes comments on
    Brahms the man and composer, his musical style and links to
    past tradition.

96 #Berten, Walter. "Johannes Brahms. 7. Mai 1833 geb[oren].
    in Hamburg - in Wien gest[orben]. 3. April 1897" Deutsche
    Musiker-Zeitung (Berlin) 58/15 (9.4.1927) pp. 326-29. ill.
    Surveys Brahms's life with comments on Brahms as a composer
    and a romantic.

97 Biernatzki, Johannes. "Johannes Brahms" Illustrirte Zeitung
    (Leipzig) Bd. 66/1717 (27.5.1876) p. 421. Includes comments
    on Brahms the composer and his musical style.

98 Blom, Eric. "Brahms" in Blom. Some Great Composers. London,
    New York [et al]: Oxford University Press, 1944. pp. 98-
    106.
    *issues: 1945-49.
    *[New Edition with reset text:] 1961.
    *issues: 1962-79. pp. 113-22. [from 1979 issue]
    (b) *Spanish translation by Ricard Boadella (of ? Edition):
    Galeriá de grandes compositores. (Colleccion el mástil
    5) Barcelona: Editorial Miguel Arimany, [1962].

99 *Bouws, Jan. "Johannes Brahms" Ruiter 1/39 (30.1.1948) pp.
    44-45. ill.

100 *Bouws, J[an]. "Johannes Brahms. (Musiekmeesters 5)"
     Huis [en haard] 42/2182 (17.1.1964) pp. 46-49. ill.

101 *[Otto Neitzel] "Brahms" Kölnische Zeitung (4.4.1900?).

102 "Brahms (Little Biographies for Club Meetings no. 21)" Etude
     47/10 (10.1929) p. 778. ill. Includes comments on Brahms
     the composer.

103 *Brauer, Max. "Johannes Brahms" Badische Presse (Karlsruhe)
(25.2.1911).

104 Brian, Havergal. "Johannes Brahms. Birth Centenary. Born
1833. Died 1897." Musical Opinion and Music Trade Review
56/667 (4.1933) pp. 596-98. ill. Discusses Brahms's life
up to 1862 and comments on Brahms the man.
(d) continued by: Brian. "Johannes Brahms. The
Musician. Born 1833. Died 1897." Musical Opinion
and Music Trade Review 56/668 (5.1933) pp. 688-89.
ill. Continues account of Brahms's life and death
up to the settling of his Nachlass. Also discusses
reception accorded orchestral works, and Brahms's
opinion of his musical contemporaries.

105 Buenzod, Emmanuel, see 2810.5

106 Burch, Gladys and John Walcott. "Johannes Brahms. Thinker
in Music. Born 1833-Died 1897" in Burch and Wolcott. A
Child's Book of Famous Composers. New York: A. S.
Barnes & Company, 1939. pp. 131-36. ill.
Reissued as: Burch and Wolcott. Famous Composers for Young
People. New York: Dodd, Mead & Company, 1939. Juvenile
literature with discussion of selected works.
*issue (of Dodd Mead reissue): 1945.

107 #Charles, M. [Max Chop] "Dr. Johannes Brahms" in Charles.
Zeitgenössische Tondichter. Studien und Skizzen. Leipzig:
Verlag der Rossberg'schen Buchhandlung, 1888. pp. 167-92.
Includes comments on Brahms the man and composer, and his
historical position. Includes reprint of 317.

107.5#Cherbuliez, A. -E. [Antoine Elisée] "Johannes Brahms geboren
am 7. Mai 1833. Ein Gang durch sein Leben und Werk"
Schweizerische musikpädagogische Blätter 22 (1933) pp. 130-
35, 150-54. ill. Overview of life, focusing on how environ-
mental factors affected Brahms and how they are reflected
in his music; includes discussion of Brahms's features over
the years, based on photographs and drawings in 721.
(a) *reprint: Cherbuliez. "Brahms. Wege zum Verständnis
seiner Kunst" Bündner Haushaltungs- und Familienbuch (1934).
(a) *reprint: Cherbuliez. Johannes Brahms. Wege
... Kunst. Chur: Bischofberger & Co.,
1934. 31 pp. ill.

108 *Church, Richard. "Brahms" Radio Times [before 1931].
(d) *incorporated into: Church. "Brahms" in The Men
Behind the Music. C[larence]. Henry Warren, ed.
London: G. Routledge & Sons Ltd., 1931. pp.
31-40.

(a) reprint: Port Washington, N.Y./London: Kennikat Press, 1970. Focuses on life prior to 1862; includes comments on Brahms the man and composer.

109 *Ciomac, Emanoil. Poeţii armoniei. Bucureşti: Fundatia pentru literatura si arta Regele Carol II, 1936. 264 pp. *Ediţia a 2-a: Ingrijita de Silviu Gavrilă. Bucureşti: Editura muzicala, 1974. 247 pp.

110 "The Composer of the Month" Etude 71/5 (5.1953) p. 3. ill.

111 Cooke, James Francis. "Johannes Brahms" in Cooke. Music Masters Old and New. A Series of Educational Biographies of the Greatest Musicians. Philadelphia: Theo[dore]. Presser Co., 1918. pp. 13-14. ill., facsim., notes. Includes very brief comments on Brahms's family, Brahms the man and composer (also excerpt of 39) and the Brahms-Wagner controversy
(d) *Cooke. Johannes Brahms. A Short Biography. (Etude Musical Booklet Library) Philadelphia: Theodore Presser Co., 1928. 16 pp.

112 *Dahl, Titt Fasmer. [Mathilde Fasmer Dahl] Eventry i toner. Chopin, Schumann, Brahms. Tegninger av Chrix Dahl. Oslo: Aschehoug, 1950. 183 pp. ill. [Juvenile literature.]
(b) *Swedish translation by Ulrika Widmark?: Musikens trollmakt. (Samlung 3: Chopin, Schumann, Brahms.). (Barnbiblioteket saga. 256) Stockholm: Svensk Läraretidning, 1954. 255 pp.

113 *_____. Musikkens store B'er. Bach, Beethoven, Brahms. Tegninger av Chrix Dahl. Oslo: Gyldendal Norsk Forlag, n.d.
Ny revidert utgave: 1970. "Johannes Brahms": pp. 85-134, [1] pp. ill. Juvenile literature.

114 Davey, Henry. "Johannes Brahms" Musical Herald (London) no. 866 (1.5.1920) pp. 199-200. Also discusses Brahms the man and Brahms and Wagner.

115 Davidson, J. A. "Johannes Brahms" Musical Standard Illustrated Series 23/592 (68/2127) (6.5.1905) p. 280. Includes comments on Brahms's musical style and historical position.

116 #De Gibert, Vicents M.a. "Johannes Brahms" Revista musical catalana 30/360 (12.1933) pp. 489-95. Includes discussion of Brahms's relationships with Dvořák and Wagner.

117 *Deiters, Hermann. "Johannes Brahms" Sammlung musikalischer Vorträge Neue Reihe [2. Reihe]/23 u[nd]. 24 [(1880)] pp.

[319]-74. notes. [from 117.a]
(a) reprint (of Sammlung): Nendeln: Kraus Reprint,
1976. Discusses Brahms's life and his works up
to the time of Op. 79; also discusses and evaluates
Brahms as a composer.
(b) i) English translation, with Additions by Rosa Newmarch.
Edited with a Preface by J[ohn] A[lexander] Fuller-
Maitland: Deiters. Johannes Brahms. A Biographical Sketch. London: T. Fisher Unwin, 1888.
160 pp. ill., notes. Includes postscript by editor
containing descriptive analysis of Opp. 80-97.
(c) i) excerpt: in 2894. p. 6 (volume p. 246).
ii) excerpt: in 1871.
(e) report: "Johannes Brahms" Spectator [61]/3110
(4.2.1888) pp. 174-75.
ii) French translation by Mme. H. Fr.: Deiters.
Johannes Brahms. Leipzig et Bruxelles: Breitkopf
& Haertel, éditeurs, 1884. 100 pp. Includes postscript by translator containing an updated list of
published works.
(d) *continuation: Deiters. "Johannes Brahms. II"
Sammlung musikalischer Vorträge VI Bd. [6. Reihe]
/63 [(1898)] pp. [73]-112. notes. [from 117.d.a]
(a) reprint: see 117.a. Updates account of life
and discusses more recently published
works.
(e) i) report: see 618.a.e.ii.
ii) report: see 618.a.e.iii.
(e) i) report: Chr. [Friedrich Chrysander] "H. Deiters
über Johannes Brahms" Allgemeine musikalische
Zeitung 16/22, 23 (1.,8.;6.; 1881) cols. 337-39,
353-57. notes.
ii) *report: Hanslick, Eduard. "Neuestes über Brahms"
Neue freie Presse (Wien) (17.3.1880).

118 *Dettelbach, H[ans v.]. "Johannes Brahms" Alpenländische
Monatshefte (Graz) [5?] (1927/28) pp. 503-06.

119 *Dole, Nathan Haskell. "Johannes Brahms (1833-1897)" in Dole.
Famous Composers. Revised and Enlarged Edition. New
York: Thomas Y. Crowell Company, [1925].
3rd Edition Revised and Enlarged: 1929. pp. 547-71. ill.
Includes comments on Brahms the man and his musical style.
*issue: 1934.
*4th Edition with Appendix by David Ewen: 1936.
(a) reprint (of 4th Edition): (Essay Index Reprint Series)
Freeport, N.Y.: Books for Libraries Press, 1968.

120 #Druskin, M[ihail]. "Brams" Sovetskaia muzyka [18]/12 (12.1954)
pp. 73-83. mus., notes.

121 *Ehrlich, Heinrich. "Johannes Brahms" Nord und Sud Bd. 21

(1880) pp. 242-51.

(d) reworked: Ehrlich. in Ehrlich. Aus allen Tonarten.
Studien über Musik. Berlin: Verlag von Brachvogel
& Ranft, 1888. pp. 73-86. notes. Surveys life
up to 1863 and takes a philosophical look at the
contemporary state of music and Brahms as composer.

122 #Ehrmann, Alfred von. "Brahms'sche Weihnachten" Die Musik
(Berlin) 29/3 (12.1936) pp. 161-64. Traces Brahms's life
by describing his Christmases: where they were spent and
with whom.

123 #Elling, Catherinus. "Johannes Brahms" Ringeren [2]/3 (1899)
pp. 26-29.

124 *Elson, Louis C[harles]. "Johannes Brahms" in Elson. Great
Composers and Their Work. [(Music Lovers' Series)]
Boston: L. C. Page and Company (Incorporated), 1898.
pp. 252-61. ind. [from 124.a]
*issue: 1910.
(a) reprint (of 1898 Edition): (Essay Index Reprint Series)
Freeport, N.Y.: Books for Libraries Press, 1972.
Includes comments on Brahms the man and his historical position.

125 Erb, J[ohn]. Lawrence. "1833 Johannes Brahms 1897. The
Classical Spirit in Modern Music" Etude 25/6 (6.1907) pp.
359-61. ill., facsim. Includes comments on Brahms the man
and his historical position.

126 *Ferris, George T[itus]. "Brahms and Gade" in Ferris. Great
German Composers. Bach to Dvorak. New Edition Revised
and Illustrated. New York: D. Appleton and Company,
1895. [total paging: vi, [2], [7]-244 pp.] ill.
*issues: 1897-1899, 1911.

127 Forsblom, Enzio, see 1760.5

128 *Fuller-Maitland, J[ohn]. A[lexander]. "Johannes Brahms" in
Fuller-Maitland. Masters of German Music. (Masters of
Contemporary Music) London: Osgood, McIlvaine & Co.,
1894. pp. 1-95. ill., facsim. [from New York 1895 issue]
*also: New York: Charles Scribner's Sons, 1894.
*issue (London Edition): 1895.
issues (New York Edition): 1895-1896. series omitted. Includes comments on Brahms's character, influence, musical
style and historical position.
(a) i) *reprint (of New York 1894 Edition): Boston:
Milford House, [1973].
ii) *reprint (of New York 1894 Edition): Boston:
Longwood Press, 1977.

(e) report (on New York 1894 Edition): [Henry T. Finck]
"Brahms and Brahmsian" Nation (New York) 59/1529
(18.10.1894) pp. 289-90. Also comments on evaluating
Brahms's position as composer.

129 *Funk, Heinrich. "Brahms" Das Orchester (Berlin) 6/13 (1929).

130 *Furtwängler, Wilhelm. "Der grosse Brahms" Ochsenkopf (Hof)
no. 2 (1952/53) pp. 1-2.

131 *Furtwängler, W[ilhelm]. "Johannes Brahms" Der Türmer 43
(1940/41) p. 547.

132 Gale, Harlow. "Johannes Brahms" The Critic 29[39]/[6]
(12.1901) pp. 523-28. ill., notes.

133 *Glover, Cedric Howard. "Johannes Brahms" Parents Review.
(d) incorporated into: Glover. "Johannes Brahms" in
Glover: The Term's Music. (The Musicians Bookshelf)
London: Kegan Paul, Trench, Trubner & Co. Ltd.,
J. Curwen & Sons Ltd.; New York: E. P. Dutton &
Co., 1925. pp. 89-100.

134 *Gröhn, W., see 2376.5

135 Groves, Cecil T. "Johannes Brahms" London Quarterly and
Holborn Review 158/[3] (6th Series--vol. 2) (7.1933) pp.
342-50. Includes comments on Brahms's character and
historical position; Op. 45 highlighted.

136 Gumprecht, Otto. "Johannes Brahms" Westermanns illustrierte
deutsche Monatshefte für das gesamte geistige Leben der
Gegenwart Bd. 63/373,374 (Jahrg. 32) (10.,11.;1887) pp.
109-21, 233-43. Includes comments on Brahms the composer.

137 *Guttmann, Alfred. "Johannes Brahms" Deutsche Arbeiter-
Sängerzeitung (Berlin) 28/11 [(1927)].

138 *Hadow, Sir W[illiam]. H[enry]. "Johannes Brahms" in Hadow.
Studies in Modern Music. Second Series. Frederick Chopin,
Antonin Dvořák, Johannes Brahms. New York: Macmillan
Company?, 1894. pp. [227]-304. Ill., notes. [from London
1926 Edition]
10th Edition: New York: The Macmillan Company, [1923].
Includes comments on Brahms's historical position and musical
style.
*[11th Edition: 1925]
12th Edition: [193-?].
*also: London: Seeley, 1895.
*? Edition: London: Seeley and Co., Limited, 1897.
4th Edition: 1902.

*5th-8th Editions: London: Seeley and Co., 1904-1910.
*9th-10th Editions: London: Seeley, Service and Co., 1913-
1923.
11th Impression. Pocket Edition: London: Seeley, Service
and Co., Limited, 1926.
(a) *reprint (of London 1926 Edition): Port Washington,
N.Y.: Kennikat Press, [1970].
(c) excerpt (of ? Edition): in 2821 pp. 9-10 (volume pp.
201-02). notes.

139 *Hampe, Johann Christoph. "Später Dank an Johannes Brahms"
Sonntagsblatt. Unabhängige Wochenzeitung für Politik,
Wirtschaft und Kultur (Hamburg) no. 20 (1958) p. 12.

140 *Hasse, Karl. "Johannes Brahms" in Hasse. Von deutschen
Meistern. Zur Neugestaltung unseres Musiklebens im neuen
Deutschland. Ausgewählte Aufsätze. (Von deutscher Musik.
Bd. 44) Regensberg: Gustav Bosse Verlag, 1934. [total
paging: 131 pp.]

141 #Hess, Viktor. "Meister Brahms" Die Garbe. Schweizerisches
Familienblatt (Basel) 16 (1933) pp. 458-61. ill. Includes
comments on Brahms's milieu.

142 *Hoffmann, E. "Brahms" Freiburger Theaterblätter (1935/36)
p. 138.

143 *Hohlbaum, Robert. Brahms-Bruckner-Strauss. (Deutsche
Jugendbücherei 436) Berlin: Hillger, 1933. 31 pp.

144 Holl, Karl. "Johannes Brahms. Zum 100. Geburtstag" Frankfurter Zeitung 77/338 (7.5.1933) 2. Morgenblatt. Dreimalige
Ausgabe. p. 5. ill., facsim. A chronicle of Brahms's
life.

145 #Huettner, Dr. "Niedersachsens Seele in der Musik. Ein Erinnerungsblatt an den 25. Todestag von Johannes Brahms
(3. April 1897)" Weser-Zeitung (Bremen) 29/274 (20.4.1922)
Morgenausgabe pp. 1-2 [across page bottoms]. Fiction:
presents Brahms reminiscing on his life; author focuses
on Brahms's Germanic nature.

146 Huneker, James [Gibbons]. "Johannes Brahms" Musician
(Boston) 20/10 (10.1915) pp. 623-24, 675. ill. Includes
comments on Brahms the man. Article consists of excerpts
from Huneker's remarks in J. Brahms. Forty Songs and
J. Brahms. Selected Piano Compositions, both in The
Musicians Library series, (Boston: O. Ditson Co., n.d.).

147 Imbert, Hugues. "Johannes Brahms (Profils de musiciens)"
L'Indépendance musicale et dramatique 1/5,8 (1.5. and 15.6.;

1887) pp. 147-56, 230-37. notes. Includes comments on
Brahms in relation to Wagner and Beethoven, and on Brahms's
musical style.
(a) #reprint: Imbert. "Johannes Brahms" in Imbert.
Profils de musiciens. P. Tschaikowsky.-J. Brahms.
E. Chabrier.-Vincent d'Indy. J. Fauré.-C. Saint-Saëns.
Avec une préface par Edouard Schuré. Paris: Librairie Fischbacher, Librairie Sagot, 1888. pp. 9-24.
(d) i) #incorporated into: Imbert. Etude sur Johannès
Brahms. Avec le catalogue de ses oeuvres. Paris:
Librairie Fischbacher, 1894. 32 pp. notes. Text to
p. 17. Also includes comments on 968 and on Brahms's
works as played in Paris.
ii) see: 37.
iii) Imbert. "Johannes Brahms. (1833-1897).
L'Avènement d'une renommée musicale" Revue bleue 40^e
année - 4e série 19/3 (17.1.1903) pp. 79-84. Includes
comments on Brahms's musical style and historical
position.

148 *"Jan Brahms" Tygodnik ilustrowany no. 177 (1893) p. 316. ill.

149 *[Richard Heuberger] "Johannes Brahms" Deutsche Kunst- und
Musikzeitung (Wien) [20] (15.5.1893).
(a) *reprint: Heuberger, Richard. "Johannes Brahms.
(Zu seinem 60. Geburtstage.)" in Heuberger.
Musikalische Skizzen. (Musikalische Studien VI.)
Leipzig: [H.] Seemann [Nachfolger], 1901. pp. 56-65.
notes. [from 241 and 149.a.a]
(a) reprint: Heuberger. In Musikalische Studien
VI in Musikalische Studien [10 nos. in 2 vols.]
Nendeln: Kraus Reprint, 1976. Surveys
Brahms's life and milieu; includes comments
on musical style, historical position, and compares Brahms with Wagner.
(d) Heuberger, Richard. Universum 10/21 (1894) cols.
2025-27. Surveys Brahms's life up to the 1850's;
includes comments on Brahms the composer and his
musical style.

150 [Hermann Kretzschmar] "Johannes Brahms. 1.-[4.]" Die Grenzboten 43[29-33] (Bd. 3) ([21.,28.;7. and 12.,19.;8.;]
1884) pp. 123-32, 167-79, 276-84, 314-28. notes. Includes
comments on Brahms's musical style and his historical position.
(a) reprint: Kretzschmar, Hermann. "Johannes Brahms
(1884)" in Kretzschmar. Gesammelte Aufsätze über
Musik und Anderes aus den Grenzboten. Alfred
Heuss, ed. Bd. 1. Leipzig: Fr. Wilh. Grunow,
1910. pp. 151-207.

151 "Johannes Brahms" Musician (Philadelphia) 2/5 (5.1897) p. 117.

152 "Johannes Brahms" Niederrheinische Musikzeitung 12/15 (9.4.
1864) pp. 117-19. Introduction to this "new" composer,
covering life and works to 1862; includes comments on his
reception.
(d) summary (in English): Roores, Groker. Musical
World (London) 42/19 (7.5.1864) pp. 297-99. notes.
(a) reprint: "Johannes Brahms. To The Editor
of the London Musical World" Dwight's
Journal of Music 24/8 (Whole no. 607)
(9.7.1864) p. 269. notes.
(c) *excerpt: in 2843 p. 271.

153 "Johannes Brahms" Temple Bar 132/536 (7.1905) pp. 25-28.
Includes comments on Brahms the composer.

154 [Theodor Helm] "Johannes Brahms. Geboren 7. März (sic)
1833 zu Hamburg. I. Biographisches" Musikalisches Wochenblatt 1/3 (14.1.1870) pp. 40-41. ill., notes. Discusses
Brahms's life 1853- ; describes Schumann's thoughts on
Brahms, focuses on Brahms in Wien.
(d) continued: Helm, Theodor. "Johannes Brahms. Geboren 7. März (sic) 1833 zu Hamburg. II. Charakteristik" Musikalisches Wochenblatt 1/4 (21.1.1870)
pp. 56-59. ill. Analyzes music in light of Schumann's "Neue Bahnen" article, and compares it to
the music of Rubinstein and Wagner.

155 *Johansen, David Monrad. David Monrad Johansen i skrift og
tale. Øystein Gaukstad and Ole Mørk Sandvik, eds.
Oslo: Tanum, 1968. 144 pp.

156 Jones, G, Kirkham. "Johannes Brahms. (1833-1897.)"
School Music Review 35/416 (15.1.1927) pp. 255-58. ill.,
notes. Juvenile literature: discusses Brahms's life, with
comments on his musical style and on selected songs.

157 Jullien, Adolphe. "Johannes Brahms 1833-1897" Le Courrier
musical 8/11,12 (Nouvelle série) (1.,15.;6.;1905) pp. 333-37,
361-65. Includes comments on Brahms as classisist.

158 _____. "Johannes Brahms. 1833-1897" Revue internationale
de musique [1]/2 (15.3.1898) pp. 102-14. ill., facsim. Includes comments on Brahms's historical position and his
relationship with Wagner.

159 Kelterborn, Louis. "Johannes Brahms" in Famous Composers
and Their Works. Volume 3. John Knowles Paine, Theodore
Thomas and Karl Klauser, eds. Boston: J. B. Millet
Company, 1891. pp. 503-14. ill., facsim.

160 *Klein, Ida. [Isabella Nowotny] Kritische Studien über berühmte
Persönlichkeiten. Prague: H. Mercy, 1882. 236 pp.

161 Kobbé, Gustav. "Johannes Brahms" Forum 23 (7.1897) pp.
577-85. Includes comments on Brahms and Wagner.

162 Köstlin, H. A. "Johannes Brahms" Daheim 18/16 (21.1.1882)
pp. 254-56.

163 *Krummeich, Paul. "Johannes Brahms" University of Pennsylvania
General Magazine and Historical Chronicle 34 (4.1932) pp.
377-90.

164 *Kruziński and Wincenty. "Jan Brahms" Przeglad tygodniowy
zycia społecznego, literatury i sztuk pieknych (Warszawa)
no. 32 (1869) pp. 270-71.

165 La Mara. [Ida Maria Lipsius] "Johannes Brahms" Westermann's
illustrirte deutsche Monatshefte 37/219 (3. Folge Bd. 5/27)
(12.1874) pp. 292-316. ill., notes. Focuses on early life
and discusses music up to Op. 59; includes comments on
Brahms the composer.
(a) reprint: in La Mara. Musikalische Studienköpfe aus
der Jüngstvergangenheit und Gegenwart. Charakterzeichnungen von Moscheles, David, ... Brahms,
Tausig, nebst den Verzeichnissen ihrer Werke.
[Bd. 3] Leipzig: Heinrich Schmidt & Carl Günther,
1875. pp. 233-97. omits ill., adds fig.
(d) *reworked: in La Mara. Musikalische Studienköpfe. Dritter Band: Jüngstvergangenheit
und Gegenwart. n.p., n.d.
*4. umgearbeitete Auflage: 1878.
5. umgearbeitete Auflage: [1878]. pp. 241-307.
*6. Auflage: [1894-1902].
*7. Auflage: [1910].
(b) *Russian translation by A. Zheliabuzhs-
koĭ (of ? Auflage): Muzykal'no-
kharakteristicheкĭe étiudy. Moskva:
n.p., 1889?.
(c) *excerpt (of 7. Auflage): Johannes
Brahms. Neubearbeiteter Einzel-
druck aus den Musikalischen
Studienköpfen. 8. Auflage.
(Breitkopf & Härtel Musikbücher.
Kleine Musikerbiographien) Leipzig:
Breitkopf & Härtel, 1911. 54 or
61 pp.
9. Auflage: 1919. 57 pp. series
omitted. Includes discussion of
later works, and Brahms's style
and milieu.
10. und 11. Auflage: 1921. ilL, notes.
(c) excerpt (of 1911 Auflage in
English translation by
Phoebe R[ogoff]. Cave):

Marxsen, Eduard. "A
Hard Beginning" in 758.
pp. 329-311.

166 Law, Frederic S. "Johannes Brahms" Musician (Boston) 9/6
(6.1904) pp. 207-08. Brahms's life with discussion of his
musical style.

167 *Leinburg, Mathilde v. "Wer war Joh[annes]. Brahms?"
Wiener Mode.

168 *Leonard, Richard Anthony. "Brahms 1833-97" in Leonard.
Stream of Music. Garden City, N.Y.: Doubleday Doran
and Co., Inc., 1943. pp. 252-83.
*also: London, New York, et. al.: Jarrolds Limited, 1945.

169 *Levik, B[oris]. V[eniaminovich]. "I. Brams" in Levik.
Muzykal'naia literatura zarubezhnykh stran. Izdanze 5-e.
Moskva: Muzyka, [1976].
*also: Tbilisi: Ganatleba, 1976. [total paging: 453 pp.]
ill., mus.

170 #Limbert, K. E. "Brahms, 1833-1897" Parents Review [48]
(1.1938) pp. 43-50. notes. Discusses life up to early
1850's, with comments on selected works.
(d) #reworked: Limbert. Parents Review [56] (1.1946)
pp. 10-14. Omits reference to specific recordings,
some comments changed to allow for passing of World
War II.

171 Lissauer, Ernst. "Johannes Brahms. Zum Gedächtnis seines
hundertjährigen Geburtstags am 7. Mai" Illustrierte Zeitung
(Leipzig-Berlin) Bd. 180/4599 (4.5.1933) pp. 558-64. ill.,
facsim. Discusses Brahms's life, includes comments on his
musical style.

172 *Lissy, Th. "Brahms" Kunstgarten (Wien) 5 (1927) pp. 241-46.

173 Marnold, Jean. "Dialogues des morts. I. Mendelssohn, Brahms"
Le Mercure musical (Paris) 1/2 (1.6.1905) pp. 49-56. Written
in dialogue form.

174 Mason, Daniel Gregory. "The Work of Brahms" The Outlook
70/1 (4.1.1902) pp. 84-90. ill. Focuses on life before
1855, includes comments on Brahms the composer.
(a) *reprint: Mason. "Johannes Brahms" in Mason. From
Grieg to Brahms. Studies of Some Modern Composers
and Their Art. New York: The Outlook Company,
1902. pp. [173]-201. adds notes.
*also: New York: Macmillan Company, 1908.
*issues (Outlook Edition): 1903-1908.

*issues (Macmillan Edition): 1912-1924.
*New and Enlarged Edition: New York: Macmillan
Company, 1927. issue: 1936.
(d) reworked (from Outlook Edition, ? issue):
"Johannes Brahms. Born 1833: Died 1897"
Masters in Music 5/Part 29 (5.1905) pp.
[1]-6 (volume pp. 193-98) notes. Excerpts
of 174.a. plus new material on Brahms the
man.

175 "Masters of Music" [Illustrated by Ben Stahl] Coronet 27/1
(Whole no. 157) (11.1949) pp. 61-69. Brahms: pp. 66-67.
ill. Discusses life up until 1853, and Brahms the man.

176 *Meth, B. "Johannes Brahms" Pauliner-Zeitung (Leipzig) 43
(1931) p. 128.

177 *Meyer, Wilh[elm]. "Johannes Brahms" in Meyer. Charakter-
bilder grosser Tonmeister. Persönliches und Intimes aus
ihrem Leben und Schaffen. Für junge und alte Musikfreunde.
Vierter Band. Chopin/Brahms/Bruckner/Reger. Zerstreute
Blätter. Bielefeld und Leipzig: Verlag von Velhagen &
Klasing, 1920.
#2. verbesserte und vermehrte Auflage: 1926. pp. 37-89. ill.
Discusses life and includes comments on Brahms the man.

178 #Mila, Massimo "Johannes Brahms. (1833-1897)" La Cultura.
Rivista mensile di filosofia, lettere, arte (Roma) 12 (new
series vol. 5) (1933) pp. 562-72. notes. Includes comments
on Brahms's musical style.
(a) *reprint: in Mila. Cent'anni di musica moderna. (Collezione il pensiero 6322) Milano: Ed. Rosa e ballo,
1944. 289 pp.
(a) *reprint: New Preface by the Author. Torino:
Edizioni di Torino, 1981. 212 pp.

179 Moser, Hans Joachim. "Johannes Brahms - sein Werk und sein
Weg" Universitas 21/11 (11.1966) pp. 1161-70. Includes
comments on Brahms and folksong, and on his interest in
music of the old masters.

180 Moser, Hans Joachim, see 2405.5

181 *Naaff, A. "Johannes Brahms" Lyra (Wien) 13/1,3 (1889/90).

182 "The New Etude Gallery of Musical Celebrities" Etude 47/4
(4.1929) pp. 279-80. ill.

183 *Niemann, Walter. ["Johannes Brahms"] Schleswig-Holsteinischer
Kunst-Kalender (1917).

184 *Oberborbeck, Felix. "Offener Brief" Junge Musik (1955).

185 Pirani, Eugenio di. "Johannes Brahms (Secrets of Success of Great Musicians)" Etude 39/4 (4.1921) pp. 235-36. ill. Discusses life, and comments on Brahms the man; includes personal recollections. An attempt to discover what makes Brahms "tick".

186 Pulver, Jeffrey. "Brahms: A Short Biographical Sketch" Musical Times 74/1083 (5.1933) pp. 419-22. Surveys Brahms's life.

187 -r. [August Reiser] "Johannes Brahms" Neue Musikzeitung 2/7,8.4. Auflage [1.,15.;4.;]1881) pp. 61-62, 69-70. ill.

188 Rather, Francis Taylor. "Johannes Brahms" Etude 51/5 (5.1933) p. 358. ill. Poem telling of Brahms's life and his personal characteristics.

189 Reed, E. M. G. "Brahms (Lives of Great Musicians--XXVII.)" Music and Youth 3/5 (Y. & M. Series no. 87) (5.1923) pp. 95-96. ill. Focuses on life before 1855; also discusses Brahms's musical style.

190 _____. "The Story of Johannes Brahms and His Academic Festival Overture" Music and Youth 11/3 (3.1931) pp. 55-56. ill., mus. Focuses on life before 1855; also identifies student tunes in Op. 80.

191 *Refardt, Edgar. Johannes Brahms, Anton Bruckner, Hugo Wolf. Drei Wiener Meister des 19. Jahrhunderts. Ihr Leben und Werk in kurzen Biographien. Basel: Amerbach-Verlag, [1949]. 228 pp. (?) ill.

192 Reimerdes, Ernst Edgar. "Johannes Brahms. Zu seinem 25jährigen Todestag 3. April 1897" Neue preussische Zeitung (Kreuz-Zeitung) (Berlin) [75]/157 (2.4.1922) Morgenausgabe. Beilage. p.[1].

193 *Riemann, Hugo. "Johannes Brahms" Max Hesse's Deutscher Musiker-Kalender [13] (1898) p. 136.

194 *Roubakine, Boris. "Brahms. Sa vie. Son oeuvre." Schweizerische musikpädagogische Blätter 27 (1938) pp. 156-58, 187-91, 204-07.

195 *Rüdiger, Theo. "Brahms" Der Chorleiter (Hildburghausen) [8]/4 (1927).

196 S. B. [Selmar Bagge] "Johannes Brahms" Allgemeine musikalische Zeitung Neue Folge 1/27 (1.7.1863) cols. 461-67. notes. An introduction to Brahms and his music.

197 #Schabacher-Bleichröder, Anna. "Johannes-Brahms-Erinnerungen.
    Zum 25. Todestag, 4 April" Deutsche Musiker-Zeitung
    (Berlin) 53/12 (25.3.1922) p. 100. Focuses on pre-1862
    period; includes comments on Brahms the man.

198 #Scherwatzky, Robert. "Der Ausgang des 19. Jahrhunderts.
    Brahms und Reger/Bruckner/Hugo Wolf." in Scherwatzky.
    Die grossen Meister deutscher Musik in ihren Briefen und
    Schriften. Göttingen: Deuerlichsche Verlagsbuchhandlung,
    1939. pp. 292-319. Brahms: pp. 292-95, 298-306. notes.
    Includes excerpts from 816, 819, 1179.
    *3., wesentlich veränderte und vermehrte Auflage: [1942?].

199 *Schmid, Otto. "Johannes Brahms" Das Orchester (Dresden)
    [3] (10.6.1886).

200 *Schöne, A. "Grosse Musikergestalten der Romantik: Franz
    Schubert, Johannes Brahms, Frédéric Chopin, Robert Schu-
    mann" Welt-Stimmen (Stuttgart) 26 (1957) pp. 547-49.

201 Scholes, Percy A. "A Lesson in Brahms (Born 1833. Died
    1897)" School Music Review 31/362 (1.7.1922) pp. 22-24.
    Juvenile literature; includes comments on Brahms the man
    and his relationship with Wagner.

202 *Schonberg, Harold C. New York Times.
    (a) reprint: Schonberg. "Keeper of the Flame. Johannes
    Brahms" in Schonberg. The Lives of the Great
    Composers. New York: W. W. Norton & Co. Inc.,
    1970. pp. 274-88. ill. Includes comments on
    Brahms the man and composer, his milieu, and
    historical position.
    Revised Edition: New York, London: W. W. Norton
    & Co., 1981. pp. 296-310.

203 Schuricht, Carl. "Brahms. 1833-1897" in Les Musiciens
    celebres. Jean Lacroix, ed. (La Galerie des homme celebres
    1) Geneve: Editions d'Art Lucien Mazenod, 1948. pp. 228-
    31. ill. Includes comments on Brahms's musical style.
    (d) #Schuricht, Carol. "Itinerario de Brahms (1833-1897)"
    Ars. Revista de arte 17/79 (1957) pp. [2-8]. adds
    facsim.

204 Schwab, Frederick A. "Johannes Brahms" in The Music of the
    Modern World. Volume One. Text. Anton Seidl, ed.
    New York: D. Appleton and Company, 1895. pp. 176-78.
    ill. Includes comments on Brahms's historical position and
    Brahms in Bad Ischl, [Austria].

205 *Seibert, Willy. "Brahms" Rheinische Musik- und Theaterzeitung
    (Köln) 13/3 (1912) (?).

206 *Sharp, Robert Farquharson. Makers of Music. Biographical
     Sketches of the Great Composers with Chronological Summar-
     ies of Their Works, Portraits, Facsimiles of Their Composi-
     tions and a General Chronological Table. New York:
     Charles Scribner's Sons, 1898. 337 pp.
     *2nd Edition, revised: 1901. 3, [2], 237 pp.
     *3rd Edition, revised: 1905.
     *4th Edition, revised and enlarged: [1913]. 4, [2], 245 pp.
     Brahms: pp. 224-29.
     *also: London: W. Reeves, [1898]. 237 pp.
     *2nd Edition, revised: 1901.
     *3rd Edition, revised: 1905.
     *4th Edition, revised and enlarged: 1913. 245 pp.
     (a) reprint (of [which?] 1898 Edition): Sharp. "Johannes
          Brahms (1833-1897), Edvard Grieg (B. 1843)" in
          Sharp. (Essay Index Reprint Series) Freeport,
          N.Y.: Books for Libraries Press, 1972. pp. 200-12.
          Brahms: pp. 200-05, 211. ill., facsim., fig. An
          overview of his life; includes comments on Brahms
          the man.

207 *Sherwood, Percy. "Johannes Brahms" Dresdner Nachrichten
     (27.10.1911).

208 *_____. (Shewood) "Vortrag über Brahms im Brahms-Abende
     des Musikpädagogischen Vereins zu Dresden" Dresdner
     Nachrichten (29.1.1912).

209 "Some Living Composers" Dwight's Journal of Music 35/21 (Whole
     no. 907) (22.1.1876) p. 168. "Johannes Brahms": p. 168.
     Reprint of biographical notes from the program book "Carl
     Retter's Six Performances of Pianoforte Music in Strictly
     Chronological Order."

210 *Sorgoni, Angelo. "Joh[annes]. Brahms" Le Cronache musicali
     2/14 (1901).

211 *Streatfeild, Richard Alexander. ["Johannes Brahms"] in Streat-
     feild. Modern Music and Musicians. New York: Macmillan
     Company, 1906. pp. 297-311. ill.
     *issue: 1908.
     *also: London: Methuen & Co., [1906].
     *2nd Edition: [1907].
     (b) *French translation by Louis Pennequin (of ? Edition):
          Streatfeild. "Johannes Brahms" in Streatfeild.
          Musique et musiciens modernes. Paris: H. Falque,
          1910.
     (d) *Streatfeild. "Johannes Brahms" Revue du temps
          présent (1910).

212 *Talbot. "Study of Brahms" Music Student 6 (1914) p. 8.

213 "Tonmeister der Gegenwart. I" Illustrirte Zeitung (Leipzig)
Bd. 58/1503 (20.4.1872) p. 287. Includes comments on
Brahms the composer.

214 *Weber, Gustav. Schweizerische Musikzeitung und Sängerblatt
[21] (30.11. and 15.,31.;12.;1881).

215 *Widmann, J[osef]. V[iktor]. "Johannes Brahms" Neue Zürcher
Zeitung (4.1907).

216 *Wöhler, Willi. "Liebe zu Brahms" Salve hospes 8 (1958) pp.
40-41.

217 Zschorlich, P., see 756.d.ii.

See also 5.d, 312, 315, 319, 321, 385, 404, 412.5, 413, 418, 420,
436-38, 461, 469, 470, 492.5, 507, 655, 709, 732, 789, 825, 827,
830, 863, 1316, 1329, 1346, 1352, 1392.d., 1409, 1425, 1759, 1785,
1803, 1812, 1837, 1882, 1912, 1933, 1972, 1991, 2022, 2135, 2225,
2237, 2309.d.ii., 2451, 2485, 2572, 2821, 2836, 2843, 2849, 2979.

B. BRAHMS STUDY

1. General Appreciation

218 Bruyr, José. "Le Cas Brahms" La Revue musicale belge 9/5
(5.3.1933) pp. 2-3. Urges the French to become more
aware of Brahms and his music; also discusses his relationship with Wagner.

219 Dumesnil, René. "Le Cas de "Brahms"" Le Monde (Paris)
10/2052 (5.8.1953) p. 7. Explains Brahms and his music
to the French.

220 *Finck, H. [Henry T. Finck] Looker-On [3/1] (7.1896)
(d) see: 2479

221 Gunn, Glen Dillard. "An Appreciation of Brahms" Music
(Chicago) 19/[3] (1.1901) pp. 246-48. Discusses the greatness of Brahms's music, and the difficulties of understanding
it.

222 "A modern composer named Brahms, ..." in Laughable Limericks.
Sara and John E. Brewton, comps. Ingrid Fetz, illustrator.
New York: Thomas Y. Crowell Company, 1965. p. 108.
A limerick on the difficulty of understanding Brahms's
music.

223 Patterson, Grace Dickinson. "Mme. Julie Rivé-King on the Study of Brahms" Musician (Boston) 23/7 (7.1918) p. 460. On the growing popularity of Brahms's music, especially the solo piano works; also mentions Reményi and his relationship with Brahms.

224 Ritter, William. "Johannes Brahms" La Revue générale (Bruxelles) 58/1 (year 59/1) (7.1893) pp. 80-89. Discusses Brahms in relation to Wagner and Bruckner, his reception in Vienna and the author's personal impressions of various Brahms works.

225 Scott, Hugh Arthur. "A Word on Brahms" The Chord no. 2 (9.1899) pp. 55-62. Describes the qualities of Brahms's music that require diligence in its appreciation.

225.5#Thomas-San-Galli, Wolfgang A[lexander]. "Brahmsiana. Erlebtes, Erhörtes, Erlesenes" Rheinische Musik- und Theaterzeitung (Köln) 11/5 (1910) pp. 77-78. Author describes his methods for becoming familiar with Brahms's music and Brahms as composer; includes comments on the change in Brahms's critical reception and a report on 1853.

See also 1416, 1553, 1577, 1817, 2006, 2387.

See also "Commemorative Pieces" and "Evaluation" in VII.

2. Classroom Study

See 201, 1339, 1360, 1364, 2044, 2282.

3. Musicological Research

226 Batka, Richard. "Der Monatsplauderer" Neue Musikzeitung 28/13 (4.4.1907) pp. 282-84. facsim. Discusses the need for an objective reassessment of Brahms's historical position.

226.5#Bekker, Paul. "Brahms-Studien. Zur Aufführung des "Deutschen Requiems" durch den Philharmonischen Chor" Berliner neueste Nachrichten 28/586 (16.11.1908) Unterhal-tungs-Beilage p. [?]. notes. Calls for more study of Brahms in order to further the understanding of his music; discusses the German romantic period in music together with Brahms's place in that period.

227 Bopp, Wilhelm. "Johannes Brahms" Deutsche Rundschau 55/3 (Bd. 217) (12.1928) pp. 233-47. notes. Uses contemporary literature to cast new light on some of Kalbeck's findings [see 39].

228   Chop, Max. "Bewusste und unbewusste Brahms-Heuchelei"
       Signale für die musikalische Welt 76/40/41 (2.10.1918) pp.
       643-46. Discusses the need to distinguish between legend
       and reality in historical studies.

229   Kulenkampff, Hans-Wilhelm. "Warum ist Brahms berühmt?
       Provokation eines unzeitgemässen Themas" Neue Zeitschrift
       für Musik 130/9 (9.1969) pp. 414-18. Discusses the need
       to re-evaluate Brahms's historical position relative to the
       20th century. Speech given during Baden-Baden Brahmsta-
       gen, 1969.

230   McCorkle, Donald M. in collaboration with Margit L. McCorkle.
       "Five Fundamental Obstacles in Brahms Source Research"
       Acta musicologica 48/2 (1976) pp. 253-72. notes. Points
       out limitations of currently available research, to be sur-
       mounted before a better understanding of Brahms can be
       achieved.

231   Riemer, Otto. "Zum Brahmsbild unserer Zeit" Musica (Kassel)
       1/2 (3.-4.1947) pp. 90-96. Outlines areas in Brahms re-
       search that need to be investigated.

See also 358, 635, 712, 1009.d., 1179.e.i., 2524, 2884, 3020, 3120.

C. RESEARCH TOOLS

See also "Creative Process" in V.C.

1. Bibliography

Contains significant compilations of Brahms literature.

232   *Aber, Adolf. "Johannes Brahms" in Aber. Handbuch der
       Musikliteratur in systematisch-chronologischer Anordnung.
       (Kleine Handbücher der Musikgeschichte nach Gattungen.
       Bd. 13. Handbuch der Musikliteratur) Leipzig: Breitkopf
       & Härtel, 1922. cols. 254-56.
       (a) reprint: Hildesheim: Georg Olms, 1967. 38 items.

233   Bekker, Paul, see 226.5

234   [Daniel Gregory Mason] "Brahms Bibliography" Masters in
       Music 5/part 30 (6.1905) p. 16 (volume p. 256). 34 items,
       mainly magazine articles.

235 #Ehrmann, Alfred v. "Noch einmal Brahms" Die Musik (Berlin)
     27/7 (4.1935) pp. 481-84. Presents an overview of the
     literature on Brahms, and compares it with that for Wagner
     and Beethoven.

236 *Franke, H. "Zur Brahms-Literatur" Rheinische Musik- und
     Theaterzeitung (Köln) 8/5/6 (1907).

237 *"Johannes Brahms anlässl[ich]. seines 70. Todestages am
     3.4.1967" Bibliographische Kalenderblätter [10]/Folge 4
     (1967) pp. 13-27.
     (d) continued: "75. Todestag des deutschen Komponisten.
          Johannes Brahms geb[oren]. am 7.5.1833 in Hamburg
          gest[orben]. am 3.4.1897 in Wien. Nachtrag zu dem
          Bibliographischen Kalenderblatt über Johannes
          Brahms anlässl[ich]. seines 70. Todestages am
          3.4.1967 (Jg. 1967, Folge 4, s. 13-27)" Bibliograph-
          ische Kalenderblätter 14/Folge 4 (1972) pp. 6-11.
          ill. 58 items: includes a discography, which is
          the major section.

238 #"Johannes Brahms-Literatur (mit Ausschluss der Musikalien)"
     Börsenblatt für den deutschen Buchhandel und die verwandten
     Geschäftszweige 64/95 (Bd. 2) (24.4.1897) pp. 3090-91. 23
     items.

239 [Musikantiquariat Hans Schneider, comp.] Johannes Brahms.
     Leben und Werk. Seine Freunde und seine Zeit. (Katalog
     no. 100) Tutzing: Hans Schneider, 1964. 229, [3] pp. ill.,
     facsim. Auction catalog: pp. 27-228. 1750 items including
     many personal possessions of Brahms, memorabilia, editions
     of his and his contemporaries' music, autographs, literature
     and pictures.
     includes: Orel, Alfred. "Johannes Brahms und seine Verleger"
     pp. 19-24. Overview of Brahms's relationships with his
     music publishers.
     includes: Schneider, Hans. "Nachwort" pp. 229-[2]. In-
     cludes a discussion on Kalbeck and his links with Brahms.

240 Keller, Otto. "Johannes Brahms-Literatur" Die Musik (Berlin)
     12/2 (Bd. 45) (10.1912) pp. 86-101. 466 items.
     (d) i) see: 241.
         ii) continued: Seidl, Arthur. "Nachtrag (bis Ende
             Oktober 1912) zu Otto Kellers "Johannes Brahms-
             Bibliographie"" Die Musik (Berlin) 12/5 (Bd. 45)
             (12.1912) pp. 287-91. 110 items.

241 *Koch, Lajos [Louis]. "Brahms-Bibliográfia" A Fovárosi könyvtár
     evkönyve 12 (1942) pp. 65-149.
     (a) reprint: Koch. Brahms-Bibliográfia. Brahms-Biblio-
          graphie. [Budapest:] Budapest Szélesfőváros

Házinyomdája, 1943. 87 pp. 1544 items. Includes
summary of Elősző [Introduction] in German translation.

242 *Liepmannssohn, Leo. [auction house] Katalog 232: Johannes
Brahms. Zum 7. Mai 1933. Berlin: Author, [1933]. 18
pp. 291 items. [from Jahrbuch der Musikbibliothek Peters
40 (1933) p. 78]

243 Lübbe, Ingrid. "Das Schrifttum über Johannes Brahms in den
Jahren 1933-1958" (Hamburgisches Welt-Wirtschafts-Archiv)
Prüfungsarbeit Hamburger Bibliotheksschule, 1960. [1],
83, [3] pp. ind. 700 items; includes a history of Brahms
commemorations in Hamburg, and describes recent Brahms
acquisitions at the Universität Hamburg.

244 *Struck, Ingrid. "Johannes Brahms Stiftung. Zeitungsaus-
schnitte, Konzert programme und andere Druckschriften"
Jahresarbeit der Hamburger Bibliotheksschule, 1961. 63
pp.

245 Tapper, Thomas. "Brahms in Literature" in "Johannes Brahms
(The New Education--The Mastery of Teaching Material)"
Musician (Philadelphia) 3/5 (5.1898) p. 128. Presents an
overview of available literature.

246 *[Dresden. Städtische Bücherei und Lesehalle] Verzeichnis
der in der städtischen Bücherei und Lesehalle vorhandenen
Literatur über Johannes Brahms. Dresden: Städtische
Bücherei und Lesehalle, 1933. 9 pp.

See also 13, 225.5, 317, 1245, 1329, 2437, 2813, 2976.

2. Discography

Contains compilations and comparative studies of recordings of Brahms's
music.

247 *[[R. Rufener]] Phono 5/2,4 [(1958-59)]. For instrumental
works. [from S096]

248 *[[E. Werba]] Phono 5/3 [(1959)]. For Op. 121. [from S096]

249 *[[Gerhard Wienke]] Phono 7/4;8/1 [(1950-51)]. For instrumental
works. [from S096]

250 Affelder, Paul. "The Chamber Music of Brahms on Records
(High Fidelity Discography no. 12)" High Fidelity 4/7;5/1
(9.1954;3.1955) pp. 75-76, 78-85; 72-82.

"Part I: Sextets; Quintets; Quartets; Trios."
"Part II: Sonatas, Keyboard Music; Instrumental Miscellany."
    Includes descriptive comments on the musical works,
    and on Brahms the composer and his musical style. Part
    II includes Op. 122 and Ungarische Tänze arranged for
    violin and piano.

251   Bagar, Robert C. Brahms on Records. With Foreword by
       Dimitri Mitropoulos. New York: The Four Corners, 1942.
       91 pp. ill. Only deals with recordings on the Columbia
       label. Includes overview of life and works, and comments
       on performers' interpretations of Opp. 11, 24, 35, 56a,
       68, 73, 77, 80, 81, 87, 90, 98, 108, and miscellaneous songs
       and solo piano works.

252   "Brahms on the Gramophone" Music Teacher 12/4 (M.S. Series
       26/7) (4.1933) p. 189.

253   Brewsangh, V. G. "Recorded Piano Music of Brahms" American
       Music Lover 4/7 (11.1938) pp. 232-34, 247. ill. Includes
       discussion of keyboard instruments in the 19th century.

254   Burke, C. G. "Brahms. The Orchestral Music on Microgroove
       (Hi Fidelity Discography no. 24)" Hi Fidelity 6/4,9 (4.,9.;
       1956) pp. 97-105; 77-84. ill.
       "Part I: Overtures; Symphonies; Serenades."
       "Part II: Concertos; Works with Chorus; Miscellany." In-
       cludes comments on Brahms the composer, his musical
       style and orchestration. Part II includes Opp. 45, 50,
       53, 54, 56a, 82, 89, Ungarische Tänze.

255   *Darrell, R. D. "The Recorded Works of Brahms" Music Lover's
       Guide 1/9 (5.1933) pp. 258-64, 272.

256   Deppisch, Walter. "Vergleichende Diskographie der Klavier-
       Konzerte von Johannes Brahms" Brahms-Studien Bd. 2 (1977)
       pp. 47-78. ill. Using Wilhelm Backhaus for a standard,
       compares 20 other soloists' recordings of Opp. 15 and 83
       with respect to interpretation and performance.

257   *Gallois, Jean. "La Première symphonie de Brahms: enregistre-
       ments confrontes" Diapason (Paris) no. 211 (11.1976) pp.
       32-34.

258   Gilbert, Richard. "Phonograph Discs of Brahms Offer Manifold
       Delights to the Music-Lover" Musical Courier 106/18 (Whole
       no. 2769) (6.5.1933) pp. 20-21. notes. For all currently
       available recordings of the works.

259   *Halbreich, Harry. "Discographie comparée" Harmonie no. 41
       (12.1968) pp. 69-72. [citation for discography only?]
       For the symphonies. [from S096]

260 *Junghanns, Franz. fono forum [9]/1 (1.1964) p. 31. [citation
     for discography only?] For Op. 90. [from S096]

261 * _____. fono forum [10]/3 (3.1965) p. 100. [citation for
     discography only?] For Op. 98. [from S096]

262 *Konold, Wulf. "Eine vergleichende Diskografie des Doppel-
     konzerts a-moll von Johannes Brahms" fono forum [18]/7
     (7.1973) p. 606. [citation for discography only?] [A
     comparative study for Op. 102.]

263 *Kraus, Gottfried. "Diskografie" fono forum [15]/4 (4.1970)
     p. 217. [citation for discography only?] For Op. 45. [from
     S096]

264 * _____. "Diskografie" fono forum [16]/8 (8.1971) p. 559.
     [citation for discography only?] For Op. 77. [from S096]

265 *Kroher, Ekkehart. fono forum [13]/2 (2.1968) p. 78. [citation
     for discography only?] For the instrumental works. [from
     S096]

266 Lawry, Martha. "Recordings of Brahms Rhapsodie (Op. 53)"
     [Association for Recorded Sound Collections [ARSC]. Journal]
     11/1 (1979) pp. 29-36. notes. Includes comments on the
     best available recording.

267 Morse, Peter, comp. Schubert/Schumann/Brahms Choral Music.
     (Discography Series V) Utica, N.Y.: J. F. Weber, 1970.
     [ii], 8, 6, 12 pp. ind. "Brahms": 12 pp. [3rd paging]
     Includes all vocal/choral material with orchestra, together
     with deliberate abridgements or excerpts; arranged by opus
     number.

268 *"Music on Record: Johannes Brahms" Audio and Record Review
     8/9 (5.1968) pp. 346-47. [citation for discography only?]

269 #Szersnovicz, Patrick. "Discographie comparée--Brahms: Le
     Concerto pour violon" Harmonie no. 137 (5.1978) pp. 110-15.
     ill., notes. A descriptive analysis of Op. 77 and a compari-
     son of performances on available recordings.

270 * _____. (P.) "Discographie comparée: Les Symphonies de
     Brahms" Harmonie no. 156 (3.1980) p. 132.

271 Weber, J. F., comp. Brahms Lieder (Discography Series IV)
     Utica, N.Y.: Author, 1970. [3], 20 pp. Songs arranged
     alphabetically by title, except for Opp. 33, 91, 103, 121
     and Volkslieder which are treated as separate units.
     Addenda: May 1971.

See also 6, 13, 14, 42, 50, 60, 76, 237.d., 757, 1357, 1400, 1401, 1586, 1749, 1845, 1879, 1909, 2032, 2269, 2385, 2471, 2600, 2813.

3. Editions

a. Johannes Brahms. "Sämtliche Werke." 26 Bde. Leipzig: Breitkopf & Härtel, [1926-27].

272 *Brahms, Johannes. Sämtliche Werke. Ausgabe der Gesellschaft der Musikfreunde. [Hans Gal and Eusebius Mandyczewski, eds.] 26 Bde. Leipzig: Breitkopf & Härtel, [1926-27]. ill., facsim. Contains Revisionsberichte and music in score format. [from 1949 reprint]
    (a) i) *reprint (of Bd. 7): Gloucester, Mass.: Peter Smith Publisher Inc., n.d.
      ii) reprint: [With some corrections by Hans Gal] (Edwards Music Reprints. Series A. Complete Works and Monumenta. no. 3) Ann Arbor, Mich.: J. W. Edwards, 1949.
      iii) *reprint: Wiesbaden: Breitkopf & Härtel, [1964-65].
        (a) *reprint: Brahms. Complete Collected Works. Microfiche Reprint Edition. New York: University Music Editions, Inc., [196-?].
      iv) reprint (of Bd. 7): Brahms. Complete Chamber Music for Strings and Clarinet Quintet. The Vienna Gesellschaft der Musikfreunde Edition. [Dover Edition] Hans Gal, ed. (Dover Series of Study Editions. Chamber Music, Orchestral Works, Operas in Full Score) New York: Dover Publications, Inc., 1968. viii, 262 pp. Includes English translation of Revisionsberichte and adds a Table of Contents.
      v) *reprint: [Microform Edition] New York: Datamics Inc., [197-].
      vi) reprint (of Bd. 13): Brahms. Complete Sonatas and Variations for Solo Piano. The Vienna Gesellschaft der Musikfreunde Edition. [Dover Edition] Eusebius Mandyczewski, ed. [(Dover Series of Playing Editions)] New York: Dover Publications, Inc., 1971. xi, 178 pp. ill. Includes English translation of Revisionsberichte and English translation only of the original's Inhalt.
      vii) reprint (of Bd. 14): Brahms. Complete Shorter Works for Solo Piano. The Vienna Gesellschaft der Musikfreunde Edition. [Dover Edition] Eusebius Mandyczewski, ed. (Dover Series of Playing Editions) New York: Dover Publications, Inc., 1971. x, 180 pp. Includes English translation of Revisionsberichte and English translation only of the original's Inhalt.

viii) reprint (of Bd. 15): Brahms. Complete Transcrip-
tions, Cadenzas and Exercises for Solo Piano. The
Vienna Gesellschaft der Musikfreunde Edition.
[Dover Edition] Eusebius Mandyczewski, ed. (Dover
Series of Playing Editions) New York: Dover Publi-
cations, Inc., 1971. [3], vii-xii, 178 pp. Includes
English translation of Revisionsberichte and English
translation only of original's Inhalt.

ix) reprint (of Bde. 1,2): Brahms. Complete Symphonies in Full Orchestral Score. The Vienna Gesellschaft der Musikfreunde Edition. [Dover Edition]
Hans Gal, ed. (Dover Series of Study Editions.
Chamber Music, Orchestral Works, Operas in Full
Score) New York: Dover Publications Inc., 1974.
[6], 344 pp. ill. Contains English translation only
of Revisionsberichte.

x) reprint (of Bd. 12): Brahms. Complete Piano
Works for Four Hands. The Vienna Gesellschaft
der Musikfreunde Edition. [Dover Edition] Eusebius
Mandyczewski, ed. New York: Dover Publications,
Inc., 1976. [4], 2-217 pp. Includes English
translation of Revisionsberichte and English translation only of the original's Inhalt.

xi) *reprint: [Microform Edition] Washington, D.C.:
Library of Congress Photoduplication Service,
[1977].

xii) reprint (of Bde. 23-26): Brahms. Complete Songs
for Solo Voice and Piano. Series I-Series IV. 4
vols. From the Breitkopf & Härtel Complete Works
Edition. Eusebius Mandyczewski, ed. With a New
Prose Translation of the Texts by Stanley Appelbaum.
[Dover Edition] New York: Dover Publications,
Inc., 1979-80. Original Verzeichnis and Inhalt
broken down for each volume, with separate title
and first line indexes. Adds poet index and glossary
of German musical terms; has English translation
only of Revisionsberichte.

(c) excerpt: 55 vols. (Kalmus Study Scores) (Kalmus
Miniature Orchestra Scores) Huntington Station,
N.Y.: Edwin F. Kalmus, [1971]. Music only, in
miniature score format.

(d) *index: see 311.

(e) #report: Pfannenstiel, Alexander. "Eine Kulturtat
ersten Ranges. Gesamtausgabe der Werke von
Brahms" Rheinisch-Westfälische Zeitung (Essen) no.
751 (2.12.1925) Morgenausgabe. p. 6.

b. Editing, Popular Editions and Publication Rights

Contains bibliographies of Brahms's works and comments on the

editing of Brahms's music and the ending of copyright limitations
on the original editions.

273 Beninger, Eduard. "Pianistische Herausgebertechnik" Zeitschrift
für Musikwissenschaft 12/5 (2.1930) pp. 281-98. Brahms:
p. 291. mus. Describes the layout process for piano music
in score, with Op. 79, no. 2 as example.

274 *Borschel, Roswita. "Verzeichnis der Erst- und Frühdrucke
von Johannes Brahms" [Prüfungsarbeit der Hamburger
Bibliotheksschule,] 1971.

275 Deutsch, Otto Erich. "The First Editions of Brahms" Introduction and Postscript translated by Percy H. Muir. Music
Review 1/2,3 (5.,7.;1940) pp. 123-43, 255-78. notes. Bibliographic list, includes published collections of the works.

276 Fr. Sch. "Der Kampf um den funfzigjährige Schutzfrist. Der
Fall Brahms" Germania (Berlin) no. 558 (30.11.1927) p.
[?]. Presents arguments for authors' rights to continue for
50 years after their deaths; uses Brahms as an example
of what could happen if this time period isn't accepted.

277 Hofmann, Kurt. Die Erstdrucke der Werke von Johannes Brahms.
Bibliographie mit Wiedergabe von 209 Titelblättern. (Musikbibliographische Arbeiten 2) Tutzing: Hans Schneider,
1975. xl, 414 pp. ill., notes. Detailed bibliographic
description of editions, with introductory remarks on Brahms
and his music publishers, and general comments on the
publication history of the editions.
(e) i) #report: Biba, Otto. "Wie Brahms seine Werke
publizieren liess" Musikblätter der Wiener Philharmoniker 34/6 (1980) pp. 167-72. facsim., ill.
ii) report: Jong, W. C. de. "Brahms' complete oeuvre
chronologisch geinventariseerd" Mens en melodie
30/[12] (12.1975) pp. 389-92. ill., notes.

278 *[Dresden. Städtische Bücherei und Lesehalle] Katalog der
in der städtischen Musikbücherei und ihren Deposita vorhandenen Werke von Johannes Brahms. Dresden: Städtische
Bücherei und Lesehalle, 1933. ii, 39 pp.

279 Kirstein, Gustav. "Brahms, Bruckner und die Schutzfrist"
Vossische Zeitung (Berlin) Unterhaltungsblatt nr. 173
(27.7.1926) p.[2]. Speculates on the effect of the end of
copyright limitations on publication of Brahms's music.

280 Lessmann, Otto. "Eine neue Brahms-Ausgabe und Anderes"
Allgemeine Musikzeitung 28/45 (8.11.1901) pp. 728-29. Reviews Eulenburg edition and comments on Brahms's historical
position.

281   Schnirlin, Ossip. "Die neue Ausgabe der Brahmsschen Kammer-
      musikwerke" Die Musik (Berlin) 19/2 (11.1926) pp. 93-98.
      mus., notes.   Comments on his editing of Simrock's Neue
      revidierte Ausgabe of Brahms's works (1927-28). [contains
      the chamber music with piano, the string sextets, quintets
      and Op. 115]
      (e) report: Altmann, Wilh[elm]. "Schnirlins Neuausgaben
      Brahmsscher Kammermusikwerke" Allgemeine Musik-
      zeitung 55/[12] (1928) p. 317.

282   Wiesengrund-Adorno, Theodor. "Eduard Steuermanns Brahms-
      Ausgabe" Anbruch 14/1 (1.1932) pp. 9-11. Discusses the
      problems of editing music, using as an example Op. 79,
      no. 1 from Brahms. Klavierwerke. Neu revidiert von
      Eduard Steuermann (Wien, n.d.).

See also 13, 230, 239, 1136, 1393, 1749, 1752, 1757, 1768, 2317.5,
2343, 2838. See also "Textual Criticism" and "Works Catalogues and
Indexes" in I.C.; individual publishers in III.B.2.; and "Creative
Process" in V.C.

4. Manuscripts and Manuscript Studies

See also "Creative Process" in V.C.

a. Autograph Facsimiles

      Contains guides to finding facsimiles and cross-references to
complete facsimiles.

283   Dedel, Peter. Johannes Brahms: A Guide to His Autographs
      in Facsimile. (MLA Index and Bibliography Series no. 18)
      Ann Arbor, Mich.: Music Library Association, 1978. 86
      pp. facsim., ind., notes. Contains reference to facsimiles
      for 115 works and 108 examples of Brahms's correspondence;
      also 16 examples from Brahms's manuscript copies of other
      composers' works, and 26 nonmusical miscellaneous items.

See also 721, 798, 1103.d., 1379, 1442, 1500, 1544.d., 1697, 1935,
1992, 2042, 2162, 2163, 2241, 2317.5.

b. Manuscripts--Music and Letters

      Contains descriptions of Brahms's manuscripts and lists exhi-
bitions featuring Brahms's manuscripts of his own works or his copies
of others' works. Includes comments on the process of tracing dis-
persed manuscripts. Cross-reference is made to discussions of individual manuscripts.

Austria: 288, 289, 293, 298, 302, 304, 309, 310.
Germany: 287, 290, 291, 292, 297, 305, 308.
Poland: 307.
Sweden: 300.
Switzerland: 306.
United States of America: 284, 285, 286, 294, 295, 301, 303.

284   Albrecht, Otto E. "Adventures and Discoveries of a Manuscript
       Hunter" Musical Quarterly 31/4 (10.1945) pp. 492-503.
       Brahms: pp. 500-01. Relates background to 286, calling
       attention to the extent of manuscript collections in the U.S.A.,
       with systematic indication of Brahms manuscript locations.
       (b) German translation: Albrecht. "Erlebnisse und Ent-
           deckungen eines Manuskript-Jägers in USA" Musica
           (Kassel) 2/3/4 (1948) pp. 129-38. Brahms: pp.
           136-37.

285   _____ "Autographs of Viennese Composers in the U.S.A."
       in Beiträge zur Musikdokumentation. Franz Grasberger zum
       60. Geburtstag. Günter Brosche, ed. Tutzing: Hans
       Schneider, 1975. pp. 17-25. Brahms: pp. 20-22. Lists
       important autographs of Brahms and their locations.

286   _____. "Brahms, Johannes, 1833-1897" in Albrecht. A
       Census of Autograph Music Manuscripts of European Com-
       posers in American Libraries. Philadelphia: University of
       Pennsylvania Press, 1953. pp. 49-67. notes. 89 items--
       detailed particulars, including manuscript information (des-
       cription, provenance) included.

287   *"Autographen berühmter Meister (Versteigerung bei Ernst
       Henrici, Berlin)" Münchner neueste Nachrichten (8.9.1910).

288   Biba, Otto. "Haydn-Abschriften von Johannes Brahms" Haydn-
       Studien Bd. 4/2 (5.1978) pp. 119-22. facsim., mus., notes.
       Brhams's copies of works by Haydn: manuscript description
       and historical background.

289   _____. "Neuerwerbungen des Archivs der Gesellschaft
       der Musikfreunde" Osterreichische Musikzeitschrift 36/12
       (12.1981) pp. 647-49. facsim. Describes recent acquisitions
       --3 letters, plus manuscripts for Op. 21 no. 2 and nos. 3
       and 4 from the Fünf Klavierstudien [Hofmann nr. 130;
       McCorkle Anhang Ia, nr. 1]

290   Elvers, Rudolf. "Die Brahms-Autographen in der Musikabteilung
       der Staatsbibliothek Preussischer Kulturbesitz, Berlin"
       Brahms-Studien Bd. 2 (1977) pp. 79-83. 16 items--a com-
       plete list of music manuscripts and letters with historical
       background and description.

291   Heyer, Wilhelm. "Brahms (1833-1897)" in Heyer. Musikhistor-
      isches Museum von Wilhelm Heyer in Cöln. Katalog. Bd. 4.
      Musik-Autographen. By Georg Kinsky, Konservator des
      Museums. Frau Wilhelm Heyer, ed. Leipzig: Kommissions-
      Verlag von Breitkopf & Härtel, 1916. pp. 789-806. facsim.,
      mus., notes. 9 items--description, textual criticism and
      historical background.

292   Koch, Louis. "Johannes Brahms (1833-1897)" in Koch.
      Manuskripte, Briefe, Dokumente, von Scarlatti bis Stravinsky.
      Katalog der Musikautographen-Sammlung Louis Koch.
      Beschrieben und erläutert von Georg Kinsky. [After
      Kinsky's death, finished by Marc André Souchay] Stuttgart:
      Hoffmannsche Buchdruckerei Felix Kraus, 1953. pp. 287-99,
      347-48. facsim., mus., notes. Describes 11 items, both
      music and letters.

293   #Kraus, Hedwig. "Los Autógrafos de Brahms en la sociedad de
      amigos de la música de Viena" Ars. Rivista de Arte 17/79
      (1957) pp. [112-19] ill., facsim. Describes Brahms's manu-
      scripts at the Gesellschaft der Musikfreunde in Wien--original
      works and his copies of others' music.

294   *Kromer, Julius von. "An Index of Brahms Autographs prepared
      for the Library of Congress" 1938.

295   *[United States.] Library of Congress. Music Division. [=United
      States. Library of Congress. Gertrude Clarke Whittall
      Foundation] Autographs. Music and Letters. Prepared by
      Edward N. Waters. Washington, D.C.: Gertrude Clark
      Whittall Foundation, 1951. 17 pp.
      Revised Edition: 1953. [[1, 18, 1]] pp. "Brahms, Johannes
      (1833-1897)": pp. [[4-9]]. Descriptive comments for 38
      manuscripts and the collection of Levi-Brahms correspondence.

296   McCorkle, Margit L. "Die erhaltenen Quellen der Werke von
      Johannes Brahms. Autographe. Abschriften. Korrekturab-
      züge" in Musik. Edition. Interpretation. Gedenkschrift
      Günter Henle. Martin Bente, ed. München: G. Henle Verlag,
      1980. pp. 338-54. notes. An inventory giving the location
      and function of manuscripts for original works and arrange-
      ments by Brahms; includes comments on the research.

297   Maasz, Gerhard. "Clara Schumanns Weihnachtsgeschenk vor
      100 Jahren: Erinnerung an Brahms" Hamburger Abendblatt
      7/295 (20.12.1954) p. 11. ill. Describes circumstances
      concerning gift of Brahms manuscripts from Marie Böje née
      Völckers to him: Opp. 23; 33, no. 13; 47, no. 5; and letter
      from Clara Schumann-Brahms Briefwechsel.
          (d) i) #Maasz. "Erinnerung an Brahms. Seltsames
              Schicksal einer alten Ledermappe" Der junge

Musikfreund [Beilage zur Kontakte] 2 (1964) pp.
89-91. ill. Describes his friendship with Betty
Völckers [member of Brahms's Frauenchor] and her
gift to him of Brahms manuscripts.

ii) *_____. "Meine Brahms-Erinnerungen" Hamburger
Hafennachrichten 11/9 (1958) p. 28.

298   Maier, Elisabeth. "Die Brahms-Autographen der Osterreichischen
National-Bibliothek" Brahms-Studien Bd. 3 (1979) pp. 7-34.
facsim., notes. Lists 32 items--includes manuscripts of
music and letters.

298.5 Mendelssohn Bartholdy, P. The Times (London) Late London
Edition no. 51,466 (22.8.1949) p. 5. "Missing Mozart Scores."
Elaborates on Carleton Smith's work [see 305, 307] and reports that formerly missing manuscript for Op. 77 has been
located.

299   *Mies, P[aul]. "Johannes Brahms in der Handschrift" Lied und
Chor 50 (1958) p. 81.

300   Mühlhäuser, Siegfried. "Brahms, Johannes (1833-97)" in Mühlhäuser. Die Handschriften und Varia der Schubertiana-
Sammlung Taussig in der Universitätsbibliothek Lund.
(Quellenkataloge zur Musikgeschichte 17) Wilhelmshaven:
Heinrichshofen's Verlag, 1981. pp. 89-93. notes. Describes
5 manuscripts, including 3 of different arrangements of Op.
39, and 1 letter.

301   Mumford, L. Quincy and Edward N. Waters. "Musical Vienna
in the Library of Congress" in Festschrift Josef Sturmvoll.
Josef Mayerhöfer and Walter Ritzer eds. unter Mitarbeit
von Maria Razumovsky. (Museion. Neue Folge. 2. Reihe.
4 Bd.) Wien: Verlag Brüder Hollinek in Komm., 1970.
2. Teil. pp. 593-615. "Johannes Brahms": pp. 598-603.
facsim. Historical background and manuscript description
of 9 items.

302   Österreichische Nationalbibliothek. "Johannes Brahms" in
Osterreichische Nationalbibliothek. Katalog des Archivs
für Photogramme musikalischer Meisterhandschriften Widmung
Anthony van Hoboken. Teil 1. Agnes Ziffer, ed. (Museion.
Neue Folge. 3. Reihe. Bd. 3) Wien: Georg Prachner Verlag,
1967. pp. 95-115, 441-42. ind., notes. Lists 93 items,
manuscripts of both music and letters.

303   Pierpont Morgan Library. The Mary Flagler Cary Music
Collection. Printed Books and Music. Manuscripts. Autograph
Letters. Documents. Portraits. [Otto E. Albrecht, Herbert
Cahoon and Douglas C. Ewing, comps. Herbert Cahoon,
general editor] New York: Author, 1970. xii, 108, 49 pp.

Brahms: pp. 19-21, 59, 103. facsim., notes. 7 items
described; includes provenance and publication history.
(d) Rigbie Turner, J. "Nineteenth-Century Autograph
Music Manuscripts in the Pierpont Morgan Library:
A Checklist [(I)] (II)" 19th Century Music 4/1,2
(Summer, Fall 1980) pp. 49-69, 157-83. notes.
"Brahms, Johannes, 1833-97": pp. 58-59. notes.
Detailed description and provenance of 18 items; in-
cludes Albrecht identification [see 286].
(a) reprint: Rigbie Turner. Nineteenth-Century
Autograph Music Manuscripts in the Pierpont
Morgan Library. A Check List. New York:
Pierpont Morgan Library, 1982. 53 [1, 17]
pp. Brahms: pp. 16-17. adds facsim.

304 Santner, Inge. "Brahms-Schätze in Abfalleimern. Unbekannter
Nachlass entstieg de Vergangenheit. Das Erbe der Frau
Celestine" Hamburger Abendblatt 19/72 (26./27.3.1966) p.
13. ill. Discusses Frau Truxa's savings of Brahms's "rejected" compositional materials, and its inheritance by her
sons; describes contents of the collection and her sons'
relationship with Brahms.
(a) *reprint: Santner. Der Musiker (München) [=Der
Berufmusiker] [17?]/5 (5.1966) pp. 5-6.

305 "Search for Music Manuscripts. German Collections Still
Missing" The Times (London) Late London Edition no. 51,479
(6.9.1949) p. 4. Reports on Carleton Smith's search for
music manuscripts formerly in the possession of the Preussischer Staatsbibliothek; includes works of Brahms.
(d) i) "Lost Musical Mss. American Search Unsuccessful"
The Times (London) Late London Edition no. 51,818
(10.10.1950) p. 5. Continues to follow Smith's efforts.
ii) see: 307.

306 Seebass, Tilman. "Brahms, Johannes" in Seebass. Musikhandschriften in Basel aus verschiedenen Sammlungen.
Ausstellung im Kunstmuseum Basel vom 31. Mai bis zum
13. Juli 1975. [Basel:] Kunstmuseum Basel, [1975]. pp.
69-70. facsim. 6 items: Op. 8, songs from Opp. 14 and
49, Liebeslieder Walzer arranged with orchestral accompaniment; includes manuscript description and historical background.

307 Smith, Carleton. "Music Manuscripts lost during World War
II" Book Collector 17/1 (Spring 1968) pp. 26-36. Brahms:
p. 33. Relates the background of materials originally housed
in the Preussischer Staatsbibliothek Musikabteilung, their
dispersement, and attempts at their recovery. 3 Brahms
manuscripts listed in a catalog of manuscripts stored at
Książ/Wałbrzych, Poland.

308   Springer, Hermann. "Bach-Beethoven-Brahms-Autographen
        in der Berliner Königlichen Bibliothek" Allgemeine Musikzeitung
        40/17 (25.4.1913) pp. 534-35. Brahms: p. 535. Provenance
        of manuscripts for Opp. 15 and 55.

309   Szmolyan, Walter. "Brahms schreibt ab" Osterreichische Musik-
        zeitschrift 26/3 (3.1971) p. 157. Reports on a lecture by
        R[udolf]. Klein on music manuscripts copied out by Brahms,
        held in the Gesellschaft der Musikfreunde in Wien.

310   *Wiener Stadtbibliothek. Meisterhandschriften aus der Musiks-
        ammlung der Wiener Stadtbibliothek. [Fritz Racek, ed.]
        [Wien: Author, 1963].

See also 68.e., 230, 239, 243, 313, 627, 1058, 1103.d.d., 1308,
1325, 1348, 1363, 1380, 1397, 1454, 1485, 1496, 1500, 1544.d., 1592,
1634, 1639, 1648, 1662, 1683, 1697, 1718, 1727, 1749, 1773, 1791,
1935, 1938, 1942, 1945, 1948, 1992, 2033, 2040, 2093, 2109, 2133,
2135, 2139, 2146, 2162, 2163, 2200.d., 2241, 2305, 2322, 2331, 2343,
2450, 2595.

See also "Autograph Facsimiles" and "Textual Criticism" in I.C.;
and "Creative Process" in V.C.

c. Textual Criticism

        Contains comparisons of editions of Brahms's music with relevant
manuscript sources, or manuscript-to-manuscript comparisons. Cross-
reference is made to studies of individual works.

See 1415, 1552, 1681, 1789, 1894, 2052.

See "Manuscripts--Music and Letters" in I.C.; and "Creative Process"
in V.C.

5. Works--Catalogs and Indexes

        Contains publishers' and thematic catalogues, commercially pre-
pared indexes to the works, and systematically arranged lists of
Brahms's music.

311   *Breitkopf & Härtel. [music publisher] Brahms Werkverzeichnis.
        Verzeichnis sämtlicher Werke von Johannes Brahms. Ausgabe
        der Gesellschaft der Musikfreunde in Wien. Kritische
        Gesamtausgabe, Band- und Einzelausgaben für die praktische
        Gebrauch. Leipzig: Author, [1933]. 50 pp.

312   Dufflocq, Enrico Magni. "Johannes Brahms. Cenni biografici"
        Bollettino bibliografico musicale 4/12 (12.1929) pp. 1-16.
        Includes sketch of Brahms's life.

313 *Ehrmann, Alfred von. Johannes Brahms. Thematisches Ver-
     zeichnis seiner Werke. Ergänzung zu Johannes Brahms.
     Weg, Werk und Welt. Leipzig: Breitkopf & Härtel, 1933.
     vi, [2], 180, [1] pp. mus., ind.
     (a) reprint: Walluf-Nendeln: Sändig, 1977. Also includes
         information on first performances, time and place of
         composition, date of first edition, place in Sämtliche
         Werke, and autograph manuscript owners.
     (d) see: 320.d.iv.

314 *[Eugen Eunike. [music publisher]] Johannes Brahms. Verzeich-
     niss seiner Werke, mit Angabe der Verleger, des Preises,
     sämmtlicher Arrangements, der Titel und der Textanfänge
     aller Gesänge. Weimar: Musikhandlung von Eugen Eunike,
     [1878].

315 *Lengnick, Alfred. [music publisher] A Complete Catalog of
     Johannes Brahms' Works, Original and Arrangements.
     London: Alfred Lengnick & Co., 1906. [4], 68 pp. Pub-
     lisher's catalog: includes English translation of biographical
     sketch in 319. [from 320.a.]

316 ‡Orel, Alfred. "Ein eigenhändiges Werkverzeichnis von Johannes
     Brahms. Ein wichtiger Beitrag zur Brahmsforschung" Die
     Musik (Berlin) 29/8 (5.1937) pp. 529-41. notes. A des-
     cription and transcription of Brahms's own catalog of works,
     Opp. 1-79, including also the Ungarische Tänze [Hofmann
     nr. 128; McCorkle WoO posthum 1] and Fünf Studien für
     Pianoforte [Hofmann nr. 130; McCorkle Anhang Ia, nr.1]

317 *Pabst, P. [music publisher?] Verzeichniss der im Druck er-
     schienenen Compositionen von Johannes Brahms. Leipzig:
     Author, n.d.
     4. Auflage: 1890. 32 pp. ind. Also includes list of books
     on Brahms and list of available pictures of him.
     (a) #reprint (of 1. Auflage?): in 107.

318 Peters, C. F. [music publisher] Johannes Brahms. Verzeichnis
     seiner Werke. Mit Einführung von Adolf Aber. (Edition
     Peters no. 3960) Leipzig: Author, [1928]. xxiii, 49 pp.
     ill., ind. Publisher's catalog. Includes: Aber, Adolf. "Das
     Werk von Johannes Brahms": pp. vii-xxiii. Surveys the
     works with descriptive and stylistic commentary.

319 *Rieter-Biedermann, J. [music publisher] Verzeichniss der
     Compositionen von Johannes Brahms nebst ihren Bearbeitungen
     aus dem Verlage von J. Rieter-Biedermann in Leipzig.
     [Edmund Astor, ed.] Leipzig: Author, 1898.
     ? Auflage: 1905. 16 pp. Publisher's catalog; includes a
       biographical sketch.
     (a) *reprint (of 1898 Auflage): Katalog des Musikalien-

Verlages von J. Rieter-Biedermann in Leipzig. [Leip-
zig: Author,] 1909. pp. 22-30.
(b) *English translation (of biographical sketch only): in
315.

320 *Simrock, N. [music publisher] Thematisches Verzeichniss der
bisher im Druck erschienenen Werke von Johannes Brahms.
Nebst systematischen Verzeichniss und Registern. Berlin:
Author, 1887. [6], 134 pp.
*2. Auflage: Thematisches Verzeichniss sämmtlicher im
Druck ... Registern. 1897. [6], 175 pp.
*Neue Ausgabe [3. Auflage]: 1902.
*4. Auflage: Simrock G.m.b.H., N. 1903.
*Neue vermehrte Ausgabe [5. Auflage]: 1904.
*6. Auflage: 1910.
[for bibliographical history see 320.a. pp. xxxvii-ix.]
(a) reprint (of 1897 Auflage): Simrock. The N.
Simrock Thematic Catalog of The Works of Johannes
[[Thematisches Verzeichniss sämmtlicher im Druck
erschienenen Werke von Johannes Brahms.]] New
Introduction, including Addenda and Corrigenda by
Donald M. McCorkle. (Da Capo Press Music Reprint
Series) New York: Da Capo Press, 1973. 1 [roman
numeral], [6], 175 pp. ind., notes. Includes
introduction on the bibliographic history of this
catalog, Brahms and his music publishers, and
bibliographic descriptions for all catalog issues.
(d) i) *Simrock. Vollständiges Verzeichniss sämmtlicher
Werke und sämmtlicher Arrangements der Werke von
Johannes Brahms. Berlin: Author, 1897. 32 pp.
publisher's catalogue.
  ii) *Simrock G.m.b.H., N. Vollständiges Verzeichniss
aller im Druck erschienenen Werke von Johannes
Brahms. Berlin: Author, 1908.
  iii) *_____. Vollständiges Verzeichniss sämmtlicher
Gesangswerke von Johannes Brahms. Berlin:
Author, [1903?].
  iv) [Simrock] Thematic Catalog of the Collected Works
of Brahms. Enlarged Edition. Edited with Foreword
by Joseph Braunstein. [New York:] Ars Musica
Press, 1956. [5], 187 pp. ill., ind. Revision and
enlargement of 1907 (?) Auflage, with inclusion of
materials from 313.
    (e) report: R. S. "Brahms Catalogue Edited by
Braunstein" Musical America 76/16 (15.12.
1956) p. 34. report (on 1887 Auflage):
(e) report (on 1887 Auflage): Ed. H. [Eduard Hanslick] "Der
neue Brahms-Katalog" Neue freie Presse (Wien) no.
8486 (10.4.1888) Morgenblatt pp. 1-3 [across page
bottoms].
    (a) *reprint: Hanslick, Eduard. "1. Der

neue Brahms-Katalog. (1888)."
in 2948. pp. 131-41. [from 2.
Auflage]

321   Tschierpe, Rudolph. Johannes Brahms. 7. Mai 1833-3. April
1897. Hamburg: Hamburger öffentlichen Bücherhallen,
1958. 29 pp. ill., facsim., ind., notes. Discusses Brahms's
life, together with a list of works.

322   *Verzeichniss der im Druck erschienenen Compositionen von
Johannes Brahms. Mit Angabe der Arrangements, Preise
und Verlagsfirmen. [printed in 1878 by Brückner & Niemann
in Leipzig. 8 pp.]

323   "Vollständige Liste der im Druck erschienenen Werke von
Joh[annes]. Brahms" Dur und Moll 1/8 (1897) pp. 127-28.

See also 274-76, 278.

PART II. BRAHMS HIMSELF

Contains materials that focus on specific periods in Brahms's life; places he visited in his travels; comments he made about other countries; and on his personality, physical condition and, in general, relationships with other people.

A. LIFE

This subsection is arranged chronologically.

1. Family History, Childhood (1833-1853), and Links to Hamburg

Brahms and Hamburg: 332, 340, 347, 348, 355, 365, 367, 372.
Genealogy: 329, 330, 332-34, 340, 343, 344, 349, 353, 357, 361, 364, 368, 371.

324 *"Aus der Jugendzeit von Johannes Brahms" Hamburger Nach-
       richten Beilage no. 20 (1905).

325 #"Aus Johannes Brahms' Schulzeit" Hamburger Nachrichten
       (8.9.1915) Morgen-Ausgabe [2 pages] [across page bottoms].
       report on 358.

326 "A Back-Ally Musical Shrine in Hamburg" Etude 50/1 (1.1932)
       p. 7. ill. Brahms's humble beginnings are used as an
       example of the importance of developing talents rather than
       relying on a favorable position from birth.

327 *Becker C. "Aus Brahms Jugendzeit" Schweizerische Zeitung
       für Gesang? (St.-Gallen) 8/20 (1915).
         (d) *Becker. "Aus Johannes Brahms Jugendzeit" Hamburger
             Fremdenblatt [(1915)].

328 "Birthplace of Johannes Brahms" Musical Courier 34/22 (Whole
       no. 900) (2.6.1897) p. 19. ill. Picture caption with informa-
       tion on Brahms's childhood.

329 *Brahms, Adolf. "Die Familie Brahms" Leuchtfeuer. Heimatblatt
    für die Jugend zwischen Niederelbe und Ems 26 Folge 14
    (28.12.1974).

330 #_____. "Ist Johannes Brahms ostfriesischer Herkunft?
    (Musikgeschichte und Genealogie 37)" Genealogie. Deutsche
    Zeitschrift für Familienkunde 24/4 (Bd. 12) (4.1975) pp.
    481-84. notes. Genealogical problems in tracing the Brahms
    family. Author hypothesises that Ottendorf, not Horsten,
    is the family ancestral home.

331 "Brahms's Birthplace" Musical Courier 52/25 (Whole no. 1369)
    (20.6.1906) p. 15. ill. Reports on the unveiling of the
    memorial tablet at Brahms's birthplace.

332 [Fred Hamel] "Brahms und seine Heimat Hamburg" Die Zeit
    (Hamburg) 13/19 (8.5.1958) p. 4. ill. Discusses the family
    and Brahms's childhood; also his links to Hamburg through-
    out his life.

333 *Brenner, Franz. "Uber die aus Tondern stammenden Ahnen
    des Komponisten Johannes Brahms" Die Heimat (Kiel) 39
    (1929) pp. 273-80.

334 Broesicke-Schoen, Max. "Die Ahnenreihe von Johannes Brahms"
    Kölnische Zeitung no. 534 (21.10.1937) Abendblatt p. 2.
    Traces family back to 1430.
    (a) *reprint: Die Musik-woche 5/51 (1937) p. 2.

335 *Coit, Lottie Ellsworth and Ruth Bampton. The Child Brahms.
    (Childhood Days of Famous Composers) Philadelphia:
    Theodore Presser Co., 194-?. [juvenile literature]

336 #Crawshaw, J. E. "Birthplaces of Mendelssohn and Brahms"
    The Choir and Musical Journal 3/36 (12.1912) pp. 225-26.
    Brahms: p. 225. ill. Describes searching for the house;
    includes comments on Brahms's relations with his parents.

337 Deucher, Sybil. The Young Brahms. Illustrated by Edward
    and Stephani Godwin. [(Great Musicians Series)] New York:
    E. P. Dutton & Company Inc., 1949. 152 pp. ill., mus.
    Juvenile literature; historical fiction on Brahms from ages
    6 - 15.
    *also: London: Faber & Faber, [1951].

338 *Duckstein, H. "Das 100jährige Brahms-Haus" Gut Ton (Dresden)
    28/29 (1941) p. 165.

339 E. M. G. [Eva M. Grew] "The Childhood of Great Musicians.
    VIII. Brahms" British Musician and Musical News no. 89
    (9/5) (5.1933) pp. 106-09. ill. Discusses the environment
    in which Brahms was raised.

340 Ebrard, Friedrich. "Vom Hamburger jungen Brahms" Schweiz [erische]. Musikzeitung. Revue musicale suisse 86/11 (1.11.1946) pp. 397-402. ill., notes. Presents details on the family background and residences; also Brahms's milieu and its influence on him.

341 *Fietsch, R. "Brahms--Dirigent der Schullehrer von Winsen" Preussische Lehrerzeitung (Magdeburg) no. 69 (1933).

342 Frankenfeld, Alfred. "Brahms in Hamburg" Berliner Tageblatt 62/211 (7.5.1933) Ausgabe A p.[27]. Provides details on where Brahms and his friends lived, and where he went to school.

343 *Freitag, E. "Geschichte der Familie Brahms" Dithmarschen 8 (1932) pp. 80-82.

344 Gebhardt, [Peter] von. "[Fragen] 830. Brahms" Familienge-schichtliches Such- und Anzeigenblatt 2/9 (5/9) (15.9.1926) p. 110. Queries the place of origin for the Brahms family name, prior to 1750 in Hannover.

345 "Das Geburtshaus von Johannes Brahms" in 2667. pp. 59-60. ill. Text from 39A Bd. 1. Erster Halbband (? Auflage).

346 Gerber, Walther. "Der Brunsbüttler Brahmsstamm" Brahms-Studien Bd. 4 (1981) pp. 97-103. Traces the Brahms family tree up through the 1900's.

347 #Hermann, László. "Brahms ifjúkora" [Brahms's Youth] A Zene [2] (1910) pp. 133-36, 154-56. Discusses Brahms's life in Hamburg and his relationship with Reményi; includes comments on other family members.

348 #Hübbe, Walter. Brahms in Hamburg. (Hamburgische Liebhaber-bibliothek) Hamburg: Gedruckt bei Lütcke & Wulff [Vertrieb durch die Commetersche Kunsthandlung], 1902. [3], 67 pp. ill., ind. Describes links with Hamburg from 1853- ; includes information on Brahms's local musical activities and relationships.

349 #Janssen, Georg. "Ist Johannes Brahms ostfriesischer Herkunft?" Familiengeschichtliche Blätter 31/10/11 (1933) pp. 261-62. notes. Compares known genealogies to date; gives Horst as the family ancestral home.
(a) *reprint: Janssen. Zeitschrift für niedersächsische Familienkunde 15 (1933) pp. 65-68.

350 *Kalbeck, Max. "Brahms-Häuser" Neues Wiener Tagblatt (7.5. 1905).
(a) #reprint: Kalbeck. "Brahms-Häuser" Rheinische Musik-

und Theaterzeitung (Köln) 6/11 (1905) pp. 255-57.
notes. Surveys the cities where Brahms spent time
during his life, together with comments on the
houses where he stayed being established as memorial
sites.

351 *_____. "Vom jungen Brahms" Neues Wiener Tagblatt (7.,
8.;5.;1897).

352 Kerr, Caroline V. "Brahms' Birthplace" Musician (Boston)
11/12 (12.1906) p. 595. ill. Author describes visit to the
house.

353 Keyserlingk, Botho, Graf von. "Brahms und seine Ahnen"
Signale für die musikalische Welt 96/2 (12.1.1938) pp. 25-26.
Examines Brahms's family tree to show that there are no non-
Germanic elements in his line.

354 Koch, F[riederike]. C[hristiane]. "Der 15jährige Brahms gibt
sein erstes Konzert" Mitteilungen der Brahms-Gesellschaft
Hamburg e.V. no. 4 (4.1973) p. 10. notes. Gives the
concert programme and comments from contemporary sources.

355 Kulenkampff, Hans-Wilhelm. "Brahms und Hamburg" Die Musik
(Berlin) 30/1 (10.1937) pp. 17-21. Discusses Brahms's
links to Hamburg in his personal and artistic development.
(a) *reprint: Kulenkampff. in Deutsche Brahms-Gesellschaft.
9. Brahmsfest Programmbuch. [Hamburg: n.p.,
1937] pp. 4-13.

356 Leinburg, Mathilde von. "Wo blisst denn bloss de leebe Gott?
Eine Erzählung aus Johannes Brahms' Kindheit" Daheim 48/11
(16.12.1911) pp. 22-24. An anecdote from Brahms's childhood illustrating his faith in God.

357 #Marquard, Gertrud. "Wohnten die Ahnen von Brahms in
Döse?" "Der Deichwanderer". [Cuxhavener Presse.
Heimatbeilage] (13./14.8.1960) pp. [1-2]. ill. Reviews
genealogy and proposes that the family ancestral home is
Ritzebüttel/Cuxhaven.

358 Meisner, Robert. "Aus Johannes Brahms' Schulzeit. Zur
Kritik der Darstellung von Max Kalbeck.--Der Schullehrer
Johann Friedrich Hoffmann." Mitteilungen des Vereins für
Hamburgische Geschichte Bd. 12 Heft 2/4 (8.1915) pp. 193-
203. notes. Corrects Kalbeck's account of Hamburg's private schools; discusses Brahms and Hoffmann.
(a) reprint: Meisner. Brahms-Studien Bd. 2 (1977) pp.
85-94.
(e) i) #report: see 325.
ii) #report: Wiepking, H[enny]. "Wo ging Johannes

Brahms zur Schule?" Vom Jungfernstieg zur Reeperbahn Ausgabe Mitte no. 6 (1962) pp. 5-6.
(a) reprint: Wiepking, Henny. Mitteilungen der
Brahms-Gesellschaft Hamburg e.V. no. 2
(4.1971) pp. 9-10. ill.

359 Murdoch, William J. "The Musical Problem Child" Etude 68/3
(3.1950) p. 54. ill. Brahms as a piano student, and his
near escape from becoming a touring prodigy.

360 Nadeau, Roland. "With Perfect Pitch. Brahms: 1833-1897"
Christian Science Monitor 56/210 (1.8.1964) p. 5. notes.
Historical fiction concerning how Brahms became interested
in the piano, and about his lessons with Cossel.

361 *Purnhagen, Wilhelm. "Ein Beitrag zur Namenskunde. Der
Name Brahms" Leuchtfeuer. Heimatblatt für die Jugend
zwischen Niederelbe und Ems 26 Folge 14 (12.12.1974).

362 *Sittard, J[osef]. Hamburgischer Korrespondent [(before
10.1902)].[from 39A.d.i.]

363 #Spengel, Julius. "Johannes Brahms. Jugend- Lehr- und
Wanderjahre" Die Musikwelt (Hamburg) 2/9 (1.6.1922) pp.
6-11 (volume pp. 226-31). ill. Reviews his life up to
1862, focusing on relationships with his contemporaries.

364 #Stange, Hermann. "Johannes Brahms in seinen Beziehungen
zu unserer engeren Heimat" Die Heimat (Kiel) 8/10 (10.1898)
pp. 193-98. ill. Family background, affinity to the region's
poets particularly to Klaus Groth.

365 Stephenson, Kurt. "Die Wohnungen der Familie Brahms 1830
bis 1883" Mitteilungen der Brahms-Gesellschaft Hamburg e.V.
no. 3 (3.1972) pp. 5-7. Lists Hamburg residences for
Brahms family.

366 Tenne, Otto. "Johannes Brahms und seine niederdeutsche
Heimat" Mitteilungen aus dem Quickborn 48/3 (7.1958) pp.
58-60. Traces Brahms's family tree and discusses his affinity with North Germany; includes comment on his links
with Klaus Groth and "Dar geiht ein Bek" [Hofmann nr.
193].

367 *Tschierpe, Rudolf.[Rudolph Tschierpe] "Brahms und Hamburg"
Die Volksbühne (Hamburg) 8/11 (1958) pp. 213-15.

368 Wagener, Conrad. "Aus Brahms' Jugendzeit" Neue Musikzeitung
18/10 (1897) p. 125. ill. Information on the Brahms family
background, his birthplace, scholarly and musical education
and childhood activities.

369 #Weinrich, Otto. "Das Geburtshaus von Johannes Brahms"
       Nationalzeitung (Berlin) Sonntagsbeilage no. 336 (29.5.1904)
       pp. 3-4. Describes birthplace as well as other Brahms
       family residences in Hamburg.
       (d) Weinrich. "Brahms' Geburtshaus" Signale für die
            musikalische Welt 62/40/41 (13.7.1904) pp. 725-29.
            A reprint of article, with the opening paragraph
            omitted.

370 #Wild, Irene. "Johannes Brahms' Geburtshaus. Ein Mahnwort"
       Hamburger Nachrichten (17.3.1904) p. [?] Describes her
       reactions during a visit to Brahms's birthplace and repri-
       mands the city of Hamburg for not showing any interest
       in commemorating this site.

371 *Witt, Kl. "Neues über die Ahnen von Johannes Brahms"
       Dresdner Anzeiger (5.5.1936).

372 *Zinne, Wilhelm. "Brahms in Hamburg" Neue freie Presse (Wien)
       (11.11.1903?).

See also 20.d., 21, 22, 39A, 39D, 48, 58, 73, 104, 107.5, 108, 121,
145, 149, 152, 165, 170, 174, 175, 189, 190, 197, 445.5, 488, 545,
617, 618.a.e.i., 638, 683, 716, 721, 732, 736, 790, 799, 827, 844.5,
883, 958, 995, 1061, 1071, 1082, 1083, 1084, 1107, 1109, 1138, 1152,
1165, 1173, 1211, 1400, 1403.d., 1590, 2136, 2375.5, 2468, 2478,
2487, 2706, 2862, 3007, 3044.

See also "Brahms Family" in III.B; and "Memorial Activities" in VII.

2. In Transition (1853-1862)

373 *"Aus seiner Düsseldorfer Zeit" Das Tor. Düsseldorfer Heimat-
       blätter 31/10 (1965) pp. 185-91.

374 [Anna Gildemeister] "Der Efeukranz" Vossische Zeitung (Berlin)
       Unterhaltungsblatt no. 125 (7.5.1933) p. [4]. Author
       describes being at the recital, in Lüneburg, where Brahms
       and Reményi performed Beethoven's Op. 30 on concert tour,
       and Brahms transposed the piano part to compensate for
       an out-of-tune piano.

375 "Der Hamburger Frauenchor des jungen Johannes Brahms"
       Hamburger Abendblatt 11/104 (6.5.1958) p. 7. ill. Presents
       background on the choir, its members, and their repertoire.

376 *Herrmann, Feliz. "Wie Brahms entdeckt wurde" Deutsche
       Musikerzeitung (Berlin) 56/30+ (1925).

377 *Kordt, Walter. "Johannes Brahms am Rhein. Aus Brahms

rheinischer Zeit in Düsseldorf" Das Tor. Düsseldorfer Heimatblätter 31/9 (1965) pp. 178-82.

378   Müller-Dombois, Richard. Die Fürstlich Lippische Hofkapelle. Kulturhistorische, finanzwirtschaftliche und soziologische Untersuchung eines Orchesters im 19. Jahrhundert. (Studien zur Miskgeschichte des 19. Jahrhunderts. Bd. 28) Regensburg: Gustav Bosse Verlag, 1972. 255 pp. notes. Brahms: pp. 125-27 + passim. Discusses his connection with the court orchestra during his time in Detmold.

379   #off. "Berühmte Musiker in Düsseldorf" Die Heimat (Düsseldorf) [9]/9 (9.1958) pp. 269-71. Brahms: p. 271. Discusses Brahms's connections with Düsseldorf, 1853-57, and mentions the offering of the post of Musikdirektor to him in 1876.

380   #Schramm, Willi. Johannes Brahms in Detmold. Leipzig: Verlag von Fr. Kistner & C. F. W. Siegel, 1933. viii, 64 pp. ill., facsim., notes. Focuses on the period 1857-59, but includes connections with the city after 1860. Includes comments on works written during this period, and influences on his composing activities.

See also 22, 39A.c.v., 39A.e.iv., 48, 58, 104, 107.5, 108, 121, 149.d., 152, 154, 165, 170, 174, 190, 197, 297, 347, 363, 544, 570, 606, 607, 638, 680, 686, 716, 721, 732, 797, 894, 899, 918, 996, 997, 1015, 1060, 1061, 1075, 1089, 1090, 1103, 1121, 1126, 1132, 1143, 1150, 1153, 1161, 1162, 1165, 1171, 1176, 1178, 1185, 1186, 1188, 1247, 1400, 1590, 1617, 1730, 1748.d., 2128, 2135, 2187.c., 2193, 2283, 2343, 2349, 2468, 2525, 2526, 2527, 2628, 3058.

See also "F. A. E. Sonatensatz" and "Piano Trio in A Major" in IV.A.1.a. specific works.

3. Brahms and Vienna (1862-1894)

Brahms and the Rote Igel: 384, 386, 401, 403, 406, 408.
Involvement with Viennese Institutions: 388, 391, 392, 397, 399.

381   *[Otto Keller] "Brahms' erstes Auftreten in Wien" Die Zeit [Tageszeitung] (Wien) (14.11.1902) Abendblatt p. 2.

382   Cloeter, Hermine. "Johannes Brahms in Wien" Neue freie Presse (Wien) no. 25,785M (23.6.1936) Morgenblatt pp. 1-3 [across page bottoms]. Discusses Brahms's accomplishments in Wien's musical life; also includes descriptions of his residences there.
      (d) i) *Cloeter. Gut Ton (Dresden) 26 (1939).
           ii) *Cloeter, H. Der Merker (Berlin) 26 (1937) pp. 127-29, 141-43.

383 "Erinnerungen an Johannes Brahms. Von einem alten Lübecker" Zeitschrift für Musik 97/6 (6.1930) pp. 474-75. Brahms in Wien: his activities, affinity for the city, and milieu.

384 Ewen, David. "Dreams of Old Musical Vienna. How Musical History Was Made Over Cups of Coffee" Etude 58/1 (1.1940) pp. 10, 49. Brahms: p. 49. Describes the place of Viennese coffeehouses in the social and cultural life of the city--Brahms and the Rote Igel.

385 Gartenberg, Egon. "The Good Taverns" in Gartenberg. Vienna. Its Musical Heritage. University Park, Penn., and London: Pennsylvania State University Press, 1968. Brahms: pp. 117-27. ill. [no. 19] life from 1862- ; includes comments on his milieu, the Viennese attitude towards him and his music, also includes anecdotes.

386 Geiringer, Karl. "Brahms' Prickly Pet" Etude 59/2 (2.1941) pp. 82, 134, 139. ill. Brahms and the Rote Igel.

387 *Graener, Paul. "Wien, die Damenkapelle und Brahms" Die Oper (Breslau) no. 7 (1932/33).

388 Grasberger, Franz. "100 Jahre Musikvereinsgebäude" Oster-reichische Musikzeitschrift 25/5/6 (5.-6.1970) pp. 282-89. Brahms: pp. 284-85. Discusses Brahms's connection with the Gesellschaft der Musikfreunde, including his letter to Präsident Dr. Franz Egger, 12.1871.

389 #Gutmann, Albert. Aus dem Wiener Musikleben. Künstler-Erinnerungen. 1873-1908. Band 1. Wien: Verlag der k.u.k. Hofmusikalienhandlung Albert J. Gutmann, 1914. "Johannes Brahms": pp. 29-35. ill., facsim. anecdotes of Brahms in Wien and Thun. "Brahms' letzter Silvesterabend": pp. 36-37. Describes activities from New Year's Eve, 1896. "Johannes Brahms' letzte Handschrift": pp. 38-40. facsim. background to letter that Brahms wrote to Gutmann from his deathbed.

390 Helm, Theodor. "Brahms' erstes und letztes künstlerisches Auftreten in Wien" Musikalisches Wochenblatt 34/19 (7.5.1903) pp. 262-64. Discusses concerts in which Brahms participated: 11.1862 and 1.1895.

391 #Hernried, Robert. "Brahms und sein Wiener Kunstkreis" Oster-reichische Rundschau. Land-Volk-Kultur 3/6 (1937) pp. 269-75. Covers 1862-97: Brahms's milieu, his involvement with Viennese institutions and organizations, and the contrast between the spirit of the city and Brahms's nature.

392 Heuberger, Richard. "Brahms als Vereinsmitglied" Der Merker
     (Wien) 3/2 (1.1912) pp. 64-71. notes. Brahms as a member
     of the Wiener Tonkünstler-Verein.
     (a) reprint: in 991.

393 Höcker, Karla. "Wiener Hausmusik der achtziger Jahre. I"
     Velhagen und Klasings Monatshefte 54/3 (11.1939) pp. 222-26.
     Brahms: pp. 222-24. Discusses private concerts at the
     residences of Theodor Billroth and the Fellinger family.

394 #Hoffmann, Rud[olph]. St[ephan]. "Brahms und wir" Die
     Musikwelt (Hamburg) 2/9 (1.6.1922) pp. 13-[15] (volume pp.
     233-[35]). ill. Describes Brahms in Wien and performances
     of his works.

395 *Kalbeck, Max. "Brahms in Wien" Neues Wiener Tagblatt (21.
     11.1907).

396 *_____. "Brahms und Wien" Neues Wiener Tagblatt (7.,8.;
     5.;1908).

397 Kobald, Karl. "Brahms und Wien" Die Musik (Berlin) 25/8
     (5.1933) pp. 567-71. from 1862-97; the city's reception
     of Brahms and his music, the character of Wien, Brahms's
     milieu, and his involvement with Viennese institutions.
     (a) reprint: in 3186.c. pp. 7-11.

398 *Korngold, J[ulius]. "Der Wiener Brahms" in 2745.

399 Mitringer, Hedwig and Otto Biba. "Die Gesellschaft der Musik-
     freunde und die Wiener Festwochen 1976" Osterreichische
     Musikzeitschrift 31/4/5 (4./5.1976) pp. 216-22. Brahms:
     pp. 216-17. facsim. [pp. 217, 219] discusses his involve-
     ment with the Gesellschaft.

400 "Musik in Haus" Vossische Zeitung (Berlin) Unterhaltungsblatt
     nr. 125 (7.5.1933) p. [3]. Anecdote concerning Brahms's
     search for lodgings in Wien, using a household's level of
     musical activity as criterion.

401 *P.V.S. "Der Igel" [Wiener] Abendpost (11.4.1905).

402 *Paumgartner, Bernhard. "Johannes Brahms und das musikal-
     ische Wien um die Jahrhundertwende" Musica (Wien) 8/11
     (1936/37) pp. 5-9.

403 *Promintzer. "Brahms, Bruckner und der "Rote Igel"" Volk
     und Heimat 6/14 (1953) [Beilage to Burgenländische Sänger-
     zeitung 3 (1953)] pp. 8-9.

404 Rickett, Richard. "Johannes Brahms 1833-1897" in Rickett.

Music and Musicians in Vienna. Wien: Georg Prachner
Verlag, 1973. pp. 89-98. ill. Gives an account of Brahms's
life and musical works, focusing on post-1862 period; includes comments on his musical style.

405 *Schneider, Otto. "Die Philharmonischen Konzerte vor 100
Jahren. Ihr Programm im Spiegel der zeitgenössischen
Presse" Musikblätter der Wiener Philharmoniker 36/1,2
(9.,11.;1981) pp. 19-22, 102-06. ill. Discusses concerts
arranged and conducted by Hans Richter during the 1881-82
season, and how he got caught in partisan groups' crossfire
in the local press as a result of his decision to perform the
works of Brahms or Wagner. [from S202]

406 *Schönthan, Paul v. "Alte Wiener Wirtshäuser: Der Rote Igel"
[Wiener] Abendpost (7.1905).

407 #Servaes, Franz. "In der Brahms-Wohnung" Neue freie Presse
(Wien) no. 13,481 (6.3.1902) Morgenblatt pp. 1-3 [across
page bottoms]. Describes Brahms's last Viennese residence:
exterior, interior layout and contents of each room.
  (e) *report: "Wiener Kunstwanderungen (In der Wohnung
      von Brahms)" Neues Wiener Tagblatt (10.3.1902).

408 "(Die Wiener Stammlokale Johannes Brahms'.)" Neue freie
Presse (Wien) no. 24,658 (7.5.1933) Morgenblatt p. 9.
Describes Brahms's visits to the Prater and the cafes that
he frequented.

409 Wisoko-Meytsky, Karl. "Brahms und Wien" Osterreichische
Musikzeitschrift 2/4/5 (4./5.1947) pp. 88-90. Describes
first and last public appearances in Wien, Brahms's role as
conductor, and his love for Austria.

See also 32, 39D, 104.d., 152, 154, 224, 293, 309, 544, 657, 684,
695, 706, 715, 721, 732, 738, 749, 759, 778, 812, 829, 844.5, 879,
880, 899, 916, 949.b., 953, 958, 968, 971, 982, 990, 1024, 1054,
1064, 1074, 1108, 1109, 1114, 1126.5, 1128.5, 1138, 1139, 1190,
1234, 1243, 1246, 1249, 1286, 1403.d., 2135, 2296.d., 2580, 2815,
2836, 2887, 2943-50, 3048.

See also "Last Years, Death, Nachlass and Testament" in II.A.;
"Hubay Family" in III.B.; and "Memorial Activities" in VII.

4. Last Years, Death, Nachlass and Testament (1894-1902)

Last Days (8.1896-4.1897): 412, 412.5, 414, 421, 432, 436, 441,
443, 448, 455, 459, 477, 480, 482, 485, 486, 495, 499, 506, 526.
Death and Funeral: 423, 429, 431, 443.c.ii., 446, 451-55, 471, 480,
485, 486, 490, 491, 495, 504.

Obituaries/Death Notices: 410, 412.5, 415, 417-20, 424, 433, 434,
    437-40, 445, 452, 457, 458, 461, 467-70, 471, 473, 474, 476, 483,
    487, 492, 493, 497, 508-10, 515, 517, 520, 521, 524, 528, 530-32.
Nachlass: 412.5, 416, 425, 426, 428, 431, 443.c.ii., 444, 449, 450,
    460, 463, 464, 466, 498, 511, 519, 533.
Testament and Its Settlement: 422, 426, 430, 462, 463, 475, 498,
    500-03, 505, 511-13, 523, 525, 527.

410   *L'Echo musical (Bruxelles) [27] (18.4.1897).

411   *Musical Herald (London) (1897).

412   *Pester Lloyd (Budapest) no. 80 (3.4.1897) Reports on Brahms's
        illness. [from 241]

412.5 "† Johannes Brahms" Neue freie Presse (Wien) no. 11,715
        (3.4.1897) Abendblatt p. 2. Describes Brahms's last days,
        his Viennese professional positions and circle of friends,
        and the Nachlass contents; also gives an overview of his
        life and works and comments on Brahms the man and his
        philosophy.
        (c) excerpt: "Aus den Zeitungen" Signale für die musika-
              lische Welt 55/24 (9.4.1897) pp. 372-75.
        (e) reports: see 695?, 729?.

413   #Abel, Hedwig. "Johannes Brahms" Dur und Moll 1/8 (1897)
        pp. 122-27. ill., facsim. [after p. 116] Surveys Brahms's
        life and works; also discusses the influence and use of older
        musical forms in his music.
        (d) i) #reworked: Abel. Gegenwart Bd. [51]/16 (17.4.
              1897) pp. 247-48. Includes comments on Brahms's
              relationship with Wien, his ties with musical tradition,
              and his personal character.
            ii) see: 418.

414   "Aus dem Johannes Brahms-Archiv der Staats- und Universi-
        tätsbibliothek Hamburg veröffentlichen wir den nachstehenden
        Bericht von Anastasia Tettinek, der Hausgehilfin von Frau
        Truxa, über seinen Sterbetag" Mitteilungen der Brahms-
        Gesellschaft Hamburg e.V. no. 3 (3.1972) p. 3. Description
        of Brahms's last day, taken from a letter of 1.5.1902.

415   "Aus Wien kommt ..." Musikalisches Wochenblatt 28/15 (8.4.
        1897) p. 209. Notice of Brahms's death.

416   "Aus Wien wurde unlängst berichtet, dass ein neuerlicher
        Streit ..." Allgemeine Musikzeitung 29/4 (24.1.1902) p. 84.
        Reports on correspondence in Brahms's Nachlass and how
        its writers want their letters returned.

417   #B. [Carl Krebs] "Johannes Brahms †" Die Umschau (Frankfurt)

1/16 (1897) pp. 286-87. notes. Notice of death; surveys
Brahms's music and the characteristics of individual works.

418 B. T. [Hedwig Abel?] "Johannes Brahms. Ein Nachruf" Die
Gartenlaube [45]/9 (1897) pp. 288, 290. ill. Memorial
article: overview of Brahms's life and works.

419 *Beer, August. "Johannes Brahms" Pester Lloyd (Budapest)
(10.4.1897). Obituary and evaluation. [from 241]

420 Berggruen, O. "Johannes Brahms" Le Ménestrel 63/15 (11.4.
1897) pp. 113-15. ill., facsim., notes. Discusses Brahms's
life and works, focusing on the songs; also discusses his
general musical style and characteristics.

421 *"Brahms betegsége" Egyetértés (Budapest) (3.4.1897). Report
on Brahms's illness. [from 241]

422 "Brahms hat seinen letzten Willen ..." Der Klavierlehrer 21/9
(1.5.1898) p. 121. A transcription of Brahms's letter to
N. Simrock which contains his will.

423 *"Brahms' Leichenbegängniss" Neue freie Presse (Wien) no.
11,719 (7.4.1897) p. 6.

424 *"Brahms meghalt" [Pesti] hirlap (Budapest) (7.4.1897). Notice
of death. [from 241]

425 *"Brahms' Nachlass" Neues Wiener Tagblatt (24.10.1901). [con-
cerning disposition of private correspondence in the Nachlass]

426 *"Brahms' Nachlass" Pester Lloyd (Budapest) no. 89 (14.4.1897).
Reports on Brahms's will. [from 241]

427 "Brahms Programs" Music (Chicago) 12/[3] (7.1897) p. 378.
Outlines memorial concert programmes in Berlin.

428 #"Brahms' Reliquien" Musikhandel und Musikpflege (Leipzig)
3/5 (3.11.1900) pp. 37-38. Lists Nachlass contents.

429 *"Brahms temetése" Egyetértés (Budapest) (7.4.1897). Report
on Brahms's funeral. [from 241]

430 *"Brahms végrendelete" Egyetértés (Budapest) (7.4.1897).
Reports on the situation regarding Brahms's will. [from 241]

431 "Brahmsiana" Allgemeine Musikzeitung 24/16 (16.4.1897) pp.
245-47. Describes funeral (from Neue freie Presse [Wien]);
includes excerpts from 443, anecdotal material and comments
on Brahms and Goldmark, and discussion of the Nachlass.
(c) excerpt: A.Br. "Brahmsiana" Neue Zeitschrift für

Musik 64/16,17 (Bd 93) (21.,28.;4.;1897) pp. 181-83,
193-95. Also includes excerpts from 412.5, 530,
755, 775, 1098.d.d., 1235; more anecdotes, and a
transcription of the will.
(e) *report: Werner, Hildegard. Newcastle Journal
(1897).
(e) report: "Numerous Brahms anecdotes
have, of course, been current ..."
Musical News (London) 12/324
(15.5.1897) pp. 457-58. presents
anecdotes.
(e) report: m. "Einige Brahms-
Anekdoten veröffentlicht
Miss Hildegard Werner ..."
Neue Musikzeitung 18/17
(1897) p. 214. Adds new
anecdotes to those reported.

432 "Brief von Frau Celestina Truxa, der Hauswirtin von Johannes
Brahms, an Frau Marie Böie anlässlich seines Todes am 3.
April 1897--aus dem Besitz von Herrn Gerhard Maass
[Maasz], Ronco s. Ascona--" Mitteilungen der Brahms-
Gesellschaft Hamburg e.V. no. 3 (3.1972) pp. 4-5. Letter
dated 29.4.1897; describes Brahms's last days.

433 Bruneau, Alfred. "Brahms" Le Figaro (Paris) 3e série 43/84
(4.4.1897) p. 3. Discusses Brahms the composer.

434 Cobbett, W[alter]. W[illson]. "Johannes Brahms" Musical
News (London) 12/319 (10.4.1897) pp. 345-46. Discusses
Brahms and the characteristics of his music.

435 Collan, M. "Johannes Brahms" Finsk tidskrift 43/6 (12.1897) pp.
444-50. Comments on Brahms's death with an overview of
Brahms the man and musician.

436 "Death of Brahms, Special Memoir" Daily News (London) no.
15,920 (5.4.1897) p. 7. Reviews Brahms's last days and
summarizes his life; also comments on Brahms and England
and the English reception of his work, and Brahms the composer and his music.
(a) reprint: "Death of Johannes Brahms" Musical Opinion
and Music Trade Review 20/236 (1.5.1897) p. 537.
ill.

437 "Death of Johannes Brahms" New York Times 46/14,235 (4.4.
1897) p. 16. Summarizes life and works; also discusses
Brahms the composer.

438 "Death of Johannes Brahms" The Times (London) no. 35,169
(5.4.1897) p. 10. Presents overview of life and work.

439 *Dobrowolski, Adam. "Zgon Jana Brahmsa" Bluszcz (Warszawa)
     no. 14 (1897) p. 111.
     (d) *Dobrowolski. Wedrowiec (Warszawa) ⌈series 5] no.
     15 (1897) p. 288. ill.

440 *[Theodor Helm] "Dr. Johannes Brahms gestorben" Deutsche
     Zeitung (Wien) (6.4.1897) Morgenblatt p. 2.

441 e.klbg. "Aus Wien meldet unser Berichterstatter: ..."
     Neue Musikzeitung 18/8 (1897) p. 101. Reviews Brahms's
     life since Clara Schumann's death, and reports on his last
     public appearances in Wien.

442 E. U. "Gedächtnissfeier für Brahms. [[Wiesbaden, 8. Mai.]]"
     Neue Zeitschrift für Musik 64/21/22 (Bd. 93) (26.5.1897)
     p. 258. Notes on memorial programme.

443 Ed. H. [Eduard Hanslick] "Von Johannes Brahms' letzten Tagen"
     Neue freie Presse (Wien) no. 11,716 (4.4.1897) Morgenblatt
     pp. 1-2 [across page bottoms]. notes. Discusses Brahms's
     life and activities from August 1896 until his death.
     (a) *reprint: Hanslick, Eduard. "Johannes Brahms. Die
          letzten Tage. (Wien, 3. April 1897.)" in 2943.
          pp. 365-72. [from 2. Auflage]
     (c) i) excerpt: in 431.
         ii) excerpt (in English translation): J. B. K. "Brahm-
             siana" Musical Opinion and Music Trade Review
             20/239, 240; 21/241, 245-48 (1.;8.-10.;1897 and
             1.;2.-5.;1898) pp. 745-46, 825-26; 26-27, 324, 390-
             91, 465-66, 542. Includes excerpts of 431.c.,
             534.c., 969, 1294.c.; also reports on Brahms's
             funeral, the settling of the Nachlass, proposed
             memorials, and contains comments by Frau Heyer on
             Brahms in Karlsbad.
        iii) excerpt: "Von Johannes Brahms' letzten Tagen
             berichtet uns ..." Neue Zeitschrift für Musik 64/15
             (Bd. 93) (14.4.1897) pp. 177-78.
     (d) see: 969.c.

444 "The Estate of Brahms" Music (Chicago) 18/[4] (9.1900) pp.
     490-91. Describes the Nachlass.

445 *Fourcaud, Louis de. Le Gaulois (Paris) (7.4.1897).

445.5 #F.Pf. [Ferdinand Pfohl] "Johannes Brahms" Hamburger
     Nachrichten (4.1897) p. [?]. In memoriam article: Discusses
     Brahms as a North German, reviews his childhood, describes
     qualities of his music that reflect North Germany; includes
     comments on Brahms as composer, and the qualities of his
     music in general, together with comments on the relationship
     between Brahms and Schumann.

446 "The Funeral of Herr Johannes Brahms ..." The Times (London)
     no. 35,171 (7.4.1897) p. 12. Describes the ceremony in Wien.

447 G. E. B. "Johannes Brahms. 1833-1897" Musical Opinion and
     Music Trade Review 20/236 (1.5.1897) p. 518. Poem in
     memorium.
     (a) reprint: G. E. B. Musician (Philadelphia) 2/5 (5.1897)
          p. 147.

448 Geiringer, Karl. "Johannes Brahms: Aus der letzten Lebens-
     zeit. Nach Tagebuchaufzeichnungen Olga von Millers"
     Anbruch 19/3 (3.1937) pp. 40-43. notes. Covers 11.1896-
     4.1897, including notes on Brahms's activities and milieu.

449 *Gesellschaft der Musikfreunde. Inventur und Schätzung der
     Musikalien im Nachlasse von J[ohannes]. Brahms. Wien:
     Author, 1897.

450 *_____. Verzeichnis der von der Wiener Städtischen Samm-
     lungen. Bücher und Musikalien aus dem Nachlass von
     Johannes Brahms. Wien: Author, 1932.

451 "Gossip from Gay Vienna" New York Times 46/14,265 (9.5.1897)
     p. 23. Report on Brahms's death and funeral; includes
     anecdotes about Brahms and J. Strauss, Brahms's dislikes,
     and comments on his milieu.

452 *H., Dr. [Eduard Hanslick] Phoenix (Wien) [10]/5 (1897) cols.
     153-54. Obituary. [from Music Library, British Library]

453 *Haas, Rudolf and Wolfgang Münkel. Wegweiser zu den Grab-
     stätten bekannter Persönlichkeiten. Mannheim: n.p.,
     1981.

454 *Helm, Theodor. "Wiener Musikbrief: Trauerfeier für Brahms"
     Pester Lloyd (Budapest) no. 89 (14.4.1897).

455 _____. (Th.) "Zum Tode Johannes Brahms'." Musikalisches
     Wochenblatt 28/16 (15.4.1897) pp. 229-30. Reports on
     Brahms's last days and the planned memorial activities.

456 *Herzfeld, Viktor. "Johannes Brahms" Neue musikalische Presse
     [6] (2.4.1897).

457 *Heuberger, Richard. "Johannes Brahms" [Neues] Wiener Tag-
     blatt (6.4.1897).
     (a) reprint: Heuberger. "Johannes Brahms. († 3. April
          1897.) in 149.a. pp. 84-92. notes. Discusses
          Brahms's early beginnings as a composer, his re-
          ception; also includes anecdotes together with an
          assessment of Brahms as a composer.
     (e) report?: see 729.

458 *Heulhard, M. Le Courrier musical 1 (1897).

459 "The Illness of Herr Brahms" Daily News (London) no. 15,918
(3.4.1897) p. 5. Reports on Brahms's condition; also discusses his influence on Viennese musical life.

460 "Im Nachlass Johannes Brahms' ..." Musikalisches Wochenblatt
33/3 (9.1.1902) p. 43. Reports that letters in Brahms's
Nachlass will be returned to their authors.

461 Imbert, Hugues. "Johannès Brahms" Le Guide musical (Bruxelles) 43/15 (11.4.1897) pp. 283-85. Obituary notice; surveys
Brahms's life and works.
(e) report: [Theodore Thomas] "Concerning Brahms"
Music (Chicago) 12/[2] (6.1897) pp. 239-42. Includes report on 495.
(c) excerpt: in 2894. pp. 6-7 (volume pp. 246-
47).

462 "In dem Process um die Erbschaft Johannes Brahms ..." Musikalisches Wochenblatt 31/28 (5.7.1900) p. 381. Announces
court's decision on the beneficiaries of Brahms's Nachlass,
overturning decision reported in 475.

463 "In einem Briefe, den Johannes Brahms seiner Zeit ..."
Neue Musikzeitung 18/10 (1897) p. 132. Reporting on
Viennese newspapers' comments on Brahms's will and Nach-
lass.

464 "In Wien hat kürzlich ... gerichtliche Verhandlung ..." Allgemeine Musikzeitung 29/14 (4.4.1902) p. 263. On the
success of Frau Joachim's legal action for the return of
her letters to Brahms, and the ramifications for other correspondents.

465 *"János Brahms 1833-1897" Vasárnapi újság (Budapest) no. 15
(1897).

466 *"Joh[annes]. Brahms' Nachlass" Neue freie Presse (Wien)
(25.,26.;6.;1900).

467 "Johannes Brahms" The Athenaeum no. 3624 (10.4.1897) pp.
487-88. A memorial article: surveys Brahms's works and
comments on Brahms the man.

468 "Johannes Brahms" The Critic 30/790 [old series] 27 [new
series] (10.4.1897) p. 259. An obituary.

469 "Johannes Brahms" Musical Times 38/651 (1.5.1897) pp. 297-99.
An obituary; gives an overview of Brahms's life and works,
discusses the man and his milieu, and comments on his merit

as a composer.
(c) *excerpt: in 2915. p. 279. [from reprint]

470   "Johannes Brahms" Musician (Philadelphia) 2/5 (5.1897) p. 117.
Obituary: discusses Brahms's life, musical output and
historical position.

471   "Johannes Brahms" Signale für die musikalische Welt 55/24
(9.4.1897) pp. 369-72. Obituary: discusses the funeral
arrangements, Brahms the musician, Brahms and Wien,
and surveys his musical output.

472   *"Johannes Brahms" Die Umschau (Frankfurt) 1/16 (1897).

473   *"Johannes Brahms †" Pester Lloyd (Budapest) no. 81 (4.4.1897).

474   *"Johannes Brahms †" Pester Lloyd (Budapest) no. 82 (6.4.1897).

475   "Johannes Brahms auf 300.000 M geschätztes Nachlassver-
mögen ..." Musikalisches Wochenblatt 30/4 (19.1.1899) p.
56. Announces court's decision on the beneficiaries of
Brahms's Nachlass. See also 462.

476   [Otto Neitzel] "Johannes Brahms, geb[oren]. am 7. Mai 1833
in Hamburg, gest[orben]. am 3. April 1897 in Wien"
Kölnische Zeitung no. 307 (4.4.1897) p. [1]. Relates what
Schumann, Nietzsche, Speidel and Wüllner thought of Brahms;
comments on his sense of humour, surveys his works and
discusses his relationship with Wien.
(b) *French translation by Th. Lindenlaub: Le Temps
     (Paris) (1897).
     (e) *report: see 3167.
(e) *report: see 3167.

477   "Johannes Brahms ist schwer erkrankt ..." Neue freie Presse
(Wien) no. 11,715 (3.4.1897) Morgenblatt p. 7. Reports
on Brahms's physical condition.

478   *Joncières, Victorin. La Liberté (11.4.1897).

479   Kähler, Otto, see 844.5.

480   Kahler, O[tto]. H[ans]. "Brahms's Finale" Münchener medizinische Wochenschrift 122/36 (5.9.1980) pp. 1199-1200.
ill., notes. Reviews Brahms's last days from a medical perspective, Winter 1896- ; disagrees with 485 as to cause of
death, presents evidence for his own theory of death as
a result of jaundice.

481   *Kalbeck, Max. "Neues über Brahms" Neues Wiener Tagblatt
(2.,5.;4.;1898).

182 Karpath, Ludwig. "Vom kranken Brahms" Die Musik (Berlin)
2/15 (Bd. 7) (5.1903) pp. 225-26. Describes being with
Brahms in Bad Ischl (7.1896) and Wien (9.-10.1896).
(d) incorporated: 1028.

483 *Kauders, A. "Johannes Brahms" Neues Wiener Journal (4.4.
1897).

484 *Keller, Otto. "Johannes Brahms" Deutsche Kunst- und Musikzeitung (Wien) [24] (15.4.1897).

485 Kerner, D[ieter]. "Wie Johannes Brahms starb" Münchener
medizinische Wochenschrift 121/16 (20.4.1979) pp. 565-68.
ill., notes. Reviews Brahms's last days from medical perspective, Winter 1896- ; speculates that cause of death was
cirrhosis of the liver. See 480 for another opinion.
(d) Kerner, Dieter. "Letzter Brahms" Das Orchester
(Mainz) 29/7/8 ([7./8.] 1981) pp. 642-45. ill. Reviews Brahms's last days from a medical perspective,
Winter 1896- .

486 *Körbler, Juraj. "Krankheit und Tod des Komponisten Johannes
Brahms" Gesnerus (Aarau) Bd. 17 (1960) pp. 163-65.

487 Krebs, Carl. "Johannes Brahms" Deutsche Rundschau 23/8
(Bd. 91) (5.1897) pp. 300-02. A memorial article: expounds
on the greatness of Brahms and his work.

488 #La Mara. [Ida Maria Lipsius] "Johannes Brahms. Zu seinem
Geburtstag (7. Mai)" Wissenschaftliche Beilage der Leipziger
Zeitung no. 54 (6.5.1897) pp. 213-16. notes. Memorial
article: surveys his life up to 1853; discusses Brahms as
a composer with comments on his technique and the qualities
of his music, together with an examination of his position
in music history; includes comments on Brahms's relation to
opera and to folkmusic.

489 *Le Borne, Fernand. Le Monde artiste [37] (18.4.1897) p. 58.

490 *"Das Leichenbegängniss Johannes Brahms'" Pester Lloyd (Budapest) no. 83 (7.4.1897). Reports on Brahms's funeral.
[from 241]

491 Leinburg, Mathilde v. "Die Beerdigung von Johannes Brahms.
Persönliche Erinnerungen" Der Türmer 24/6 (3.1922) pp.
427-29. Describes her personal reaction to Brahms's
death, from when she paid her last respects to when she
attended his funeral.

492 #Lessmann, Otto. "Johannes Brahms †" Allgemeine Musikzeitung
24/15 (9.4.1897) pp. 229-30. ill. A memorial article: discusses Brahms's works and his historical position.

492.5 #Lewinsky, Josef. "Johannes Brahms †" Harmonie (Hannover)
      10/[8] (15.4.1897) pp. 1845-46. Summarizes Brahms's life
      and major works; includes comments on his place in music
      history.

493   Lindenlaub, Th. "Johannes Brahms" Le Temps (Paris) 37/13,091
      (5.4.1897) p. [3]. Notice of Brahms's death; comments on
      Brahms and Robert Schumann, Brahms as a composer, his
      classical tendencies and musical style.

494   Loewenfeld, Hans. "Johannes Brahms" Monatsschrift für neue
      Litteratur und Kunst (Berlin) 1/7 (4.1897) pp. 565-73.
      Discusses Brahms the composer, his historical position,
      Brahms in relation to Wagner and Nietzsche.

495   M. K. [Maurice Kufférath] "Le Mal qui a emporté Brahms ..."
      Le Guide musical (Bruxelles) 43/15 (11.4.1897) pp. 285-86.
      Describes Brahms's last days from 9.1896- and the funeral
      in Wien.
      (e) i) report: see 461.e.
          ii) report: "Le Guide Musicale (sic) gives the following
              anecdote about Brahms ..." Musical News (London)
              12/322 (1.5.1897) p. 422. Concerns Brahms's circum-
              vention of his doctor's advice.

496   #Marsop, Paul. "Johannes Brahms" Gegenwart [Bd. 51]/18
      (1.5.1897) pp. 277-80. Discusses Brahms as a pessimist,
      and his musical style.
      (d) reworked: Marsop. in Marsop. Musikalische Essays.
           Berlin: Ernst Hofmann & Co., 1899. pp. 184-95.

497   -n. "Johannes Brahms †" Vossische Zeitung (Berlin) no. 159
      (4.4.1897) Morgenausgabe 1. Beilage p. [3]. Discusses
      Brahms the composer.

498   n. "Der Nachlass von Johannes Brahms" Neue freie Presse
      (Wien) no. 12,892 (15.7.1900) Morgenblatt p. 9. Discusses
      resolution of Brahms's will and summarizes Nachlass contents.

499   *Nelsbach, Hans. "Die letzte Krankheit Johannes Brahms"
      Hamburger Fremdenblatt (8.9.1928).

500   #"Neuerlicher Streit um den Nachlass von Joh[annes]. Brahms"
      Musikhandel und Musikpflege (Leipzig) 4/6 (9.11.1901) p.
      40. Report on 501.

501   "Neuerlicher Streit um den Nachlass von Johannes Brahms"
      Neue freie Presse (Wien) no. 13,334 (8.10.1901) Morgenblatt
      p. 7. Reports on status of will contestation.
      (e) #report: see 500.

502 *"Nochmals der Nachlass von Johannes Brahms" Hamburgischer Correspondent no. 497 (1901).

503 O. L. [Otto Lessmann] "Das Testament Johannes Brahms'" Allgemeine Musikzeitung 25/16 (22.4.1898) pp. 235-36. Transcribes the letter Brahms wrote to Simrock, which was his will.

504 Ober, William B. "De Mortibus musicorum--Some Cases Drawn From a Pathologist's Notebook" Stereo Review 25/5 (11.1970) pp. 79-84. Brahms: pp. 83-84. A medical report on the cause of Brahms's death.

505 "Par un jugement récent ..." La Revue musicale (Paris) 4/21 (1.11.1904) p. 520. Reports on attempt to have estate tax repealed.

506 *Perger, Richard v. "Brahms' letzte Tage" Die Zeit(?) (Wien) [3] (3.4.1897) (?).
    (a) reprint: Perger. Musikbuch aus Osterreich 5 (1908) pp. 41-45. notes. A record of Brahms from 8.1896--7.1897; describes his activities and conversations with the author, in both Wien and Bad Ischl.

507 Pfohl, Ferdinand. "Johannes Brahms. Ein Denkblatt" Daheim 33/31 (1.5.1897) pp. 496-98. ill. Gives overview of Brahms's life and works; discusses musical style, influences, and historical position.

508 Pfohl, Ferdinand, see 445.5.

509 *Pirani, Eugenio von. [Eugenio di Pirani] "Johannes Brahms †" Charlottenburger Zeitung (Berlin) no. 94 (5.4.1897) p. 1.
    (e) report: "Noch waren die irdischen Ueberreste des ebenso grossen ..." Musikalisches Wochenblatt 28/16 (15.4.1897) p. 235. Gives a negative evaluation of Brahms's musical status.

510 *Poliński, Aleksander. "Sp[iacy]. Jan Brahms" Tygodnik ilustrowany no. 15 (1897) pp. 295-96. ill.

511 Prime-Stevenson, Irenaeus. "A Music Maker's Treasures" The Independent (New York) 53/2721 (24.1.1901) pp. 207-09. Reports on estate contestation and describes contents of Brahms's library.

512 "Der Process um den Nachlass J[ohannes]. Brahms ..." Musikalisches Wochenblatt 32/44 (24.10.1901) p. 586. Reports on new development in estate litigation.

513 r.h. "Der Streit um Johannes Brahms' Nachlass" Frankfurter

Zeitung und Handelsblatt 45/309 (8.11.1900) 2. Morgenblatt
p. 1. Reports on the contesting of the will.

514 Remenyi, Edouard. [Eduard Reményi] "Johannes Brahms Dead"
Julius Rosenberg, translator. Music (Chicago) 15/1 (11.1898)
pp. 43-46. A memorial article: discusses Brahms the composer and surveys the works.

515 s.- "Johannes Brahms ist ..." Neue Musikzeitung 18/8 (1897) pp.
99-100. Discusses Brahms the composer and the man.

516 *Schenker, Heinrich. "Johannes Brahms" Neue Revue (Wien)
[8] (4.1897).

517 *Schönaich, Gustav. "Joh[annes]. Brahms" Reichswehr (Wien)
(4.4.1897).

518 Schuster, Heinrich. "Johannes Brahms" Allgemeine Zeitung
(München) Beilage no. 102 (7.5.1897) pp. 1-3. notes.
Focuses on Brahms the composer and his musical style; also
discusses his historical position.

519 *Smekal, Richard. "Unbekanntes von Johannes Brahms. Relikvien und Briefe aus seinem Nachlass" Neues Wiener Journal
(6.1930).

520 Söhle, Carl. [Karl Söhle] "Johannes Brahms todt!" Musikalisches Wochenblatt 28/15 (8.4.1897) pp. 210-11. Discusses
the qualities of Brahms's music.
(d) #Söhle, Karl. "[Johannes Brahms]" Der Kunstwart
10/14 (1896-97) p. 216.

521 *Speidel, L[udwig]. Wiener Fremdenblatt (6.4.1897).
(a) reprint: "Johannes Brahms. 1833-1897" Signale für
die musikalische Welt 55/25 (14.4.1897) pp. 385-87.
Gives an assessment of Brahms as composer, and
describes the qualities of his music.

522 Stobbe, A. "Nachruf an Brahms" Neue Zeitschrift für Musik
64/21/22 (Bd. 93) (26.5.1897) p. 258. A poem on Brahms's
death, a loss to the musical world.

523 "Suivant les renseignements que publient les journaux de
Vienne ..." Le Guide musical (Bruxelles) 43/15 (11.4.1897)
pp. 286-87. Relates the background in regards to Brahms's
will.

524 *T. H. "Johannes Brahms" [Wiener] Fremdenblatt (4.4.1897).

525 #"Das Testament von Johannes Brahms" Berliner Tageblatt 30/404
(1900) p.[?]. Contains the text of the will and describes
the circumstances under which it was written.

526 Truxa, Celestina. "Am Sterbebette Brahms" Neue freie Presse
(Wien) no. 13,899 (7.5.1903) Morgenblatt p. 8. Describes
Brahms's last day.
(e) report: "In Wien wurde am 7. d[ieses]. M[onats].,
..." Allgemeine Musikzeitung 30/20 (15.5.1903) p.
351. Includes report on 3097.

527 "Verlassenschaftsprocess Brahms vor dem Ober-Landesgerichte"
Neue freie Presse (Wien) no. 13,005 (6.11.1900) Morgenblatt
p. 6. Gives background and reports opening positions as
will contestation goes before the court.

528 Vogel, Bernhard. "Johannes Brahms" Illustrirte Zeitung
(Leipzig) Bd. 108/2806 (8.4.1897) p. 448. ill. [on issue
cover] On the loss of Brahms; surveys his works, musical
style, and his links to Beethoven.

529 _____. "Zur Erinnerung an Johannes Brahms" Neue Zeitschrift für Musik 63/14 (Bd. 93) (7.4.1897) p. 157. A
poem on the loss of Brahms.

530 *"Vom Meister Johannes Brahms" Neues Wiener Tagblatt (4.4.1897).

531 *Wallaschek, Richard. "Johannes Brahms" Die Zeit [Wochenschrift]
(Wien) 3/198 (10.4.1897) pp. 26+.

532 *Widmann, J[osef]. V[iktor]. Der Bund (Bern) no. 95
(6.4.1897). [from 2394.5]
(a) i) #reprint: Widmann. "Johannes Brahms" in Widmann.
Ausgewählte Feuilletons. Max Widmann, ed. Frauenfeld: Huber & Co., 1913. pp. 180-85. A memorial
article: assesses Brahms's historical position and
discusses Brahms the man.
ii) reprint: Widmann, Josef Viktor. "Nekrolog" in
72. pp. 254-59, 261-62.

533 "Wien. Ein neuerlicher Streit um die in Joh[annes]. Brahms'
Nachlass ..." Zeitschrift der Internationalen Musikgesellschaft 3/5 (1902) p. 206. Reports on court battle over
publication of letters in the Nachlass.

534 *Wüllner, Franz. "Zu Johannes Brahms' Gedächtniss. Worte
der Erinnerung" [speech given on 2.5.1897 at the Köln
Konservatorium der Musik]
(c) excerpt: Wüllner, F[ranz]. Neue Zeitschrift für Musik
64/19 (Bd. 93) (12.5.1897) pp. 218-19. Discusses
first meeting Brahms in 1853 and Brahms as his
friend, Brahms as an orchestrator, and Brahms's
connections with Köln.

See also 32, 87.c., 104.d., 389, 402, 409, 580-83, 608, 620, 638, 657,

674, 680, 683, 684, 695, 721, 728, 732, 738, 778, 813, 829, 856,
868, 890, 897, 898, 917, 951, 953, 969, 971, 981, 1027, 1028, 1036.5,
1054, 1087, 1101, 1121, 1127, 1139, 1154, 1182, 1211, 1212, 1224,
1243, 1246, 1279, 1285, 1288, 1302, 1312, 1313, 1373, 1403.d.,
1748.d., 1766, 2172, 2289, 2453, 2606, 2623.

See also "Memorial Activities" in VII.

B. BRAHMS THE TRAVELLER

This subsection is divided alphabetically by country. Cross
references include reference to national attitudes towards Brahms
and his music.

See also 350, 721, 732, 987.

---Austria

General Remarks: 537, 538, 545.
Bad Ischl: 539, 541, 543, 544.
Graz: 540.
Mürzzuschlag: 535.
Pörtschach: 536, 542, 546.
Wien: See "Brahms and Vienna" and "Last Years, Death, Nachlass
and Testament" in II.A.

535 *Böhm, F. J. "Brahms in Mürztal" Deutscher Volkskalender
(Wien) [25] (1937) p. 93. [Discusses Brahms and Mürzzuschlag.]

536 Fuchs, Anton. "Johannes Brahms. Auf seinen Spuren in
Kärnten" Die Brücke (Klagenfurt) 2/4 (Herbst 1976) pp.
235-51. [text ends on p. 250] ill., facsim. Issue title:
"Festausgabe zum Jubiläumsjahr des Landes Kärnten." Discusses Brahms and Pörtschach: his compositional activities,
lodgings, and friends there.

537 Grasberger, Franz. "Brahms' Sommerreisen" Osterreichische
Musikzeitschrift 26/5/6 (5./6.1971) pp. 290-95. ill. Discusses where Brahms spent the summer after he settled
in Wien; focuses on towns in Austria.

538 *Hernried, Robert. "Brahms und die österreichische Landschaft"
Die Osterreichische Schule (1937) pp. 248-50.

539 Hutton, Winfield. "Bad Ischl (Byways of Europe -2)" Opera

News (17.2.1968) pp. 27, 29. Brahms: p. 29. ill.
Describes places in Bad Ischl Brahms frequented, and his
relationship with J. Strauss.

540   Ivichich, Max v. "Kleine Geschichten über Wagner, Bruckner
      und Brahms" Neue freie Presse (Wien) no. 18,834 (28.1.1917)
      Morgenblatt pp. 13-14 [across page bottoms]. Brahms:
      p. 14. Relates anecdotes of Brahms visiting Graz, 10.1882
      and 11.1884, and experiences he had with the young ladies
      there.

541   *Kalbeck, Max. "Brahms in Ischl" Neues Wiener Tagblatt
      (1913?).
      (b) English translation: Kalbeck. New Music Review
           and Church Music Review 13/145 (12.1913) pp. 10-14.
           ill. Describes Brahms's visits 1889- : lodgings,
           friends present, daily and compositional activities.

542   Kalbeck, Max and Hans Müller. "Johannes Brahms in Pört-
      schach" in 3123. [pp. 9-33]. Describes Brahms's visits
      1877-78: lodgings, friends there, daily and compositional
      activities.

543   *Prochaska, Heinrich. "Chronik von Ischl über Brahms' Som-
      meraufenthalte in den Jahren 1882-1896" in Prochaska.
      Geschichte des Badeortes Ischl. Linz: n.p., 1924.

544   Sp-r. [Daniel Spitzer] "Wiener Spaziergänge (Aus Ischl)"
      Neue freie Presse (Wien) no. 8973 (18.8.1889) Morgenblatt
      p. 5. Describes Brahms in the Cafe Walter in Bad Ischl.

545   Schneider, Constantin. "Johannes Brahms und Osterreich.
      Zum hundertsten Geburtstage des Meisters am 7. Mai 1933"
      Bergland 15/4 ([4.] 1933) pp. 21-24, 46-47. ill., facsim.,
      notes. Traces early life, then discusses Brahms in Wien,
      and his summer residences in Austria, pointing out what
      he composed in each place.

546   *Th. Grazer Tagespost [(3.? 1899)].
      (a) #reprint: Th. "Eine Erinnerung an Johannes Brahms"
           Neue musikalische Presse [8]/14 (2.4.1899) pp. 6-7.
           Describes Brahms in Pörtschach, Summer 1879,
           and his first meeting with Marie Soldat.

See also 107.5, 204, 550.d.i., 684, 738, 812, 868, 890, 898, 971, 974,
982, 1028, 1117, 1131, 1147.5, 1224, 2627, 3071, 3094, 3095, 3098,
3099, 3112, 3113, 3116, 3123, 3127, 3128, 3140, 3154, 3156.

See also "Brahms and Vienna" and "Last Years, Death, Nachlass
and Testament" in II.A.

--Belgium

See 37.

--Czechoslovakia

See also 801.

547 *Hrabussay, Zoltán. "Johannes Brahms a Bratislava [in Brahms's
      time: Pressburg]" Slovenská hudba 2 (5.1958) pp. 209-12.

548 #_____. "Johannes Brahms a naša hudobná minulosť" Hudobný
      zivot 4/6 (1972) p. 8. ill. Discusses Brahms's ties to
      Bratislava [in Brahms's time: Pressburg]: Describes per-
      formances given there and friends from the city.

--England

General Remarks: 550-52, 554.
Cambridge: 549,553-56.

549 *Daily News (London) (9.3.1877). On Brahms and the offer
      of an honorary degree by Cambridge [from 241].

550 Blair, David Hunter. "The Ideals of Brahms" The Times
      (London) Late War Edition no. 41,569 (29.8.1917) p. 9.
      Letter to the editor: comments on Brahms's dislike and
      contempt for England, with evidence
      (d) i) comment: May, Florence. The Times (London) Late
              War Edition no. 41,575 (5.9.1917) p. 9. Refutes
              Blair's claims with description of incident with Brahms,
              Bad Ischl, Summer 1894.
          ii) comment: Stanford, [Sir] Charles V[illiers]. The
              Times (London) Late War Edition no. 41,572 (1.9.1917)
              p. 9. Refutes Blair's claims with personal comments
              on Brahms.
         iii) comment: Walker, Ernest. The Times (London)
              Late War Edition no. 41,570 (30.8.1917) p. 9.
              Refutes Blair's claims with example of letter by
              Brahms to Oxford University Musical Club and Union.

551. "Brahms and England" Music and Youth 10/11 (11.1930) p. 251.
      Brahms didn't visit England because of his aversion to
      wearing dress clothes, not fear of seasickness.

552 "Brahms on British Music" The Times (London) Late War
      Edition no. 40,843 (1.5.1915) p. 11. Comments on a favorable
      comment by Brahms on English music; also discusses Brahms's
      knowledge of England.

553   Norris, Gerald. "Brahms" in Norris. Stanford, The Cambridge
      Jubilee and Tschaikovsky. Newton Abbot et al.: David &
      Charles, 1980. pp. 66-100. ind., notes. Traces attempts
      to invite Brahms to England by various individuals and
      groups (1873-92), particularly Stanford's attempt to invite
      him to Cambridge in 1893 for the University Musical Society's
      Jubilee. Also includes anecdotes and comment on English
      reaction to Brahms's music and the composer's feelings
      towards England.

554   Pulver, Jeffrey. "Brahms and England" Monthly Musical Record
      58/685 (2.1.1928) pp. 3-4. ill. Discusses the Cambridge
      honorary degree incident, England's enthusiasm for Brahms's
      music, his interpreters there, Brahms and Florence May,
      and Brahms's interest in older English music.

555   Pulver, Jeffrey. "Brahms and the Doctorate" Sackbut 14/5
      (12.1933) pp. 127-29. Relates why Brahms refused the
      Cambridge degree and accepted the degree from Breslau.

556   Schenkman, Walter. "Music on the Academic Bandwagon"
      American Music Teacher 26/2 (11.-12.1976) pp. 26-27, 30.
      Brahms: p. 30. notes. Discusses the Cambridge, Breslau
      degree incidents.

See also 48.e.ii., 436, 879, 1015, 1212, 1217, 1238, 1349, 1886, 1898,
1899, 1914, 1915, 2250, 2497, 2935, 3043.

--France

See 27, 37, 76, 147.d.i., 218, 219, 1224, 2036, 2099, 2359, 2614,
2773, 2810.5, 2886, 2922, 2985, 2987, 3001, 3027.

--Germany

Bad Neuenahr: 593, 595.
Baden-Baden: 561, 588, 600, 601.
Berlin: 568, 573, 576, 590, 592, 605, 608.
Breslau: 559.5, 560, 566, 569.
Detmold: See "In Transition" in II.A.
Düsseldorf: 558, 570, 607. See also "In Transition" in II.A.
Ebernburg: 586.
Essen: 559.
Frankfurt a.M.:   568.
Hamburg: See "Family History, Childhood, and Links to Hamburg"
   in II.A.
Karlsbad: 580-83.
Karlsruhe: 565, 603.
Kiel: 575.
Köln: 571.

Königsberg: 585.
Krefeld: 562, 574, 597, 598.
Leipzig: 563, 564, 606.
Mannheim: 602, 609.
Meiningen: 577, 599.
München: 578, 587, 596.
Sassnitz: 604.
Sondershausen: 572.
Stuttgart: 591.
Tutzing: 589.
Wiesbaden: 579.
Ziegelhausen: 557, 567, 584.

557   A. H. "Ein Landaufenthalt des Meisters Johannes Brahms"
      Neue Musikzeitung 18/13 (1897) p. 164. Describes Brahms's
      stay in Ziegelhausen 4.-10.1876: daily activities and his
      milieu.

558   #"Als Johannes Brahms Musikdirektor in Düsseldorf werden sollte.
      Briefdokumente aus der Zeit um 1876" Die Heimat (Düssel-
      dorf) [9?]/9 (9.1958) pp. 271-73. Uses correspondence
      from 1009, 1170, 1179, and miscellaneous letters to Clara
      Schumann to trace the period 4.1875-2.1877, when Brahms
      was asked to take up a permanent conducting position in
      Düsseldorf.

559   #Altmann, Wilh[elm]. "Brahms-Erinnerungen eines alten Esseners"
      Allgemeine Musikzeitung 44/[21] (1917) pp. 338-39. notes.
      Describes Brahms while in Essen for a conducting engagement,
      2.-3.1884: what he said and did, as well as his personal
      qualities.

559.5#Andreae, Friedrich. "Brahms und die Universität Breslau"
      Schlesische Zeitung (Breslau) no. 227 (6.5.1933) Unterhal-
      tungsbeilage pp. [1-2]. Surveys Brahms's musical and
      personal links to Breslau; corrects 39 on the people behind
      the Universität's presentation of a degree to Brahms; in-
      cludes comments on Op. 80.

560   *Andreas, F. "Brahms in Breslau" Schlesische Monatshefte
      (Breslau) 10 (1933) p. 212.

561   Baser, Friedrich. "Clara Schumann, Brahms in seiner Baden-
      Badener "Komponierhöhle"" in Baser. Grosse Musiker in
      Baden-Baden. Tutzing: Hans Schneider, 1973. pp. 97-108.
      ill., facsim., notes. Describes his compositional activities,
      lodgings and friends.

562   #Beckerath, Heinz von. "Erinnerungen an Johannes Brahms.
      Brahms und seine Krefelder Freunde" Die Heimat (Krefeld)
      29/[1-4?] (1958) pp. 81-93. ill. Reports on Brahms in

Krefeld in the 1880's and 1890's: his activities, and friends there, focusing on his relationship with the von Beckerath family.
(a) *reprint [separatdruck]: Beckerath. Erinnerungen an Johannes Brahms. Brahms und seine Krefelder Freunde. n.p., [1958]. 12 pp.

563 #Bose, Fritz v. "Brahms und die Musikstadt Leipzig" Leipziger neueste Nachrichten (5.5.1933) p.[?]. Traces Brahms's links to Leipzig through first performances of his works there.

564 *"Brahms Musik im Gewandhaus" Pauliner-Zeitung (Leipzig) 45 (1933) pp. 105-07.

565 *"Brahms und Karlsruhe" Residenz-Anzeiger (?) (Karlsruhe) (21.1.1933).

566 #E. G. "Brahms-Erinnerungen an Breslau. Bei der Kegelpartie-Begeisterung im ersten Sinfonie-Konzert unter seiner Leitung Ehrendoktor der Friedrich-Wilhelms-Universität" Schlesische Zeitung (Breslau) (1.5.1943) p. [1]. Describes Brahms's visits, 1874-81, focusing on 1.1877 concert where he conducted; also discusses his receipt of an honorary degree from the University.

567 Eberts, Karl. "Joh[annes]. Brahms in Ziegelhausen" Neue Musikzeitung 37/2 (21.10.1916) pp. 30-32. ill. Describes Brahms's connections from 1875- : his lodgings and milieu.

568 Egidi, Arthur. "Johannes Brahms in Berlin. Persönliche Erinnerungen" Berliner Tageblatt 59/542 (16.11.1930) Morgen-ausgabe. 6. Beiblatt p. [23]. Describes Brahms's circle of friends in Berlin 1880- ; also Brahms in Frankfurt a.M., summer 1888.

569 #Enderwitz, F. M. C. "Johannes Brahms' Beziehungen zu Bres-lau" Schlesische Zeitung (Breslau) nos. 648(?), 650, 652 (20.(?), 21.,22.;11.;1918) [one page in each issue]. notes. Surveys Brahms's private and professional visits to Breslau, 1874-1886; includes comments on Brahms and Scholz.

570 Eulenberg, Herbert. "Brahms und das Rheinland" Neue freie Presse (Wien) no. 24,667 (16.5.1933) Morgenblatt pp. 1-2 [across page bottoms]. Describes Brahms's connections with the region and his friends there, in particular Düssel-dorf and the Schumanns, respectively; also comments on Rhenish influences in his music and his use of texts by Rhenish poets.

571 #Fremery, Fritz. "Kleine Ursachen--grosse Wirkungen. Eine

wahrhaftige Ballade" in "Johannes Brahms in Köln" Kölner
Stadt-Anzeiger Abendblatt no. 566 (5.11.1942) p.[?].
Describes Brahms going on a potluck picnic in Köln, 1886.

572 *Gresky, W. "Johannes Brahms nach Sondershausen" Thüringer
Heimatkalender (1964) pp. 71-74.

573 *Grindel, Gerhard. "Brahms in Berlin. Zu seinem 50. Todestag
am 3. April" Sie. Die führende Zeitung für die Frau 2/13
(1947) p. 7.

574 Hiebert, Elfrieda Franz. "Johannes Brahms and His Mennonite
Friends" Mennonite Life 13/4 (10.1958) pp. 156-59. ill.,
notes. Describes Brahms's connection to Krefeld 1880- ,
especially his relationship with the von Beckerath and von
der Leyen families; also comments on his interest in Mennonite
philosophy and writings.

575 Hofmann, Kurt. Johannes Brahms und Kiel. Ein Beitrag zur
Musikgeschichte Kiels. Hamburg: Brahms-Gesellschaft
Hamburg e.V., 1973. 31, [1] pp. ill., facsim., notes.
Describes Brahms's visits and performances from 1856- ,
together with his circle of friends there.

576 Kalbeck, Max. "Brahms in Berlin" in 2667. pp. 3-16. ill.
Discusses Brahms's relationship to Berlin; also comments
on the nature of these Deutsche Brahms-Gesellschaft concerts
and compares Brahms to Beethoven.

577 *_____. "Brahms in Meiningen" Appenzellische Jahrbücher
(Trogen [or St. Gallen?]) 3. Folge Heft 11 no. 284 [p.
284?].

578 *_____. "Brahms in München" in 2745.

579 *_____. "Brahms in Wiesbaden" Neues Wiener Tagblatt
(5.,7.;6.;1912).
(d) Kalbeck, Max. [Max Kalbeck] "Brahms in Wiesbaden.
(Mit ungedruckten Briefen) (Aus dem Festbuch des
2. Deutschen Brahmsfestes in Wiesbaden im Jahre
1912)" Signale für die musikalische Welt 79/22
(1.6.1921) pp. 568-77. Taken from Deutsche Brahms-
fest Programmbuch. Focuses on 1883-84 and his
work on Op. 90, leading up to its first performance.
Contains letters from Brahms to von Beckerath,
Billroth, Hanslick, Rauenstein, and Wegeler: some
letters reprinted in 804, 816.

580 #Karell, Viktor. "Johannes Brahms als Karlsbader Kurgast"
Sudetendeutsche Monatshefte (1937) pp. 197-202.
Describes Brahms's stay, 9.-10.1896: lodgings, activities,
friends there; also describes the city's memorial activities.

581 *Karpath, Ludwig. "Johannes Brahms in Karlsbad" Neues Wiener
     Tagblatt (17.8.1897). Describes Brahms's stay in the city
     for medical reasons. [from 241]
     (d) incorporated: 1028.
     (e) report: see 969.c.

582 Kaufmann, M. "Brahms als Karlsbader Kurgast" Der Auftakt
     2/4 (1922) pp. 119-20. Related to 583.

583 _____. "Ernstes und Heiteres aus Johannes Brahms' Kurau-
     fenthalt in Karlsbad 1896" Neue Zeitschrift für Musik 79/17
     (25.4.1912) pp. 236-38. ill., notes. Describes Brahms's
     stay, 9.1896- : his lodgings, milieu and musical activities.
     (d) see: 582.

584 Koch, Adolf. "Johannes Brahms in Ziegelhausen. Ein Erinner-
     ungsblatt" Frankfurter Zeitung und Handelsblatt 46/104
     (15.4.1902) 1. Morgenblatt pp. 1-2 [across page bottoms].
     Describes Brahms's visit in 1875: his lodging, milieu,
     compositional and daily activities.

585 Kroll, Erwin "Königsberg und Brahms" in 2732. pp. 28-37.
     ill., facsim. Describes Brahms's friendship with local resi-
     dents Gustav Dömpke and Louis Köhler, his visit in 1880,
     and visits of his friends; also comments on performances
     there of his music.
     (d) Kroll. "Königsberg als Brahmsstadt" in Kroll.
               Musikstadt Königsberg. Geschichte und Erinnerung.
               Freiburg i. Br. und Zürich: Atlantis Verlag, 1966.
               pp. 212-17. omits ill., facsim.

586 *Krumbach, Wilhelm "Johannes Brahms an der Ebernburg"
     Pfälzische Heimatblätter (Neustadt, Aisch) 12/5 (1964) pp.
     38-39.

587 Leinburg, Mathilde v. "Brahms in München. Zum 25. Tode-
     stage des Meisters" Münchner neueste Nachrichten 75/140
     (1./2.4.1922) Abendblatt pp. 8-9 [across page bottoms].
     Reports on Brahms's visits and personal connections with
     München and Tutzing; also discusses München as a Wagner
     centre and its reaction to Brahms.

588 _____. "Johannes Brahms in Baden-Baden. Unveröffent-
     lichtes ..." Neue Musikzeitung 26/14 (20.4.1905) pp. 309-12.
     notes. Author describes her relationship with Brahms;
     where he stayed in Baden-Baden, his friends there, es-
     pecially Clara Schumann, and his compositional activity.
     (a) *reprint: Atlant[isches]. Tageblatt (5.1911).

589 _____. "Johannes Brahms in Tutzing. Ein Beitrag zur
     Brahmsbiographie" Neue Musikzeitung 28/13 (4.4.1907) pp.

286-87. Describes Brahms's lodgings, compositional and daily activities, and his friends there.

(a) *reprint: Münchner illustrierte Zeitung. Süddeutsche Woche [2]/36 (1909).

590   Linn, Catherine C. "A Story or Two" Music Magazine/Musical Courier 164/6 (7.1962) p. 39. Tells anecdote of Brahms at a concert of his own works in Berlin [1894-95?], and the irritation of audience members disturbed by his behavior during the performance.

591   *Mall, Hermann. "Johannes Brahms und seine schwäbischen Freunde" [Schwäbische Heimat (Schwäbischer Heimatbund) (Stuttgart)] 9 (1958) pp. 151-52.

592   Manz, Gustav. "Brahms und Berlin. Ein Gedenkblatt zum 25 jährigen Todestag des Künstlers" Velhagen und Klasings Monatshefte 36/8 (36/Bd. 2) (4.1922) pp. 146-52. ill. Describes Brahms's visits to Berlin and his friends there.

593   #Matthäus, Wolfgang. "Vor 95 Jahren ... Johannes Brahms konzertierte in Bad Neuenahr" Heimatjahrbuch für den Landkreis Ahrweiler (Rheinberg) 21 (1964) pp. 18-22. ill. Describes stay from 5.-8.1868, during which time Brahms and Stockhausen performed a concert on 25.7.1868.

594   #Münster, Robert. Brahms in München. Ausstellung zum 75. Todestag des Komponisten. Bayerische Staatsbibliothek Musiksammlung, 11. April bis 31. Juli 1972. [(Kleine Ausstellungsführer 19) München: Bayerische Staatsbibliothek, 1972. 10 pp.] ill. Describes Brahms's visits from 1864-1877; also discusses local performances of his music, and people with whom he associated.

595   *Ottendorff-Simrock, Walther and Erich Rütten. "Bad Neuenahr hundert Jahre Heilbad" Heimatjahrbuch für den Landkreis Ahrweiler (Rheinberg) [14] (1958) pp. 17-23.

596   *Otto, Eberhard. "Johannes Brahms und Bayern" Bayerische Staatszeitung (München) Unser Bayern, Heimatbeilage (1.1975) pp. 1-3.

597   #Pieper, Carl. "Johannes Brahms und sein Freundeskreis. Nach einem Briefe von Gustav Ophüls vom 6. Oktober 1892" Die Heimat (Krefeld) 17 (1938) pp. 398-400. ill. Describes a Brahms visit to Krefeld, his activities and friends there.

598   #_____. "Krefelder Musiker" Die Heimat (Krefeld) 2/2 (1922) pp. 61-65. Brahms: p. 62. ill. Summary of Brahms's ties to the city and to his friends there.

599   Potts, Joseph E. "The Meiningen Court Orchestra" The Strad
      79/939 (7.1968) pp. 97, 99, 101, 103. Brahms: pp. 99,
      101. Brahms's association with the orchestra and its per-
      formances of his works, 1881-85.

600   #Reiss, Wolfgang [wf(?)]. "Johannes Brahms komponierte und
      dirigierte in Baden-Baden. Erinnerungen an die Aufenthalte
      des grossen Komponisten in der Kurstadt und in Lichtental"
      Badisches Tagblatt no. 134 (Baden-Baden) (12.6.1968)
      p. [?]. Describes Brahms in Baden-Baden, 1862-1887:
      circle of friends, lodgings, compositional activity, perform-
      ances of his works. Includes anecdote concerning Brahms
      writing poetry.

601   Rössler, Oskar. "Johannes Brahms in Baden-Baden" Frankfurter
      Zeitung 54/113 (25.4.1910) Morgenblatt p. 1. Describes
      visits to Baden-Baden and Lichtental in the 1860's: friends
      there and activities.

602   #Scheuenstuhl, Fred. "Mannheim und Brahms" Mannheimer
      Tageblatt (6./7.5.1933) p. 7. ill. Discusses Brahms's links
      to Mannheim, 1855-1895: visits, friends there, works
      performed there. Includes comments on Brahms and Hecht.

603   *Schulz, Ekkehard. "Johannes Brahms und Karlsruhe. Urauf-
      führungen im Hoftheater und im Museum" Badische neueste
      Nachrichten (Karlsruhe) (21./22.2.1976).

604   Stahmer, Klaus. "Brahms auf Rügen. Der Sommeraufenthalt
      eines Komponisten" Brahms-Studien Bd. 3 (1979) pp. 59-68.
      ill., notes. Describes Brahms's stay at Sassnitz a. Rügen,
      6.-8.1876: discusses work on Op. 68, as well as his recre-
      ational activities.

605   Vecchio-Verderame, Angelo. "Un Certo suonatore d'organetto"
      La Scala (Milan) no. 113 (4.1959) p. 72. Describes incident
      in Berlin when Brahms hears Op. 49 no. 4 played on an
      organ; also comments on Brahms and Wagner.

606   #Weinhold, Liesbeth. "Geschäftsbriefe von grossen Musikern,
      persönlich und historisch betrachtet. Ungedruckte Briefe
      von Schumann, Brahms und Reger an das Leipziger Konser-
      vatorium und Gewandhaus" Leipziger Jahrbuch (1940) pp.
      55-62. Brahms: pp. 58-60. ill. Discusses Brahms's links
      with Leipzig and this institution, focusing on his concert
      of 10.1.1856; includes two letters 12.1855 and 1.1856.

606.5 wf (?) [Wolfgang Reiss], see 600.

607   Wiens, Erich. "Johannes Brahms und die Rheinlande"

Kölnische Zeitung no. 437 (25.4.1909) 2. Beilage p. [1].
Discusses Brahms's relationship to Düsseldorf, 1850-1870's,
and his friends there, especially the Schumanns and
Joachims.

608 *Wintzer, Richard. "Eine Generalprobe unter Brahms. Zum
letzten Konzert des Meisters in Berlin" Hamburger Nachrichten
(5.1. or 1.5.;1932).
   (a) *reprint: Wintzer. "Eine ... Brahms. Das Letzte
      Konzert des Meisters in Berlin" Die Musik-Woche
      4/31 (1936) pp. 17-18.
   (d) #condensed: Wintzer. Die Musik (Berlin) 25/8 (5.1933)
      p. 608. Describes a rehearsal of the Berliner
      Singakademie Orchester 10.1896 with Brahms con-
      ducting, d'Albert as soloist.

609 *Zobeley, Fritz. "Johannes Brahms und Mannheim" Neue badische
Landes-Zeitung Morgen-Ausgabe no. 225 (6.5.1933) p. 6.

See also 107.5, 443.c.ii., 534, 537, 555, 556, 803, 804, 873, 879,
888, 939, 963, 964, 974, 979, 991, 997, 1024, 1025, 1066, 1067, 1078,
1100, 1111, 1112, 1117, 1132, 1140, 1141, 1144, 1154, 1182, 1202,
1205, 1208, 1212, 1239, 1241, 1247, 1288, 1307, 1311.5, 1321, 1943,
2405.5, 2657, 2664, 2776, 2796, 2907, 2909, 3026, 3027, 3063, 3073,
3076, 3089, 3107, 3159.

See also "Family History, Childhood and Links to Hamburg" and "In
Transition" in II.A.

--Holland

See The Netherlands

--Hungary

General Remarks: 610, 611.
Budapest: 612-14.

610 *Batári, Gyula. "Brahms in Ungarn" Budapester Rundschau
    no. 31 (2.8.1968) p. 10.

611 *Koch, Lajos. [Louis Koch] "Brahms Magyarországon. Brahms
    in Ungarn" A Fővárosi könyvtár évkönyve 2 (1932).
      (a) *reprint: Brahms Magyarországon. Brahms in Ungarn.
          (Tanulmányok. Kiadja a Fővárosi könyvtár, Budapest.
          II) [Budapest: Budapest székesfővárosi házinyomdája,
          1933]. 25 pp. Includes summary in German.
          [from 241]

612 *Radó, Richard. "Brahms János pesti hangversenyei. Viss-
     zaemlékezések a zeneköltő centenáriuma alkalmából" Pesti
     hirlap (Budapest) (11.9.1932). Discusses Brahms's first
     concerts in Budapest and the critics' reaction to him.
     [from 241]

613 *Sebestyén, Ede. "Brahms budapesti hangversenyei" A Zene
     15 (1933-34) pp. 94-99. Discusses Brahms's relationship
     with Budapest and the city's reaction to his work; includes
     comments on his interest in Hungarian folkmusic. [from 241]

614 *Sebestyén, Ede. "Brahms és a filharmónikus társaság" Magyar
     hirlap (Budapest) (28.3.1933). Discusses Brahms's links
     with the Budapest Philharmonic: its performances of his
     music, and his guest appearances. [from 241]

See also 19.b., 1125, 1249.
See also "Hubay Family" in III.B.; and "Ethnic and Folksong Influ-
     ences" in V.D.

--Italy

General Remarks: 615, 618.
Rome: 617.

615 *Leinburg, Mathilde [v.]. ""Prussiano" Brahms in Italien"
     Völkischer Beobachter (Berlin) (24.8.1940?).

616 Levi, Lionello, see 2397.5.

617 *Münz, Sigmund. "Johannes Brahms" in Münz. Römische Remi-
     niscenzen und Profile. (Allgemeiner Verein für deutsche
     Litteratur, Berlin [Veröffentlichungen]. Abt. XXVI) Berlin:
     Allgemeiner Verein für deutsche Litteratur, 1900. pp. 42-
     59. ind.
     2. Auflage: 1900. omits series.
         Describes Brahms in Rome with Widmann, 1888; also
         incorporates 1096.
     (c) *excerpt (of ? Auflage): Münz. "Brahms in
             Rom" Hamburger Correspondent 170/575
             (1900) p. 13.
     (d) Münz, S. "Wiener Brahms-Erinnerungen. Zum
             25. Todestag des Meisters" Hamburger
             Fremdenblatt 94/158 (3.4.1922) Abendausgabe
             p. 1. Includes comment on Brahms and
             religion, and trips to Italy with Münz.
     (e) i) report (on ? Auflage): see 39A.d.e.ii.
         ii) report (on ? Auflage): "Höchst interessante
             Beiträge zu dem Charakterbild von
             Johannes Brahms ..." Allgemeine Musik-
             zeitung 29/41 (10.10.1902) pp. 680-81.

618 Widmann, J[osef]. V[iktor]. "Erinnerungen an Johannes
     Brahms. Brahms in Italien" Deutsche Rundschau 23/10 (Bd.
     92) (7.1897) pp. 89-106. notes. Describes trips with
     Brahms in 1889, 1890, 1893.
     (a) *reprint in: Johannes Brahms in Erinnerungen. Berlin:
         Verlag von Gebrüder Paetel, 1898. 180 pp.
         additional notes.
         2. Auflage: 1898.
             also includes 2631 and reprint of 1302.
         *3. Auflage: 1910.
         *4. Auflage: 1921. 176 pp.?
         [New Auflage:] Neu herausgegeben und ergänzt
             von Willi Reich. Basel: Amerbach-Verlag,
             1947. 131, [2] pp. ill., additional notes.
             Includes an Anhang of letters Brahms to
             Widmann, 1888 (1) [from 1297]; Widmann-
             Gottfried Keller, 1888 (3) [from Gottfried
             Keller. Gottfried Keller und J. V. Widmann:
             Briefwechsel. Max Widmann, ed. Zürich:
             O. Füssli, [1922]] and Widmann to Max
             Kalbeck, 1897 (1) [from ?].
         [New Auflage:] Widmann, Josef Viktor. Erinnerungen
             an Johannes Brahms. Einleitung von Samuel
             Geiser. Zürich und Stuttgart: Rotapfel-
             Verlag, 1980. 165, [3] pp. facsim. Omits
             1302 and 2631; Anhang of 1947 Auflage not
             included.
     (b) English translation by Dora Hecht
              (of 1898 Auflage): see 894.b.
     (c) i) excerpt (of 1898 Auflage): Stgl,
              R. "Brahms' Deutschtum" Zeitschrift
              für Musik 100/5 (5.1933) p. 476.
         ii) *excerpt (of 1947 Auflage): Widmann.
              "Johannes Brahms" Amerbach Bote:
              Almanach (Basel) Bd. 1 (1947)
              pp. 245-51.
     (e) i)#report (on 1898 Auflage): "Erinner-
              ungen an Johannes Brahms. Altes
              und Neues aus seinem Leben"
              Neues Wiener Journal no. 3130
              (12.7.1902) p. 10. Also includes
              reports on 479, 667; includes
              comments on Brahms and Hamburg,
              as well as Brahms and Wagner.
         ii) report (on 1898 Auflage): Paetow,
              Walter. "Neuere Brahms-Literatur"
              Deutsche Rundschau 24/12 (Bd.
              96) (9.1898) pp. 470-74. Includes
              reports on 73, 117, 894, 1346, 2540.
         iii) report (on 1898 Auflage): R. B.
              "Brahmsiana" Der Kunstwart

[=Deutsche Zeitschrift] 11/22
(8.1898) pp. 302-07. Includes
reports on 73, 85, 117, 816, 894,
1346.

(d) *expanded: Sizilien und andere Gegenden Italiens. Reiseerinnerungen.
Frauenfeld: [T.] Huber & Co.,
1898. viii, 338 pp. notes. [from
1912 Auflage]

*2. Auflage: Sizilien und ... Italiens.
Reisen mit Johannes Brahms. 1903.
vi, 338 pp.

3. Auflage: 1912. viii, 299 pp. Only
contains a more detailed accounting
of trips with Brahms.

(e) *report (on 1898 Auflage):
"Johannes Brahms var ..."
Neue Musikzeitung 19/2
(1898) pp. 17-19.

(e) report: "Erinnerungen an Johannes
Brahms" Neue Musikzeitung 18/15
(1897) pp. 186-87. Includes report
on 969.

See also 107.5, 755, 868, 1294, 1295, 2397.5, 2815, 2832.

--The Netherlands

619   "Brief von Professor Engelmann aan Mevrouw Engelmann-
Brandes" Caecilia (Utrecht) 79/12 (10.5.1922) pp. 185-87.
ill. Reports on letter written in Utrecht, 1.1882, which
describes a Brahms concert on 21.1., and its preparation:
Brahms conducted Op. 73 and was the soloist for a performance of Op. 83.

620   "Johannes Brahms in Holland. Persönliche Erinnerungen von
Julius Röntgen" Neue Musikzeitung 41/15 (29.4.1920) pp.
236-38. ill., mus. Describes Brahms's trips, 1876-85,
and the reception of his music; author also comments on
Brahms's relationship with the Engelmann family and his
own personal friendship with Brahms.

621   *Röntgen, Julius. "Brahms in Holland" Die Musikwelt (Hamburg)
3/1 (1922).

See also 920, 1193, 2812, 2884.

--Rumania

Braşov [=Brassó=Kronstadt]: 622, 623, 625.

Cluj [=Kolozsvár=Klausenburg]: 622-25.
Sibiu [=Nagyszeben=Hermannstadt]: 622, 623, 625.
Sighișoara [=Segesvár=Schässburg]: 622, 625.
Timișoara [=Temesvár]: 622, 625.

622 #Bickerich, Viktor and Norbert Petri. "Johannes Brahms în
Transilvania. O informare pe bază de documente" Studii
de muzicologie 6 (1970) pp. 259-81. notes. Includes French
summary. Traces preparation and route of Brahms-Joachim
tour of 9.1879 with excerpts from 1009 and the contemporary
local presses.

623 *"Brahms és Joachim 1879 IX. 19-én Brassöban, 21-én Szebenben,
23-én Kolozsvárott hangversenyezett" Fővárosi lapok (Budapest) (20.9.1879). Brahms and Joachim performing on
19.9.1879 in Kronstadt, 21.9.1879 in Hermannstadt, 23.9.1879
in Klausenburg. [from 241]

624 *"Brahms és Joachim kolozsvári hangversenyének elözetes jelentése" Kelet (Kolozsvár) (12.9.1879). Announcement of the
Brahms-Joachim concert in Klausenburg. [from 241]

625 *Lakatos, István. "Brahms és Joachim erdélyi hangversenykörútja" Pásztortűz 18/2 (1942). Discusses the Brahms-
Joachim "Siebenbürger" concert tour. [from 241]
  (b) *German translation: Lakatos, Stefan. "Brahms in
       Siebenbürgen" Ungarn (Budapest) no. 5 (1942).
    (a) reprint: Lakatos. in Deutsch-Ungarische
         Begegnungen. Béla Pukánszky, ed.
         (Ungarn-Bücherei Bd. II) Budapest-Leipzig-
         Milano: Verlag Danubia, 1943. pp. 194-97.
         Presents a record of the Brahms-Joachim
         concert tour, 9.1879, and its affiliated
         activities.

See also 241 pp. 21-25 for concert tour reviews.

--Scotland

See 2532.

--Switzerland

General Remarks: 630, 631, 633.
Basel: 629, 633.d.ii.
Bern: 633.d.i., 634.
Thun: 627.5, 628.
Winterthur: 634.
Zürich: 626, 627, 632, 634.

626   E. I. "Johannes Brahms und Zürich. Zum hundertsten Ge-
      bürtstag des Meisters" Neue Zürcher Zeitung 154/823
      (7.5.1933) 2. Sonntagausgabe Blatt 5 pp. [1,2] [across
      page bottoms]. Discusses Brahms's links to Switzerland,
      particularly Zürich: his visits, his friends, local perform-
      ance of his works.

627   Erismann, Hans. "Johannes Brahms in Zürich" in Musiker-
      Handschriften. Zeugnisse des Zürcher Musiklebens. Martin
      Hürlimann, ed. [Zürich:] Atlantis Verlag, [1969]. pp.
      30-34. ill., facsim. text: pp. 30, 32. Discusses Brahms's
      visits, his friends and musical activities; also describes 4
      manuscripts: Opp. 45 (2), 98, Kleine Hochzeitskantate
      [Hofmann nr. 190; McCorkle WoO posthum 16]; and an edition
      of Op. 45.
      (d) *Erismann. Johannes Brahms und Zürich. Ein Beitrag
           zur Kulturgeschichte von Zürich. (Zürcher Druck
           40) Zürich: Gebrüder Fretz AG, 1974. 129 pp. ill.

627.5 Guinzburg, Juana. "Peregrinaje suizo con los grandes músicos:
      Johannes Brahms" Buenos Aires musical 28/455 (1.9.1973) p.
      5. Summarizes Brahms's links to Switzerland, focusing on
      Thun area--what he wrote there, his Swiss friends--and
      contrasts the city of 1973 with the city of Brahms's time.

628   *Kunz, Paul and Ernst Isler. "Brahms in Thun" Rheinische
      Musik- und Theaterzeitung (Köln) 16/29,30 (1915).

629   *Löw, R. Basler Nachrichten (15.6.1924).

630   *Otto, Eberhard. "Johannes Brahms und die Schweiz" Winter-
      thurer Tagblatt? [=Winterthurer Stadtanzeiger?] (1.3.1974).

631   *_____. "Zu Johannes Brahms' Schweizer Aufenthalten"
      Neue Zürcher Zeitung (3.3.1974).

632   P.Pf. "Eine Brahms-Reminiszenz aus dem Jahre 1866" Neue
      Zürcher Zeitung 177/2835 (10.10.1956) Abendausgabe p.
      [1]. [=Neue Zürcher Zeitung 177/2822 (10.10.1956) Morgen-
      ausgabe p. 14.] Describes Brahms's stay in Zürich: his
      lodgings, friends there, daily activities and work on Op. 45.

633   Refardt, Edgar. "Brahms in der Schweiz. (Zum 100. Ge-
      burtstag des Komponisten am 7. Mai 1933)" Schweizerische
      Musikzeitung und Sängerblatt. Gazette musicale suisse
      73/9 (1.5.1933) pp. 341-50. ill., mus., notes. Describes
      visits Brahms made to Switzerland and his activities there;
      includes comment on Swiss performances of Brahms's music.
      (a) *reprint: in Refardt. Musik in der Schweiz. Aus-
           gewählte Aufsätze. [Herausgegeben im Auftrag
           der Ortsgruppe Basel der Schweizerischen Musik-
           forschenden Gesellschaft von Hans Ehinger und

Ernst Mohr] Bern: P. Haupt, 1952.

(d) i) *Refardt. "Brahms in Bern" Der kleine Bund
(Bern) 14/19 (1933).

  ii) *Refardt. "Brahms und Brahms-Musik in Basel"
Basler Nachrichten Sonntagsblatt no. 19 (1933).

634 #Tiénot, Yvonne. "Brahms à Zurich, Winterthur et Berne"
Revue musicale de Suisse Romande 22/2 (5.-6.1969) pp.
2,3,5. ill., notes. Describes his lodgings, daily and
compositional activities, friends there; also contains anecdotal
material.

See also 27.c.i., 389, 537, 618.a., 755, 824, 958, 1057, 1080, 1129,
1130, 1302, 1318, 2297, 2850, 2960, 3133.

--Union of Soviet Socialist Republics

See 2354.5.

--United States of America

See 1354, 1365, 1908, 2952, 2993.

C. BRAHMS THE MAN

1. Physical/Emotional Being and Lifestyle

Brahms the bibliophile: 672, 673, 689, 690, 719, 728.
Brahms the conductor: 685, 706, 713, 735, 737.
Brahms the pianist: 638, 639, 642, 647, 650, 651, 657, 658, 674,
692, 713, 715, 727, 747, 754.
Brahms the teacher: 687, 691, 694, 697, 724.

635 *Musical Courier (1.3.1893) p. 9.
(a) i) *reprint: Etude(?)
(a) reprint: Huneker, James [Gibbons]. "Musical
Biography Made to Order" in Huneker. Old
Fogy. His Musical Opinions and Grotesques.
With an Introduction by James Huneker.
Philadelphia: Theodore Presser Co., 1913.
pp. 147-59. Brahms: pp. 151-52. Discusses
the coloring of biographical facts with historical fiction: example, Wagner's report
that Brahms hated cats.
  ii) reprint: "Brahms' Hatred of Cats" In Theory Only
2/5 (8.1976) p. 26.

636 *Musik im Unterricht 49/9 (1958).

637 A.F-nn. "Aus dem Leben von Johannes Brahms" Neue Musik-
     zeitung 18/8 (1897) 1. Beilage p. 103. Relates anecdotes
     illustrating Brahms's character: Brahms and children,
     Brahms and autograph collectors; Brahms and Wagner;
     examples of his sharp wit.

638 Abell, Arthur M[aynard]. "Brahms As I Knew Him" Etude
     49/12 (12.1931) pp. 851-52. Describes meetings with Brahms
     in 1891, 1893, 1896: relates the composer's comments on
     his early days [c. 1853]; composing for the violin/piano
     medium, and his own works for that combination; religion
     and its effect on music. Includes Abell's comments on
     Brahms's piano-playing technique.
     (d) i) Abell. "Brahms, The Man and Musician" New York
            Times 82/27,497 (7.5.1933) Section 9 pp. 5, 6.
            Describes meetings with Brahms in 1891 and 1896,
            with additional comments by Brahms on how he com-
            poses.
        ii) incorporated: 2453.

639 Amory, A. H. "Brahms als pianist" Caecilia (Utrecht) 79/11
     (10.4.1922) pp. 169-71. Discusses Brahms's piano teachers
     and their backgrounds, and describes his capabilities as a
     pianist, including performance of his own works.

640 [Daniel Gregory Mason] "Anecdotes of Brahms" Masters in Music
     5/part 30 (6.1905) pp. [1]-5 (volume pp. [241-45]). notes.
     Uses excerpts from 880, 894.b., 978 to illustrate various
     sides of Brahms's character.

641 Antcliffe, Herbert. "Brahms: Light and Sombre" Musical
     Opinion and Music Trade Review 76/904 (1.1953) pp. 211,
     213. Refutes the customary view of Brahms as being a
     solemn person, with examples of lightheartedness in his
     music and life.

642 #"Bei Meister Brahms" Deutsche Militärmusikerzeitung 33/5
     (3.2.1911) p. 51. Relates anecdote of Brahms accompanying
     and drowning out a cellist.

643 Belleau, André. "Avez-vous lu Brahms?" Liberté 7 (9./10.1965)
     pp. 433-37. notes. States the opinion that to understand
     Brahms the person, one needs to study his music.

644 Berger, Fred. "The Big Bear" Coronet 39/2 (Whole no. 230)
     (12.1955) pp. 142, 144. ill., discog. Presents anecdotes
     from throughout Brahms's life to describe his character.

645 Berry, Leland J. "Brahms and His Music" Calcutta Review

Third Series 33/2/3 (11./12.1929) pp. 256-59. Illustrates Brahms's nature with anecdotes; also discusses Brahms as composer, and his links to Schubert.

646 Birt, Th. "Noordwyk und Brahms. Ein Reisebrief" Frankfurter Zeitung 54/249 (8.9.1909) 1. Morgenblatt pp. 1-2 [across page bottoms]. Aspects of the author's trip to Noordwyk remind him of qualities of Brahms and his music; also discusses links between Rembrandt and Brahms.

647 Bose, Fritz [v.]. "Die einzige Schallaufnahme von Brahms" Musica Schallplatte. Zeitschrift für Schallplattenfreunde [Beilage to Musica (Kassel)] no. 3 (1958) pp. 33-35. notes. Concerning the only known recording of Brahms playing Ungarische Tänze no. 1 [Hofmann nr. 128; McCorkle WoO 1]: gives its circumstances, provenance of the disc, and comment on the performance.

648 Bossert, Audrey. "An Intransigeant Egotist. "A Thundering Stream ... Voices of Nightingales"" Music. The A.G.O. and R.C.C.O. Magazine 4/4 (4.1970) pp. 35, 58-59. Describes what Brahms was really like, through the eyes, i.e. the writings, of his contemporaries: uses excerpts from 969, 983, 1013, 1179, 1302, 3013 and Wagner's writings.

649 Brahms. Bilder aus seinem Leben. [Text by Ludwig Berger. Picture captions by Philipp Harden-Rauch] Stuttgart: E. Schreiber, 1968. 64 pp. ill., facsim., notes. text: pp. 3-16, discusses Brahms's life. 55 ill.

650 "Brahms at the Piano. A Gramophone Record" The Times (London) Late London Edition no. 48,969 (4.7.1941) p. 6. Presents circumstances of Brahms recording Ungarische Tänze no. 1 [Hofmann nr, 128; McCorkle WoO 1], the provenance of the disc, and a comment on Brahms's playing.

651 "Brahms Record Discovered" Musical Courier 110/11 (Whole no. 2852) (16.3. 1935) p. 5. Reports on discovery in Berlin of disc containing Brahms playing Ungarische Tänze no. 1 [Hofmann nr. 128; McCorkle WoO 1].

652 "Brahms the Stoic. The Horn Tune" The Times (London) Late London Edition no. 51,701 (26.5.1950) p. 8. Describes how Brahms's choice of song texts reveals his stoicism; also comments on the dichotomy of Brahms's personality as seen in his music, and the significance of the alpine horn tune that Brahms sent to Clara Schumann.
(d) Hamand, L. A. "Brahms's Horn Tune" The Times (London) Late London Edition no. 51,706 (1.6.1950) p. 7. Letter to the editor: gives background on horn tune as noted in 1139.d.ii.

653   Bührig, Wilhelm. "Buchstaben- und Notenschrift" Zeitschrift
      für Menschenkunde 3/2 (7.1927) pp. 116-20. Brahms:
      pp. 117-18. facsim. Comments on Brahms's handwriting
      using a specimen from 2.1897, contained in Karl Geigy-
      Hagenbach. Album von Handschriften berühmter Persön-
      lichkeiten von Mittelalter bis zur Neuzeit. (Basel: R.
      Geering, 1925).

654   C. K. "An eine Brahms-Anekdote ..." Allgemeine Zeitung
      (München) 110/364 (8.8.1907) Vorabendblatt p. 3. Relates
      anecdote showing the violent side of Brahms when he was
      angry.

655   Comini, Alessandra. "The Visual Brahms: Idols and Images"
      Arts Magazine 54/2 (10.1979) pp. 123-29. ill., notes. Ex-
      amines photographs and pictures of Brahms to see what they
      reveal of his life and music.

656   Crawshaw, Edith A. H. "Brahms--As Seen By Others. A
      Selection of Recollections & Reflections" Music Teacher 12/4
      (M.S. [Music Student] series 26/7) (4.1933) pp. 187, 189.
      ill. Comments and opinions on Brahms the man, the musician,
      and on his works: excerpts from 18, 23, 48, 73, 82, 138,
      211, 871, 1109, 1179, 1208, 1336, 1392, 1816, 2486, 2935,
      3048, and comments by Smyth, Grove, Brodsky, and
      Tchaikovsky.

657   Davies, Fanny. "Some Personal Recollections of Brahms as
      Pianist and Interpreter" in Cobbett's Cyclopedic Survey
      of Chamber Music. Walter Willson Cobbett, comp. and ed.
      London: Humphrey Milford, Oxford University Press, 1929.
      pp. 182-84. Describes Brahms in the period 1884-86, focuses
      on a performance he gave of Op. 101.
      2nd Edition: London, New York, Toronto: Oxford University
      Press, 1963.

658   Decsey, Ernst. Die Spieldose. Musiker-Anekdoten. Leipzig,
      Wien, Zürich: E.P. Tal & Co. Verlag, 1922. 185, [4] pp. notes.
      "Brahms als Kritiker": p. 131.
         Brahms criticizing the music of Scholz.
      "Die letzte Welle": p. 168.
         Mahler walking with Brahms, trying to read great sig-
         nificance into Brahms's simple, literal remarks.
      *2. veränderte Auflage: (Musikalische Volksbücher) Stutt-
         gart: J. Engelhorns Nachf[olger]., [1928]. 186, [4]
         pp. ill., mus.
      "Brahms als Brahmsbegleiter": p. 132. [from 241]
      "Der Stern": p. 133. [from 241]
      "Die letzte Welle": pp. 169-70. [from 241]

659 Diesterweg, Adolf. ""Bürger" Brahms" Allgemeine Musikzeitung
59/20 (20.5.1932) pp. 270-71. Evaluates Brahms's character.
(d) see: 2989.

659.5 #dp.[Walter Deppisch] "Einmal schlief das Modell ein" Die Welt
(Hamburg) no. 146 (27.6.1970) p. [?]. ill. Discusses the
Brahms-Archiv's acquisition of paintings of Brahms by Ludwig Michalek; includes comments on Brahms sitting for the
works.
(a) reprint: Deppisch. Mitteilungen der Brahms-Gesellschaft
Hamburg e.V. no. 1 (10.1970) p. 7. ill. [p. 6]

660 Dresden, Sem. "Brahms, een der groote figuren?" Caecilia
(Utrecht) 79/12 (10.5.1922) pp. 182-85. Discusses Brahms's
character as seen in his works; also comments on Brahms
as the extension of Beethoven's musicality.

661 *Egidi, A[rthur]. "Brahms in Momentaufnahmen" Musik in
Zeitbewusstsein 1 (1933/34) pp. 16-18.

662 Ehrmann, Alfred von. "The "Terrible" Brahms" G. R. translator Musical Quarterly 23/1 (1.1937) pp. 64-76. notes.
Describes Brahms's attitude towards his contemporaries and
their musical works. Focuses on Joachim, Grimm, Scholz,
Bruch, and Herzogenberg.

663 Engelbrecht, Kurt, see 2368.5.

664 *Erler, Katharina. "Johannes Brahms Stiftung, Bilder" Jahresarbeit der Hamburger Bibliotheksschule, 1961. 55 pp.

665 Ernest, Gustav. "Johannes Brahms" Die Musik (Berlin) 25/8
(5.1933) pp. 561-66. Discusses Brahms's character: its
evolution, and its reflection in his music.
(a) reprint: in 3186.c. pp. 1-6.

666 #"Ernstes und Heiteres um Brahms" Deutsche Musiker-Zeitung
(Berlin) 58/15 (9.4.1927) pp. 528-29. Comments on Brahms
the man, including materials from 618.a., 1067.a., 1090,
and 1180.

667 *Fellinger, Maria. Brahms-Bilder. Leipzig: Breitkopf & Härtel,
1900. ill.
2. vermehrte Auflage: (Breitkopf & Härtels Musikbücher)
1911. 40 leaves. ill. Text on leaf 1, pictures leaf 3-40.
Contains 38 photographs of Brahms either by himself or with
friends, out of doors, 1887- . Includes pictures of Marxsen,
Fritz Schnack and a drawing by Menzel.
(e) i) report (on 1900 Auflage): see 618.a.e.i.
ii)*report (on 1900 Auflage): Kalbeck, M[ax]. Neues
Wiener Tagblatt (12.10.1900).
iii) report (on 1900 Auflage): see 2022.e.ii.

668 Fleischer, Herbert. "Brahms--ein Bürger?" Vossische Zeitung
(Berlin) Unterhaltungsblatt nr. 125 (7.5.1933) pp. [2-3]
[across page tops]. Examines Brahms's music and background
and concludes that an intellectual streak is prevalent in
Brahms's work.

669 *Fodor, Gyula. Zenéloóra. Történetek zenéröl és zenészekröl.
Budapest: Singer és Wolfner, 1941. 307 pp. Brahms:
pp. 39, 60-61, 63-64, 69, 139, 152-54, 254. anecdotes.
[from 241].

670 Friedland, Martin. "Brahms und der Pessimismus I-III" Allgemeine Musikzeitung 52/44, 45 (30.10. and 6.11.;1925)
pp. 899-901, 919-21. Discusses pessimism as shown by
Brahms in his person and music, draws parallels between
Brahms and Schopenhauer.

671 Gauer, Oscar. "Beethoven and Brahms" Musical Opinion and
Music Trade Review 31/361 (1.10.1907) p. 28. Points
out similarity between sketch of Beethoven by Johann Peter
Lyser in Die Musik (Berlin) 6/16 (Bd. 23) (5.1907) [Beilagen,
p. 4] and the Otto Böhler cutout paper silhouette of Brahms.

672 Geiringer, Karl. "Brahms as a Reader and Collector" M.D.
Herter Norton translator Musical Quarterly 19/2 (4.1933)
pp. 158-68. mus., notes. Discusses the types of materials
in Brahms's personal library.
(d) see: 25.b.i. (1982 Edition).

673 Geiringer, Karl and Irene Geiringer. "Die Bibliothek von
Johannes Brahms. Anlässlich ihrer Neuaufstellung in Wien"
Neue Zürcher Zeitung 194/164 (Fernausgabe no. 96) (8.4.
1973) pp. 51-52. ill. Describes exhibit and cites some of
Brahms's marginalia and notes from the items.
(d) Geiringer and Geiringer. "The Brahms Library in the
"Gesellschaft der Musikfreunde", Wien" Notes 30/1
(9.1973) pp. 7-14. ill., notes. Describes musically
related materials in Brahms's personal library.

674 Geisler-Schubert, Carola. "Memories of Brahms" The Times
(London) Late London Edition no. 48,976 (12.7.1941) p. 5.
A letter to the editor describing occasions where she heard
Brahms play, as well as seeing him in his final public ap-
pearance in Wien.

675 Gerdes, Karl. "Brahms als Tröster" Signale für die musikalische Welt 88/7 (12.2.1930) pp. 173-75. Describes how
Brahms's experience with sorrow in his life helped him in
the emotion's musical realization, with examples from the
choral works.

676 Glock, W. F., see 2633.5.

677   Goodwin, Amina. "Memories of Brahms" The Times (London)
      Royal Edition no. 45,742 (9.2.1931) p. 8. Relates anecdotes
      about Brahms and his love of good food, from her days of
      study with Clara Schumann.

678   #Der grösste Komponist" Schlesische Zeitung (Breslau) (1.5.1943)
      p. [1]. Relates an anecdote about Brahms's avoidance of
      a toast to himself at a dinner, by his toasting Mozart instead.

679   *Grosser, F. "Brahms, der Ungastliche" Volksgesundheitskalen-
      der (Zürich) 6 (1933) p. 70.

680   *Grun, Bernard. Private Lives of the Great Composers, Con-
      ductors and Musical Artistes of the World. London, New
      York: Rider, 1954. 300 pp. also: New York:
      also: New York: Library Publishers, 1955.
         Brahms: pp. 31-32, 60, 70, 73-74, 78-79, 110, 122, 150,
         185, 204, 209-11, 239-41, 277, 281. ill., facsim., mus.,
         ind. Relates anecdotes of Brahms with his family and
         contemporaries; his character and sharp wit; public
         reaction to his music; his relationship with women; and
         allusions in his music.

681   Hadden, J[ames]. Cuthbert. "Stars Among The Planets" in
      Hadden. Master Musicians. A Book for Players, Singers &
      Listeners. London & Edinburgh: T. N. Foulis, [1909].
      pp. 229-54. "Brahms": pp. 242-46. Describes Brahms the
      man, and the characteristics of his piano music.
      *also: Boston: L. Phillips, [1909].
      *also: Chicago: A. C. McClurg & Co., 1911.
      *also: London & Edinburgh: T. N. Foulis; Boston: Le Roy
         Phillips, 1913.
      issues (of London & Edinburgh 1909 Edition): 1911, 1913,
         1917, 1919.

682   #Hansen, W. "Anecdotes de musiciens" L.M.-C. translator.
      Revue musicale de suisse romande 20/1 (3.1967) pp. 5-8.
      Brahms: pp. 6, 8. ill. Presents anecdotes as a window on
      Brahms's personality: Brahms and R. Strauss, examples
      of some of his dislikes, and his flair for sarcasm.

683   Heimann, Wilhelm. "Johannes Brahms als Künstler und Mensch.
      Ein Erinnerungsblatt auf das Grab des deutschen Meisters
      zu seinem 30. Todestage am 3. April 1927" Signale für
      die musikalische Welt 85/15 (13.4.1927) pp. 577-81. Describes
      Brahms the man; includes comment on his childhood, last
      days, and his worth.

684   "Heiteres von Joh[annes]. Brahms" Schweizer Musiker-Revue
      9/12 (15.6.1934) pp. 4-5. Relates anecdotes of Brahms in
      Bad Ischl with Menzel: his love of food and avoidance of

doctors, his thoughts on memorials, and his method for
seeking appropriate lodgings.

685   *Helm, Theodor. "Brahms als Dirigent" Osterreichische Musik-
und Theaterzeitung (Wien) [11] (15.1.1898).

686   Henschel, Maria. "Studie über zwei Musikerhandschriften
(Brahms und Chopin)" Die Schrift (Brünn) 3/4 (1937) pp.
167-87. Brahms: pp. 170-79. facsim., notes. Graphologi-
cal analysis of 3 letters written by Brahms in 1859, 1863,
1878; also discusses changes in his handwriting over the
years.

687   *Hernried, Robert. "Brahms und die Musikpädagogik. Mit
ungedruckte Ausserungen der Meisters" Schweizerische
musikpädagogische Blätter 26 (1937) pp. 98-100.

688   #Heuberger, Richard. "Zum Gedächtnis an Brahms bei der
zehnten Wiederkehr seines Todestages" Der Kunstwart 20/13
(4.1907) pp. 6-10. Discusses Brahms in relation to his
colleagues and relates his opinions of them: Wagner,
Meyerbeer, Bizet, Dvořák, Smetana, Verdi, Strauss, Fuchs.

689   Hirschfeld, Robert. "Brahms und seine Bücher. Zur sieb-
zigsten Wiederkehr seines Geburtstages am 7. Mai 1903"
Frankfurter Zeitung und Handelsblatt 47/126 (7.5.1903)
1. Morgenblatt pp. 1-2 [across page bottoms]. Discusses
what his library holdings tell us about Brahms the man;
includes comments on the sources he owned that he used
for song texts.

690   Hofmann, Kurt. Die Bibliothek von Johannes Brahms. Bücher-
und Musikalienverzeichnis. (Schriftenreihe zur Musik)
Hamburg: Verlag der Musikalienhandlung Karl Dieter
Wagner, 1974. xxxiv, 171 pp. ill., facsim., notes. Discusses Brahms the bibliophile and the history of his library;
presents newly compiled indices for nonmusic material, and
previously overlooked music material; contains reprint of
728.

691   *Huschke, Konrad. "Brahms als Lehrer" Deutsche Tonkünstler-
Zeitung (Berlin) 31 (1931?) p. 83.
(d) #incorporated: Huschke. Johannes Brahms als Pianist,
Dirigent und Lehrer. Karlsruhe in Baden: Friedrich
Gutsch Verlag, [1935]. 116 pp. ill., ind. Work
is based on available documentation and personal
comments from those contemporaries of Brahms who
are still living. Incorporates 692 as well.

692   _____. "Brahms als Pianist" Die Musik (Berlin) 23/3 (12.1930)
pp. 176-82.
(d) #incorporated: 691.d.

693 #_____. "Johannes Brahms' Nationalgefühl" Völkischer Beobachter (Berlin) Norddeutscher Ausgabe no. 317 (13.11.1935)
Unterhaltungsbeilage p. [?]. Discusses patriotic Brahms,
focuses on Op. 55.
    (a) *reprint: Huschke. Deutsche Sängerbundeszeitung
        (Berlin) 28 (1936) pp. 369-70.

694 Jenner, G[ustav]. "Brahms als Mensch, Lehrer und Künstler"
Die Musik (Berlin) 2/15,17 (Bd. 7) (5.,6.;1903) pp. [171]-98,
389-403. notes. Author describes studying composition
with Brahms 1887-88 and Brahms's thoughts on various
topics relating to composition.
    (a) reprint: Jenner, Gustav. Johannes Brahms ... Künstler.
        Studien und Erlebnisse. Marburg in Hessen: N. G.
        Elwert'sche Verlagsbuchhandlung, 1905. [2], 78
        pp. ill., facsim.
        *2. Auflage: 1930.
        (c) #excerpt (of 1905 Auflage): see 697.
        (e) i) *report (on 1905 Auflage): Leipziger Zeitung
              57/41 (1906).
           ii) report (on 1930 Auflage): see 61.e.i.
    (c) *excerpt?: Jenner, Gustav. Russkaia muzykalnaia
        gazeta [20]/34,35 (1913). [Discusses Brahms as
        a teacher]
    (e) report: Peyser, Herbert F. "Johannes Brahms. The
        Master as Teacher" Musical America 67/3 (2.1947)
        pp. 3, 224, 357. ill. Describes Jenner's period
        of study with Brahms.

695 "Johannes Brahms" Neue Musikzeitung 18/9 (1897) pp. 114-15.
    Kl. "Es hat wenige grosse Künstler gegeben": pp. 114-15.
    Discusses Brahms as composer and other people's reaction
    to him; Brahms and opera; his last words on his death-
    bed.
    A.Frn. "Zu Brahms' 60. Geburtstag": p. 115.
    Discusses the medallion presented by the Gesellschaft
    der Musikfreunde to Brahms, and his comments on it.
    "Die Neue freie Presse bringt ebenfalls ...": p. 115.
    Report on 412.5.

696 "Johannes Brahms (The New Education--The Mastery of Teaching
Material)" Musician (Philadelphia) 3/5 (5.1898) pp. 126-27.
Manchester, Arthur L. "The Man": pp. 126-27. Also
discusses Brahms the composer.

697 #"Johannes Brahms als Kompositionslehrer" Musik im Unterricht
[Ausgabe A] 54/6 (6.1963) p. 195. excerpt of 694.a.

698 *"Johannes Brahms rauh und gütig" Der Bau und die Bauindustrie. Beilage. Der Baukasten (Düsseldorf) 6/8 (1954)
p. 7.

699 *"Johannes Brahms und das Vaterland" Deutsche Zeitung in
Norwegen (Oslo) (25.8.1943).

700 *Kalbeck, Max. "Brahms als Briefsteller" Neues Wiener Tagblatt
(28.11.1906).

701 *_____. "Brahms als Patriot" Berliner Tageblatt (3.11.1913).

702 _____. "Ein deutscher Meister der Tonkunst. Zum 20.
Jahrestage von Brahms' Tode" Über Land und Meer Bd.
118/30 (Jahrgang 59) (1917) pp. 560-61. Discusses the
patriotic Brahms, focuses on Op. 55.

703 *_____. "Ein Passionsweg. Aus Tagebuchblättern" Neues
Wiener Tagblatt (3.,4.;4.;1907).

704 Karpath, Ludwig. Lachende Musiker. Anekdotisches von
Richard Wagner, Richard Strauss, Liszt, Brahms, Bruckner,
Goldmark, Hugo Wolf, Gustav Mahler und anderen Musikern.
Erlebtes und nacherzähltes von ... München: Verlag Knorr
& Hirth G.m.b.H., 1929. 131, [1] pp.
"Johannes Brahms": pp. 31-41. Anecdotes.
"Brahms und Goldmark": pp. 43-47. Anecdotes.
(c) excerpt: "Anekdoten" Vossische Zeitung (Berlin)
Unterhaltungsblatt nr. 125 (7.5.1933) p. [2].

705 #Köhler, Louis. Johannes Brahms und seine Stellung in der
Musikgeschichte. Hannover: Verlag von Arnold Simon,
1880. 48 pp. Examines Brahms's music as a key to understanding his character; also discusses his historical position.

706 Komorn, Maria. Johannes Brahms als Chordirigent in Wien und
seine Nachfolger bis zum Schubert-Jahr 1928. (U.E. nr.
8821) Wien-Leipzig: Universal-Edition, 1928. 143 pp.
Brahms: pp. 17-62. ill., notes. Discusses Brahms as
conductor of the Gesellschaft der Musikfreunde and its
Singverein: his programming, rehearsal techniques,
character; also includes 2267.
(d) condensed in English translation by W. Oliver Strunk:
Komorn. "Brahms, Choral Conductor" Musical
Quarterly 19/2 (4.1933) pp. 151-57.

707 *Krebs, Carl. "Brahms als Sammler" Der Tag (Berlin) (29.5.
1912).

708 #_____. "Der Politiker Brahms" Der Tag (Berlin) Ausgabe
B no. 111 (13.5.1914) Illustrierter Teil pp. [1-3] [across
page bottoms]. Presents an example of Brahms's thoughts
on politics; includes comments on 39.

709 Kretzschmar, Hermann. "Johannes Brahms. Eine Charakterstudie aus der Componistenwelt der Gegenwart." Die

Gartenlaube [28]/14 (1880) pp. 220-24. ill. Presents an overview of Brahms's life and examines his music for insight into his character.

710   L. Musical Courier 52/26 (Whole no. 1370) (27.6.1906) pp. 23-24. Brahms: p. 24. on the "idiotsyncrasies" of great musicians-- a parody on articles that describe obvious or inconsequential characteristics of composers.

711   #Laaff, Ernst. "Zwei Photo-Platten mit Brahms-Aufnahmen gefunden" Musik im Unterricht 49/5 (1958) p. 141. ill. Describes 2 photographs of Brahms taken by Maria Fellinger c. 1895.

712   Leinburg, Mathilde v. "Der anekdotenhafte Brahms" Neue Musikzeitung 43/13 (6.4.1922) pp. 205-07. ill. Gives correct versions of anecdotes distorted by their recurrent telling, plus new anecdotes on Brahms with friends, together with Brahms's comments on Beethoven, Mozart, Bach, Bruckner.

713   *_____. (von Leinburg) "Brahms als Klavierspieler und Dirigent" Daheim 70/31 (1933).
       (a) *reprint: Die Propyläen? (München) 34 (1937) pp. 221-22.

714   *_____. (Leinburg) "Brahms als möblierter Zimmerherr" Der Tag (Berlin) (23.3.1922).
       (a) *reprint: Leinburg. Hamburger Nachrichten (3.4.1922).

715   #_____. (von Leinburg) "Johannes Brahms als Mensch" Bergstadt 13/1 (3.1925) pp. 619-23. ill. Discusses Brahms's personality as shaped by his experiences in life; with anecdotes on topics such as Brahms and religion, his piano playing, and Brahms and Wien.
       (e) #report: "Brahms am Klavier. Aus neuen Erinnerungen" Hamburger Nachrichten (6.3.1925) Morgenausgabe p. [?].

716   #Leinburg, Mathilde v. "Der lachende Brahms. Zum 3. April, dem 25. Todestag des Meisters" Germania (Berlin) no. 220 (2.4.1922) p. [1]. Relates anecdotes to show that Brahms had a sense of humor.
       (a) i) #reprint: Leinburg. "Der lachende Brahms" Die Unterhaltung. Literarische Beilage zum Hannoverschen Kurier (2.4.1922) [2 pages].
           iii) *reprint: [von Leinburg] Chemnitzer Tageblatt (2.4.1922).

717   Lissauer, Ernst. "Der Schwierige" Vossische Zeitung (Berlin) Unterhaltungsblatt nr. 125 (7.5.1933) p. [4]. Provides

examples from Brahms's life to show that he was not as
difficult a person as he made himself out to be.

718   Lyle, Watson. "Brahms Himself" Review of Reviews (London)
      84/527 (10.12.1933) pp. 57-60. Describes Brahms's person-
      ality as expressed in his daily life and music, with anecdotes.
      Based on discussion with living contemporaries of Brahms
      and available documentation.

719   Mandyczewski, Eusebius. "Die Bibliothek Brahms" Musikbuch
      aus Osterreich 1 (1904) pp. 7-17. Describes Brahms as
      bibliophile and the types of materials in his personal library.

720   *Mandyczewski, Eusebius, ed. Drei Meister Autographe. Wien:
      n.p., 1923.
      (d) *The Autograph of Three Masters (Beethoven, Schubert,
            Brahms). (Harrow Replicas 1) London: Chiswick
            Press, 1942. [4], 1, 1 pp. facsim. Includes fac-
            simile of Brahms's signature. [from Notes 37/3
            (3.1981) p. 539]

721   Miller zu Aichholz, Viktor von, ed. Ein Brahms-Bilderbuch.
      Mit erläuterndem Text von Max Kalbeck. Wien: R. Lechner
      (Wilh. Müller) k.u.k. Hof- und Universitats-Buchhandlung,
      [1905]. iii, [1], 119 pp. ill., facsim. Photographs with
      explanatory notes, covering Brahms's life and including the
      memorials struck after his death.

722   *Müller-Marein, Josef and Hannes Reinhardt. Das musikalische
      Selbstporträt von Komponisten, Dirigenten, Instrumentalisten,
      Sängerinnen und Sängern unserer Zeit. [Hamburg:]
      Nannen-Verlag, [1963]. 508 pp. ill.

723   *Nägele, H. "Der schlagfertige Brahms. Eine dutzend Anek-
      doten" Hamburger Fremdenblatt (5.4.1927).

724   *Neuda-Bernstein, Rosa. "Brahms als Lehrer" Neue frei Presse
      (Wien) (11.5.1908). [Describes Brahms as a piano teacher.]

725   Newman, Ernest. "A Note on Brahms" New Music and Church
      Music Review 5/56 (7.1906) pp. 1011-13. Discusses the
      contrast between the physical and spiritual Brahms.

726   #Nussac, Sylvie de. "Aimez-vous Brahms?" Musica (Chaix)
      no. 70 (1.1960) pp. 18-21. ill., discog. Presents a series
      of anecdotes on Brahms, showing his character and his
      relationship with various contemporaries.

727   "Only Record by Brahms Goes to Reich Institute" New York
      Times 84/28,128 (28.1.1935) p. 1. Describes Brahms's re-
      cording of Ungarische Tänze no. 1 [Hofmann nr. 128;

McCorkle WoO 1] and the circumstances behind its being made.

728 • Orel, Alfred. "Johannes Brahms' Musikbibliothek" N. Simrock Jahrbuch 3 (1930-34) pp. 18-47. ill., notes. A transcription of Brahms's own inventory, plus an appendix of materials found in the Nachlass but not listed.
(a) reprint: in 690.

729 "Personal" New York Times 46/14,255 (27.4.1897) p. 6. Relates anecdotes taken from Viennese papers [412.5, 457, 755?] illustrating Brahms's cruel wit and discussing why he never married or wrote an opera.

730 Peschnig, Emil. "Die Melancholie des Unvermögens" Signale für die musikalische Welt 82/48 (26.11.1924) pp. 1825-27. Discusses Brahms as an example of a stoical person.

731 #Pfordten, [Hermann] von der. "Brahms als Mensch und Künstler. Zu seinem 40. Todestag am 3. April 1897" Deutsche Volksbildung 11 (1937) pp. 57-58. ill. Discusses Brahms's character and how it is revealed in his music.

732 "Pictorial Biography of Johannes Brahms, May 7, 1833-April 3, 1897" [Editorial Preface by Leonard Liebling] Musical Courier 95/24 (Whole no. 2488) (15.12.1927) pp. 20-25. ill. 35 photographs covering Brahms's life, with remarks on his historical position and an overview of his life.

733 *Pischel, Maria. "Johannes Brahms. Eine Persönlichkeit als Künstler und Mensch" Wochenschrift für katholische Lehrerinnen (Paderborn) 46 (1933) pp. 159-60.

734 *Pl., Consul. Lübecker Zeitung (1897).
(c) excerpt: "Aus den Zeitungen" Signale für die musikalische Welt 55/25 (14.4.1897) p. 388. [total pp. 387-88]. Relates anecdote of a gypsy woman telling Brahms's fortune and how in retrospect, it was accurate; includes 755.c.

735 Pulver, Jeffrey. "The Choral Activities of Johannes Brahms" Musical Opinion and Music Trade Review 59/699 (12.1935) pp. 211-12. Describes Brahms's relationship to choirs he conducted, together with a list of his choral works.

736 #R.W.W. "Bei einem Festmahl ..." Berliner Börsenzeitung 85/3 (3.1.1940) Morgenausgabe p. 3. Relates anecdote involving a conversation between Brahms and Klaus Groth, 1878: conversation reveals Brahms's feelings on being passed over for the position of leader of Hamburger Singakademie and Philharmoniker.

737   Racek, Fritz. "Die Künstlerpersönlichkeit im Spiegel der
       Notenhandschrift" Osterreichische Musikzeitschrift 1/8
       (8.1946) pp. 269-78. Brahms: p. 276. facsim. Presents
       a character analysis based on graphological research.

738   *Reimers, Gerd. Beethoven flyttlass och andra essäer: Kring
       musiker och deras boningar i österrike. (Profilresan 1)
       Stockholm: Edition Reimers, 1977. 249 pp. ill. Contains
       descriptions of Brahms's residences in Austria. [from S202]

739   Robinson, Edward. "The Solitary Brahms" New Music Review
       and Church Music Review 32/377 (6.1933) pp. 245-47. mus.
       Discusses Brahms in respect to the emotions of love and
       death, and traces a "death motif" in his music, focusing
       on Opp. 121, 122.

740   Roner, Anna. "Zum 3. April 1897" Neue Zürcher Zeitung
       no. 436 (2.4.1922) 3. Blatt [pp. 1-2, across page bottoms].
       Describes Brahms from times she saw him, both privately
       and in public, 1880's-1895.

741   *Schmidt, Leopold. "Brahms als Mensch" in 2745.
           (a) reprint: Schmidt. in Schmidt. Erlebnisse und Bet-
               rachtungen. Aus dem Musikleben der Gegenwart.
               Berlin: A. Hofmann & Comp., 1913. pp. 206-14.
               Discusses the problem of understanding Brahms the
               man and what is known about his character.

742   *Schnapp, Friedrich. "Handschriften berühmter Musiker"
       Skizzen [5]/5 (5.1931) pp. 5-8.

743   *Scholz, Bernhard. "Ein Scherzwort von Brahms" Dresdner
       Nachrichten (30.12.1911).

744   Spengel, Julius. Johannes Brahms. Charakterstudie.
       (Hamburgische Liebhaberbibliothek) Hamburg: Lütcke &
       Wulff, 1898. 52 pp. Attempts to present a picture of
       Brahms the man and the composer.

745   "Staatsbibliothek erwarb vier Brahms-Bilder", see 659.5.

746   #Suter, Ernst. "Landschaft und Charakter" Deutsche Zeitung
       (Berlin) (2.4.1922) p. [?]. Describes Brahms's North
       German roots and how they are reflected in his music;
       includes comments on Brahms's historical position in the
       19th century.

747   Symonds, Frederic. "Brahms's Record" Musical Opinion [94]/
       1123 (4.1971) p. 359. Letter to editor, correcting dating
       of recording Brahms made of Ungarische Tänze no. 1
       [Hofmann nr. 128; McCorkle WoO 1] and describing its
       quality.

748 *"Teczka wedrowiec" Wdrowiec (Warszawa) [series 5]/17 (1897).
"Szczęsliwy!": p. 334. Anecdotes from Brahms's life.
[from S204]

749 Thiel, Rudolf. "Umgang mit Brahms" in Theil. Der Himmel
voller Geigen. Das Leben der grosser Symphoniker. Wien,
Berlin, Stuttgart: Paul Neff Verlag, 1951. pp. 599-668.
ill. Anecdotes about Brahms and the people around him;
Brahms in Wien.
*also: Berlin, Darmstadt: Deutsche Buch-Gemeinschaft, 1955.

750 Thomas, Wolfgang. [Wolfgang Alexander Thomas-San-Galli]
"Brahms-Selbstporträt. Nach seinen Briefen" Der Merker
(Wien) 4/12,14,15 (6.,7.,8.;1913) pp. 441-45, 521-23, 561-64.
Discusses Brahms the man, as seen in Brahms Briefwechsel
vols. 1-7 [954, 983, 1009, 1062, 1122] and 969.a.

751 Thomas-San-Galli, Wolfgang A[lexander]., see 1442.5.

752 "Three Composers. Psychology and Criticism" The Times
(London) Late London Edition no. 51,155 (20.8.1948) p. 7.
Presents a psychological analysis of Schumann, Bizet and
Brahms in an attempt to view them as romantic composers.

753 *Vogelsang, J. "Ein Berufener" Junges Leben. Zeitschrift
für die Jugend (Berlin) 3/5 (1947) p. 10.

754 *Weiss, Josef. "The Virtuoso Technic of Brahms's Playing"
The Century Library of Music. Vol. 8. Ignace Jan Paderew-
ski, ed. New York: The Century Co., 1900. pp. 260-72.

755 Widmann, J[osef]. V[iktor]. "Persönliches über Brahms"
Die Nation (Berlin) 14/28 (10.4.1897) pp. 427-29. Presents
impressions and anecdotes of Brahms, 1865-97; also discusses
Brahms and opera, Brahms as a patriot, Brahms and marriage.
(c) excerpt: "Aus den Zeitungen" Signale für die musikalische Welt 55/25 (14.4.1897) pp. 387-88. [total
pp. 387-88] anecdotes on Brahms and marriage,
outline of his typical day. Includes 734.c.
(d) Slonimsky, Nicolas. "Musical Oddities" Etude 73/6
(6.1955) pp. 4-5. Brahms: p. 4. why Brahms
never married, as well as his comments on memorial
monuments.
(e) i) report?: see 729.
ii) report: "Why Brahms Never Married" Music (Chicago)
12/[2] (6.1897) pp. 242-43.

756 Wohlfahrt, Frank. "Johannes Brahms der Prototyp einer
Persönlichkeit" Die Musik (Berlin) 18/1 (10.1925) pp. 5-20.
Examines music to obtain idea of Brahms's personality; in-
cludes a detailed look at Opp. 68 and 90.

(d) i) Misch, Ludwig. "Der Brahmskenner von Fiesole"
   Allgemeine Musikzeitung 52/50 (11.12.1925) pp. 1022-
   23. notes. Negative remarks on Wohlfahrt's efforts.
   ii) reply: #Zschorlich, Paul. "Ein Wort für Brahms!"
   Deutsche Zeitung (Berlin) (13.12.1925) p. [?].
   Author feels that Brahms deserves better recognition,
   suggests that Wohlfahrt's choice of musical examples
   was too limited.

757 Wooldridge, David. "Mendelssohn, Liszt and Brahms" in Wooldridge. Conductor's World. London: Barrie & Rockliff,
   The Cresset Press, 1970. pp. 35-47. ind., notes., discog.
   Brahms: pp. 42-47. Discusses Brahms as a conductor,
   examines his orchestral writing for evidence of his conducting
   practice; also comments on performance practice in Brahms's
   music.

758 Zoff, Otto. "Johannes Brahms" in Great Composers Through
   the Eyes of Their Contemporaries. Zoff, ed. Phoebe Rogoff
   Cave, translator and assistant editor. New York: E. P.
   Dutton & Company, Inc., 1951. pp. 328-49. Contains
   excerpts as indicated from 39A, 165.d.c., 886, 894.b.,
   1322.b., 3013.
   (b) *German translation: Zoff. Die grossen Komponisten
      gesehen von ihren Zeitgenossen. Bern: A. Scherz,
      [1952].
      *2. Auflage: Bern, Stuttgart, Wien, 1959.
      *also: [Düsseldorf:] Deutsche Bücherbund; [Stutt-
      gart:] Stuttgarter Hausbücherei, [1960].
      *also: [Zürich:] Buchergilde Gutenberg, [1965].

759 "Zu unserer Musik- und Notenbeilage" Neue Zeitschrift für
   Musik 95/4 (4.1928) pp. 220-22. ill. [facing p. 209]
   Brahms: pp. 220-21. Relates background to two pictures:
   Brahms in his Viennese residence, Brahms with Stocker and
   Mandyczewski.
   (b) English translation: "Two Rare Brahms Portraits"
      Musical Opinion and Music Trade Review 52/620 (5.
      1929) p. 741. ill.

760 "Der zwanzigjährige Brahms" in 2667. p. 61. ill. On portrait
   done by Laurens: background, provenance, description.
   Text from 39A Bd. I. Erster Halbband (? Auflage).

761 "Der zwanzigjährige Brahms" Zeitschrift für Musik [88]/11
   (6.1921) p. 277. ill. On portrait done by Laurens: background, provenance, description. Text from 39A Bd. I.
   Erster Halbband (? Auflage).

See also 1, 4, 8, 18, 20, 24-26, 33, 36, 39-41, 44, 46, 48, 50, 57,
61, 62, 70, 72, 73, 75, 76.d., 78, 90, 95, 104, 107, 107.5, 108,
111, 114, 119, 124, 125, 128, 135, 145, 174.d., 175, 177, 185, 188,

197, 202, 206, 239, 316, 317, 320.a., 326, 341, 348, 354, 356, 359,
374, 375, 378, 387, 391, 397, 398, 400, 404, 407, 409, 412.5, 413.d.i.,
431, 435, 451, 457, 467, 469, 476, 495, 496, 511, 515, 532, 540,
550, 553, 559, 566, 571, 574, 590, 599, 600, 606, 608, 609, 617,
618, 708, 794, 795, 801, 812, 813, 819.c.ii.e.ii, 819.c.ii.e.iii, 825,
827, 830, 842, 844.5, 848, 850, 856, 860, 863, 866, 878, 880, 926,
929, 931, 953, 963, 971, 979, 983.e.ii., 989.d.i., 991, 993, 995,
1001, 1007, 1024, 1030, 1061, 1063, 1067, 1071, 1072, 1086, 1096,
1108, 1110, 1111, 1116, 1122.e.ii., 1132, 1138, 1142, 1144, 1160,
1172, 1179.c.i., 1180, 1181, 1190, 1202, 1205, 1208, 1211, 1217,
1224, 1224.5, 1232, 1243, 1246, 1255, 1257, 1266, 1288, 1294, 1302,
1310, 1312, 1317, 1318, 1322, 1341, 1349, 1400, 1425, 1440, 1441,
1568, 1581, 1588, 1808, 1943, 1952, 1957, 2089, 2109, 2117, 2128,
2164, 2187.c., 2200, 2212, 2216, 2238, 2267.d., 2286, 2290, 2299,
2317.5, 2330, 2353, 2405.5, 2432, 2438, 2452, 2453, 2467, 2470, 2473,
2525-27, 2580, 2583, 2585, 2607, 2621, 2625, 2630, 2631, 2636, 2657,
2806, 2815, 2821, 2825, 2831, 2838, 2845, 2849, 2854, 2862, 2868,
2880, 2891, 2899, 2900, 2903, 2925, 2984, 2989, 2990, 3000, 3002,
3013, 3032, 3049, 3077, 3106, 3130, 3132, 3156.

See also "Brahms and the "Fair Sex"" and "Friedrich Eckstein" and
"Eduard Hanslick" in III; "Des Jungen Kreislers Schatzkästlein" in
IV.C.2.; "Editing" and "Texts and Text Setting" in V.B.;
"Creative Process" in V.C.; "Music Previous to the Classical Period"
in VI.A.; and "Religion" in VI.B.

2. Visual Images and Iconography

See 7, 9, 48, 107.5, 317, 649, 655, 659.5, 664, 667, 711, 721, 732,
760, 761, 787, 804, 1060, 1127.

See also VII.E.

PART III.   BRAHMS'S RELATIONS TO OTHER PEOPLE

Contains materials that discuss Brahms's physical, emotional, or musical relationship with other individuals from any time, on any level.   See also 72, 844.5.

A.   BRAHMS AND THE "FAIR SEX"

Contains materials that discuss the subject generally, or in terms of specific groupings of individual women.

762   *Decsey, Ernst.   "Frauen um Brahms" Schwaben-Spiegel (Stutt-
      gart) 27 (1933) p. 139.

763   #H.-W., Susanne.   "Die Frauen im Leben von Johannes Brahms.
      Zu seinem 100. Geburtstag am 7. Mai" Neue preussische
      Zeitung. Kreuz-Zeitung nr. 125 2. Beiblatt [Beiblatt titled
      "Die Frau unserer Zeit"] (7.5.1933) p. [1].   Describes
      Brahms's loves, focusing on Clara Schumann, but also dis-
      cussing Agathe von Siebold and Elisabet von Herzogenberg.

764   Hitschmann, Eduard.   "Johannes Brahms und die Frauen"
      Psychoanalytische Bewegung 5/2 (3./4.1933) pp. 97-129.
      notes.   A psychoanalytical study of Brahms and his attitude
      towards women and sexuality; also, how this is reflected
      in his music.
      (b) i) English translation: Hitschmann, Edward.   "Johannes
             Brahms and Women" American Imago 6/2 (6.1949)
             pp. 69-96.
             (a) reprint: Hitschmann. in Great Men. Psycho-
                  analytic Studies.   Sydney G. Margolin, ed.
                  with the assistance of Hannah Gunther.
                  Foreword by Ernest Jones.   New York:
                  International Universities Press, 1956. pp.
                  199-224.
                  *2nd Issue: 1956.
          ii) *Italian translation: Hitschmann.   Archivio

generale di neurologia psichiatria, e piscoanalisi
(Naples) [16?] (1934).

iii) #Spanish translation: Hirtschmann, Eduardo.
"Brahms y las mujeres" Ars. Revista de arte 17/79
(1957) pp. [28-55]. adds ill., facsim.

765 *Huschke, Konrad. "Brahms und die Frauen" Westermanns
illustrierte deutsche Monatshefte [160] (5.1933) pp. 233-37.
  (b) *Hungarian translation: Huschke, Conrad. "Brahms
     és a nők" A Zene 14 (1932/33) pp. 204-13.
  (c) #excerpt: Huschke. Mannheimer Tageblatt (6./7.5.
     1933) p. 7. Describes Brahms's feelings about
     marriage; includes comments on Brahms and Clara
     Schumann.
  (d) #reworked: Huschke. Frauen um Brahms. Karlsruhe
     in Baden: Friedrich Gutsch Verlag, [1936]. 234
     pp. ill., ind. Presents a systematic account of
     Brahms's relationships with individual women, based
     on interviews by the author and available documenta-
     tion.
  (d) Huschke. "Die erste Geigerin, die das
     Brahmssche Violinkonzert meisterte. Zum
     75. Geburtstag von Marie Röger-Soldat am
     25. Marz" Allgemeine Musikzeitung 66/12/13
     (24.3.1939) pp. 199-200. Describes her
     relationship with Brahms, 1879-97.
  (e) report: Willers, Anni. "Brahms und Elisabeth
     v. Herzogenberg" Kölnische Zeitung no. 549
     (28.10.1936) Ausgabe C Morgenblatt p. [6].
     Focuses on her role as musical adviser to
     Brahms.

766 *Jemnitz, Sándor. "A Művészet rabszolgája" A Zene 16 (1935)
pp. 254-57. Discusses Brahms, Clara Schumann and Agathe
von Siebold. [from 241]

767 Long, Raymond. "The Unmaid Bed" Fugue 4/5/6 (2.1980)
pp. 31-32, 34. Brahms: pp. 31-32. Describes Brahms's
approach towards women.

768 Prilipp, E. "Johannes Brahms und die Frauen" Kölnische
Zeitung no. 15 (7.1.1925) Abendausgabe p. [2].; no. 20
(9.1.1925) 2. Morgenausgabe p. [2]. Discusses Brahms's
relationships with women, and their effect on his composing.

769 #Schemann, Bertha. Drei Frauen um Johannes Brahms. Ein
Gedenkwort zu seinem 50. Todestag. Berlin: Afas, Musik-
verlag Hans Dünnebeil, 1948. 23 pp. ill., notes. Describes
Brahms's relationship with Clara Schumann, Agathe von
Siebold and Elisabet von Herzogenberg; includes excerpts
from 983, 1013, 1179.

770 *"Von Brahms-Sängerinnen" Wiener Mode (7.11.1907). (?)

See also 20.d., 39A.e.iv., 78, 283, 297, 375, 387, 540, 680, 682,
729, 755, 786, 1061, 1127, 1208, 1302, 1321, 2117.d., 2193, 2525-
27, 2585.

B. BRAHMS AND PARTICULAR INDIVIDUALS

1. Persons Not Identified

771 *Kölnische Zeitung (1908).
     (e) report?: see 774.

772 *"Ein Besuch bei Brahms" Deutsche Musikerzeitung (Berlin)
     [37] (1906).

773 "Brahms and a Young Composer" Music (Chicago) 13/[3]
     (1.1898) pp. 373-74. Anecdote relating that Brahms gave
     a very negative critique on a composer's music, and how
     this person never composed again.

774 #"Eine Brahms-Erinnerung" Neues Wiener Journal (10.9.1908)
     p. 4. Describes Brahms in Ziegelhausen, 1875.

775 *"Briefe von Johannes Brahms" Pester Lloyd (Budapest) no. 82
     (6.4.1897). 6 letters, 1867-71. [from 241]
     (c) excerpt: in 431.c. p. 195. Only reprints letters
         1, 3-5; 1867, 1869.

776 *F-n A. "Aus dem Leben von Johannes Brahms" Harmonie
     (Hannover) [14] (20.9.1901).

777 *Fein, Heidi. "Johannes Brahms Stiftung, Briefe. Staats- und
     Universitätsbibliothek Hamburg, Brahms-Briefe" Jahresarbeit
     der Hamburger Bibliotheksschule, 1961. 57 pp.

778 #H.M. "Erinnerungen an Brahms" Wiener Konzertschau 1/3 (1911)
     p. 14. Anecdotes about Brahms in Wien: meeting the
     composer at the Tonkunstlerverein 1896- , suggesting that
     he write a new choral work.

779 *Krüger, Eduard. Musikalische Briefe aus der neuesten Zeit.
     Münster: Russel, 1870.

780 *Meinardus, Ludwig. Des einigen deutschen Reiches Musikzustände.
     12 Briefe. (Kulturgeschichtliche Briefe über deutsche
     Tonkunst. Bd. 1) Oldenburg: Schulze'sche Buchhandlung,
     [1872]. 176 pp. Brahms: pp. 165ff. [from 241]
     *2. Auflage: 1873.

781 *"Neues von Brahms. Unbekannte Briefe, ein Lied und ein
     Denkmalsentwurf" Musikblätter 7 (1953) p. 44.

782 Reinecke, Carl. "Eine Plauderei über Dedikationen musikalischer
     Werke" Deutsche Revue (Stuttgart) 27/Bd. 2 (5.1902) pp.
     205-11. Brahms: p. 210. On the practice of making dedi-
     cations to musical works, and how Brahms contributed little
     to this practice.

783 *Simms, Marguerite. "Neuerwerbungen des Brahms-Archivs
     der Staats- und Universitätsbibliothek Hamburg" [Prüfung-
     sarbeit der Hamburger Bibliotheksschule] 1970.

784 *V. H. "Brahms und ich. Eine Jugenderinnerung" Die Lesestunde
     14 (1938) pp. 314-15.

785 *Willige, Jochen. "Neuerwerbungen des Brahms-Archivs der
     Staats- und Universitätsbibliothek Hamburg" [Prüfungsarbeit
     der Hamburger Bibliotheksschule] 1967.

786 #"Zwei ungedruckte Briefe von Johannes Brahms" Wiener Almanach
     20 (1911). p. 171. Letters to a woman in Pressburg (7.1867),
     and a Frau v.B. (2.1868).

See also 383, 559, 3154.

2. Persons Identified

     This subsection is divided alphabetically by individual family
name. If more than one person is mentioned in a citation, the item
is filed under the name of the first person referred to, with cross
references from the other people discussed. See also 72.

--Abell, Arthur M. (1868-1958)

See 638, 2453.

--Abraham, Max, Dr. (1831-1900)

See 848.

--Ahle, Johann Rudolph (1625-1673)

See 2346.

--Albert, Eugen d' (1864-1932)

787   Abell, Arthur M[aynard]. "A Picture of Brahms" New York
       Times 87/29,149 (14.11.1937) Section 11, p. 9. ill. Dis-
       cusses Brahms and d'Albert and Julius Klengel.

--Allgeyer, Julius (1829-1900)

788   Orel, Alfred. "Johannes Brahms und Julius Allgeyer" N.
       Simrock Jahrbuch 1 (1928) pp. 24-40. facsim., notes.
       Describes their knowledge of each other, their personal
       relationship, 1850's-90's, and their correspondence, especially
       on the subject of an opera text. Also discusses Hermann
       Levi and Anselm Feuerbach.
       (e) report: Becker, Harry Cassin. "When Brahms Con-
            sidered Writing An Opera" Musical America 47/25
            (7.4.1928) p. 9. Discusses this particular aspect
            of the Allgeyer-Brahms letters.

789   Orel, Alfred. Johannes Brahms und Julius Allgeyer. Eine
       Künstlerfreundschaft in Briefen. Tutzing: Hans Schneider,
       1964. 152 pp. ill., fig. 76 letters, 1855-95, with com-
       mentary; includes sketches of both men's lives.
       (c) excerpt: see 1179.c.i.

--Allmers, Hermann (1821-1902)

See 2149.

--Arnim, Gisela von (1827-1889)

See 1012, 1013.

--Assmann [fl. 19th century]

See 1222.

--Astor, Edmund [fl. 19th century]

See 848.

--Auer, Leopold [von] (1845-1930)

See 1016.

--Avé-Lallemant, Johann Theodor Friedrich (1805?-1890)

790 *Avé-Lallemant, Johann Theodor Friedrich. Rückerinnerungen
eines alten Musikanten. In Veranlassung des fünfzigjährigen
Bestehens der philharmonischen Concerte für deren Freunde.
Hamburg: Langhoff, 1878. iv, 107 pp. Includes information
on Hamburger Philharmoniker concerts 1828-78 [from S032].

--B., Frau v. [fl. 19th century]

See 786.

--Bach, Carl Philipp Emanuel (1714-1788)

See 793.

--Bach, Johann Sebastian (1685-1750)

791 Abert, Hermann. "Bach, Beethoven, Brahms" Frederick H.
Martens, translator. Musical Quarterly 13/2 (4.1927) pp.
329-43. Brahms: pp. 339-42. Explains this grouping,
and compares Brahms to the other two: discusses their
influences on him; also comments on Brahms's historical
position.

792 Altmann, Wilhelm. "Brahmssche Urteile über Tonsetzer" Die
Musik (Berlin) 12/1 (Bd. 45) (10.1912) pp. 45-55. notes.
Reprints Brahms's comments, with editorial remarks, on 27
composers, Bach to Wagner, from the literature [871, 894,
954, 983, 1009, 1062, 1122, 1170].

793 Helms, Siegmund. "Johannes Brahms und Johann Sebastian
Bach" Bach-Jahrbuch 57 (1971) pp. 13-81. mus., notes.
Discusses numerous aspects of the subject: editorship of
works of Bach and his sons, arranging and performing of
Bach's music, ownership of Bach editions and manuscripts,
performance practice, and Bach's influence on Brahms's
own music.

794 Kendall, Raymond. "Brahms's Knowledge of Bach's Music"
in Papers of the American Musicological Society. Annual
Meeting, 1941. Minneapolis, Minnesota. Gustave Reese,
ed. Richmond: AMS, 1946. pp. 50-56. notes. Discusses
what Brahms studied, owned, played, taught, and conducted
of Bach's works; describes Brahms's comments on Bach in
his correspondence.

See also 712, 967, 1180.c.ii., 1193, 1461, 1474, 1556, 1679, 1701,
1757, 1760.5, 1761, 1770, 1819, 1994, 2014, 2030, 2116, 2178,
2216, 2220, 2235, 2252, 2258, 2285, 2325, 2346, 2447-49, 2454,
2469.5, 2539, 2598, 2630, 2675, 2880, 2918, 2993.

--Bach, Wilhelm Friedemann (1710-1784)

See 793.

--Bachrich, Sigismund (1841-1913)

795   Bachrich, S[igismund]. "Erinnerungen eines Musikers. III.
        (Brahms-Goldmark-Bruckner-Richter)" Frankfurter Zeitung
        50/179 (1.7.1906) 2. Morgenblatt p. 1. Describes his first
        meeting with Brahms, and the contrast to what he had
        expected. Contrasts the three composers: public's view
        of them and the manner in which premieres of their works
        were acknowledged.
        (e)   report: "In der "Frankfurter Zeitung" ..." Allgemeine
              Musikzeitung 33/28/29 (13./20.7.1906) pp. 477-78.

--Backhaus, Wilhelm (1884-1969)

See 256.

--Bagge, Selmar (1823-1896)

See 2925.

--Barbi, Alice (1860?-1948)

796   *Huschke, K[onrad]. "Johannes Brahms' letzte Liebe" Leipziger
        neueste Nachrichten (10.11.1931).
        (d)   see: 765.d.

See also 953, 1222, 3102.

--Bargheer, Carl Louis (1831-1902)

797   *Bargheer, Carl. "Erinnerungen an Johannes Brahms in Detmold
        1857-1865" 16 pp. [from Lippische Landesbibliothek, Detmold]
        (d)   *[another copy?:] 8 pp. [from Lippische Landesbibliothek,
              Detmold]

See also 1016.

--Bargiel, Waldemar (1828-1897)

See 1733.

--Barth, Richard (1850-1923)

798 *Barth, Richard. Meine Lebensgeschichte. n.p.: 1916. Contains Brahms-Barth correspondence and facsimile of Op. 100, 1st movement [from S094].

799 Hofmann, Kurt. Johannes Brahms in den Erinnerungen von Richard Barth. Barths Wirken in Hamburg. Hamburg: J. Schuberth & Co., 1979. 124 pp. ill., facsim., ind., notes. Includes Barth-Brahms correspondence, 16 letters, 1880-96.

See also 1016.

--Bartók, Bela (1881-1945)

800 Goebels, Franzpeter. "Klaviermusik des jungen Bartók--eine Orientierung" Musik und Bildung 13/4 (72) (4.1981) pp. 237-42. Brahms: pp. 239-41. mus. [p. 239] traces the influence of Brahms's Opp. 9 and 10, no. 4 on Bartók's Op. 18 [DD50] and DD64, respectively.

See also 1513, 2608, 2991.

--Batka, Johann [fl. 19th century]

801 Zagiba, Franz. "Johannes Brahms als "Dirigenten-Promoter." Unbekannte Briefe des Meisters" Musikerziehung 9/4 (6.1956) pp. 238-39. notes. Describes Brahms's link with Batka and Pressburg; includes 2 letters from Fall 1883.

--Beck, Julius [fl. 19th century]

802 *Beck, Julius. "Erinnerungen an Brahms" Der Sammler [Beilage zu Augsburger Abendzeitung?] (7.1911).

803 _____. "Originelle Kritik. Eine Erinnerung an Johannes Brahms" Neue freie Presse (Wien) no. 11,815 (15.7.1897) Morgenblatt pp. 1-4 [across page bottoms]. Relates incident from Summer 1872: meeting Brahms at Starnberger See, asking for an opinion on some music, and Brahms's reply.

--Beckerath Family, von [fl. 19th century]

804 Stephenson, Kurt. Johannes Brahms und die Familie von Beckerath. [Brahms-Gesellschaft Baden-Baden, ed.] Hamburg: Christians Verlag, 1979. 80, [23] pp. ill., facsim., ind.,

notes. Describes their friendship, 1874-97. Includes correspondence between Brahms and Rudolf, Laura [wife], and Kurt [son] von Beckerath; excerpts from Laura's diary; comments on Willy von Beckerath as a painter of Brahms. Includes 60 letters, 1874-97.

See also 562, 574, 579.d., 598, 891, 1066, 2160.

--Beethoven, Ludwig van (1770-1827)

805 Barry, Barbara. "In the Shadow of Beethoven" Music and Musicians 25/10 (no. 298) (6.1977) pp. 30-32, 34, 36. Brahms: pp. 34, 36. Discusses Beethoven's influence on Brahms and the symphonic works.

806 *Hartmann, H[ans]. "Beethoven und Brahms" Deutsche Tonkünstler-Zeitung 25/446 (1927) p. 49.

807 #"Johannes Brahms" Kasseler Volksblatt 4. Beilage zu nr. 77 (1.4.1927) p. [?]. ill. Compares Brahms with Beethoven; includes comment on Brahms the composer.

808 *Nagel, Wilibald. [Willibald Nagel] "Johannes Brahms als Nachfolger Beethoven's" Schweizerische Musikzeitung und Sängerblatt [31] (14.5.1892).
      (a) #reprint: Nagel. Johannes Brahms als Nachfolger Beethoven's. Leipzig & Zürich: Gebrüder Hug, [1892]. 32 pp. notes. Points out parallels between Brahms's and Beethoven's time, examines Brahms's music to compare both composers' approach to composition, as well as the character of their work; discusses Brahms's study of Beethoven and how his influence is revealed in Brahms's work.

809 Pousseur, Henri. "Esquisse pour une rhapsodie pathétique" L'Arc no. 40 [(1970)] pp. 65-76. notes. Brahms: pp. 72-74. Compares Brahms and Beethoven and traces the musical lineage from one to the other.
      (a) *reprint: Pousseur. Musique de tous les temps no. 53 (1970) pp. 65-76.

810 Siegmund-Schultze, Walther. "Beethovens Nachwirkung bei bedeutenden Komponisten des 19. Jahrhunderts" in Bericht über den Internationalen Beethoven-Kongress 10.-12. Dezember 1970 in Berlin. Heinz Alfred Brockhaus and Konrad Niemann, eds. Berlin: Verlag Neue Musik, 1971. pp. 107-14. Brahms: pp. 111-13. notes. Discusses the influence of Beethoven on Brahms, as seen in Brahms's music.

811 Wurm, Ernst. "Beethoven und Brahms" Allgemeine Musikzeitung

64/43 (22.10.1937) pp. 621-23. Comments on the social
background of their respective times and philosophizes on
the two men.

See also 147, 235, 374, 528, 576, 660, 671, 680, 712, 749, 791, 792,
967, 969.a.c., 1277, 1340, 1357, 1367, 1402, 1405, 1433, 1448,
1497.d., 1513, 1517, 1556, 1600, 1610, 1625, 1701, 1776, 1819,
1822, 1826, 1895, 1896, 1903, 1932, 1949, 1954, 1994, 2013, 2014,
2123, 2168, 2235, 2314, 2330, 2403.a., 2413, 2415.d.i., 2422, 2427,
2509, 2513, 2551, 2553, 2554, 2572, 2600, 2630, 2646, 2675, 2749,
2837, 2880, 2993, 3141.

--Behm, Eduard (1862-1946)

812   #Behm, Eduard. "Aus meinem Leben. (Wien und Ischl 1890).
      Plauderei" Deutsche Tonkünstler-Zeitung 9/222-31 (15.;
      1.-10.;1911) pp. 5-7, 29-31, 59-61, 85-86, 107-08, 125-27,
      148-49, 167-68, 189-91, 209-12. Describes his friendship
      and instruction under Brahms, 1.-6. 1890. Includes 2
      letters, 1891, and many anecdotes revealing Brahms the man.
      (d) i) *Behm. "Brahms, der Kinderfreund" Neues Wiener
               Journal (13.9.1912).
          ii) _____. (Ed.) "Mein Unterricht bei Brahms"
               Allgemeine Musikzeitung 49/13 (31.3.1922) pp. 244-45.
               Describes his first composition lesson with Brahms,
               2.1890.
               (a) reprint: Behm. "Studien bei Brahms" Allgemeine
                    Musikzeitung 64/13/14 (26.3.1937) pp. 183-85.
                    notes.
         iii) #"Brahms als Kinderfreund" Hamburgischer Cor-
               respondent (16.9.1911) Morgenausgabe p. 2.
               Describes Brahms at the Prater in Wien.

--Behrend, William (1861-1940)

813   Behrend, William. "Hos Johannes Brahms. Et rejseminde"
      Tilskueren 14 (5.1897) pp. 427-39. Describes Behrend's
      visit to Brahms in Wien, Christmas 1895; provides a detailed
      account of their conversation, a description of Brahms, and
      comments on Brahms as composer and on his historical po-
      sition.
      (b) German Translation: Behrend, Wilhelm. "Ein Besuch
           bei Johannes Brahms. Eine Reiseerinnerung"
           Wiener Rundschau Bd. 4/13 (15.5.1898) pp. 481-91.

--Berg, Alban (1885-1935)

See 1791.

--Berlioz   Hector   (1803-1869)

See 2403, 3009.

--Bernstein, Leonard (1918-   )

See 2974.

--Billroth, Theodor (1829-1894)

814   *Journal of the American Medical Association 103-04(?) (1934) (?)
         (a)   reprint: "Dr. Brahms and Dr. Billroth" Etude 53/2
               (2.1935) p. 70.   Describes their friendship 1866-93.

815   #Begegnung mit Johannes Brahms" Weltwacht der Deutschen
         (Hellerau) 10/8 (1943) p. 3.   Historical fiction--describes
         first meeting of Brahms and Billroth, excerpted from Ludwig
         Weiler. Carl Theodor Billroth. (Essen: Fels-Verlag, 1942).

816   *Billroth, Theodor. Briefe. Georg Fischer, ed. Hannover und
         Leipzig: Hahnsche Buchhandlung, 1895.   viii, 464 pp.
         2. vermehrte Auflage: 1896.   viii, 600 pp. ind., notes.
              Contains 35 letters Brahms-Billroth, 1866-94.
       *3. vermehrte Auflage: 1896.   xii, 623 pp.
         4. vermehrte Auflage: 1897.   xii, 627 pp.
       *5. vermehrte Auflage: 1899.   604 pp.
       *6. vermehrte Auflage: 1902.   xii, 600 or 605 pp.
         7. vermehrte Auflage: 1906.   xii, 622 pp.
              Text to p. 597.   Contains 36 letters.
         8. veränderte Auflage: 1910.   xii, 523, [3] pp.
       *9. Auflage: 1922.   xii, 525 pp.
         (c)   i)   excerpt (of ? Auflage):   see 818.
              ii)   excerpt in English translation (of ? Auflage):   see
                    821.
         (d)   see: 819.
         (e)   i)   report (on ? Auflage):   see 618.a.e.ii.
              ii)   report (of ? Auflage):   Weber, Wilh[elm].   "Brahms
                    und Billroth.   Ein Gedenkblatt zu Brahms' siebzigstem
                    Geburtstage (7. Mai)" Neue Musikzeitung 24/12
                    (30.4.1903) pp. 150-52.   notes.
              iii)   report (of ? Auflage):   see 831.

817   Bogusz, Józef.   "Brahms i Billroth" Muzyka (Warszawa) 6/9/10
         (1955) pp. 62-74. ill., notes.   Describes their friendship,
         1866-93, and Billroth's comments on Brahms's works.

818   Bokay, Johann v.   "Billroth und Brahms.   Zum Brahms-
         Zentenarium" Pester Lloyd (Budapest) 80/57 (10.3.1933)
         Morgenblatt pp. 1-3 [across page bottoms].   Discusses their
         friendship, 1866-93; includes quotations from 816.

819 #Brahms, Johannes. Billroth und Brahms im Briefwechsel.
Mit Einleitung. [Einleitung von Otto Gottlieb-Billroth]
Berlin und Wien: Urban & Schwarzenberg, 1935. viii,
528 pp. ill., ind., notes.
"Theodor Billroth und Johannes Brahms": pp. 3-176. Includes correspondence of Brahms to Billroth and his
wife, and of Billroth to Brahms, from 816: total of
332 letters, 1865-94.
  *[Neu Auflage?:] Wien: Urban und Schwartzenberg [Urban
  und Schwarzenberg], 1957.
    (c) i) excerpt (of ? Auflage): Billroth im Briefwechsel mit
       Brahms. Aloys Greither, ed. München, Berlin:
       Urban und Schwarzenberg, 1964. 130, [1] pp.
       ill., ind., notes. 78 letters, 1865-94; includes essay
       on Billroth's life and his friendship with Brahms.
         (c) *excerpt: "Billroth und Brahms. Aus dem von
            Aloys Greither herausgegebenen Briefwechsel"
            Deutsches Arzteblatt 62/42 (1965) pp. 2166-
            69.
      ii) excerpt in English translation by Hans Barkan (of
       1935 Auflage): Brahms. Johannes Brahms and
       Theodor Billroth. Letters from A Musical Friendship.
       Barkan, ed. Norman, Okla.: University of Oklahoma
       Press, 1957. xxi, [1], 264 pp. ill., ind., notes.
       Includes letters only.
         (a) *reprint: Westport, Conn.: Greenwood Press,
            1977.
         (e) i) *report: Böttger, Herbert. "Johannes
            Brahms und Theodor Billroth" Therapeutische
            Berichte 29 (1957) pp. 296-301.
           ii) #report: Goldron Romain. "Johannes Brahms
            épistolier" Schweizerische musikpädogogische
            Blätter 46/2 (1958) pp. 83-86. Describes
            Brahms's character as seen in the Billroth-
            Brahms correspondence.
          iii) report: Kern, Ernst. "Dokumente der
            Freundschaft. Johannes Brahms und Theodor
            Billroth" Musica (Kassel) 12/5 (5.1958) pp.
            270-75. ill. Discusses Billroth as a critic
            of Brahms's music and the character of the
            two men.
     iii) excerpt (of ? Auflage): see 1179.c.i.
      iv) #excerpt (of 1935 Auflage): see 1179.c.ii.
       v) *excerpt (of ? Auflage): see 1009.c.x.
      vi) excerpt (of 1935 Auflage in English translation by
       Daphne Woodward): "Johannes Brahms" in The
       Musicians World. Great Composers in Their Letters.
       Hans Gal, ed. London: Thames and Hudson, 1965.
       pp. 301-22. Billroth Briefe: pp. 309, 311, 315-
       17. 9 letters, 1876-81.
         #excerpt (of 1935 Auflage): see 198.

(e) i) report (on 1935 Auflage): Grolman, Adolf von. "Billroth und Brahms im Briefwechsel" <u>Kölnische Zeitung</u> no. 116 (4.3.1935) Ausgabe C. Abendblatt p. [4].
    ii) report (on 1935 Auflage): see 25.e.
    iii) report (on 1935 Auflage): Stefan, Paul. "Important Brahms Correspondance (sic) Issued" <u>Musical America</u> 55/4 (25.2.1935) p. 8.

820   Class, F. Morris. "Brahms' Family Doctor" <u>Harvard Musical Review</u> 4/2 (11.1915) pp. 2-7. Surveys Billroth's life and relations with Brahms.

821   *Garrison, Fielding H. "Medical Men Who Have Loved Music" <u>Bulletin of the Society of Medical History of Chicago</u> 2/158 (10.1920) pp. 158-76.
    (a) i) reprint: Garrison. <u>Musical Quarterly</u> 7/4 (10.1921) pp. 527-48. Billroth and Brahms: pp. 541-48. Describes their friendship, 1866-93, with excerpts from 816 in English translation.
        ii) reprint: Garrison. In <u>Music and Medicine</u>. Dorothy M. Schullian and Max Schoen, eds. New York: Henry Schumann Inc., 1948. pp. 190-217. Billroth and Brahms: pp. 208-17. [annotation as for 821.a.i]

822   #Jagic, Nikolaus von. "Theodor Billroth und Johannes Brahms" Vortrag, 2. Medizinischen Universitätsklinik, Wien. Lecture given on the 50th anniversary of Billroth's death, 11.2. 1944: reviews the two men's lives and describes their friendship, 1866-93, relates some personal memories of Brahms from the 1890's, and comments on Brahms and Bruckner, and on Brahms's music.

823   Jirásek, Arnold. "Billroth a Brahms" <u>Vesmír</u> 45/6 (1966) p. 183. Surveys their friendship, 1866-93.

824   Kahler, Otto-Hans. [Otto Hans Kahler] "Billroth und Brahms in Zürich" <u>Brahms-Studien</u> Bd. 4 (1981) pp. 63-76. ill. Discusses Billroth as music critic and his reaction to Brahms's works; also comments on first performances of Brahms's works in Zürich and the beginning of the two men's friendship.

825   Marx, Rudolph. "Billroth and Brahms" <u>Surgery, Gynecology & Obstetrics</u> 100/1 (1.1955) pp. 121-25. Gives an overview of the two men's lives and discusses like and contrasting aspects of their personalities; also includes comments on Billroth's role in the dispute between the Viennese champions of Wagner, Bruckner and Brahms.

826 #Mulach, G. A. "Berühmte Freundschaften. Billroth und
     Brahms, Allmers und Haeckel" Hannoverscher Kurier. Kurier
     Tägeblatt no. 117 (28.4.1942) p. 5. Article is report on
     2 books; Billroth-Brahms section is report on Ludwig Weiler.
     Carl Theodor Billroth. (Essen: Fels-Verlag, 1942).

827 Strohl, E. Lee. "The Unique Friendship of Theodor Billroth
     and Johannes Brahms" Surgery, Gynecology & Obstetrics
     131/4 (10.1970) pp. 757-61. ill., notes. Presents an over-
     view of their lives and friendship, 1866-93; also contrasts
     their upbringing and appearance.

828 Sunderman, F. William. "Medicine, Music and Academia"
     American String Teacher 20/2 (Spring 1970) pp. 42, 44-47.
     ill., mus., notes. Discusses the furthering of the Billroth-
     Brahms friendship through music, with the evolution of Op.
     80 as example: how much of the work reflects contributions
     by Billroth, how much, Brahms?

829 _____. "Theodor Billroth as Musician" Bulletin of the
     Medical Library Association 25/4 (5.1937) pp. 209-20.
     Brahms: pp. 211-18. ill., notes. Surveys their friendship,
     1866-94, focusing on Viennese period.

830 Weir, Neil F. "Theodor Billroth and Johannes Brahms--A Thirty
     Year Friendship" History of Medicine 6/3-4 (Autumn/Winter
     1975) pp. 8-14. notes. Describes their friendship, 1866-94,
     and personalities; also surveys the lives of both.

831 Wiedemann, E. "Theodor Billroth und die Musik. Zu seinem
     100. Geburtstage am 26. April" Zeitschrift für Musik 96/5
     (5.1929) pp. 265-67. Brahms: pp. 265-66. Describes
     Billroth's relations with Brahms and Hanslick and comments
     on Billroth's opinions concerning Brahms's music [as recorded
     in 816].

832 *Worbs, Hans Christoph. "Arzt von Profession, Musiker aus
     Passion. Der Chirurg Theodor Billroth und die Musik"
     Musik + Medizin (Neu-Isenburg) 3 (1977) pp. 45-56, 49-50.

833 #Zebrowski, Bernhard. "Die Freunde. Theodor Billroths Leistung
     und Brahms' Musik" Berliner Börsen-Zeitung 87/117 (11.3.
     1942) 2. Ausgabe p. 2. Surveys Billroth's life, emphasizing
     its musical side; includes discussion of his friendship with
     Brahms.

See also 393, 579.d.

--Binder, Fritz [fl. 19th century]

834 *Binder, Fritz. "Es war einmal!" Lied und Heimat (Sollingen)

12 (1936) p. 3, p. 47. Reminisces about Brahms in Wien, 1893. [from S177]

--Bizet, Georges (1838-1875)

See 688, 726, 752, 792, 3009.

--Bloch, Ernest (1880-1959)

See 1625.

--Blume [fl. 19th century]

835 *"Zwei bisher unbekannte Briefe von Brahms" Lüneburgsche Anzeigen no. 75 (29.3.1901) pp. 2-3. Contains 2 letters from Brahms to Blume, 9.1853 and 8.1854. [from Ratsbücherei der Stadt Lüneburg]
(b) reprint in English translation by Florence May: in 48 (2nd Edition) pp. 120, 171-72.

--Böhler, Otto (?-1913)

See 671.

--Böie, Frau Marie [fl. 19th century]

See 432.

--Brahms, Otto (1856-1912)

See 993.

--Brahms Family

Karoline Brahms (1823-1902): 837, 843, 844.5, 845, 846.
Christiane Brahms (1889-1865): 837, 841, 847.
Elise Brahms (183-?-1892): 837, 841.d.ii., 847.
Fritz Brahms (1835-1885): 837, 841.d.ii., 844.5, 847.
Johann Jakob Brahms (1806-1872): 837-39, 841.d.ii., 842, 844-47.

836 Brahms, Johannes. [Briefwechsel. 16 Bde.]
See 983 (I, II); 1122 (III); 954 (IV); 1009 (V, VI): 1062 (VII): 1297 (VIII); 1204 (IX, X); 1203 (XI, XII); 920 (XIII); 848 (XIV); 1314 (XV); 1215 and 892 (XVI).

837   . Johannes Brahms' Heimatbekenntnis in Briefen an
seine Hamburger Verwandten. Eingeleitet und herausgegeben
von Kurt Stephenson. Hamburg: Paul Hartung Verlag,
1933. 104 pp. ill., facsim., ind., notes. Contains 76
letters, 1864-97, and an introduction on Brahms and Hamburg.
*2., um 74 Briefe vermehrte Auflage: (Die kleinen Musikbücher
2) (Drei Türme Edition) Hamburg: Hoffmann &
Campe, 1948. 182 pp.
    (c) i) #excerpt (of 1933 Auflage): see 1179.c.ii.
       ii) excerpt (of 1933 Auflage): Brahms. Das
         Vaterhaus. Briefe von Johannes Brahms an
         seinen Vater Johann Jakob Brahms und an
         seine Stiefmutter Karoline. (Imprimatur.
         Bd. VII, Beilage) Hamburg: Genzsch &
         Heyle Schriftgiesserei A-G, 1937. 14, [1]
         pp. notes.
      iii) #excerpt (of 1933 Auflage): see 1179.c.vi.
    (d) i) incorporated: Brahms. Johannes Brahms
         in seiner Familie. Der Briefwechsel. Kurt
         Stephenson, ed. (Veröffentlichungen aus
         der Hamburger Staats- und Universitäts-
         bibliothek Bd. 9) Hamburg: Dr. Ernst
         Hauswedell & Co., 1973. 309, [2] pp.
         ill., fig., ind., notes. Includes a family
         history and all family letters (548, 1853-97)
         with editorial comment.
        (c) excerpt: see 1179.c.i.
      ii)*Stephenson, Kurt. "Brahms und seine Vater-
         stadt Hamburg. Zum 100. Geburtstag des
         Komponisten am 7. Mai" Hamburger Fremden-
         blatt (4. or 5.;5.;1933) Abendausgabe pp.
         1-2.
    (e) *report (on 1933 Auflage): Pfister, Kurt.
        "Johannes Brahms schreibt an seine Eltern"
        Beobachter deutsche Brenzlande (Potsdam)
        13 (1934) pp. 219-22.

838 "Brahms' Father" Music (Chicago) 12/[3] (7.1897) p. 379.
    Relates a comment by a friend of Johann Jakob, on his
    character.

839 "The Fathers of Great Musicians" Musical Times 47/756 (1.2.1906)
    pp. 91-95.
    "Brahms": pp. 94-95. ill. Describes his life.

840 "Four Brahms Relatives Hear Composer's Work First Time"
    Musical America 55/3 (10.2.1935) p. 132. Reports on the
    reaction of Brahms's great-grand nephews and nieces in
    Duluth, Minnesota, [U.S.A.] upon hearing Op. 68 at a
    symphony concert.

841 Geiringer, Karl. "Brahms' Mutter. Briefe von Christiane

Brahms an Johannes aus den Jahren 1853-1856" Schweizerische
Musikzeitung und Sängerblatt. Gazette musical suisse 76/1,
2,4 (1.,15.;1. and 15.2.; 1936) pp. 1-6, 42-47, 107-12.
notes. Contains 22 letters, 1853-56.
(d) i) incorporated: into 837.d.i.
    ii) Geiringer. "The Brahms Family. With Hitherto
    Unpublished Letters" H. B. Weiner, translator.
    Musical Opinion and Music Trade Review 60/709,
    710, 712, 713, 715 (10.,11.;1936 and 1.,2.,4.;
    1937) pp. 21-22, 120-21, 308-09, 405-07, 595-96.
    notes. Includes letters to Brahms from Christiane
    (9; 1853-56); Johann Jakob (8; 1865-70); Fritz
    (11;1853-84); and Elise (7; 1854-77), together with
    background on each correspondent.
    (c) excerpt: Geiringer. "Vater Brahms schreibt
    an Johannes (mit unbekannten Briefen)"
    Anbruch 19/2 (2.1937) pp. 42-46. notes.
    Includes introduction and 6 letters from
    11.1936 and 1.1937 issue of Musical Opinion.
(d) incorporated: into 837.d.i.

842 Hoecker, Karla. "Johann Jakob Brahms" Deutsche allgemeine
Zeitung (Berlin) 78/323/324 (9.7.1939) Reichsausgabe. Unterhaltungsblatt p. [9]. Historical fiction: describes life
of Brahms's father; includes comments on father's relationship
with son, and how he felt towards his son.

843 Hofmann, Kurt. "Ein neuaufgefundener Brief von Johannes
Brahms an seine Stiefmutter" Brahms-Studien Bd. 4 (1981)
pp. 94-96. notes. Provides transcription and background
information, description: letter dated 22.12.1885.

844 Hübbe, Thomas. "Brahms-Anekdoten" Zeitschrift für Musik
108/8 (8.1941) pp. 532-33. Presents stories about young
Brahms and his father.

844.5#Kähler, Otto. "Altes und Neues von Brahms" Hamburger
Nachrichten no. 159 (9.7.1902) Morgen-Ausgabe. 2. Beilage
[2 pages] [across page bottoms] Discusses Brahms's relationship with his father, and stepfamily; Hamburg's attitude
toward Brahms; Brahms and Wien; and reports many anecdotes
and observations on Brahms's interpersonal relationships
throughout his life.
(e) report: see 618.a.e.i.

845 *Kalbeck, Max. Neues Wiener Tagblatt (1902).
    (e) report: "In Hamburg starb kürzlich die Stiefmutter
    ..." Allgemeine Musikzeitung 29/18 (2.5.1902) p.
    330. Discusses her relationship with Brahms and
    his father.

846 *Ritz, Erika. "Die Briefe von Johannes Brahms an seinen Vater
     und Caroline Brahms" [Prüfungsarbeit der Hamburger Bib-
     liotheksschule,] 1963.

847 *Wolff, Felix. Auf dem Berliner Bahnhof. Das Leben einer
     Hamburger Familie um 1860. (Hamburgische Hausbibliothek)
     Hamburg: G. Westermann, 1925. 96 pp.

     See also 21, 39D, 111, 618.a.e.i., 667, 680, 2298.
     See also "Family History, Childhood, and Links to Hamburg" in II.A.

--Breitkopf & Härtel [music publisher]

848 *Brahms, Johannes. Johannes Brahms im Briefwechsel mit
     Breitkopf & Härtel, Bartolf Senff, J. Rieter-Biedermann,
     C. F. Peters, E. W. Fritzsch, und Robert Lienau. Heraus-
     gegeben von Wilhelm Altmann. (Johannes Brahms. Brief-
     wechsel XIV) Berlin: Verlag der Deutsche Brahms-Gesell-
     schaft m.b.H., 1920. xliii, [1], 431 pp. ind., notes.
     [from 848.a.]
     (a) reprint: (Brahms-Briefwechsel Band XIV) Tutzing:
         Hans Schneider, 1974. 435 private and business
         letters in one chronological sequence, 1853-96:
         Breitkopf & Härtel (139); Senff (20); Rieter-
         Biedermann (166); C. F. Peters (47); Fritzsch (52);
         Robert Lienau (9); Richard Linnemann (1) and
         excerpt from 1170.
     (c) i) excerpt: see 1179.c.i.
        ii)#excerpt: see 1179.c.ii.
       iii) excerpt: see 849.
     (d) i) Altmann, Wilh[elm]. "Aus neu veröffentlichten
         Briefen von Brahms" Allgemeine Musikzeitung 48/13/
         14-16 (1.,8.,15.;4.;1921) pp. 193, 195, 236-37,
         253-54. Discusses the relationship between Brahms
         and his publishers.
        ii) _____. (Wilhelm) "Brahms und seine Verleger"
         Zeitschrift für Musik 100/5 (5.1933) pp. 430-34.
         notes. Discusses the relationship between Brahms
         and his publishers.

849 *Hase, Oskar von. "[Musikalienverlag. Führer der Romantik]
     Johannes Brahms" in von Hase. Breitkopf & Härtel. Gedenk-
     schrift und Arbeitsbericht. Zweiter Band: 1828 bis 1918.
     Teil 1. 4. Auflage. Leipzig: Breitkopf & Härtel, 1919.
     pp. 125-38. ill., facsim. [from 5. Auflage]
     5. Auflage: Wiesbaden, 1968. Discusses Brahms's relationship
         with the firm, with quotations from 848.

     See also 239, 320.a.

--Brode, Max (1850-1917)

See 887, 2517.

--Brodsky, Adolf (1851-1929)

See 656.

--Browning, Robert (1812-1889)

850   Bannard, Joshua. "Browning and Brahms (Occasional Parallels
       III)" Monthly Musical Record 44/521 (1.5.1914) pp. 123-24.
       Traces similarities in their lives and personalities.

See also 2621.

--Bruch, Max (1838-1920)

See 662, 1100, 1122, 1122.c.iv., 1122.e.iii.

--Bruckner, Anton (1824-1896)

851   *Bienenfeld, Elsa. "Bruckner und Brahms" Sang und Klang:
       Almanach (Berlin) [4] (1923).

852   "Bruckner Catches Up With Brahms" The Times (London) no.
       55,929 (7.2.1964) p. 15. Compares Bruckner's 8th Symphony
       to Brahms's Op. 68, reflecting on the Bruckner-Brahms
       controversy.

853   *Decsey, Ernst. "Brahms und Bruckner" Grazer Tagespost
       (10.1900).

854   Floros, Constantin. Brahms und Bruckner. Studien zur
       musikalischen Exegetik. Wiesbaden: Breitkopf & Härtel,
       1980. 246 pp. ill., facsim. ind., notes. Discusses bio-
       graphical, historical, and artistic connections between the
       two composers; includes a section on Brahms and Robert
       Schumann.

855   _____. "Zur Antithese Brahms-Bruckner" Brahms-Studien
       Bd. 1 (1974) pp. 59-90. notes. Examines their backgrounds
       for influences, their opinions of each other, and respective
       historical positions; also discusses their sacred choral works
       and compositional methods.

856   Franck, Hans. Die vier grossen B. Musikergeschichten.

Freiburg/Breisgau: Dikreiter Verlagsgesellschaft, 1955.
127 pp.
"3. Unüberbrückber?" [chapter in "Der Meister von St.
Florian" section]: pp. 93-98. Records a meeting of
Brahms and Bruckner in Wien, 10.1889.
"Wellen im Strom": pp. 122-27. Brahms and Mahler walking
in Wien; contrasts the young, idealistic Mahler with the
old, cynical Brahms. Includes discussion on being
remembered after death.
(d) see: 658.

857 *Grasberger, F[ranz]. "Anton Bruckner und Johannes Brahms.
Ein Vergleich" Musikblätter der Wiener Philharmoniker 5
(1951) pp. 19+.

858 Huschke, Konrad. Unsere Tonmeister unter Einander. [Bd.
4.] Johannes Brahms, Anton Bruckner und Hugo Wolf.
Pritzwalk: Verlag von Adolf Tienken, 1928. 89, [3] pp.
ill., ind., notes. Discusses Brahms and Bruckner as composers and Bruckner's comments on Brahms; also discusses
Wolf as a critic of Brahms. Includes reprinted material
from 3048.
(d) i) Huschke. "Brahms, Bruckner und Hugo Wolf" in
Huschke. Musiker, Maler und Dichter als Freunde
und Gegner. Leipzig: Helingsche Verlagsanstalt,
1939. pp. 237-66.
ii) *Huschke. "Wolf über Brahms" Deutsche Militärmusikerzeitung 54/46,47 (1932).

859 *Perger, Richard von. "Brahms und Bruckner" Schweizerische
Musikzeitung und Sängerblatt 46/1,2 (1907).

860 Pfordten, Hermann von der. "Brahms und Bruckner" Deutsche
Revue (Stuttgart) 47/Bd. 2 (4.1922) pp. 43-47. Traces
parallels in their character, compositional technique and
schools of musical influence.

861 *Pisk, P. A. "Johannes Brahms und Anton Bruckner" Almanach
für Arbeitersänger (Wien) [1] (1930).

862 Rietsch, Heinrich. "Brahms-Bruckner" Almanach der deutschen
Musikbücherei (Regensburg) (1926) pp. 92-102. notes.
Compares and contrasts their lives, their work as composers;
also discusses both as exponents of romanticism and their
views on religion.

863 Schönzeler, Hans-Hubert. "The Romantic Classicists: Brahms
and Bruckner" in Of German Music. A Symposium. Edited
and Introduced by Hans-Hubert Schönzeler. London:
Oswald Wolff; New York: Barnes & Noble Books, 1976.
pp. 219-45. Brahms: pp. 221-27, 233-45. ill. Surveys

both men's lives, then concentrates on the similarities and differences in their characters and approaches to composition. Attempts to achieve a more balanced perspective of these two men.

864 *Stoverock, D[ietrich]. "Brahms und Bruckner" Völkische Musikerziehung 6 (1940) pp. 167-72.

865 Würzl, Eberhard. "Das Verhältnis Bruckners-Brahms und der Musikerzieher von Heute" in Anton Bruckner in Lehre und Forschung. Symposium zu Bruckners 150. Geburtstag. Linz a.d. Donau, September 1974. Regensburg: Gustav Bosse Verlag, 1976. pp. 33-38. Author reviews the Bruckner-Brahms controversy from the point of view of reminiscences of his teachers and other contemporaries; includes a comparison of both composers' symphonic works.

866 #Zoellner, Heinrich. "Brahms und Bruckner. Nachklänge zum letzten Gewandhauskonzert" Leipziger Tagblatt (13.11.1904) p. [?]. Author points out differences between the two men both in their approaches to composition and in their personalities.

See also 39C.c.iii., 60, 224, 403, 712, 792, 795, 822, 825, 917, 953, 989.e.d., 1054, 1209, 1261, 1535, 1826, 1835, 1836, 2025, 2387, 2392, 2625, 2655, 2749, 2871, 2996, 3009, 3025.a.c.

--Brüll, Ignaz (1846-1907)

867 Ganghofer, Ludwig, see 937.

868 Schwarz, Hermine. "Erinnerungen an meinem Bruder Ignaz Brüll, Brahms und Goldmark" Deutsche Revue (Stuttgart) 53/Bd.2-3 (5.-9.1918) pp. 146-57, 239-49, 24-35, 136-48, 271-84. Brahms: (6.,8.,9.;1918) pp. 244-45; 136-37, 139-42, 144;273-74. Focuses on the meeting of Brüll and Brahms in Bad Ischl, 1870's-1896; includes comments on Brahms's trips to Italy and on Brahms and opera.
(a) reprint: Ignaz Brüll und sein Freundeskreis. Erinnerungen an Brüll, Goldmark und Brahms. Vorwort von Felix Salten. When et al.: Rikola-Verlag, 1922. 128 pp.
(c) excerpt: "Erinnerung an Ignaz Brüll und Brahms" Hamburger Nachrichten 127/283 (5.6.1918) 1. Abendausgabe p. [2]. Taken from the 6.1918 section.

--Bülow, Hans von, Freiherr (1830-1894)

869 Albrecht, Otto E. "Johannes Brahms and Hans von Bülow"

University of Pennsylvania Library Chronicle 1/3 (10.1933) pp. 39-46. facsim., notes. Discusses their relationship, focusing on a letter from Brahms to Bülow, 1.1883.

870 *"Brahms und Bülow" Hamburger Nachrichten (16.1.1882). [discusses the change in Bülow's attitude towards Brahms as a composer]

871 Bülow, Hans von. Briefe und Schriften. Marie von Bülow, ed. 8 Bde. Leipzig: Breitkopf & Härtel, 1895-1908. Bd. 3 is collected writings, other volumes are correspondence. Work covers the time period 1841-93. Brahms mentioned passim; also includes Brahms-Bülow correspondence in Bd. 6-8: 49 letters, 1877-93.
　　*Bde. 1,2.: 2. Auflage: 1899.
　　*Bd. 3.: 2. vermehrte Auflage: 1911.
　　*Bd. 4.: 2. Auflage: 1936.
　　(c) i) excerpt (of 1. Auflage): see 792.
　　　　ii) excerpt (of Bd. 3, 1. Auflage in English translation by Daniel Gregory Mason): "The Art of Brahms" Masters in Music 5/part 29 (5.1905) p. 10 (volume p. 202).
　　　iii) *excerpt (of Bde. 1-2?, 1. Auflage): Early Correspondance of Hans von Bülow. Edited by His Widow. Selected and Translated into English by Constance Bache. London: T. F. Unwin, [1895]. xiv, 266 pp. [covers 1854-55? Brahms mentioned passim]
　　　　*also: New York: D. Appleton & Co., [1895].
　　　　*issues (London Edition): 1896.
　　　　*issues (New York Edition): 1896-98.
　　　　　(a) *reprint (of New York 1896 issue): New York: Vienna House, 1972.
　　　　　(c) excerpt (of London 1896 issue): "Hans von Bülow" in Musicians on Music. F[erruccio]. Bonavia, ed. London: Routledge and Kegan Paul, 1956. pp. 194-98. "Brahms": p. 195. 2 items, 1853-54.
　　　iv) excerpt (of Bd. 8, 1. Auflage in English translation by Karl Geiringer): see 25.b.i. (2nd Edition). 1 letter, Brahms to Bülow, 3.1887.
　　　　v) excerpt (of 1. Auflage): see 872.
　　(d) *Bülow. Ausgewählte Briefe. Marie v. Bülow, ed. Leipzig: Breitkopf & Härtel, 1919. xvi, 600 pp. ind., notes.
　　(e) i) *report (on Bd. 6?, 1. Auflage): "Brahms und Hans von Bülow. Neue Briefe" Deutsche Musikdirektoren-Zeitung 9/47 (1907).
　　　　ii) report (on Bd. 6, 1. Auflage): Korngold, Julius. "Brahms und Bülow" Neue freie Presse (Wien) no. 15,487 (3.10.1907) Morgenblatt pp. 1-3 [across page bottoms]. notes.

872   Göhler, Georg. "Brahms und Bülow" Der Türmer 24/12 (9.1922)
      pp. 409-11. Describes the change in how Bülow felt about
      Brahms, with quotations from 871.

873   #Langer, Wolfhart. "Johannes Brahms in Krefeld. Eine ergän-
      zende Randbemerkung" Die Heimat (Krefeld) 44 (1973) pp.
      100-01. ill., notes. Relates incident in which Brahms and
      Bülow discuss who will conduct a performance of Op. 98 in
      Frankfurt, 1885-early 1887.

874   Lessmann, Otto. "Hans von Bülow und seine Stellung zu
      Brahms" Allgemeine deutsche Musikzeitung 9/4 (27.1.1882)
      pp. 32-34. Examines Bülow's change from championing
      Wagner to supporting Brahms.

875   *Patrick, Susan Bess. "Hans von Bülow as Music Critic" Ph.D.
      diss., Music, University of North Carolina at Chapel Hill,
      1973. 161 or 162 pp. notes.

876   *Rösch, Friedrich. Musik-ästhetische Streitfragen. Streiflichter
      und Schlagschatten zu den ausgewählten Schriften von Hans
      von Bülow. Ein kritischer Waffengang. Leipzig: Kommissions-
      Verlag von F. Hofmeister, 1897. 239 pp.

877   #"Unbekannte Brahms-Briefe" Schweizer Musiker-Revue 9/11
      (15.5.1934) pp. 1-2. Discusses letters from Brahms to
      Bülow, 7.1881 and 2.1883.

See also 65.d., 592, 599, 680, 1109, 1111, 1137, 1210, 1225, 1232,
1903, 1954, 3009.

--Bungert, August (1845 or 1846-1915)

See 1123.

--Busch, Fritz (1890-1951)

See 1880.

--Busnois, Antoine (d. 1492)

See 1683.

--Buths, Julius (1851-1920)

See 792.

--Cady, Calvin Brainard (1851-1928)

See 2967.

--Carreño, Theresa (1853-1917)

See 987.e.d.

--Chaikovskiĭ, Petr Il'ich see Tchaikovsky, Peter Ilyich

--Cherubini, Luigi (1760-1842)

See 792, 2551.

--Chopin, Frédéric (1810-1849)

878 #Antcliffe, Herbert. "Chopin and Brahms" Musical News (London)
     40/1058 (10.6.1911) pp. 565-66. Discusses their differences
     as persons together with their similarities as composers;
     includes comments on Chopin's influence on Brahms, as seen
     in Brahms's Opp. 4 and 10.

See also 686, 792, 1122.e.iv., 1557, 1599, 1600, 1625, 1663, 1674,
1679, 1733-36, 2131, 2553, 2608.

--Chrysander, Friedrich (1826-1901)

879 Geiringer, Karl. "Brahms and Chrysander" Monthly Musical
     Record 67/787, 788, 790; 68/795 (6.,7.-8.;10.;1937 and
     3.-4.1938) pp. 97-99, 131-32, 178-80; 76-79. notes. In-
     cludes 17 letters Chrysander-Brahms, 1869-94. Subjects
     covered include the questions of Brahms obtaining an ap-
     pointment as a Music Director, Brahms visiting England,
     and Brahms editing the Händel vocal duets [Hofmann nr.
     197, 165, 198; McCorkle Anhang Ia nr. 10, 11].
     (c) *excerpted: Fock, Gustav. "Brahms und die Musik-
            forschung im besonderen Brahms und Chrysander"
            in Beiträge zur hamburgischen Musikgeschichte.
            Festgabe des Musikwissenschaftlichen Instituts der
            Universität Hamburg an die Teilnehmer des Inter-
            nationalen Musikwissenschaftlichen Kongresses Ham-
            burg 1956. Heinrich Husmann, ed. Hamburg:
            Musikwissenschaftlichen Instituts der Universität
            Hamburg, 1956. pp. 46-69. ill., facsim., notes.
         also: Hamburg: Verlag der Musikalienhandlung Karl
            Dieter Wagner, n.d. Discusses Brahms's interest

in the musical past. Includes: "Brahms und
Chrysander. Persönliche Beziehungen zueinander":
pp. 49-69. Contains, in excerpt and entirely, 13
new letters and postcards, Brahms to Chrysander,
10.1876-2.1881; also excerpt from 879 and 1079.
Topics covered include Brahms and Wien, Brahms
and Hamburg, Brahms and England, and Brahms
being asked to accept the post of Musikdirektor in
Düsseldorf.

--Clark, Frederic Horace (1860-1917)

See 2623.

--Conrat, Hugo [fl. 19th century]

880   Conrat, Hugo. "Brahms, wie ich ihn kannte" Neue Musikzeitung
       24/1,2 (27.11. and 11.12.;1903) pp. 4-5, 17-18. Describes
       their friendship from 1887-97, focusing on Brahms in Wien;
       includes comment on Brahms the man.
       (a) reprint: Conrat. Bühne und Welt 6/13 (1904) pp.
           546-50. notes.
       (d) reworked in French translation: Conrat. "Johannes
           Brahms (Souvenirs Personnels)" La Revue musicale
           (Paris) 4/21 (1.11.1904) pp. 514-20. notes.
       (c) excerpt (in English translation by Daniel
           Gregory Mason): "Anecdotes of Brahms"
           Masters in Music 5/part 30 (6.1905) p. 3
           (volume p. [243]).

--Copland, Aaron (1900-)

See 1644

--Cornelius, Peter (1824-1874)

881   Huschke, Konrad. "Peter Cornelius und Johannes Brahms"
       Allgemeine Musikzeitung 64/28/29 (9.7.1937) pp. 439-40.
       Discusses their relationship, 1853-74.
       (d) Huschke. "Hebbel, Brahms und Cornelius" in 858.d.i.
           pp. 180-91. Brahms: pp. 189-91. ill., ind.
           Includes comment on Cornelius's opinion of Brahms's
           music [taken from Cornelius. Ausgewählte Schriften
           und Briefe. Paul Egert, ed. (Klassiker der Musik
           in ihren Schriften und Briefen [9]) Berlin: B.
           Hahnefeld, [1938]?]

882   Lederer, Josef-Horst. "Cornelius und Johannes Brahms" in

Peter Cornelius als Komponist, Dichter, Kritiker und Essayist. Vorträge, Referate und Diskussionen. Hellmut Federhofer and Kurt Oehl, eds. (Studien zur Musikgeschichte des 19. Jahrhunderts. Bd. 48) Regensburg: Gustav Bosse Verlag, 1977. pp. 57-63. notes. Discusses these two composers as representatives of contrasting movements in music history; includes comments on their personal relations.

See also 792, 1259, 2537.

--Cossel, Otto [fl. 19th century]

883 #Falke, Agnes. "Erinnerungen an Johannes Brahms" Hamburger Nachrichten no. 494 (4.11.1921) p. 2. Describes Brahms as a student of Cossel's, and Brahms in Hamburg.
      (a) *reprint: Falke, A. Rheinisch-Westfälische Zeitung (Essen) (4.11.1921).

884 Pulver, Jeffrey. "The Teachers of Johannes Brahms" Sackbut 6/9 (4.1926) pp. 251-53. Discusses Otto Cossel and Eduard Marxsen: their backgrounds and connection with Brahms.

See also 39A.c.i., 359, 363, 639.

--Couperin, François [le grand] (1668-1733)

See 1737, 1738.

--Crumb, George (1929-)

See 2608

--Daumer, Georg Friedrich (1800-1875)

885 Otto, Eberhard. "Georg Friedrich Daumer und Johannes Brahms--Ein fränkischer Dichter und sein Komponist" Musik in Bayern no. 21 (1980) pp. 11-18. Gives an overview of Daumer's life and work, with comments on Brahms's settings of his poems interspersed.

See also 2038, 2081, 2530.

--David, Ferdinand (1810-1873)

See 1016.

--Davies, Fanny (1861-1934)

See 657, 718, 2594.

--Debussy, Claude (1862-1918)

886   De Ternant, Andrew. "Debussy and Brahms" Musical Times
      65/977 (1.7.1924) pp. 608-09. Describes the two composers'
      meeting in Wien, 1887. [fiction?]
      (c) excerpt: de Ternant. "Debussy Visits Old Brahms"
          in 758. pp. 340-44.

See also 1398, 2116, 2431.5.

--Deiters, Hermann (1833-1907)

887   #Heuberger, R[ichard]. "Briefe von Johannes Brahms" Allgemeine
      Zeitung (München) Beilage nr. 260 (14.11.1899) pp. [1]-3.
      notes. Discusses Deiters's relationship to Brahms; includes
      4 letters: Brahms to Dieters (2; 1869) and (2;1880) [re-
      printed in 1122]; also single letters from Brahms to J.
      Hübner, Graf Wimpffen, and M. Brode.
      (c) excerpt (of Brode letter): in 2517.

See also 1122, 1205, 2925.

--de Lara [Tilbury], Adelina (1872-1961)

888   de Lara, Adelina. "Brahms and the Teaching of Clara Schumann"
      in de Lara. Finale. In collaboration with Clare H-Abrahall.
      London: Burke, 1955. pp. 48-60. Brahms: pp. 48-53.
      ill. Describes meeting Brahms in Frankfurt in the 1870's;
      includes comments on Brahms and Clara Schumann.

--Denninghof, Elise [fl. 19th century]

889   "Ungedruckte Briefe von Johannes Brahms (Nachdruck nur mit
      genauer Quellenangabe gestattet)" Allgemeine Musikzeitung
      27/32/33 (10./17.8.1900) pp. 473-74. notes. Presents 5
      letters: Brahms to Deninghof, 10.1880-6.1890.

--Derenburg, Mrs. Carl [Ilona Eibenschütz] (1873-1967)

890   Derenburg, Mrs. Carl. "My Recollections of Brahms" Musical
      Times 67/1001 (1.7.1926) pp. 598-600. notes. Describes
      Brahms at Bad Ischl 1891, 1892, 1896.

See also 684.

--Dessoff, Otto (1835-1892)

891 *Bauer, Elfriede. "Johannes Brahms im Briefwechsel mit Otto
   Dessoff und Rudolf und Laura von Beckerath" Jahresarbeit
   der Hamburger Bibliotheksschule, 1962. 94 pp.

892 *Brahms, Johannes. Johannes Brahms im Briefwechsel mit Otto
   Dessoff. Carl Krebs, ed. ([Johannes Brahms. Briefwechsel]
   XVI. Teil II) Berlin: Verlag der Deutschen Brahms-Gesellschaft m.b.H., 1922. pp. [111]-222. mus., ind., notes.
   [from 1215.a]
   (a) *reprint: in 1215.a.
       Brahms and Dessoff: [second paging] pp. [4],
       114-222. 87 letters, 3.1863-10.1892. [from 1215.a.a.]
   (c) i) excerpt: see 1179.c.i.
       ii) #excerpt: see 1179.c.ii.
       iii) excerpt (in English translation by Karl Geiringer):
           see 25.b.i. (2nd Edition).

--Detmering, Christian (1830-1892)

See 340.

--Diest, v. [fl. 19th century]

893 *"Ein Freund von Brahms" Leipziger Tageblatt (9.3.1911).

--Dietrich, Albert (1829-1908)

894 Dietrich, Albert. Erinnerungen an Johannes Brahms in Briefen
   besonders aus seiner Jugendzeit. Leipzig: Verlag von Otto
   Wigand, 1898. iv, 76 pp. ill., notes. Consists of recollections of Brahms 1853-89, letters between Brahms and
   Dietrich and his wife, and letters between Dietrich and other
   members of the Brahms circle.
   (b) *English translation by Dora Hecht: Dietrich. Recol-
       lections of Johannes Brahms by Albert Dietrich and
       J[osef]. V[iktor]. Widmann. London: Seeley and
       Co., Lmt., 1899. vi, 211 pp. ill. Includes 618.a.b.
       (c) i) excerpt: [Daniel Gregory Mason] "Anecdotes
              of Brahms" Masters in Music 5/part 30
              (6.1905) pp. [1], 4-5 (volume pp. [241,
              244-45]). Dietrich: p. [1]; Widmann:
              pp. 4-5.
           ii) excerpt: Dietrich. "Brought to Light" in

758. pp. 333-36.
iii) excerpt: Dietrich. "Recollections of Johannes
    Brahms" Musician (Philadelphia) 5/2 (2.1900)
    pp. 50-51.
iv) excerpt: Garbett, A. S. "The Musical
    Scrap Book" Etude 41/9 (9.1923) p. 598.
    "Why Brahms Never Married": p. 598.
    States reasons as related by Brahms to
    Widmann.
 v) excerpt: in 913. p. 327. 1 letter, before
    9.1862.
(e) i) report: "Brahms: The Man and The
       Musician" Musical Opinion and Music Trade
       Review 23/272 (1.5.1900) p. 554.
   ii) report: Swayne, Egbert. "Glimpses of
       Johannes Brahms" Music (Chicago) 17/[4]
       (2.1900) pp. 382-90.
(c) i) excerpt: see 792.
   ii) #excerpt: see 1179.c.ii.
  iii) excerpt: see 3077.
(e) i) report: "Johannes Brahms in seiner Jugend" Neue
       Musikzeitung 19/11 (26.5.1898) pp. 130-31.
   ii) report: see 618.a.e.ii.
  iii) report: see 618.a.e.iii.

See also 1730.

--Dobzanska, Mlle [fl. 19th century]

895 Slonimsky, Nicolas. "Musical Oddities" Etude 72/10 (10.1954)
    p. 4. Discusses Brahms and Mlle Dobzanska: his comments
    on her piano compositions, together with a Brahms comment
    on Raff.

--Dömpke, Gustav (1851-1923)

896 *Dömpke, G[ustav]. "Erinnerungen an Brahms" Königsberger
    hartungsche Zeitung (4.4.1922).

See also 585, 1102.

--Dohnányi, Ernő (1877-1960)

897 "Dohnanyi recalls his first meeting with Johannes Brahms"
    The Musician (New York) 35/10 (10.1930) p. 12. Describes
    meeting Brahms in Bad Ischl in 1894.

898 Holley, Joan. "Dr. Ernst Von Dohnanyi, Florida State University,

Cites Some Incidents in His Personal Acquaintance with
Brahms ..." Southwestern Musician 20/5 (1.1954) pp. 7, 28.
Covers time period Summer 1895- : describes a visit to
Brahms, and his interest in what was to be Dohnányi's
Op. 1.

See also 2378.

--Door, Anton (1833-1919)

899   Door, Anton. "Persönliche Erinnerungen an Brahms" Die Musik
       (Berlin) 2/15 (Bd. 7) (5.1903) pp. 216-21. mus. Includes
       reminiscences from mid-1850's, but mostly 1872- in Wien.
       (c) i) excerpt: Door. "Erinnerungen an Brahms" Die
            Musik (Berlin) 25/8 (5.1933) pp. 601-02.
            (a) reprint: in 3186.c. pp. 41-42.
           ii) excerpt: "Johannes Brahms" Frankfurter Zeitung
               47/126 (7.5.1903) 2. Morgenblatt p. 1.

--Dunkel, Johann [fl. 19th century]

900   *Dunkel, Norbert. "Unbekannte Briefe von Brahms" Neues
       Wiener Journal (12.2.1932). Presents 3 letters, Dunkel to
       Brahms. [from 241]
       (a) reprint: Dunkel. Die Musik (Berlin) 25/8 (5.1933)
            pp. 612-13. Relates anecdotes of Brahms in 1867,
            1874- ; includes 4 letters from Brahms to Dunkel,
            1867-69.
       (d) #Dunkel. "Brahms Johannes" in Dunkel. A Világ
            urai. Visszaemlékezések és intimitások világnirai
            művészek életéből. Számos ismeretlen levéllel.
            Budapest: Egyetemi ny., 1933. pp. 112-17. ill.
            Contains anecdotes and first 3 letters from 900.a.

--Dunkl, Johann Nepomuk (1832-1910)

901   *Dunkl, J[ohann]. N[epomuk]. Aus den Erinnerungen eines
       Musikers. Wien: Rosner, 1876. 68 pp. Brahms: pp.
       51-54. [from 241]

--Dvořák, Antonín (1841-1904)

902   *Beveridge, David Ralph. "Romantic Ideas in a Classical Frame:
       The Sonata Forms of Dvořák" Ph.D. diss., University of
       California (Berkeley), 1980. 415 pp. Includes comparisons
       between the compositional methods of Dvořák and composers
       who influenced him, including Brahms and Schubert.
       [from S202]

903 *Biba, Otto. "Brahms und Dvořák" Musikblätter der Wiener
Philharmoniker 33/7 (1979) pp. 179-200.

904 *"Brahms und Dvorak" Neue Militärmusikzeitschrift (?) (Hannover)
11/29 (1904). Discusses their correspondence. [from 241]

905 Cerný, Miroslav K. "Ad vocem Dreigestirn Wagner-Brahms-
Mahler in der Beziehung zur tschechischen Musik" in Collo-
quim musica bohemica et europaea Brno 1970. Rudolf
Pečman, ed. (Colloquia on the History and Theory of
Music at the International Music Festival in Brno. vol. 5/
Musikwissenschaftliche Kolloquien der Internationalen Musik-
festspiele. Bd. 5) Brno: International Musical Festival/
Internationale Musikfestspiele [Mezinárodní Hudební Festival],
1972. pp. 389-96. notes. Brahms: pp. 392-93. notes.
Discusses the influence of Brahms on Dvořák.

906 Clapham, John. "Dvořák's Relations with Brahms and Hanslick"
Musical Quarterly 57/2 (4.1971) pp. 241-54. Discusses
Brahms as a supporter of Dvořák; includes two new letters
Dvořák to Brahms: 3.1878, 12.1894.
(b) Czech translation: Clapham. "Dvořákovy vztahy k
Brahmsovi a Hanslickovi" Hudební věda 10/3 (1973)
pp. 213-24. notes.
(d) condensed in German translation: "Brahms und Dvorak"
Mitteilungen der Brahms-Gesellschaft Hamburg e.V.
no. 3. (3.1972) pp. 7-8

907 Geiringer, Karl. "Brahms und Dvořák (Mit ungedruckten
Briefen Anton Dvořáks.)" Der Auftakt 17/7-8 ([7.-8.]
1937) pp. 100-02. Describes the encouragement that Brahms
gave Dvořák; includes 4 letters: Dvořák to Brahms (3),
Brahms to Dvořák (1) from 1877-79.

908 #Graf, Harry. "Brahms y Antonin Dvorak" Ars. Revista de arte
17/79 (1957) pp. [94-103]. ill., facsim., notes. Describes
how Brahms helped Dvořák become established.

909 *Kalbeck, Max. "Dvořák à Brahms" Hudební revue 4 (1911)
pp. 465-67.

910 *Schmidt, Leopold. Berliner Tageblatt (1898).
(a) #reprint: in Schmidt. "Brahms" in 3022. pp. 255-67.
"Brahms und Dvorak": pp. 263-65. Review of a
concert featuring music of both composers.

911 *Sourek, Otaker. "Freundschaft zwischen Brahms und Antonin
Dvořák" Bulletin der diplomatischen Mission der Tschechoslowskischen Republik (Berlin) no. 7 (1955).

912 *Stoverock, Dietrich. "Brahms-Dvořák, eine Musikerfreundschaft"
Philharmonische Blätter [10]/2 (1972/73) pp. 8-11.

913 Weiss, Piero, compiler, editor, translator. Letters of Composers
Through Six Centuries. Foreword by Richard Ellmann.
Philadelphia, New York, London: Chilton Book Company,
1967. pp. 359-61. 2 letters, 12.1877, from Dvořák. Antonín
Dvořák: Letters and Reminiscences. Otakar Sourek, ed.
Roberta Finlayson Samsour, tr. (Prague: Artia, [1954]).

See also 116, 688, 792, 1145, 2943.c., 2974, 3009.

--Eames, Henry (1872-1950)

See 2967.

--Ebner, Ottilie [fl. 19th century]

914 Balassa, Ottilie von. Die Brahmsfreundin Ottilie Ebner und Ihr
Kreis. Wien: Kommissionsverlag Franz Bondy, 1933. 151,
[1] pp. Brahms: pp. 38-123. ill., notes. Describes
Brahms and Ebner and her circle, 1862-97.

--Eckhardt, Julius von. [fl. 19th century]

915 Eckhardt, Julius von. "Erinnerungen aus meinem Leben"
Deutsche Rundschau 36/5,6 (Bd. 142) (2.,3.;1910) pp. 171-
93, 374-99. Brahms: p. 192. Describes meeting Brahms
and Feuerbach in Karlsruhe.
(a) i) reprint: Eckhardt. Halbmonatshefte der Deutschen
Rundschau Jahrgang 1909/10/10,11 (Bd. 2) (2.,3.;
1910) pp. 294-316, 430-55. Brahms: pp. 315-16.
ii) *reprint: Eckhardt. Neues Wiener Journal (31.1.
1910).

--Eckstein, Friedrich [fl. 19th century]

916 *Eckstein, Friedrich. "Bruckner, Brahms und Wolf. Erinnerungen"
Rhein-Mainische Volkszeitung (Frankfurt a.M.) (25.7.1931).
Describes meeting Brahms while walking in Wien and Eck-
stein's impressions of him. [from 241]

917 #Selinko, Annemarie. "Begegnungen mit Johannes Brahms. Die
Geschichte vom Leben und Sterben eines einsamen Mannes"
Wienr Bühne 13/445 (1937) pp. 2-5. ill. Describes meetings
between Eckstein and Brahms in the 1880's, 1894-96?; includes comments on Bruckner and Brahms, and anecdotes
showing Brahms to be a solitary individual.

--Edmunds [fl. 19th century]

See 992.

--Egger, Franz [fl. 19th century]

See 388.

--Egidi, Arthur (1859-1943)

See 568.

--Ehrlich, Heinrich (1822-1899)

918 Ehrlich, Heinrich. Dreissig Jahre Künstlerleben. Berlin:
     Verlag Hugo Steinitz, 1893. 416, viii pp. Brahms: pp.
     184-87, 189-91. notes. Relates his impressions of Brahms
     at their first meeting in 1853, describes their relationship
     and evaluates Brahms's music.

See also 1059.

--Eibenschütz, Ilona

See Derenburg, Mrs. Carol

--Eldering, Bram (1865-1943)

919 "Bram Eldering und Joh[annes]. Brahms" Zeitschrift für
     Musik 102/8 (8.1935) pp. 894-95. Describes their first
     meeting and subsequent relationship, 1887-

--Elgar, Edward, Sir (1857-1934)

See 2462, 2622.

--Engelmann, Theodor Wilhelm (1843-1909)

920 *Brahms, Johannes. Johannes Brahms im Briefwechsel mit
     Th[eodor]. Wilhelm Engelmann. Mit einer Einleitung von
     Julius Röntgen. (Johannes Brahms. Briefwechsel XIII)
     Berlin: Verlag der Deutschen Brahms-Gesellschaft, 1918.
     182 pp. notes.
     also: Leipzig: Verlag von Wilhelm Engelmann, 1918.
     Contains 174 letters, 1874-97.
     (a) reprint (of Berlin Auflage): (Brahms-Briefwechsel
         Band XIII) Tutzing: Hans Schneider, 1974.
     (c) i) excerpt (of Berlin Auflage): see 1179.c.i.
        ii) #excerpt (of Berlin Auflage): see 1179.c.ii.

(e) #report (on Berlin Auflage): Altmann, Wilh[elm]. "Der Briefwechsel zwischen Brahms und Professor Dr. Th[eodor]. Wilhelm Engelmann" Allgemeine Musikzeitung 45 (1918) pp. 403-04. Discusses various aspects of the two men's relationship as revealed in their letters.

See also "The Netherlands" in II.B.

--Epstein, Julius (1832-1918)

921 *Bauer-Lechner, Natalie. Fragmente--Gelerntes und Gelebtes. Wien: R. Lechner, 1907. iv, 236 pp.

922 *Menczigar, Maria. "Julius Epstein. Sein Leben und Wirken unter besonderer Erforschung seiner Beziehung zu Johannes Brahms" Phil.F. diss., Universität Wien, 1957. xxvi, 579 pp.

--Erkel, Sánderhoz (1846-1900)

923 Isóz, Kálmán, ed. Zenei kéziratok. I. Kötet. Zenei levelek. (A Magyar Nemzeti Múzeum Konyvtárának. Cimjegyzéke. VI) Budapest: Kiadja A Magyar Nemzeti Múzeum könyvtára, 1924. Brahms: pp. 128-29. Describes 3 letters Brahms to Erkel: 1879, 1881, ?.

--Eunike, Eugen [music publisher]

See 314.

--Faber, Bertha [fl. 19th century]

See 39A.e.iv., 2136.
See "Op. 49" in IV.B.1. Specific Works.

--Falke, Agnes [fl. 19th century]

See 883.

--Fall, Leo[póld] (1873-1925)

924 *Willner, A. M. "Brahms und "Die Dollarprinzessin"" Nord und Sud 32/10 (11.1908).
(a) *reprint: Willner. Deutsche Militärmusikerzeitung 31 (15.1.1909).

--Fauré, Gabriel (1845-1924)

See 2099, 2116, 2401, 2488.

--Fehr [fl. 19th century]

See 1318.

--Fellinger Family [fl. 19th century]

925 Fellinger, Richard. Klänge um Brahms. Erinnerungen. Berlin:
Verlag der Deutschen Brahms-Gesellschaft, 1933. 135 pp.
Describes relations with Brahms and the Brahms circle
1881- ; includes the Fellinger family history and comments
on memorial events for Brahms.
(c) #excerpt: Fellinger. "Klänge um Brahms. Erinnerungen"
Die Musik (Berlin) 26/2 (11.1933) pp. 107-11. notes.

926 #Horovitz-Barnay, Ilka. "Brahms-Briefe" Neue freie Presse
(Wien) no. 14,882 [(18.1.1906?)] Beilage pp. 31-32. notes.
Discusses letters from Brahms to Maria and Richard Fellinger
and what they reveal of Brahms the man. Letters from
8.1887-9.1896, all included in 1062.

See also 393, 667, 711, 999, 1062, 3089.

Feuerbach Family
Anselm (1829-1880): 929-32.
Henriette (1812-1892): 927-29, 931, 932.

927 Ebert, H. "Briefe von Anselm Feuerbach und Johannes Brahms"
Süddeutsche Monatshefte 4/3 (4/Bd. 1) (3.1907) pp. 301-12.
Brahms: pp. 310-11. notes. 2 letters to Henriette
Feuerbach, 8.1881.

928 *Feuerbach, Henriette. Henriette Feuerbach. Ihr Leben in
ihren Briefen. Hermann Unde-Bernays, ed. Berlin: Meyer
& Jessen, 1912. 490 pp.
*also: München: Kurt Wolff Verlag, n.d.
*Auflagen (Berlin Ausgabe): [9.-13.;] 1913.
Auflagen (München Ausgabe): 4.-8.;1920. Contains 9 letters
Feuerbach to Brahms, 1875-88 and references passim; in-
cludes libretto for proposed opera.
Auflagen (München Ausgabe): 15.-19.; 1926.

929 Huschke, Konrad. "Anselm Feuerbach und Johannes Brahms"
Die Kunst (München) [=Kunst und das schöne Heim] Bd.
63/5,6 (2.,3.;1931) pp. 154-55, 171-81. Describes Feuerbach's
rise as an artist and his relationship with Brahms; includes

comments on their philosophies, description of Brahms sitting
for a portrait by Feuerbach, and reference to Brahms and
Henriette Feuerbach with respect to the dedication of Op.
82.
(d) i) Huschke. "Anselm Feuerbach und Johannes Brahms"
        Zeitschrift für Musik 100/5 (5.1933) pp. 434-40.
        (d) reworked: see 929.d.ii.
     ii) reworked: Huschke. "Brahms--Feuerbach und
        Menzel" in 858.d.i. pp. 165-80. ill. Includes
        discussion of Brahms's relationship with Menzel,
        1890's.
(e) #report: "Brahms und Feuerbach" Berliner Börsenzeitung
        (7.3.1931) p.[?].

930 #Leinburg, Mathilde v. "Johannes Brahms und seine Künstler-
     freundschaften. Zum 3. April, der 25. Wiederkehr seines
     Todestages" Daheim 57/27/28 (1922) pp. 10-13. ill. Dis-
     cusses Brahms and his relationship with Feuerbach and
     Klinger, includes comments on memorials built after his
     death.

931 Michelmann, Emil. Feuerbach und Brahms. Eine psychologische
     Skizze. Berlin: Ed. Bote & G. Bock, 1940. 13, [2] pp.
     ill. Compares their backgrounds and personalities; includes
     comment on Brahms's relationship with Henriette Feuerbach.

932 *Stettner, Thomas. "Brahms in seinem Beziehungen zu Anselm
     und Henriette Feuerbach" Pauliner-Zeitung (Leipzig) 45
     (1933) pp. 107-11.
     (d) i) Stettner. "Johannes Brahms in seinem Beziehungen
        zu Anselm und Henriette Feuerbach" Fränkische
        Heimat (Nürnberg) 15/11/12 ([11./12.] 1936) pp.
        270-73. Discusses Brahms's relationship with the
        two Feuerbachs, especially with respect to Op. 82
        and its dedication.
     ii) reworked: Stettner. "Johannes Brahms in seinem
        Beziehungen zu Anselm und Henriette Feuerbach.
        Erinnerungen zu Johannes Brahms' 40. Todestag
        am 3. April 1937" Zeitschrift für Musik 104/4 (4.1937)
        pp. 382-85. notes.

See also 788, 915, 994, 1877.

--Fortner, Wolfgang (1907-)

See 2318.

--Franck, Cesar (1822-1890)

See 2608.

--Frank, Ernst (1847-1889)

933 Einstein, Alfred. "Briefe von Brahms an Ernst Frank" Zeitschrift für Musikwissenschaft 4/17 (4.1922) pp. 385-416. notes. Includes 63 letters between the two men, 1875-86; also 3 letters Brahms to Frank family, 1888-89. (e) report: see 3180.e.

See also 947.

--Franz, Robert (1815-1892)

934 *Müller, Erich H. "Robert Franz über Johannes Brahms" Schweizerische Musikzeitung und Sängerblatt 66 (10.-11.1926). (a) i) *reprint: Müller. Leipziger neueste Nachrichten (5. or 19.; 11.;1926). ii) *reprint: Müller. Deutsche Tonkünstler-Zeitung 26/473 (1928).

See also 2064.

--Fribberg, Franz [fl. 19th century]

935 *Fribberg, Franz. "Brahms Erinnerungen" Berliner Tageblatt (18.12.1898).

--Friedberg, Carl

936 "Brahms and Friedberg" New York Times 81/27,154 (29.5.1932) Section 8, p. 6. Reminiscences of Brahms by Friedberg [from 1880's-90's].

--Friedman, Ignacy (1882-1948)

See 1645.

--Fritzsch, Ernst Wilhelm (1840-1902)

See 320.a., 848.

--Fröhlich, Friedrich Theodor (1803-1836)

See 2318.

--Fuchs, Robert (1847-1927)

See 688.

--Furtwängler, Wilhelm (1886-1954)

See 2267, 2698.

--Gabrieli, Giovanni (c1553-1612)

See 2216.

--Gade, Niels (1807-1890)

See 1176.

--Ganghofer, Ludwig [fl. 19th century]

937 Ganghofer, Ludwig. "Das Ringtheater. Wiener Erinnerungen" Süddeutsche Monatshefte 9/10,11 (Bd. 1) (10.,11.;1911) pp. 73-100, 197-225. Brahms: pp. 91-92. Recounts a meeting with Brahms in Summer 1881, together with an anecdote from a later time.
(e) #report: "Wiener Theater- und Künstlererinnerungen von Ludwig Ganghofer" Leipziger neueste Nachrichten (20.9.1911) p. [?].

--Garbe, Laura [fl. 19th century]

See 48, 375, 1061, 2193.

--Gehring, Franz (1838-1884)

938 #Schiedermair, Ludwig. "Johannes Brahms und Franz Gehring" Kölnische Zeitung Literatur- und Unterhaltungsblatt nr. 616 (18.9.1927) pp. [1-2]. Describes Gehring's background and the Gehring family connection with Brahms.

--Georg II, Herzog von Sachsen-Meiningen (1826-1914)

939 Müller, Herta. "Brahms's Briefwechsel mit Meiningen" Beiträge zur Musikwissenschaft 20/2 (1978) pp. 85-132. notes. 55 letters, between Georg II, the Freifrau von Heldburg, and Brahms, 1881-97.

940 *Widmann, J[osef]. V[iktor]. "Meininger Erinnerungen" Neue
    freie Presse (Wien) (1906).
    (e) report: "Anlässlich des 80. Geburtstages des Herzogs
        Georg II ..." Allgemeine Musikzeitung 33/17 (27.4.
        1906)p. 294. Discusses Brahms's relation with Georg II.

See also 3105, 3141.

--Gericke, Wilhelm (1845-1925)

See 989.e.d.

--Gernsheim, Friedrich (1839-1916)

See 1062.

--Gildemeister Family [fl. 19th century]

See 374.

--Girzick, Rosa [fl. 19th century]

See 1222.

--Gluck, Christoph Willibald (1714-1787)

See 1739, 2330, 2630.

--Godowsky, Leopold (1870-1938)

See 3037.

--Goethe, Johann Wolfgang von (1749-1832)

941 *Graevenitz, G[eorge von]. "Brahms und Goethe" Die Propyläen
    (München) 19 (1922) p. 202.
    (a) *reprint: Graevenitz, George von. "Goethe und
        Brahms" Berliner Zeitung(?) [Berliner Börsen-
        Zeitung(?)] (28.8.1924).

942 *Kockegey, Annegret. "Brahms und Goethe" Phil.F. diss.,
    Humboldt-Universität Berlin, 1948. 88 pp. mus.

943 #Luithlen, Victor [J.]. "Brahms und Goethe" Chronik des Wiener
    Goethe-Vereins Bd. 47 (1942) pp. 59-61. Describes Brahms's
    knowledge and opinion of Goethe's work; includes an overview
    of Brahms's settings of his poetry.

944 *Vogt, Paul. "Brahms und Goethe" Hamburger Nachrichten
    (26.;5. or 6.;1932). Examines Brahms's settings of Goethe's
    poetry. [from 241]
    (c) #excerpt: Vogt. Die Musik (Berlin) 25/8 (5.1933)
        p. 609. Discusses Brahms's knowledge of the work
        of Goethe and his contemporaries; also looks at
        Op. 81 as a possible Faust Overture.

See also 2309, 2312, 2534.

--Goetz, Hermann (1840-1876)

945 *Hunziker, Rudolf. "Hermann Goetz und Johannes Brahms"
    Neue Zürcher Zeitung nr. 1852 (1940).
    (a) *reprint: Hermann Goetz und Johannes Brahms.
        Zürich: Neue Zürichische Zeitung, 1940. 13 pp.

946 *Huschka, K. [Konrad Huschke] "Hermann Goetz und J[ohannes].
    Brahms. Zu Goetz' 100. Geburtstag" Warschauer Zeitung
    (7.12.1940).

947 Schorn, Hans. "Brahms und die Oper" Neue Musikzeitung
    40/3 (1919) pp. 36-37. Discusses how Goetz' last wish was
    that Brahms and Ernst Frank should finish his Francesca
    di Rimini, and why Brahms would have nothing to do with
    the project.

948 Weigl, Bruno. "Johannes Brahms und Hermann Götz" Neue
    Musikzeitung 28/13 (4.4.1907) pp. 284-86. ill., notes.
    Discusses their relationship, both personal and through cor-
    respondence, and contrasts their professional careers; in-
    cludes a letter Brahms to Goetz' widow, [12.1876].

See also 1302, 2320.

--Goldmark, Carl (1830-1915)

949 *Goldmark, Karl [Carl]. Erinnerungen aus meinem Leben.
    [Vorwort von Ferdinand Scherber] Wien: Rikola Verlag,
    1922. 153, [13] pp. Brahms: pp. 84-96, 139-40. [from
    241]
    *also: Wien: Amalthea-Verlag, 1922.
    (b) English translation by Alice Goldmark Brandes:
        Notes from The Life of a Viennese Composer.
        Karl Goldmark. [Epilogue by F.S.] New York:
        Albert and Charles Boni, 1927. xv, [3], 19-280 pp.
        Brahms: pp. 152-70. Describes their first meeting
        in 1860-61, focuses on anecdotes of Brahms in Wien,
        1870's.

(e) report: Schonberg, Harold C. "Brahms Spoke
Up--To Knock a Jew" New York Times
119/40,965 (22.3.1970) Section 2, p. 21.
Reports on a disparaging remark Brahms
made about Goldmark.

(c) excerpt (of ? Auflage): "Goldmarks Erinnerungen
an Wagner und Brahms" Neue freie Presse (Wien)
no. 20,715 (2.5.1922) Nachmittagblatt pp. 1-2
[across page bottoms].

(b) English translation: "Goldmark's Memories of
Wagner and Brahms" Living Age 313/4068
(24.6.1922) pp. 791-93.

950 *_____. (Carl) "Johannes Brahms-Erinnerungen" Wiener
Fremdenblatt (1906/07).

(b) English translation: "Brahms as a Practical Joker"
Etude 25/6 (6.1907) p. 362. Relates anecdote of
sloppy piano playing by an incognito Brahms as a
joke on Goldmark's wife.

(d) *incorporated: into 949.

(e) i) report: "Goldmark erzählte kürzlich ..." Neue
Zeitschrift für Musik 73/29/30 (Bd. 102) (25.7.1906)
p. 626.

ii) report: "Eine heitere Brahms-Anekdote hat Karl
Goldmark ..." Allgemeine Musikzeitung 33/30/31
(27.7./3.8.;1906) p. 494.

iii) report: "[[Johannes Brahms als miserabler Bub]]"
Frankfurter Zeitung 50/183 (5.7.1906) 2. Morgenblatt
pp. 1-2 [across page bottoms].

951 *"Johannes Brahms †" Pester Lloyd (Budapest) no. 77 (5.4.1897)
Abendblatt.

See also 431, 704, 795, 868, 989.e.d., 1142.

--Goodwin, Amina (1867-1942)

See 655, 718.

--Gounod, Charles (1818-1893)

See 2630.

--Graener, Paul (1872-1944)

952 *Graener, Paul. "Besuch bei Brahms" Magdeburger Bühnenblät-
ter. Spielzeit (1936/37) pp. 50-52.

--Graf, Max (1873-1958)

953 Graf, Max. "Recollections of Johannes Brahms" in Graf.
Legend of a Musical City. New York: Philosophical Library,
1945. pp. 97-114. ill. Describes meetings and activities
with Brahms in Wien, late 1880's-90's.
(a) *reprint: New York: Greenwood Press Publishers,
1969.
(b) i)*German translation: Legende einer Musikstadt.
Illustrationen von Carry Hauser. (Auszug für die
österreichische Buchgemeinschaft. Bd. nr. 13)
Wien: Osterreichische Buchgemeinschaft, [1949].
476 or 478 pp.
ii) *Spanish translation: Leyenda de una cuidad musical,
la historia de Viena. Buenos Aires: Editorial
Futuro, [1947]. 269 pp.
(d) i) reworked in German translation: Graf. "Johannes
Brahms in Wien. Zum 125. Geburtstag des Komponisten. Erinnerungen" Frankfurter allgemeine Zeitung
no. 108 (10.5.1958) Feuilleton p. [1].
ii) reworked: Graf. "Recollections of Brahms" Musical
America 80/3 (2.1960) pp. 73-74.

--Greef, Arthur de (1862-1940)

See 718.

--Grieg, Edvard (1843-1907)

See 1239, 1398, 1625, 2400, 2551.

--Griffes, Charles T. (1884-1920)

See 1625.

--Grillparzer, Granz (1791-1872)

See 1074.

--Grimm, Julius Otto (1827-1903)

954 *Brahms, Johannes. Johannes Brahms im Briefwechsel mit J. O.
Grimm. Richard Barth, ed. (Johannes Brahms. Briefwechsel
IV) Berlin: Verlag der Deutschen Brahms-Gesellschaft m.b.H.,
1908. xvi, 165 pp. ill., ind., notes. [from 954.a.]
*2. durchgesehene Auflage: 1912. xvi, [2], 165 pp.

(a) reprint (of 1912 Auflage): (Brahms-Briefwechsel Band
    IV) Tutzing: Hans Schneider, 1974. 128 letters,
    12.1853-3.1897.
(c) i) excerpt (of 1912 Auflage): see 792.
    ii) excerpt (of ? Auflage): see 1179.c.i.
    iii)#excerpt (of ? Auflage): see 1179.c.ii.
    iv) excerpt (of 1912 Auflage): Bücken, Ernst. "Johan-
        nes Brahms" in Musikerbriefe. Bücken, ed. (Samm-
        lung Dieterich. Bd. 36) Leipzig: Dieterich'schen
        Verlagsbuchhandlung, 1940. pp. 204-25. ill., mus.,
        notes. 2 letters, Brahms to Grimm; includes ex-
        cerpts from 983, 1122, 1179.
        *[Auflage:] Wiesbaden, [1952].
    v) excerpt (of 1912 Auflage in English translation by
       Karl Geiringer): see 25.b.i. (2nd Edition).
    vi) excerpt (of 1908 Auflage in English translation by
        Jacques Barzun): see 1930.
(e) i) report (on 1908 Auflage): Bergh, Rudolph [S.].
       "Johannes Brahms' Brevvexling" Tilskueren [28]/1.
       Halvbind (3.1911) pp. 287-94. notes. also reports
       on 983, 1009, 1062.
    ii) *report (on 1908 Auflage): "Brahms, J. O. Grimm,
        und Joachim" National Zeitung (Berlin) Sonntags-
        Beilage no. 19 (1907).
    iii) *report (on 1908 Auflage): Friedrich, W. "Johannes
         Brahms und J. O. Grimm" Zeitschrift für Literatur,
         Kunst und Wissenschaft [Beilage des Hamburgerischer
         Correspondent] no. 23 (1907).
    iv) report (on ? Auflage): see 750.
    v)#report (on 1908 Auflage): see 1195. 1196.

954.5 #Preising, Dr. "Julius Otto Grimm" Rheinische Musik- und
      Theaterzeitung (Köln) 6/25 (9.12.1905) pp. 573-74. Includes
      comments on Brahms's relationship with Grimm, 1854-1860.

See also 68.e., 662.

See also "Gisela von Arnim" in III.B.2.

--Grosser, Julius [fl. 19th century]

955 Holde, Artur. "Unpublished Letters by Beethoven, Liszt and
    Brahms" Musical Quarterly 32/2 (4.1946) pp. 278-88.
    Brahms: pp. 284-88. facsim., notes. Contains one letter
    to Grosser (28.1.1886) and one to Siegfried Ochs (8.9.1891).
    (b) *German translation: Holde, A. "Brief aus New York.
        Unbekannte Briefe von Beethoven, Liszt und Brahms"
        Die amerikanische Rundschau 2 (1946) pp. 86-92.

--Groth, Klaus (1819-1899)

956 Brahms, Johannes. Briefe der Freundschaft. Johannes Brahms-
Klaus Groth. Volquart Pauls, ed. Heide in Holstein: Westholsteinische Verlagsanstalt Boyens & Co., 1956. 168 pp.
ill., ind., notes. Contains 83 letters, 1868-96, and a note
from Groth.
(c) #excerpt: see 959.

957 #Fink, Hermann. "Klaus Groth und Johannes Brahms. Ein
Freundschaftsbild" Niedersachsen [29] (1924) pp. 178-80,
182. notes. Examines how their friendship originated;
includes comments on how Brahms set various poems by
Groth.
(a) *reprint: Fink. "Brahms und Klaus Groth" Niederdeutsche Monatshefte 8 3.1933) pp. 118-24.
(c) #excerpt: Fink. Die Musik (Berlin) 25/8
(5.1933) pp. 611-12.

958 #Groth, Klaus. "Erinnerungen an Johannes Brahms" Gegenwart
Bd. 51/45-47 (6.,13.,20.;11.;1897) pp. 295-99, 307-10,
327-29. notes. Gives a history of the links between the
Groth and Brahms families and describes their friendship;
Brahms in Wien and Thun, Brahms the man, and Brahms and
opera.
(d) #reworked: in 959.
(e) *report: see 3102.

959 #Miesner, Heinrich, ed. Klaus Groth und die Musik. Erinnerungen an Johannes Brahms. Briefe, Gedichte und Aufzeichnungen nebst einem Verzeichnis von Vertonungen Grothscher
Dichtungen. (Beiträge zur Heimat- und Wohlfahrtskunde 12)
Heide in Holstein: Westholsteinische Verlagsanstalt, Heider
Anzeiger G.m.b.H., 1933. 148 pp. ill., ind., notes.
Includes reminiscences of Brahms, an overview of their correspondence with excerpts, and examines Brahms's settings
of Groth poems.
(d) *Miesner. "Groths Musikbibliothek" Dithmarschen 8
(7./8.1932) pp. 113-24.
(e) report: see 61.e.i.

960 #Sannemüller, Gerd. "Die Freundschaft zwischen Johannes
Brahms und Klaus Groth" [Klaus-Groth-Gesellschaft.
Jahresgabe] (1969) pp. 114-27. Examines their relationship
and their affinity for and opinions of each other, their
correspondence, and Brahms's settings of Groth poems.

961 Stolz, Heinz. "Brahms und Klaus Groth. Eine Begegnung zu
Pfingsten." Rheinisch-Westfälische Zeitung (Essen) 180/421
(27.5.1917) p. 1. Describes a meeting of Brahms and Groth
in Düsseldorf, early 1850's, and compares their backgrounds.

See also 364, 366, 736, 1214, 1492, 2092, 2530.

--Grove, George (1820-1900)

962   Geiringer, Karl. "Brahms, Grove and Pohl. Two Unpublished
       Letters" The Times (London) no. 47,448 (8.8.1936) p. 8.
       Contains 2 letters, Grove to Brahms, 10.1884 and 5.1887;
       includes comments on their friendship and how Pohl acted
       as an intermediary between the other two.

See also 656.

--Grünberg, Eugene [fl. 19th century]

See 2967.

--Grüters Family [August and Emilie] [fl. 19th century]

963   #[Heinrich Melsbach] "Erinnerungen an Johannes Brahms. Nach
       Aufzeichnungen von Frau Prof. August Grüters" Die Heimat
       (Krefeld) 10 (1931) pp. 126-29. Relates a series of anecdotes
       about Brahms and his Krefeld friends, and about Brahms's
       character.

964   #Melsbach, Heinrich. "Crefelder Brahmserinnerungen. Ein
       Beitrag zu Geschichte des Crefelder Musiklebens" Die Heimat
       (Krefeld) 5 (1925) pp. 126-30. notes. Discusses the link
       between August Grüters and Brahms and Brahms's visits
       to Krefeld; includes 9 letters, 1879-1880's.

See also 598.

--Guinzburg, J. [fl. 20th century]

965   Guinzburg, J., see 627.5.

--Gund, Robert (1865-1927)

966   *Gund, Robert. "Meine Erinnerungen an Brahms" Musikbote
       [1] (1925).

--Gutmann, Albert [fl. 19th century]

See 389.

--Haas, Bela [fl. 19th century]

See 684.

--Händel, Georg Friedrich (1685-1759)

967   Antcliffe, Herbert. "Handel and Brahms" Musical Opinion and
      Music Trade Review 27/321 (1.6.1904) pp. 699-700. Compares
      their lives and musical styles; also includes a comparison
      of the personal characteristics of Beethoven and Bach, with
      those of Brahms.

See also 792, 879, 1023, 2325, 2522, 2630.

See also "Op. 24" in IV.A.1.a. Specific Works.

--H"rtel, Hermann (1803-1875)

See 848.

--Härtel, Raymund (1810-1888)

See 848.

--Hanslick, Eduard (1825-1904)

968   Hanslick, Eduard. "Aus meinem Leben" Deutsche Rundschau
      20/4 (Bd. 78) (1.1894) pp. 58-60. Describes Brahms's
      first appearance in Wien, and compares him with Wagner;
      also looks at Brahms the man and his friendship with Hans-
      lick.
      (a) *reprint: in Hanslick. Aus meinem Leben [2 Bde.]
            Berlin: Allgemeiner Verein für deutsche Litteratur,
            1894.
            (a) reprint (2 Bde. in 1): Westmead: Gregg In-
                  ternational Publishers Limited, 1971. Brahms:
                  Bd. 2, pp. 14-20.
      (c) excerpts (in French translation): Hanslick, Edward.
            "Souvenirs d'un critique musical Viennois" Revue
            bleue 4e série 1/9,10 (3.,10.;3.;1894) pp. 279-82,
            312-14. Brahms: p. 312.
            (e) report: see 147.d.i.

969 * _____. "Johannes Brahms, Erinnerungen und Briefe" Neue
      freie Presse (Wien) (27. and 29.,6.;1. and 6.,7.;1897).
      (a) *reprint: Hanslick. "[Johannes Brahms. Die letzten
            Tage] II. Erinnerungen und Briefe" in 2943. pp.

372-409.   notes.   Describes Brahms as a letterwriter,
with the correspondence between Marie Lipsius,
Hanslick and Brahms, 16 letters, 1863-96; also describes Brahms's final year and includes anecdotes
about Brahms the man and his milieu.
- (b)   Italian translation by Paola Tonini: Hanslick,
   E.   "Johannes Brahms.   Lettere e ricordi"
   Il Convegno musicale 2/3-4 (1965) pp. 3-21.
- (c)   *excerpt (of 2943, 3. Auflage):   Brahms, Johannes.   "Beethovens frühe Kantaten" in
   Der Kritische Musikus.   Musikkritiken aus
   drei Jahrhunderten.   Horst Seeger, ed.
   (Reclams Universal-Bibliothek Bd. 136)
   Leipzig: Verlag Philipp Reclam jun., 1964.
   pp. 177-79.
   - (e)   report (on ? Auflage):   see 750.
- (c)   excerpt (in English translation):   J. B. K. "Brahmsiana"
   Monthly Musical Record 28/334 (1.10.1898) pp. 219-
   20.   Relates incidents from 1884, 1889, 1891; also
   includes excerpt and reports of 581 and 1235.
   - (e)   i)   report: "The late Johannes Brahms detested letter-
      writing ..." Nation (New York) 65/1678 (26.8.1897)
      p. 169.
      - (d)   continued: "It must be admitted that most of
         Brahms's letters ..." Nation (New York)
         65/1678 (26.8.1897) p. 169.
      ii)   report: -n. "Hofrat Hanslick veröffentlicht ..."
      in 618.e. p. 187.

970   Korngold, Julius.   "Ein Brief Hanslicks an Brahms" Der Merker
(Wien) 3/2 (1.1912) pp. 57-58.   1 letter, [2.1890?]:   contains
Hanslick's opinion on the revised version of Op. 8.
- (e)   report: "Beethoven and Brahms" Monthly Musical
   Record 42/498 (1.6.1912) pp. 150-51.

See also 39C.c.ii., 579.d., 680, 831, 906, 1229, 1265, 2160, 3047,
3051.

--Hatch, Earl [fl. 20th century]

See 2608.

--Haupt, Leopold [fl. 19th century]

See 2129.

--Hauptmann, Moritz (1792-1868)

See 2448.

--Hausegger, Friedrich von (1837-1899)

971   Hausegger, Friedrich von. Gedanken eines Schauenden.
       Gesammelte Aufsätze. Siegmund von Hausegger, ed.
       München: Verlagsanstalt F. Bruckmann A.-G., 1903.
       "Johannes Brahms": pp. 231-36. Memorial article, describes
       strength and qualities of Brahms's music; includes personal
       reminiscences of Brahms in Wien (1862), and Graz (1867, 1882).
       "Die E-moll-Sinfonie von Joh[annes]. Brahms": pp. 237-39.
       Review of a local Graz performance, Brahms conducting.

--Hausmann, Robert (1852-1909)

See 1016, 1112.

--Haydn, Franz Joseph (1732-1809)

972   Wirth, Helmut. "Nachwirkungen der Musik Joseph Haydns
       auf Johannes Brahms" Musik. Edition. Interpretation.
       Gedenkschrift Günter Henle. Martin Bente, ed. München:
       G. Henle Verlag, 1980. pp. 455-62. mus., notes. Examines
       Brahms's study and playing of Haydn works and traces
       allusions to Haydn's music in his own, focusing on Opp. 56a
       and 56b.

See also 288, 1826, 2330, 2539, 2630, 3070, 3091.

--Hebbel, Friedrich (1813-1863)

973   *Frillinger, Elfriede. ""Grosse Erinnerungen einer kleinen
       Stadt" [Gmunden] Erinnerungen an Friedrich Hebbel und
       Johannes Brahms" Zeitschrift Oberösterreich (Linz) (Sommer-
       heft 1963).

See also 1074.

--Hecht Family [fl. 19th century]

See 602, 1062.

--Heermann, Hugo (1844-1935)

974   Heermann, Hugo. Meine Lebenserinnerungen. Leipzig: F. A.
       Brockhaus, 1935. 44, [2] pp. Brahms: pp. 20-22, 24-26,
       28, 36-37. Describes his relationship with Brahms, 1860's
       (Germany), 1889-90's (Germany, Austria).

See also 1016.

--Hegar, Friedrich (1841-1927)

975 "Ein Brief von Johannes Brahms an Friedrich Hegar" Schweizer-
    ische Musikzeitung. Revue musicale suisse 98/5 (1.5.1958)
    p. 202. Describes 1 letter, 6.1883.

976 Pulver, Jeffrey. "Personal Contacts with Brahms. I. II."
    Monthly Musical Record 65/764,765 (2.,3.-4.;1935) pp. 35-36,
    57-58. Cites memories of Frau Hegar on her husband's
    relationship with Brahms; also describes 3 letters from Brahms
    to Hegar, 1893, 1895.

See also 340, 1302.

--Heimsoeth, Friedrich (1814-1877)

See 1122.

--Heine, Heinrich (1797-1856)

See 2067, 2101, 2530.

--Heldburg, Helene, Freifrau von [fl. 19th century]

See 939.

--Hellmesberger, Joseph (1828-1893)

See 1016.

--Henschel, George (1850-1934)

977 Geiringer, Karl. "Brahms and Henschel: Some Hitherto Un-
    published Letters" Musical Times 79/1141 (3.1938) pp. 173-74.
    notes. Describes 5 letters Henschel to Brahms, 1878-82,
    together with their replies from 979.

978 *Henschel, George. ["Erinnerungen an Johannes Brahms"]
    Neues Wiener Tagblatt (4. or 5.;1898). [mus., notes]
    [gives excerpts from his journal, 2.-7.1876]
        (d) incorporated in English translation: Henschel. "Per-
            sonal Recollections of Johannes Brahms" Century
            Magazine 61/5 (New Series 39/5) (3.1901) pp. 725-36.
            ill., facsim., mus., notes. Also includes recollections
            from 5.1874-3.1875.
        (c) excerpt: [Daniel Gregory Mason] "Anecdotes

of Brahms" <u>Masters in Music</u> 5/part 30
(6.1905) pp. 2-3 (volume pp. 242-43).
(d)   incorporated: Henschel. [Royal Institution
of Great Britain. Proceedings] 18 (1905-07)
pp. 136-51. mus. only.   Also includes
recollections for 1878 and 1890's.
(d)   incorporated: into 979.

979   _____ . Personal Recollections of Johannes Brahms.
<u>Some of His Letters to and Pages from a Journal kept by
George Henschel</u>. Boston: Richard G. Badger, 1907.
95 pp.   ill., facsim., ind., notes.   Includes all recollections,
journal, plus 21 letters, 1874-92.
(a)   *reprint: New York: AMS Press, 1978.
(c)   i)   excerpt: see 1380.
      ii)   excerpt (in German translation):   "Brahms über
            das musikalische Schaffen" <u>Der Merker</u> (Wien) 3/6
            (3.1912) p. 211.
      iii) excerpt: Garbett, A. S.   "The Musical Scrap Book"
            <u>Etude</u> 42/5 (5.1924) p. 312.   "Brahms's Way of
            Composing"
      iv)   excerpt: in 977.
      v)   excerpt: Norman, Gertrude and Miriam Lubell
            Shrifte.   "Johannes Brahms.   Hamburg, 1833--Vienna,
            1897" in Norman and Shrifte. <u>Letters of Composers.
            An Anthology.   1603-1945</u>. New York: Alfred A.
            Knopf, 1946. pp. 224-25.   1 letter, 2.1880.
      vi)   excerpt: "Sayings of Brahms" <u>Etude</u> 25/6 (6.1907)
            pp. 361-62.
(d)   i)   see: 977.
      ii)   incorporated: Henschel. <u>Musings & Memories of
            a Musician</u>. London: Macmillan and Co., Limited,
            1918.   mus., notes.   Brahms: pp. 44-48, 54-55,
            73-75, 82-131.   Includes recollections and journal.
            [journal entries only for 1876, previous entries
            incorporated into recollections]
            *also: New York: Macmillan and Co., Limited, 1919.
            (a)   *reprint (of New York Edition):   With a New
                  Table of Contents prepared by Roy Chernus.
                  (Da Capo Press Reprint Series) New York:
                  Da Capo Press, 1979.
      iii) *incorporated: Henschel, Helen.   "The Brahms
            Recollections of Sir George Henschel" in Henschel.
            <u>When Soft Voices Die.   A Musical Biography</u>. London:
            John Westhouse Ltd., 1944.
            also: London: Methuen & Co., Ltd., 1949. pp. 127-
            54. only mus., notes.   Includes recollections and
            journal.   [journal only set apart for 1876]
      iv)   see: 981.
(e)   *report: Tucholsky, Berta.   "Erinnerungen an Johannes
      Brahms" <u>Pester Lloyd</u> (Budapest) (4. and 5.;3.;1908).

(c) excerpt: "Erinnerungen an Johannes Brahms"
Frankfurter Zeitung und Handelsblatt 52/68
(8.3.1908) 5. Morgenblatt pp. [1]-2 [across
page bottoms].

980 *Linke, Norbert. "Die schlesische musikalische Romantik und
der Brahms-Freund Sir Georg Henschel" Schlesien 22 (1977)
pp. 178-80.

981 #Zuidberg-Jkvr. Strick van Linschaten, Dido. "Herinnerungen
aan Brahms als vriend en collega van George Henschel"
Symphonia 16/5 (5.1933) pp. 87-89. ill. Describes their
friendship, 1874-97; includes excerpts from 979.

See also 1222.

--Herder, Johann Gottfired (1744-1803)

See 2112, 2532.

--Hermenau [fl. 19th century]

982 Hermenau, San.-Rat Dr. "Erinnerungen an Brahms" in 2732.
pp. 45-47. Describes meeting Brahms in Bad Ischl and Wien.

--Herzogenberg, von, Family

Elisabet (1847-1892): 983, 984.
Heinrich (1843-1900): 983, 985, 986.

983 *Brahms, Johannes. Johannes Brahms im Briefwechsel mit Heinrich und Elisabet von Herzogenberg. Max Kalbeck, ed. 2
Bde. (Johannes Brahms. Briefwechsel I, II) Berlin:
Verlag der Deutschen Brahms-Gesellschaft m.b.H., 1907.
ill., ind., notes.
*2. durchgesehene Auflage: 1908.
*3. durchgesehene Auflage: 1912.
*4. durchgesehene Auflage: 1921.
(a) reprint (of 1921 Auflage): (Brahms-Briefwechsel Band
I, II) Tutzing: Hans Schneider, 1974. Contains
181 letters, 8.1876-3.1897.
(b) English translation by Hannah Bryant (of 1907 Auflage):
Brahms. The Herzogenberg Correspondence. Max
Kalbeck, ed. London: John Murray, 1909. xix,
[1], 425 pp. ill., notes. The two original volumes
are joined to make one.
*also: New York: E. P. Dutton & Co., 1909.
(a) *reprint (of London Edition): New York: Vienna
House, 1972.

(c) excerpt (of London Edition): in 1380.
(c) i) excerpt (of ? Auflage): see 792.
ii) excerpt (of ? Auflage): see 1179.c.i.
iii) *excerpt (of ? Auflage): see 1179.c.ii.
iv) excerpt (of ? Auflage): see 954.c.iv.
v) excerpt (of ? Auflage in English translation by Karl Geiringer): see 25.b.i. (2nd Edition)
vi) excerpt (of ? Auflage): see 1179.c.vi.
vii)*excerpt (of ? Auflage): see 1009.c.x.
viii) excerpt (of 1907 Auflage in English translation by Daphne Woodward): in "Johannes Brahms" in 819. c.vi. pp. 301-22. Herzogenberg Briefe: pp. 314-15, 317-32. 10 letters, 1880-92.
ix)#excerpt (of 1908 Auflage): Kalbeck, Max, ed. "Aus dem Briefwechsel zwischen Johannes Brahms mit Heinrich und Elisabet von Herzogenberg" in 3178. pp. 73-89. ill., mus., notes. Based on letters no. 261-end.
x) excerpt (of ? Auflage): see 769.
xi) excerpt (of ? Auflage): see 81.d.
(e) i) *announcement: Neue frei Presse (Wien) (1906).
(e) report: "Ueber den demnächst in der Oeffentlichkeit erscheinenden Briefwechsels Johannes Brahms ..." Allgemeine Musikzeitung 33/51/52 (21./28.12.1906) pp. 828-29.
ii) report (on 1907 Auflage): Altmann, Wilhelm. "Brahms im Briefwechsel mit dem Ehepaar Herzogenberg" Die Musik (Berlin) 6/16 (Bd. 23) (5.1907) pp. 228-33. notes. Gives examples of Brahms's opinions, as seen in these letters.
iii) report (on 1907 Auflage): Andro, L. "Johannes Brahms im Briefwechsel mit Heinr[ich]. und Elisabeth v. Herzogenberg (Erste Publikation der Deutschen Brahms-Gesellschaft)" Neue Musikzeitung 29/4 (21.11.1907) pp. 83-84.
iv) announcement: "Der Briefwechsel ..." Allgemeine Musikzeitung 33/48 (30.11.1906) p. 764.
v) *report (on 1907 Auflage): K. A. "Johannes Brahms" [Wiener] Fremdenblatt (3.4.1907).
vi) *report (on 1907 Auflage): Kalbeck, Max. "Johannes Brahms" Neues Wiener Tagblatt (4.4.1907).
vii) Köstlin, H. A., see 986.d.
viii) report (on 1907 Auflage): Prelinger, Fritz. "Der Briefwechsel zwischen Johannes Brahms und dem Ehepaar v. Herzogenberg" Signale für die musikalische Welt 65/51 (28.8.1907) pp. 891-95.
ix) *report: (on 1907 Auflage): Schmidt, Leopold. "Johannes Brahms in Briefen an des Ehepaar Herzogenberg" Berliner Tageblatt (1907).
(a) #reprint: in Schmidt. "Brahms" in 3022. pp. 255-67. "Brahms in Briefen": pp. 265-67.

"Brahms in Briefen": pp. 265-67.

x) report (on ? Auflage): see 750.

xi) #report (on 1907 Auflage): Wilfferodt, Felix. "Brahms in seinen Beziehungen zu Heinrich und Elisabet v. Herzogenberg" Neue Militärmusikzeitung 14/26,27 (1907). [1 page per issue; across page tops].

984 Huschke, Konrad. "Johannes Brahms und Elisabeth v. Herzogenberg" Die Musik (Berlin) 19/8 (5.1927) pp. 557-73. notes. Describes their relationship and her comments and influence on his composing.
    (a) #reprint: in Huschke. Unsere Tonmeister unter Einander. [Band 5] Pritzwalk: Verlag von Adolf Tienken, 1928. pp. 110-36. ill.
    (d) reworked: into 765.d.

985 Kühn, Hellmut. "Brahms und sein Epigone Heinrich von Herzogenberg (Zur Musik in der Gründerzeit und im Fin de siècle (I))" Musica (Kassel) 28/6 (11.-12.1974) pp. 517-21. ill., notes. Discusses von Herzogenberg as a disciple of Brahms.

986 *Smend, Julius. "Johannes Brahms und Heinrich von Herzogenberg" Deutsche Monatsschrift für das gesamte Leben der Gegenwart Bd. 11 (6/6) (3.1907) pp. 761-71. notes. Describes Brahms's friendship with the von Herzogenbergs and the two men's attitude towards religion.
    (d) #comment: Köstlin, H. A. "Johannes Brahms und Heinrich von Herzogenberg" Korrespondenzblatt des evangelischen Kirchengesangvereins für Deutschland (Leipzig) 21/6 (30.5.1907) pp. 73-77. notes. Includes discussion on Brahms as a composer of sacred works and contrasts him with von Herzogenberg in this respect.

See also 592, 662, 749, 763, 765.d.e., 769, 1013, 1208, 1952, 1993, 2030.

--Hessen, von, Family [fl. 19th century]

987 Hessen, Alexander Friedrich von. "Aus meinen Erinnerungen an Brahms" Frankfurter Zeitung 77/333-34 (6.5.1933) Dreimalige Ausgabe p. 1. Describes their friendship, 1881-95, and his travels with Brahms; includes 1 letter, Brahms to von Hessen, 1892.

988 *Pessenlehner, R. "Anna Landgräfin von Hessen, ein Leben in Musik. Zur 40. Widerkehr ihres Todestages (†. 12. Juni 1918)" Fuldaer Geschichtsblätter 34 (1958) pp. 81-128.

--Heuberger, Richard (1850-1914)

989 *Hernried, Robert. "Richard Heuberger, seine Brahms-Erinnerungen und sein Briefwechsel mit Künstlern seiner Zeit"
3 teile.
(c) excerpt: Hernried. "Unbekannte Aufzeichnungen über
Johannes Brahms" Anbruch 18/2 (3./4.1936) pp.
34-38. notes. Describes the friendship between
Heuberger and Brahms.
(d) i) #see: Hernried. "Johannes Brahms. Unbekannte
Anekdoten um den Meister" Der Funk (Berlin) no.
19 (5.5.1933) pp. 73-74. Uses anecdotes to reveal
various aspects of his character.
ii) see: 2587.
iii) superceded: by 991.
(e) report: Peyser, Herbert F. "Richard Heuberger's
Diary of Brahms" New York Times 86/28,918 (28.3.
1937) Section 11, p. 6. Brahms's opinions on Wagner
and Wagner's music.
(d) continued: Peyser. "Heuberger's Diary of
Brahms" New York Times 86/28,925 (4.4.
1937) Section 10, p. 5. Brahms's opinions
of various contemporaries.
(d) see: 1134.

990 Heuberger, Richard. "Aus der ersten Zeit meiner Bekanntschaft
mit Brahms" Die Musik (Berlin) 2/5 (Bd. 5) (12.1902) pp.
323-29. notes. Describes their friendship, 1876-80; also
relates Brahms's opinions on various topics.
(a) #reprint: Heuberger. in 3178. pp. 52-58. adds ill.
(b) English translation: Heuberger. "My Early Acquaintance
with Brahms" Musical World (Boston) 3/3 (3.1903)
pp. 38-41.

991 _____. Erinnerungen an Johannes Brahms. Tagebuchnotizen
aus den Jahren 1875 bis 1897. Kurt Hofmann, ed. Tutzing:
Hans Schneider, 1971. 182 pp. ill., facsim., ind., notes.
Contains recollections and diary entries from 1867-97, bio-
graphy of Heuberger and additional material from his diary.
Also includes:
"Johannes Brahms als Pianist": pp. 128-30. Heuberger
describes seeing Brahms as a pianist.
"Johannes Brahms bei Landpartien": pp. 130-32.
Describes day trips with Brahms from Wien.
2. überarbeitete und vermehrte Auflage: 1976. 204 pp.
"Johannes Brahms als Pianist": pp. 131-33.
"Johannes Brahms bei Landpartien": pp. 135-36. Adds a
reprint of 392; diary entries, 1897-1911, that include
comments on Brahms; also additional diary material.

See also 687, 1134, 2473.

--Heyer, Wilhelm (1849-1913)

See 291.

--Heyse, Paul (1830-1914)

See 2589.

--Hiller, Ferdinand (1811-1885)

992   Hiller, Ferdinand. Aus Ferdinand Hillers Briefwechsel. Beit-
       räge zu einer Biographie Ferdinand Hillers. Reinhold Sietz,
       ed. 7 Bde. (Beiträge zur rheinischen Musikgeschichte.
       Hefte 28, 48, 56, 60, 65, 70, 92) Köln: Arno Volk-Verlag,
       1958-70. notes. Brahms-Hiller correspondence in Bde.
       1-5: 65 items, 1858-84. Includes 3 letters between Brahms
       and Edmunds, 1875, and an excerpt from 1179.

See also 792.

--Hindemith, Paul (1895-1963)

See 2991.

--Hirschfeld, Georg (1873-1942)

993   Hirschfeld, Georg. "Zu Tisch mit Brahms" Vossische Zeitung
       (Berlin) Unterhaltungsblatt no. 145 (24.6.1927) p. [1].
       Describes dining with Brahms in 1896; also describes a
       meeting of Brahms and Otto Brahm.

--Hölderlin, Johann Christian Friedrich (1770-1843)

994   #Fehrle-Burger, Lili. "Hölderlin und Feuerbach--durch Chor-
       gesänge Brahms geehrt" Ekkhart. Jahrbuch für das Badener
       Land (1972) pp. 36-62. ill. Compares the two artists
       and how their relationship with Brahms keeps their names
       from obscurity.

See also 2318, 2321, 2322, 2534.

--Hölty, Ludwig (1748-1776)

See 2530.

--Hoffmann, E. T. A. [Ernst Theodor Amadeus] (1776-1822)

995   Kross, Siegfried. "Brahms--der unromantische Romantiker"
        Brahms-Studien Bd. 1 (1974) pp. 25-43. mus., notes.
        Traces through his music and writings the change in Brahms
        from his early affinity with romantic ideals to his becoming
        a pragmatist and pessimist.
        (d) Kross. "Brahms and E[rnst]. T[heodor]. A[madeus].
            Hoffmann" 19th Century Music 5/3 (Spring 1982)
            pp. 193-200. facsim., notes. Discusses Brahms's
            identification with the Kreisler character, and its
            consequences.
            (d) "Jacob Lateiner has ..." 19th Century Music
                6/2 (Fall 1982) pp. 182-83. facsim. Pre-
                sents another Johann Kreisler signature.

See also 854, 2619.

See also "Des jungen Kreislers Schatzkästlein" in IV.C.2.; "Romanticism" in VI.B.

--Hoffmann, Johann Friedrich [fl. 19th century]

See 358.

--Hoffmann von Fallersleben, August Heinrich (1798-1874)

996   Schäfer, Rudolf. "-(Der jugendliche Brahms.)" Neue Musik-
        zeitung 15/19 (1894) 2. Beilage p. 231. Relates Hoffmann
        von Fallersleben's description of meeting Brahms in 9.1853;
        excerpted from Hoffmann von Fallersleben. Mein Leben.
        In verkürzter form herausgegeben und bis zu des Dichters
        Tode fortgeführt von Dr. H. Gerstenberg. 2 Bde. (Berlin:
        F. Fontane & Co., 1892-94).

See also 2091, 2132.

--Holst, Gustav (1874-1934)

See 1841.

--Holstein, Hedwig von [fl. 19th century]

997   *Kalbeck, Max. "Neues über Brahms" Neues Wiener Tagblatt
        (7.5.1897).
        (a) reprint: [Hedwig von Holstein] Eine Glückliche. Hedwig
            von Holstein in ihren Briefen und Tagebuchblättern.
            Leipzig: Verlag von H. Haessel, 1901. pp. 114-17.

Relates the von Holsteins's description of Brahms
at the Schumanns, Spring 1854.

--Horovitz-Barnay, Ilka [fl. 19th century]

998 [Ilka Horovitz-Barnay] "Erinnerungen an Robert Volkman"
Neue freie Presse (Wien) no. 13,888 (26.4.1903) Morgenblatt. Beilage pp. 35-38 [across page bottoms]. Brahms:
pp. 37-38. Relates Brahms's comments on the author as
a composer.

999 #Ilias. [Ilka Horovitz-Barnay] "Von Johannes Brahms" Deutsche
Revue (Stuttgart) 23/Bd. 4 (10.1898) pp. 67-75. mus.
Relates first meeting with Brahms, and anecdotes involving
Brahms and the Fellinger family, including Fellinger-Brahms
letters. [all letters in 1062] notes.
  (a) reprint: Horovitz-Barnay. in Horovitz-Barnay.
     Berühmte Musiker. Erinnerungen. Berlin: Con-
     cordia Deutsche Verlags-Anstalt, 1900. pp. 33-50.
     adds mus.
     (c) excerpt: Horovitz-Barnay. Deutsche Dichtung
       Bd. 27/[2] [(1899)] pp. 47-51.
     (e) #report: Reijen, Paul van. "De muzikale
       memoires van Ilka Horovitz-Barney (I)"
       Mens en melodie 20/5,6 (5.,6.;1965) pp.
       147-50, 176-79. Brahms: pp. 149-50.
       notes.
  (b) #Hungarian translation: Horovitz-Barnay, Ilka.
     "Brahmsról" Zeneirodalmi füzetek [Supple-
     ment to Szimfónia (Budapest)] no. 7
     (9.1917) pp. 57-64.
  (e) report: "Einige amüsante Anekdoten über
     Brahms ..." Allgemeine Musikzeitung
     25/51 (23.12.1898) pp. 775-76.

--Hubay, von, Family

Andor (?): 1001.

Jenő (1858-1937): 1000, 1002-05.

1000 *Haraszti, Emil. Hubay Jenő élete és munkái. Budapest:
     Singer & Wolfner, 1913. 206 pp. Brahms: pp. 31, 108-12,
     118, 137-38. [from 241]

1001 Hubay, Andor von. "Minner om Brahms" Dansk Musiktidsskrift
     34/4 (5.1959) pp. 91-94. Describes meeting Brahms in
     Wien and Budapest, 1866-97; includes Brahms's comments
     on his own music.

1002 Hubay, Eugène de. [Jenő von Hubay] "My Memories of
Brahms, Liszt and Massanet" Musical Times 71/1046 (1.4.1930)
pp. 316-17. Brahms: p. 317. Describes meetings with
Brahms in Budapest and Wien.

1003 *Hubay, Jeno [von]. "Misserfolge. Erinnerungen an Brahms"
in Menschen und Menschenwerke. Men of To-day and
Their Work. Hommes et oeuvres du temps présent. Arpád
Keitner, ed. 3 vols. in 5 Wien: Verlag "Menschen und
Menschenwerke", 1924-28. vol. 2, p. 146.

1004 *Hubay, Jenő [von]. "Visszaemlékezés Brahmsra" A Zene 14
(1932-33) pp. 199-202.
(d) i) Hubay, Eugen v. [Jenő von Hubay] "Erinnerungen
an Brahms. Zur hundertsten Jahreswende seines
Geburtstages" Pester Lloyd (Budapest) 80/101
(5.5.1933) Morgenblatt pp. 1-3 [across page bottoms].
Describes their friendship, 1872-97, meetings with
Brahms in Budapest and Wien and Brahms's interest
in Hungarian folkmusic.
ii) *Hubay Jenő [von]. "Brahms és a magyarok"
Uj idök [38 or 39] (1933) pp. 582-83.

1005 *Neubauer, Pál. Hubay Jeno. Egy élet szimfóniája. 2 vols.
Budapest: Helikon kiad., 1941. Brahms: vol. 1, pp.
206-11, 277-84, 384-85; vol. 2., pp. 39, 322. [from 241]

See also 2378.

--Hübner, Julius [fl. 19th century]

See 887.

--Humperdinck, Engelbert (1854-1921)

See 2630.

--Hunnius, Monika [fl. 19th century]

1006 *Hunnius, Monikus. Mein Weg zur Kunst. Heilbronn: E.
Salzer, 1925. 356 pp.
*2. Auflage: 1925. [2], 351 pp.
*5.-11. Auflage: 1927-30. [2], 352 pp.
*also: 1.-7. Tsd. der Volksausgabe; 51.-57. Tsd. der Gesam-
tauflage: 1935. 349 pp.
*8.-13. Tsd. der Volksausgabe; 58.-63. Tsd. der Gesamtauflage:
1936.
*14.-18. Tsd. der Volksausgabe; 64.-68. Tsd. der Gesamtauflage:
1937.

*19.-24. Tsd. der Volksausgabe; 69.-74. Tsd. der Gesamtau-
    flage: 1938.
*25.-28. Tsd. der Volksausgabe; 75.-78. Tsd. der Gesamtau-
    flage: 1941.
*Berichtigte und gekürzte Ausgabe (79.-84. Tsd. der Gesam-
    tauflage): Heilbronn, Stuttgart: Salzer, 1948. 345 pp.
*85.-86. Tsd. der Gesamtauflage: Heilbronn. 1951.
*87.-89. Tsd. der Gesamtauflage: 1953. 312 pp.

--Jagic, Nikolaus von [fl. 19th century]

See 822.

--Jenner, Gustav (1865-1920)

1007 *Kohleick, Werner. "Gustav Jenner 1865-1920. Ein Beitrag
        zur Brahmsnachfolge" Phil.F. diss., Universität Marburg,
        1943.
    (a) reprint: Kohleick. Gustav Jenner 1865-1920. Ein
        Beitrag zur Brahmsnachfolge. (Musik und Schrifttum
        Heft 2) Würzburg: Konrad Triltsch Verlag, 1943.
        [4], 91, [2] pp. Brahms: pp. 9-17, 41-80. mus.,
        notes. Describes Jenner first meeting Brahms
        and studying with him, and traces Brahms's in-
        fluence in Jenner's works.

See also 694, 1084.

--Jensen, Frau [fl. 19th century]

1008 #Lepel, Felix von. "Ein unbekannter Brahms-Brief" Signale
        für die musikalische Welt 96/2 (12.1.1938) pp. 27-28.
        Presents 1 letter Brahms to Jensen's widow, 2.1879.

--Joachim Family

Amalie (1839-1898): 1009-11.

Joseph (1831-1907): 1009-21.

1009 Brahms, Johannes. Johannes Brahms im Briefwechsel mit
        Joseph Joachim. Andreas Moser, ed. 2 Bde. (Johannes
        Brahms. Briefwechsel V,VI) Berlin: Verlag der Deutschen
        Brahms-Gesellschaft m.b.H., 1908. mus., ind. [Bd. 2],
        notes. 525 letters in total, 5.1853-3.1897: Bd. 1, nos.
        1-250; Bd. 2, nos. 251-525.
    *2. durchgesehene und vermehrte Auflage: 1912.
        546 letters in total: Bd. 1, nos. 1-251; Bd. 2, nos. 252-
        546.

*3. durchgesehene und vermehrte Auflage [Bd. 1 only]: 1921.
  (a) reprint (of Bd. 1, 1921 Auflage; Bd. 2, 1912 Auflage):
    (Brahms-Briefwechsel Band V,VI) Tutzing: Hans
    Schneider, 1974.
  (c) i) excerpt (of ? Auflage): see 729.
    ii) excerpt (of 1908 Auflage): "Aus dem Briefwechsel
     zwischen Johannes Brahms und Joseph Joachim"
     Deutsche Rundschau 35/1 (Bd. 137) (10.1908)
     pp. 66-76. mus., notes. Contains 7 letters, 1853-
     54.
     (a) reprint: "Aus ... Joachim" Halbmonatshefte
       der Deutschen Rundschau Bd. 138 (10.
       1908) pp. 45-55.
    iii) excerpt (of ? Auflage): see 1179.c.i.
    iv)#excerpt (of ? Auflage): see 1179.c.ii.
    v) excerpt (of 1908 Auflage): "Briefe von Johannes
     Brahms und Joseph Joachim" Süddeutsche Monatshefte
     5/10 (5/Bd. 2) (10.1908) pp. 423-30. mus., notes.
     6 letters, 1854-56.
    vi) excerpt (of ? Auflage): "Drei Briefe an Joseph
     Joachim" Osterreichische Musikzeitschrift 2/4/5
     (4./5.1947) pp. 94-95. 3 letters from 1856.
    vii) excerpt (of ? Auflage in English translation by
     Karl Geiringer): see 25.b.i. (2nd Edition).
    viii) excerpt (of 1912 Auflage in English translation by
     Nora Bickley): see 1013.c.i.
    ix)*excerpt (of ? Auflage): see 1179.c.vi.
    x)*excerpt (of 1908 Auflage): "Johannes Brahms" in
     Hans Gal. In Dur und Moll. Briefe grosser Kompon-
     isten von Orlando di Lasso bis Arnold Schönberg.
     Frankfurt a.M.: G. B. Fischer, 1966. pp. 361-86.
     ill., facsim., mus. Includes excerpts from 819,
     983, 1179. [from the Music Division, Library of
     Congress]
    xi) excerpt (of 1908 Auflage in English translation by
     Daphne Woodward): in "Johannes Brahms" in
     819.c.vi. pp. 301-22. Joachim Briefe: pp. 302-08,
     310-13, 320-22. 27 letters, 1854-96.
  (d) Holde, Artur. "Suppressed Passages in the Brahms-
    Joachim Correspondence Published for the First
    Time" Willis Wager, translator. Musical Quarterly
    45/3 (7.1959) pp. 312-24. facsim., notes. Details
    9 instances where omitted materials may claim con-
    siderable interest, 1854-93: comments on Joachim-
    Brahms relationship, the Joachims' dispute, Brahms
    and Clara Schumann. Also mentions 5 other places
    where slight omissions were made.
  (e) i)*report (on 1908 Auflage): "Briefe von J[ohannes].
    Brahms und J[oseph]. Joachim" Tägliche Rundschau
    (Berlin) no. 455 (27.9.1908).
    ii) *report (on 1908 Auflage): Daffner, Hugo. "Johannes

Brahms und Josef Joachim in Briefen" Königsberger
allgemeine Zeitung nos. 457, 459 (1908).
iii) *report (on 1908 Auflage): es. [Heinrich Ehrlich]
"Neues von Johannes Brahms" Leipziger Volkszeitung
no. 227 (1908).
iv) *report (on 1908 Auflage): Hirschfeld, Robert.
"Künstlerbriefe. Brahms und Joachim" Pester Lloyd
(Budapest) (15.2.1908).
v) *report (on 1908 Auflage): "Joachim und Brahms
in ihrem Briefwechsel" Der Bund (Bern) (10.2.1909).
vi) *report (on 1908 Auflage): "Joachim und Brahms in
ihrem Briefwechsel" Dresdner Anzeiger (23.5.1909).
vii) *report (on 1908 Auflage): Korngold, Julius.
"Brahms und Joachim" Neue freie Presse (Wien)
(11.12.1908).
viii) report (on 1908 Auflage): Prelinger, Fritz.
"Johannes Brahms im Briefwechsel mit Joseph
Joachim" Signale für die musikalische Welt 67/16
(21.4.1909) pp. 581-84. notes.
ix) report (on 1908 Auflage): Prelinger, Fritz.
"Johannes Brahms und sein Violinkonzert. Nach
seinem Briefwechsel mit Jos[eph]. Joachim"
Schweizerische Musikzeitung und Sängerblatt 50/2,3
(8.,15.;1.;1910) pp. 15-16, 21-22.
x) *report (on 1908 Auflage): Schmidt, Leopold.
Berliner Tageblatt (1909).
(a) #reprint: in Schmidt. "Brahms" in 3022.
pp. 255-67. "Brahms und Joachim": pp.
259-60.
xi) report (on ? Auflage): see 750.

1010 *Felzer, Cornelia. "Die Briefe Joseph Joachims an seine
Frau Amalie Joachim von 1865-1874" [Prüfungsarbeit der
Hamburger Bibliotheksschule?] 196-?.

1011 *Fesefeldt, Hedda. "Johannes Brahms-Archiv. Briefe von
Amalie Joachim an Joseph Joachim 1863-1879" [Prüfungsarbeit
der Hamburger Bibliotheksschule?] 1967.

1012 *Hannover, Dorothea. "Die Briefe Joseph Joachims an Gisela
von Arnim" [Prüfungsarbeit der Hamburger Bibliotheksschule?]
1967.

1013 Joachim, Joseph. Briefe von und an Joseph Joachim. Andreas
Moser & Johannes Joachim, ed. 3 Bde. Berlin: Julius Bard,
1911-13. Thirdhand accounts of Brahms's activities,
volumes's dates: 1842-1907.
(c) i)*excerpt (in English translation by Nora Bickley):
Letters From and To Joseph Joachim. Nora Bickley,
ed. With A Preface by J[ohn]. A[lexander].
Fuller-Maitland. London: Macmillan and Co.,

Limited, 1914. xiii, [1], 470 pp. ill., mus., notes.
(a) reprint: New York: Vienna House, 1972.
    Includes c. 25 letters from 1009 (1912
    Auflage), 1853-96.
(c) i) excerpt (with extensive revisions by Piero
    Weiss to reflect original letter in 1009
    (1912 Auflage)): in 913. pp. 317-18.
    1 letter, [1.1859].
  ii) excerpt (in English translation by Daphne
    Woodward): in "Johannes Brahms" in
    819.c.vi. pp. 301-22. Joachim Briefe:
    pp. 302, 304, 307, 321. 7 letters, 1853-
    93; Joachim to Clara Schumann, Herzogen-
    berg and Gisela von Arnim.
  iii) excerpt: see 769.

1014   Moser, Andreas. Joseph Joachim. Ein Lebensbild. Berlin:
        B. Behr's Verlag (E. Bock), 1898. viii, 301, [2] pp. ill.,
        facsim., mus. Includes reference to Brahms and his music
        and to his relationship with Joachim, passim.
        *2. Auflage: 1900.
        *3. Auflage, Neue wohlfeile Volksausgabe: 1904.
        *Neue, umgearbeitete und erweiterte Ausgabe: 2 Bde. Berlin:
        Verlag der Deutschen Brahms-Gesellschaft m.b.H., 1908-10.
        (b) *English translation by Lilla Durham (of 1898 Auflage?):
        Joseph Joachim. A Biography (1831-1899). Intro-
        duction by J[ohn]. A[lexander]. Fuller-Maitland.
        London: P. Wellby, 1901. xvi, 336 pp. ill.,
        facsim., mus.

1015   Pulver, Jeffrey. "Brahms and the Influence of Joachim"
        Musical Times 66/983 (1.1.1925) pp. 25-28. Describes the
        beginnings of their relationship in the 1850's: Joachim
        as a promoter of Brahms, and services he did for Brahms;
        includes comments on Brahms and England.

1016   Pulver, Jeffrey. "Brahms's Violinists and 'Cellists" The Strad
        64 [44]/522, 523 (10.,11.;1933) pp. 224, 226; 258-59.
        Notes on Brahms's contemporaries.

1017   *Röper, Ady. "Die Musikalien aus dem Nachlass von J[oseph].
        Joachim im Besitz der Staats- und Universitätsbibliothek
        Hamburg" [Prüfungsarbeit der Hamburger Bibliotheksschule?]
        1967.

1018   *Roftmann, L. "Joseph Joachim und Johannes Brahms" Königs-
        berger hartungsche Zeitung (26.6.1931).

1019   *Schaper, Karin. "Die Briefe Joseph Joachims an Johannes
        Brahms aus dem Briefnachlass der Staats- und Universitäts-
        bibliothek Hamburg" Jahresarbeit der Hamburger Bibliotheks-
        schule, 1962. xvii, 66 pp.

1020 *Schwartz, Elke. "Die Briefe von Johannes Brahms an Joseph
Joachim in der Staats- und Universitätsbibliothek Hamburg"
Jahresarbeit der Hamburger Bibliotheksschule, 1962. 61
pp.

1021 *Wackernagel, Peter. "Viotti's Violinkonzert in a-moll als
"Versohnungswerk" für Joachim und Brahms" Philharmonische
Blätter [10]/6 (1973/74).

See also 65.d., 464, 607, 662, 792, 1112, 1123, 1137, 1172, 1176,
1188, 1208, 1210, 1222, 1247, 1544, 1791, 1829, 1935, 1939, 1948,
2378, 2453, 2504, 2594, 2735, 3043, 3058.

See also "Rumania" in II.B.

--Jonas, Oswald (1897-1978)

See 1669.

--Kahn, Robert (1865-1951)

1022 *Musikrevy 30/5 (1975) p. 247. (?)

1023 [Helmuth Rilling] "From Johannes Brahms to Robert Kahn:
1887 (Litterae ab musicis)" BACH 6/4 (10.1975) pp. 20-22.
ill., facsim. Relates an anecdote of Brahms giving Kahn
a copy of Händel's Israel in Egypt.

1024 Kahn, Robert. "Der gute Freund. Erinnerungen" Vossische
Zeitung (Berlin) Unterhaltungsblatt no. 125 (7.5.1933)
pp. [3-4]. Describes Brahms in Mannheim (1886), Wien
(1887), Berlin (1888), with comments on the Wagner-Brahms
polarity, on Brahms as a piano teacher; also relates Brahms's
views on other musicians and music in general.
(b) English translation by Jeanne Day: Kahn. "Memories
of Brahms" Music and Letters 28/2 (4.1947) pp.
101-07. mus., notes.

--Kaiserfeld, Mortiz von [fl. 19th century]

1025 Kaiserfeld, Mortiz von. "Ein Brahms-Erinnerung" Neue Musikzeitung 19/16 (1898) p. 193. Describes a visit by Brahms
to Alt-Aussee in 8.1882.

--Kalbeck, Max (1850-1921)

1026 *Kalbeck, Max. "Persönliches über Brahms" Badener Buch
(1923) pp. 112-19.

1027 #Kalbeck, Max. "Persönliches über Johannes Brahms" Der
    Lotse 1/8, 15 (24.11.1900; 12.1.1901) pp. 238-47, 480-89.
    Discusses their friendship from first meeting in 1874,
    but focuses on last half of 1896: describes their activities,
    circle of friends.
    (e) report: "Erinnerungen an Brahms ..." Allgemeine
        Musikzeitung 28/21 (24.5.1901) p. 356.

See also 239, 618.a., 680.

--Karpath, Ludwig (1866-1936)

1028 *Karpath, Ludwig. "Bekanntschaft mit Johannes Brahms" in
    Karpath. Begegnung mit dem Genius. Denkwürdige
    Erlebnisse mit Johannes Brahms--Gustav Mahler--Hans
    Richter--Max Reger--Puccini--Mascagni [--] Leoncavallo--
    Fürstin Marie Hohenlohe [--] Fürstin Pauline Metternich--
    Franz Lehár und vielen anderen bedeutenden Menschen.
    Zahlreiche unbekannte Briefe und Abbildungen. Wien-
    Leipzig: Fiba-Verlag, [1934].
    2. Auflage: 1934. pp. 325-37. ind. Describes their friend-
        ship 1894- ; incorporates 482, 581.

--Kauffmann, Adolf [fl. 19th century]

See 1102.

--Keats, John (1795-1821)

See 1897.

--Kegel, M. (1819-1890)

See 2706.

--Kélér, Béla [fl. 19th century]

See 1721.

--Keller, Gottfried (1819-1890)

1028.5*Pfister, K[urt]. "Gottfried Keller und Johannes Brahms.
    (Ein unbekannter Brief)" Berliner Börsenzeitung no. 604
    (1931).

See also 618.a.

--Keller, Otto (1861-1928)

1029 *Keller, Otto. "Meine Erinnerungen an Brahms" Schweizerische
      musikpädagogische Blätter 12/4 (1923) p. 50.

See also 2033.

--Kempe, Rudolf (1910-1976)

See 2596.

--Kienzl, Wilhelm (1857-1941)

1030 Kienzl, Wilhelm. "Johannes Brahms. 1833-1896" in Kienzl.
      Meine Lebenswanderung. Erlebtes und Erschautes.
      Stuttgart: J. Engelhorns Nachf[olger]., 1926. pp. 234-39.
      ind., notes. Describes their relationship from 1880- ;
      also discusses Brahms's character.
      (d) *Kienzl. Wilhelm Kienzls "Lebenswanderung". Im
           Auszug, neu eingelegt und hinsichtlich der letzten
           17 Lebensjahre biographisch ergänzt; Kienzls Brief-
           wechsel mit Peter Rosegger, eingelegt und kommen-
           tiert, nebst einem Namen-, Brief- und vollständigen
           Werkverzeichniss von Hans Sittner. Zürich, Leipzig,
           Wien: Amalthea-Verlag, 1953. 479 pp.

--Kiesekamp [fl. 19th century]

See 1222.

--Kirchner, Theodor (1823-1903)

1031 Hofmann, Kurt. "Die Beziehungen zwischen Johannes Brahms
      und Theodor Kirchner. Dargestellt an den überlieferten
      Briefen" in Festschrift Hans Schneider zum 60. Geburtstag.
      Rudolf Elvers and Ernst Vögel, eds. München: Verlag
      Ernst Vögel, 1981. pp. 135-49. ill., facsim., notes.
      Describes their relationship, includes 5 letters, 1875-95.

1032 Sietz, Reinhold. "Johannes Brahms und Theodor Kirchner.
      Mit ungedruckten Briefen Th[eodor]. Kirchners" Die
      Musikforschung 13/4 (10.-12.1960) pp. 396-404. notes.
      Discusses their meeting and friendship 1856-97; includes
      15 letters, 1875-97.
      (d) Sietz. Theodor Kirchner. Ein Klaviermeister der
           deutschen Romantik. (Studien zur Musikgeschichte
           des 19. Jahrhunderts Bd. 21) Regensburg:
           Gustav Bosse Verlag, 1971. 167 pp. Includes
           excerpts of first 7 letters, 1875-83.

--Kitzler, Otto (1834-1915)

1033   *Kitzler, Otto. Musikalische Erinnerungen. Mit Briefen von
       Wagner, Brahms, Bruckner und Rich[ard]. Pohl. Brünn:
       C. Winiker, 1904. 39 pp. facsim.

--Kjerulf, Halfdan (1815-1868)

See 1176.

--Klengel, Julius (1859-1933)

See 787.

--Klinger, Max (1857-1920)

1034   Avenarius, Ferdinand. "Brahmsphantasie" in Avenarius.
       Max Klinger als Poet. Mit einem Briefe Max Klingers und
       einem Beitrage von Hans W. Singer. Herausgegeben vom
       Kunstwart. München: Kunstwartverlage G. D. W. Callwey,
       [1917]. pp. 91-107. ill., notes. Text to p. 96: describes
       artist's rendering of work.
       *2. Auflage: [1917?].
       *3. Auflage: [1918].
       *Kriegsausgabe [4. Auflage]: 1919.
       *5. Auflage: [1921]. Mit einem Briefe Max Klingers, einem
       Nachruf von F. Avenarius und einem Beitrage von Hans
       W. Singer.
       *6. Auflage: [1923].

1035   *Brahms, Johannes. Johannes Brahms an Max Klinger. [Hans
       Schulz and Ernst Eggebrecht, comps. Leipzig: n.p.,
       1924]. 13 pp. Contains 7 letters, 1886-96. [from S037]

1036   Brieger-Wasservogel, Lothar. "Brahms-Phantasie" in Brieger-
       Wasservogel. Max Klinger. [(Männer der Zeit. Neue
       Folge. 12 Bd.)] Leipzig: Hermann Seemann Nachfolger,
       1902. pp. 233-46. Presents an explanation of the painting,
       along with the appropriate texts.

1036.5#E.G.(?) "Klinger und Brahms. Das Widmungsexemplar der
       "Brahmsphantasie" wird in der Schweiz versteigert" Neue
       Leipziger Zeitung (12.5.1935) p. [?]. Surveys their re-
       lationship through their correspondence, 1886-97; describes
       Klinger visiting Brahms in Wien, 1894; and discusses
       Brahms's reaction to Klinger's Brahmsphantasie.

1037   #Friedrich, Paul. "Musikalische Griffelkunst. Zu Max Klingers

"Brahms-Phantasie"" Kunst für Alle (München) 48/9 (6.1933)
pp. 263-64. Discusses Klinger's affinity with Brahms,
their common use of motifs and Op. 121; describes Brahms's
opinion of Klinger's work.
(a) reprint: Friedrich. Die Kunst (München) [=Kunst
und das schöne Heim] Bd. 67/9 (6.1933) pp. 263-64.

1038 Heyne, Hildegard. "Brahms und Klinger" Illustrierte Zeitung
Bd. 180/4599 (4.5.1933) pp. 564, 582. ill. [pp. 561-62]
Discusses Klinger's Brahms-Phantasie.

1039 #Huschke, Konrad. "Max Klinger und Johannes Brahms. Ein
Gedenken zu Brahms' 100. Geburtstag" Kunst für Alle
(München) 48/9 (6.1933) pp. 257-62. ill. Describes their
relationship; Klinger's Brahms-Phantasie, and what Brahms
thought of it and other Klinger works.
(a) i) Huschke. "Max Klinger und die Musik. 3. Klinger
und Brahms" Die Kunst (München) [=Kunst und
das schöne Heim] Bd. 67/9 (6.1933) pp. 257-62.
ii) Huschke. Zeitschrift für Musik 103/12 (12.1936)
pp. 1465-69. omits ill.
(d) reworked: Huschke. "Klinger--Beethoven, Brahms,
Reger und Wagner" in 868.d.i. pp. 318-38.
Brahms: pp. 324-30. adds ind.

1040 #Kalbeck, Max. "Klinger und Brahms" Rheinische Musik- und
Theaterzeitung (Köln) 4/2-4 (9.,16.,23.;1.1903) pp. 12-13;
20-21; 26-28. Describes their relationship, focuses on
Klinger's artwork for Opp. 96, 97 and his Brahms-Phantasie.

1041 *Klinger, Max. Brahms-Phantasie. 41 Stiche, Radierungen und
Steinzeichnungen zu Compositionen von Johannes Brahms.
Op. XII. Leipzig: n.p., 1894.
*also: Berlin: Amsler & Ruthardt, n.d. 37 pp.
(e) report (on ? Auflage): Bie, O[scar]. "Es wird
unsere Leser interessiren, dass Max Klinger ..."
Allgemeine Musikzeitung 20/51/52 (22./29.12.1893)
p. 677.

1042 *"Klinger an Brahms. Aus unveröffentlichten Briefen" Neue
Leipziger Zeitung (16.5.1935).

1043 Lehrs, Max. "Max Klinger's "Brahms-Phantasie"" Zeitschrift
für bildende Künste N.F. 6/5 ([5.] 1895) pp. 113-18.
An analysis of the work.

1044 *Lützow, K. v. "Max Klingers Brahms-Phantasie" Neue freie
Presse (Wien) (12.2.1904).

1045 "Max Klinger und Brahms", see 1036.5.

1046 *Mayer-Pasinski, Karin. Max Klingers Brahmsphantasie. Frankfurt a.M.: Rita G. Fischer, Verwaltungsgesellschaft mbH
& Co. Verlags KG, 1982. 324 pp.

1047 Museum Villa Stuck, [München]. "Brahmsphantasie Opus XII"
in Museum Villa Stuck. Max Klinger. Die graphischen
Zyklen. 28 November 1979 bis 17 Februar 1980. [Joachim
Poetter, catalogue] München: Stuck-Jugendstil-Verein,
1979. pp. 64-75. ill., notes. An exhibition catalogue;
provides historical background to this work.

1048 *Pastor, Willy. Max Klinger. Berlin: Verlag von Amsler &
Ruthardt, 1918.
2. vermehrte Auflage: 1919. Brahms: pp. 129-50. ill.,
mus. Discusses Brahms and Klinger and compares
Klinger's artworks to Brahms's settings of the same
texts.
3. Auflage: 1922.

1049 Richter, Kurt W. "Brahms und Klinger. Drei unveröffentlichte
Briefe Max Klingers an Johannes Brahms aus dem Brahms-
Archiv" Mitteilungen der Brahms-Gesellschaft Hamburg e.V.
no. 4 (4.1973) pp. 3-6. Describes their relationship, with
letters from 1880, 1894, 1896.

1050 *Still, L. H. "The Concepts of Gesamtkunstwerk and Corres-
pondences in Max Klinger's 'Brahmsphantasie'" M.A. diss.,
Queens College, City University of New York, 1975.

1051 *Strzygowski, Josef. "Klingers Brahmsphantasie in öffentliche
Vorführung" Kunst für Alle (München) 31/11/12 (3.1916)
pp. 214-20.

See also 44D.d., 930, 2518, 3062, 3081, 3085, 3103, 3106, 3142, 3149,
3174.

--Köhler, Louis (1820-1886)

See 585.

--Koessler, Hans (1853-1926)

1052 Stöckl, Rudolf. "Ein unveröffentlicher Brahms-Brief" Neue
Zeitschrift für Musik 119/11 (11.1958) pp. 647-48. facsim.
1 letter, Brahms to Koessler, after 1889.

--Kraft, William (1923-)

See 2608.

--Krančević, Dragomir [fl. 19th century]

1053   Djurić-Klajn, Stana. "Correspondance inédite de Johannes
        Brahms" in Bericht über den Siebenten Internationalen
        Musikwissenschaftlichen Kongress Köln 1958. Gerald
        Abraham, Suzanne Clercx-Lejeune, Hellmut Federhofer,
        Wilhelm Pfannkuch, eds. Kassel [et al]: Bärenreiter, 1959.
        pp. 88-91. Describes their relationship and correspondence,
        1862-80's, with synopses of 3 letters, 1879, 1881 and 1884,
        Brahms to Krančević.

--Kraus, Felix von (1870-1937)

1054   Kraus, Felix von. Begegnungen mit Anton Bruckner, Johannes
        Brahms, Cosima Wagner. Aus den Lebenserinnerungen von
        Dr. Felix von Kraus (1870-1937). Zusammengestellt und
        ergänzt von Felicitas von Kraus. Wien: Dr. Franz Hain,
        [1961?]. 202, [1] pp. Brahms: pp. 23-49. ill., notes.
        Describes friendship with Brahms and other members of
        Brahms's circle, in Wien 1894-97.

--Krause, Emil (1840-1916)

1055   *Krause, Emil. "Brahms und einige Erinnerungen aus seinem
        Leben" Hamburger Fremdenblatt no. 2 (1903).
        (d) see: 2976.

See also 2976.

--Kreisler, Fritz (1875-1962)

See 1938, 1945.

--Kreisler, Johann

See Hoffmann, E.T.A.

--Kretschmann, Theobald (1850-1919)

1056   #Kretschmann, Theobald. "Johannes Brahms" in Kretschmann.
        Tempi passati. Aus den Erinnerungen eines Musikanten.
        2 Bde. Wien, Teschen, Leipzig: Verlag von Karl Prochaska,
        1910-13. Bd. 1, pp. 148-53. Author first heard of Brahms
        in 1874, describes their friendship 1874- .

--Kretzschmar, [August Ferdinand] Hermann (1848-1924)

See 2989.

--Kretzschmer [fl. 19th century]

See 2573.

--Krolop, F. [fl. 19th century]

See 1222.

--Künzelmann [fl. 19th century]

1057 sp. "Thuner Erinnerung an Brahms" Zeitschrift für Musik 93/2
      (2.1926) pp. 99-100. Relates an anecdote from Summer 1886
      of Brahms listening to the Kurorchester.

--Kugler, Franz Theodor (1808-1858)

See 2530.

--Kundmann, Carl [fl. 19th century]

See 3085.

--Kupfer, Wilhelm (1843-?)

1058 *"Brahms' Notenschreiber" Neues Wiener Tagblatt (12.2.1906).
      (a) reprint: in 39D (Zweiter Halbband, 1. or 2. Auflage).
      pp. 549-51. Describes Kupfer's life and association with
      Brahms, 1872- .

--Lamond, Frederic[k] (1868-1948)

See 1074.

--Langer, Hermann (1819-1889)

1059 #Grabau, Carl. "Zwei Brahmsbriefe (Zum 7. Mai)" Pauliner-
      Zeitung (Leipzig) 43/5 (1931) pp. 105-08. notes. Describes
      correspondence: Brahms to Langer, 1.1874; and to Ehrlich,
      1882?.

--Lanner, Joseph (1801-1843)

See 2142.

--Lara, Adelina de

See de Lara, Adelina

--Lassen, Eduard (1830-1904)

See 792.

--Laurens, Jean-Joseph Bonaventure (1801-1890)

1060   Herrmann, Marcelle. "J[ean].-J[oseph].B[onaventure].
       Laurens' Beziehungen zu deutschen Musikern" Schweizerische
       Musikzeitung. Revue musicale suisse 105/5 (9./10.1965)
       pp. 257-66. Brahms: pp. 264-65. Describes their meeting
       at the Schumanns, 10.1853, the picture Laurens engraved
       of Brahms, Brahms's manuscript gift of Op. 3, no. 1 to
       Laurens.

See also 760, 761, 2109.

--Leinburg, Mathilde von [fl. 19th century]

See 491, 588.

--Leistner, Albrecht [fl. 19th century]

See 3132.

--Lemacher, Heinrich (1891-1966)

See 2344.

--Lengnick, Alfred [music publisher]

See 315.

--Lentz, Franzisca [fl. 19th century]

1061   #"Brahms-Erinnerungen. Aus dem Tagebuch von Frau Wasser-
       baudirektor Lentz, geb. Meier" Jahrbuch der Gesellschaft
       Hamburgischer Kunstfreunde [8] (1902) pp. [41]-60. ill.
       Covers 8.-9.1859: time of the Hamburger Frauenchor ac-
       tivities.

See also 48, 375, 2193.

--Lessing, Karl Friedrich (1808-1880)

See 2384.

--Levi, Hermann (1839-1900)

1062 *Brahms, Johannes. Johannes Brahms im Briefwechsel mit
      Hermann Levi, Friedrich Gernsheim sowie den Familien
      Hecht und Fellinger. Leopold Schmidt, ed. (Johannes
      Brahms. Briefwechsel. VII) Berlin: Verlag der Deutschen
      Brahms-Gesellschaft m.b.H., 1910. ix, [1], 324 pp.
      facsim., mus., notes. [from 1062.a.]
      (a) reprint: (Brahms-Briefwechsel Band VII) Tutzing:
          Hans Schneider, 1974. Contains Levi: 121 letters,
          11.1864-2.1878; Gernsheim: 9 letters, 11.1870-2.
          1884; Hecht: 20 letters, 5.1884-1.1897; Fellinger:
          145 letters, 5.1882-3.1897.
      (c) i) excerpt: see 729.
          ii) excerpt: see 1179.c.i.
          iii)#excerpt: see 1179.c.ii.
      (d) see: 926.
      (e) #report: J.V.W. [Josef Viktor Widmann] "Brahms im
          Briefwechsel mit Hermann Levi und andern Zeit-
          genossen" Der Bund (Bern) 61/81 (17./18.2.1910)
          Abendblatt pp. 1-2 [across page bottoms].

1063 Ettlinger, Anna. "Johannes Brahms und Hermann Levi" Neue
      Musikzeitung 34/2 (17.10.1912) pp. 29-32. Describes their
      connections, 1870-97; includes comments on their personal
      relationship, their characters, as well as on their relation-
      ship as composers.

See also 295, 788.

--Lewing, Adele (1866-1943)

1064 Lewing, Adele. "Personal Reminiscences of Johannes Brahms"
      Etude 51/8 (8.1933) pp. 509-10. ill. Describes meeting
      Brahms in Wien.

--Lewinsky, Joseph (1835-1907)

1065 *Lewinsky, Joseph. "Eine Brahms-Reminiszenz" Berliner Tage-
      blatt (1897).

--Leyen, Rudolf von der [fl. 19th century]

1066 #Fellmann, Walter. "Johannes Brahms und seine Beziehungen

zu Krefelder Mennoniten" Christlicher Gemeindekalender
48 (1939) pp. 82-85. notes. Describes the relationship
between Brahms and the von der Leyen and von Beckerath
families.

1067   Leyen, R[udolf]. von der. "Johannes Brahms als Mensch und
       Freund" Die Freude [4] (1905) pp. 155-223. Describes
       their personal contact and letters, 1880-96.
       (a) #reprint: Leyen, Rudolf von der. Johannes Brahms
           als Mensch und Freund. Nach persönliche Erin-
           nerungen. Düsseldorf und Leipzig: Verlag von
           Karl Robert Langewiesche, 1905. 99 pp. facsim.
       (c) #excerpt: Leyen. "Johannes Brahms als
           Mensch und Freund" in 3178. pp. 64-72.
           ill. [contains pp. 40-59 of 1067.a.]
       (e) #report: m.f. "Neue Brahms-Erinnerungen"
           Neues Wiener Journal no. 4298 (10.10.1905)
           p. 3.

See also 574, 598.

--Lienau, Robert Ernst (1838-1920)

1068   Lienau, Robert. Erinnerungen an Johannes Brahms. Berlin-
       Lichterfelde: [Lienau'schen Musikverlage], 1934. 48 pp.
       notes. Describes his association with Brahms and his
       circle, from 1890- .
       (b) English translation by H. B. [H.B. Weiner]: Lienau.
           "Recollections of Brahms" Musical Opinion and Music
           Trade Review 58/690-95 (3.-8.1935) pp. 499-500,
           594-95, 686-87, 762-63, 845-46, 925. notes.
       (c) excerpt: Lienau. "Erinnerungen an Johannes Brahms"
           Deutsche Musikkultur 2/5(12.-1.1937/38) pp. 275-80.

--Lind, Jenny (1820-1887)

See 989.e.d.

--Linnemann, Richard (1845-1909)

See 848.

--Lipsius, Ida Maria (1837-1927)

1069   *La Mara. [Ida Maria Lipsius] Musikerbriefe aus Fünf Jahrhun-
       derten. Leipzig: Breitkopf & Härtel, [1886]. 2 Bde.
       [Brahms: Bd. 2, p. 348. 1 letter, 5.1885]

(a) i) *reprint: in 1179.c.vi.
   ii) *reprint: in 969.
(b) i) English translation by Daphne Woodward: in 819.
    c.vi. pp. 9-10.
   ii) English translation by Piero Weiss: in 913. pp.
       380-81.

--Liszt, Franz (1811-1886)

1070 *Andreae, H. "Brahms, Liszt und Schumann" Bayrische Staats-
     zeitung (München) (6.5.1933).

1071 Antcliffe, Herbert. "Liszt and Brahms" Monthly Musical
     Record 39/457 (1.1.1909) pp. 7-8. Compares the two men
     in terms of character, background, also as composers.

1072 Aronson, Maurice. "Brahms in His Relation to Liszt and
     Wagner" Musical Courier 75/26 (27.12.1917) (Whole no. 1970)
     p. 38. Discusses the three composers' personal relation-
     ship, their characters, and musical style.

1073 *L.H-i. [Ludwig Hevesi] "Wiener Brief: Liszt und Brahms. --
     Bülowiana" Pester Lloyd (Budapest) (25.2.1882). Discusses
     the reconciliation between the two composers. [from 241]

1074 #Lamond,Frederic[k]."Liszt und Brahms, wie ich sie sah" Neues
     Wiener Journal no. 14,082 (2.2.1933) p. 8. Compares
     Liszt and Brahms; includes his own memories of Brahms in
     Wien c. 1885, and Brahms with Grillparzer and Hebbel.
     (c) #excerpt: Lamond, Frederick. Die Musik (Berlin)
     25/8 (5.1933) pp. 608-09.

1075 Mason, William. "Memories of A Musical Life" Century Magazine
     60/3-6 (7.-10.1900) pp. 438-49, 569-74, 763-76, 848-64.
     Brahms: pp. 772-75, 856. Describes the first meeting
     of Brahms and Liszt in 1853; includes author's memories
     of Brahms from 1880, and his comments on his world pre-
     miere of Op. 8 in New York, 1855.
     (d) Mason. Memories of A Musical Life. New York:
         The Century Co., 1901. xii, 306 pp. ind. Brahms:
         pp. 127-32, 135-42, 193-95, 267-68. Includes
         comments on Brahms's arrangements of other com-
         posers' works.
         issue: 1902.
         (a) *reprint (of 1901 Edition): New York: AMS
             Press, [1970].

1076 [Moritz Rosenthal] "Opera and Concert Asides" New York
     Times 87/29,191 (26.12.1937) Section 10, p. 7. Describes
     the day, after Brahms met Liszt for the first time.

See also 60, 680, 726, 792, 1002, 1185, 1289, 1625, 1645, 1701, 1718, 1726, 2378, 2400, 2838, 3009.

--Löw, R. [fl. 19th century]

1077 *Löw, R. "Persönliches aus Brahms' Leben" Basler Nachrichten (5.3.1916).

--Loewe, Karl (1796-1869)

See 2330, 2630.

--Lohse, Otto (1858-1925)

See 2967.

--Lübke, Wilhelm (1826-1893)

1078 #"Ein unveröffentlichter Brief von Brahms aus den Zeiten der Stuttgarter Erstaufführung seines Requiems" Schwäbischen Merkur (Stuttgart) Sonntags-Beilage no. 67 (19.3.1933) p. [1]. One letter from Brahms to Lübke, 10.1871; also contains excerpts from 2277.

--Lyser, Johann Peter (1803-1870)

See 671.

--Maccallum, Frank [fl. 20th century]

See 2608.

--Maasz, Gerhard (1906-)

See 297, 432.

--Mahler, Gustav (1860-1911)

See 658, 680, 856, 1289, 1356, 1836, 1961, 2168, 2974.

--Mandyczewski, Eusebius (1857-1929)

1079 Geiringer, Karl. "Johannes Brahms im Briefwechsel mit

Eusebius Mandyczewski" Zeitschrift für Musikwissenschaft
15/8 (5.1933) pp. 337-70. mus., notes. Includes 99
letters, 1882-96.
(a) *reprint: Brahms, Johannes. Johannes Brahms im
   Briefwechsel mit Eusebius Mandyczewski. Mitgeteilt
   von Karl Geiringer. Leipzig: Breitkopf & Härtel,
   1933. pp. [337]-70.
(c) i) excerpt: see 1179.c.i.
   ii) excerpt: see 879.c.
(e) report: Altmann, Wilhelm. "Brahms und Mandyczew-
   sky" Allgemeine Musikzeitung 61/1 (5.1.1934) pp.
   2-4. notes.

See also 759, 953.

--Manz, Gustav [fl. 19th century]

1080 *Manz, Gustav. "Brahms-Erinnerungen. Nach eigenen Erlebnissen erzählt von Gustav Manz" Pester Lloyd (Budapest)
(11.4.1897). Describes Brahms in Thun, 1887. [from
241]

--Marks, G. B. [pseud.]

1081 Alexander, Arthur. "The Strange Case of Mr. Marks" Music
Teacher and Piano Student 31/[5] (5.1952) p. 244. States
the case for Brahms carrying on the Marks "tradition,"
with stylistic analysis of 2 Potpourris as evidence.

1082 Zakariasen, William. "Pop Music by Classical Composers" High
Fidelity and Musical America 24/1 (1.1974) pp. 96-100.
Brahms: p. 97. ill. Discusses Brahms as a youth, to-
gether with his works composed under the Marks pseudonym.

See also 55.d.ii., 1708.

--Marteuz [fl. 19th century]

See 3037.

--Martucci, Giuseppe (1856-1909)

See 1398.

--Marxsen, Eduard (1806-1887)

1083 Dietrich, Rudolf Adrian. "Brahms' Lehrer Eduard Marxsen"

Zeitschrift für Musik 114/5 (5.1953) pp. 284-85. Describes
Marxsen's background, and his personal and professional
relationship to Brahms.

1084   Jenner, Gustav. "War Marxsen der rechte Lehrer für Brahms?"
        Die Musik (Berlin) 12/2 (Bd. 45) (10.1912) pp. 77-83.
        notes. Refutes Kalbeck's negative opinion on this matter,
        with Jenner's own recollections of Brahms's comments on
        the matter; includes comments on Marxsen's background
        and on how he taught his pupils.

See also 39A.d.i., 340, 363, 639, 667, 884, 2478.

--Mason, William (1829-1908)

See 1075.

--Massanet, Jules (1842-1912)

1085   *L'Echo de Paris
            (b) *German translation: "Die Memoiren Massenets.
                Erinnerungen an Wien" Die Zeit [Tageszeitung]
                (Wien) (26.2.1911) Morgenblatt p. 3.

See also 989.e.d., 1002.

--May, Florence (1845-1915)

1086   *May, Florence. Musical Magazine or Musical Gazette [10]
            (1902).
            (d) incorporated: in 48. Personal recollections of Brahms
                1871, 1881-82, 1888-89, 1894-95, including Brahms
                as a teacher.

See also 48, 550.d.i., 554.

--Meier, Franzisca

See Lentz, Franzisca

--Meiningen, Herzog von

See Georg II, Herzog von Sachsen-Meiningen

--Mendelssohn, Arnold (1855-1933)

1087   Mendelssohn Bartholdy, A[rnold]. "Centenary of Brahms" The

Times (London) Royal Edition no. 46,443 (13.5.1933) p. 13.
Provides a summary of occasions when he was with Brahms
or saw him in concert, late 1880's-90's.

See also 2974.

--Mendelssohn, Felix (1809-1847)

See 1239, 1822, 1826, 1946, 2043, 2064, 2209, 2386, 2490, 2630.

--Menzel, Adolf (1815-1905)

See 667, 684, 929.d.ii.

--Metzenger, Edward M.

See 2600.

--Meyer [fl. 19th century]

See 3085.

--Meyer-Dustmann, Marie [fl. 19th century]

1088   Huschke, Konrad. "Marie Luise Meyer-Dustmann und Johannes
       Brahms" Allgemeine Musikzeitung 59/15 (15.4.1932) p. 207.
       Describes their relationship, 1862-97.

--Meyerbeer, Giacomo (1791-1864)

See 688, 2919.

--Meysenbug Family [fl. 19th century]

1089   *Meysenbug, Hermann, Freiherr von. "Aus Johannes Brahms'
       Jugendtagen" Neues Wiener Tagblatt (9.,11.;5.;1901)
       Describes Brahms in Detmold. [from 241]

1090   *Meysenbug, Karl von. "Aus Johannes Brahms' Jugendtagen"
       Neues Wiener Tagblatt (3.,4.;4.;1902). Describes Brahms
       in Detmold. [from 241]

--Michalek, Ludwig (1857-1942)

See 659.5.

--Milhaud, Darius (1892-1974)

See 2974.

--Miller, Olga von [fl. 19th century]

See 448.

--Miller-Aichholz [fl. 19th-20th centuries]

See 3099, 3154, 3156.

--Miyoshi, Akira (1933-)

See 2608.

--Mörike, Eduard (1804-1875)

See 2066, 2144.

--Moscheles, Ignaz (1794-1870)

See 2013.

--Mozart, Wolfgang Amadeus (1756-1791)

1091 *Meckna, Michael. "The Legacy of Wolfgang Amadeus Mozart"
      Music Journal 39/1 (?) (1.1981) (?) pp. 11-14. Discusses
      Mozart's influence on those who followed him, influence
      either through direct contact or through studying his music.
      Brahms discussed along with 10 others. [from S202]

See also 678, 712, 792, 1325, 1405, 1496, 1516, 1538, 1543, 1644, 1701,
   1826, 2015, 2330, 2347, 2413, 2509, 2521, 2523, 2630.

--Mühlfeld, Richard (1856-1907)

1092 Fellinger, Imogen. "Johannes Brahms und Richard Mühlfeld"
      Brahms-Studien Bd. 4 (1981) pp. 77-93. ill., facsim.,
      notes. Discusses their relationship, 1891-97, and traces
      the evolution of Opp. 114, 115, 120.

1093 Portnoy, Bernard. "Brahm's Prima Donna" Woodwind Magazine
      1/5 (3.1949) pp. 3,8. Discusses Mühlfeld's influence on

Brahms's composing, as well as their relationship, 1891-97.
(a) #reprint: Portnoy. Woodwind World 4/9 (1963) pp.
12-13.

1094 #Winston, Edmund W. "Virtuosity and the Contributions of
Müller and Klose-Buffet to the Development of the Clarinet.
Part III. Mühlfeld and Brahms" NACWPI [National Association of College Wind and Percussion Instructors] Journal
24/4 (Summer 1976) pp. 34-35. Discusses the relationship
between Brahms and Mühlfeld, focusing on Mühlfeld as a
clarinetist.

--Müller, Wilhelm (1794-1827)

1095 #Lissauer, Fritz. "Brahms und Wilhelm Müller" Deutsche Tonkünstlerzeitung 17/343 (5.9.1919) pp. 83-84. Discusses
Müller as poet, with descriptive comments on Brahms's
settings of Müller in Opp. 20, 42, 44.
(a) i) *reprint: Lissauer. Schweizerische musikpädagogische Blätter 9/7 (1920) p. 101.
ii) *reprint: Lissauer. Rheinische Musik- und Theaterzeitung (Köln) 21/12 (1920).

--Münz, Sigmund (1859-?)

1096 *Münz, Sigmund. "Erinnerungen an Brahms" Neue freie Presse
(Wien) (3.4.1898) or no. 12,069 (30.3.1898). Describes
meeting with Brahms in Wien, 1890- , and his Germanic
character. [from 617]
(d) incorporated: into 617.
(e) report: "In der "N[eue]. fr[eie]. Pr[esse]."
veröffentlichte kürzlich ..." Allgemeine Musikzeitung
25/14/15 (8./15.4.1898) p. 221.

--Muffat, Georg (1653-1704)

See 792.

--Musser, Clair Omar [fl. 20th century]

See 2608.

--Neitzel, Otto (1852-1920)

See 1725.

--Neuda-Bernstein, Rosa [fl. 19th century]

See 724.

--Nietzsche, Friedrich (1844-1900)

1097   Thatcher, David S. "Nietzsche and Brahms: A Forgotten
       Relationship" Music and Letters 54/3 (7.1973) pp. 261-80.
       notes. Describes parallels in their background and lives;
       Nietzsche's interest in Brahms's, music, especially Op. 55,
       and his subsequent disavowal; also discusses Wagner and
       Brahms.
       (d) Thatcher. "Nietzsches Totengericht über Brahms"
           Nietzsche-Studien Bd. 7 (1978) pp. 339-61. notes.
           Discussion: pp. 357-61. Describes Nietzsche's
           interest in Brahms's music and Brahms and Wagner
           as seen through his eyes.

1098   *Widmann, J[osef]. V[iktor]. Der Bund (Bern) ([4. or 5.]
       1897).
       (d) i) Gast, Peter. "Nietzsche und Brahms" Die Zukunft
              (Berlin) Bd. 19/[6] [(5/19)] (8.5.1897) pp. 266-69.
              Corrects Widmann's account of Brahms's opinion
              of a choral work by Nietzsche.
              (d) Widmann, J[osef]. V[iktor]. "Brahms und
                  Nietzsche" Die Zukunft (Berlin) Bd.
                  19/[7] [(5/20)] (15.[5.]1897) pp. 326-28.
                  Reply to above.
           ii) see: 3167.

See also 476, 494, 680, 726, 792.

--Noorden, Carl von [fl. 19th century]

See 2971.

--Nothingham, Ethel [fl. 19th century]

See 2627.

--Novák Vítězslav (1870-1949)

See 1398.

--Ochs, Siegfried (1858-1929)

1099   Reznicek, Emil, see 1126.5.

1100   Ochs, Siegfried. Geschehenes, Gesehenes. Leipzig und
       Zürich: Grethlein & Co., 1922. 427, [2] pp. Brahms:
       pp. 296-304. facsim., mus. Describes meeting Brahms
       in Berlin and their conversation; reports Brahms's comments
       on the music of Bruch.

See also 955, 1210.

--Ophüls, Gustav [fl. 19th - 20th centuries]

1101   #Ophüls, Gustav. Erinnerungen an Johannes Brahms. Berlin:
       Verlag der Deutschen Brahms-Gesellschaft m.b.H., 1921.
       77 pp. ill. Describes his spending time with Brahms,
       1896- ; includes comments on 2540 and Op. 89.
       (c) excerpt: "Brahms über sein Chorwerk "Gesang der
                     Parzen"" Zeitschrift für Musik [88]/11 (6.1921)
                     pp. 279-80. adds mus., notes.
       (e) report: Niemann, Walter. "Brahms' "Gesang der
                     Parzen" und Ophüls' Brahms-Erinnerungen" Zeit-
                     schrift für Musik 89/7 (4.1922) pp. 156-60. mus.,
                     notes only.

See also 597.

--Otten, Georg Dietrich (1806-1890)

1102   Callomon, Fritz. "Some Unpublished Brahms Correspondence"
       Arthur Mendel, translator. Musical Quarterly 29/1 (1.1943)
       pp. 32-44. facsim., notes. Contains transcriptions of 4
       letters: Brahms to Otten (2.1856); to Adolf Kauffmann
       (4.1879); to Bernhard Scholz (11.1873); and to Gustav
       Dömpke (10.1886).

1103   Stephenson, Kurt. "Johannes Brahms und Georg Dietrich
       Otten" in Festschrift Karl Gustav Fellerer. Zum sechzigsten
       Geburtstag zm 7. Juli 1962. Heinrich Hüschen, ed. Regens-
       burg: Gustav Bosse Verlag, 1962. pp. 503-18. facsim.,
       notes. Discusses their relationship during the 1850's; also
       includes 6 letters from Brahms to Otten, 1855-63, and dis-
       cussion of the gift of a Sarabande manuscript to Frau
       Otten.
       (d) reprint: Stephenson. Johannes Brahms und Georg
                     Dietrich Otten. In Verbindung mit einem Faksimile-
                     Druck der Brahms-Urschrift "Sarabande" (h-moll).
                     (Jahresgabe Brahms-Gesellschaft Hamburg e.V.
                     1972) [Hamburg:] Brahms-Gesellschaft Hamburg
                     e.V., 1972. 16pp. + Beilagen. facsim., notes.
                     (d) Stephenson. "Brahms' Klavier-Sarabande in
                         h-moll" Mitteilungen der Brahms-Gesellschaft

Hamburg e.V. no. 4 (4.1973) pp. 6-9.
Presents work's background and an analysis; includes manuscript description.

--Paganini, Nicolò (1782-1840)

See "Op. 35" in IV.A.2.a. Specific Works

--Palestrina, Giovanni Pierluigi da (1525?-1594)

See 2344.

--Paumgartner, Bernhard (1887-1971)

1104 *Paumgartner, Bernhard. "Kindheitserinnerungen an Brahms,
      Bruckner und Hugo Wolf" Atlantis Almanach (Zürich) (1946).
      (d) incorporated: Paumgartner. Erinnerungen. Salzburg:
      Residenz Verlag, 1969. 209, [2] pp. Brahms:
      pp. 20-21. Relates memories of Brahms from Paum-
      gartner's childhood.

--Paur, Emil (1855-1932)

1105 Kenny, Ellen, ed. "Some Letters to Emil Paur" Notes Second
      series 8/4 (9.1951) pp. 631-49. Brahms: pp. 633-37, 639.
      facsim., notes. Presents 2 letters: Brahms to Paur:
      Summer 1886 or 1887 and 12.1888-1.1889.

--Pepping, Ernst (1901-)

See 1761.

--Perger, Richard von (1854-1911)

1106 *Perger, Richard [von]. "Vor zehn Jahren. Brahms und
      Bruckner--Erinnerungen und Bekenntnisse" Die Zeit
      [Tageszeitung] (Wien) (24.10.1906) Morgenblatt p. 1.
      (a) *reprint: Perger. Schweizerische Musikzeitung und
          Sängerblatt 45/31/36? (1906).
      (d) #incorporated: into 68.

--Peterffy, Jenő v. [fl. 19th century]

See 2868.

--Peters, C. F. [music publisher]

See 239, 318, 320.a., 848.

--Petersen Family [fl. 19th century]

1107   Hofmann, Kurt. "Brahmsiana der Familie Petersen. Erinner-
        ungen und Briefe" Brahms-Studien Bd. 3 (1979) pp. 69-105.
        ill., facsim., notes. Includes: Petersen, Toni. "Erin-
        nerungen an Brahms": pp. 76-83. Describes Brahms in
        Hamburg, 1878-93. Includes 20 letters between Brahms
        and Carl (9), Toni (10) and Anna (1) Petersen, 1889-94.

--Petőfi, Sándor (1823-1849)

See 2038.

--Petzold-Angermünde, Max. [fl. 19th century]

1108   #Petzold-Angermünde, Max. "Eine Erinnerung an Brahms zum
        7. Mai. Plauderei" Halbmonatsschrift für Schulmusikpflege
        18/3 (1.5.1923) pp. 17-18. Relates anecdotes about Brahms
        the man, in Wien 1887.

--Pfitzner, Hans (1869-1949)

See 2054.

--Pirani, Eugenio di (1852-1939)

See 185.

--Platen-Hallermunde, August, Graf von (1796-1835)

See 2115.

--Plessing [fl. 19th century]

1109   #Plessing, Generalkonsul. "Erinnerungen an Johannes Brahms"
        Die Salzspeicher (Lübeck) (1929) pp. 20, 24. Presents
        impressions of Brahms as a child in Hamburg, as well as
        later in Wien; includes anecdotes on Brahms and Bülow.

--Pohl, Carl Ferdinand (1819-1887)

1110   Geiringer, Karl. "Der Brahms-Freund C[arl]. F[erdinand].
        Pohl. Unbekannte Briefe des Haydn-Biographen an Johannes
        Brahms" Zeitschrift für Musik 102/4 (4.1935) pp. 397-99.
        Includes transcription of letters in excerpt (7) and in full
        (2) 4.1871-5.1885, as means of shedding light on the letter
        writers' characters.

--Pohl, Louise [fl. 19th century]

1111   Pohl, Luise. "Brahms-Erinnerungen" Frankfurter Zeitung
        51/103 (14.4.1907) 5. Morgenblatt p. 1. mus. Describes
        Brahms in Baden-Baden: his personality and activities.
        (a) reprint: Pohl. Allgemeine Musikzeitung 34/19
        (10.5.1907) pp. 339-40.

1112   _____. (Louise) "Eine Brahms-Joachim-Hausmann-Erinnerung"
        Allgemeine Musikzeitung 36/13 (26.3.1909) pp. 268-69.
        Describes the rehearsal of a new piano trio in Baden-Baden.

See also 962.

--Pohlig, Carl (1858-1928)

1113   *Pohlig, Carl. Bühnen-Blättern von Landestheater (Braun-
        schweig) (1920).

1114   #Pohlig, Carl. "Ein Besuch bei Johannes Brahms" Salve hospes
        10/7 (7.1960) pp. 53-54. Describes meeting Brahms in
        Wien, 1.1878.

--Popper, David (1843-1913)

See "Hubay Family" in III.B.

--Porubsky, Bertha

See Faber, Bertha.

--Premyslav Leopold [fl. 19th century]

See 2594.

--Proffen, Elisabeth

See Roesing, Elisabeth

--Raabe, Wilhelm (1831-1910)

1115 *Prahm, Adolf. "Johannes Brahms und Wilhelm Raabe" Mitteil-
       ungen der Raabe-Gesellschaft 42 (1955) pp. 63-64.

--Raff, Joachim (1822-1882)

1116 Huschke, Konrad. "Joachim Raff--Bülow, Wagner, Brahms und
       Cornelius" in 858.d.i. pp. 202-17. ind. Brahms: pp.
       212-14. ill. Describes the relationship of Brahms and Raff,
       1853-82, together with Raff's opinion of Brahms's music
       and his piano playing.

See also 792, 895.

--Rappoldi, Adrian (1876-1949)

1117 Rappoldi, Adrian. "Meine Erinnerungen an Brahms" Zeitschrift
       für Musik 100/5 (5.1933) pp. 446-48. Describes Brahms's
       visit to the Rappoldi family in Dresden during the author's
       childhood; also their meeting in Bad Ischl and Mannheim.

--Rauenstein [fl. 19th century]

See 579.d.

--Ravel, Maurice (1875-1937)

See 1676.

--Reger, Max (1873-1916)

1117.5#Lindner, Adalbert. "Max Reger und Johannes Brahms u.a."
       in Lindner. Max Reger. Ein Bild seines Jugendlebens und
       künstlerischen Werdens. Stuttgart: J. Engelhorns Nachf.,
       1923. pp. 100-04. notes. Brahms: pp. 100-02. Describes
       their acquaintance through their letters; includes 1 letter,
       1 postcard, both Brahms to Reger, c. 1895.

1118 Riemer, Otto. "Vom alten Brahms zum jungen Reger" Allge-
       meine Musikzeitung 65/19 (6.5.1938) pp. 293-95. Discusses
       their personal and musical links.

1119   Wirth, Helmut. "Johannes Brahms und Max Reger" Brahms-
        Studien Bd. 1 (1974) pp. 91-112. mus., notes. Describes
        parallels in their lives and personal opinions, comments
        on their correspondence and on Brahms's musical influence
        on Reger.

See also 1518, 1638, 1702, 1949, 2178, 2341, 2386, 2416, 2444, 2461,
    2609, 2610, 2695, 2723, 2974.

--Rehberg, Willy (1863-1937)

1120   Rehberg, Willy. "Brahms-Erinnerungen" Der Weihergarten nos.
        3/6, 7/10 (3./6.,7./10.;1933) [Beilage to Melos 12 (1933)]
        pp. 19-20, 25-26. ill. Describes his friendship with
        Brahms, 1880's.

--Reinecke, Carl (1824-1910)

1121   #Reinecke, C[arl]. "Meine letzten Begegnungen mit Johannes
        Brahms" Dur und Moll 1/8 (1897) pp. 128-30. ill., mus.
        Describes period 3.1896-4.1897; also discusses their first
        meeting, Summer 1853.
        (d) reworked: Reinecke. "Johannes Brahms" in Reinecke.
        "und manche liebe Schatten steigen auf." Gedenk-
        blätter an berühmte Musiker. Leipzig: Verlag von
        Gebrüder Reinecke, 1900. pp. 109-19. ill., mus.

See also "Karl Reinthaler" in III.B.

--Reinthaler, Karl (1822-1896)

1122   *Brahms, Johannes. Johannes Brahms im Briefwechsel mit
        Karl Reinthaler, Max Bruch, Hermann Deiters, Friedr[ich].
        Heimsoeth, Karl Reinecke, Ernst Rudorff, Bernhard und
        Luise Scholz. Wilhelm Altmann, ed. (Johannes Brahms.
        Briefwechsel III) Berlin: Verlag der Deutschen Brahms-
        Gesellschaft m.b.H., 1908. vii, 237 pp. facsim., ind.,
        notes.
        *2. durchgesehene und vermehrte Auflage: 1912. vi, [2],
        241 pp.
        (a) reprint (of 1912 Auflage): (Brahms-Briefwechsel
            Band III) Tutzing: Hans Schneider, 1974. Rein-
            thaler: 77 letters (10.1867-2.1896); Bruch: 15
            letters (9.1864-6.1894); Deiters and Heimsoeth: 9
            letters (5.1868-1.1897); Reinecke: 11 letters
            (2.1869-6.1883); Rudorff: 25 letters (1.1865-
            12.1886); Scholz: 43 letters (3.1872-12.1882).
        (c) i) excerpt (of ? Auflage): see 792.

ii) excerpt (of ? Auflage): see 1179.c.i.

iii)#excerpt (of ? Auflage): see 1179.c.ii.

iv) excerpt (of ? Auflage): see 954.c.iv.
Includes 1 letter Bruch to Brahms; 1,
Brahms to Reinthaler; 1, Scholz to Brahms;
and 1, Brahms to Rudorff.

(e) i)*report (on 1908 Auflage): Altmann, Wilhelm. "Aus
dem Briefwechsel von Brahms mit B[ern-
hard]. und L[uise]. Scholz" Osterreichische
Rundschau (Brünn) 13 (1908) pp. 50-56.

ii) report (on 1908 Auflage): Altmann, Wilhelm. "Aus
dem Briefwechsel von Johannes Brahms
mit Karl Reinthaler" Die Musik (Berlin)
7/2 (Bd. 25) (10.1907) pp. 98-106. notes.
Describes characteristics of correspondence.

iii) *report (on 1908 Auflage): Altmann, W[ilhelm].
"Aus dem Briefwechsel von Johannes
Brahms mit Max Bruch und Ernst Rudorff"
National-Zeitung (Berlin) Sonntags-Beilage
no. 14 (1907).

iv) report (on 1908 Auflage): "Brahms als Philologe"
Allgemeine Musikzeitung 34/42 (18.10.1907)
pp. 686-89. Uses correspondence to show
Brahms's principles on editing the music
of Chopin and Schumann.

v) report (on 1908 Auflage): Kohut, Adolf. "Max
Bruch und Johannes Brahms. Zu Max
Bruchs 70. Geburtstag" Berliner Börsen-
Courir (5.1.1908) pp. 6-7. Describes
their friendship through excerpts from
their correspondence.

vi) report (on 1908 Auflage): Prelinger, Fritz. "Johannes Brahms. Briefwechsel, Band III
und IV" Signale für die musikalische
Welt 66/1 (1.1.1908) pp. 11-14. Includes
report on 954.

vii) report (on ? Auflage): see 750.

1123 #Wessling, Berndt W. "Das Bremer Fünfkönigstreffen--Karl
Martin Reinthaler in Bremen" Radio Bremen Hausbuch
(1967) pp. 82-88. Discusses Brahms, Joachim, Reinecke,
Bungert and Reinthaler: their activities and their comments concerning each other.

--Rembrandt [Rembrandt Harmensz van Rijn] (1606-1669)

See 646.

--Reményi, Eduard (1830-1898)

1124 #"Der Komponist der "Ungarischen Tänze" ... " Deutsche

Wacht (Dresden) (21.5.1898) p. 2. Contains reference to
Reményi's quarrel with Brahms over the Ungarische Tänze
[Hofmann nr. 128; McCorkle WoO 1].
(e) #report: "Immer wieder versuchen es gewisse Bieder-
    männer ... " Musikalisches Wochenblatt 29 (1898)
    pp. 320-21.

1125 *Lestyán, Sandor. Repülj fecském ... Reményi Ede regényes
    élete. [Budapest:] Renaissance kiadó, [1942]. 202, [2]
    pp. Brahms: pp. 31-32, 34-44. [from 241]

1126 "A Twenty-Five Years' Secret. Revelations That Will Stir
    the Musical World. Remenyi and Johannes Brahms. Who
    Composed "Brahms' Celebrated Hungarian Dances?"" New
    York Herald no. 15,489 (18.1.1879) p. 10. Reményi on
    his relationship with Brahms in the 1850's; also discloses
    the attributions for the Ungarische Tänze [Hofmann nr.
    128; McCorkle. WoO 1].
    (a) reprint: "Remenyi, Liszt and Brahms" in Gwendolyn
        Dunlevy Kelley [Gwendolyn (Kelley) Hack] and
        George P. Upton. Edouard Remenyi. Musician,
        Litterateur, and Man. An Appreciation. Chicago:
        A. C. McClurg & Co., 1906. pp. 79-95. ill.,
        ind., notes.
    (c) i) excerpt: "Brahms and Remény" Etude
            24/7 (7.1906) pp. 462-63.
        ii) excerpt: Garbett, A. S. "The Musical
            Scrap Book" Etude 41/12 (12.1923) p. 830.
            "A Poor Piano Teacher Named Brahms."
            The circumstances behind Reményi and
            Brahms's first meeting.
    (e) *report: Goldstein, Max. New Yorker Musik- und
        Unterhaltungsblätter [22]/5 (1.2.1879).

See also 233, 347, 374, 638, 680, 1016, 1718, 1727, 1730, 2378, 2559.

--Reti, Rudolph (1885-1957)

See 2391.

--Reuter, Marie [fl. 19th century]

See 48, 375, 1061, 2193.

--Rezniček, Emil Nikolaus von (1860-1945)

1126.5#Rezniček, E[mil]. N[ickolaus] v. "Gott Brahms" in Reznicek.
    "Von Brahms bis zur Prinzessin Ululani Nui. Geschichten

aus einem Musikerleben (1860-1930)." Deutsche allgemeine
Zeitung (Berlin) no. 205-06 (6.5.1930) Beiblatt p. [1].
Relates anecdote of author meeting Brahms in Wien, 1872.

--Ribarz-Hermala, Henriette [fl. 19th century]

1127   Sanford, Ralph S. ""Oh No!"" New York Times Magazine
        (13.4.1969) pp. 104, 106. ill. Describes the circumstances
        behind the taking of a photograph of Ribarz-Hemala and
        Brahms, 1895.

--Richter, Hans (1843-1916)

See 989.e.d., 1279.

--Riemann, Hugo (1849-1919)

See 2418.

--Rieter-Biedermann, Jakob Melchior (1811-1876)

1128   Hunziker, Rudolf. "Ein Brief von Johannes Brahms an seinen
        Verleger Rieter-Biedermann in Winterthur" Schweizerisches
        Jahrbuch für Musikwissenschaft Bd. 2 (1927) pp. 107-09.
        notes. 1 letter, 7.1861.

See also 239, 320.a, 848.

--Rietsch, Prof. [fl. 19th century]

1128.5#Rietsch, Prof. "Eine kleine Brahmserinnerung" Der Auftakt
        2/4 (1922) pp. 120-21. Letter to editor describing a visit
        made to Brahms in Wien, 1890.

--Riggenbach-Stehlin Family [fl. 19th century]

1129   #Schanzlin, Hans Peter. "Basels private Musikpflege im 19.
        Jahrhundert" Neujahrsblatt der Gesellschaft zur Beförderung
        des Guten und Gemeinnützigen (Basel) no. 139 (1961).

1130 #_____. "Brahms-Briefe aus Basler Privatbesitz" Basler
        Stadtbuch. Jahrbuch für Kultur und Geschichte (1966)
        pp. 207-17. facsim. Discusses Brahms and Switzerland;
        includes 5 letters to Riggenbach-Stehlin family, 1.-Fall
        1866, 10.1893.

--Rilke, Rainer Maria (1875-1926)

1131 "Rainer Maria Rilkes "Begegnung" mit Brahms" Das Inselschiff
15/2 (Frühjahr 1934) pp. 95-97. Describes in a letter
written in 1912, meeting Brahms at Bad Aussee in 1891-92.

--Röger-Soldat, Marie

See Soldat, Marie

--Röntgen, Julius (1855-1932)

See 792.
See also "The Netherlands" in II.B.

--Roesing, Elisabeth [fl. 19th century]

1132 "Aus der Zeit des jungen Brahms. Nach Erinnerungen von
Elisabeth Proffen, geb. Roesing. Zu unserer Bilderbeilage"
Zeitschrift für Musik 94/7/8 (7./8.1927) pp. 416-18.
[Beilage between pp. 400-01] Describes Brahms in Spring
1861 when he stayed with Roesing; includes her comments
on Op. 26.

--Romberg, Bernhard (1767-1841)

See 1475.

--Roner, Anna [fl. 19th century]

See 740.

--Rosé, Arnold (1863-1946)

See 340.

--Rosegger, Peter [Petri] (1843-1918)

1133 *Rosegger, Peter. Der Heimgarten (1894)
(a) i) *Neue Musikzeitung (189-?).
(b) English translation by Ernst Held: Held,
Ernst. "An Episode in the Life of Johannes
Brahms" Musician (Philadelphia) 2/5
(5.1897) pp. 117-18. Rosegger describes

meeting Brahms during a summer the
composer spent at Mürzzuschlag.

  ii) *Rosegger, Peter. "Ein fremder Herr (1886)" in
Rosegger. Mein Weltleben. Neue Folge. Erinnerungen eines Siebzigjährigen. Leipzig: L. Staackmann, 1914.

    (a) reprint: Rosegger. "Mein fremder Herr" in
Rosegger. Aus dem Weltleben des Waldbauernbuben. Erinnerungen und Bekenntnisse. Ausgewählt und mit einem Nachwort
herausgegeben von Bruno Gloger. Il-
lustriert von Kurt Eichler. Berlin: Union
Verlag, 1969. pp. 315-19. ill.

    (d) *Rosegger. in Rosegger. Mein Weltleben.
Erinnerungen eines Siebzigjährigen.
(Rosegger. Gesammelte Werke. Bd. II)
1924. pp. 207-10.

--Rosenthal, Moritz (1862-1946)

1134   Snowdon, Edward W. "Brahms Reminiscences" New York
Times 86/28,953 (2.5.1937) Section 11, p. 7. Describes
connection between Brahms and Rosenthal, correcting it as
described in 989.e.d.

See also 989.e.d.

--Rott, Hans (1858-1884)

1135   *Marschner, Franz. "Brahms--Hans Rott" Osterreichische
Revue no. 1 (1903).

--Rubinstein, Anton (1829-1894)

See 154.d., 1185, 1289, 1860, 2979.

--Rudorff, Ernst (1840-1916)

1136   Reich, Nancy B. "The Rudorff Collection" Notes 31/2 (12.
1974) pp. 247-61. Brahms: pp. 256, 260. ill., notes.
Describes the relationship of Brahms and Rudorff and lists
Rudorff's holdings of Brahms editions.

1137   Rudorff, Ernst. "Johannes Brahms. Erinnerungen und
Betrachtungen" Schweizerische Musikzeitung. Revue
musicale suisse 97/3-5 (1.;3.-5.; 1957) pp. 81-86, 139-45,
182-87. mus., notes. Comments on Brahms's music and

his historical position, describes meeting Brahms in 12.1878
and 1.-2.1884, as well as the Joachim, Brahms and Bülow
relationship.

See also 1122, 1733, 1736.

--Sachau, Eduard [fl. 19th century]

1138   Sachau, Eduard. "Brahms als Mensch. Persönliche Erinner-
        ungen" Deutsche allgemeine Zeitung (Berlin) 61/143 (25.
        3.1922) Morgenausgabe 2. Beiblatt p. [7]; 61/145 (26.3.1922)
        Morgenausgabe 2. Beiblatt p. [9]. Describes relationship
        with Brahms in Wien 1869-76; also discusses the derivation
        of the Brahms surname.
        (a) reprint: Sachau. Münchner neueste Nachrichten
             75/141 (3.4.1922) Abendblatt pp. 1-2. [across
             page bottoms]

--Sachsen-Meiningen, Herzog von

See Georg II, Herzog von Sachsen-Meiningen

--Sauer, Emil von (1862-1942)

1139   Sauer, Emil. Meine Welt. Bilder aus dem Geheimfache
        meiner Kunst und meines Lebens. Stuttgart: Verlag
        von W. Spemann, 1901. 292 pp. Brahms: pp. 192-96.
        Describes their first meeting (1889) and last meeting
        (1897), both in Wien.
        (d) *Sauer. "Meine Bekanntschaft mit Brahms" Wiener
             Konzertschau [1]/10 (1912).
             (d) #Sauer. "Ismeretségem Brahms-szal" A Zene
                  [3] (1912) pp. 254-55.

--Scarlatti, Domenico (1685-1757)

See 792, 2091.

--Scharwenka, Xaver (1850-1924)

1140   *Scharwenka, Xaver.
        (d) Zobel, Bertha. "Brahms on the Baltic: A Romance
             and A Dedication" Musical Courier 141/5 (Whole
             no. 3206) (1.3.1950) pp. 6-7. ill. Provides
             background on Scharwenka's Op. 33 and its dedi-
             cation to Brahms; also discusses Brahms in Sassnitz,
             1877.

1141 #-ten-. "Brahms und Scharwenka" <u>Königsberger hartungsche</u>
      <u>Zeitung</u> Sonntagsblatt nr. 577/578 (?) (10.12.1922) pp. 3-4.
      Describes first meeting Brahms in Sassnitz, 1877; includes
      letter Brahms to Scharwenka, on occasion of Scharwenka's
      Op. 33 being dedicated to Brahms [1879?]. Excerpted
      from Scharwenka. <u>Klänge aus meinem Leben. Erinnerungen</u>
      <u>eines Musikers</u> (Leipzig: K. F. Köhler, 1922).

--Scheidt, Samuel (baptized 1587-1654)

See 1644.

--Schenkendorf, Max von (1793-1817)

See 2530.

--Schenker, Heinrich (1868-1935)

1142 Schenker, Heinrich. "Erinnerungen an Brahms" <u>Deutsche</u>
      <u>Zeitschrift</u> [=Der Kunstwart] 46/8 (5.1933) pp. 475-82.
      notes. Discusses Brahms's significance, Brahms as person
      and teacher, includes anecdotes about Brahms and Goldmark.

See also 1597, 1669, 1692, 2353.

--Schmaltz, Susanne [fl. 19th century]

1143 *Schmaltz, Susanne. <u>Beglückte Erinnerung. Lebenslauf eines</u>
      <u>Sonntagskindes</u>. Dresden, Leipzig: Verlag Deutsche
      Buchwerkstätten, [1925]. 288 pp. ill. Contains remi-
      niscences about Brahms from the time of the Hamburger
      Frauenchor. [from 2343]

See also 48, 375, 1061, 2193.

--Schnirlin, Ossip [fl. 19th century]

See 1943.

--Schnitzler, Victor [fl. 19th century]

1144 Schnitzler, Victor. "Johannes Brahms" in Schnitzler. <u>Erin-</u>
      <u>nerungen aus meinem Leben</u>. Köln: [Author], 1921. pp.
      46-59. ill. Describes their relationship from 1874- and
      Brahms's visits to Köln; transcribes 4 letters to the

Schnitzler family: 1886-96; includes comments on Brahms
the man.
*[? Auflage:] Köln a. Rh.: Tischer & Jagenberg G.m.b.H.,
1935.

--Schoenberg, Arnold (1874-1951)

1145 *Gerlach, Reinhard. "War Schönberg von Dvořák beeinflusst?"
in Colloquium musica cameralis Brno 1971. Rudolf Pečman,
ed. (Colloquia on the History and Theory of Music at the
International Musical Festival in Brno 6) Brno: Mezinárodní
hudební festival, 1977. pp. 157-76. Analyzes the influences
of Dvořák and Brahms in Schoenberg's D major String
Quartet (1897).

1146 *Musgrave, Michael Graham. "Schoenberg and Brahms: A
Study of Schoenberg's Response to Brahms's Music as
Revealed in His Didactic Writings and Selected Early Com-
positions" Ph.D. diss., University of London, 1980.

1147 *Pfisterer, Manfred. "Brahms's Bedeutung für die Entwicklung
der neuen Musik dargestellt am Verhältnis Schönberg-
Brahms" Philharmonische Blätter [13]/3 (1975/76) pp. 14-16.

See also 1366, 1457, 1459, 1461, 1518, 1669, 1680, 1791, 1850, 2362,
2368, 2372, 2491, 2991.

--Scholz Family [fl. 19th century]

See 569, 658, 662, 1102, 1122.

--Schopenhauer, Arthur (1788-1860)

See 670.

--Schubert, Franz (1797-1828)

See 267, 645, 680, 792, 902, 1339, 1365.5, 1444, 1496, 1600, 1702,
1740, 1741, 1826, 2036, 2043, 2064, 2098, 2142, 2168, 2193, 2348,
2348.5, 2415.d., 2427, 2446, 2465, 2490, 2537, 2630, 2837.

--Schubring, Adolf (1817-1893)

See 1297, 2925.

--Schütz, Heinrich (1585-1672)

See 2216, 2285.

--Schütz, Max [fl. 19th century]

1147.5*Schütz, Max. "Regentage in Ischl. (Mit Musikbegleitung)"
        Pester Lloyd (Budapest) (19.,20.;10.;1880). Describes a
        visit with Brahms in Bad Ischl. [from 241]

--Schumann, Georg (1866-1952)

See 2862.

--Schumann Family

Clara (1819-1896): 1149, 1151, 1154-65, 1167, 1169, 1170, 1172-79,
     1181, 1182, 1184-87.
Eugenie (1851-1938): 1158, 1179, 1180.
Felix (1854-1879): 1158.
Ferdinand (1849-1891): 1154, 1182.
Marie (1841-1925): 1179.
Robert (1810-1856): 1150-53, 1158, 1160-62, 1165-73, 1175, 1176,
     1178, 1179, 1183, 1185, 1186, 1188.

1148   *Frankfurter allgemeine Zeitung (6.8.1979) (?).

1149   *Bockemühl, Erich. "Brahms und Clara Schumann" Preussische
        Lehrerzeitung (Magdeburg) no. 56 (1933).

1150   #Boetticher, Wolfgang. "Robert Schumann in seinen Beziehungen
        zu Johannes Brahms" Die Musik (Berlin) 29/8 (5.1937)
        pp. 548-54. notes. Uses Schumann's diary as source
        for description of Brahms's first meeting with Schumann
        in 1853; also comments on Brahms as a musical disciple of
        Schumann.

1151   Cheiner, Sophie. "El trio patetico" Heterofonia no. 57 (10/6)
        (11.-12.1977) pp. 14-18. ill. Discusses Brahms, Robert
        and Clara Schumann: the circumstances of their meeting
        and the evolution of their friendship.
        (d)   summary (in English): Cheiner. "The Pathetical
              Trio" Heterofonia no. 57 (10/6) (11.-12.1977) pp.
              46-47.

1152   DAS. [Adolf Schubring] "Schumanniana Nr. 11. Die
        Schumann'sche Schule. Schumann und Brahms. Brahms'
        vierhändige Schumann-Variationen" Allgemeine musikalische

Zeitung 3/6,7 (5.,12.;2.;1868) pp. 41-42,49-51. mus., notes.
Describes Brahms's life up to his first involvement with
the Schumanns; includes review of Brahms's Op. 23.

1153 Ed.H. [Eduard Hanslick] "Aus Robert Schumann's letzten
Tagen. Mit ungedruckten Briefen von ihm. I.,II." Neue
freie Presse (Wien) no. 11,558;11,560 (27.,29.;10.;1896)
Morgenblatt [both parts] pp. 1-4; 1-3 [both parts across
page bottoms]. Brahms: Part II. Contains 4 letters
Schumann to Brahms, 1854-55. All included in 1179.
(a) *reprint: Hanslick, Eduard. "Robert Schumann in
Endenich. Mit ungedruckten Briefen von ihm.
I.,II." in 2943. pp. 317-42. Brahms: pp. 336-41.

1154 "Erinnerungen an Clara Schumann. Tagebuchblätter ihres
Enkels Ferdinand Schumann" Neue Zeitschrift für Musik
84/9-13 (1.-29.;3.;1917) pp. 69-72, 77-80, 85-88, 93-96,
101-04. ill., mus. Covers the time period 4.1894-5.1896.
Use with 1182.
(d) *English translation, edited [condensed?] by June M.
Dickinson: Schumann, Ferdinand. Reminiscences
of Clara Schumann as found in the Diary of her
Grandson, Ferdinand Schumann. [Rochester:
Schumann Memorial Foundation, 1949.] 41 pp.
omits mus.
2nd Edition: New York: Musical Scope Publishers,
1973. omits ill., adds notes.

1155 *Eulenberg, Herbert. "Brahms" in Eulenberg. Letzte Bilder.
Berlin: Bruno Cassirer, 1915. [total paging: xiv, 305
pp.]
*4. bis 6. Auflage: 1916.
*10. bis 13. Auflage: 1918. [total paging: xiv, 332 pp.]
*19. bis 23. Auflage: 1919. [total paging: xiv, 331 pp.]
*24. bis 30. Auflage: 1920.
31. bis 37. Tausend: 1922. pp. 247-57. [total paging:
[5], 341 pp.] fiction describing Brahms at Clara Schumann's
funeral, and his reflections on their relationship.
*[? Auflage:] 1923.
(a) i) *reprint: Eulenburg. Ergebnisse der Immunitatsforschung (1916) pp. 247-57.
ii) *reprint: in Eulenberg. Das deutsche Angesicht.
Berlin: Bruno Cassirer, 1917. pp. 135-45.

1156 *Franck, Hans. Dur und Moll. Erzählung um Johannes Brahms
und Clara Schumann. (Der Eckart-Kreis, Bd. 30) Witten,
Berlin: Eckart-Verlag, 1971. 108 pp.

1157 *_____. "Der getreue Johannes" in Franck. Du holde Kunst.
Gesammelte Musikergeschichten. Berlin: Union Verlag,
[1964]. pp. 241-337.

1158 *Frazeni, Titus. [Alfred Schumann] Johannes Brahms der
Vater von Felix Schumann, das Mysterium einer Liebe.
Eine sehr ernste Parodie auf die "Erinnerungen" von Eugenie
Schumann. Mit einem geleitwort von Alfred Schumann und
sechs Originalschnitten von Fritz Steinau. 1. Auflage
Bielefeld: Manfred-Verlag, Schumann & Steinau, 1926.
95 pp. ill.
(e) i) report: Diesterweg, Adolf. "Clara Schumann und
Johannes Brahms als Opfer einer Hintertreppenphantasie" Allgemeine Musikzeitung 53/32/33 (6.8.1926)
pp. 625-26. notes.
ii) report: Ernest, Gustav. "Klara Schumann und
Johannes Brahms. Ein unwürdiger Nachkomme"
Berliner Tageblatt 56/32 (20.1.1927) Morgenausgabe
1. Beiblatt pp. [3].
iii) *report: Hernried, Robert. "Schumann-Brahms
Schändung" Das Orchester (Berlin) 3 (15.6.1926)
p. 133.
(d) *Hernried, Robert. Rheinisch-Westfälische
Zeitung (Essen) 189/372 (1926).
iv) *report: Schumann, [Ferdinand or Alfred (?)].
"Schumann-Brahms-Schändung" Das Orchester
(Berlin) 3/20, [21] (1926) pp. 299+, 243+.
(d) #Schumann, Ferdinand. "Schusswort zum
Kapitel: "Schumann-Brahms-Schändung""
Rheinisch-Westfälische Zeitung (Essen)
189/548, 552 (8.,10.;8.1926) pp. [?;
1-2] [across page bottoms]. Scathing
remarks on book; refutes its conclusions
with evidence from his own observations
of Clara Schumann and Brahms, her letters,
the Schumann family.

1159 #Gallwitz, S[ophie]. D[orothea]. "Clara Schumann und Brahms"
Bunte Truhe 1 (6.10.1919) p. [1]. [Beilage to Weser-
Zeitung (Bremen) 26/681 (6.10.1919) Mittags-Ausgabe]
Comments on their relationship.

1160 Geiringer, Karl. "Schumanniana in der Bibliothek von Jo-
hannes Brahms" in Convivium musicorum. Festschrift
Wolfgang Boetticher zum sechzigsten Geburtstag am 19.
August 1974. Heinrich Hüschen and Dietz-Rüdiger Moser,
eds. Berlin: Verlag Merseburger, 1974. pp. 79-82. notes.
Surveys Brahms's holdings of Schumann editions, autograph
manuscripts, and books given to him as gifts by Clara
Schumann.

1161 Ginder, C. Richard. "Great Musical Women of Yesterday"
Etude 59/9 (9.1941) pp. 603, 632. Brahms: p. 632.
Describes Brahms and the Schumanns, focusing on Brahms
and Clara.

1162 Hagen, Hans W[ilhelm]. "Treue. Clara Wiecks Schicksal zwischen Robert Schumann und Johannes Brahms" in Hagen. Musikalisches Opfer. Ein Altar in Worten mit vier Seitentafeln um den Mittelschrein. München: Türmer Verlag, 1960. pp. 135-58. Brahms: pp. 147-50, 153-58. Describes his first arrival in Düsseldorf and how Clara can only resolve her feelings for both her husband and Brahms through her musicmaking.

1163 *Havemann, Hans. Frankfurter Zeitung (1926?-1927).

1164 *Henning, Laura. [Lore Schmidt-Delbrück] Die Freundschaft Clara Schumanns mit Johannes Brahms. Aus Briefen und Tagebuchblättern. Zürich: Werner Classen Verlag, [1946]. 147 pp. ill.
   2. Auflage: 1952. 156 pp. adds notes. Traces the history of their relationship, including quotations from 1170 and 1179.

1165 *Hubbard, Elbert. Little Journeys to the Homes of Great Musicians: Brahms. East Aurora, N.Y.: The Roycrofters, 1901. pp. 129-49. ill.
   (a) i) *reprint: Brahms. (Little Musicians 9/12). n.p., n.d.
      ii) reprint: Hubbard. "Johannes Brahms" in Hubbard. Little Journeys to the Homes of Great Musicians. 2 vols. (His Little Journeys vol. 8-9) vol. 2, pp. 129-49. Describes Brahms's early life, focuses on meeting the Schumanns and on his relationship with them.
      [New Edition:] New York & London: G. P. Putnam's Sons, 1903. pp. 117-37.
      *issues: 1905-06.
      *issue: 1909. pp. 391-422.
      *Memorial Edition: (His Little Journeys vol. 14) East Aurora, N.Y.: The Roycrofters; New York, Chicago: Wm.H. Wise & Co., [1916].
      *[Tower Books Edition] New York: World Publishers, 1928.
      *issue: 1943.

1166 *Kerner, D[ieter]. Bunte Illustrierte (Offenburg in Baden) (10.4.1980).

1167 Kross, Siegfried. "Brahms und Schumann" Brahms-Studien Bd. 4 (1981) pp. 7-44. ill., notes. Discusses the personal relationship of these two men and presents the theory that Brahms and Clara were linked by music, not by romance.

1168 La Mara. [Ida Maria Lipsius] "Briefe von Brahms an Robert Schumann. Nach den Originalen ... (Zum Geburtstage

Brahms', 7. Mai)" Neue freie Presse (Wien) no. 11,747
(7.5.1897) Morgenblatt pp. 1-3 [across page bottoms].
notes. Includes 9 letters, 1853-55. All in 1179.
(e) i)   report: J. B. K. "Letters from Brahms to
       Schumann" Monthly Musical Record 28/333 (1.9.1898)
       pp. 195-97.
  ii) *report: Legge, R. H. Musician (Boston)
     (a) *reprint: Legge. in Studies in Music. Robin
        Grey, ed. London: Simpkin, Marshall,
        Hamilton, Kent & Co. Lmt., 1901. pp.
        45-51. notes.
     also: New York: Scribner's Sons, 1901.
     (a) *reprint (of ? Edition): New York:
        n.p., 1976.

1169 *Liebert, Paul. Den die Götter lieben. Episoden aus der Leben
berühmter Männer und Frauen. Illustrationen von Willy
Röttges. Nürnberg: L. Liebel, 1948.
"Träumerei": pp. 139-45.
"Brahms bei Schumann": pp. 145-48.

1170 *Litzmann, Berthold, ed. [Clara Schumann. Ein Künsterleben
nach Tagebüchern und Briefen.]
(c) i)   excerpt (of ? Auflage): see 792.
  ii) *excerpt (of ? Auflage): see 848.
  iii) *excerpt (of ? Auflage): see 1164.
(d) i)   abridgement of 4. Auflagen (in English translation
    by Grace Hadow): Litzmann, ed. Clara Schumann.
    An Artist's Life. Based on Materials Found in
    Diaries and Letters. With a Preface by W[illiam].
    H[enry], Hadow. 2 vols. London: Macmillan &
    Co., Ltd., 1913.
  *also: Leipzig: Breitkopf & Härtel, 1913.
    (a) i) *reprint (of London Edition): New York:
        Vienna House, 1972.
      ii) *reprint (of London Edition): With New
        Introduction by Elaine Brody. New York:
        Da Capo Press, Inc., 1979.
  ii)*Schiedermair, Ludwig. Clara Schumann. Frauenliebe
   und Leben. Aus Tagebüchern und Briefen nach
   der Biographie von Berthold Litzmann. München,
   Wien: Langen-Müller, 1978. 229 pp. ill.

1170A Band I.

*Litzmann, ed. Clara Schumann. Ein Künstlerleben nach
Tagebüchern und Briefen. Erster Band. Mädchenjahre.
1819-1840. Leipzig: Breitkopf & Härtel, 1902. ill., ind.,
notes.
3. durchgesehene Auflage: 1906. vii, [1], 431 pp.
*5., aufs neue durchgesehene Auflage: 1912. ix, 431 pp.
*7. Auflage: [1920?]. x, 431 pp.
8. Auflage: 1925. ix, 431 pp.

1170B Band II.

*Litzmann, ed. Clara Schumann. Ein Künstlerleben nach
Tagebüchern und Briefen. Zweiter Band. Ehejahre.
1840-1856. Leipzig: Breitkopf & Härtel, 1905. [4], 416
pp. ill., ind., notes.
*3. durchgesehene Auflage: 1907.
*4., unveränderte Auflage: 1910. v, 416 pp.
*6. Auflage: [1920?].
7. Auflage: 1925. iv, [2], 416 pp.
(e) report (on 1905 Auflage): Stoecklin, Paul de.
"Ménage d'Artistes. Robert et Clara Schumann"
Le Courrier musical 9/18,19 (15.9. and 1.10.;1906)
pp. 550-57, 573-79. Brahms: pp. 575-79. Describes
the period of Schumann's death and the relationship
between Brahms and Clara as seen in 1170.

1170C Band III.

Litzmann, ed. Clara Schumann. Ein Künstlerleben nach Tagebüchern und Briefen. Dritter Band. Clara Schumann und
ihre Freunde. 1856-1896. Leipzig: Breitkopf & Härtel,
1908. vi, [2], 642 pp. ill., ind., notes.
*3. durchgesehene Auflage: 1910.
*4. unveränderte Auflage: [192-?].
5. und 6. Auflage: 1923.
(e) i) report (on ? Auflage): Segnitz, Eugen. "Clara
Schumann und Johannes Brahms" Allgemeine Musikzeitung 39/50,51/52 (13.,20.;12.;1912) pp. 1342-44,
1372-74. Surveys their relationship.
ii) report (on 1908 Auflage): Stoecklin, Paul de.
"Clara Schumann. Les Années de veuvage" Le
Courrier musical 12/17-18,19 (1.,15.;9. and
1.10.;1909) pp. 517-24, 541-46. ill. Brahms:
pp. 542-46. ill. Describes the nature of Clara
Schumann's relationship with Brahms as seen in
1170C.

1171 M.H. [A.V. Winterfeld] "Schumann und Brahms" Neue Musikzeitung 13/12 (1892) Beilage p. 141. Describes their first
meeting, quotes 3013 in full.

1172 Melkus, Eduard. "Zur Revision unseres Schumann-Bildes"
Osterreichische Musikzeitschrift 15/4 (4.1960) pp. 182-90.
ill., facsim. Presents a new look at Robert Schumann's
last years, as well as the involvement of Joachim and
Brahms with the Schumann family.

1173 Munte, Frank. "Robert und Clara Schumann in Hamburg"
Brahms-Studien Bd. 2 (1977) pp. 7-46. notes. Describes
visits, concert performances, also performances of Schumann's works, 1835-81.

1174 #Quednau, Werner. Die grosse Sinfonie. Roman einer Künstler-
Freundschaft. [Gütersloh:] S. Mohn, [1963]. 204 pp.

1175 #Ronde, H. W. de. "Brahms en Schumann" Symphonia 16/5
(5.1933) pp. 96-97. Discusses Brahms's relationship with
Robert and Clara Schumann, focuses on the "Neue Bahnen"
article. [3013]

1176 Schjelderup-Ebbe, Dag. "Some Recollections by Two Norwegian
Artists of German Musical Life in the 1850's" Studia musicologica norvegica 2 (1976) pp. 123-34. Brahms: pp.
132-33. notes. Excerpts from letters between Gade and
Halfdan Kjerulf, 1851-56, with their comments on the
Schumanns, Joachim and Brahms. Norwegian summary:
p. 134.

1177 Schmitz, Eugen. "Clara Schumann and Johannes Brahms.
Eine chronologische Darstellung" Zeitschrift für Musik
89/17 (9.1922) pp. 368-71. Presents an overview of their
relationship.

1178 #Schoeppl, Grete. "Schumann und Brahms" Gelbe Hefte 15/11
(8.1939) pp. 605-07. Describes Brahms's relationship with
the Schumanns, 1853-Robert Schumann's death.

1179 *Schumann, Clara. Clara Schumann. Johannes Brahms.
Briefe aus den Jahren 1853-1896. Im Auftrage von Marie
Schumann herausgegeben von Berthold Litzmann. 2 Bde.
Leipzig: Breitkopf & Härtel, 1927. mus., notes.
(a) reprint: Hildesheim, New York: Georg Olms Verlag,
1970. Contains 759 letters, 1853-96; includes 11
letters Robert Schumann to Brahms, 1854-55; 2
letters Brahms-Eugenie Schumann, 1896; and 5
letters Brahms-Marie Schumann, 1876.
(c) i) excerpt: Brahms, Johannes. Johannes Brahms
Briefe. Hans Gal, ed. Originalausgabe ([Fischer
Taschenbuch allgemeine Reihe] 2139) Frankfurt/M.:
Fischer Taschenbuch Verlag, 1979. [6], 7-210,
[1] pp. ill., ind., notes. Letters with commentary;
purpose of collection is to show that Brahms was
not a "loner", but capable of significant friendships.
Includes excerpts from 789, 819, 837.d.i., 848,
892, 920, 954, 983, 1009, 1062, 1079, 1122, 1203,
1204, 1215, 1297, 1314.
ii) #excerpt: Brahms, Johannes. Johannes Brahms
in seinen Schriften und Briefen. Richard Litterscheid, ed. (Klassiker der Tonkunst in ihren
Schriften und Briefen [10]) Berlin: Bernhard
Hahnefeld Verlag, 1943. 480 pp. ill., facsim.,
ind., notes. Traces Brahms's life through his
correspondence, includes excerpt from 819, 837,

848, 892, 894, 920, 954, 983, 1009, 1062, 1122,
1203, 1204, 1215, 1297, 1314.
iii) excerpt: "Brahms an Clara Schumann" Vossische
Zeitung (Berlin) Unterhaltungsblatt no. 12 (15.1.
1927) p. [1]. 1 letter, 10.1857.
iv) excerpt: "Brahms an Clara Schumann. Stichproben
aus ihrem Briefwechsel" Frankfurter Zeitung 71/41
(17.1.1927) Morgenblatt p. 1. notes. Contains 4
letters, Brahms to Clara Schumann, 1855-56, 1886;
attempts to prove that they were lovers.
(b) English translation: "New Brahms Letters"
New York Times 76/25,222 (13.2.1927)
Section 7, p. 8.
v) excerpt: see 954.c.iv.
vi)*excerpt: in Einstein, A[lfred]. "Johannes Brahms"
in Einstein, ed. Briefe deutscher Musiker. (Forumbücher) [Amsterdam: Querido-Verlag, 1939].
*Verbilligter Sonderdruck für deutsche Kriegsgefangene
[Unveränderte und ungekürzte Ausgabe]:
(Bücherreihe Neue Welt Bd. 12) 1945 [1938].
2. Auflage: [omits book series] Zürich/Stuttgart:
Pan-Verlag, 1955.
"Johannes Brahms 1833-1897": pp. 280-99. Includes
excerpts from 39, 837, 983, 1009, 1069, 1203, 1204.
vii) *excerpt: see 1009.c.x.
viii) excerpt: see 1164.
ix) excerpt: see 992.
x) excerpt (in Russian translation by V. Tarasovoj):
Levina, V. and V. Tarasovoj. "Iz perepiski
Johannesa Brahmsa s Klaroj i Robertom Schumann"
Sovetskaia muzyka [36]/9 (9.1972) pp. 83-97.
ill., notes. 28 letters, 1853-88.
xi) excerpt: M[ueller]. von Asow, Hedwig. "Weinacht-
liche Musiker-Briefe" Österreichische Musikzeitschrift
12/12 (12.1957) pp. 464-72. Brahms: pp. 465-68.
notes. Discusses musicians and how they celebrate
Christmas; 3 letters: 12.1854, 12.1864, 12.1865.
(a) *reprint: in Reich, Etta, ed. Weihnachtsbriefe
(von Goethe, Claudius, Brahms [u.a.])
Zürich: Verlag der Arche, [1973]. 63
pp. ill.
xii) excerpt: see 53.
xiii) excerpt: see 769.
xiv) excerpt (in French translation by Marguerite and
Jean Alley): Schumann. Une Amitié passionée:
Clara Schumann--Brahms. (Collection musicale)
Paris: Robert Laffont, 1955. 246, [1] pp. Contains 129 letters, 1853-96, with commentary. An
attempt to bring out, through their correspondence,
these two people's feelings for each other.
(b) English translation by Mervyn Savill:

Schumann. A Passionate Friendship.
Clara Schumann and Brahms. London:
Staples Press Limited, 1956. 214 pp.
(a) *reprint: St. Clair Shores, Mich.:
Scholarly Press, n.d.
xv) excerpt: see 81.d.
xvi) excerpt (in English translation by Piero Weiss): in
913. pp. 296, 297, 302-306, 390-91. notes. 4
letters, 1853, 1855 and 1894.
(d) i) see: 1168.
ii) selection and abridgement (in English translation):
Schumann. Letters of Clara Schumann and Johannes
Brahms 1853-1896. Dr. Berthold Litzmann, ed.
2 vols. New York: Longmans, Green and Co.;
London: Edward Arnold & Co., 1927. adds ind.
452 letters, examples from all original correspondence
included.
*also: London: Edward Arnold & Co., 1927.
(a) i) reprint (of New York Edition): New York:
Vienna House, 1973.
ii) *reprint (of New York Edition): (Encore
Music Editions) Westport, Conn.: Hyperion
Press Inc., 1979.
(c) i) excerpt (of ? Edition): in Bonavia,
F[erruccio]. "Johannes Brahms" in Musicians
on Music. Bonavia, ed. London: Routledge & Kegan Paul Ltd., 1956. pp. 199-
202. 1 letter, 1855.
ii) excerpt (of ? Edition): in 979.c.iv. pp.
222-24, 225-26. notes. 2 letters, 1857
and 1894.
iii) excerpt: Morgenstern, Sam. "Johannes
Brahms 1833-1897" in Composers on Music.
An Anthology of Composers' Writings from
Palestrina to Copland. Morgenstern, ed.
New York: Pantheon Books, 1956. pp.
210-13. notes. 3 letters: 1856, 1870,
1877.
(e) report (on London Edition): "Brahms's Letters.
The Quality of Reticence" The Times
(London) Royal Edition no. 44,826 (25.2.
1928) p. 10.
i) report: Bauer, Moritz. "Einige Bemerkungen über die Brahms und den Brahms-
kreis betreffende neue Literatur" Zeitschrift für Musikwissenschaft 10/5 (2.1928)
pp. 300-08. Also reports on 58, 1180,
1223 with short comments on other contemporary studies; includes survey of
lacunae in Brahms research.
ii) report: Diesterweg, Adolf. "Der Briefwechsel zwischen Clara Schumann und

Johannes Brahms" Allgemeine Musikzeitung
54/30/31 (29.7.1927) pp. 855-56. notes.
iii) *report: Jansen, Ferdinand. "Brahms-
Erlebnisse" Schweizerische Musikzeitung
und Sängerblatt 67/1+ (1927).
iv) #report: Manx, Gustav. "Ein Denkmal
der Freundschaft" Velhagen und Klassings
Monatshefte 42/Bd. 1 (1928) pp. 574-76.
v) #report: Roner, Anna. "Clara Schumann
und Johannes Brahms in ihren Briefen"
Schweizerische Musikzeitung und Sängerblatt 67/28-30 (?;?;10.12.1927) pp. ?,
439-40, 453-54.
vi) report: Virneisel, Wilhelm. "Johannes
Brahms e Clara Schumann nell'epistolario
recentement pubblicato" Musica d'oggi
10/12 (12.1928) pp. 437-41. mus., notes.
vii) report: Wetzel, Justus Hermann. "Der
Briefwechsel zwischen Brahms und Clara
Schumann" Zeitschrift für Musik 94/7/8
(7./8.1927) pp. 400-04.
viii) *report: Wetzel, Justus Hermann. "Clara
Schumann und Johannes Brahms" Musikpädagogische Blätter [49]/6 ([8./9.]1927).

1180   Schumann, Eugenie. "Brahms" in Schumann. Erinnerungen.
(Musikalische Volksbücher) Stuttgart: J. Engelhorns
Nachf[olger]., 1925. pp. 228-72. ill., mus., ind.
Describes her relationship with Brahms, 1872-95, including
having Brahms as a piano teacher; includes comments on
Brahms the man.
*issue: 1927.
*[Neu Auflage:] Stuttgart: J. Engelhorns Nachf[olger].,
A. Spemann, [1943]. omits series.
*also: Stuttgart: Engelhornverlag, 1943. pp. 168-203.
*issues: 1944, 1948.
(b)   English translation by Marie Busch: Schumann.
"Brahms" in Schumann. Memoirs of Eugenie Schumann. London: William Heinemann Ltd., 1927.
pp. 141-73. omits ind.
*also: Schumann. The Schumanns and Johannes
Brahms. The Memoirs of Eugenie Schumann. New
York: L. MacVeagh, The Dial Press, 1927.
(a)   i) *reprint (of New York Edition): (Select
Bibliographies. Reprint Series. Facsimile
Editions (?)) Freeport, N.Y.: Books
for Libraries Press, [1970].
ii) *reprint (of New York Edition): (Encore
Music Editions) Westport, Conn.: Hyperion
Press, 1979.
(c)   excerpt (of New York Edition): Garbett, A. S.

"The Musical Home Reading Table" Etude
48/6 (6.1930) p. 447. "A Glimpse of
Brahms".
(c) i) #excerpt (of 1943 Engelhornverlag Auflage): "Musikerzieher von einst: Wie gab Brahms der Tochter
Schumanns Klavier-Unterricht?" Musik im Unterricht 41/4 (1950) p. 116. mus.
ii) excerpt [(of 1943 Engelhornverlag Auflage)]: "Wie
Brahms das Bach-Spielen lehrte..." Musik im Unterricht 41/12 (1950) p. 352-53.
(e) i) report (on 1925 Auflage): see 1179.e.i.
ii) report (on 1925 Auflage): R.Wr. "Neues von
Robert und Klara Schumann und Brahms" Neue
preussische Zeitung (Kreuz-Zeitung) (Berlin)
79/328 (17.7.1926) Abendausgabe p. [9].
iii) report (on 1925 Auflage): Wetzel, Justus Hermann.
"Eugenie Schumanns Erinnerungen" Musikpädagogische
Blätter 48/5 (6./7.1926) pp. 53-54. notes.

1181 #Schumann, Ferdinand. "Brahms als Künstler und Mensch"
Signale für die musikalische Welt 83/9 (4.3.1925) pp. 327-33.
notes. Refutes 730 on question of Brahms and Clara
Schumann having been lovers. Based on 1154, 1182.

1182 _____. "Erinnerungen an Johannes Brahms. 1894, 1895,
1896" Neue Zeitschrift für Musik 82/26-28 (1.-15.;7.;1915)
pp. 225-28, 233-36, 241-43. Brahms in Frankfurt a.M.,
9.1894-5.1896; taken from author's diary. Use with 1154.
(c) i) excerpt: "Johannes Brahms in Frankfurt. Erinnerungen von Ferdinand Schumann" Frankfurter Zeitung
60/201 (22.7.1915) 1. Morgenblatt pp. 1-3 [across
page bottoms]. 1894-95 material only.
ii) excerpt (in English translation by Jacques Mayer):
Schumann. "Brahms and Clara Schumann" Musical
Quarterly 2/4 (10.1916) pp. 507-15. notes.

1183 *Schumann, Robert. Robert Schumanns Briefe: Neue Folge.
2. vermehrte und verbesserte Auflage. F. Gustav Jansen,
ed. Leipzig: Breitkopf & Härtel, 1904.
(c) excerpt (in English translation by Piero Weiss): in
913. pp. 307-08. 1 letter, Schumann to Brahms,
3.1855.
(e) #report: rs. "Schumann und Brahms" Hagener Zeitung
no. 182 (5.8.1905) p. 1. Gives examples of Schumann's comments on Brahms, from letters written
to people other than Brahms.

1184 *Sehlmeyer, G. "Johannes Brahms und Clara Schumann. Zum
100. Geburtstag des Meisters am 7. Mai" Preussische
Volksschullehrerinnenzeitung 26 (1933) pp. 27+.

1185   Spry, Walter. "The Hey Day of Brahms und Schumann"
       Etude 60/6 (6.1942) pp. 368, 416. ill. Discusses Brahms
       and the Schumann family, also Brahms in connection with
       Liszt and Rubinstein; includes a method for teaching
       Brahms's piano works.

1186   Struck, Michael. "Gerüchte um den "späten" Schumann"
       NZ-Neue Zeitschrift für Musik 143/5 (15.5.-15.6.;1982)
       pp. 52-56. notes. Details Schumann's last days; also
       Clara's relationship with Brahms and their suppression of
       Schumann's last work.

1187   *Susskind, Pamela Gertrude. "Clara Wieck Schumann as Pianist
       and Composer: A Study of Her Life and Works" Ph.D.
       diss., Music, University of California (Berkeley), 1977.
       2 vols. mus., fig., notes.

1188   *Ulmann, Hellmuth von. "Ein Meisterwerk wurde nicht begehrt"
       Hamburger Anzeiger (20.7.1956).
       (d) Ulmann. Die veruntreute Handschrift. Robert
            Schumanns Violinkonzert und seine Tragödie.
            Geschichte einer Recherche. (Salzers Volksbücher
            236) Heilbronn: Eugen Salzer Verlag, 1981. 74,
            [1] pp. Describes Brahms's and Joachim's involve-
            ment in the evolution of Schumann's concerto and
            in its consequent suppression.

See also 39A.c.v., 39A.e.iv., 65.d., 154.d., 267, 297, 476, 493,
561, 570, 588, 607, 680, 718, 726, 749, 752, 763, 765.c., 766, 769,
792, 854, 888, 997, 1009.d., 1013, 1060, 1070, 1111, 1205, 1208,
1239, 1252, 1317, 1332, 1339, 1367, 1402, 1447, 1586, 1600, 1616-18,
1620, 1701, 1742, 1762, 1770, 1822, 1826, 1835, 1861, 1896, 1993,
2043, 2064, 2066, 2072, 2076, 2091, 2103, 2109, 2121, 2131, 2160,
2166, 2168, 2169, 2285, 2298, 2350, 2403, 2453, 2454, 2465, 2469.5,
2472, 2490, 2492, 2498, 2505, 2525, 2527, 2585, 2628, 2630, 2678,
2682, 2806, 2872, 2924, 2926, 2957, 2969, 2974, 2998, 3009, 3019.5,
3035, 3043.

--Schwartz, Hermine [fl. 19th century]

See 868.

--Seligmann, A. F. [fl. 19th century]

1189   *Seligmann, A. F. "Brahms-Erinnerungen eines Wiener Musik-
       freundes" Neue freie Presse (Wien) (3.5.1908).

1190   _____. "Der hundertste Geburtstag von Johannes Brahms.
       Letzte Begegnung" Neue freie Presse (Wien) Beilage zur no.

24,658 (7.5.1933) Morgenblatt p. 21. Describes meeting
Brahms in Wien in the early 1880's.

--Senff, Bartholf (1815-1900)

1191   A. K. "Ungedruckte Briefe von Joh[annes]. Brahms" Neue
        Musikzeitung 32/17 (1.6.1911) pp. 350-52. Provides ex-
        cerpts and descriptions of 18 letters, Brahms to Senff,
        1853-78, that were put up for auction. Letters included
        in 848.

1192   O. L. [Otto Lessmann] "Ungedruckte Briefe von Joh[annes].
        Brahms" Allgemeine Musikzeitung 35/41 (9.10.1908) pp. 711-
        12. Report on contents of 18 letters, Brahms to Senff,
        1853-78, sold at auction. Letters included in 848.
        (a)   reprint: "Ungedruckte Briefe von Joh[annes]. Brahms"
               Hamburger Nachrichten 117/719 (11.10.1908) 2.
               Morgenausgabe 1. Beilage p. [3].
        (b)   English translation: Lessmann, Otto. "Some Unpub-
               lished Brahms' Letters" New Music Review and
               Church Music Review 8/86 (1.1909) pp. 72-74.
        (e)   #report: Wilfferodt, Felix. "Ungedruckte Brahms-
               briefe" Leipziger Tageblatt 102/304 (3.11.1908) 3.
               Beilage p. 1.

See also 320.a., 848.

--Shakespeare, William (baptized 1564-1616)

See 2182.

--Sibelius, Jean (1865-1957)

See 1240.

--Sibmacher Zijnen, W.N.F.F. [fl. 19th century]

1193   Sibmacher Zijnen, W.N.F.F. "Brahms-herdenking" Caecilia
        (Utrecht) 79/11 (10.4.1922) pp. 167-69. Presents remini-
        scences about Brahms in Holland, reflects on Brahms's
        music and discusses Bach in relation to Brahms.

--Siebold, Agathe von (1835-1909)

1194   Bonavia, Ferruccio. "Dialogues in Elysium. II: Brahms and
        Agathe von Siebold" Monthly Musical Record 66/774 (2.1936)

pp. 34-35. Fiction about their meeting in Heaven: their feelings for each other, why they didn't marry.
(a) reprint: Bonavia. "Brahms and Agathe von Siebold" in Bonavia. Musicians in Elysium. With Illustrations by Beatrice MacDermott. London: Secker & Warburg, 1949. pp. 63-69. ill.

1195 #"Johannes Brahms Göttinger Liebe" Neue Militärmusikzeitung 15/20 (14.5.1908) pp. 153-54. [across page tops] Report on 954, focuses on relationship of Brahms and von Siebold.

1196 #K. "Johannes Brahms' Göttinger Liebe" Leipziger neueste Nachrichten (5.5.1908) p. [?]. Traces relationship of Brahms and von Siebold as recorded in 954.

1197 Kaufmann, Paul. "Die Jugendliebe von Johannes Brahms. Zum hundertsten Geburtstag von Agathe von Siebold" Die Musik (Berlin) 27/10 (7.1935) pp. 753-54. Describes von Siebold's life and Brahms coming into it, together with the effect she had on him.

1198 Lange, Wilhelm H. "Johannes Brahms' grosse Liebe" Zeitschrift für Musik 102/8 (8.1935) pp. 895-96. Comments on Brahms and Agathe von Siebold.

1199 *Michelmann, Emil. Agathe von Siebold. Johannes Brahms' Jugendliebe. Göttingen: Verlag Dr. Ludwig Häntzschel & Co. G.m.b.H., 1930. 419 pp. ill., facsim., mus., ind. [from 2. Auflage]
2. Auflage: 1930.
Brahms: pp. 139-210. Describes their relationship 1856-60, and her influence on his composing.
*2[2. neubearbeitete und erweiterte Auflage:] Stuttgart: J. G. Cotta'sche Buchhandlung Nachf[olger]., 1930. 407 pp.
(c) excerpt (of 1. Auflage): Michelmann. "Agathe von Siebold. Johannes Brahms' Jugendliebe" Die Musik (Berlin) 22/3 (12.1929) pp. 171-77.
(e) i) report (on 1. Auflage): Ernest, Gustav. "Johannes Brahms' Jugendliebe" Allgemeine Musikzeitung 56/51/52 (20.12.1929) pp. 1257-58. ill., notes.
ii) report (on 1. Auflage): Jacobs, Robert [L.]. "Brahms in Love" Monthly Musical Record 60/713 (1.5.1930) pp. 138-39.
iii) report (on 2. Auflage): x.x.x. "Johannes Brahms und Ungarn. Liebesroman der Agathe von Siebold" Pester Lloyd (Budapest) 78/28 (5.2.1931) Morgenblatt pp. 1-3 [across page bottoms]. Focuses on items that would interest Hungarian readers.

1200 _____. "Agathe von Siebold. Rede bei der Gedenkfeier am hundertsten Geburtstag der Jugendliebe von Johannes

Brahms im Geburtshause am Geismartor 5. Juli 1935" <u>Mitteil-</u>
<u>ungen des Universitätsbundes Göttingen</u> 17/1 (1935) pp.
7-16. Brahms: pp. 9-13. Discusses his relationship with
von Siebold and music he wrote at that time.
(a) *reprint: <u>Agathe von Siebold</u>. Berlin-Schöneberg:
    Verlag der Deutschen Brahms-Gesellschaft m.b.H.;
    Max Hesse, [1935]. 18 pp. ill.

See also 39A.e.iv., 726, 763, 766, 769, 2136, 2526.

--<u>Siloti, Alexander Il'yich</u>

See Ziloti, Alexander Il'yich

--<u>Simrock Family</u>

Clara (?): 1202, 1205.
Friedrich August [Fritz] (1837-1901): 1201, 1203, 1204, 1206, 1207.
P.J. (1792-1868): 1204, 1206.

1201   Altmann, Wilhelm. "Eine vergessene Postkarte von Johannes
        Brahms" <u>N. Simrock Jahrbuch</u> 3 (1930-34) pp. 90-92.
        Brahms to Fritz Simrock, 10.1889.

1202   Bock, Alfred. "Erinnerungen an Clara Simrock und Johannes
        Brahms" <u>Zeitschrift für Musik</u> 98/6 (6.1931) pp. 477-78.
        Relates her anecdotes of Brahms in Berlin and Lichtenthal;
        Brahms with Wegeler in Koblenz; includes comment on
        Brahms the man, and on his religious nature.

1203   *Brahms, Johannes. <u>Johannes Brahms Briefe an Fritz Simrock</u>.
        Max Kalbeck, ed. Bde. 3,4 (Johannes Brahms. Brief-
        wechsel. XI,XII) Berlin: Verlag der Deutschen Brahms-
        Gesellschaft m.b.H., 1919. mus., ind., notes [from 1203.a.]
        (a) reprint: (Brahms-Briefwechsel Band XI,XII) Tutzing:
                Hans Schneider, 1974. 939 letters [total number
                for 1204 and 1203], dates for material in these 2
                volumes: 11.1882-3.1897.
        (c) i) excerpt: see 1179.c.i.
          ii) #excerpt: see 1179.c.ii.
         iii) *excerpt: see 1179.c.vi.
         iv) excerpt (in English translation by Karl Geiringer):
            see 25.b.i. (2nd Edition).
        (e) i) *report: Altmann, Wilhelm. "Brahms' Briefe an
            seinen Verleger Fritz Simrock" <u>Allgemeine Musik-</u>
            <u>zeitung</u> 47 (1920) pp. 541+, 551+, 564+.
         ii) *report: Altmann, [Wilhelm]. "Brahms in seinen
            Briefen" <u>Deutsche Musikzeitung</u> (Berlin) 1/2 (1919?).
        iii) #report: see 1204.e.ii.

1204 *Brahms, Johannes. Johannes Brahms Briefe an P. J. Simrock
und Fritz Simrock. Max Kalbeck, ed. Bde. 1, 2 (Johannes
Brahms. Briefwechsel. IX, X) Berlin: Verlag der
Deutschen Brahms-Gesellschaft m.b.H., 1917. mus., [ind.
in 1203], notes. [from 1204.a.]
    (a) reprint: (Brahms-Briefwechsel Band IX, X) Tutzing:
Hans Schneider 1974. 939 letters [total number
for 1203 and 1204]; letters to P. J., 5.1860-11.1866;
letters to Fritz, 1867-11.1882.
    (c) i) excerpt: see 1179.c.i.
      ii) #excerpt: see 1179.c.ii.
     iii) *excerpt: see 1179.c.vi.
     iv) excerpt (in English translation by Karl Geiringer):
see 25.b.i. (2nd Edition).
    (e) i) report: Altmann, Wilhelm. "Brahms und der Verlag
Simrock" Allgemeine Musikzeitung 44/3 (19.1.1917)
pp. 31-33, 49+. notes.
      ii) report: Krebs, Carl. "Brahms an Simrock" Der
Tag (Berlin) Ausgabe B no. 88 (17.4.1917)
Illustrierter Teil pp. [1-3] [across page bottoms].
     iii) *report: Liebscher, A. "Brahms und der Verlag
Simrock" Dresdner Anzeiger (25.2.1917) (?).

1205 #Kaufmann, Paul. "Brahms-Erinnerungen" Die Musik (Berlin)
25/10 (7.1933) pp. 749-54. ill. Describes Clara Simrock
and Brahms, 1884- : Brahms's comments on marriage,
also his activities when he visited the Simrocks in Berlin.
Also relates secondhand accounts of Brahms and the Schumanns, as well as Deiters and Brahms.

1206 Simrock, Fritz. Johannes Brahms und Fritz Simrock. Weg
einer Freundschaft. Briefe des Verlegers an den Kompon-
isten. Kurt Stephenson, ed. (Veröffentlichungen aus der
Hamburger Staats- und Universitäts-Bibliothek Bd. 6)
Hamburg: Verlag J. J. Augustin, 1961. [4], 261 pp.
mus., ind., notes. 5 letters from P.J., 161 from Fritz
Simrock to Brahms, 10.1862-3.1897.
    (e) i) report: Dreimüller, Karl. "Verlegerbriefe an einen
Komponisten. Fritz Simrock schreibt an Johannes
Brahms" Börsenblatt für den deutschen Buchhandel
Frankfurter Ausgabe 18/45 (5.6.1962) pp. 1121-22.
notes.
    (e) ii) Lucius. "Brahms als Beruf. Die Verlegerbriefe
Fritz Simrocks" NZ-Neue Zeitschrift für Musik
122/12 (12.1961) pp. 534-36. ill.

1207 *Treichel, Christiane. "Johannes Brahms Archiv. Briefe von
Fritz Simrock an Johannes Brahms" Jahresarbeit der Hamburger Bibliotheksschule, 1963.

See also 239, 320, 509, 592, 749, 848.d.ii., 1725, 1943, 2033.

--Sittard, Josef (1846-1903)

See 2590.

--Smetana, Bedřich (1824-1884)

See 688.

--Smyth, Ethel, Dame (1858-1944)

1208 *Smyth, Ethel. "Brahms" in Smyth. Impressions That Reminded.
        Memoirs. 2 vols.
        London: Longmans Green & Co., 1919.
        3rd Edition: 1920. vol. 1, pp. 261-70; also pp. 179-80.
        Describes meeting Brahms in 1878, and further meetings
        in Leipzig at the von Herzogenbergs, and under other cir-
        cumstances.
        *also: New York: Longmans Green, 1919.
        Issue (of New York Edition): 1920.
        *New Edition: London, New York: Longmans Green, 1923.
        *[New Edition:] Introduction by Ernest Newman. New York:
        A. A. Knopf, 1946. xxxv, 509, xi, [2] pp.
        (a) reprint (of 1946 Edition): With New Introduction by
            Ronald Crichton. (Da Capo Press Music Reprint
            Series) New York: Da Capo Press, 1981. 556,
            [32] pp. ill., ind.
        (c) excerpt (of London 1919 Edition): Smyth. "Impressions
            of Brahms" in The Music Lover's Companion. Ger-
            vase Hughes and Herbert van Thal, eds. London:
            Eyre & Spottiswoode, 1971. pp. 151-58. notes.
        (d) *incorporated: Smyth. "Recollections of Brahms" in
            Smyth. Female Pipings in Eden. [London:] P.
            Davies, 1933.
            *[2nd Edition Revised:] P. Davies, Limited, 1934.
            (d) i) Smyth, Ethel, Dame. "Brahms. 'I Knew
                   A Man'" The Listener 15/364 (1.1.1936)
                   pp. 18-19. ill. Describes their relation-
                   ship 1878-84, with comments on Brahms's
                   character and on Brahms and Wagner.
               ii) #_____. "Brahms As I Remember Him"
                   Radio Times 10 (5.5.1933) pp. 266-68.
                   ill.
              iii) _____. (Ethel) "Recollections of
                   Brahms" The Fortnightly N.S. 139/833
                   (5.1936) pp. 548-58.

See also 656, 718.

--Soldat, Marie (1863-1955)

See 546, 765.d.d., 1016.

--Spe, Friedrich von (1591-1635)

See 2175.

--Specht, Richard (1870-1932)

1209 *Specht, Richard. "Ein Gespräch mit Brahms" Die Zeit (Wien)
(7.5.1903). Relates details of meeting Brahms in 1897:
presents Brahms's comments on the music of Bruckner and
Wagner. [from 241]
(a) *reprint: Specht. Tägliche Rundschau (Berlin) Unterhaltungsbeilage no. 107 (8.5.1903).

See also 82, 3176.

--Spee, Friedrich von

See Spe, Friedrich von

--Speidel, Ludwig [fl. 19th century]

See 476.

--Spengel, Julius (1853-1936)

1210 *Braker, Doris. "Neuerwerbungen des Brahms Archiv, Staats-
und Universitätsbibliothek Hamburg" Jahresarbeit der
Hamburger Bibliotheksschule, 1965. Describes letters to
Brahms from Spengel, Joachim, Bülow, Ochs. [from 243]

1211 #[Julius Spengel] "Erinnerungen an Johannes Brahms" Deutsche
Musik-Zeitung (Köln) 37;38 (1937;1938) pp. 95-96; 2-3.
Describes Brahms in various cities, and comments on his
personality.
(d) incorporated: Brahms, Johannes. Johannes Brahms
an Julius Spengel. Unveröffentlichte Briefe aus
den Jahren 1882-1897. Zusammengestellt und erläutert von Annemari Spengel. Hamburg: Gesellschaft der Bücherfreunde, 1959. 45 pp. ill.
Contains letters and reminiscences covering the
period 1859-97.

See also 2698.

--Speyer, Edward [Eduard] (1839-1934)

1212   Speyer, Edward. "Johannes Brahms (1833-1897)" in Speyer.
       My Life and Friends. With a Foreword by H[enry]. C[ope].
       Colles. London: Cobden-Sanderson, 1937. pp. 86-115.
       ill. Describes their meetings and activities 6.1887-1895,
       especially in Frankfurt and Meiningen; also includes 5
       letters, Brahms to Speyer, 1889-94, and an account of an
       attempt to get Brahms to England.

--Spies, Hermine (1857-1893)

1213   #Dorn, Otto. "Hermine Spies und Johannes Brahms" Rheinische
       Musik- und Theaterzeitung (Köln)   6/4 (18.2.1905) pp.
       73-74. notes. Report on 1214; includes a new letter Spies
       to Brahms, 12.1891.

1214   *[Minna Spies] Hermine Spies. Ein Gedenkbuch für ihre Freunde
       von ihrer Schwester. Mit einem Vorwort von Hans Bulthaupt.
       Mit eine Reihe ungedruckter Briefe von J[ohannes].
       Brahms und K[laus]. Groth. Leipzig: G. J. Göschen,
       1905.
       (e) #report: see 1213.

See also 1222, 2587.

--Spitta, Philipp (1841-1894)

1215   *Brahms, Johannes. Johannes Brahms im Briefwechsel mit
       Philipp Spitta. Carl Krebs, ed. ([Johannes Brahms.
       Briefwechsel] XVI. Teil I) Berlin: Verlag der Deutschen
       Brahms-Gesellschaft m.b.H., 1920. 107, [1] pp. mus.,
       ind., notes. [from 1215.a.a.]
       (a) *reprint: Brahms, Johannes Brahms im Briefwechsel
           mit Philipp Spitta und Otto Dessoff. Carl Krebs,
           ed. (Johannes Brahms. Briefwechsel XVI) Berlin:
           Verlag der Deutschen Brahms-Gesellschaft m.b.H.,
           1922. Includes 892.a.
           (a) reprint: Johannes Brahms im Briefwechsel mit
               Philipp Spitta [und Otto Dessoff]. (Brahms-
               Briefwechsel Band XVI) Tutzing: Hans
               Schneider, 1974. Brahms and Spitta, 49
               letters, 11.1868-4.1894: [first paging]
               pp. 7-107, [1].
           (e) report: Altmann, Wilh[elm]. "Der 16.
               Band des Brahmsschen Briefwechsels"
               Allgemeine Musikzeitung 50/34/35, 36/37
               (31.8.;and 14.9.;1923) pp. 545-46, 560-61.
               notes.

(c) i) excerpt: see 1179.c.i.
    ii) #excerpt: see 1179.c.ii.
    iii) excerpt: see 81.d.

1216 Krebs, Carl, ed. "Johannes Brahms und Philipp Spitta. Aus
    einem Briefwechsel" Deutsche Rundschau 35/7 (Bd. 139)
    (4.1909) pp. 15-40. Describes their relationship with
    excerpts from letters. Letters included in 1215.
    (d) Krebs. "Zum Briefwechsel Brahms-Spitta im Aprilheft"
        Deutsche Rundschau 35/8 (Bd. 139) (5.1909) p.
        315. Announces publication in Brahms Briefwechsel
        series and lists corrections for previous article.
    (e) report: "Johannes Brahms und Philipp Spitta" Frank-
        furter Zeitung und Handelsblatt 53/93 (3.4.1909)
        2. Morgenblatt p. 1.

See also 793.

--Spry, Walter (1868-1953)

See 1673.

--Stanford, Sir Charles Villiers, (1852-1924)

1217 *Stanford, Sir Charles Villiers. "A Few Memories of Johannes
    Brahms" The Outlook no. 74 (25.7.1903) pp. 743-46.
    (a) i) reprint: Stanford. Leisure Hour [53/2] (12.1903)
        pp. 123-26. ill., facsim., notes. Describes first
        hearing of Brahms in 1867, their meeting in 1873,
        1877-78, 1880's; includes anecdotes and comments
        about Brahms and England.
      ii) reprint: Stanford, C[harles]. V[illiers]. in Stan-
        ford. Studies and Memories. London: Archibald
        Constable and Co. Ltd., 1908. pp. 107-16. ill.
        (a) *reprint: Portland, Me.: Longwood Press,
        1976.
    (e) *report: "Erinnerungen an Brahms" Neues Wiener
        Journal (28.11.1903).

See also 550.a.d.ii., 553.

--Steinbach, Fritz (1855-1916)

1218 *Berliner Börsen-Courier (1897).
    (a) #reprint: "Der "Berliner Börsen-Courier" theilt zwei
        Briefe ..." Neue freie Presse (Wien) no. 11,927
        (5.11.1897) Morgenblatt p. 8. Contains 2 letters
        from Brahms to Steinbach, 9.1895 and 2.1897.

1219   Huschke, Konrad. "Fritz Steinbach und Joh[annes]. Brahms.
        Erstgenannten zum Gedenken in seinen 20. Todesjahr"
        Allgemeine Musikzeitung 63/41 (9.10.1936) pp. 625-26.
        Presents an overview of Steinbach's life, focusing on his
        relationship with Brahms, 1875-97; includes comments on
        Steinbach as conductor of Brahms's music.

See also 65.d., 1781, 2603, 2798.

--Stocker, S. [fl. 19th century]

See 759.

--Stockhausen, Julius (1826-1906)

1220   d. "[[Johannes Brahms und Julius Stockhausen.]]" Frankfurter
        Zeitung 50/185 (7.7.1906) Abendblatt p. 1. Reports on
        Stockhausen presenting Frankfurt a.M. with bust of Brahms,
        together with comments on their relationship.
        (e) report: "In Frankfurt a.M. ..." Allgemeine Musik-
                zeitung 33/28/29 (13./20.7.1906) p. 475.

1221   *Fries, Hildegaard. "Johannes Brahms in Briefwechsel mit
        Julius Stockhausen" Jahresarbeit der Hamburger Bibliotheks-
        schule, 1966.

1222   Pulver, Jeffrey. "Brahms's Contemporary Singers" Monthly
        Musical Record 64/754 (2.1934) pp. 35-36. Presents an
        overview of 12 people: Stockhausen, Henschel, Spies,
        Joachim, Barbi, Wilt, Viardot-Garcia, Girzick, Kiesekamp,
        Assmann, Krolep, Walter.

1223   Stockhausen, Julius. Julius Stockhausen, der Sänger des
        deutschen Liedes. Nach Dokumenten seiner Zeit dargestellt
        von Julia Wirth-Stockhausen. (Frankfurter Lebensbilder
        10) Frankfurt am Main: Verlag Englert und Schlosser,
        1927. [7], 536, [1] pp. ill., mus., ind., notes. Includes
        48 letters between Brahms and Stockhausen, 1862-96.
        (e) report: see 1179.e.i.

See also 593.

--Stojowski, Sigismond [Zygmunt] (1870-1946)

1224   Stojowski, Sigismond. "Recollections of Brahms" Musical
        Quarterly 19/2 (4.1933) pp. 143-50. Describes meetings
        with Brahms in Wien and Bad Ischl during the 1890's;
        includes comment on the French attitude towards Brahms
        and reports on Tchaikovsky's acquaintance with Brahms.

--Stone, Minna, geb. Völkers [fl. 19th century]

1224.5#Stone, Minna, geb. Völkers. "Johannes Brahms als Lehrer.
      Zum Gedächtnis an seinen 25. Todestag am 3. April.
      Erinnerungen von ..." Hamburger Nachrichten (3.4.1922)
      Abend-Ausgabe. Beilage [Beilage called Zeitschrift für
      Wissenschaft, Literatur und Kunst] p. [?]. Author
      describes being a piano pupil of Brahms; includes comments
      on their relationship 1861-1893.

--Storm, Theodor (1817-1888)

See 2530.

--Strakergan, Maurice [fl. 19th century]

See 2969.

--Strauss, Johann (1825-1899)

1225 #Huschke, Konrad. "Johannes Brahms, Johann Strauss, und
      Hans von Bülow" Neue Musikzeitung 48/8 (1.1927) pp. 157-
      61. Describes the three persons in Baden-Baden, 1872.
      (d) reworked: Huschke. in Huschke. Unsere Tonmeister
          unter Einander. [Bd. 5] Pritzwalk: Verlag von
          Adolf Tienken, 1928. pp. 69-82.

1226 *"Johannes Brahms und Johann Strauss" Gut Ton (Dresden) 26
      (1939) p. 26.

1227 Kalbeck, Max. "Von Schreibtisch und aus den Atelier.
      Erinnerungen an Johann Strauss" Velhagen und Klasings
      Monatshefte 22/1 (9.1907) pp. 129-36. Brahms: pp. 132,
      134. ill. Describes the friendship of Brahms and Strauss.

1228 Lamb, Andrew. "Brahms and Johann Strauss" Musical Times
      116/1592 (10.1975) pp. 869-71. ill., notes. Presents an
      account of their friendship; includes anecdotes.

1229 #Pilcz, Alexander. "Johann Strauss und Johannes Brahms"
      Monatsschrift für Kultur und Politik 2 (3.1937) pp. 42-46.
      Presents Brahms's opinions on Strauss and his music;
      includes comment on Strauss and Hanslick.

1230 Weidemann, Alfred. "Johann Strauss und Brahms" Zeitschrift
      für Musik 95/10 (10.1928) pp. 557-58. Gives Strauss's
      opinion of Brahms's music, as seen in an excerpt from
      Johann Strauss. Johann Strauss schreibt Briefe. Mitgeteilt
      von Adele Strauss. (Berlin: Verlag für Kulturpolitik,

1926); includes information on Tchaikovsky's reference to
Brahms in same letter.
(d) *Weidemann. "Brahms und Johann Strauss" Skizzen
    7/1 (1.1933) p. 10.

1231 #Ziegler, Günther. "Brahms und Johann Strauss" Hallische
      Nachrichten no. 126 (1.6.1929) pp. 2-3 [across page
      bottoms]. Overview of the two men's relationship, focuses
      on Brahms's interest in Strauss's music.

See also 451, 539, 688, 1111, 2142, 2507.

----Strauss, Richard (1864-1949)

1232 #Strauss, Richard. "Persönliche Erinnerungen an Hans v.
      Bülow" Neue freie Presse (Wien) no. 16,288 (25.12.1909)
      Weinachtsbeilage pp. 33-34. Brahms: p. 34. Describes
      seeing Brahms in 1885 and Brahms's comments on Strauss's
      conducting; also discusses Bülow's opinion of Brahms,
      together with the influence of Brahms on Strauss's music.
      (e) #report: L. A. "Richard Strauss über Johannes
          Brahms und Hans v. Bülow" Allgemeine Musikzeitung
          37/2 (14.1.1910) p. 37.

See also 680, 682, 989.e.d., 1836.

--Streicher, Emil (1836-1916)

1233 #Lepel, Felix v. "Sieben unbekannte Briefe von Brahms. Aus
      der Handschrift erstmalig veröffentlicht" Signale für die
      musikalische Welt 94/36/37 (2.9.1936) pp. 509-10. Contains
      7 letters, 1869 and late 1870's, Brahms-Streicher.

--Suk, Joseph (1874-1935)

1234 Suk, Joseph. "Aus meiner Jugend. Wiener Brahms-Erinner-
      ungen" Der Merker (Wien) 2/4 (25.11.1910) pp. 147-50.
      Describes encounters with Brahms in Wien, 1893.

--Tausig Family

Carl (1841-1871)
Seraphine (1841-1931)

1235 *Berliner Tageblatt (1897).
       (a) i) reprint: in 431.c. p. 194. Contains a letter of
              Brahms to Frau Tausig, 1867.

ii) reprint: "(Ein Konzertprogramm von Joh[annes].
Brahms.)" Neue Musikzeitung 18/9 (1897) pp. 115-
16.
(b) English translation: in 969.c. p. 220.

See also 792, 1259.

--Tchaikovsky, Peter Ilyich [Chaikovskii, Petr Il'ich] (1840-1893)

1236   Altmann, Wilh[elm]. "Tschaikowsky als Beurteiler anderer
Komponisten. (Ein Gedenkblatt anlässlich seines Todestages
(6. November 1893))" Zeitschrift der Internationalen
Musikgesellschaft 5/2 (1903) pp. 58-62. Brahms: pp.
61-62. Presents an opinion about Brahms as given in Modest
Chaikovskii. Das Leben Peter Iljitsch Tschaikowsky. 2
Bde. Paul Juon, translator (Moskau-Leipzig: P. Jurgenson,
[1901]-03).

1237   *"Begegnung von Brahms und Tschaikowsky in Hamburg 1889"
in 125 Jahre Philharmonie. Philharmonische Staatsorchester.
Hamburg: Philharmonische Gesellschaft, 1953. Excerpt
from Herbert Weinstock. Tschaikowsky. Reinhold
Scharnke, translator (München: Winkler-Verlag, 1948)
[this is a translation of the 1943 New York: A. A. Knopf,
1943 edition.] [section describes the two composers' feelings
towards each other and their meeting in Hamburg, 3.1889.]
[Annotation supplied from London: Cassell, 1946 edition of
Weinstock.]

1238   "Brahms Night. Tschaikowsky as Critic" The Times (London)
Royal Edition no. 45,914 (29.8.1931) p. 13. Discusses
Tschaikovsky's opinion of Brahms, as well as the merits
of both composers; includes comments on the English interest
in Brahms's music.

1239   *Chaikovskii, Petr Il'ich.
(a) *reprint: in Chaikovskii. P[etr]. I[li'ch]. Chaykov-
sky: muzikal'noye feletoni i zametki. Herman
Laroche [German Augustovich Larosh] redaktor.
Moscow: S. P. Yaklovev, 1898.
(b) German translation by Heinrich Stümcke: Tschaikowsky,
Peter. Musikalische Erinnerungen und Feuilletons.
Berlin: "Harmonie" Verlagsgesellschaft für Literatur
und Kunst, [1899]. v, [1], 125, [2] pp. ind.
"Erinnerungen an Leipzig, Berlin und Hamburg,
1888": pp. 17-71. Brahms: pp. 33-37. Describes
meeting Brahms in Leipzig, 1888.
"Mendelssohn, Schumann und Brahms". pp. 86-89.
Brahms: pp. 88-89. Relates his impressions of
Brahms's music.

(c) i) excerpt: "Peter Tschaikowsky über Johannes Brahms" Neue Zeitschrift für Musik
66/18/19 (Bd. 95) (10.5.1899) pp. 198-99.

ii) excerpt: Tschaikowski, Peter Jijitsch.
"Erinnerungen an Brahms und Grieg"
Bühne und Welt 1/14 (1899) pp. 635-38.
Brahms: pp. 635-36.

(d) English translation: Tschaikovsky, Peter.
"On Brahms" in The Critical Composer.
The Musical Writings of Berlioz, Wagner,
Schumann, Tschaikovsky and Others. Irving
Kolodin, ed. New York: Howell, Soskin
& Co., 1940. pp. 202-05. Excerpts from
2 letters, 1880, 1888; and his diary,
1886, 1888.

1240   *Glinski, M. "Brahms-Ciaikovski-Sibelius" L'Osservatore romano
no. 63 (1952) p. 3.

1241   Huschke, Konrad. "Peter Tschaikowsky über andere grosse
Musiker" Allgemeine Musikzeitung 67/18 (3.5.1940) pp. 138-
39. Brahms: p. 139. Describes their meeting in Leipzig,
1888 and their thoughts on each other's music.

See also 553, 656, 1224, 1230, 1885, 2400, 2480, 2494, 2974, 2993, 3009.

--Tennyson, Alfred, Lord (1809-1892)

1242   Highet, Gilbert. "The Poet and the Musician" in Highet. A
Clerk of Oxenford. Essays on Literature and Life. New
York: Oxford University Press, 1954. pp. 149-55. Traces
parallels in the work, lives, and character of Brahms and
Tennyson.

--Tettinek, Anastasia [fl. 19th century]

See 414.

--Thewman, Samuel [fl. 19th century]

1243   Wollstein, R. H. "Brahms--A Portrait in New Colors" Musical
America 48/36 (22.12.1928) pp. 5, 28-29. ill. Thewman's
reminiscences of Brahms in Wien, 1890, 1896-97; includes
numerous comments on Brahms the man.

--Thibaut (1201-1253)

See 2112.

--Thomas, Theodore (1835-1905)

1244   Thomas, Rose Fay. Memoirs of Theodore Thomas. New York:
        Moffat, Yard and Company, 1911. Brahms: p. 420. Con-
        tains letter Brahms to Thomas, 9.1892.

See also 2967.

--Thomas-San-Galli, Wolfgang Alexander (1874-1918)

1245   Thomas-San-Galli, Wolfgang Alexander, see 225.5

--Tieck, [Johann] Ludwig (1773-1853)

See "Op. 33" in IV.B.1. Specific Works.

--Toscanini, Arturo (1867-1957)

See 1797.

--Tournemire, Charles (1870-1939)

See 1748.

--Tovey, Donald, Sir (1875-1940)

See 2594.

--Truxa, Celestine [fl. 19th century]

1246   Fock, Gustav. "Wie Frau Celestina Truxa mit Johannes Brahms
        bekannt wurde--Brahms als Hausgenosse" Brahms-Studien
        Bd. 3 (1979) pp. 53-57. Includes note by Kurt Hofmann:
        p. 57. Describes Brahms's search for lodgings, 9.1887,
        in Wien; includes comments on Brahms as a lodger, and on
        his last days.

See also 304, 414, 432, 526.

--Turgenev, Ivan (1818-1883)

See 2591.

--Uhland, Ludwig (1787-1862)

See 2530.

--Unger, William [fl. 19th century]

1247 Unger, William. Aus meinem Leben. Wien: Gesellschaft für
      vervielfältigende Kunst, 1929. 205, [1] pp. ind. Brahms:
      p. 21. Describes Brahms in Göttingen, early 1850's.

--Urio, Francesco Antonio (1631 or 1632?-1719 or later)

See 792.

--Verdi, Giuseppe (1813-1901)

See 688, 2494.

--Vetter Family [fl. 19th century]

Ellen
Ferdinand

See 1297.

--Viardot[-Garcia], Pauline (1821-1910)

See 1222.

--Viotti, Giovanni Battista (1755-1824)

See 792, 1021.

--Völckers Family [fl. 19th century]

Betty, Minna

See 48, 297, 375, 1061, 1224.5, 2193, 2343.

--Volkmann, Robert (1815-1883)

1248 *Horovitz-Barnay, Ilka. "Erinnerungen an Robert Volkmann"
      Neue freie Presse (Wien) (26.4.1903).

B.   Brahms and Particular Individuals / 235

1249   Volkmann, Hans. "Johannes Brahms' Beziehungen zu Robert
       Volkmann. Mit bisher ungedruckten Schreiben beiden
       Meister" Die Musik (Berlin) 11/13 (Bd. 43) (4.1912) pp.
       3-13. ill., facsim., notes. Describes their meeting in Pest,
       1869, and Wien, late 1870's; includes letters from Brahms
       to Volkmann (2; 1874, 1882) and from Volkmann to Brahms
       (1; 1874).
       (c) reprint: Volkmann, Robert. Briefe von Robert
                 Volkmann. Hans Volkmann, herausgegeber. Leip-
                 zig: Breitkopf & Härtel, 1917. pp. 402-04. notes.
                 Only includes the letter of Volkmann to Brahms.

--Wagner, Cosima (1837-1930)

See 443.c.ii., 1279.

--Wagner, Friedchen (1831-1917)

See 48, 375, 1061, 2193.

--Wagner, Richard (1813-1883)

1250   *Aldrich, Richard. New York Times.
          (a) reprint: Aldrich. "Wagner and Brahms On Each
                 Other" in Aldrich. Musical Discourse from the New
                 York Times. New York [et al.]: Oxford Univer-
                 sity Press; London: Humphrey Milford, 1928.
                 pp. 85-102. Examines Wagner's writings for ref-
                 erences to Brahms; Brahms's reaction to Wagner,
                 as well as his thoughts on Wagner's music; describes
                 the Tannhäuser manuscript incident; also Wagnerian
                 allusions in Brahms's music.

1251   Altmann, Wilhelm. "Brahms und Wagner" Allgemeine Musikzeit-
       ung 49/13 (31.3.1922) pp. 245-47. notes. Examines con-
       temporary documentation for what Brahms thought of Wagner
       and his music; also discusses their personal acquaintance,
       together with allusions to Wagner's music in that of Brahms.

1252   *Beringer, Karl [or Geiringer, Karl?]. "Musiker untereinander.
       Schumann, Brahms, Wagner" Die Propyläen (München) 18
       (1921) pp. 324+.

1253   Bos, W[illem]. H[endrik]. van den. "Richard Wagner en
       Johannes Brahms" Die Nuwe brandwag 5/3 (8.1933) pp.
       145-49. Compares them as composers.

1254   C.S. [Cesar Saerchinger] "The Wagner-Brahms Year" Musical

Courier 105/15 (Whole no. 2739) (8.10.1932) p. 16. Reviews the Wagner-Brahms controversy and compares them
as composers.

1255 #Einstein, Alfred. "Das neue Jubiläumsjahr. Wagner, Brahms
und wir" Berliner Tageblatt 61/621 (31.12.1932) Abend-
Ausgabe pp. 1-2. Discusses the two men as composers
and as people; includes comments on their historical positions.
(a) reprint: Einstein. "Wagner Brahms und wir. Eine
Neujahrs-Betrachtung" in Einstein. Nationale
und Universale Musik. Neue Essays Zürich/Stutt-
gart: Pan-Verlag, 1958. pp. 110-15.
(d) English translation: Einstein. "Wagner and Brahms"
Living Age 344/4400 (5.1933) pp. 259-62. Discusses the importance of both composers in music
history.

1256 Ernst, Erich. "Brahms und Wagner" Vossische Zeitung
(Berlin) Sonntagsbeilage no. 15 (11.4.1897) [zur Vossische
Zeitung no. 171 (11.4.1897) Morgenausgabe] p. [3]. Discusses the two schools of music and their supporters;
includes comments on Brahms and opera, and Wagner's
thoughts on Brahms.

1257 Fuller, Roy. "Brahms Peruses The Score of Siegfried. The
Photograph by von Eichholz" in Fuller. Buff. London:
Andre Deutsch, 1965. pp. 41-42. Poem that describes
a scene in terms of Brahms's appearance, surroundings,
and wonders at his non-reaction to the 'new music'
(a) reprint in: Fuller. New and Collected Poems 1934-84.
London: Secker & Warburg in association with
London Magazine Editions, 1985. pp. 249-50.
(a) reprint: Fuller. "Brahms Peruses The Score
of 'Siegfried'" in John Bishop, comp.
Music and Sweet Poetry. A Verse Anthology. London: John Baker, 1968.
p. 147.

1258 Gallwitz, S[ophie Dorothea]. "Brahms und Wagner" Die Hilfe
39/11 (3.6.1933) pp. 304-06. Compares the two men as
composers.

1259 Geiringer, Karl. "Wagner and Brahms, with Unpublished
Letters" M. D. Herter Norton, translator. Musical Quarterly
22/2 (4.1936) pp. 178-89. notes. Discusses Wagner's
and Brahms's relationship, 1860-63; also includes letters
to Brahms from Peter Cornelius (2; 1864-65); Carl Tausig
(2; 1867-68); and Mathilde Wesendonck (2; 1867-68).

1260 Graf, Max. "Johannes Brahms" Bühne und Welt 6/3 (1903) pp. 101-05. ill. Contrasts Brahms and Wagner: their lives and their approaches to music.

1261 Grasberger, Franz. "Das Jahr 1868" Österreichische Musikzeitschrift 23/4 (4.1968) pp. 197-200. Compares Wagner, Brahms and Bruckner through works that appeared in this year: Brahms's Op. 45, Bruckner's 1st symphony, and Wagner's Die Meistersinger.

1262 *Grolman, A[dolf]. von. "Zwischen Brahms und Wagner" Krakauer Zeitung Reichsausgabe (17.9.1944).

1263 *Hadow, Sir William Henry. "Wagner, Brahms and Their Contemporaries" Music (London) [=Music, Art and Trade Journal and Talking Machine Review] [30] (1925).

1264 *Herwig, Hans. "Wagner und Brahms" Deutsche Musikzeitung (Köln) 34/4+ (1933).

1265 Howes, Frank. "Brahms versus Wagner" The Listener 73/1878 (25.3.1965) pp. 443-44. ill., notes. Discusses the Brahms-Wagner controversy from an aesthetic point of view; includes comments on Hanslick and Wagner.

1266 Huschke, Konrad. Unsere Tonmeister unter Einander. [Bd. 2]. Pritzwalk: Verlag von Adolf Tienken, 1928. 97, [3] pp. ill., ind. "Richard Wagner und Johannes Brahms" discusses their lives, relationship to, and thoughts on each other.
　　　(d) i) Huschke. "Brahms über Wagner" Allgemeine Musikzeitung 62/10 (8.3.1935) pp. 148-50. Describes Brahms's opinions of Wagner.
　　　　　ii) reworked: Huschke. "Wagner und Brahms" in 858.d.i. pp. 132-65. ill. only.

1267 #Istel, Edgar. "Wagner und Brahms" Münchner neueste Nachrichten (11., 12.;9.;1909) pp. 2;2. Describes their relationship and what Wagner wrote about Brahms; includes 4 letters Wagner-Brahms, Brahms-Wagner, 6.1875.

1268 *Kalbeck, Max. "Brahms und Wagner" Neues Wiener Tagblatt (7.4.1901).

1269 *Kalcik. "Richard Wagner und Brahms" Musikleben (Wien) [3]/5 (1933) p. 3.

1270 *Kokkonen, Joonas. "Brahmsin suhteesta Wagneriin" Uusi musiikkilehti [2]/5 (1955).

1271 *Kretschmer, Emanuel. "Brahms und Wagner" Das Schwalbennest (Erfurt) 9/8 (1927).

1272 #Latzko, Ernst. "Wagner und Brahms in persönlichem Verkehr
und Briefwechsel" Der Auftakt 13/7-8 ([7.-8.] 1933) pp.
91-97. Describes their personal relationship, focusing on
the Tannhäuser manuscript incident.

1273 Leinburg, Mathilde v. "Wagnerianer und Brahmsianer" Der
Türmer 13/1 (10.1910) pp. 151-56. Describes the history
of the Brahms-Wagner camps and the relationship of the
two composers; includes comment on Brahms's historical
position and on his views concerning Wagner.

1274 #Pilcz, Alexander. "Brahms über Wagner, Wagner über Brahms"
Die Kultur 11/3 (1910) pp. 285-95. notes. Presents a
list of their written comments about each other, with comparative remarks on where and when the comments were
written, and on the two composers' writing styles.

1275 *Pretzsch, Paul. "R[ichard]. Wagner und Johannes Brahms"
Chemnitzer Tageblatt no. 111 (1912).

1276 Schmitz, Eugen. "Brahms und Wagner" Hochland 9/8 (5.1912)
pp. 220-27. notes. Traces the history of the Brahms-
Wagner camps; includes comments on what each composer
thought of the other's music, and describes the influence
that Wagner's music had on Brahms's.

1277 #Segnitz, Eugen. "Beethoven, Wagner und Brahms" Rheinische
Musik- und Theaterzeitung (Köln) 17/11/12 (1916) pp. 80-81.
Discusses their common characteristics as composers, together with their historical positions; includes comments
on the qualities of each composer's music.

1278 Taylor, Deems. "Two Masters" in Taylor. Of Men and Music.
New York: Simon & Schuster, 1937. pp. 14-15. ind.
Compares Wagner and Brahms as composers.
*issues: 1938-45.

1279 *Wagner, Cosima. "Briefliche Ausserung über Joh[annes].
Brahms an Hans Richter" (7.4.1897).
(e) report: "Frau Cosima Wagner hat folgendes seltsame,
fast komische schreiben ..." Neue Zeitschrift für
Musik 64/17 (Bd. 93) (28.4.1897) p. 202. Transcribes a letter from Cosima Wagner to Richter,
7.4.1897, which contains her reaction to the news
of Brahms's death.

1280 *Wagner, Richard. Richard Wagners Briefe in Originalausgaben.
2. Folge. Bd. XVII. An Freunde und Zeitgenossen. Erich
Kloss, ed. Leipzig: Breitkopf & Härtel, 1912. Contains
2 letters, Wagner to Brahms, 6,1875. [from Library of
Congress. Music Division]

(a) i) reprint: see 39B. Also includes 2 letters, Brahms
to Wagner, 6.1875.

ii) reprint: see 81.d. Also includes 2 letters, Brahms
to Wagner, 6.1875.

iii) reprint: see 1283. Also includes 2 letters, Brahms
to Wagner, 6.1875.

1281 Weidemann, Alfred. "Brahms und Wagner" Neue Musikzeitung
43/13-15 (6. and 20.,4.; and 4.5.;1922) pp. 200-05, 217-20,
235-39. ill., mus., notes. Describes their relationship
1860- ; the Tannhäuser manuscript episode; Brahms's
comments on Wagner's musical ideas; examples of the influence of Wagner's music on Brahms's work.

1282 *_____. (A.) "Brahms und Wagner" Skizzen [7]/4 (1933).

1283 Weismann, W. "Wagner und Brahms. Ein beinahe tragikomischer Briefwechsel" Der Türmer 33/8 (7/8) (Bd. 2) (5.5.
1931) pp. 121-25. Describes the two men's thoughts concerning each other and discusses the Tannhäuser manuscript
episode; includes 4 letters Brahms-Wagner, 6.1875.

See also 39.e.ii., 39B.c., 60, 111, 114, 116, 147, 149, 154.d., 158,
161, 201, 218, 224, 235, 405, 494, 587, 605, 618.a.e., 635, 648,
680, 688, 792, 825, 968, 989.e., 1024, 1054, 1072, 1097, 1208.d.d.i.,
1209, 1413, 1823, 1896, 2131, 2330, 2387, 2397.5, 2403.a., 2408,
2446, 2461, 2468.5, 2469.5, 2487, 2494, 2498, 2507, 2552, 2584, 2586,
2606, 2630, 2643, 2655, 2657, 2764, 2786, 2806, 2808, 2826, 2832,
2838, 2843, 2862, 2871, 2872, 2899, 2910, 2918, 2919, 2921, 2968,
2975, 2993, 2997, 3003, 3009, 3019.5, 3047.
See also "Hans von Bülow" and "Cosima Wagner" in III.B.2.

--Wallaschek, Richard (1860-1917)

1284 *Wallaschek, Richard. "Erinnerungen an Johannes Brahms" Die
Zeit [Wochenschrift] (Wien) [4] (16.6.1898) pp. 42+.

--Wallisch, Frau [fl. 19th century]

1285 Wallisch, Friedrich. "Symphonie in e-moll" Deutsche Rundschau 89/9 (9.1963) pp. 63-66. Describes how Brahms
wrote Wallisch's mother a letter, telling her that she was
the inspiration for Op. 98, and requesting a visit; also
includes an account of Brahms's last appearance at a public
concert in Wien.

--Wallnöfer, Adolf (1854-1946)

1286 Müller, Erich H. "Der erste Brahms-Abend in Wien" N.

Simrock Jahrbuch 3 (1930-34) pp. 86-89. ill., notes.
Describes a concert given 24.4.1880 by Wallnöfer, its
preparation and aftermath; includes comments on Brahms
and Wallnöfer, together with 1 letter.

--Walter, Gustav (1834-1910)

See 1222.

--Walther, Johann (1684-1748)

See 1761.

--Wasielewski, Wilhelm Joseph von (1822-1896)

1287   Wasielewski, Wilhelm Joseph von. "Briefe von und an Johannes
        Brahms (1833-1897)" in Wasielewski. Wilhelm Joseph von
        Wasielewski (1822-1896) im Spiegel seiner Korrespondenz.
        Renate Federhofer-Königs, ed. (Mainzer Studien zur
        Musikwissenschaft Bd. 7) Tutzing: Hans Schneider, 1975.
        pp. 163-78. ind., notes. Traces their relationship, with
        14 letters, 11.1879-12.1882.

--Weber, Carl Maria von (1786-1826)

See 2064, 2330, 2630.

--Webern, Anton (1883-1945)

See 1679.

--Wegeler [fl. 19th century]

See 579.d., 1202.

--Weigl, Karl (1881-1949)

See 1320.

--Weingartner, Felix (1863-1942)

1288   *Weingartner, Felix. Neues Wiener Journal (1919-21)
            (a) *reprint: in Weingartner. Lebenserinnerungen. Wien,

Leipzig: Wiener literarische Anstalt A.G., 1923.
2, [2], 466, [1] pp.
*also: Wien: [Wila-Verlag K. Fiedler], 1923. 467 pp.
#also: 2 Bde. Zürich und Leipzig: Orell Füssli Verlag,
1928-29. "Nach München": Bd. 2, pp. 60-93.
[only a few scattered references in Bd. 1] Brahms:
pp. 62-70. facsim. Describes their meeting in Berlin
and Wien, 1896; includes 1 letter Brahms to Weingartner.
Bd. 1: *2., umgearbeitete Auflage: ?.
    (c) excerpt (of 1928-29 Auflage in English transla-
        tion by Robert Lorenz): "Extracts from
        the Reminiscences of Felix Weingartner.
        III--Some Brahms Memories" Musical Times
        74/1083 (5.1933) pp. 422-24.
    (d) i) *Weingartner. "Begegnung mit Brahms"
        München-Augsburger Abendzeitung (11.4.
        1929).
     ii) *abridgement (of ? Auflage in English
        translation by Marguerite Wolff): Wein-
        gartner. Buffets and Rewards. A Mu-
        sician's Reminiscences. London: Hutchin-
        son & Co., [1937]. [4], 13-383. ill.,
        facsim.

See also 2594, 2606.

--Weis, Karel (1862-1944)

See 39C.c.i.

--Weiss, Joseph [fl. 19th century]

1289 *Weiss, Jos[eph]. "Erinnerungen an Liszt, Rubinstein, Brahms,
    Mahler u.a." Der Energetiker. Blätter für musikalische
    Hand- und Willenskultur (Berlin) 3/5/6+ (1922).

--Weiss, Karel

See Weis, Karel

--Wendt, Gustav [fl. 19th century]

1290 *Wendt, Gustav. "Lebenserinnerungen eines Schulmannes"
    Deutsche Militärmusikerzeitung [32] (28.10.1910).

--Wenzel, Anna [fl. 19th century]

1291 *Decsey, E[rnst]. Neues Wiener Tagblatt (11.2.1930).
      (e) #report: "Brahms und das Steirerlied" Deutsche
            Volkslied 32 (1930) p. 85. Relates how Brahms met
            Wenzel in 1885, describes their friendship and
            how Brahms encouraged her to become a professional
            singer.

--Wesendonck, Mathilde (1828-1902)

1292 Brahms, Johannes. Johannes Brahms und Mathilde Wesendonck.
      Ein Briefwechsel. [Erich H. Müller von Asow, ed.] Wien:
      I. Luckmann Verlag, 1943. 128 pp. ill., facsim., ind.,
      notes. Describes their relationship 1865-97; includes 10
      letters, 1867-69, 1873-74.
      (d) *Maag, Otto. National-Zeitung (Basel) (9.2.1960).

1293 *Huschke, Konrad. "Asyl der Komponisten. Die Freundschaft
      zwischen Mathilde Wesendonck und Johannes Brahms" Die
      Wochenpost. Zeitfragen, Kultur, Kunst, Unterhaltung 3/49
      (1948) p. 4.

See also 1259.

--Wichmann, Hermann (1824-1905)

1294 *Wichmann, H[ermann]. "Alte Typen im neuen Rom". (?)
      (c) excerpt: Wichmann. "Noch ein Beitrag zur Charak-
            teristik von Brahms" Allgemeine Musikzeitung 24/18
            (30.4.1897) pp. 270-71. Relates anecdotes of
            Brahms in Rome.
      (e) report: m. "Herr H. Wichmann, ein intimer
            Freund ..." Neue Musikzeitung 18/18 (1897)
            p. 226.

1295 *Wichmann, Hermann. Frohes und Ernstes aus meinem Leben.
      Leipzig: Rom, Loescher [C.G. Röder], 1898. iv, 271, 64
      pp.

--Widmann, Josef Viktor (1842-1911)

1296 *Der Bund (Bern) (5.7.1932).

1297 *Brahms, Johannes. Johannes Brahms Briefe an Joseph Viktor
      Widmann, Ellen und Ferdinand Vetter, Adolf Schubring.
      Max Kalbeck, ed. (Johannes Brahms. Briefwechsel. VIII)
      Berlin: Verlag der Deutschen Brahms-Gesellschaft m.b.H.,

1915. 244, [1] pp. ill., facsim., ind., notes.
(a) reprint: (Brahms-Briefwechsel Band VIII) Tutzing:
Hans Schneider, 1974. Widmann: 138 letters,
11.1877-12.1896; Vetter Family: 6 letters, 7.1886-
9.1896; Schubring: 34 letters, 1.1856-3.1893.
(c) i) excerpt: see 1179.c.i.
ii) #excerpt: see 1179.c.ii.
iii) excerpt (in English translation by Karl Geiringer):
see 25.b.i. (2nd Edition).
(e) report: Kalisch, Alfred. "Some New Brahms Letters"
Musical Times 57/879 (1.5.1916) p. 244.

1298　*Denhoff, E. "Eine Morgenmusik bei J[osef]. V[iktor].
Widmann. Zu Brahms 30. Todestag" Der Bund (Bern)
(1.4.1927).

1299　Heuberger, Richard. "Briefe Joseph Victor Widmanns" Der
Merker (Wien) 3/2 (1.1912) pp. 59-63. Presents excerpts
from Widmann's correspondence to the author, 15 letters,
1885-97, concerning Brahms and his activities.

1300　*"Joseph Victor Widmann und Johannes Brahms" Schweizer
Musiker-Revue 18/10 (1942) p. 2.

1301　*Otto, Eberhard. "Johannes Brahms und J[osef]. V[iktor].
Widmann" Der Bund (Bern) (4.8.1974).

1302　Widmann, J[osef]. V[iktor]. "Erinnerungen an Johannes
Brahms: I. Erste Begegnungen; II. Eine Oper; III. Die
Sommer in Thun (1886, 1887 und 1888); IV. Die letzten
Jahre" Deutsche Rundschau 24/1,2 (Bd. 93) (10.,11.;1897)
pp. 120-41, 210-27. notes.
I.: pp. 120-27.
Describes their relationship, 1865-72, and Brahms's visits to
Switzerland.
II.: pp. 127-33.
Reports on Brahm's attempts at writing opera; why he
never married.
III.: pp. 133-41, 210-14.
Describes Brahm's activities.
IV.: pp. 215-27.
Describes Brahms and his activities, 12.1889-4.1897.
(a) reprint: in 618.a.
(e) i) report: "J[osef]. V[iktor]. Widmann über
Johannes Brahms" Neue Musikzeitung 18/20 (15.10.
1897) pp. 248-49.
ii) report: "J[osef]. V[iktor]. Widmann über Jo-
hannes Brahms" Neue Musikzeitung 18/23 (1897)
pp. 286-87.

1303　*Widmann, J[osef]. V[iktor]. "42 millionen Deutsche auf der
Strecke" Der Bund (Bern) (19.8.1888).

See also 617, 618, 716, 755, 868, 2586, 2589.

--Wilbrandt, Adolf (1837-1911)

1304 *Wilbrandt, Adolf. "Johannes Brahms--Wiener Erinnerungen"
     Neue freie Presse (Wien) no. 14,391 (1904).

--Wilt, Marie (1833-1891)

See 1222.

--Wimpffen, Graf [fl. 19th century]

See 887.

--Winkel, Fritz [fl. 19th century]

1305 *Winkel, Fritz. Klangwelt unter der Lupe. Berlin: n.p.,
     1952.

--Winkler, Julius [fl. 19th century]

1306 *Moser, Karl. "Erlebnisse mit Brahms" Neues Wiener Journal
     (5.2.1933).
     (d) condensed: Moser. Die Musik (Berlin) 25/8 (5.1933)
              p. 610. Contains anecdotes from 1886.

--Witte, Georg Hendrik (1843-1929)

1307 #Witte, C. H. [Georg Hendrik Witte] "Erinnerungen an Johannes
     Brahms. Zur 25. Wiederkehr seines Todestages am 3.
     April. I.II." Rheinisch-Westfälische Zeitung (Essen)
     185/290 [289], 295 (2.,4.;4.;1922) pp. [?]; [?]. Describes
     their contact, which was mainly by correspondence, 1867-
     1887; includes 6 letters, Brahms to Witte, 1867-1884, to-
     gether with descriptions of visits by Brahms to Essen,
     1884, 1885.
     (d) *Witte. "Erinnerungen an Johannes Brahms" Hellweg
              2 (1924) p. 268.

--Wittgenstein Family

Ludwig (1889-1951)
Paul (1887-1961)

1308 Flindell, E. Fred. "Ursprung und Geschichte der Sammlung
      Wittgenstein im 19. Jahrhundert" Die Musikforschung 22/3
      (7.-9.1969) pp. 298-314. ill., facsim., fig., notes.
      "Brahms und sein Kreis": pp. 305-07. Describes his
      friendship with the Wittgensteins, 1854- and Brahms
      commemorative activities on the part of the family; also
      includes a list of the Wittgenstein collection's contents,
      including holdings of 59 items of Brahmsiana [pp. 310-14].

--Wittman, Karl Friedrich [fl. 19th century]

1309 *W. [Karl Friedrich Wittmann] "Stammtischabende. Erinnerung
      an Brahms" Neue freie Presse (Wien) (10.5.1908).

--Wolf, Hugo (1860-1903)

1310 Ehrmann, Alfred von. "Johannes Brahms and Hugo Wolf:
      A Biographical Parallel" Barbara Lattimer, translator.
      Musical Quarterly 29/4 (10.1943) pp. 458-65. Discusses
      their lives, their personalities and their work as composers.

1311 Grasberger, Franz. "Johannes Brahms und Hugo Wolf"
      Osterreichische Musikzeitschrift 15/2 (2.1960) pp. 67-69.
      Describes their first meeting, and gives their opinions of
      each other personally and professionally, as seen in their
      writings.

See also 858, 989.e.d., 2043, 2054, 2064, 2066, 2082, 2108, 2541,
2543, 2561, 2630, 2642, 2871, 2974, 2983, 2995, 3009, 3048, 3062.
See also "Op. 19" in IV.B.1. Specific Works.

--Wolff Family

Hermann (1845-1902): 1313

1311.5*Rembert, K. "Die Krefelder Familie Wolff, ein Beitrag zur
      Musikgeschichte unserer Stadt und zur Verehungslehre"
      Die Heimat (Krefeld) 12/3/4 (1933) pp. 140-59. Brahms:
      pp. 150-52. Discusses Brahms in context of his friendship
      with Wolff family and various other Krefeld families. [from
      Library of Congress]

1312 Stargardt-Wolff, Edith. "Zusammensein mit Johannes Brahms"
      in Stargardt-Wolff. Wegbereiter grosser Meister. Unter
      Verwendung von Tagebuchblättern, Briefen und vielen
      persönlichen Erinnerungen von Hermann und Louise Wolff,
      den Gründern der ersten Konzertdirektion, 1880-1935.
      Berlin, Wiesbaden: Ed. Gote & B. Bock, 1954. pp. 140-44.

ind. Relates Louise Wolff's meetings with Brahms in 1891, 1895 as she recorded in her diary, together with 1 letter Louise Wolff to Brahms, 1895.

1313 Wolf, Werner, ed. "Der verschmähte Taktstock. Unveröffentliche Brahms-Briefe" Vossische Zeitung (Berlin) Unterhaltungsblatt no. 125 (7.5.1933) pp. [1-2]. Contains 7 letters, Brahms to Hermann Wolff, 1897.

--Wordsworth, William (1770-1850)

See 2934.

--Wüllner Family

Franz (1832-1902): 1314, 1316.
Ludwig (?-1939): 1315.

1314 *Brahms, Johannes. Brahms im Briefwechsel mit Franz Wüllner. Ernst Wolff, ed. (Johannes Brahms. Briefwechsel. XV) Berlin: Verlag der Deutschen Brahms-Gesellschaft m.b.H., 1922. 194 pp. notes.
(a) reprint: (Brahms-Briefwechsel Band XV) Tutzing: Hans Schneider, 1974. 141 letters, 9.1853-10.1896. Includes: Wüllner. "Zu Johannes Brahms' Gedächtnis. Worte der Erinnerung": pp. 186-91. In memoriam speech given in Köln.
(c) i) excerpt: in 1179.c.i.
   ii) #excerpt: in 1179.c.ii.
   iii) excerpt (in English translation by Karl Geiringer): see 25.b.i. (2. Edition)
(e) #report: Altmann, Wilh[elm]. "Brahms und Franz Wüllner" Allgemeine Musikzeitung 50/2 (12.1.1923) pp. 92-94. Includes comments on Brahms the man.

1315 "Der verstorbene Sänger und Rezitator Ludwig Wüllner ..." Allgemeine Musikzeitung 66/46 (17.11.1939) p. 618. Describes Wüllner's Nachlass and its Brahmsiana as transferred to the Preussische Staatsbibliothek.

1316 Wüllner, Josepha. "Johannes Brahms in seiner Lebensfreundschaft mit Franz Wüllner" Die Musik (Berlin) 34/6 (5.1942) pp. 192-97. notes. Describes Brahms's life, as well as his relationship with Wüllner, 1852-

See also 476, 534, 1348.

--Wurm, Mary (1860-1938)

1317 Wurm, Mary. "Playing Duets with Brahms" Etude 51/7 (7.1933)

p. 441. ill. Describes an impromptu performance of Op.
52 at Clara Schumann's residence in Frankfurt, 1881,
together with Clara's reaction.

See also 2139.

--Ysäye, Eugène (1858-1931)

See 1514.

--Z.-F., L. [fl. 19th century]

1318   A. S. "Erinnerungen an Brahms" Neue Zürcher Zeitung
133/28 (28.1.1912) 3. Blatt (No. 125) p. [1]. Relates
L.Z.-F.'s account of Brahms's stay with her family at
Nidelbad-Rüschlikon, Summer 1874.
(a) *reprint: "Brahms als Hausgenosse" Neues Wiener
Journal (2.2.1912).
(e) report: "Erinnerungen an Brahms ..." Neue Zeitschrift
für Musik 79/7 (15.2.1912) p. 86.

--Zemlinsky, Alexander von (1871-1942)

1319   *"Brahms und Zemlinszky [Zemlinsky]" Münchner neueste Nachrichten (28.5.1909).
(a) *reprint: [same title] Neues Wiener Tagblatt (1909).

1320   Zemlinsky, Alexander v. and Karl Weigl. "Brahms und die
neuere Generation. Persönliche Erinnerungen" Musikblätter des Anbruch (4/5.-6.;3.1922) pp. 69-70. Describes
personal meetings, and comments on Brahms the composer.
(e) report: see 3180.e.

--Ziloti, Alexander Il'yich (1863-1945)

See 3037.

--Zöllner, Heinrich (1854-1941)

1321   Zöllner, Heinrich. "Eine Erinnerung an Johannes Brahms"
Zeitschrift für Musik 89/9/10 (5.1922) p. 226. Relates an
incident in Köln, 1886/87 where Brahms used Zöllner as
an intermediary to a lady.

--Zuccalmaglio, Anton Wilhelm Florentin von (1803-1869)

See 2177, 2573.

PART IV. WORKS

Contains historical background and analytical discussions for the works. To facilitate the placing of references in this section, it is organized according to instrumental genres. Within each section provision has been made for subsections to deal with general remarks, or to focus on individual opus numbers. The following chart shows the principal genres used and their relation to each other:

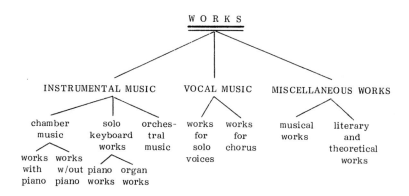

For example, an article on one of the string quartets would be located in IV.A.1.b., "Chamber Music," "Works without Piano," "Specific Works," under the respective opus number. An article on all the piano and string quartets would be located in IV.A.1., "Chamber Music," "General." An article on one of the string quartets and a piano sonata would be located in IV.A., "Instrumental Music," "General." An article on all the chamber music, two of the symphonies, and the Triumphlied would file in IV. "Works," "General."

Citations at the "General" level within each genre are for the most part cross-referenced to particular opus numbers at the "Specific" level. Only when the citation is a broad overview of Brahms's works is cross-referencing not provided.

Identification for works without opus number is given in accordance with two Brahms bibliographies: Kurt Hofmann, Die

Erstdrucke der Werke von Johannes Brahms: Bibliographie mit Wieder-
gabe von 209 Titelblättern. Musikbibliographische Arbeiten 2. (Tutzing:
Hans Schneider, 1975): and Margit L. McCorkle, Johannes Brahms:
Thematisch-Bibliographisches Werkverzeichnis. Herausgegeben nach
gemeinsamen Vorarbeiten mit Donald M. McCorkle † (München: G. Henle
Verlag, 1984).

WORKS--GENERAL

1322 Adler, Guido. "Weiheblatt zum 100. Geburtstag des Johannes
Brahms: Wirken, Wesen und Stellung. Mitgliedes unserer
leitenden Kommission" Studien zur Musikwissenschaft (Wien) 20
(1933) pp. 6-27. ill., mus., notes. Defines Brahms's personality
as a man and composer with a summation of his historical position.
Includes summary of works, surveys their quantity and when
they appeared; also discusses Brahms's style
    (a) *reprint: Adler. Johannes Brahms. Wirken, Wesen und
        Stellung. Gedenkblatt zum 100. Geburtstag ge-
        widmet ihrem Mitgliede von der leitenden Kommission
        der "Denkmäler der Tonkunst in Österreich".
        Wien: [Universal Edition, 1933.] 21 pp.
    (b) English translation by W. Oliver Strunk: Adler.
        "Johannes Brahms. His Achievement, His Personality
        and His Position" Musical Quarterly 19/2 (4.1933)
        pp. 113-42. omits ill., adds fig.
    (c) excerpt: Adler. "The Personality of Brahms"
        in 758. pp. 344-49.

1323 Altmann, Wilhelm. "Geschichtliches und Bibliographisches
über die zur Aufführung kommenden Werke" in 2667. pp.
20-58. facsim. Descriptive programme notes.

1324 Anderson, William Robert. Introduction to the Music of Brahms.
(Introduction to the Music of [Masters]) London: D.
Dobson, [1949]. 78, [6] pp. mus., ind. Gives an over-
view of Brahms's works in the context of his life.

1325 Badura-Skoda, Paul. "Eine Brahms-Kadenz zu Mozarts d-Moll
Konzert KV 466 und andere unbekannte Musikerhandschriften
aus der Leipziger Universitätsbibliothek" Das Orchester
(Mainz) 28/11 ([11.] 1980) pp. 887-90. facsim., mus.,
notes. Provides historical background and manuscript
descriptions; includes Op. 92, no. 1 and cadenza to 1st
movement, Mozart's KV 466 [McCorkle Anhang IV, nr. 4]
    (d) "leicht veränderter Form": Badura-Skoda. "Eine
        ungedruckte Brahms-Kadenz zu Mozarts d-moll-
        Konzert KV 466" Österreichische Musikzeitschrift
        35/3 (3.1980) pp. 153-56. omits facsim.

1326 *Barth, Richard. Johannes Brahms und seine Musik. Hamburg:
      Otto Meissners Verlag, 1904. 61 pp.
      #2. Auflage: 1904. Describes the state of music when Brahms
      first began to compose; includes descriptive analysis of
      his works.

1327 Br., v. Deutsche Musikzeitung (Wien) 1/12 (17.3.1860) pp.
      92-94. Brahms: pp. 93-94. Reviews of Opp. 6, 10.

1328 *Bruyck, Karl Debrois van. "Federstiche [Federstriche?]
      zur Charakterisierung des gegenwärtigen Standes der Tonkunst
      in einigen ihrer renomierten [renommierten?] Vertreter"
      Wiener Zeitung (25.9.1857). Reviews Opp. 1-10. [from
      241]

1329 Burkhardt, Max. Johannes Brahms, Ein Führer durch seine
      Werke mit einer einleitenden Biographie, zahlreichen Noten-
      beispielen sowie einer Anzahl Illustrationen u[nd]. einem
      Überblick über die Brahmsliteratur. Berlin: Globus Verlag
      G.m.b.H., [1912]. 223 pp. ill., facsim., mus., ind.,
      notes. Focuses on descriptive analysis of Brahms's music;
      includes comments on his historical position.
      (c) #excerpt (in Spanish translation): Burkhart, Max.
          "La Posición de J. Brahms en la historia de la
          música" Ars. Revista de arte 17/79 (1957) pp.
          [130-35]. Omits mus., ind., notes.

1330 Cherbuliez, Antoine Elisée, see 107.5.

1331 Colles, H[enry]. C[ope]. Brahms. (The Music of the Masters)
      London: John Lane, The Bodley Head, 1908. x, 168 pp.
      ill., mus., fig., notes. Descriptive analysis of the works,
      with comment on Brahms's historical position.
      *also: New York: Brentano's, 1908.
      *2nd Edition (of London Edition): J. Lane, 1920.
      (a) *reprint (of New York Edition): [Edited by Wakeling
          Dry] New York: AMS Press, 1978.
      (b) German translation by A. W. Sturm (of London Edition):
          Colles. Johannes Brahms' Werke. Bonn: Carl
          Georgi Universitäts-Buchdruckerei und Verlag
          G.m.b.H., 1913. vii, [1], 129 pp. ill., mus., ind.
          also: Leipzig: Breitkopf & Härtel, [191-?].

1332 DAS. [Adolf Schubring] "Schumanniana Nr. 8. Die Schu-
      mann'sche Schule. IV. Johannes Brahms" Neue Zeitschrift
      für Musik Bd. 56/12-16 (21.3.-18.4.; 1862) pp. 93-96,
      101-04, 109-12, 117-19, 125-28. mus., notes. Introduction
      to Brahms and his music, including analysis and evaluation
      of Opp. 1-18, together with comments on Brahms's relation-
      ship with Schumann.
      (d) comment: "Der Verfasser des von uns jüngst ausge-
          zeigten Artikels ..." Deutsche Musikzeitung (Wien)

3/18 (3.5.1862) p. 142. Remarks that Brahms's
"new" harmonic style is nothing more than chromaticism.

1333 Dickinson, A. E. F. "Brahms the Musical Architect" Music
Teacher 12/4 (M.S. Series 26/7) (4.1933) pp. 181, 183,
185. ill., mus. Discusses Brahms's style, together with
an overview of his works.

1334 *Dömpke, Gustav. "Brahms' D-dur Symphonie und Lieder"
Wiener allgemeine Zeitung (27.3.1885).

1335 _____. (Doempke, G.) "Johannes Brahms und seine
neuesten Werke" Gegenwart Bd. 23/24,25 (16.,23.;6.;
1883) pp. 374-77, 396-98. notes. Reviews Opp. 84-89.

1336 Ehlert, Louis. "Brahms" Deutsche Rundschau 6/9 (Bd. 23)
(6.1880) pp. 341-57. Describes his historical position,
characteristics of his music in general and individual works
in particular.
(a) *reprint: Ehlert. in Ehlert. Aus der Tonwelt. Essays.
Neue Folge Berlin: B. Behr, 1884. pp. 213-48.
*Wohlfeile Ausgabe: B. Behr (E. Bock), 1898.
(b) *English translation by Helen D. Tretbar (of
? Auflage): Ehlert. "Johannes Brahms"
in Ehlert. From the Tone World. A Series
of Essays. n.p., n.d.
*2nd, Enlarged Edition: New York: C. F.
Tretbar, [1892].
(c) excerpt (of 1892 Edition): [Daniel
Gregory Mason] "The Art of
Brahms" Masters in Music 5/part
30 (6.1905) p. 7 (volume p. 247)

1137 #Ehrmann, Alfred von. "Zahlenspiele um Brahms" Die Musik
(Berlin) 30/9 (6.1938) pp. 616-18. mus. Presents mnemonic
devices for remembering works' opus numbers, when they
were published, their sequence, the number of works in
each genre, etc.

1138 *Evans, Edwin. Historical, Descriptive and Analytical Account
of the Entire Works of Johannes Brahms. 4 vols. London:
W. Reeves, 1912-[36]. [reprint of 1386, 1387.d., 2022]
(a) *reprint: New York: Somerset Publishers, n.d.

1339 Freitag, Siegfried. "Musik grosser Gefühlstiefe und Volks-
verbundenheit. Hinweise zur Stoffeinheit 2 der Klasse 10
des neuen Lehrplans" Musik in der Schule 23/7 ([7.] 1972)
pp. 282-89. Brahms: pp. 284-89. mus., notes. focuses
on Opp. 56a and 62, no. 3; also includes music by Schubert
and Schumann for classroom study.

1340   Gablentz, Otto Heinz v.d. "Johannes Brahms" Deutsches
        Volkstum [27]/1 (Bd. 1) (1.1925) pp. 42-48. notes. Dis-
        cusses his links with Beethoven and surveys his musical
        output.

1341   Goodfriend, James. "Johannes Brahms" Stereo Review 29/2
        (8.1972) pp. 54-61. ill. Defines Brahms's personality by
        looking at his musical development and the types of works
        that he wrote.

1342   H. D. [Hermann Deiters] Allgemeine musikalische Zeitung
        4/14 (7.4.1869) pp. 106-09. mus. Reviews Opp. 46-49
        and the Ungarische Tänze Hefts 1 and 2 [Hofmann nr. 128;
        McCorkle WoO 1].

1343   Henckell, Karl. "Johannes Brahms" in Henckell. Buch der
        Kunst. (Henckell. Gesammelte Werke. Bd. 4) München:
        J. Michael Müller Verlag, 1921. pp. 138-39. Poem that
        describes poet's feelings when he hears Brahms's music.

1344   *Hewitt, Helen [Margaret]. "The Organ and Sacred Choral
        Works of Johannes Brahms" M.S.M. diss., Union Theological
        Seminary (New York), 1932. [ii, 63 pp.] mus., notes.
        Contains brief appreciations, together with circumstances
        of composition; includes comments on Opp. 54, 91, 121,
        Deutsche Volkslieder [Hofmann nrs. 127,133; McCorkle
        WoO 34,33] and Volks-Kinderlieder [Hofmann nr. 125;
        McCorkle WoO 31]. [from Union Theological Seminary
        (New York)]

1345   [Carl von Noorden]. "Johannes Brahms" Deutsche Musikzeitung
        (Wien) 1/34 (18.8.1860) pp. 265-68. notes. Discusses Opp.
        1-10.

1346   *Johannes Brahms. Erläuterungen seiner bedeutendsten Werke
        von C. Beyer, R. Heuberger, J. Knorr, H. Riemann, J.
        Sittard, K. Söhle und G. H. Witte nebst einer Darstellung
        seines Lebensganges mit besonderer Berücksichtigung
        seiner Werke von A. Morin. (Musiker und ihre Werke)
        Leipzig: Seemann, 1897. xliv, 307 pp. [reprints of 1429,
        1520, 1526, 1833, 1856, 1858, 1872, 1874, 1892, 1926,
        1940, 1964, 1981, 2002, 2012, 2203, 2219, 2236, 2327]
        *also: Frankfurt a.M.: H. Bechhold, [1897].
        *also: Leipzig: H. Seemann Nachf[olger]., n.d.
        *also: Stuttgart: J. Schmitt Verlag, n.d.
        *also: Berlin: Schlesinger, n.d.
        (e) i) report (on ?): see 618.a.e.ii.
            ii) report (on ?): see 618.a.e.iii.

1347   *"Johannes Brahms in der Hausmusik" Sächsische Sängerbundes-
        Zeitung (Leipzig) 4 (1933) pp. 342-44.

1348   Kämper, Dietrich. "Ein unbekanntes Brahms-Studienblatt aus
        dem Briefwechsel mit F[ranz]. Wüllner" Die Musikforschung
        17/1 (1.-3.1964) pp. 57-60. facsim., mus., notes. Dating
        and study of 3 canons.

1349   Keeton, A. E. "Johannes Brahms 1833-1897" Monthly Review
        no. 76 (26/1) (1.1907) pp. 95-103. notes. An overview
        of Brahms's music, its characteristics and how it reflects
        Brahms the man; includes comments on the English interest
        in Brahms's music.
        (a) reprint: Keeton. Living Age 252/3267 (Seventh
            Series vol. 34) (16.2.1907) pp. 410-15.

1350   #Ker. [Louis Köhler] "Johannes Brahms und seine sechs ersten
        Werke" Signale für die musikalische Welt 12/18 (4.1854)
        pp. 145-51. Reviews Opp. 1-6.

1351   Killer, Hermann. "Zur Vortragsfolge des zweiten Orchester-
        Konzerts" in 2732. pp. 22-28. mus. Descriptive programme
        notes for Opp. 55, 56a, 81, 83.

1352   Krause, Emil. Johannes Brahms in seinen Werken. Eine
        Studie. Mit Verzeichnissen sämtlicher Instrumental- und
        Vokal-Komponistionen des Meisters. Hamburg: Lucas
        Gräfe & Sillem, 1892. 107 pp. ind., notes. Provides
        background and descriptive analysis for Brahms's works
        up to Op. 73; includes biographical introduction. Incorpo-
        rates 1396, 2068, 2206.
        (e) report: ""Johannes Brahms in seinen Werken"" Neue
            Musikzeitung 12/21 (1891) p. 250.

1353   *Kretzschmar, Hermann. Führer durch den Concertsaal.
        (d) see also: 1893, 1928, 1977, 2000, 2270, 2311, 2319.

1353A   I. Abtheilung
        *Kretzschmar. Führer durch den Concertsaal. I. Abtheilung:
        Sinfonie und Suite. Leipzig: A. G. Liebeskind, 1887.
        2. Auflage: 1890. "Die moderne Suite und die neueste Ent-
            wickelung der classischen Sinfonie.": pp. 247-309. Brahms:
            pp. 255-62, 289-307. mus., notes. Descriptive notes for
            Opp. 11, 16, 68, 73, 90, 98.
        *3. Auflage: 1895, 1898. Leipzig: Breitkopf & Härtel.
        *4. vollständige neubearbeitete Auflage: 1913. Führer durch
            den Konzertsaal.
        *5. neudurchgesehene Auflage: 1919.
        *6. Auflage: 1921.
        *7. Auflage:
            a) *Kretzschmar. Führer durch den Konzertsaal. Die
               Orchestermusik: Bd. I. Sinfonie und Suite (von
               Gabrieli bis Schumann). Bearbeitet und ergänzt
               von Friedrich Noack. 1932.

b) *Kretzschmar. Führer durch den Konzertsaal. Die
Orchestermusik: Bd. II. Sinfonie und Suite (von
Berlioz bis zur Gegenwart). Bearbeitet und ergänzt von Hugo Botstiber. 1932.
c) *see also: 1384, 1437.

1353B II. Abtheilung, Theil I.
*Kretzschmar. Führer durch den Concertsaal. II. Abtheilung,
Theil I. Kirchliche Werke: Passionen. Leipzig: A. G.
Liebeskind, 1888. Brahms: pp. 244-52, 329-30, 353-58.
Descriptive notes for Opp. 45, 30, 74, 27, 29 no. 2. [from
Boston Public Library. Music Department]
*2. Auflage: [1895-99. Leipzig: Breitkopf & Härtel?]
*3. vollständige neubearbeitete Auflage: 1905. Führer durch
den Konzertsaal. Leipzig: Breitkopf & Härtel.
*4. vollständige neubearbeitete Auflage: 1916.
*5. Auflage: 1921. Brahms: pp. 314-28, 441-42, 520-21.
Order of presentation altered to Opp. 45, 27, 29 no. 2,
74, 30. [from Boston Public Library. Music Department]

1353C II. Abtheilung, Theil II.
*Kretzschmar. Führer durch den Concertsaal. II. Abtheilung,
Theil II. Oratorien und weltliche Chorwerke. Leipzig:
A. G. Liebeskind, 1890. Brahms: pp. 359-61, 369-74.
Descriptive notes for Opp. 50, 53-55, 82, 89. [from Boston
Public Library. Music Department]
*2. Auflage: [1895-99. Leipzig: Breitkopf & Härtel?]
*4. vollständige neubearbeitete Auflage: 1920.
Brahms: pp. 659-60, 672-76. Omits reference to Op. 55.
[from Boston Public Library. Music Department]

1354 *Lahee, Henry C. Annals of Music in America. A Chronological
Record of Significant Events, from 1640 to the Present Day,
with Comments on the Various Periods into which the Work
is divided. Boston: Marshall Jones Company, 1922. vii,
[2], 298 pp. ind.
(a) reprint: New York: AMS Press, 1969. Records first
performances of Brahms's works in the United
States of America.

1355 *Lewinski, Wolf-Eberhard von. "Der späte Brahms--der wahre
Brahms" Philharmonische Blätter [14]/7 (1976/77) pp. 1-3.

1356 McGuinness, Rosamund. "Mahler und Brahms: Gedanken zu
"Reminiszenzen" in Mahlers Sinfonien" Melos/NZ für Musik
3/3 (5.1977) pp. 215-24. mus., notes. Describes rhythmic
and thematic allusions to Brahms's Opp. 73, 82, 68, 90
in the symphonies of Mahler.

1357 Mackenzie, Compton. "Editorial" Gramophone 18/214 (3.1941)
pp. 215-19. "And More About Brahms": pp. 215-18.

Discusses Op. 68 and its relationship to Beethoven's work,
Opp. 121 and 43 no. 1; describes available phonorecordings
of Brahms's music.

1358　Mathews, W.S.B.　"The Works of Brahms" in "Johannes Brahms
(The New Education--The Mastery of Teaching Material)"
Musician (Philadelphia) 3/5 (5.1898) p. 127.　Lists Brahms's
musical output, focusing on the piano works.

1359　*Müller-Reuter, Theodor.　"Johannes Brahms" in Müller-Reuter.
Lexikon der Deutschen Konzertliteratur.　Nachtrag zu Band
I.　Leipzig:　C. F. Kahnt, 1921.　pp. 153-214.　mus., notes.
(a)　reprint:　(Da Capo Press Music Reprint Series) New
York:　Da Capo Press, 1972.　For c. 60 works
provides performance duration, background on
composition and publication, information on first
performance, relevant literature.

1360　*Oberborbeck, Felix.　"Brahms in der Schule" Zeitschrift für
Schulmusik (Wolfenbüttel) 6 (1933) p. 49.

1361　"Opus 1-4 von Joh[annes].　Brahms" Süddeutsche Musikzeitung
(Mainz) 3/18-20 (1.,8.,15.;5.;1854) pp. 69-70, 73-74, 77-
79.　mus.　Reviews.

1362　*Paumgartner, H.　"Die e-moll-Symphonie und das Triumphlied"
[Wiener] Abendpost (18.1.1887).

1363　*Preising.　(?) Rheinische Musik- und Theaterzeitung (Köln) 7
(1.1906 (?)).
(e)　report:　"Wie wir in der "Rheinischen Musik- und
Theater-Zeitung" ... Nachlasse J. O. Grimms ..."
Allgemeine Musikzeitung 33/5 (2.2.1906) p. 86.
Describes Grimm's Nachlass, focusing on holdings
of Brahms manuscripts:　Missa canonica, Opp. 1,
3 no. 1.

1364　Roy, Otto.　"Brahms in der Schulmusik" Die Musikpflege 3/10
(1.1933) pp. 420-35.　notes.　Presents a proposal for
teaching the music of Brahms in school [Grade School and
High School], with points to be made about the characteristics of his music, and suggestions for performance.
(c)　excerpt:　Roy.　Die Musik (Berlin) 25/8 (5.1933)
pp. 610-11.
(d)　#continued:　Thiessen, Hermann.　"Eine kleine Ergän-
zung zum Artikel "Brahms in der Schulmusik""
Die Musikpflege 3 (1933) pp. 523-24.　notes.　More
suggestions for works to perform.

1365　#S. T.　"Amerika liebt Brahms. Interessante Zahlen aus dem
Konzertleben der USA" Hamburger Abendblatt 11/110 (13.5.

1958) p. 7. facsim. Reports on speech made by David
von Vactor in Hamburg, on Brahms in the Chicago Symphony's repertoire, and on the general interest in Brahms's
music throughout the United States of America.

1365.5*Schmidt, Leopold. Berliner Tageblatt.
(a) #reprint: in Schmidt. "Brahms" in 3022. pp. 255-67.
"Vom Nachlass": pp. 257-59. Reviews Op. 122,
the Deutsche Volkslieder (1894) [Hofmann nr. 133;
McCorkle WoO 33] and Brahms's arrangement of
Schubert's Ellens zweiter Gesang [Hofmann nr. 140;
McCorkle Anhang Ia, nr. 17].

1366 *Scott, James Copland. "Structural Principles in Schoenberg's
Song Cycle, Opus 15, and Their Anticipation in Some Late
Works of Brahms" Ph.D. diss., Peabody Institute of Balti-
more, 1973.

1367 *Smith, David Hills. "Formal Coherence in Nineteenth-Century
Variations: A Study of Selected Works of Beethoven,
Schumann and Brahms" Ph.D. diss., Theory, Yale Univer-
sity. In Progress.

1368 *Spaeth, Sigmund [Gottfried]. "So This is Brahms" in Spaeth.
Stories Behind The World's Great Music. New York:
McGraw-Hill Book Company Inc.; London: Whittlesey House,
[1937]. pp. 209-27. mus., notes.
*issue (of New York Edition): 1938.
*also: New York: Garden City Publishing Co., Inc., [1940].

1369 Spitta, Philipp. "Johannes Brahms" in Spitta. Zur Musik.
Sechzehn Aufsätze. Berlin: Verlag von Gebrüder Paetel,
1892. pp. 385-427. Discusses Brahms the composer,
with an overview of his works; includes comments on Brahms
and folkmusic.
(b) *English translation by Mrs. Clara Bell: Musician
Boston (?).
(a) *reprint: Spitta. in 1168.e.ii.a. pp. 1-44.
(c) excerpt (in English translation by Alfred Einstein):
in 1380. [source of excerpt is Einstein's Music in
the Romantic Era. (New York: W. W. Norton &
Company, Inc., 1947)]

1370 *Stromenger, Karol. "Z "Przewodnika koncertowego"" in
Stromenger. Czy należy spalić Luwr? Felietony muzyczne.
Kraków: Polskie wydawnictwo muzyczne, 1970. pp. 106-27.

1371 Taylor, Deems. "The Devil and the Deep Sea" in Taylor.
The Well Tempered Listener. New York: Simon and Schuster, 1940. pp. 150-53. Discusses problems with concert
programming, using Brahms's works as examples.

*issues: 1943, 1945.
   (a) *reprint: Westport, Conn.: Greenwood Press, [1972].

1372   Tovey, Donald Francis. Essays in Musical Analysis.
       *[New Edition:] 2 vols. (Oxford Paperbacks) London, New
       York: Oxford University Press, 1981.
       Vol. 1: Symphonies and Other Orchestral Works. xi, 561 pp.
       mus.
       Vol. 2: Concertos and Choral Works.
       [essays on works no longer in the repertory have been
       dropped.]

1372A Volume I.
       Tovey. Essays ... Analysis. Volume I. Symphonies. London:
       Oxford University Press, Humphrey Milford, 1935. mus.
       "Brahms": pp. 84-137. mus. Descriptive notes for Opp.
       68, 73, 90, 98, 11, 16.
       15th Impression: 1976.
       *also: London, New York: Oxford University Press, 1935.
          (c) *excerpt (of ? Edition): see 1372 (1981 Edition).

1372B Volume II.
       Tovey. Essays ... Analysis. Volume II. Symphonies (II),
       Variations and Orchestral Polyphony. London: Oxford
       University Press, Humphrey Milford, 1935. "Brahms":
       pp. 136-39, 151-56. mus. Descriptive notes for Opp.
       56a, 81, 80.
       12th Impression: 1972.
       *also: London, New York: Oxford University Press, 1935.
          (c) *excerpt (of ? Edition): see 1372 (1981 Edition).
          (d) see: 1372E.

1372C Volume III.
       Tovey. Essays in Musical Analysis. Volume III. Concertos.
       London: Oxford University Press, Humphrey Milford, 1936.
       "Brahms": pp. 114-47. mus. Descriptive notes for Opp.
       15, 83, 77, 102.
       12th Impression: 1972.
       *also: London, New York: Oxford University Press, 1936.
          (c) *excerpt (of ? Edition): see 1372 (1981 Edition).

1372D Volume V.
       Tovey. Essays ... Analysis. Volume V. Vocal Music.
       London: Oxford University Press, Humphrey Milford, 1937.
       "Brahms": pp. 211-29. mus., notes. Descriptive notes
       for Opp. 45, 53, 54.
       2nd Impression: 1938.
       11th Impression: 1977.
       *also: London, New York: Oxford University Press, 1937.
          (c) *excerpt (of ? Edition): see 1372 (1981 Edition).

1372E Volume VI.
Tovey. Essays ... Analysis. Volume VI. Miscellaneous Notes.
Glossary and Index. London: Oxford University Press,
Humphrey Milford, 1939. ind. "A Further Note on Brahms's
Tragic Overture (Op. 81)": pp. 55-57. mus.
10th Impression: 1972.
*also: London, New York: Oxford University Press, 1939.
(c) *excerpt (of ? Edition): see 1372 (1981 Edition).

1372F Volume VII.
Tovey. Essays ... Analysis. [Volume VII.] Chamber Music.
With an Editor's Note by Hubert J. Foss. London: G.
Cumberlege, Oxford University Press, [1944]. ind.
"Brahms": pp. 167-214. mus. Descriptive notes for Opp.
24, 35, 25, 26, 60.
7th Impression: 1972.
*also: London: Oxford University Press, Humphrey Milford,
1944.
issue: 1945.
*also: London, New York: Oxford University Press, 1944.

1373 W. S. B. M[athews]. "When the great heart of Johannes
Brahms ..." Music (Chicago) 12/1 (5.1897) pp. 67-71.
An obituary with examination of Brahms's music, focusing
on the solo piano works; includes comments on his historical
position.

1374 *Warburton, A[nnie] O. Music Teacher and Piano Student 48
(1.1969) pp. 16, 37. Analysis of Op. 45 mvts. 1,4,5 and
Op. 119 nos. 1,4.[from 1374.a]
(a) reprint: see 1375C.

1375 Warburton, Annie O. Analyses of Musical Classics. Contains
reprints of 1374, 1604, 1705, 1907, 1956, 1960, 2104.

1375A Book 1
Warburton. Analyses of Musical Classics. Book 1. London:
Longman, 1963.
"German Lieder": pp. 237-53. Brahms: pp. 251-53.
Analysis of songs from Opp. 7, 19, 43, 49, 86, 91, 96, 106,
and Volks-Kinderlieder [Hofmann nr. 125; McCorkle WoO
31].
"Chopin, Schumann and Brahms: Piano Works": pp. 254-
78. Brahms: pp. 276-78. Analysis of Opp. 79 no. 2,
and 118 nos. 2, 3.
"Overtures": pp. 279-301. Brahms: pp. 299-300.
Analysis of Op. 80.
*3. Impression: 1970.

1375B Book 2.
Warburton. Analyses of Musical Classics. Book 2. London:

Longman, 1967. Brahms: pp. 225-38. Analysis of Opp.
68, 81, 56a, 119 nos. 2, 3.
*2. Impression: 1969.
*4. Impression: 1975.

1375C Book 3.
Warburton. Analyses of Musical Classics. Book 3. London:
Longman, 1971. Brahms: pp. 196-212. Analysis of Opp.
45 mvts. 1, 3, 5 and 119 nos. 1, 4.

1376 #Whitwell, David. "Brahms--His Music for Winds" Instrumentalist
20/7 (2.1966) pp. 59-60. notes. Examines works featuring
wind instruments; also comments on tempi.

1377 Zopff, Hermann. "Werke von Johannes Brahms im Verlage
von Rieter-Biedermann. Leipzig und Winterthur" Neue
Zeitschrift für Musik Bd. 63/43 (18.10.1867) pp. 373-77.
mus. Reviews Opp. 32-35, 37, 39, 44.

See also 218, 251, 252, 255, 258, 268, 417, 467, 471, 476, 488, 492,
514, 528, 1785, 2004, 2107, 2375, 2376, 2376.5, 2393, 2397.5, 2399,
2403, 2406, 2415, 2435, 2469, 2478, 2500, 2555, 2568, 2572, 2646,
2673, 2704, 2774, 2785-87, 2815, 2849, 2850, 2862, 2888.d., 2933,
2943-49, 2993, 2994, 2997, 2998, 3048. See also I.A. and "Editions",
"Manuscripts and Manuscript Studies", and "Works Catalogues and
Indexes" in I.C.

A. INSTRUMENTAL MUSIC--GENERAL

1378 *[Ed.H.] Neue freie Presse (Wien) (1889).
(a) *reprint: Hanslick, Eduard. "Brahms' neueste In-
strumental-Compositionen (1889)." in 2948. pp.
149-56. [paging from reprint of 2. Auflage]
Reviews Opp. 99, 100, 102, 108. [from 2948.a.]

1379 Brahms, Johannes. Opus 24. Opus 23. Opus 18. Opus 90.
New York: Robert Owen Lehman Foundation, 1967. [10],
164 pp. [Starting with Op. 23, each facsimile has an individual paging, as well as a paging for the whole work.]
Facsimile edition of 4 Library of Congress manuscripts.
The Op. 18 manuscript is for the piano 2-hand arrangement
of that work's 2nd movement. Op. 24: pp. 1-24; Op. 23:
pp. 25-52; Op. 18: pp. 53-60; Op. 90: pp. 61-164.

1380 Brahms, Johannes. Variations on a Theme of Haydn for
Orchestra, Op. 56a and for Two Pianos, Op. 56b. The
Revised Scores of the Standard Editions. The Sketches.
Textual Criticism and Notes. Historical Background.

Analytical Essays. Views and Comments. Donald M.
McCorkle, ed. (Norton Critical Scores) New York: W. W.
Norton & Company Inc., 1976. ix, [3], 3-221, [2] pp. ill.,
facsim., mus., notes. Includes excerpts from 24.b.,
39B, 979, 983.b., 1369, 1879, 2946, and Heinrich Schenker.
Der freie Satz (Wien: Universal--Edition, 1935) with ac-
companying explication by Murray J. Gould. Includes reprint of 1390.

1381   [James Gibbons Huneker] "The Brahms Piano Music" Musical
        Courier 34/26 (30.6.1897) pp. 24-25. Discusses solo piano
        music and the piano concertos; also comments on Brahms's
        historical position.
        (d) incorporated: see 1392.

1382   *Carney, Horace Richard, Jr. "Tonality and Structure in the
        Instrumental Works of Johannes Brahms" Ph.D. diss., Uni-
        versity of Iowa, 1981. 495 pp. Examines tonal systems
        of 35 orchestral and chamber works, and what effect on
        form these systems have. [from S156]

1383   *Czesla, Werner. "Studien zum Finale in der Kammermusik
        von Johannes Brahms" Phil.F. diss., Rheinischen Friedrich-
        Wilhelms-Universität Bonn, 1968. 252 pp. mus., fig.,
        notes.
        (a) #reprint: Studien ... Brahms. Bonn: n.p., 1968.
            252, [1] pp. Structural analytical study of Opp.
            1, 2, 5, 8 [both versions], 18, 25, 34, 36, 38, 40,
            51 nos. 1 and 2, 60, 88, 111.
        (d) Czesla. "Motivische Mutationen im Schaffen von
            Johannes Brahms" in Colloquium amicorum. Joseph
            Schmidt-Görg zum 70. Geburtstag. Siegfried Kross
            and Hans Schmidt, eds. Bonn: Beethovenhaus,
            1967. pp. 64-72. mus. Examines Brahms's method
            for transforming motifs, as seen in the finales of
            Opp. 2, 25, 51 no. 1.

1384   *Engel, Hans. Das Instrumentalkonzert. (Hermann Kretzschmar.
        Führer durch den Konzertsaal. Die Orchestermusik. Bd.
        III.) Leipzig: Breitkopf & Härtel, 1932.

1385   Epstein, David. "Ambiguity as Premise" in Epstein. Beyond
        Orpheus. Studies in Musical Structure. Cambridge, Mass.,
        and London: MIT Press, 1979. pp. 161-77. mus., notes.
        Studies the structural possibilities of ambiguity using Opp.
        73, 118 no. 2 as examples.

1386   Evans, Edwin. Handbook to the Chamber and Orchestral
        Music of Johannes Brahms. Historical and Descriptive Ac-
        count of Each Work with Exhaustive Structural, Thematic
        and Rhythmical Analyses, and a Complete Rhythmical Chart

of Each Movement. Complete Guide for Student, Concert-
goer and Pianist. 2 vols. [(Evans. Historical, Descriptive
and Analytical Account of the Entire Works of Johannes
Brahms. vols. 2, 3)] London: William Reeves Bookseller
Limited, [1933-35]. mus., fig.
[Volume 2:] First Series to Op. 67 inclusive.
[Volume 3:] Second Series. Op. 68 to the end.
General comments on Brahms as a composer in these genres,
with systematic analysis of respective works.
(a) i) *reprint: see 1338.
     ii) *reprint: ([Original series]) (Burt Franklin Research
          and Source Works Series, 557) New York: B[urt].
          Franklin, [1970].

1387 _____ . "The Piano Works of Brahms" Musical Standard
     (London) 31/793, 795, 797, 799, 801, 803 Illustrated Series
     [Full (volume/issue) no. 76/2328, 2330, 2332, 2334, 2336,
     2338] (13.,27.;3. and 10.,24.;4. and 8.,22.;5.;1909)
     pp. 169-70, 196-98, 228-30, 261-62, 293-95, 324-25. Dis-
     cusses Brahms as a composer for the piano, together with
     the qualities of this music; includes an overview of these
     works.
     (d) incorporated: Evans. Handbook to the Pianoforte
          Works of Johannes Brahms. Comprising the Complete
          Solo Works; Works for Piano and Orchestra; also
          Works for Piano Duet and Organ Works as Applicable
          to Pianoforte Solo. Complete Guide for Student,
          Concert-goer and Pianist. [(Evans. Historical,
          Descriptive and Analytical Account of the Entire
          Works of Johannes Brahms. vol. 4)] London:
          William Reeves Bookseller Limited, [1936]. xv, 327
          pp. mus., ind., notes. Includes systematic analysis
          for the respective works.
          (a) i) *reprint: see 1338.
               ii) *reprint: [(Original series)] (Burt Franklin
                    Research and Source Works Series, 557)
                    New York: B[urt]. Franklin, [1970].

1388 Fontaine, Paul. Basic Formal Structures in Music. New York:
     Appleton-Century-Crofts, 1967. x, 241 pp.
     "Theme with Variations": pp. 93-123. Brahms: "Section-
          alized Variations": pp. 96-103. mus. Analyses Op. 24.
     "The Passacaglia and the Chaconne": pp. 104-20. Brahms:
          pp. 105-20. mus. Analyses Op. 98, 1st movement.

1389 #Fontenla, Jorge. "Brahms y su obra para piano" Ars. Revista
     de arte 17/79 (1957) pp. [82-83, 85-93]. ill., facsim.
     Comments on the state of piano music when Brahms first
     began composing; presents descriptive comments on the
     works for piano solo and duet, concertos, cadenzas, etc.

1390   Forte, Allen. "The Structural Origin of Exact Tempi in The
        Brahms-Haydn Variations" Music Review 18/2 (5.1957) pp.
        138-49. mus., fig., notes. Uses Opp. 56a, 56b to show
        the interrelationship of tempo, rhythm and melody.
        (a) reprint: see 1380.

1391   Howard-Jones, E[vlyn]. "Brahms in His Pianoforte Music"
        Proceedings of the Musical Association. 37th Session (1910-
        11) pp. 117-28. notes. Appraises musical idea and musical
        and instrumental expression in the piano concertos and works
        for solo piano as an attempt to understand Brahms's music;
        includes discussion.

1392   *Huneker, James [Gibbons]. "The Music of The Future" in
        Huneker. Mezzotints in Modern Music. Brahms, Tschaikow-
        sky, Chopin, Richard Strauss, Liszt and Wagner. New
        York: Charles Scribner's Sons, 1899. pp. 1-[80]. ind.
        *2nd Edition: 1899.
        *issue: 1901.
        *3rd Edition: 1905.
        *issue: 1906.
        *4th Edition: 1910.
        *issue: 1912.
        *5th Edition: ?.
        *6th Edition: 1915.
        *issues: 1920-27.
        also: London: William Reeves, 1928.
        Posits reasons why Brahms should be considered a great
        composer, presents descriptive analysis of solo piano works
        and piano concertos, comments on Brahms's historical
        position. Incorporates 1381.
        (a) i) *reprint (from ? Edition): Huneker. In Huneker.
                Essays by James Huneker. Selected with an Intro-
                duction by H[enry]. L[ouis]. Mencken. New
                York: Charles Scribner's Sons, 1929. pp. 70-120.
                ind.
                issue: 1932.
              *also: London: T. Werner Laurie, 1930.
                (a) *reprint (of New York 1929 Edition): New
                    York: AMS Press, 1976.
            ii) *reprint (of New York 1905 Edition): New York:
                AMS Press, [1971].
           iii) *reprint (of New York 1925 Edition): St. Clair
                Shores, Mich.: Scholarly Press, 1972.
        (c) i) excerpt (of New York 1899 Edition): [Daniel
                Gregory Mason] "The Art of Brahms" Masters in
                Music 5/part 29 (5.1905) pp. 7-9 (volume pp.
                [199-201]).
             ii) excerpt (of New York 1899 Edition): [Daniel
                Gregory Mason] "The Art of Brahms" Masters in
                Music 5/part 30 (6.1905) p. 6 (volume p. [246]).

(d) reworked: Huneker. "[Preface]" in Johannes Brahms.
Selected Piano Compositions. Rafael Joseffy, ed.
With a Preface by James Huneker (The Musicians
Library) Boston: Oliver Ditson Company et al,
[1910]. pp. vii-xv. Includes survey of Brahms's
life.
(e) report (on New York 1899 Edition): Swayne, Egbert.
"James Huneker's "Mezzotints in Modern Music""
Music (Chicago) 16/1 (5.1899) pp. 17-27. ill.

1393 *Hutcheson, Ernest. "Johannes Brahms (1833-97)" in Hutcheson.
The Literature of the Piano. A Guide for Amateur and
Student. New York: Alfred A. Knopf, 1948. pp. 225-41.
mus., notes.
2nd Edition Revised: 1949. mus., notes. Describes the
style of Brahms's piano music, provides an overview of
works for solo piano and piano duet as well as the piano
concertos; includes comments on works' editions and a
list of the piano chamber music.
*issue: 1952.
3rd Edition, Revised and Brought Up to Date by Rudolph
Ganz: 1964. pp. 251-69.
*also: London, New York: Hutchinson, [1950?] [=New York
2nd Edition].
2nd Edition [=New York 3rd Edition]: Revised and Brought
Up to Date by Rudolph Ganz. London: Hutchinson, 1969.
pp. 251-69.
*issue: 1974.

1394 *Ismer, Ursula and Hanna John. "Studien zur Entwicklung
der Variation vom 19. Jahrhundert bis zur spätbürgerlichen
Musik" Phil.F. diss., Martin-Luther Universität, Halle,
1976. 2 vols. mus., notes. Discusses and compares works
in variation form by composers from Beethoven through
Stravinsky. [from S202]

1395 *Knepler, Georg. "Die Form in den Instrumentalwerken Johannes Brahms" Phil.F. diss., Universität Wien, 1930.

1396 Krause, Emil. "Johannes Brahms als Instrumentalcomponist.
I. Claviermusik; II. Die Kammermusikwerke; III. Die Or-
chester- und Concert-Compositionen" Neue Zeitschrift für
Musik 58/9-15 (Bd. 87) (4.,11., 18.,25.;3. and 1.,8.,
15.;4.;1891) pp. 97-99, 109-11, 121-23, 134-36, 147-48,
159-60, 169-70. notes. Provides historical background
and descriptive analysis for each work.
(d) incorporated: into 1352.

1397 Lamberton, Elizabeth Jean. "Brahms's Piano Quintet, Op. 34,
and Duo-piano Sonata, Op. 34bis: A Critical Study" M.A.
thesis, Musicology, University of British Columbia, 1978.
xi, 260, [2] pp. mus., fig., notes. Reviews the history

of the original quintet and its successors; examines extant
manuscripts for insight into Brahms's creative processes
and for establishing a chronology of revisions; includes a
revised text for the 1st movement of each work.

1398   Leoni, Sergio. "Johannes Brahms" in Leoni. L'Arte pianistica
        in Martucci, Brahms, Grieg, Novák, Debussy. Padova:
        Edizioni Carturan, 1915. pp. 43-68. Presents descriptive
        comments on the solo piano and piano concerto works;
        includes comment on Brahms the composer.

1399   Linke, Oskar. "Klavierwerke von Johannes Brahms" Neue
        Musikzeitung 12/13,14 (1891) pp. 151-52, 163. Presents
        an overview of the works for solo piano and piano concertos;
        includes a description of the characteristics of this literature.

1400   Mackenzie, Compton. "Editorial" Gramophone 18/211 (12.1940)
        pp. 147-50. "Brahms": pp. 147-50. Comments on the
        Germanic Brahms and his life up to the time of Op. 15;
        contrasts Op. 15's reception with that of Op. 83. Provides
        historical background for Opp. 77, 102, 68 and 73, and
        comments on available recordings.

1401   _____. "Editorial" Gramophone 18/212 (1.1941) pp. 169-72.
        "Brahms": pp. 170-72. Provides historical background
        and analysis of Opp. 90, 98, and the solo piano works;
        includes comments on available recordings.

1402   _____. "Editorial" Gramophone 18/213 (2.1941) pp. 193-96.
        "Brahms": pp. 195-96. Describes allusions in Op. 68
        to Beethoven's music; Op. 60 and its background; also
        Brahms's relationship with the Schumanns.

1403   Mason, Daniel Gregory. "Great Modern Composers. No. 12.
        Brahms" New Music Review and Church Music Review
        14/165 (8.1915) pp. 292-96. mus., notes. Analysis of
        Op. 10, no. 1, and the 1st movement of Op. 73.
        (d) *incorporated: Mason. "Johannes Brahms" in Mason.
                Great Modern Composers. Biographical Sections by
                Mary L. Mason (The Appreciation of Music. Vol.
                II) New York: H. W. Gray Company, 1916.
            *issues: 1918, 1924-25.
                (a) reprint (of 1918 issue): (Essay Index Reprint
                        Series) Freeport, N.Y.: Books for Libraries
                        Press, 1968. pp. 182-97. mus., notes.
                        Discusses Brahms as a classical composer
                        and his characteristic methods of compo-
                        sition; describes his early and late life
                        with analysis of two representative works
                        [Op. 10, no. 1 and Op. 73, 1st movement].

1404 Matthews, Denis. Brahms's Three Phases. An Inaugural
Lecture-Recital delivered before the University of Newcastle
upon Tyne on Monday 24. January 1972 and repeated on
Wednesday 2. February 1972. Newcastle upon Tyne: University of Newcastle upon Tyne, 1972. 19 pp. notes.
Describes Brahms's compositional phases and musical style,
focusing on the works for solo piano and piano concertos.
(d) i) Matthews. "Beethoven, Schubert and Brahms" in
Keyboard Music. Matthews, ed. New York, Washington: Praeger Publishers, 1972. pp. 166-208.
ind. "Brahms (1833-1897)": pp. 198-208. mus.
Overview of solo piano works demonstrating the
characteristics of Brahms's writing.
*also: Newton Abbot: David & Charles, 1972.
also: (Crescendo Book) New York: Taplinger Publishing Company, 1978.
Paperback Edition (of New York 1972 Edition): Harmondsworth: Penguin, 1972.
ii) Matthews. Brahms Piano Music. (BBC Music
Guides) London: BBC, 1978. 76 pp. mus., ind.
Presents historical background and descriptive
analysis for the solo piano works.
*also: Seattle: University of Washington Press, 1978.

1405 Mies, Paul. "Die Konzertkadenz bei Johannes Brahms" in
Mies. Das Konzert im 19. Jahrhundert. Studien zu Formen
und Kadenzen. (Abhandlungen zur Kunst- , Musik- und
Literaturwissenschaft Bd. 126) Bonn: Bouvier, Verlag
Herbert Grundmann, 1972. pp. 7-30. mus., ind., notes.
Analyses the cadenzas in Brahms's own chamber and or-
chestral works, and those that he wrote for the piano
concertos of Beethoven and Mozart.

1406 Mohr, Wilhelm. "Johannes Brahms' formenschöpferische Origi-
nalität, dargestellt am ersten Satz seiner Violinsonate Op.
108, und seiner Rhapsodie, Op. 79, nr. 2" in Bericht über
den Internationalen Musikwissenschaftlichen Kongress, Leipzig 1966. Carl Dahlhaus, Reiner Kluge, Ernst H. Meyer,
Walter Wiora, eds. Kassel [et al.]: Bärenreiter; Leipzig:
VEB Deutscher Verlag für Musik, 1970. pp. 322-24. notes.
An analysis to show the originality of Brahms's use of form
in his music.

1407 Newman, William S. "Brahms and Others in Austria From About
1850 to 1885." In Newman. The Sonata Since Beethoven.
The Third and Final Volume of A History of the Sonata Idea.
Chapel Hill: University of North Carolina Press, 1969. pp.
319-52. "Brahms: Output, Resources and Chronology":
pp. 321-48. ill., facsim., mus., fig., ind., notes. Provides historical background and commentary on the piano
sonatas and ensemble sonatas: Opp. 1, 2, 5, 34bis, 38,

78, 99, 100, 108, 120 nos. 1 and 2, and the destroyed
sonata for violin and piano [McCorkle Anhang IIa, nr. 8].
[Paperback Edition:] New York: W. W. Norton & Co., 1972.

1408 Pulver, Jeffrey. "The String Music of Johannes Brahms"
The Strad 63 [43]/516;64 [44]/517-19 (4.-7.1933) pp. 536,
538;28, 30, 59-60, 99-100. Provides historical background
and comments on ensemble and solo chamber music, the
concertos with string soloist, and the string arrangements
of the Ungarische Tänze [Hofmann nr. 133; McCorkle WoO 33].

1409 Range, Hans-Peter. "Johannes Brahms" in Range Von
Beethoven bis Brahms. Einführung in die konzertanten
Klavierwerke der Romantik. Lahr: Moritz Schauenburg
Verlag, 1967. pp. 191-213. ind., notes. Descriptive
analysis and historical background for Opp. 1, 2, 4, 5, 9,
10, 15, 24, 35, 76, 79, 83, 116-19; also includes survey
of Brahms's life.

1410 Rehberg, Walter. "Brahms als Klavierkomponist" Münchner
neueste Nachrichten. 75/193 (6./7.5.1922) p. 8. Surveys the works for solo piano and piano concertos, with
descriptive comments.
(d) *Rehberg: "Klavierwerke von Johannes Brahms"
Frankfurter Zeitung (6.5. or 5.6. ?;1922).

1411 *Schmidt, Christian Martin. "Verfahren der motivischthematischen
Vermittlung in der Musik von Johannes Brahms, dargestellt
an der Klarinetten-Sonate f-moll, Op. 120, 1" Phil.F. diss.,
Freie Universität West Berlin, 1970. 186 pp. notes.
(a) reprint: Verfahren ... Op. 120, 1. (Berliner musikwissenschaftliche Arbeiten 2) München: Musikverlag
Emil Katzbichler, 1971. Motivic-thematic processes
and their relationship to harmony and form, as seen
in late works of Brahms; includes analysis of Op.
118, no. 2.

1412 Sielmann, Herbert. "Zur Vortragsfolge der kammermusikalischen
Morgenfeier" in 2732. pp. 14-19. Provides historical background and descriptive analysis for Opp. 51, no. 2; 79,
no. 2; 115; 117, no. 1; 119, no. 4.

1413 Sopeña [Ibáñez], Federico. "En torno a la musica de camara
de Brahms" in Sopeña. Ensayos musicales. Madrid:
Editora nacional, 1945. pp. 177-93. Presents an overview
of the chamber and piano music; includes comments on
Brahms and Wagner, and Brahms's affinity for folkmusic.

1414 *Stark, Helmut Volker. "Das Variationsprinzip in den Instrumentalwerken von Johannes Brahms" Phil.F. diss., Johannes
Gutenberg-Universität Mainz. In Progress.

1415 Szigeti, Joseph. "Druck- und Lesefehler in der Violin-Literatur" NZ-Neue Zeitschrift für Musik 127/4 ([4.] 1966) pp. 136-39. Brahms: pp. 137, 139. mus. Points out differences between manuscript sources and printed edition text for Opp. 77, 78.

1416 Thomas-San-Galli, Wolfgang A[lexander]. "Eine Brahms-Betrachtung" in 2544. pp. 25-28. Presents a general analysis of the instrumental music as an appreciation of Brahms's work.

1417 "Uebersicht neu erschienener Musikwerke. A. Instrumental-Musik" Leipziger allgemeine musikalische Zeitung 1/6, 7,10,16,19 (7.,14.;2. and 7.;3. and 18.;4. and 9.;5.; 1866) pp. 47-48, 56-57, 80, 128-29, 153-54. Brahms: pp. 48, 56-57. Short reviews of Opp. 34 and 35.

1418 Walker, Ernest. "Brahms's Variations" Monthly Musical Record 70/814 (2.1940) pp. 33-36. notes. Groups the works in which variations appear chronologically, analyses, and discusses each group's qualities.

1419 Wessem, Constant van. "Over Brahms' klaviermuziek en haar studie" Caecilia (Utrecht) 70/12 (15.12.1913) pp. 337-42. mus. Presents descriptive analysis for Opp. 24, 15, 118; includes comments on Brahms as composer, and on his influences.

1420 #Zonderland, Willem. "Johannes Brahms als klavierdichter" Symphonia 16/5 (5.1933) pp. 98-99. Surveys the works for solo piano and piano concertos, with descriptive comments.

See also 247, 249, 265, 2042, 2355, 2381, 2409, 2436, 2439, 2442, 2444, 2531.

1. Chamber Music--General

1421 Monthly Musical Record 1/4 (1.4.1871) pp. 48-49. Reviews Opp. 18, 8, 26, 40.
(c) *excerpt: in 2915 pp. 271-72.

1422 Antcliffe, Herbert. "The Chamber Music of Brahms" Monthly Musical Record 36/427 (1.7.1906) pp. 146-47. Surveys the chamber music for 3 or more parts; includes comments on Brahms the composer and classicist.

1423 *Brand, Friedrich. "Das Wesen und Charakter der Thematik

im Brahmsschen Kammermusikwerk" Phil.F. diss., Universität Berlin, 1937. xii, 156 pp.
(a) reprint: Brand. Das Wesen der Kammermusik von Brahms. Berlin: Deutsche Brahms-Ges[ellschaft] m.b.H., 1937. xii, 155 pp. mus., ind., notes. Contains systematic analysis movement-by-movement, also discusses the types of thematic material Brahms used.

1424 Colles, H[enry]. C[ope]. The Chamber Music of Brahms. (The Musical Pilgrim) London: Humphrey Milford, Oxford University Press, 1933. 64 pp. mus., notes. Descriptive analysis.
(a) *reprint: New York: AMS Press, 1976.

1425 *Drinker, Henry S[andwith]., Jr. The Chamber Music of Johannes Brahms. Philadelphia: Elkan-Vogel Co., 1932.
(a) reprint: Westport, Conn.: Greenwood Press Publishers, 1974. [2], 130 pp. ill., notes. Presents historical and descriptive information; includes sketch of Brahms's life and comments on the man and his music in general.
*issue: 1976.

1426 Fenske, David Edward. "Texture in the Chamber Music of Johannes Brahms" Ph.D. diss., Music, University of Wisconsin, 1973. iv, 540, [1] pp. fig., notes. A systematic study of texture in the trios, quartets, quintets, and sextets as a contribution towards a stylistic understanding of Brahms's musical composition process.
(d) Fenske, David. "Contrapuntal Textures in the String Quartets, Op. 51, No. 2 and Op. 67 of Johannes Brahms" in Music East and West. Essays in Honor of Walter Kaufmann. Thomas Noblitt, ed. ([Pendragon Press] Festschrift Series no. 3) New York: Pendragon Press, 1981. pp. 351-69. notes. Movement-by-movement textual analysis.

1427 Ferguson, Donald N. "Johannes Brahms. 1833-1897" in Ferguson. Image and Structure in Chamber Music. Minneapolis: University of Minnesota Press, 1964. pp. 175-218. mus., ind., notes. Structural and descriptive analysis of the chamber works; includes some comments on Brahms's musical background.

1428 *Hawn, Margaret Elizabeth. "Melodic Relationships in Selected Chamber Works of Brahms" M.M. thesis, Music Theory, Indiana University, 1969. 83 pp. mus., notes. Discusses the construction of thematic and accompaniment materials, and the relationships between musical ideas in same, or different movements in: Opp. 18, 34, 51, no. 2, 87, 115.
[from S202]

1429 Heuberger, Richard. Johannes Brahms, I. Trio für Pianoforte,
      Klarinette (oder Bratsche) und Violoncello, op. 114   II.
      Quintett für Klarinette (oder Bratsche) 2 Violinen, Bratsche
      und Violoncello, op. 115. (Der Musikführer. no. 45)
      Frankfurt a/M.: Verlag von H. Bechhold, [1895]. 21 pp.
      mus. Op. 114; pp. 3-10; Op. 115: pp. 11-21. Descriptive
      analysis with some background of the works.
      *also: Berlin: Schlesinger, n.d.
      *also: Stuttgart: Schmitt, n.d.
      (a) *reprint: in 1346.

1430 "[Übersicht neu erschienener Musikwerke.] Kammermusik"
      Leipziger allgemeine musikalische Zeitung 1/40 (3.10.1866)
      pp. 322-23. Brahms: p. 323. Reviews Opp. 36 and 38.

1431 #Kell, Reginald. "The Clarinet Music of Johannes Brahms"
      Woodwind World 4/3 (12.1961) p. 5. Opp. 114, 115, and
      120: personal impressions as well as comments on perform-
      ance practice.

1432 Keys, Ivor. Brahms Chamber Music. (BBC Music Guides)
      London: BBC, 1974. pp. [1-4], 5-68. mus., ind., notes.
      Descriptive analysis.

1433 #Kint, Cor. "Brahms' kamermuziekwerken" Symphonia 16/5
      (5.1933) pp. 100-02. Surveys the works with descriptive
      comments.

1434 *Kroher, Ekkehart. "Beethoven im Rücken und überflüssige
      Noten under dem Tisch. Der "unbekannte, kammermusik-
      alische" Johannes Brahms" Musik + Medizin (Neu-Isenburg)
      7/10 (1981) pp. 60, 63-64, 66.

1435 Leyensdorff, H. "Eenige aanteekeningen over kamermuziek-
      werken van Brahms" Caecilia (Utrecht) 79/12 (10.5.1922)
      pp. 187-89. mus. Presents an overview of the chamber
      works; includes comments on Brahms the composer and the
      current status of the composer.

1436 Mason, Daniel Gregory. The Chamber Music of Brahms.
      New York: Macmillan Company, 1933. xii, 276 pp. ill.,
      facsim., mus., ind., notes. Analytical study. Reprints
      1460, 1463, 1529, 1532; incorporates 1456.c., 1480, 1489,
      1521, 1528.
      (a) i) *reprint: New York: AMS Press, [1970].
          ii) *reprint: (Select Bibliographies. (?) Reprint
              Series) Freeport, N.Y.: Books for Libraries
              Press, [1970].
      (d) "Reprinted with Corrections": (Edwards Music Re-
          prints. Series B. No. 3) Ann Arbor, Mich.:
          J. W. Edwards, 1950.

1437 Mersmann, Hans. Die Kammermusik. Band III. Deutsche
Romantik. (Hermann Kretzschmar. Führer durch den
Konzertsaal) Leipzig: Breitkopf & Härtel, 1930. Brahms:
pp. 85-113. mus. Descriptive notes.

1438 "Mr. Surette on Brahms" The Times (London) no. 39,733
(3.11.1911) p. 11. A report on Surette's lecture on
Brahms's chamber works for violin.

1439 #Montefal, Heriberto. "La Música de cámara de J[ohannes].
Brahms" Ars. Revista de arte 17/79 (1957) pp. [120-28].
facsim. Presents historical background and descriptive
analysis.

1440 Sharp, J. Wharton. "Brahms & His Chamber Music" The
Strad 21/244 (8.1910) pp. 140-42. Discusses Brahms's
character and chamber music composing style; includes
comments on his historical position.

1441 #Söhle, Karl. "Johannes Brahms in seiner Kammermusik (Die
Werke und wir. 5)" Der Kunstwart 20/13 (4.1907) pp. 10-15.
Describes how the chamber music reflects Brahms as composer, his position as composer, and character; surveys the
works with descriptive comments, focusing on Opp. 34
and 36.

1442 *Stahmer, Klaus. "Musikalische Formung in soziologischem
Bezug. Dargestellt an der instrumentalen Kammermusik
von Johannes Brahms" Phil.F. diss., Christian-Albrechts-
Universität, 1968. xvii, [3], 222 pp. ill., facsim., mus.,
notes.
(a) reprint: Musikalische ... Brahms. Kiel: n.p., 1968.
Examines the chamber music in relation to the social
setting in which it was created; includes a facsimile
manuscript of an unpublished chamber work. [see
1544]

1442.5#Thomas-San-Galli, Wolfgang A[lexander]. "Brahms als Künstler"
Rheinische Musik- und Theaterzeitung (Köln) 11/18 (1910)
pp. 312-14. Analyses Opp. 26 and 67 for general qualities
of Brahms's music.

1443 Tovey, Donald Francis. "Brahms, Johannes" in Cobbett's
Cyclopedic Survey of Chamber Music. Walter Willson Cobbett,
comp. and ed. London: Humphrey Milford, Oxford University
Press, 1929. pp. 158-82. mus. Descriptive analysis,
includes detailed comparison of the two versions of Op. 8.
2nd Edition: London, New York; Toronto: Oxford University
Press, 1963.
(a) reprint (from 1929 Edition): Tovey. "Brahms's
Chamber Music" in Tovey. The Main Stream of

Music and Other Essays. Collected with Introduction
by Hubert [J.] Foss. New York: Geoffrey Cumberlege, Oxford University Press, 1949. pp. 220-
70.
*also: London, New York: Oxford University Press,
1949. Title: Essays and Lectures on Music.
(a) i) reprint (of New York Main Stream ...
Edition): New York: Meridian Books,
Inc., 1959.
ii) reprint (of New York Main Stream ...
Edition): New York: AMS Press, 1979.

1444   Webster, James. "Schubert's Sonata Form and Brahms's First
Maturity" 19th Century Music 2/1, 3/1 (7.1978;7.1979)
pp. 18-35;52-71. mus., fig., notes. Describes the characteristics of Schubert's use of sonata form and traces the
development of Brahms's appreciation for Schubert in his
chamber works of the 1860's.

See also 20, 1382, 1386, 1396, 1408, 1418, 1453, 2379, 2405, 2415.d.,
2431, 2466, 2511, 2593, 2601, 2602, 2884.

a. Works with Piano--General

1445   *Groathouse, Daniel Lynn. "Johannes Brahms's Treatment
of Sonata-form in the Opening Movements of the Piano
Trios" M.M.A. thesis, Musicology, University of Wisconsin,
1975. 81 pp. mus., notes. Analysis focusing on melodic
treatment; also discusses relationship between the trios,
and their historical background. [from S202]

1446   Knights, E. Spurgeon. "Brahms's 'Cello Sonatas" The Strad
51/612 (4.1941) pp. 283-84. Historical background and
comments on the balance between cello and piano part.

1447   Pauer, F. X. "Uber Brahms' Geigensonaten" Zeitschrift
für Musik 89/7 (4.1922) pp. 160-63. mus., notes. General
analysis to show the evolution of the literature from Schumann's time; examines the interaction of the violin and
piano parts in Brahms's works.

1448   *Pierce, Esther Mayo. "A Comparative Study of the Styles
of Beethoven and Brahms as Exemplified in the Sonatas
for Piano and Violoncello" M.A. thesis, Music, University
of North Carolina, 1947.

1449   *Prohaska, Carl. Johannes Brahms, 1. und 2. Violin-Sonaten,
op. 78 und 100. (Schlesinger'sche Musikbibliothek. Der
Musikführer nr. 298) Berlin: Schlesinger (R. Lienau),
[1908]. 15 pp.

1450 *R. M. "Brahms-trió́k" Szimfónia (Budapest) [1/7] (1917) p.
      55.

1451 S. B. [Selmar Bagge] "Neue Kammermusik-Werke von Johannes
      Brahms" Leipziger allgemeine musikalische Zeitung 2/1-3 (2.,
      9.,16.;1.;1867) pp. 4-6, 15-17, 24-25. mus., notes. Re-
      views Opp. 38 and 40.

1452 *Threlfall, Sheila Marzolf. "Unity and Variety in the Piano
      Quartets of Johannes Brahms" D.M.A. diss., Piano Per-
      formance, University of Cincinnati, 1981. 173 pp. mus.,
      ind., notes. Historical background and systematic analysis
      of each piano quartet with overall discussion of certain
      characteristic unifying and varying devices in each work;
      includes a historical survey of the piano quartet. [from
      S202]

See also 57, 281, 638, 1112, 1386, 1393, 1396, 1422, 2451.

a. Works with Piano--Specific

See also 1386.

--Op. 8

1453 Eccarius-Sieber, A. "Johannes Brahms' H-dur-Trio (Meister-
      werke der Kammermusik und ihre Pflege)" Neue Musikzeitung
      28/13 (4.4.1907) pp. 277-82. ill., mus., notes. Formal
      analysis, also points out harbingers of Brahms's style;
      includes an overview of all the chamber music.

1454 Herttrich, Ernst. "Johannes Brahms--Klaviertrio H-dur opus
      8, Frühfassung und Spätfassung. Ein analytischer Verg-
      leich" in Musik. Edition. Interpretation. Gedenkschrift
      Günter Henle. Martin Bente, ed. München: G. Henle
      Verlag, 1980. pp. 218-36. mus., notes. Presents the
      historical background of the work, lists the significant
      changes by Brahms in the copyist's manuscript and Hand-
      exemplar (A-Wn), and compares both versions.

1455 Ker. [Louis Köhler] Signale für die musikalische Welt 13/12
      (3.1855) pp. 89-90. Review.

1456 Mason, Daniel Gregory. "Brahms's B major Trio" New York
      Times 81/27,077 (13.3.1932) Section 8, p. 8. Gives the
      circumstances of the first performance of Op. 8 in North
      America, compares both versions.
      (c) excerpt: Mason. "The First Chamber Music Work
          of Brahms. The B Major Trio" Musical Courier

106/2 (Whole no. 2753) (14.1.1933) pp. 6-7. ill.,
mus., notes.
(d) incorporated: in 1436.

See also 250, 272.a., 306, 970, 1075, 1332, 1345, 1359, 1383, 1421,
1437, 1443, 1445, 1509, 1510, 2343, 2372, 2525, 2899.

--Op. 25

1457 Gülke, Peter. "Über Schönbergs Brahms-Bearbeitung" Beiträge
zur Musikwissenschaft 17/1 (1975) pp. 5-14. mus., notes.
Examines how Schoenberg orchestrated Brahms's Op. 25.
(a) reprint: Gülke. in Sonderband Arnold Schönberg
(Musik-Konzepte [17]) München: edition text kritik
GmbH, 1980. pp. 230-42.

1458 H. D. [Hermann Deiters] Allgemeine musikalische Zeitung
N.F. 3/11 (15.3.1865) cols. 182-88. mus., notes. Review.

1459 Jacob, Gorden. "Schoenberg and Brahms's Op. 25" Music
and Letters 32/3 (7.1951) pp. 252-55. notes. Describes
the instrumentation that Schoenberg used in his arrangement.

1460 Mason, Daniel Gregory. "The Pianoforte Quartet of Brahms
in G minor, Op. 25" Musical Times 73/1075 (1.9.1932)
pp. 785-89. mus., notes. Historical background and
analysis.
(a) reprint: in 1436.

1461 *Velten, Klaus. "Schönbergs Instrumentationen Bachscher
und Brahmsischer Werke als Dokumente seines Traditions-
verständnisses" Phil.F. diss., Universität Köln, 1976.
185 pp.
(a) reprint: Velten. "Schönbergs Instrumentation des
Klavierquartetts in g-moll op. 25 von J[ohannes].
Brahms" in Velten. Schönbergs ... Traditions-
verständnisses. (Kölner Beiträge zur Musikforschung Bd. 85) Regensburg: Gustav Bosse Verlag,
1976. pp. 50-105. mus., notes. Traces the influence of Brahms on Schoenberg's work, and
analyses that composer's orchestration of Brahms's
Op. 25.
(d) Velten. "Das Prinzip der entwickelnden Variation bei
Johannes Brahms und Arnold Schoenberg" Musik
und Bildung 6 (10.1974) pp. 547-55. mus., notes.
Discusses how Schoenberg's work on his Op. 38
was influenced by his work orchestrating Brahms's
Op. 25.

See also 250, 1359, 1372F, 1383, 1405, 1437, 1452, 2343, 2372.

--Op. 26

1462   a. [Selmar Bagge] Allgemeine musikalische Zeitung N.F. 1/37
         (9.9.1863) cols. 625-28. mus., notes. Review.

1463   Mason, Daniel Gregory. "The Pianoforte Quartet of Brahms
         in A major, Op. 26" Musical Times 73/1076 (1.10.1932)
         pp. 881-85. mus., notes. Historical background and
         analysis.
         (a) reprint: in 1436.

See also 250, 1132, 1359, 1372F, 1421, 1437, 1442.5, 1452, 1634,
2372, 2422, 2547, 2899.

--Op. 34

1464   Monthly Musical Record 2/19 (1.7.1872) p. 103. Review.

1465   #Altmann, Wilhelm. "Entstehungsgeschichte von Brahms' op.
         34. Eine Quellenstudie" Die Musikwelt (Hamburg) 2/9
         (1.6.1922) pp. 16-19. (Volume pp. 236-39). notes. Cites
         references from primary documentation to trace evolution
         of Op. 34 from string quintet through duo piano sonata
         to final form as piano quintet.

1466   *Ambros, A. W. "Ein neues Klavierquintett von Brahms, op.
         34" [Wiener] Abendpost (30.12.1875).

1467   *Brahms, Johannes. Quintet in F minor for Strings. [Con-
         jectural reconstruction of the destroyed manuscript by
         Sebastian H. Brown, made from Opp. 34 and 34bis] London:
         Stainer and Bell, [1947]. 5 parts.
         (d) Brown, Sebastian H. "The Missing Brahms Quintet"
              The Gramaphone 24/278 (7.1946) pp. 16-18. mus.,
              notes. Relates the history of Opp. 34 and 34bis,
              and describes the method used in reconstructing
              the original quintet version.

1468   Dunhill, Thomas F. "Brahms's Quintet for Pianoforte and
         Strings" Musical Times 72/1058 (1.4.1931) pp. 319-22.
         mus., notes. Historical background and formal movement-
         by-movement commentary.

1469   H. D. [Hermann Deiters] Leipziger allgemeine musikalische
         Zeitung 1/17,18 (25.4. and 2.5.;1866) pp. 134-37, 142-45.
         mus. Review.

1470   *Helm, Theodor. "Wiener Musikbrief: Brahms' Klavierquintett
         f-moll, op. 34a (sic)" Pester Lloyd (Budapest) (29.3.1879).

1471   Mason, Daniel Greogry. "The Pianoforte Quintet of Brahms

in F minor, Op. 34" Musical Times 74/1083 (5.1933) pp.
413-18. mus., notes. Historical background and analysis.
(d) incorporated: into 1436.

1472   Newbould, Brian. "Brahms: Piano Quintet in F Minor, Op.
34 (Analysis in the Sixth Form. 5)" Music Teacher 54/7
(7.1975) pp. 16-17. mus., notes. Detailed analytical
study.

1473   *Prohaska, Karl. Johannes Brahms, Klavierquintett für Pianoforte, zwei Violinen, Viola und Violoncell, op. 34. (Schlesinger'sche Musikbibliothek. Der Musikführer no. 293)
Berlin: Schlesinger (R. Lienau), [1908]. 12 pp.

See also 250, 301, 988, 1359, 1377, 1383, 1397, 1417, 1428, 1437,
1441, 1586, 2372, 2415.c., 2605.

--Op. 38

1474   Altmann, Wilhelm. "Bach-Zitate in der Violoncello-Sonate op.
38 von Brahms" Die Musik (Berlin) 12/2 (Bd. 45) (10.1912)
pp. 84-85. mus., notes. Points out parallels between
passages in the cello part and music in Bach's Kunst der
Fuge.

1475   Klenz, William. "Brahms, Op. 38; Piracy, Pillage, Plagiarism
or Parody?" Music Review 34/1 (2.1973) pp. 39-50. mus.
Discusses the possible relationship of Op. 38 to one of
Romberg's trios in his Op. 38.

1476   Pascall, Robert. "Brahms' Sonata in E minor for Piano and
Cello, Op. 38 (Set Works for 'O' Level)" Music Teacher
60/5 (5.1981) p. 18. notes. Historical background and
analysis.

1477   Stanfield, M[illy]. B. "Some 'Cellistic Landmarks" The
Strad 54/648; 55/649-50, 652-54 (4.-6. and 8.-10.;1944)
pp. 273-74; 9-10, 36, 38, 81-82, 105-06, 129-30. Discusses
Brahms's style and the technique needed to play Op. 38.
(a) reprint: Stanfield, Milly B. Violins and Violinists
9/7-9; 10/1 (10.-12.1948;1.1949) pp. 304-05, 348-49,
392-93; 28-29.

See also 250, 1359, 1383, 1407, 1430, 1437, 1446, 1448, 1451.

--Op. 40

1478   Elliott, David G. "The Brahms Horn Trio and Hand Horn
Idiom" Horn Call 10/1 (10.1979) pp. 61-73. mus., notes.,

discog. Discusses the historical background and compositional processes related to Op. 40, as well as the manner in which Brahms wanted the horn part played; includes discussion on the evolution of the horn.

1479 *King, John Robert. "The Technique of Writing for the French Horn as Illustrated in the Trio Opus 40 by Johannes Brahms" M.Mus. thesis, University of Rochester (Eastman School of Music), 1946.

See also 301, 1359, 1376, 1383, 1421, 1437, 1451, 2515-17, 2523.

--Op. 60

1480 Mason, Daniel Gregory. "The Pianoforte Quartet of Brahms in C minor, Op. 60" Musical Times 74/1082 (4.1933) pp. 311-16. mus., notes. Historical background and analysis. (d) incorporated: into 1436.

1481 Schlösser, L. "Besprechungen neuer Werke" Allgemeine deutsche Musikzeitung 4/47 (16.11.1877) pp. 361-62. Brahms: pp. 361-62. mus. Review.

1482 Webster, James. "The C Sharp Minor Version of Brahms's Op. 60" Musical Times 121/1644 (2.1980) pp. 89-93. ill., mus., notes. Discusses the first version of Op. 60, and its relationship to the final, published version, based on available documentation.

See also 94, 250, 1359, 1372F, 1383, 1402, 1437, 1452, 2368, 2525.

--Op. 78

1483 Beythien, Jürgen. "Die Violinsonate in G-Dur, Op. 78, von Johannes Brahms--ein Beitrag zum Verhältnis zwischen formaler und inhaltlicher Gestaltung" in 1406. pp. 325-32. fig., notes. Examines links between the work's historical background and its form.

1484 #dpa. ""Regen-Lied". Wiederentdeckte Brahms-Sonate für Cello in Wien vorgestellt" General-Anzeiger (Bonn) (16.5. 1974) Feuilleton p. 10. Discusses the discovery of the cello arrangement of Op. 78; includes comments on its textual relationship to Op. 78.

1485 Fellinger, Imogen. "Brahms' Sonate für Pianoforte und Violine Op. 78. Ein Beitrag zum Schaffensprozess des Meisters" Die Musikforschung 18/1 (1.-3.1965) pp. 11-24. facsim., notes. Historical background and detailed

comparison of manuscript (A-Wst) with edition, noting
crossed out materials in particular.

1486 #"Für die entfernte Kusine" Er 24/10 (1974) p. 9. Discusses
the cello arrangement of Op. 78.

1487 *Helm, Theodor. "Wiener Musikbriefe: Brahms' Piano-Violin
Sonate G-dur, op. 78" Pester Lloyd (Budapest) (12.12.1886).

1488 Hollander, Hans. "Der melodische Aufbau in Brahms' "Regen-
lied"-Sonate" NZ-Neue Zeitschrift für Musik 125/1 (1.1964)
pp. 5-7. mus. Discusses the use of motifs from Op. 59,
no. 3, in this work.

1489 Mason, Daniel Gregory. "Brahms, The Master: His Violin
Sonata in G" Musical America 53/3 (10.2.1933) pp. 10-11.
ill., mus. Analysis.
(d) incorporated: into 1436.

1490 #"Le Point de vue de Antoine Goléa" Guide du concert no.
394 (6.-19.;7.;1963) p. 18. Comments on the importance
of balance between the two parts in Op. 78.

1491 Schonberg, Harold C. "Happiness is Playing a "Lost" Brahms
Cello Sonata" New York Times Late City Edition 123/42,561
(4.8.1974) Section 2, p. 13. ill., mus. Reports on the
cello arrangement of Op. 78: relates how manuscript was
discovered and compares it with the original version.

1492 Stephenson, Kurt. "Zur "Regenliedsonate", op. 78" Mitteilungen der Brahms-Gesellschaft Hamburg, e.V. no. 2 (4.
1971) pp. 1-5. Discusses the relationship of Brahms and
Groth, and includes descriptive analysis of Op. 78.

1493 "Uncovered Masterpiece" Time Canadian Edition 104/6 (5.8.1974)
p. 39. ill. Reports on discovery of manuscript of cello
arrangement for Op. 78.
American Edition: pp. 76, 78.

1494 *Weiss, F[erdinand]. "Cu privire la unele probleme de inter-
pretare ale sonatei nr. 1 in sol major pentru pian si vioara
op. 78 de J[ohannes]. Brahms" Lucrari de muzicologie 1
(1965) pp. 211-23. Summaries in Russian, French, German
and Italian. [from S198]

See also 250, 1359, 1407, 1415, 1437, 1447, 1449, 2372, 2404, 2601,
2605.

--Op. 87

1495 Musical Times 24/[480] (1.2.1883) p. 92. Review.

See also 250, 251, 301, 680, 1335, 1359, 1428, 1437, 1445.

--Op. 99

1496　#Mies, Paul. "Notation und Herausgabe bei einigen Werken
　　　　von W[olfgang]. A[madeus]. Mozart, Franz Schubert
　　　　und Johannes Brahms" in Festschrift Joseph Schmid-Görg
　　　　zum 60. Geburtstag. Dagmar Weise, ed. Bonn: Beetho-
　　　　venhaus, 1957. pp. 213-23. Brahms: pp. 219-23. mus.,
　　　　notes. Compares manuscript (A-Wgm) with edition in order
　　　　to study composer's intent.

See also 250, 1359, 1378, 1407, 1437, 1446, 1448, 2372.

--Op. 100

1497　Robjohns, Sydney. "Familiar Difficult Passages on the Violin.
　　　　Brahms Sonata in A--First Movement" Music and Youth 7/10
　　　　(Y. & M. Series. No. 140) (10.1927) p. 232. mus.
　　　　Performance hints for the first movement.
　　　　(d) continued: Robjohns. "Familiar Difficult Passages
　　　　　　on the Violin. Brahms Sonata in A (Concluded);
　　　　　　Beethoven Romance in G" Music and Youth 7/11
　　　　　　(Y. & M. Series. No. 141) (11.1927) p. 257. mus.
　　　　　　Performance suggestions for the second and third
　　　　　　movements.

See also 250, 680, 798, 1359, 1378, 1407, 1437, 1447, 1449, 2404, 2601,
2631.

--Op. 101

See 250, 657, 1359, 1437, 1445.

--Op. 108

1498　Fischer, Richard S. "Brahms' Technique of Motive Development
　　　　in His Sonata in D minor, Opus 108 for Piano and Violin"
　　　　D.M.A. diss., Performance, University of Arizona, 1964.
　　　　iii-viii, 178 pp. mus., notes. Detailed analytical study.

1499　*Prohaska, Carl. Johannes Brahms dritte Violin-Sonate, Op.
　　　　108. (Der Musikführer no. 360) Berlin: Carl Schles-
　　　　inger'sche Buch- und Musikhandlung (R. Lienau), [1907?].
　　　　11 pp. mus.

See also 250, 251, 1359, 1378, 1406, 1407, 1437, 1447, 2404, 2552,
2601, 2604.

--Op. 114

1500 Brahms, Johannes. Trio für Pianoforte, Clarinette und Violon-
      cell Opus 114. Alfons Ott, ed. Tutzing & München: Hans
      Schneider, 1958. 14, [2], [26] pp. ill. Facsimile edition:
      Includes information on the background and publication
      history of the work, its first performances, together with
      description of the manuscript.

1501 *Eppich, Dennis Fred. "A Comprehensive Performance Project
      in Piano Literature and an Essay on the Trio in A minor,
      Op. 114 by Johannes Brahms" D.M.A. diss., University of
      Iowa, 1980.

1502 *Paumgartner, H. "Das Trio für Klavier, Violoncell und
      Klarinette" [Wiener] Abendpost (23.12.1891).

See also 250, 1359, 1376, 1429, 1431, 1437.

See also "Richard Mühlfeld" in III.B.2.

--Op. 120

1503 *Aasmundstad, John. "Part I: Motion, Direction, Shape and
      Gesture as Ingredients of Convincing Musical Performance.
      Part II: A Performance Score Analysis of Brahm's "Sonate
      für Klarinette und Klavier" Op. 12, (sic) #2" D.M.A. diss.,
      Catholic University of America, 1978.

1504 Oppelt, Robert. "A Passage of Brahms. Clarinet vs. Viola"
      American String Teacher 30/1 (Winter 1980) pp. 38-39.
      mus. Points out differences between the two versions of
      Op. 120, with suggested fingerings for passages in the
      viola transcription.

See also 250, 1359, 1376, 1407, 1411, 1431, 1437, 2372, 2450, 2548.

See also "Richard Mühlfeld" in III.B.2.

--F.A.E. Sonatensatz [Hofmann nr. 134; McCorkle WoO posthum 2]

1505 Altmann, Gustav. "Ein unbekanntes Werk von Brahms?"
      Neue Musikzeitung 34/4 (21.11.1912) p. 76. Describes
      the work's characteristics.
      (d) comment: G. "Ein unbekanntes Werk von Brahms"
           Neue Musikzeitung 34/6 (19.12.1912) p. 114. Re-
           lates history of F.A.E. Sonata, as given in 39
           and 1014.

1506 "Sonata of Sentiment" New York Times 86/28,813 (13.12.1936)
Section 11, Part II, p. 9. Review of F.A.E. Sonata.

1507 Valentin, Erich. "Die FAE-Sonate. Das Dokument einer
Freundschaft" Zeitschrift für Musik 102/12 (12.1936) pp.
1337-40. mus., notes. Presents the history of the work,
with discussion of each movement.
(d) comment: Düsterbehn, Heinrich. "Ein Beitrag zur
Entstehung der FAE-Freundschafts-Sonate" Zeitschrift für Musik 103/3 (3.1936) pp. 284-86.
Author relates Albert Dietrich's version of work's
history, and compares it with Valentin's version.

See also 250, 894, 1172, 1359, 1365.5.

--Piano Trio in A major [Hofmann nr. 140; McCorkle Anhang IV, nr.
5]

1508 Altmann, Wilhelm. "Das kürzlich veröffentlichte Brahmssche
Klaviertrio in A-dur" Allgemeine Musikzeitung 65/42 (21.
10.1938) pp. 636-37. mus. Presents the work's history
and manuscript provenance; includes a descriptive analytical
discussion that points out those details that prove the
work was composed by Brahms.

1509 #Brand, Friedrich. "Das neue Brahms-Trio" Die Musik (Berlin)
31/5 (2.1939) pp. 321-27. mus., notes. Pairs this work
with the 1st version of Op. 8, pointing out similarities
between the two works. Asserts that Brahms is the composer.

1510 #Bücken, Ernst. "Bedeutender Brahms-Fund in Bonn. Ueber
ein ungedrucktes Klaviertrio des Meisters" Rheinische
Heimatblätter 14/4 (1936) pp. 8-9. mus. Relates work's
history, pointing out evidence of Brahms's style and a
possible connection to Op. 8.
(d) #Bücken. "Ein neuaufgefundenes Jugendwerk von Johannes Brahms" Die Musik (Berlin) 30/1 (10.1937)
pp. 22-25. mus. Presents historical background,
descriptive analysis and relationship of the work
to Op. 8.

1511 "Concert and Opera Asides" New York Times 88/29,667 (16.
4.1939) Section 10, p. 7. Report on background of the
work.

1512 Fellinger, Richard. "Ist das Klaviertrio in A-dur ein Jugendwerk von Johannes Brahms?" Die Musik (Berlin) 34/6
(5.1942) pp. 197-98. Presents Brahms's personal situation
at that time, and 1014, as evidence of this work being by
him.

See also 250.

--Sonata for Violin and Piano in A minor [McCorkle Anhang IIa, nr. 8]

See 1407.

b. Works without Piano--General

1513 *Fisher, John Frederic. "Cyclic Procedures in the String Quartet from Beethoven to Bartok" Ph.D. diss., Theory, University of Iowa, 1981. xi, 233 pp. mus., fig., notes. Brahms: pp. 83-96. Descriptive analyses of Opp. 51 and 67 with regard to their levels of cyclic thematic affinity. [from Fisher]

1514 *Greenspan, Bertram. "No. 1: The Six Sonatas for Unaccompanied Violin and Musical Legacy of Eugène Ysaÿe. No. 2: The Sextets by Brahms: An Analysis" Mus.D. diss., Violin Music, History and Literature, Theory, Indiana University, 1969. 205 pp. ill., mus., notes., discog.

1515 H. D. [Hermann Deiters] "Streichquartette von Johannes Brahms" Allgemeine musikalische Zeitung 13/28-30 (10., 17.,24.;7.;1878) cols. 433-39, 449-53, 465-72. mus., notes. Review of Opp. 51, nos. 1 and 2, and 67.

1516 Johnson, Martin. "Return to Mozart" Music and Letters 25/2 (4.1944) pp. 77-86. "IV. Relevance of the Brahms Quartets to Mozart's": pp. 82-84. Shows how Brahms's works resemble Mozart's in mood, style, and background.

1517 *Schmidt, Erik. "Den formale opbygning af Brahms' strygekvartetter og på basis heraf en sammenligning med Beethovens anvendelse af sonateformen i strygekvartetterne op. 59, 1-3" Specialeafhandlinger til skoleembedseksamen i musik, Københavns Universitet, 1955.

1518 *Wilke, Rainer. "Brahms. Reger. Schönberg. Streichquartette. Motivischthematische Prozesse und formale Gestalt" Fachbereich Kulturgeschichte und Kulturkunde, diss., Universität Hamburg, 1980. 233 pp. mus., notes.
　(a) reprint: Brahms. Reger ... Gestalt. (Schriftenreihe zur Musik Bd. 18) Hamburg: Verlag der Musikalienhandlung Karl Dieter Wagner, 1980.
　"Brahms, op. 51.2": pp. 33-62.
　"Brahms, op. 51.1": pp. 62-83.
　"Brahms, op. 67": pp. 83-97.
　"Brahms, Zusammenfassung": pp. 98-105.

Discusses the evolution of the string quartet from Brahms to Schönberg: analysis of selected movements from Opp. 51 no. 1 and 67; all of Op. 51 no. 2. Also discusses Reger's Opp. 74, 54 no. 1, 121; also Schoenberg's Op. 7 and Quartet in D major (1897).

See also 281, 1386, 1422, 2451.

b. Works Without Piano--Specific

See also 1386.

--Op. 18

1519   Br., v. "Kritische Revüe" Deutsche Musikzeitung (Wien) 3/6 (8.2.1862) pp. 46-47. Brahms: p. 46. Review.

1520   Knorr, Jwan. Johannes Brahms. Sextett in B-dur. Op. 18. (Der Musikführer no. 23) Frankfurt a/M.: Verlag von H. Bechhold, [1895]. 20 pp. mus. Descriptive analysis with short background on the work.
     *also: Stuttgart: Schmitt, n.d.
     *also: Berlin: Schlesinger, n.d.
     (a) *reprint: in 1346.

1521   Mason, Daniel Gregory. "Brahms's First Sextet" Disques (Philadelphia) 3/11 (1.1933) pp. 466-71. ill., mus., notes. Historical background and descriptive analysis.
     (d) incorporated: into 1436.

1522   N. [Carl von Noorden] Deutsche Musikzeitung (Wien) 3/23 (7.6.1862) pp. 179-82. mus., notes. Review.

1523   Truscott, Harold. "Brahms and Sonata Style" Music Review 25/3 (8.1964) pp. 186-201. mus. Analyzes Op. 18, 1st movement, to observe Brahms's mastering of sonata form.

See also 250, 1332, 1359, 1379, 1383, 1421, 1428, 1437, 1514, 2415.

--Op. 36

1524   Monthly Musical Record 3/26 (1.2.1873) pp. 21-22. Review.

1525   H. D. [Hermann Deiters] Leipziger allgemeine musikalische Zeitung 2/11,12 (13.,20.;3.;1867) pp. 87-90, 95-98. mus., notes. Review.

1526 *Knorr, Jwan. Johannes Brahms, Sextett für Streichinstrumente.
      (No. 2, G-dur, Op. 36). (Der Musikführer. No. 57)
      Frankfurt a/M.: Verlag von H. Bechhold, [1897]. 22 pp.
      *also: Stuttgart: Schmitt, n.d.
      *also: Berlin: Schlesinger, n.d.
      (a) *reprint: in 1346.

See also 250, 1348, 1359, 1383, 1430, 1437, 1441, 1514, 2526.

--Op. 51

1527 Hill, William G. "Brahms' opus 51--A Diptych" Music Review
      13/[2] (5.1952) pp. 110-24. mus., notes. Examines both
      quartets to see what unifying devices are used within each
      one, as well as between the two works.

1528 Mason, Daniel Gregory. "The String Quartet of Brahms in
      C minor, Op. 51, No. 1" Musical Times 73/1077 (1.11.1932)
      pp. 978-83. mus., notes. Historical background and
      descriptive analysis.
      (d) reworked: into 1436.

1529 _____. "The String Quartets of Brahms: No. 2, in A
      minor" Musical Times 74/1079 (1.1933) pp. 23-27. mus.,
      notes. Historical background and descriptive analysis.
      (a) reprint: in 1436.

1530 *Mayhew, Mary Elizabeth. "A Comparative Analysis of the
      Quartets, Opus 51 by Johannes Brahms" M.M. diss., Music,
      University of Illinois [(Urbana)], 1950. 102 pp. ill.,
      notes.

1531 Sharp, J. Wharton. "Brahms's First String Quartet" The
      Strad 21/245-48 (9.-12.1910) pp. 177-79, 191-92, 241-42,
      280-82. mus. General analysis for Op. 51, no. 1.

See also 250, 1359, 1383, 1412, 1426.d., 1428, 1437, 1513, 1515-18,
2372, 2493, 2546.

--Op. 67

1532 Mason, Daniel Gregory. "The String Quartets of Brahms:
      No. 3, in B flat, Op. 67" Musical Times 74/1081 (3.1933)
      pp. 209-14. mus., notes. Historical background and
      descriptive analysis.
      (a) reprint: in 1436.

See also 250, 1359, 1426.d., 1437, 1442.5, 1513, 1515-18.

--Op. 88

1533   Musical Times 24/[480] (1.2.1883) p. 93. Review.

1534   Ravizza, Victor. "Möglichkeiten des Komischen in der Musik.
Der letzte Satz des Streichquintetts in F dur, Op. 88 von
Johannes Brahms" Archiv für Musikwissenschaft 31/2 (1974)
pp. 137-50. mus., notes. Discusses how comic effects
are possible in music, with examples from Op. 88.

1535   Redlich, Hans F. "Bruckner and Brahms Quintets in F"
Music and Letters 36/3 (7.1955) pp. 253-58. mus. Brahms:
pp. 257-58. Describes parallels in the backgrounds of
both works, also compares the two composers' styles.

See also 250, 1335, 1359, 1383, 1437, 1592.

--Op. 111

1536   *e. [Eusebius Mandyczewski] "Ein neues Quintett von Brahms,
Op. 111" Deutsche Kunst- und Musikzeitung (Wien) [18]
(1.12.1891).

1537   *Paumgartner, H. "Ein neues Quintett von Brahms op. 111"
[Wiener] Abendpost (19.11.1890).

See also 250, 1359, 1383, 1437.

--Op. 115

1538   Boyce, Janice L. "Musical Interpretation: One Important
Aspect" School Musician 42/3 (11.1970) pp. 6, 8, 59.
Discusses the relationship between ensemble and soloist
as seen in the first movements of Brahms's Op. 115 and
Mozart's KV 581, and its implications for interpreting the
two works.

1539   Dyson, George. "Brahms's Clarinet Quintet, Op. 115" Musical
Times 76/1106 (4.1935) pp. 315-19. mus., notes. General
remarks on the work with broad movement-by-movement
analysis.

1540   Häfner, Roland. Johannes Brahms. Klarinettenquintett.
(Meisterwerke der Musik. Werkmonographien zur Musikgeschichte 14) München: Wilhelm Fink Verlag, 1978. 54,
[2] pp. ill., mus., fig., notes. Historical background
and analysis of work; includes documentation for first
performances.

1541 *Maas, Gary L. "Problems of Form in the Clarinet Quintet of
Johannes Brahms" M.M. thesis, Musicology, University of
Wisconsin, 1967. 88 pp. mus., notes. Describes changes
Brahms made within formal structure in this work. [from S202]

1542 *Paumgartner, H. "Das h-moll Quintett, op. 115" [Wiener]
Abendpost (23.1.1892).

1543 *Ratterree, Jack L. "The Clarinet and Its Use in the String
Trios and String Quintets by Mozart and Brahms" M.A.
thesis, American University, 1964. 61 pp. Discusses the
clarinet's evolution, with analysis showing its technical
and musical possibilities. [from S155]

See also 250, 1359, 1376, 1412, 1428, 1429, 1431, 1437, 3029.

See also "Richard Mühlfeld" in III.B.2.

--Hymne zur Verherrlichung des grossen Joachim
[McCorkle Anhang III, nr.1]

1544 #Stahmer, Klaus. "En musikalsk spøg" [Ebbe Knudsen, trans-
later] Musik (København) 3/4 (1.1969) pp. 3-5. facsim.,
notes. Historical background for this work.
(d) incorporated: Brahms, Johannes. Hymne zur Verherrlichung des grossen Joachim. Walzer für
zwei Violinen und Kontrabass oder Violoncello.
Klaus Stahmer, ed. 1. Ausgabe Hamburg: J.
Schuberth & Co., 1976. 19 pp., 3 parts. ill.,
facsim., mus. Historical background, manuscript
facsimile and transcription of the work; includes
parts which have been edited/transcribed. German/
English text.

See also 1442.

--Quintet in F minor for Strings [earlier version of Op. 34]

See 1397, 1465, 1467.

c. Brahms's Editing and Arranging of Other Composers' Chamber
Music

See 793.

2. Solo Keyboard Works

a. Piano Works--General

1545 Masters in Music 5/part 29 (5.1905). [3], 48 pp. (volume
pp. 193-240) ill., mus.
Issue Title: Brahms. Piano Works. Contains 174.a.d.,
871.c.ii., 1548.d.c., 1605. Includes music for selections
from Opp. 1, 10, 76, 79.

1546 Musical Times 35/614 (1.4.1894) p. 246. Reviews Opp. 118,
119.

1547 Aronson, Maurice. "Brahms Variations" Musical Courier 76/9
(Whole no. 1979) (28.2.1918) pp. 35-36. ill. A general
discussion of the solo piano works containing variations,
that focuses on Brahms's skills at this form.

1548 Bie, Oscar. Das Klavier und seine Meister. München: Verlagsanstalt F. Bruckmann A.-G., 1898. viii, 312pp. +
Beilagen. Brahms: p. 290. Describes the character of
Brahms's solo piano music.
(d) *English translation and Revision by E. E. Kellett
and E. W. Naylor; Bie. A History of the Pianoforte
and Pianoforte Players. London: J. M. Dent &
Company; New York: E. P. Dutton & Company,
1899. xi, 336 pp.
(a) reprint: Da Capo Reprint Edition with Foreword by Aube Tzerko. New York: Da
Capo Press, 1966. viii, xi, 366 pp.
Brahms: pp. 322-23.
(c) excerpt: [Daniel Gregory Mason] "The Art
of Brahms" Masters in Music 5/part 29
(5.1905) p. 10 (volume p. 202)

1549 Boughton, Rutland. "Brahms' Variations for Piano Solo:
Musical Opinion & Music Trade Review 22/254 (1.11.1898)
pp. 109-10. notes. Descriptive analysis for Opp. 9, 21,
24, 35; includes comments on Brahms as composer in this
form.

1550 "The Brahms Piano Technics" Musical Courier 42/18 (Whole
no. 1101) (1.5.1901) pp. 21-22. Reports on Fuller-Maitland's opinion of Brahms the composer, as seen in his
solo piano works.

1551 *Brandes, Alan Charles. "The Solo Piano Variations of Johannes Brahms" Ph.D. diss., Boston University, 1968.

1552 *Brinkman, Joseph and Benning Dexter. Piano Music:

Available Editions Recommended By Joseph Brinkman and
Benning Dexter. (University of Michigan Official Publication [Vol. 53, no. 38]) [Ann Arbor:] University of Michigan, [1951]. 15 pp.
*[1956 Edition:] (University of Michigan Official Publication
Vol. 57, no. 68) 19 pp.
  (d) Dexter, Benning and George Loomis. "Choosing The
       Best Edition. The Piano Works of Twelve Important
       Composers" Clavier 8/6 (9.1969) pp. 50-52. "Jo-
       hannes Brahms (1833-1897)": p. 51. A listing, with
       evaluative comments, on editorial reliability and use
       of available manuscript sources.
       (d) expanded: Dexter, Benning and Charles
          Timbrell. "Another Look at Editions. The
          Piano Works of Twelve Important Compo-
          sers." Piano Quarterly 30/116 (Winter
          1981-82) pp. 39-41. Brahms: p. 40.

1553 *Cardus, Neville. Manchester Guardian.
    (d) reworked: Cardus. "Brahms and The Piano" in
       Cardus. Talking of Music. London: Collins,
       1957. pp. 128-32. An examination of the late
       piano pieces to reawaken appreciation for Brahms.
    *also: New York: Macmillan, [1957].

1554 *Careva, E. M. "Fortepiannoe tvorchestvo Bramsa" diss.,
    [M. V. Lomonosov State University?] Moskva, 1972. 278
    pp.

1555 *Carson, H. "Brahms's Variations for Pianoforte: An His-
    torical and Analytical Study" M. A. thesis, Queen's Uni-
    versity, Belfast.

1556 [Daniel Gregory Mason] "Critical Summary" in [Mason] "The
    Art of Brahms" Masters in Music 5/part 29 (5.1905) pp.
    10-12 (volume pp. [[202-04]]). Comments on Brahms's
    ties to the past and on his classical-romantic tendencies,
    as seen in his piano works.

1557 *Dobrowolski, Janusz. "Innowacje chopinowskie w miniaturach
    fortepianowych Brahmsa" in Muzyka fortepianowa IV.
    Janusz Krassowski, ed. (Prace specjalne 25) Gdańsk:
    Państwowa Wyższa Szkoła Musyczna, 1981. pp. 93-106.
    Discusses Chopin influences in the smaller piano works
    of Brahms. Includes English summary. [from S202]

1558 Domek, Richard Charles, Jr. "A Syntactic Approach to the
    Study of Rhythm Applied to the Late Piano Works of
    Johannes Brahms" Ph.D. diss., Indiana University, 1976.
    [2], iii-xiv, 414, [1] pp. mus., fig., notes. Attempts
    to explain some systematic characteristics inherent in musical
    rhythm, focusing on Opp. 116-19.

1559 Fairleigh, James P. "Neo-classicism in the Later Piano Works of Brahms" Piano Quarterly 15/58 (Winter 1966-67) pp. 24-26. Analysis of these characteristics, as seen in the formal design of Opp. 76, 79, 116-19.

1560 Feinstein, Bernice. "The Seven Capriccios of Johannes Brahms. Op. 76, nos. 1, 2, 5, 8 and Op. 116, nos. 1, 3, 7" Ed.D. diss., Columbia University, 1972. 1-3, ii-iv, 1-237 pp. mus., notes. Structural and stylistic analysis; includes discussion of "Capriccio" as a music title from the 16th-20th centuries and comment on performance practice of these works.

1561 Ferguson, Donald N. Piano Music of Six Great Composers. (Prentice-Hall Music Series) New York: Prentice-Hall Inc., 1947. mus., fig., ind., notes.
"Johannes Brahms--The Earlier Works": pp. 251-84.
"Johannes Brahms--The Later Works": pp. 285-318.
General analysis and performance suggestions.
*also: London: Williams and Norgate Ltd., [1950]. Title: Piano Interpretation. Studies in the Music of Six Great Composers.
(a) *reprint (of New York Edition): (Essay Index Reprint Series) Freeport, N.Y.: Books for Libraries Press, [1970].

1562 Galston, Gottfried. "Brahms" in Galston. Studienbuch. Berlin: Verlag von Bruno Cassirer, 1910. pp. 173-208. mus. Performance suggestions for Opp. 24, 79, 119, 39, and 35.

1563 #Georgii, Walter. "Brahms als Klavierkomponist--im vorigen Jahrhundert und Heute" Musik im Unterricht Ausgabe A 53/12 (1962) pp. 344-47. ill., mus., notes. Compares the contemporary view (late 1800's) of the early piano works, with that of present day.

1564 *Gui, Vittorio. "Brahms" Il Pianoforte 3/3 (1922).

1565 *Haase, Rudolf. "Studien zum kontrapunktischen Klaviersatz von Johannes Brahms" Phil.F. diss., Universität Köln, 1951. 84 pp. mus.

1566 Hahn, A. Neue Berliner Musikzeitung 11/27 (1.7.1857) p. 210. Reviews the separate issue of Op. 5, 2nd movement, and Op. 10.

1567 *Hautz, Hilar. "Die Harmonik der Brahms'schen Soloklavierwerke. Teil I. Harmonische Analyse der Brahms'schen Soloklavierwerke nebst einer Darstellung des Problems harmonischer Analysen" Phil.F. diss., Universität München, 1942. 44, [2], 50-156 pp.

1568   Herrmann, Kurt. "Zur Interpretation Brahmsscher Klavier-
        werke" Musik im Unterricht [Ausgabe A?] 52/7-8 (1961)
        pp. 218-23. ill., facsim., mus. Comments on character-
        istics of piano music in general; includes comments on
        Brahms as pianist and gives performance practice suggestions.

1569   *Hirschfeld, Robert. "Neue Werke von Brahms" Die Presse
        (Wien) (20.11.1894). Discusses Opp. 116-19. [from 241].

1570   *Ignatius-Metsola, Eeva. "Tyylikehitys Johannes Brahmsin
        duosonaateissa" Pro gradu-tutkielma, moniste, Helsingin
        Yliopiston Musiikkitieteen Laitos, 1977.

1571   *Jensen, Gunver Hasseriis. "En undersøgelse af den ensatsede
        klavier-komposition hos Johs. [Johannes] Brahms, herunder
        en sammenligning mellem Brahms' og hans forgaengeres
        kompositioner inden for naevnte genre" Specialeafhandlinger
        til skoleembedseksamen i musik, Københavns Universitet,
        1940.

1572   *Jervis-Read, H[arold]. V[incent]. The Arrant Artist. Lon-
        don: Heath, Cranton, Ltd., [1939].
        (c) excerpt: in 2915. p. 285.

1573   *Kern, Edith. "Kirchentonale Wendungen in der romantischen
        Klaviermusik" Phil.F. diss., Universität Wien, 1937. 217
        pp. Brahms: pp. 110-38. [from 243]

1574   Kirby, F. E. "Brahms and The Piano Sonata" in Paul A.
        Pisk. Essays in His Honor. John Glowacki, ed. Austin:
        College of Fine Arts, University of Texas, 1966. pp. 163-
        80. mus., notes. Studies the three piano sonatas to
        determine if they are symptomatic of Brahms's style.

1575   *Kurzweil, Elisabeth Katharina. "Der Klaviersatz bei Johannes
        Brahms" Phil.F. diss., Universität Wien, 1934.

1576   Lliurat, F. "Johannes Brahms i les seves obres per a piano"
        Revista musical catalana 30/360 (12.1933) pp. 496-505.
        ill. Presents author's impressions of these works as a
        study aid for others.

1577   MacDougall, H. C. "Brahms for Piano--Study" in "Johannes
        Brahms (The New Education--The Mastery of Teaching
        Material)" Musician (Philadelphia) 3/5 (5.1898) p. 128.
        Suggests works to be studied; includes comment on the
        appreciation of Brahms's music.

1578   *McMahan, Robert Hayden. "The Late Piano Music of Brahms--
        An Essay Toward a Scientific Aesthetic" Ph.D. diss., Uni-
        versity of Chicago, 1964.

1579 Maier, Guy. "The Teacher's Round Table" Etude 60/9
(9.1942) pp. 598, 628, 636. Discusses Brahms's style
in the piano music, and how it should be interpreted.

1580 *Martin, Janet Sitges. "Motivic Unity in Selected Character
Pieces by Johannes Brahms" D.M.A. diss., Louisiana State
University and Agricultural and Mechanical College, 1978.

1581 *Martinotti, Sergio. "Il Pianoforte di Brahms" Il Pianoforte
di Schubert e di Brahms (?) 7 (1970) pp. 19-33. ill.
Discusses the composer as seen in his piano music. [from
S202]

1582 Mason, Colin. "Brahms' Piano Sonatas" Music Review 5/2
(5.1944) pp. 112-18. mus. Examines features of musical
interest in each work. [from S155]

1583 *_____. "The Pianist's Brahms" Guardian (London) [118?]
(16.4.1964) p. 8.

1584 *Matthews, Mary Lynn. "A Study of Formal Structure in
Johannes Brahms' Character Pieces for Solo Piano, Op.
116-119" M.M. thesis, University of Massachusetts, 1980.
177 pp. fig. Includes documentation of Brahms's techniques
for achieving continuity in these works. [from S155]

1585 *Meyersahm, Kjeld. "En Redegørelse for de Brahms'ske ensatsede klaverstykkers saerlige praeg, specielt en undersøgelse af tendensen mod enhed og de anvendte midler
til betoning af enheden" Specialeafhandlinger til skoleembedseksamen i musik, Københavns Universitet, 1950.

1586 *Moldenhauer, Hans. "Duo-Pianism. A Dissertation" Ph.D.
diss., Chicago Musical College, 1950.
    (a) reprint: Duo-Pianism. A Dissertation. [Chicago:]
        Chicago Musical College Press, 1950. [7], 400
        pp. notes. "Brahms": pp. 93-109. also pp.
        319-21. notes, discog. Discusses his use of
        this medium in regards to his friendship with
        Clara Schumann, and discusses those works which
        evolved through this medium, or used it in their
        final form: Opp. 15, 34, 56a, 90, 98, 39; includes
        historical background and descriptive analysis
        for Op. 56b.
    (d) Moldenhauer. "The Two Piano Medium in the Workshop
        of Johannes Brahms" Journal of the American
        Musicological Society 4/2 (Summer 1951) pp. 169-70.
        Abstract--an overview of Brahms's works in this
        genre, as well as the works evolving through its
        use.

1587   Morris, Herbert. "The Brahms" Poetry 88/4 (7.1956) p.
       218. A poem that describes the playing of Brahms's piano
       music.
       (a) *reprint: Morris. In New Poems by American Poets
           #2. Rolfe Humphries, ed. New York: Ballantine
           Books, Inc., 1957. p. 116.
           (a) reprint: (Granger Index Reprint Series) New
               York: Books for Libraries Press, 1970.

1588   #Moser, Hans Joachim. "Brahmsens Klavierspiel und Klaviersatz"
       Das Klavierspiel 6/4 (1964) pp. 18-19. Describes the charac-
       teristics of Brahms's piano music and of Brahms as pianist;
       includes comments on how to perform the works.

1589   #Nagel, Wilibald. [Willibald Nagel] "Brahms' Klaviermusik
       für Haus" Blätter für Haus- und Kirchenmusik [2] (1898)
       pp. 86-88, 101-05. Discusses Opp. 10, 76, 79, 116-19;
       includes suggestions on performance and general comments
       on Brahms's style.

1590   _____. "Die Klaviersonaten von Joh[annes]. Brahms.
       Technisch-ästhetische Analysen" Neue Musikzeitung 34/14,
       15, 18, 20, 22, 24; 35/5, 9, 11 (17.4. and 2.5. and 19.6.
       and 17.7. and 21.8. and 18.9. and 27.11.; 1913 and 29.1.
       and 5.3.; 1914) pp. 265-69, 288-91, 365-68, 404-06, 441-45,
       482-86; 85-90, 165-70, 205-10. mus. Analysis of Opp.
       1, 2, 5; includes descriptive remarks and comments on
       Brahms's early development as a composer.
       (a) reprint: Nagel. Die ... Analysen. Stuttgart:
           Verlag von Carl Grüninger (Klett & Hartmann),
           n.d. 128 pp.

1591   Niemann, Walter. "Johannes Brahms als Klavierkomponist"
       Die Musik (Berlin) 3/18 (Bd. 11) (6.1904) pp. 419-34.
       mus., notes. Examines the solo piano works; includes
       comments on Brahms's style and on his influence.

1592   Orvis, Joan. "The Smaller Piano Works of Johannes Brahms"
       M.A. thesis, Music, University of Washington, 1954.
       65, [2] pp. notes. Historical background and analysis
       of Opp. 10, 76, 79, 116-19.

1593   Pascall, Robert. "Unknown Gavottes by Brahms" Music and
       Letters 57/4 (10.1976) pp. 404-11. mus. [pp. 409-11],
       notes. Discusses a Sarabande in A major and two Gavottes
       in A minor [Hofmann nr. 137; McCorkle WoO posthum 3,5]:
       dating and genesis, manuscript description, a transcription
       of the works; includes comments on Brahms's reuse of
       thematic material.

1594   Puchelt, Gerhard. Variationen für Klavier im 19. Jahrhundert.

Blüte und Verfall einer Kunstform. Hildesheim, New York: Georg Olms Verlag, 1973. Brahms: pp. 124-36. notes. Discusses Brahms and the variation form, including comments on his variation works and variation movements within works: Opp. 1, 9, 21, 24, 35, 23, 56b.

1595 Robert, Walter. "Remarks on Brahms' Piano Style" Bulletin of the American Musicological Society no. 11-12-13 (9.1948) pp. 83-84. Abstract--general comments and placing of Brahms in 19th Century piano music.

1596 *Salocks, Madeline Katherine Bacon. "A Discussion of Selected Four-Hand Work by Brahms and Dvorak" D.M.A. diss., Stanford University, 1980. 134 pp. Discusses Op. 23 and Ungarische Tänze, no. 1 with reference to performance practice; includes analysis of available recordings.

1597 *Schenker, Heinrich. [sketches for analyses of Opp. 35, 39, 76, 79, 116-19]

1598 *Shedlock, J. S. "Schumann, Chopin, Brahms, and Liszt" in Shedlock. The Pianoforte Sonata. Its Origin and Development. London: Methuen & Co., 1895. ind.
    (a) reprint: Da Capo Reprint Edition. With a Foreword to the Da Capo Edition by William S. Newman. New York: Da Capo Press, 1964. x, vii, [1], 245 pp. ind. Brahms: pp. 209-18. mus., notes. Descriptive analyses of Opp. 1, 2, and 5.

1599 Siegmund-Schultze, Walther. "Chopin und Brahms" in The Book of The First International Congress Devoted to the Works of Frederick Chopin. Warszawa 16th-22nd February 1960. Zofia Lissa, ed. Warszawa: Pánstwowe Wydawnictwo Naukowe [PWN Polish Scientific Publishers], 1965. pp. 388-95. mus., notes. Compares style of both composers as seen in their piano music.

1600 Sterling, Eugene Allen. "A Study of Chromatic Elements in Selected Piano Works of Beethoven, Schubert, Schumann, Chopin and Brahms" Ph.D. diss., Indiana University, 1966. xii, 246, [1] pp. mus., fig., notes. An examination and comparison of chromaticism as a contribution towards understanding these composers' style, and this 19th-Century phenomenon in general. Discusses Brahms's Opp. 2, 76, 116, 118.

1601 Storer, H. J. "Brahms as Pianoforte Composer" Musician (Philadelphia) 4/7 (7.1899) p. 246. General discussion; includes suggestions for pieces to study.

1602 Szumowska, Antoinette [et al.]. "Well-known Piano Solos

and How to Play Them" The International Library of Music
for Home and Studio. Music Literature. Volume III. The
Pianist's Guide. New York: The University Society, 1925.
pp. 275-322. Brahms: pp. 280, 298, 308. Discusses
selections from Op. 39, the Ungarische Tänze [Hofmann nr.
128; McCorkle WoO 1], and Brahms's arrangement of a
Gavotte from Gluck's Iphigénie en Aulide [Hofmann nr.
159; McCorkle Anhang Ia, nr. 2].

1603   Walker, Ernest. "Brahms's Piano Music: Some Bypaths"
        Monthly Musical Record 63/746 (5.1933) pp. 73-74. notes.
        Descriptive analysis of less well-known piano works up to
        Op. 23, in an attempt to increase awareness of them.

1604   *Warburton, A[nnie]. O. Music Teacher and Piano Student
        [41 or earlier (before 1963)]. [from 1604.a]
        (a) reprint: see 1375A. Analysis of Opp. 79 no. 2,
            and 118 nos. 2, 3.

1605   [Daniel Gregory Mason] "The Works of Brahms" Masters in
        Music 5/part 29 (5.1905) pp. 12-16 (volume pp. 204-08).
        Descriptive analysis with suggestions for performance, for
        sections of Opp. 1, 10, 76, 79.

1606   *Yang, Byung Hoh. "A Study of Part Forms in the Selected
        Intermezzi (Opp. 116-119) of Johannes Brahms" M.M. thesis,
        North Texas State University, 1979" 136 pp. Analyzes the
        relationship between formal structure and the music text
        of these pieces [from S155].

See also 20, 57, 170, 223, 251, 253, 639, 681, 1185, 1358, 1373, 1381,
1387, 1389, 1391-93, 1396, 1398, 1399, 1401, 1404, 1409, 1410, 1413,
1418, 1420, 1599, 1613, 1685, 1689.d., 1710, 2405, 2431, 2456, 2608,
2623, 2892, 2893, 2951.

a. Specific Works

See also 1387.d.

--Op. 1

1607   *Rheinische Musikzeitung 4/10 (11.3.1854) pp. 78f.

1608   H.C.C. [Henry Cope Colles] "Brahms: Opus 1" Academy
        [70]/1782 (30.6.1906) pp. 625-26. Analysis.

1609   "Johannes Brahms" Niederrheinische Musikzeitung 2/9 (4.3.
        1854) pp. 65-67. mus., notes. Analysis of Op. 1 as an
        indication of Brahms's potential for greatness.

1610   Newman, William S. "Some 19th-Century Consequences of
       Beethoven's "Hammerklavier" Sonata, Opus 106. Part 2"
       Piano Quarterly 17/68 (Summer 1969) pp. 12-17. mus.,
       notes. Brahms: pp. 14-15. mus., notes. Discusses
       the relationship between Op. 1 and the Beethoven work,
       with examples of melodic, rhythmic and thematic allusions.

See also 1328, 1332, 1345, 1350, 1361, 1383, 1407, 1409, 1574, 1582,
1590, 1594, 1598, 1605, 1612, 2343, 2372, 2532, 2553.

--Op. 2

See 250, 1328, 1332, 1345, 1350, 1361, 1383, 1407, 1409, 1574,
1582, 1590, 1598, 1600, 1603, 1612, 2343, 2372.

--Op. 4

See 250, 878, 1328, 1332, 1345, 1350, 1361, 1409, 1603, 2343, 2478,
2553.

--Op. 5

1611   *Hodzhava, R. "Fortepiannaia sonata Bramsa fa-minor" in
       Vypusk III. Trudov Sbornik, ed. Tbilisi: Tbilisskaia
       Gosudarstvennaia Konservatoria, 1975. pp. 238-72. mus.,
       notes.

1612   Kraus, Detlef. "Das Andante aus der Sonate Op. 5 von
       Brahms--Versuch einer Interpretation--" Brahms-Studien
       Bd. 3 (1979) pp. 47-51. Examines slow movements in the
       other two piano sonatas, and this slow movement in rela-
       tion to the whole of Op. 5; includes suggestions for per-
       formance.

1613   Maier, Guy. "The Scherzo from the "Sonata in F Minor" of
       Brahms. A Master Lesson" Etude 57/8 (8.1939) pp. 508,
       546. ill., mus. Discusses how to interpret this movement;
       also presents suggestions for concert programmes of
       Brahms's piano music.

1614   Sutton, Wadham. "Brahms: Sonata in F minor, Op. 5"
       Music Teacher 52/8 (8.1973) pp. 12-13. ill. Descriptive
       analysis with performance practice comments.

See also 2, 250, 1328, 1332, 1345, 1350, 1383, 1407, 1409, 1566,
1574, 1582, 1590, 1598, 2343, 2372, 2523, 2552, 2619.

--Op. 9

1615   Br., v. "[Rezensionen] c. Für Pianoforte zu zwei Händen"
        Deutsche Musikzeitung (Wien) 1/14 (31.3.1860) pp. 108-09.
        Brahms: p. 108. review.

1616   Crowder, Louis. "Brahms' Early Tribute to the Schumanns"
        Clavier 5/7 (12.1966) pp. 18-25. ill., mus. Analysis
        showing allusions to Schumann piano pieces in Op. 9,
        as well as the work's relationship to Schumann's style;
        also discusses the relationship between Brahms and the
        Schumanns.

1617   Geiringer, Karl. "Ein unbekanntes Blatt aus Schumanns
        Endenicher Zeit" Anbruch 17/10 (11./12.1935) pp. 273-78.
        facsim., notes. Letter is from Schumann to Brahms, August
        1854, concerning Schumann's comment on Op. 9 which he
        wrote as marginalia.
        (d) see: 1618.

1618   Geiringer, Karl. "New Light on Schumann's Last Years"
        The Listener 21/543 (8.6.1939) p. 1237. facsim. Describes
        Schumann's reaction to Brahms's Op. 9, in a letter sent
        to Brahms, Autumn 1854.

1619   #Ker. [Louis Köhler] Signale für die musikalische Welt 13/13
        (3.1855) pp. 97-98. Review.

1620   Lacroix-Navaro, Yves. "De Schumann à Brahms" La Revue
        musicale (Paris) 17/163 (2.1936) pp. 89-94. fig., notes.
        Presents an affective analysis of Op. 9; also comments
        on Clara Schumann the woman, together with Brahms and
        Schumann as composers.

1621   Schwartz, Heinrich. "Johannes Brahms: Variationen über
        ein Thema von Schumann (op. 9) Fis-moll" Zeitschrift
        für Musik 87/10 (16.5.1920) pp. 119-21. mus. Analysis.

1622   Tetzel, Eugen. "Die Schumann-Variationen von Brahms.
        Eine Musikalische Analyse" Zeitschrift für Musik 96/6 (6.
        1929) pp. 311-16. mus. [see also Beilage no. 5 (5.1929)
        for additional mus.]

See also 250, 800, 854, 1328, 1332, 1345, 1409, 1549, 1594, 1603,
2343.

--Op. 10

1623   *Boldt, Kenwyn Guy. "The Solo Piano Ballade in the Nineteenth
        Century". D.M. diss., Piano Performance, Indiana

University (Bloomington), 1967. iii, 47 pp. fig., notes.
Discusses Op. 10 pp. 10-12 and passim, with description
of programmatic and stylistic elements with tabular analysis.
[from Music Library, Indiana University]

1624   Hambourg, Mark. "The "Ballade, Op. 10, No. 1" of Brahms.
A Master Lesson by The Renowned Piano Virtuoso" Etude
56/11 (11.1938) pp. 722, 730-31. ill., mus. [pp. 730-31]
Presents views on interpretation.

1625   *Holstad, Albert John. "I. The Ballades of Chopin, Liszt,
Brahms and Grieg; A Study of the Major Variations of
Beethoven's Second Creative Period; The Piano Sonatas
of Charles T. Griffes and Ernest Bloch. II. Performance"
D.M. diss., Performance, Piano, Northwestern University,
1973.

1626   Ker. [Louis Köhler] Signale für die musikalische Welt 14/18
(4.1856) pp. 201-02. Review.

1627   #Tiedemann, Hans-Joachim. "Die Klavier-Ballade "Edward"
Opus 10 nr 1, von Johannes Brahms" Musik im Unterricht
Ausgabe B 56 (1965) pp. 324-29. ill. Examines the poem
and how Brahms's music follows its sense.

1628   *Turrill, Pauline Venable. "The Piano Ballade in the Romantic
Era: A Categorical Study of Styles as Suggested by Genres
of Narrative Poetry" Ph.D. diss., University of Southern
California, 1977. Analysis of characteristics and stylistic
differences between three proposed categories as suggested
by their literary correlates: romance, ballad, epic. [from
S156]

1629   Wagner, Günther. "Die Klavierballaden von Brahms" in Wagner.
Die Klavierballade um die Mitte des 19. Jahrhunderts.
(Berliner musikwissenschaftliche Arbeiten Bd. 9) München-
Salzburg: Musikverlag Emil Katzbichler, 1976. pp. 71-101.
ind., notes. Compares Brahms's Op. 10 to Ballades of his
predecessors; analysis and stylistic comments included:
focus is on Op. 10 no. 1.

See also 250, 800, 878, 1327, 1328, 1332, 1345, 1403, 1409, 1566,
1589, 1592, 1603, 1605, 2147, 2532, 2619.

--Op. 21

1630   Wood, Ralph W. "Brahms's Glimpse" Music and Letters 25/2
(4.1944) pp. 98-103. Analysis to show that Op. 21 no.
1 is the high point in Brahms's writing in variation form.

See also 250, 1549, 1551, 1555, 1594, 1603.

--Op. 23

1631   D. [Hermann Deiters] Allgemeine musikalische Zeitung Neue
       Folge 1/42 (14.10.1863) cols. 708-11. Review.

1632   Witte, G[eorg]. H[endrik]. Musikalisches Wochenblatt 2/46
       (10.11.1871) pp. 725-26. Review.

See also 297, 1152, 1379, 1551, 1555, 1594, 1596, 1603.

--Op. 24

1633   Berger, Francesco. "Brahms on Handel" Monthly Musical
       Record 46/547 (1.7.1916) pp. 189-90. Performance practice
       suggestions for Op. 24.

1634   Bernstein, Jane A. "An Autograph of the Brahms "Handel
       Variations"" Music Review 34/3-4 (8.-11.1973) pp. 272-81.
       fig., notes. Examines the compositional process as seen
       in US-Wc manuscript; includes comments on sketch for
       Op. 26 found on same manuscript.

1635   Blom, Eric. "Brahms: Variations & Fugue on a Theme by
       Handel, for Piano (Op. 24)" Music Teacher 12/5 (M.S.
       series 26/8) (5.1933) pp. 257-58. ill., mus. Analysis
       of theme's treatment together with interpretation suggestions;
       includes comments on Brahms as composer for the piano.

1636   [Heinrich Schenker] "Brahms: Variationen und Fuge über
       ein Thema von Händel, op. 24" Der Tonwille 4/2/3 (Heft
       8/9 der Gesamtfolge) (1924) pp. 3-46. mus., notes.
       Schenkerian analysis and analysis of dynamic markings.

1637   *Brower, Harriette. "Brahms' Variations on a Handel Theme
       as Interpreted by Harold Bauer" Musical Observer (New
       York) 12 (1915) p. 210.

1638   Fleischer, Hugo. "Brahms-Einflüsse bei Max Reger" Der
       Merker (Wien) 8/12/13 (7.1917) pp. 446-50. Discusses
       Brahms's influence on Reger's music as seen in a comparison
       of Reger's Op. 134 with Brahms's Op. 24.

1639   Jonas, Oswald. "Die "Variationen für eine liebe Freundin"
       von Johannes Brahms" Archiv für Musikwissenschaft 12/4
       (1955) pp. 319-26. facsim., mus., notes. Discusses
       the background of the work, as well as Brahms and variation
       form; describes the manuscript (US-Wc), with a list of its

important corrections; includes textual comparison of the
Fugue with the edition.

1640 Meyer, Hans. "Der Plan in Brahms' Händel-Variationen"
Neue Musikzeitung 49/11,14,16 (1928) pp. 340-46, 437-
45, 503-12. mus., fig., notes. Discusses the work's
organization.

1641 S. B. [Selmar Bagge] Deutsche Musikzeitung (Wien) 3/41
(11.10.1862) pp. 323-35. mus. Review.

1642 *Sharon, Robert Barry. "A Performance Guide to the Variations
and Fugue on a Theme by Handel for Piano, Opus 24 by
Johannes Brahms" Ph.D. diss., New York University,
1982. 288 pp. Analytical study to guide in the interpretation of the variations; includes general discussion of
the role of variation form in solo piano music. [from S156]

1643 #Siegmund-Schultze, Walther. "Handel-Variationen des 19.
Jahrhunderts" in Siegmund-Schultze. Georg Friedrich
Händel. Thema mit 20 Variationen. Halle: n.p., [1965].
pp. 144-54. Brahms: pp. 149-50, 152-54. notes. Studies
the theme used and the method of variation.

1644 *Thompson, Loren Dean. "Comparative Aspects of Variation
Technique as Applied to the Keyboard in Selected Works
of Scheidt-Mozart-Brahms-Copland" M.A. thesis, California
State College (Fullerton), 1970. 96 pp. Analyses and
evaluates the variation techniques used in each work. [from
S155]

See also 250, 251, 1372F, 1379, 1388, 1409, 1419, 1549, 1551, 1555,
1562, 1594, 2368, 2433, 2465, 2546, 2706.

--Op. 34bis

See 1397, 1407, 1465, 1467.d., 1570.

--Op. 35

1645 *Auh, Mi Jai. "Piano Variations by Brahms, Liszt, and Friedman
on a Theme by Paganini [in his Op. 1, no. 24]" D.Mus.
diss., Piano, Indiana University, 1980. 114 pp. ill., mus.,
notes. Systematic analysis of Liszt's Etudes d'exécution
transcendante d'après Paganini no. 6 [Raabe 3a, Searle
140], Brahms's Op. 35, and Ignacy Friedman's Op. 47b?;
includes comments on performance practice. [from S202]

1646 H. E. [Heinrich Ehrlich] "Claviermusik" Neue Berliner Musikzeitung 20/43 (24.10.1866) pp. 339-40. Brahms: p. 339.
Review.

1647   Kraus, Detlef. "Die "Paganinivariationen" Op. 35--ein
        Sonderfall?!" Brahms-Studien Bd. 4 (1981) pp. 55-62.
        facsim. Presents background of work, with descriptive
        analysis of Paganini's theme [from his Op. 1, no. 24]
        and Brahms's work; includes guides for performance.

1648   Mies, P[aul]. "Zu Werdegang und Strukturen der Paganini-
        Variationen Op. 35 für Klavier von Johannes Brahms"
        Studia musicologica academiae scientiarum hungaricae 11
        (1969) pp. 323-32. fig., notes. Compares manuscript
        of Heft I (US-NYpl) and the final version of the work.
        *this volume also known as the Bence Szabolcsi Septuagenario.
        Dénes Bartha, ed. Budapest: Akadémiai Koado; Kassel:
        Bärenreiter, 1969.

1649   Sear, H. G. "The Influence of Paganini" Music Review 4/2
        (5.1943) pp. 98-111. Brahms: pp. 105-08. Work's
        background and description of the variations.

1650   Sutton, Wadham. "A Theme of Paganini" Musical Opinion
        [94]/1122 (3.1971) pp. 287-88. Brahms: p. 287. Describes
        Brahms's setting.

See also 250, 251, 1372F, 1377, 1409, 1417, 1549, 1551, 1555, 1562,
1594, 1597.

--Op. 39

1651   Anderton, Margaret. "How To Study and Play Two Brahms
        Waltzes, Op. 39, nos. 13 and 3" The Musician (New York)
        37/4 (4.1932) pp. 13-15. ill., mus. Provides suggestions
        for performance, with further suggestions for technique-
        building drills.

1652   _____. "Two Waltzes by Brahms. How To Study, How To
        Teach No. 2 and No. 9 from Opus 39" The Musician (New
        York) 38/1 (1.1933) pp. 10-12. mus. Provides suggestions
        for performance.

1653   Good, Margaret. "How To Play ... Brahms's Waltzes, Op.
        39, Nos. 15 and 2" Music and Youth 11/9 (9.1931) pp.
        177-80. ill., mus. [pp. 178-79] Provides suggestions for
        performance.

1654   Gruber, Albion. "[Some Viewpoints on Brahms:] Understand-
        ing Rhythm in the Piano Music" Clavier 13/2 (2.1974)
        pp. 9-13. ill., mus. Study of Brahms's rhythms with
        examples from the solo piano version of Op. 39.

1655   *Hanslick, Eduard. "Waffenruhe am Clavier" Neue freie Presse
        (Wien) (8.1866).

      (a) i) reprint: "Eine Feuilleton-Kritik" Leipziger allgemeine musikalische Zeitung 1/43,44(24.,31.;10.;1866) pp. 346-47, 354-55. Brahms: pp. 346-47. Review of Op. 39, four-hand version.

          ii) reprint: Hanslick. "Waffenruhe am Clavier. (Wien, im August 1866.)" in 2950. pp. 404-11. Brahms: pp. 405-07. Review of Op. 39, four-hand version.

      (b) English translation: "Music After War. Vienna" Dwight's Journal of Music 26/18,19 (Whole nos. 669,670) (24.11. and 8.12.;1866) pp. 345-46, 353-54. Brahms: p. 345. Review of Op. 39, four-hand version.

1656 *Kauffman, Larry Dale. "Rhythmic Structure in the "Sixteen Waltzes", Opus 39, by Johannes Brahms" D.M.A. diss., University of Cincinnati, 1976.

1657 Kirsch, Winfried. "Die Klavier-Walzer op. 39 von Johannes Brahms und ihre Tradition" Jahrbuch des Staatlichen Instituts für Musikforschung. Preussischer Kulturbesitz [2] (1969) pp. 38-67. fig., notes. Discusses historical antecedents and analyses work both as a complete unit, and in its individual sections.

1658 Levine, Henry. "[Some Viewpoints on Brahms:] Brahms Simplifies Brahms" Clavier 13/2 (2.1974) pp. 14-20. mus. [see also p. 21] Analyses musical and pianistic devices used in transforming the four-hand version of Op. 39 to a solo piano and solo piano simplified version.

      (d) comment: Schreuder, Frans. Clavier 13/7 (10.1974) p. 4. mus. [p. 28] Mentions the two piano four-hand version of Op. 39.

1659 Mitchell, William J. "The Waltz and Brahms' Opus 39" Etude 74/7 (9.1956) pp. 16, 60-61. mus. Discusses the history of the waltz form, together with Brahms's techniques for unifying Op. 39.

1660 S. B. [Selmar Bagge] "Vierhändige Walzer von Joh[annes]. Brahms. Op. 39" Leipziger allgemeine musikalische Zeitung 1/37 (12.9.1866) pp. 293-96. mus., notes. Review.

1661 "Ubersicht neu erschienener Musikwerke. Claviermusik zu vier Händen" Leipziger allgemeine musikalische Zeitung 1/33 (15.8.1866) pp. 265-66. Brahms: p. 265. Review.

See also 224, 250, 301, 1377, 1562, 1586, 1597, 1602, 2142, 2412.

--Op. 52a

See 2412, 2450.

--Op. 56b

1662   Orel, Alfred. "Skizzen zu Joh[annes]. Brahms' Haydn-
       Variationen" Zeitschrift für Musikwissenschaft 5/6 (3.1923)
       pp. 296-315. mus., notes. Manuscript description (A-
       Wgm), also discussion of Brahms's variation technique.

See also 250, 972, 1380, 1390, 1555, 1570, 1586, 1594.

See also "Op. 56a" in IV.A.3. Specific Works.

--Op. 65a

See 2412, 2450.

--Op. 76

1663   Horton, Charles T. "Chopin and Brahms: On A Common
       Meeting [[Middle]] Ground" In Theory Only 6/7 (12.1982)
       pp. 19, 22. mus., fig. [on pp. 20-21] Compares the
       opening of Chopin's Op. 55 no. 1 with Brahms's Op. 76
       no. 1 as an introduction to both composers' personal com-
       positional styles.

1664   Kresky, Jeffrey. "Analysis of Brahms: Intermezzo Op. 76,
       No. 7, for Piano" in Kresky. Tonal Music. Twelve Analytic
       Studies. Bloomington and London: Indiana University
       Press, 1977. pp. 120-34. mus., fig., notes. Detailed
       study of simultaneous musical events on different levels.

1665   Lewin, David. "On Harmony and Meter in Brahms's Op. 76,
       No. 8" 19th Century Music 4/3 (Spring 1981) pp. 261-65.
       mus., fig., notes. Analyses measures 1-15 with respect
       to harmony and meter as two manifestations of one formal
       organizing principle.

1666   Ohlsson, Garrick. "Cross-Rhythms in the Music of Brahms"
       Keyboard 8/9 (9.1982) p. 56. mus. Spotlights sections
       of Op. 76, no. 1 with contrasting rhythms, and explains
       how they should be performed.

1667   *Pelusi, Mario Joseph. "Contemplating a Brahms Intermezzo:
       Toward a Comprehensive Analytical Method for the Explica-
       tion and Interpretation of "Prescriptive Musical Structures""
       Ph.D. diss., Princeton University, 1982. 149 pp. Pre-
       sents his own method of musical analysis using as example
       Op. 76 no. 7: extensive musical analysis of musical events
       at all levels. [from S156]

See also 250, 1409, 1553, 1559, 1560, 1589, 1592, 1597, 1600, 1605, 2411, 3187.

--Op. 79

1668   Dommel-Dieny, Amy. "Johannes Brahms (1833-1897): Deuxième
        rhapsodie, Op. 79, No. 2 (1879)" L'Education musicale
        34/239/240 (6.-7.1977) pp. 11/325-14/328 [issue pp./volume
        pp.] mus., notes. Uses an analysis of this work to show
        Brahms's classic-romantic duality.

1669   Greenberg, Beth. "Brahms' Rhapsody in G minor, Op. 79,
        no. 2: A Study of Analyses by Schenker, Schoenberg
        and Jonas" In Theory Only 1/9-10 (12.-1.; 1975-76) pp.
        21-29. fig. [pp. 25-29], notes. Compares and evaluates
        these studies, which deal with measures 1-8 of this work.
        (d) comment: Smith, Charles J. In Theory Only 1/9-10
                (12.-1.; 1975-76) pp. 31-32.

1670   Ohlsson, Garrick. "Pedal Point in Brahms, Part 1-2" Keyboard
        8/12;9/1 (12.1982;1.1983) pp. 69;60. mus. Discusses
        this performance technique using passages from Op. 79,
        no. 1 as example.

1671   *Reti, Rudolph. The Thematic Process in Music. New York:
        Macmillan Company, 1951. x, 362 pp. mus., ind., notes.
        [New Edition:] [Prefatory Note by Donald Mitchell] London:
        Faber & Faber, 1961. vii, [5], 362 pp. Brahms: pp.
        70-72, 139-50. Uses Op. 79 as an example of thematic
        transformation and its link with a work's development.
        (a) *reprint (of New York Edition): Westport, Conn.:
                Greenwood Press, 1978.

1672   Smith, Edwin. "Brahms: Two Rhapsodies for Piano, Op.
        79" Music Teacher 55/5 (5.1976) pp. 13-14. mus. Analysis.

1673   Spry, Walter. "Master Lesson on the Brahms' Rhapsody Op.
        79, No. 2" Etude 51/2 (2.1933) pp. 96, 131, 137. ill.,
        mus. Presents suggestions for performance; includes
        personal recollections of Brahms by the author.

See also 250, 273, 282, 1375A, 1406, 1409, 1412, 1559, 1562, 1589,
1592, 1597, 1604, 1605, 2411, 2523, 2547.

--Op. 116

1674   Braun, Hartmut. "Ein Zitat. Beziehungen zwischen Chopin
        und Brahms" Die Musikforschung 25/3 (7.-9.1972) pp. 317-
        21. mus., notes. Describes parallels between Op. 116 no.
        2 and Chopin's Op. 7 no. 2.

1675   Bryant, Celia Mae. "Catching The Temperament of A Brahms
       "Caprice"" Clavier 8/4 (4.1969) pp. 29-33. mus [pp. 25-
       28]. Presents suggestions for study and performance.

1676   *Mastroianni, Thomas Owen. "1. Elements of Unity in the
       'Fantasies', Opus 116, by Brahms. 2. Pianistic Problems
       in 'Gaspard de la Nuit' by Ravel" D.M.A. diss., Piano
       Performance, Indiana University, 1970. 42 pp. mus.,
       notes.

1677   #Newman, William S. "About Brahms' Seven Fantasien Op.
       116" Piano Quarterly [6] (Spring 1958) pp. 13, 14, 17.
       ill., mus., notes. Analytical study pointing out cyclic
       unity throughout the opus.

1678   Schenker, Heinrich. Musikalisches Wochenblatt 25/4 (18.1.1894)
       pp. 37-38. Review.

1679   *Smith, Charles Justice, III. "Patterns and Strategies: Four
       Perspectives of Musical Characterization" Ph.D. diss., Uni-
       versity of Michigan, 1980. 130 pp. Examines 4 viewpoints
       that characterize analysis and the results they give. Ex-
       amples from Bach BWV 988, Chopin Op. 10 no. 1, Brahms
       Op. 116 no. 6, Webern Op. 10 no. 4. [from S202]

1680   Torkewitz, Dieter. "Die 'entwickelte Zeit'. Zum Intermezzo
       op. 116, IV von Johannes Brahms" Die Musikforschung
       32/2 ([4.-6.] 1979) pp. 135-40. mus., fig., notes.
       Analyses the use of musical phrasing; also comments on
       the same topic with respect to Schoenberg.

See also 250, 1409, 1411, 1553, 1558-60, 1569, 1584, 1589, 1592,
1597, 1600, 1606, 2397, 2411, 2428.

--Op. 117

1681   Clark, Frances. "Q & A [Question & Answer]" Clavier 14/6
       (9.1975) p. 56. mus. A query on the problem of correct
       phrasing in measures 21-27 of Op. 117 no. 1, and which
       edition to follow.
       (d) i) comment: Hinson, Maurice. Clavier 15/4 (4.1976)
                p. 5. mus.
           ii) comment: Weinberger, Jared. Clavier 15/4 (4.1976)
                pp. 4-5. mus.

1682   Cohen, Harriet. "Master Lesson: Brahms's Intermezzo, Op.
       117, No. 3" Music and Youth 10/5 (5.1930) pp. 104-07.
       mus. [pp. 105-06] Points on how to study this work.

1683   Gamer, Carlton. "Busnois, Brahms, and The Syntax of

Temporal Proportions" in A Festschrift for Albert Seay.
Michael D. Grace, ed. Colorado Springs: Colorado College,
1982. pp. 201-15. Brahms: pp. 203-15. facsim., mus.,
fig., notes. Compares the two composers' approach to
composition, together with the role of syntactic models.
Examples are Busnois's "Conditor alme siderum" and Brahms's
Op. 117 no. 3; includes comments on Brahms's creative
process as seen in the A-Wgm manuscript of this work.

1684 *Grippe, Kerry Joseph. "An Analysis of The "Three Intermezzi,
Op. 117" by Johannes Brahms" D.M.A. diss., Piano Performance, Indiana University, 1980. 57 pp. mus., notes.
Systematic analysis; includes comments on performance
practice. [from S202]

1685 Hughes, Edwin. "The Brahms Intermezzo, Op. 117, No. 1.
A Master Lesson" Etude 63/2 (2.1945) pp. 84, 113. ill.,
mus. [pp. 90-91] Suggestions for study; includes general
remarks on Brahms's piano music.

1686 [Guy Maier] "A Master Lesson By Guy Maier. Brahms' Intermezzo in E-Flat Major, Op. 117. No. 1" Etude 68/3 (3.1950)
pp. 26, 50. ill., mus. [pp. 27-28] Suggestions for study;
comments on the relationship of the music to its poetic
inscription.

1687 Schwartz, Heinrich. "Für den Klavierunterricht. Johannes
Brahms (1833-1897): Drei Intermezzi op. 117" Neue Musikzeitung 32/4, 7 (17.11.1910; 5.1.1911) pp. 81-83; 155.
mus., notes. Suggestions for study.
(a) *reprint: in Schwartz. Aus meinem Klavierunterricht.
Gesammelte Aufsätze. München: O. Halbreiter,
[1917]. pp. 124-31.
*2. Auflage: 1918.

1688 Velton, Klaus. "Entwicklungsdenken und Zeiterfahrung in
der Musik von Johannes Brahms: Das Intermezzo op. 117
Nr. 2" Die Musikforschung 34/1 (1.-3.1981) pp. 56-59.
fig., notes. Analysis demonstrating Brahms's compositional
skills in developing musical ideas.

1689 Zabrack, Harold. "Projecting Emotion. A Lesson On A Brahms
Intermezzo" Clavier 14/6 (9.1975) pp. 27-34. mus. [pp.
29-33] Using Op. 117 no. 2 to demonstrate that interpretive
decisions can be arrived at logically through score analysis.
(d) comment: Dowd, John A. Clavier 15/1 (1.1976) p.
4. On pedalling in Brahms's piano music.
(d) comment: Elder, Dean. Clavier 15/2 (2.1976)
p. 4.

See also 81.d., 250, 1409, 1411, 1412, 1553, 1558, 1559, 1569, 1584,
1589, 1592, 1597, 1606, 2411, 2532, 2546, 2548.

--Op. 118

1690   Dumm, Robert. "[Some Viewpoints on Brahms] Performer's
       Analysis. A Lesson on Brahms' Intermezzo" Clavier 5/3
       (5.-6.1966) pp. 42-44. mus. [pp. 36-39] Op. 118 no. 2
       used as an example of how analysis can be used as a basis
       for performance practice decisions.

1691   *Hicks, David. "Chronicles: Opus 118 #6 of Brahms" Ph.D.
       diss., Princeton University, 1981. 108 pp. Author's ob-
       servations--aural, analytical--form basis of study of this
       work; includes performance practice comments. [from S156]

1692   *Lamb, James Boyd. "A Graphic Analysis of Brahms, Opus
       118, with an Introduction to Schenkerian Theory and the
       Reduction Process" Ph.D. diss., Texas Tech University,
       1979. 162 pp. fig.

1693   Meyer, Hans. "Johannes Brahms: Klavierstücke op. 118"
       in Meyer. Linie und Form. Bach-Beethoven-Brahms.
       Leipzig: C. F. Kahnt, 1930. pp. 166-235. mus., notes.
       Analyses melody as a contributor to formal design in Op.
       118 nos. 2-6.

1694   *Patrick, Lynus. "From Analysis to Performance: The Musical
       Landscape of Johannes Brahms's Opus 118, no. 6" Ph.D.
       diss., University of Michigan, 1979. 161 pp. + phonorecord.
       Describes an attempt to devise a continuity scheme for
       analysis and performance study. [from S156]

1695   R. P. "Exempli gratia: A Middleground Anticipation" In Theory
       Only 2/7 (10.1976) pp. 44-45. Uses analysis to explain
       the motivation behind measures 9-10 of Op. 118 no. 1.
       (d) comment: Citron, Ronald P. In Theory Only 2/8
           (11.1976) pp. 2-3. Disagrees with R.P.'s conclusions.

1696   Schub, Andre-Michel. "Master Class: A Brahms Jewel"
       Keyboard Classics 2/6 (11./12.1982) p. 43. ill., mus. [pp.
       36-37] Suggestions for performance for Op. 118 no. 1.

See also 39D, 250, 1375A, 1385, 1409, 1411, 1419, 1546, 1553, 1558,
1559, 1569, 1584, 1589, 1592, 1597, 1600, 1604, 1606, 2360, 2411.

--Op. 119

1697   Brahms, Johannes. Intermezzi Opus 19 Nr. 2 und 3. Faksimile
       des Autographs. Mit einem Nachwort von Friedrich G.
       Zeileis. Tutzing: Hans Schneider, 1975. 16 pp. Includes
       manuscript description and background to the two works.

1698 Clements, Peter J. "Johannes Brahms: Intermezzo, Opus 119,
No. 1" CAUSM [Canadian Association of University Schools
of Music] Journal 7 (1977) pp. 31-51. mus., notes. An
analysis to determine Brahms's contribution to the development of musical language.

1699 Dumm, Robert. "[Some Viewpoints on Brahms] Playing One
of the Intermezzos. A Performer's Analysis" Clavier 13/2
(2.1974) pp. 29-32. mus. [pp. 24-28] Formal analysis
of Op. 119, no. 2, together with performance practice
comments.

1700 Hallis, Adolphe. "Notes on Playing Brahms. With Special
Reference to Rhapsody in E flat, Op. 119" Music Teacher
7/5 (M.S. series 20/8) (5.1928) pp. 303-04. ill., mus.
Describes the qualities of Brahms's music and how to perform it, focusing on Op. 119 no. 4.

1701 #Minotti, Giovanni. "Johannes Brahms" in Minotti. Die Geheimdokumente der Davidsbündler. Grosse Entdeckungen über
Bach, Mozart, Beethoven, Schumann, Liszt und Brahms.
(Ed. nr. 2630) Leipzig: Steingräber Verlag, [1934]. pp.
158-67. mus., notes. Harmonic and thematic analysis of
this opus; also points out its derivation from the works
of Beethoven and Schumann.

1702 Mitscherlich-Claus, Luise and Harald Kümmerling. "Schubert,
Brahms und Reger. Eine Sinndeutung von Regers "Sil-
houetten"" Zeitschrift für Musik 114/3 (3.1953) pp. 148-51.
mus. Analyses the relationship between Reger's Op. 53
nos. 2 and 3, and Brahms's Op. 119 nos. 1 and 4, respectively.

1703 *Nattiez, Jean-Jacques. "Fondements d'une sémiologie de la
musique" Doctorat de troisième cycle, Musique, Universite
de Paris VIII-Vincennes à St.-Denis. 3 vols.
    (a) reprint: Fondements ... musique. (Collection esthe-
        tique) ([Publisher's series no.] 1018]) Paris: Union
        Générale d'Editions, 1975. 448 pp. "III-L'Inter-
        mezzo op. 119 no. 3 de Brahms": pp. 297-330.
        mus., fig., notes. Uses measures 1-12 of Op. 119
        no. 3 to demonstrate author's theory of musical
        semiology.

1704 Newbould, Brian. "A New Analysis of Brahms's Intermezzo
in B minor op. 119, no. 1" Music Review 38/1 (2.1977)
pp. 33-43. mus., notes. Discusses the technical aspects
of this work and their musical function.

1705 *Warburton, A[nnie]. O. Music Teacher and Piano Student
[42-46 (between 1963 and 1967)].

(a) reprint: see 1375B, 1375C. Analyses Op. 119 nos.
2, 3 and Op. 119 nos. 1, 4, respectively.

See also 250, 1374, 1375B, 1375C, 1409, 1411, 1412, 1546, 1553,
1558, 1559, 1562, 1569, 1584, 1589, 1592, 1597, 1606, 2368, 2382,
2411.

--Fünf Studien für Pianoforte [Hofmann nr. 130; McCorkle Anhang Ia,
nr. I]

1706   L.K.   Signale für die musikalische Welt 27/52 (11.10.1869)
        p. 820. Reviews nos. 1 and 2.

1707   . Signale für die musikalische Welt 37/68 (12.1879)
        pp. 1073-74. Reviews nos. 3-5.

See also 1075.d., 2447, 2449.

--Klavier-Sarabande (h-moll) [Hofmann nr. 137 nr 2;
McCorkle WoO posthum 5 no. 2]

See 1103.

--Sarabandes and Gavottes

See 1593.

--Souvenir de la Russie [Hofmann nr. 123;
McCorkle Anhang IV, nr. 6]

1708   *Deutsch, Otto Erich. "Die Brotarbeiten des jungen Brahms"
        National-Zeitung (Basel) (1./2.10.1960) pp. 522+.
        (d) Deutsch. Österreichische Musikzeitschrift 15/11
            (11.1960) pp. 522-23. Concerning the question of
            Potpourris by Brahms, concludes that he didn't
            compose them.

See also "G. B. Marks" in III.B.2.

--Ubungen für Pianoforte [Hofmann nr. 132;
McCorkle WoO 6]

1709   *Bobo, Richard Lee. "Patterns in Selected Piano Studies"
        D.M.A. diss., Music, Indiana University, 1975. 3 vols.
        mus., notes.

1710   Flinsch, Erich. "Die 51 Klavierübungen von Johannes Brahms"

Der Musikerzieher 35/1 (10.1938) pp. 4-6. mus. Groups exercises by type, and gives examples of Brahms's piano pieces whose study would be facilitated by practising each exercise type.

1711 Hübbe, Thomas. "Eine Fingerübung von Johannes Brahms" Zeitschrift für Musik 109/1 (1.1942) p. 29. mus. Provides item's background and description.

--Ungarische Tänze [Hofmann nr. 128; McCorkle WoO 1]

1712 *Berliner Musikzeitung "Echo" (1876).

1713 *Berliner Zeitung (8.1876).

1714 *Illinois Staatszeitung (8.2.1879).

1715 Monthly Musical Record 10/119 (1.11.1880) p. 156. Reviews Hefts 3 and 4 [nos. 11-16, nos. 17-21, respectively].

1716 Dumesnil, Maurice. "The Hungarian Dance, No. 6 by Johannes Brahms. A Master Lesson" Etude 57/10 (10.1939) pp. 642, 681. ill., mus. Hints on how to play the two-hand piano version of this piece.

1717 Gil'bukh, Ia. and A. Moldavskii. "Novye issledovaniia o roli funktsional'noi muzyki" [New Research on the Role of Functional Music] Sotsiashstileskii trud no. 9 (9.1968) pp. 89-97. Describes the Ungarische Tänze as typical works suitable for factory background music.

1718 #Goldhammer, O. "Liszt, Brahms und Reményi" Studia musico-logica academiae scientiarum hungaricae 5 (1963) pp. 89-100. facsim., mus., notes. Reports on a Liszt-Reményi manu-script and what it reveals about Brahms and the provenance of the Ungarische Tänze materials.
*this volume also known as Bericht über den 2. Internationale Musikwissenschaftliche Konferenz Liszt-Bartok. Budapest 1961. Budapest: Akadémiai Kiadó, 1963.

1719 *Hofer, H. "Ungarische Tänze" Skizzen 12/11 (1938).

1720 *Kalbeck, Max. "Brahms und die ungarischen Tänze" Neues Wiener Tagblatt (25.5.1897).

1721 *"Kéler Béla támadása Brahms ellen a magyar táncokkal kapcso-latban" Temesi lapok (Temesvar) (6.9.1879). Kéler charges that Brahms used melody from his Op. 31 for the Ungarische Tänze no. 5. [from 241]

1722 L. K. Signale für die musikalische Welt 27/63 (22.11.1869)
      p. 997. notes. Reviews Hefts 1 and 2.

1723 Lichtenstein, G. "Hungarian Dance Composers" Monthly Musical
      Record 6/62 (1.2.1876) p. 22. Letter to the editor listing
      composers of the melodies for the Ungarische Tänze nos.
      1-10.
      (c) *excerpt: Die Tonkunst (Berlin) 1/14 (1876) p. 229.

1724 *Major, Ervin. Brahms és a magyar zene. A "magyar táncok"
      forrásai. Budapest: Arany János Nyomda, 1933. 11 pp.
      mus., notes. [from 1724.a]
      (a) #reprint: Major. "Brahms ... forrásai" in Fejezetek
          a magyar történetéböl válegatott tanulmányok.
          [Chapters From The History of Hungarian Music]
          Bóris Ferenc, ed. (Magyar zenetudomány 8) Buda-
          pest: Zeneműkiadó, 1967. pp. 82-88. Presents
          sources for melodies used in Ungarische Tänze;
          includes German summary.

1725 *Simrock, N. Zur Abwehr; Johannes Brahms und die Ungar-
      ischen Tänze. Berlin: Author, 1897. 13, [1] pp. Cor-
      respondence between Simrock and Otto Neitzel concerning
      wording of the original title. [from 241]

1726 Spur, Endre. "VIII. --Supplementary Notes on Liszt's and
      Brahms' so-called 'Gypsy' Music" Journal of the Gypsy Lore
      Society Third series 31/3-4 (1952) pp. 129-38. "2. The
      Background of Liszt's 'Rhapsodies' and Brahms' 'Gypsy
      Songs'": pp. 131-34. States that Brahms used Hungarian
      popular music, not gypsy music, in his work.

1727 Stephenson, Kurt. "Der junge Brahms und Reményis "Ungar-
      ische Lieder"" Studien zur Musikwissenschaft Bd. 25 (1962)
      pp. 520-31. facsim., mus., notes. Discusses Brahms
      and Reményi and Brahms's introduction to Hungarian music;
      includes comment on two manuscripts (D-brd-Hs and A-Wgm)
      that contain related sketch-like materials.
      *This volume also called Festschrift für Erich Schenk. Graz
      et al.: Hermann Böhlaus Nachf[olger]., 1962.

1728 *T.-E. Tribüne (Berlin) no. 292 (12.12.1880) p. 4. Reviews
      Hefts 3 and 4 [nos. 11-16, nos. 17-21, respectively].
      [from 241]

1729 Tappert, Wilhelm. "Die ungarische Tänze von Brahms. Beit-
      räge zur Geschichte derselben" Allgemeine deutsche Musik-
      zeitung 7/9 (27.2.1880) pp. 65-68. mus., notes. Compares
      Tänze no. 6 with its "source" and concludes no plagiarism
      occurs.

1730 "Ueber (sic) die Angelegenheit Brahms-Reményi theilt Albert
      [Dietrich] in Oldenburg ..." Der Klavierlehrer 2/14 (15.
      7.1879) p. 164. Relates Dietrich's recollections of first
      hearing the Tänze.

1731 "Verschiedenes" Allgemeine musikalische Zeitung 9/22 (3.6.1874)
      cols. 348-49. Names composers of tunes for Tänze nos.
      1-10.

1732 Wachtel, Aurel. "Brahms' neue Ungarische Tänze" Musikalisches
      Wochenblatt 11/47 (12.11.1880) pp. 554-56. mus. Reviews
      Hefts 3 and 4 [nos. 11-16, nos. 17-21, respectively].

See also 224, 250, 254, 647, 650, 651, 680, 727, 747, 1124, 1126, 1342,
1408, 1596, 1602, 2554, 2564, 2868, 3187.

b. Brahms's Editing and Arranging of Other Composers' Piano Music

See also 879.c.

--Bach

See 793.

--Chopin

1733 Fellinger, Imogen. "Brahms zur Edition Chopinscher Klavier-
      werke" in Musicae scientiae collectanea. Festschrift Karl
      Gustav Fellerer zum siebzigsten Geburtstag am 7. Juli 1972,
      überreicht von Kollegen, Schülern, und Freunden. Hein-
      rich Hüschen, ed. Köln: Arno-Volk-Verlag, 1973. pp.
      110-16. notes. Brahms's involvement with the Chopin
      Gesamtausgabe [Hofmann nr. 164; McCorkle Anhang VI,
      nr. 5] and his skills as editor.

1734 Higgins, Thomas. "Whose Chopin?" 19th Century Music 5/1
      (Summer 1981) pp. 67-75. Brahms: pp. 67, 73. notes.
      A comparison of editorial quality between available editions
      of Chopin piano music.

1735 Jonas, Oswald. "On The Study of Chopin's Manuscripts"
      Chopin Jahrbuch (1956) pp. 142-55. Brahms: pp. 142-44.
      facsim., mus., notes. Discusses Brahms as editor of the
      Chopin Gesamtausgabe [identification in 1733] and his edi-
      torial principles.

1736 _____. "Ein textkritisches Problem in der Ballade Op. 38
      von Frédéric Chopin" Acta musicologica 35/[3] ([7.-9.] 1963)

pp. 155-58. mus. Concerning an interpretation of rhythm as given in the Chopin Gesamtausgabe [identification in 1733].

1736.5*Zagiba, Franz. "Johannes Brahms und die erste Gesamtausgabe der Werke von Frédéric Chopin" in Zagiba. Chopin und Wien. Wien: H. Bauer Verlag, 1951. pp. 120-39.

See also 1122.e.iv.

--Couperin, François

1737   [Rob Eitner?] Monatshefte für Musikgeschichte 5/3 ([3.] 1873) pp. 46-47. Reviews Couperin's Pièces de clavecin. Livre 2. [Hofmann nr. 158; McCorkle Anhang VI, nr. 6]

1738   Eitner, Rob. Monatshefte für Musikgeschichte 2/12 ([12.] 1870) pp. 211-12. Reviews Couperin's Pièces de clavecin. Livre 1. [see 1737 for identification]

--Gluck

1739   Musical Times 15/349 (1.3.1872) p. 416. Reviews Brahms's arrangement of a Gavotte from Gluck's Iphigénie en Aulide [Hofmann nr. 159; McCorkle Anhang Ia, nr. 2].

See also 1602.

--Schubert

1740   Neue Zeitschrift für Musik Bd. 66/37 (9.9.1870) p. 339. Reviews Brahms's editions of Schubert's Ländler D366, D814. [Hofmann nrs. 155-56; McCorkle Anhang Ia, nr. 6]

1741   S. B. [Selmar Bagge] Allgemeine musikalische Zeitung 3/13 (25.3.1868) pp. 99-101. mus. Reviews Schubert's Drei Klavierstücke D946 [Hofmann nr. 154; McCorkle Anhang VI, nr. 12].

--Schumann

1742   *Stevens, Claudia A. "A Study of Robert Schumann's Impromptu's, Op. 5: Its Sources and a Critical Analysis of Its Revisions" D.M.A. diss., Boston University, 1977. 233 pp. Includes comments on Brahms as a co-editor with Clara Schumann of the Schumann. Robert Schumann's Werke. Series 1-14. (Leipzig: Breitkopf & Härtel, 1881-93) [Op. 5 is in Series 7, vol. 1 (1887)]. [from S202]

See also 1122.e.iv.

c. Organ Works--General

1743   Birkby, Arthur. "Lean Brahms Organ Output Other than
       Opus 122 Discussed" The Diapason 49/12 (Whole no. 588)
       (1.11.1958) p. 19. Reviews all other organ works; includes
       performance suggestions and analyses of chorale and fugue
       subjects.

1744   Brahms, Johannes. The Chorales from the Organ Works of
       Brahms. Edited and Harmonized ... by [Charles] Winfred
       Douglas. With an Introduction on the Organ Music of
       Brahms [by Leonard Ellinwood, based on Douglas's notes].
       New York: H. W. Gray Co., Inc., 1945. xi, [3], 15-44
       pp. facsim., mus., notes. Provides an overview of the
       backgrounds of all the works, together with comments on
       Brahms's treatment of the chorale tunes; focuses on Op.
       122 and the Choral-Vorspiel und Fugue über "O Traurigkeit,
       o Herzeleid" [Hofmann nr. 131; McCorkle WoO 7] with
       general descriptive remarks and discussion of chorale
       treatment and setting.

1745   #Busch, Hermann J. "Die Orgelwerke von Johannes Brahms"
       Ars organi 11/22 (1963) pp. 582-84. notes. An overview
       of Brahms's organ music.

1746   Byard, Herbert. "The Organ Music of Brahms" Musical Opinion
       99/1176 (10.1975) pp. 36-37. mus. Overview of the music,
       focusing on Op. 122 and the Choral-Vorspiel und Fugue
       über "O Traurigkeit, o Herzeleid" [Hofmann nr. 131;
       McCorkle WoO 7].

1747   #Farmer, Archibald. "The Organ Music of Brahms" Musical
       Times 72/1059-62 (1.;5.-8.;1931) pp. 406-08, 501-03, 596-
       98, 693-96. mus. Presents historical background, evaluation
       and descriptive analysis; focuses on Op. 122.

1748   *Gay, Harry W. "I.: Liturgical Role of the Organ in France,
       757-1750. II: Selected Organ Works of Johannes Brahms.
       III: Tournemire's L'Orgue Mystique as It Applies to the
       Problem of Relating Instrumental Music to a Worship Service"
       Ph.D. diss., Music, University of Indiana (Bloomington),
       1955.
       (d) #Gay. "Study of Brahms' Works Expanded by Vivid
            Detail" The Diapason 50/4 (Whole no. 592) (1.3.1959)
            p. 38. Describes the historical background of
            the time periods when the organ works were written.

1749   Gotwals, Vernon. "Brahms and The Organ" Music: The A.G.O.

and R.C.C.O. Magazine 4/4 (4.1970) pp. 38-55. mus.,
notes., discog. Comprehensive overview: includes comments
on the use of the organ in the choral works, on manuscript
sources, editions, ornamentation, the types of organs
Brahms played, as well as individual analyses.

1750 Martindale, James A. G. "Brahms and The Organ" Etude 57/12
(12.1939) pp. 814-15. ill. Discusses Brahms as a composer
for the organ, together with the background of Op. 122,
the A flat minor Fugue and the Choral-Vorspiel und Fugue
über "O Traurigkeit, o Herzeleid" [Hofmann nr. 126; Mc-
Corkle, WoO 8 and Hofmann nr, 131; McCorkle WoO 7,
respectively].

1751 Roberts, W. Wright. "Brahms: The Organ Works" Music and
Letters 14/2 (4.1933) pp. 104-11. mus., notes. Discusses
chorale settings and provides descriptive analysis.

1752 Schuneman, Robert. "Brahms and The Organ. Some Reflections
on Modern Editions and Performance" Music: The A.G.O.
and R.C.C.O. Magazine 6/9 (9.1972) pp. 30-34. notes.
Discusses how Brahms intended these works to be played
and how they should sound; includes recommendations for
editions published after 272. Concentrates on Op. 122.

1753 Vletter, M. "Brahms als orgelcomponist" Caecilia (Utrecht)
79/11 (10.4.1922) p. 172. Overview of the works.

See also 1344, 1387.d., 1767.5.

c. Organ Works--Specific

See also 1387.d.

--Op. 122

1754 Banta, Lorene. "Brahms in the Church Organist's Repertoire"
Journal of Church Music 2/3 (3.1960) pp. 9-12. ill. Gives
performance suggestions and traces the chorale tunes
through each prelude.

1755 #Beckmann, Gustav. "Johannes Brahms' Schwanengesang
(Elf Choralvorspiele für die Orgel, op. 122)" Monatsschrift
für Gottesdienst und kirchliche Kunst 9/2 (2.1904) pp. 57-
59. Review.

1756 Bond, Ann. "Brahms Chorale Preludes, Op. 122 (The Organist's Repertory--7)" Musical Times 112/1543 (9.1971) pp.
898-900. mus., notes. Descriptive analysis of each chorale

prelude, with background and suggestions for performance
for the opus as a whole.

1757 *Byrd, William. "The Eleven Chorale-Preludes of Johannes
Brahms" S.M.M. diss., Union Theological Seminary (New
York), 1953. ii, 65 pp. notes. Descriptive analysis,
including comparison of Brahms's setting with original Bach
chorale prelude; also comments on available editions, together with the works' historical background and religious
context. [from Union Theological Seminary Library]

1758 Coggin, Eileen. ""Mein Jesu, Der Du Mich" Chorale-Prelude
for Organ by Johannes Brahms. Analysis of the Compositional Techniques used in Building the Climax" American
Organist (New York) 53/3 (4.1970) pp. 14-20. mus. Shows
relationship between all subject and episodic material in
Chorale-Prelude no. 1, also analyses the re-appearance of
subjects in each exposition and demonstrates how these
re-appearances lead to the prelude's climax.

1759 Delli Ponti, Mario. "L'Ultima composizione di Brahms: I
'Preludi Corali' opera 122" La Scala (Milan) no. 147 (2.1962)
pp. 24-25. ill. Discusses the work's background in the
context of Brahms's life; includes comment on Brahms and
opera.

1760 Egidi, Arthur. "Meister Johannes' Scheidegruss" Die Musik
(Berlin) 2/15 (Bd. 7) (5.1903) pp. 222-24. Review.

1760.5#Forsblom, Enzio. "Piirteitä Johannes Brahmsin urkuteoksista
(Musiikkitieteellinen sarja 2)" Uusi musiikkilehti [3]/2
(1956) pp. 13-14. Discusses the influence of Bach and his
predecessors on Brahms, as seen in Op. 122.

1761 *Foster, David Lee. "1. A Study of Orchestral Concerti in
the Organ Transcriptions of J. S. Bach and Johann G.
Walther; A Study of the Cantus Firmus Organ Compositions
of Ernst Pepping; A Study of the Chorale Settings for Organ
contained in the Opus 122 Collection of Johannes Brahms.
2. Concert" D.M. diss., Performance, Organ, Northwestern
University, 1972.

1762 Heusinkveld, Frances. "Brahms Chorale Preludes" American
Music Teacher 21/6 (6.-7.1972) pp. 26-27, 29. notes.
Background and descriptive analysis; discusses the work's
links to Clara Schumann and her death, as well as the
background of each chorale tune.

1763 "Im Verlage von N. Simrock ..." Allgemeine Musikzeitung 29/14
(4.4.1902) p. 264. Review.

1764 *Isler, Ernst. "Das letzte Werk von Johannes Brahms" Schwei-
    zerische Musikzeitung und Sängerblatt 42/23 (2.8.1902).

1765 Kalbeck, Max, see 1767.5.

1766 Karpath, Ludwig. "Der musikalische Nachlass von Johannes
    Brahms (Original-Mittheilung der "Signale")" Signale für
    die musikalische Welt 60/21 (26.3.1902) pp. 353-55. Review;
    also discusses Opp. 121 and 122 as Brahms's legacy.
    (a) *reprint: Karpath. "Der musikalische Nachlass von
        Brahms" Neues Wiener Tagblatt (26.3.1902).

1767 *Kitt, Maribeth Evelyn. "The Eleven Chorale Preludes of
    Johannes Brahms" M.M. thesis, Theory, University of
    Rochester (Eastman School of Music), 1944. 3, [1 leaf]
    iii-vi, 77 pp. mus., notes. Analyses the work for fre-
    quency of occurence of various compositional techniques.
    [from Sibley Music Library, Eastman School of Music]

1767.5#Kølbeck, Max. [Max Kalbeck] "Choralvorspiele von Brahms"
    Rheinische Musik- und Theaterzeitung (Köln) 3/19 (10.5.
    1902) [2 pp.]. Describes the circumstances under which
    they were written, discusses them as examples of Brahms's
    composing skills; includes general comments on Brahms
    and organ music, the history of the chorale prelude form,
    together with discussion of Brahms's settings of the chorale
    tunes.

1768 Miller, Max B. "The Brahms Chorale Preludes. Master Les-
    son" American Organist (New York) 13/4 (4.1979) pp. 43-47.
    ill., mus., notes. Traces the settings of the chorale tunes
    and gives suggestions for performance; includes general
    comments on Brahms and the organ, and on editions.

1769 "A Posthumous Work By Brahms" Times Literary Supplement
    1/17 (9.5.1902) p. 133. Review.

1770 Senn, Kurt Wolfgang. "Johannes Brahms: Elf Choral-Vorspiele
    für Orgel, Op. 122" Musik und Gottesdienst 13/6 (11./12.
    1959) pp. 172-83. facsim., mus., notes. Discusses work's
    background and its links to J. S. Bach and Clara Schumann,
    with descriptive analysis of each prelude.

1771 Stock, Andreas. "Brahms' Opus posthumum" Signale für die
    musikalische Welt 60/23 (9.4.1902) pp. 401-03. mus., notes.
    Review.

1772 *Traber, Jurgen Habakuk. "Kitsch i den tyska krykomusiken"
    in Kritik som vapen och verktyg. Ny tysk marxistisk
    forskning och debatt kring film, teater, musik och litteratur.
    Jan Myrdal, ed. [Roland Adlerberth, translator] (En

Pan-bok) Stockholm: Pan/Norstedt, 1977. pp. 119-30. Uses Op. 122 no. 8 as an example, in an analysis of kitsch in German church music. [from S202]

See also 250, 739, 1365.5, 2300, 2349, 2387.
See also "Organ Works--General" in IV.A.2.c.

--Choral-Vorspiel und Fuge über "O Traurigkeit, o Herzeleid" [Hofmann nr. 131; McCorkle WoO 7]

See 2349, 2386, 2433.
See "Organ Works--General" in IV.A.2.c.

--Fugue in A flat minor [Hofmann nr. 126; McCorkle WoO 8]

1773　Testa, Susan.　"A Holograph of Johannes Brahms's Fugue in A-flat minor for Organ" Current Musicology no. 19 (1975) pp. 89-102. facsim., mus., notes. Discusses Brahms's compositional process, describing differences between the only available manuscript and the first edition.

See also 2349, 2433.
See also "Organ Works--General" in IV.A.2.c.

--Prelude and Fugue in A minor [Hofmann nr. 189; McCorkle WoO posthum 9]

See 2433.
See "Organ Works--General" in IV.A.2.c.

--Prelude and Fugue in G minor [Hofmann nr. 189; McCorkle WoO posthum 10]

See 2433.
See "Organ Works--General" in IV.A.2.c.

3. Orchestral Music

a. General

1774　Musical Times 22/[459] (1.5.1881) p. 258. Reviews Opp. 80 and 81 in 4-hand piano versions.

1775 "Adventurous Concertos. A Note on Brahms" The Times
(London) Royal Edition no. 45,254 (13.7.1929) p. 12. An
appreciation of Opp. 15, 77, 83, 102, with comments on
Brahms's use of form and his treatment of the soloist's
material in each of these works.

1776 Antcliffe, Herbert. "The Symphonies of Brahms" Monthly
Musical Record 34/406 (1.10.1904) pp. 186-87. Discusses
Brahms's links to Beethoven, as well as the characteristics
of Brahms's music.

1777 Benary, Peter. "Tempo und Tempoänderung. Zum Verhältnis
von Notentext und Wiedergabe" Neue Zeitschrift für Musik
131/11 (11.1970) pp. 566-68. Brahms: p. 568. Describes
problems in conducting the 4th movement of Op. 68, and
1st movement of Op. 73.

1778 Berger, Francesco. "The Pianoforte Concertos of Brahms"
Monthly Musical Record 47/561 (1.9.1917) pp. 197-99. A
negative evaluation.

1779 Besch, Otto. "Zur Vortragsfolge des ersten Orchester-
Konzerts" in 2732. pp. 6-12. Provides historical background
and descriptive analysis for Opp. 80, 102, 68.

1780 *Blom, Eric. "Snags in the Brahms Symphonies" Birmingham
Post (31.10.1938).
(a) reprint: Blom. in Blom. A Musical Postbag. London:
J. M. Dent & Sons Ltd., 1941. pp. 227-31. Discusses problems of interpretation caused by Brahms's
tempi indications.
*issues: 1943, 1945, 1949.

1781 #Blume, Walter, ed. Brahms in der Meininger Tradition. Seine
Sinfonien und Haydn-Variationen in der Bezeichnung von
Fritz Steinbach. Stuttgart: Author, 1933. 89 pp. mus.
Discusses Steinbach's notes on how he would conduct
these works.
(e) report: see 25.e.d.

1782 *Bronowicz, Teresa. [Teresa Bronowícz-Chylínska] Koncerty
Brahmsa. Kraków: Polskie Wydawnictwo Muzyczne, 1955.
85 pp. ill., fig., notes.

1783 Browne, Philip Austin. Brahms. The Symphonies. (Musical
Pilgrim) London: Oxford University Press, Humphrey Milford, 1933. 71 pp. mus., notes. Discusses the characteristics of the symphonies as a whole and provides historical
background and movement-by-movement analysis for each.
*also: London, New York: Oxford University Press, [1948].

1784   Chasins, Abram. "Brahms in D minor and B flat" in Chasins.
       Speaking of Pianists. New York: Alfred A. Knopf, 1957.
       pp. 240-45. [total paging: 291, xiv, [2] pp.] Recollects
       performances of Opp. 15 and 83, commenting on the soloists;
       also short historical background on each work.
       2nd Edition: With A Supplementary Chapter. 1961. [total
       paging: x, 312, xvii pp.]

1785   Chop, Max. Johannes Brahms Symphonien   Geschichtlich
       und musikalisch analysiert mit zahlreichen Notenbeispielen.
       [(Reclam Universal-Bibliothek nr. 6309)] (Erläuterungen zu
       Meisterwerken der Tonkunst Bd. 31) Leipzig: Philipp
       Reclam jun., [1922]. [1], 87, [1] pp. mus., notes. An
       analysis of the four symphonies; includes general remarks
       on Brahms's music and an overview of his life.

1786   Cuyler, Louise [E.]. "Brahms: A Great Mediator of Classical
       and Romantic Styles" in Cuyler. The Symphony. (The
       Harbrace History of Musical Forms) New York, Chicago,
       San Francisco, Atlanta: Harcourt Brace Jovanovich, Inc.,
       1973. pp. 104-25. facsim., mus., notes. Discusses the
       characteristics of Brahms's symphonies in general, with
       analytical comments for each one.

1787   #Dauge, Maurice. "Les Quatres symphonies de Johannes Brahms
       (1833-1897)" Le Menestrel 100/4 (28.1.1938) pp. 17-18.
       Descriptive analysis.

1788   Deas, James. "The Symphonies of Brahms" Music and Letters
       14/2 (4.1933) pp. 112-16. mus. Discusses emotional
       qualities (Op. 68), orchestration (Op. 73), performance
       difficulties (Op. 90), and compositional technique (Op. 98).

1789   Del Mar, Norman. "Confusion and Error (I), (II), (III)"
       The Score nos. 21-23 (10.1957;2.,7.;1958) pp. 14-29,
       28-40, 37-45. Brahms: (I) pp. 17; (III) pp. 41-42.
       Discusses mistakes and inconsistencies in editions of orches-
       tral works, with particular attention to Brahms's Opp. 77
       and 98; includes comment on Brahms's post-publication
       revisions.

1790   Elliot, J. H. "Brahms as Symphonist" Musical Times 70/1036
       (1.6.1929) p. 554. Discusses the symphonies as a synthesis
       of classicistic and romantic principles.

1791   Ferguson, Linda [F.]. "The Concertos of Johannes Brahms:
       An Historical and Analytical Approach to the Compositional
       Process" M.M. thesis, Texas Christian University, 1973.
       xii, 293, [3] pp. mus., fig., notes. Presents critical and
       historical commentary cum analysis of each of the four
       concertos; includes an overview of the development of the

concerto form from the Baroque period to the 20th century;
also a thematic guide, a list of locations for the Brahms
music autographs and first editions, a discussion of the
1st movement of Op. 102, Joachim's cadenza for Op. 77,
and an examination of Brahms's influence in the concertos
of Berg and Schoenberg.

1792 #Fleming, Christopher le. "Music For All Seasons. The Symphonies of Brahms" Making Music no. 52 (Summer 1963)
pp. 5-6. Correlates each symphony to a particular season:
Spring--Winter, nos. 3, 2, 4, 1, respectively.

1793 Foss, Hubert J. "Johannes Brahms (1833-1897): in The Concerto. Ralph Hill, ed. (Pelican Books A249) Melbourne,
London, Baltimore: Penguin Books, 1952. pp. 187-205.
mus. Background and descriptive analysis of Opp. 15,
77, 83, 102.
(a) *reprint: Westport, Conn.: Greenwood Press Publishers, 1978.

1794 *Frankenstein, Alfred. A Modern Guide to Symphonic Music.
New York: Meredith Press, 1966. Brahms: pp. 139-71.

1795 Fuller-Maitland, J[ohn]. A[lexander]. "Brahms's Orchestral
Music" Musical Times 74/1083 (5.1933) pp. 401-06. mus.
Background and descriptive analysis for all orchestral works.

1796 George, Graham. "Brahms' Instrumental Music" in George.
Tonality and Musical Structure. New York, Washington,
D.C.: Praeger Publishers, 1970. pp. 171-87. mus., ind.
Uses the symphonies as examples, in a discussion of the
use of tonal ambiguity within the classical structures.
*also: London: Faber, 1970.

1797 Gilman, Lawrence. "The Symphonic Brahms" in Gilman.
Toscanini and Great Music. [With An Introduction by Sir
Adrian Boult] London: John Lane, The Bodley Head, 1939.
pp. 125-50. ind. Describes the backgrounds and qualities
of the symphonies, and how Toscanini conducted them.
*also: New York, Toronto: Farrar & Rinehart, Inc., [1938].

1798 #Ginastera, Alberto. "Las Sinfonías de Brahms" Ars. Revista
de arte 17/79 (1957) pp. [18-20, 23-25]. ill. Discusses
Brahms as a symphony composer together with general
remarks and background on each symphony.

1799 *Glahn, Henrik. "På grundlag af en undersøgelse af form og
stil i Brahms' symfonier gives en redegørelse for anvendelsen
af sonateformen (satsmaessig og cyklisk) herunder benyt-
telsen af enhedsdannende elementer i de naevnte voerker"
Specialeafhandlinger til magisterkonferens i musikvidenskab,
Københavns Universitet, 1945.

1800 *Goepp, Philip H. Symphonies and Their Meaning. Second
    Series. Philadelphia & London: J. P. Lippincott Company,
    1902. mus., ind., notes.
    (a) i) reprint: Goepp. Volume Two. Classic Symphonies.
        In Goepp: Great Works of Music [[Symphonies and
        Their Meaning]]. 3 vols. in 1. Garden City,
        N.Y.: Garden City Publishing Co. Inc., [1925].
        "Brahms' First Symphony": pp. 282-322.
        "Brahms' Third Symphony": pp. 323-60.
        "Brahms' Fourth Symphony": pp. 361-400.
        Descriptive analysis.
        *issue: [1935].
        ii)*reprint: [Microfilm Edition] [Ann Arbor, Mich.:
        University Microfilms, 1967.]

1801 Goetschius, Percy. "Schumann and Brahms" in Goetschius.
    Masters of the Symphony. Fifth Year of a Study Course
    in Music Understanding, Adopted By The National Federation
    of Music Clubs.... Boston: Oliver Ditson Company;
    New York: Chas. H. Ditson & Co. [et al.], 1929. pp.
    204-57. "Johannes Brahms": pp. 223-50, also 254-56.
    ill., mus., fig., ind., notes, discog. Describes the themes
    and forms of the symphonies.
    *also: Philadelphia: Oliver Ditson Company, [1936].

1802 Haggin, B[ernard]. H. "Johannes Brahms" in Haggin. A
    Book of The Symphony. London, New York, Toronto:
    Oxford University Press, 1937. pp. 238-82. mus., notes.
    Analysis of the symphonies with musical examples; includes
    instructions on how to follow the analysis with phonorecords.
    *also: London: Methuen & Co., [1937].

1803 *Harrison, Julius. Brahms and His Four Symphonies. London:
    Chapman & Hall Ltd., [1939]. xii, 312 pp. mus., ind., notes.
    (a) reprint: (Da Capo Press Music Reprint Series) New
        York: Da Capo Press, 1971. Analytical study; in-
        cludes comments on Brahms's style, choice of keys, and
        orchestration, together with biographical information.
        (e) report: see 38.e.
    (d) Harrison. "Johannes Brahms (1833-97)" in The Sym-
        phony. Volume One. Haydn to Dvořák. Robert
        Simpson, ed. Middlesex: Penguin Books, 1966.
        pp. 316-41. mus., ind., notes.
        *issues: 1969-78.

1804 *Hauptmann, Hans. "Johannes Brahms, Der Symphoniker" Der
    Musiker. Mitteilungsblatt des Deutschen Musikerverbandes in
    der Gewerkschaft Kunst des DGB (Düsseldorf) 10(1957) p. 77.

1805 *Hendrickson, Hugh R. "Rhythmic Activity in The Symphonies
    of Brahms" M.M. thesis, Arizona State University, 1976.
    x, 48 l. mus., notes. [from Music Library, ASU]

(c) excerpt: Hendrickson, Hugh. "Rhythmic Activity
in the Symphonies of Brahms" In Theory Only 2/6
(9.1976) pp. 5-15. fig., notes. Studies rhythm
as relating to the style of the 4th movement, Op.
98, measures 1-80; also its relationship to structure
and harmony in this example.

1806 *Horney, Anna Louise. "A Study of The Derivation and Nature
of Polyphony in The Symphonies of Johannes Brahms" M.A.
thesis, Columbia University, 1930.

1807 Horton, John. Brahms Orchestral Music. (BBC Music Guides)
London: BBC, 1968. 64 pp. mus., notes. Descriptive
analysis of these works, also discusses Brahms as a composer as well as Brahms and the orchestra.
*also: Seattle: University of Washington Press, 1969.

1808 Hume, Paul. "If A Little Brahms Is Good, Then A Lot Is
Better" Washington Post 100/280 (11.9.1977) p. G3. General
comments on the orchestral works; includes comment on
Brahms in the symphonic repertoire and on Brahms's self-
criticism.

1809 Huneker, James Gibbons. "Brahms The Master Builder" New
York Times 68/22,247 (22.12.1918) Section 4, p. 6. Discusses Brahms the symphonist and his style characteristics.
(a) reprint: Huneker. "The Master Builder" in Huneker.
Variations. New York: Charles Scribner's Sons,
1921. pp. 173-80.
*also: London: T. Werner Laurie Ltd., [1921].
*issues (of New York Edition): 1922, 1924.

1810 #Hutschenruyter, Wouter. "De orkestwerken van Johannes
Brahms" Symphonia 16/5 (5.1933) pp. 84-85. A survey
with descriptive analysis of all orchestral works except the
concertos.

1811 Jacobs, Robert L. "Brahms and The Symphony" The Listener
48/1230 (25.9.1952) p. 521. Surveys Brahms as a symphonic
composer.
(a) reprint: Jacobs. In Essays on Music. An Anthology
from 'The Listener'. Felix Aprahamian, ed. London:
Cassell, 1967. pp. 60-63.

1812 Johannes Brahms. Symphonien und andere Orchesterwerke.
Erläutert von I. Knorr, H. Riemann und J. Sittard nebst
einer Einleitung: Johannes Brahms' Leben und Schaffen
von A. Morin. (Meisterführer nr. 3) Berlin: Schlesinger'sche
Buch- und Musikhandlung (Rob[ert]. Lienau); Wien:
Carl Haslinger qdm. Tobias, n.d. 158 pp. mus., notes.
Includes reprints of 1833, 1856, 1872, 1874, 1892, 1926,
1981, 2002.

1813 Klein, Rudolf. "Die konstruktiven Grundlagen der Brahms-
      Symphonien" Österreichische Musikzeitschrift 23/5 (5.1968)
      pp. 258-63. mus., notes. Discusses intermovement relation-
      ships of thematic material, with examples from each symphony.

1814 *Kozáky, István. "Brahms szimfónikus művészete" A Zene 14
      (1932/33) pp. 203-07.

1815 *Labrecque, J. Pierre. "Les Concertos pour piano de Johannes
      Brahms" Le Medecin du Quebec 9/4 (4.1974) p. 85.

1816 Lee, E[rnest]. Markham. Brahms's Orchestral Works. (The
      Musical Pilgrim) London: Oxford University Press, Hum-
      phrey Milford, 1931. 45 pp. mus. Provides historical
      background and descriptive analysis for Opp. 11, 16, 56a,
      77, 80, 81.
      *issue: 1948.
      (d) *Lee. "Brahms" Musical Mirror and Fanfare 11/3 (1931)
           (?).

1817 Leibowitz, René. "Aimez-vous Brahms?" in Leibowitz. Le
      Compositeur et son double. Essais sur l'interprétation
      musicale. (Bibliothèque des idées) [Paris:] Editions
      Gallimard, 1971. pp. 176-94. mus., notes. Refutes the
      traditional opinion that Brahms's music is incomprehensible,
      with descriptive analysis of Op. 56a and movements from
      each symphony.

1818 #Llongueres, Joan. "Les Quatre simfonies de Joan Brahms"
      Revista musical catalana 30/360 (12.1933) pp. 506-11.
      General comments on Brahms's symphonic style, with des-
      criptive analysis of each symphony.

1819 Mannheimer, Ernst. "Der Stil in der Brahms'schen Symphonie"
      Allgemeine Musikzeitung 60/18 (5.5.1933) pp. 251-53. notes.
      Discusses Brahms's symphonic style, and its roots in Bach
      and Beethoven; also looks at tonalities, types of movements,
      and their order, in each symphony.
      (d) reworked: Mannheimer. "Zur Musikerziehung. Eine
           Brahms-Analyse im Brahmsjahr" Der Auftakt 13/11-12
           ([11.-12.] 1933) pp. 168-70.

1820 *Mayer, Alois. "Die drei Symphonieen von Brahms" Wiener
      Montagszeitung (4.2.1884).

1821 *Moore, Earl V. and Theodore E. Heger. The Symphony and
      the Symphonic Poem. Analytical and Descriptive Charts
      of the Standard Symphonic Repertory. Ann Arbor, Mich.:
      [Edwards Bros.], 1949. iv, 259 pp. mus., notes.
      *2nd Revised Edition: 1952. iv, 259, 4 pp.
      *3rd Revised Edition: 1957. v, 277 pp.

*4th Revised Edition: Ann Arbor, Mich.: Ulrich's Books,
1962. 283 pp.
*5th Revised Edition: 1966. v, [1], 287 pp.
*issue: 1970.
6th Revised Edition: 1974. Brahms: pp. 61-76. mus.,
notes. also gives instrumentation of each work.

1822 Nordgren, Quentin Richards. "Texture: A Consideration of
Spacing, Doubling, Range, and Instrumentation, Based
Upon Selected Orchestral Works of Certain Nineteenth
Century Composers" Ph.D. diss., Indiana University, 1955.
xxxv, 352, [1] pp. fig., notes. "Brahms": pp. 255-32.
fig., notes. Comparative analysis of Opp. 68 and 98
together with symphonies of Beethoven (Opp. 55, 67);
Mendelssohn (Opp. 56, 90); and Schumann (Opp. 38, 120).
(c) excerpt: Nordgren, Quentin R. "A Measure of
Textual Patterns and Strengths" Journal of Music
Theory 4/1 (1960) pp. 19-31. mus., fig., notes.
Presents his methodology and the results of his
investigation.

1823 Peyser, Herbert F. "Fables in The Symphonic Literature"
Musical America 64/16 (10.12.1944) pp. 6, 10. Allusions
to Wagner in the 1st movement of Op. 90; origins of horn
tune used in the 4th movement of Op. 68.

1824 Raynor, Henry [B.]. "Form and Style. Part 1" The Chesterian
28/176 (10.1953) pp. 42-47. Brahms: pp. 45-46. Brahms's
symphonic writing seen as a balance between form and
expressiveness in the evolution of the symphony from a
form to a style.

1825 Rittenhouse, Robert John. "Rhythmic Elements in The Symphonies of Johannes Brahms" Ph.D. diss., Theory, University of Iowa, 1967. viii, 140 pp. mus., fig., notes.
Identifies the elements and their functions, and assesses
their functional significance.

1826 *Rubarth, Hermann. "Die Reprisengestaltung in den Symphonien
der Klassik und Romantik. (Haydn, Mozart, Beethoven,
Schubert, Mendelssohn, Schumann, Brahms und Bruckner)"
Phil.F. diss., Universität Köln, 1950. v, 143, 42 pp.

1827 Salmenhaara, Erkki. Tutkielmia brahmsin sinfonioista. (Acta
musicologica fennica 12) Helsinki: Suomen Musiikkitieteellinen
Seura, Musikvetenskapliga Sällskapet i Finland, 1979.
181 pp. mus., fig., notes. Historical background and
analysis.
(d) *see: 1902, 1931, 1982, 2003.

1828 *Schneider-Kohnz, Brigitte. "Motiv und Thema in den

Orchesterwerken von Johannes Brahms" Phil.F. diss.,
Universität des Saarlandes (Saarbrücken), 1982. vi, 209
pp.

1829　Schnirlin, Ossip.　"Brahms und Joachim bei der Entstehung
des Violin- und des Doppelkonzertes von Johannes Brahms"
Die Musik (Berlin) 21/2 (11.1928) pp. 97-103. mus., notes.
Describes Joachim's changes in the manuscripts of these
two works.

1830　#Schroeder, Carl.　"Der Vortrag der Brahmsschen Orchesterwerke" Der Musiksalon 5/11/12 (1913) pp. 122-40. mus.
Conductor's analysis of all symphonies, serenades, overtures, Op. 56a: discusses tempi, cueings, comments on
dynamic and expressive markings.

1831　Siegmund-Schultze, Walther.　"Johannes Brahms (1833-1897)"
in Konzertbuch. [Band 1:] Orchestermusik. Erster Teil.
17. bis 19. Jahrhundert. Karl Schoenewolf, ed. Leipzig:
VEB Deutscher Verlag für Musik, 1965. pp. 555-89.
mus. Descriptive analysis for all the orchestral works.

1832　Simon, James.　"Brahms' Orchesterwerke" Deutsche allgemeine
Zeitung (Berlin) 61/193 (26.4.1922) Morgenausgabe. Beiblatt [verso] p. [6]. Surveys Opp. 11, 16, 56a, 68, 73,
80, 81, 90, 98 with descriptive analysis and comments.

1833　*Sittard, Josef. Johannes Brahms. Akademische Fest-Ouvertüre, Op. 80. Die Tragische Ouvertüre, Op. 81. (Der
Musikführer. no. 25) Frankfurt a/M.: Verlag von H.
Bechhold, [1895]. 16 pp.
*also: Stuttgart: Schmitt, n.d.
*also: Berlin: Schlesinger, n.d.
(a)　i)　*reprint: in 1812.
　　　ii)　*reprint: in 1346.

1834　#_____. (Joseph) "Johannes Brahms als Symphoniker" in
Sittard. Künstler-Charakteristiken. Aus dem Konzertsaal.
(Sittard. Studien und Charakteristiken. II) Hamburg und
Leipzig: Verlag von Leopold Voss, 1889. pp. 106-18.
Describes the qualities of the symphonies.
(e)　report: "Johannes Brahms ist ..." Neue Musikzeitung
　　11/18 (1890) p. 214.

1835　Smith, Raymond R.　"Motivic Procedure in Opening Movements
of the Symphonies of Schumann, Bruckner and Brahms"
Music Review 36/2 (5.1975) pp. 130-34. notes. Contra-
dicts the assertion that Romantic composers had no skills
at composing within the sonata form, with an examination
of all the symphonies of the composers mentioned.

1836 Smith, Warren Storey. "Bruckner vs. Brahms, and Mahler vs. Strauss: A Study in Contrasts" Chord and Discord 2/8 (1958) pp. 33-48. Brahms: pp. 33-40. notes. Compares the qualities of their melodic inventiveness, instrumentation and harmonic idiom in the symphonic works.

1837 *Sollertinskii, Ivan Ivanovich. "Simfonii Bramsa" in Sollertinskii. Muzykal'no-istoricheskie étiudy. Leningrad: Gos. muzykal'noe izd-vo, 1956. 2. izdája: Istoricheskie étiudy. 1963. "Iogannes Brams" pp. 276-300. mus., notes, ind. Surveys orchestral works; includes biographical information.

1838 Spaeth, Sigmund [Gottfried]. "Bowing To Brahms" in Spaeth. Great Symphonies. How to Recognize and Remember Them. Garden City, N.Y.: Garden City Publishing Co. Inc., 1936. pp. 185-215. mus., notes. Informal, descriptive notes on the symphonies, with author-supplied verses to aid in the retention of the thematic materials.
*also: New York: Perma Giants, [1949].
*[Revised Edition:] Introduction by Eugene Ormandy. New York: Cornet Press Books, [1952].
*also: Garden City, N.Y.: Garden City Publishing Co., [1963].
(a) *reprint (of 1952 Edition): Westport, Conn.: Greenwood Press, [1972].

1839 Specht, Richard. "Zur Brahmsschen Symphonik" Die Musik (Berlin) 12/1 (Bd. 45) (10.1912) pp. 3-9. notes. Discusses Brahms's symphonic style; includes comments on orchestral music prior to Op. 68.
(c) excerpt: Specht. "Brahms als Sinfoniker" Die Musik (Berlin) 25/8 (5.1933) pp. 592-94. notes.
(a) reprint: in 3186.c. pp. 32-34.

1840 Stedman, Preston. "Johannes Brahms (1833-1897)" in Stedman. The Symphony. Englewood Cliffs, N.J.: Prentice-Hall Inc., 1979. pp. 143-65. ill., mus., notes. Discusses Brahms's symphonic style, with analysis of each symphony.

1841 *"Sunshine in Art: Mr. Gustav Holst and Brahm's Works" Glasgow Herald 144/15 (18.1.1926) p. 11. Report on Holst lecture during which he discusses Brahms's orchestral technique. [from S121]

1842 Swarowsky, Hans. "Marginalien zu Fragen des Stils und der Interpretation (I)" Österreichische Musikzeitschrift 24/12 (12.1969) pp. 681-90. Brahms: pp. 684-87. On the question of how a conductor interprets expressive markings in the symphonies.

1843 "The Symphonies of Brahms. Symphonic Logic" The Times

(London) Late London Edition no. 52,433 (3.10.1952) p. 9.
Discusses each symphony as a work of conflicting forces
and arguments.

1844 *Tintori, Giampiero. Il Concerto per pianoforte e orchestra
da Bach a Brahms. Note a un ciclo di audizioni. Pavia:
Ed. Orup, Organismo Rappresentativo Universitario Pavese
(Centro Universitario Musicale Pavese), 1955. 103 pp.

1845 Toledano, Ralph de. "The Best of Brahms" National Review
34/3 (19.2.1982) pp. 182-84. discog. Comments on the
value of the concertos; includes an evaluation of Brahms's
style and a look at Brahms the composer.

1846 *Valavanis, Tassos. "The Symphonies of Johannes Brahms"
The Social Monitor 1156 (21.8.1968) pp. 1-2. Discusses
the symphonies as absolute music. [from S202]

1847 #Válek, Jiří. "Nad symfonickou tvorbou J. Brahmse. K. 125.
výročí narození skladatelů" Hudební rozhledy 11 (1958)
pp. 320-22. mus., notes. Discusses compositional process
in the symphonies.

1848 *Vallis, Richard. "A Study of Late Baroque Instrumental Style
in the Piano Concertos of Brahms" Ph.D. diss., New York
University, 1978. 216 pp. Discusses the influence and
incidence of late Baroque style characteristics in these works.
[from S156]

1849 W.S.B.M[athews]. "I have a friend ..." Music (Chicago)
12/1 (5.1897) pp. 71-77. Discusses the updating of the
symphonic repertory, using Brahms as an example.

1850 Walker, Alan. "Brahms and Serialism" Musical Opinion and
Music Trade Review 82/973 (10.1958) pp. 17, 19, 21. fig.
Uses examples from Opp. 73 and 98 to show that Brahms
made conscious use of 12-tone system of composition.

1851 Watkins, Dudley. "The Symphony in Decline" Musical Opinion
and Music Trade Review 78/928 (1.1955) pp. 215, 217.
Brahms: p. 215. Traces the decline of the classical symphony form: Brahms as romanticist with no conviction as
classicist.

1852 Weigel, Hans. "Die Vierte" in Weigel. Apropos Musik. Un-
systematische und laienhafte Versuche eines Liebhabers
zur Heranführung an die Tonkunst in der zweiten Person
Einzahl. Zürich und Stuttgart: Artemis Verlag, 1965.
pp. 107-18. ill., ind. Discusses Brahms as symphonist.

1853 *Weingartner, Felix. Die Symphonie nach Beethoven. Berlin:

S. Fischer, 1898. [6], 103 pp.
*2. umgearbeitete Auflage: 1901. 109, [1] pp.
*also: Leipzig: Breitkopf & Härtel, 1901.
*3. vollständige umgearbeitete Auflage: (Breitkopf & Härtels
Musikbücher) Leipzig: Breitkopf & Härtel, 1909. [6],
113 pp. Due to considerable revision, this is practically
a new book. [from 1853.a.iii.]
*4. Auflage: 1926. 100 pp.
Brahms: pp. 42-57.
(b) i) *English translation by Arthur Bles (of 1901 Auflage): Weingartner. The Post-Beethoven Sym-
phonists. Symphony Writers Since Beethoven.
New York: Scribners, [1906]. 4, [2], 163 pp.
ill.
*also: London: W. Reeves, [1907].
*issue (of London Edition): [191-?].
*also titled: The Symphony Writers Since Beethoven
.... London: William Reeves Bookseller Limited,
[192-?]. vii, [1], 168 pp. ill. Brahms: pp.
41-61.
2nd Impression (of Reeves [192-?] Edition): With
Notice of The Author's Own No. 5 Symphony by
D.C. Parker added to this Issue. [1925].
Evaluates Brahms's symphonies.
*also: Boston: William Reeves, n.d.
(a) *reprint (of Reeves [1925] Edition): Westport,
Conn.: Greenwood Press, [1971].
ii) *English translation by Maude Barrows Dutton (of
1901 Auflage): Weingartner. The Symphony Since
Beethoven. Boston: Oliver Ditson Company;
New York: C. H. Ditson & Co., 1904. 98 pp.
*also: Boston: Oliver Ditson Company, 1914.
iii) English translation by H. M. Schott with New Notes
and Translator's Preface (of 1926 Auflage): Weingartner. "The Symphony Since Beethoven" in
Weingartner. Weingartner on Music and Conducting.
Three Essays by Felix Weingartner. New York:
Dover Publications, Inc., 1969. pp. 235-304.
"Berlioz and Brahms": pp. 262-78. Brahms:
pp. 270-78. notes.
iv) *French translation by Madame Camille Chevillard
(of 1898 Auflage): Weingartner. La Symphonie
après Beethoven. Paris: A. Durand et fils,
[1900]. 91 pp.
(d) Imbert, Hugues. "La Symphonie après Beethoven. Réponse à M. Félix Weingartner"
Le Guide musical (Bruxelles) 46/33-34 -
39 (19. u. 26.8.-30.9.; 1900) pp. 591-94,
611-14, 631-35, 647-51, 663-67, 683-86.
Brahms: pp. 631-34.
(c) excerpt (of 1898 Auflage in English translation by

Carl Armbruster): Weingartner. "The Symphony Since Beethoven. The New Classical School" Contemporary Review 75 (2.1899) pp. 271-89. Brahms: pp. 282-86. mus.
(e) #report (of 1909 Auflage?): see 225.5.

1854 "Which is Brahms's Best Symphony?" The Times (London) Royal Edition no. 54,984 (20.1.1961) p. 4. Compares these works with those of Beethoven and Sibelius; includes comments on aspects of each symphony.

1855 *Wiseman, Herbert. "Johannes Brahms (1833-1897)" in The Symphony. Ralph Hill, ed. (Pelican Books A204) Harmondsworth, Middlesex: Penguin Books, [1949]. 458 pp. mus.
*also: London, Melbourne, Baltimore: Penguin Books, 1949.
*issues (of Harmondsworth Edition): 1950. 416 pp.
*issues (of London Edition): 1950, 1951, 1954.
(a) reprint (of London 1949 Edition): St. Clair Shores, Mich.: Scholarly Press, 1978. pp. 224-46. [total pp.: 416 pp.] Historical background and analysis for each symphony.

See also 20, 61.d., 104.d., 757, 805, 865, 1382, 1386, 1387, 1396, 1418, 2398, 2405, 2415.d.ii., 2431, 2462, 2496, 2509-12, 2518, 2600, 2647, 2888.d.c., 2914.

a. Orchestral Music--Specific

See also 1386, 1387.d.

--Op. 11

1856 *Knorr, Jwan. Johannes Brahms. Serenade für grosses Orchester (D-dur, Op. 11). (Der Musikführer no. 142) Frankfurt a/M.: Verlag von H. Bechhold, [1898]. 14 pp.
*also: Berlin: Schlesinger, n.d.
*also: Berlin: Seeman Nachf[olger]., n.d.
(a) i) *reprint: in 1812.
    ii) *reprint: in 1346.

1857 N. [Carl von Noorden] Deutsche Musikzeitung (Wien) 2/15 (13.4.1861) pp. 117-19. notes. Review.

See also 251, 1332, 1353A, 1359, 1372A, 1376, 1795, 1807, 1810, 1816, 1830-32, 1839, 2451.

--Op. 15

1858 *Beyer, Carl. Johannes Brahms. Klavierkonzert in D-moll,

op. 15. (Der Musikführer no. 18) Frankfurt a/M.: Verlag
von H. Bechhold, [1895]. 18 pp. ill., mus.
*also: Berlin: Schlesinger, n.d.
*also: Stuttgart: Schmitt, n.d.
*also: Leipzig: H. Seemann Nachfolger, [c. 1900].
(a) *reprint: in 1346.

1859 Blom, Eric. "Brahms: Piano Concerto, D minor (Op. 15)"
Music Teacher 12/10 (M.S. series 27/1) (10.1933) pp.
513-14. ill., mus. Discusses its background and reception;
includes a descriptive analysis.

1860 Br., v. "Werke für Orchester und Pianoforte" Deutsche
Musikzeitung (Wien) 2/27 (8.7.1861) pp. 211-13. mus.
Reviews Brahms's Op. 15 and Rubinstein's Op. 25: the
two works are compared with each other as well as being
reviewed individually.

1861 *"Brahms d-moll-hangversenyének titka" Literatura (Budapest)
8 (5.1933) pp. 197-200. ill.

1862 Dahlhaus, Carl. Johannes Brahms. Klavierkonzert Nr. 1
d-moll, Op. 15. (Meisterwerke der Musik. Werkmonographien
zur Musikgeschichte Heft 3) München: Wilhelm Fink Verlag,
1965. 35, [1] pp. mus., fig., notes. Presents historical
background and analysis.

1863 Geeraert, Nicole. "Johannes Brahms: Konzert für Klavier und
Orchester Nr. 1 d-Moll op. 15 (Im Konzertsaal gehört)"
NZ-Neue Zeitschrift für Musik 143/8 (15.8.-15.9.;1982)
pp. 31-33. mus., notes. Provides historical background
for this work.

1864 *Gren, Donald Allen. "A Comprehensive Performance Project
in Piano Literature and An Essay on The Piano Concerto
in D Minor, Opus 15 of Johannes Brahms: Program Notes
based on Diaries, Letters and Music Reviews" D.M.A.
diss., University of Iowa, 1979.

1865 *Helm, Theodor. "Wiener Musikbrief: Brahms' d-moll Klavierkonzert" Pester Lloyd (Budapest) (12.4.1879).

1866 *James, Roberta Aileen. "Johannes Brahms: Concerto No.
1 in D minor, Op. 15" D.M.A. diss., Stanford University,
1981. 60 pp. Investigates the work's origins and studies
aspects of the work relating to performance. [from S156]

1867 Jenner, Gustav. "Zur Entstehung des d-moll Klavierkonzertes
Op. 15 von Johannes Brahms" Die Musik (Berlin) 12/1 (Bd.
45) (10.1912) pp. 32-37. notes. Traces the evolution of
Op. 15 from its genesis to its final form.

1868   Joselson, Tedd. "Brahms' Piano Concerto No. 1" <u>Contemporary</u>
        <u>Keyboard</u> 5/2 (2.1979) p. 65. mus. Suggestions for
        playing the solo part, 1st movement.

1869   Keller, Hans. "The New in Review" <u>Music Review</u> 20/3-4
        (8.-11.;1959) pp. 289-99. mus., notes. Brahms: pp.
        294-95. Suggests two textural changes to counteract
        "blemishes" in original scoring.

1870   Kretzschmar, Hermann. "Neue Werke von J. Brahms" <u>Musik-</u>
        <u>alisches Wochenblatt</u> 5/1 (2.1.1874) pp. 5-7. mus. Review.
        (d) *Kretzschmar. Johannes Brahms. Concert für das
             <u>Pianoforte mit Begleitung des Orchesters.</u> D moll,
             <u>Op. 15.</u> (Kleiner Konzertführer no. 596) Leipzig:
             Breitkopf & Härtel, n.d.

1871   W. S. B. M[athews]. "The history of this concerto ..."
        <u>Music</u> (Chicago) 17/6 (4.1900) pp. 622-26. Historical
        background and descriptive analysis; quotes from 117 for
        background.

See also 94, 256, 308, 608, 854, 1332, 1358, 1359, 1372C, 1381, 1384,
1387.d., 1391-93, 1398-1400, 1404, 1405, 1409, 1410, 1420, 1586,
1775, 1778, 1782, 1784, 1791, 1793-95, 1807, 1831, 1844, 1845, 1848,
2361, 2422, 2553, 2899.

--Op. 16

1872   *Knorr, Jwan. Johannes Brahms. Serenade für kleines Or-
             chester, op. 16. (Der Musikführer. no. 16) Frankfurt
             a/M.: Verlag von H. Bechhold, [1895]. 25 pp.
        *also: Berlin: Schlesinger, n.d.
        *also: Stuttgart: Schmitt, n.d.
             (a) i) reprint: in 1812.
                ii) *reprint: in 1346.

1873   S. B. [Selmar Bagge] <u>Deutsche Musikzeitung</u> (Wien) 2/6
        (9.2.1861) pp. 42-44. mus., notes. Review.

See also 1353A, 1359, 1372A, 1376, 1795, 1807, 1810, 1816, 1830-32,
1839, 2451, 2899

--Op. 56a

1874   *Knorr, Jwan. Johannes Brahms. Variationen über ein Thema
             von J[oseph]. Haydn für Orchester, op. 56a. (Der
             Musikführer. no. 3) Frankfurt a/M.: Verlag von H.
             Bechhold, [1894]. 21 pp.
        *also: Berlin: Schlesinger, n.d.

*also: Stuttgart: Schmitt, n.d.
  (a) i) reprint: in 1812.
     ii) *reprint: in 1346.

1875 Kretzschmar, Hermann. "Neue Werke von J[ohannes].
     Brahms. IV." Musikalisches Wochenblatt 5/13 (27.3.1874)
     pp. 164-66. mus., notes. Review.

1876 *Rost, G. W. "Chorale Sancti Antonii" Die Kirchenmusik
     (Düsseldorf) 5 (1942) pp. 6-8.

1877 Schmitz, Eugen. "Feuerbachs 'Versuchung des hl. [heiligen]
     Antonius' und die Brahmsschen Haydnvariationen" Hochland
     10/12 (9.1913) pp. 732-36. mus. Describes how Brahms
     has musically depicted Feuerbach's painting in Op. 56a.

1878 *_____. "Nochmal "Chorale Sancti Antonii"" Die Kirchenmusik
     (Düsseldorf) 5 (1942) p. 55.

1879 Stein, Leon. An Analytic Study of Brahms' "Variations On A
     Theme By Haydn" (Op. 56a). Chicago: De Paul University
     Press, 1944. 16 pp. mus., discog.

1880 *Strauss, Yair. "A Conductor's Guide to Brahms' Variations
     on a Theme by Haydn" M.M. thesis, Instrumental Conducting,
     Indiana University, 1971. 36 pp. mus., notes. Also
     examines Fritz Busch's annotated first edition of this work.
     [from S202]

1881 *Warburton, A[nnie]. O. Music Teacher and Piano Student 45
     (2.1966).
     (a) reprint: see 1375B. analysis.

See also 39B.e.iv., 254, 1339, 1351, 1359, 1372B, 1375B, 1781, 1794,
1795, 1807, 1810, 1816, 1817, 1830-32, 1839, 2548, 2573, 2899, 2980,
3038.

See also "Op. 56b" in IV.A.2.a. Specific Works.

--Op. 68

1882 Brahms, Johannes. Symphony Number One [[in C minor]]
     Opus 68. For Piano Two Hands. (Analytic Symphony
     Series. Percy Goetschius, ed. and annotator. no. 20)
     Philadelphia: Oliver Ditson Company, 1929. [[viii]], 48
     pp. ill., notes. Analysis of form and structural details;
     includes biographical information.

1883 "Brahms's Symphony" Monthly Musical Record 7/[73] (1.1.1877)
     pp. 7-8. mus. Background and descriptive analysis of

Op. 68; latter is based on a translation of a review by
Richard Pohl of a performance (Musikalisches Wochenblatt
7/49 (17.11.1876) pp. 657-68).

1884   "The C-minor Symphony by Brahms" Dwight's Journal of Music
37/19 (Whole no. 957) (22.12.1877) pp. 149-50. Translations
of German reviews of Leipzig (Signale für die musikalische
Welt 35/7 (1.1877) p. 100) and Wien performances (from ?).

1885   Carse, Adam. "First Symphonies: Studies in Orchestration.
IV. Brahms-Tschaikovsky" Musical Opinion and Music
Trade Review 43/516 (9.1920) pp. 957-58. Brahms: p.
958. notes. Analysis.

1886   Downes, Olin. "Origin of A Brahms Theme" New York Times
80/26,608 (30.11.1930) Section 9, p. 8. mus. Argues
that the horn motif from the last movement of Op. 68 is
derived from the Westminster Chimes in England.
(d)   continued: Downes. ""Thus Blew the Alphorn Today""
New York Times 80/26,748 (19.4.1931) Section 8,
p. 8. Summarizes previous article and uses excerpt
from 1179 to prove that horn motif derives from
alphorn tune.

1887   Gärtner, Gustav. "Das Terzmotiv-Keimzelle der 1. Sinfonie
von Johannes Brahms. Ein Beitrag zur Analyse des ersten
Satzes" Die Musikforschung 8/3 (1955) pp. 332-35. mus.
On the use of the interval of a third as a germ cell, with
analysis of the 1st movement showing occurrences and
variations.

1888   Grove, Geroge. "The First Symphony of Brahms" Musical
Times 46/747,748 (1.;5.-6.;1905) pp. 318-20, 397-99. mus.
Historical background and descriptive analysis.

1889   *Helm, Theodor. "Wiener Musikbrief: Brahms' Symphonie in
c-moll" Pester Lloyd (Budapest) (31.12.1878).

1890   Huschke, Konrad. "Johannes Brahms' Aufstieg zur Sinfonie.
Ein 50-Jahr-Gedenken" Allgemeine Musikzeitung 53/50 (10.
12.1926) pp. 1035-37. Discusses the genesis of Op. 68.
(d)   reworked: Huschke. "Vom Sinfoniker Brahms"
Allgemeine Musikzeitung 57/13 (28.3.1930) pp. 310-
13. notes. Includes comments on Brahms's strengths
as a symphonist with a negative opinion on Kalbeck's
drawing of programmatic allusion from Brahms's
music.

1891   JWSch. [Johann-Wolfgang Schottländer] ""Also blus das
Alphorn heut"" Deutsche Musikkultur 2/2 (4.-5.1937) pp.
51-52. facsim. Looks at alphorn motif from 4th movement

to see if theme is really compatible with the alphorn's
capabilities.
(d) [Hermann Stephani] "Zu unserem Beitrag ..." Deutsche
      Musikkultur 2/3 (8.-9.1937) p. 192. Comments on
      the alphorn's capabilities.

1892 *Knorr, Jwan. Johannes Brahms. 1. Symphonie (c-moll,
       Op. 68). (Der Musikführer. no. 73) Frankfurt a/M.:
       Verlag von H. Bechhold, [1898]. 21 pp.
       *also: Berlin: Schlesinger, n.d.
       *also: Stuttgart: Schmitt, n.d.
       (a) i) reprint: in 1812.
            ii) *reprint: in 1346.

1893 *Kretzschmar, Hermann. Brahms: Symphonie Nr. 1 (c-moll).
       (Kleiner Konzertführer no. 570) Leipzig: Breitkopf &
       Härtel, 1899. 16 pp.
       (d) *see: 1353A.

1894 #McClure, Theron. ""Bottom" Brahms" Bass World. International
       Society of Bassists Annual Journal 3/4 (1977) pp. 318-19
       (also paged J79-J80). facsim. Illustrates Brahms's
       preference for low bass parts by comparing the 4-hand
       piano version manuscript for Op. 68 with the score manu-
       script.

1895 Morgan, Bayard Quincy. "Beethoven's Signature in the "Tenth
       Symphony"" The American-German Review 5/3 (2.1939)
       pp. 9, 39. notes. Discusses the intentional plagiarism
       of Beethoven by Brahms, and speculates on its origins.

1896 Moser, Hans Joachim. "Zur Sinndeutung der Brahms'schen
       c-moll-Symphonie" Rondo [=Osterreichische Musikzeitschrift]
       8/1 (1.1953) pp. 21-24. mus. Describes allusions to the
       music of Wagner and Beethoven, use of the Clara Schumann
       theme and allusions to melodic material from earlier solo songs,
       in Op. 68.
       (a) reprint: Moser. "Zur Sinndeutung der c-Moll-
                      Symphonie von Johannes Brahms" in Moser. Musik in
                      Zeit und Raum. Ausgewählte Abhandlungen. Berlin:
                      Verlag Merseburger, 1960. pp. 220-23. mus.,
                      notes.

1897 #Neider, Charles. Brahms and Keats: A Parallel. New York:
       The Orion Press, 1946. 13 pp. mus., fig. Discusses
       formal parallels between the 2nd movement of Op. 68 and
       Keats's poem "Ode to a Nightingale".

1898 Newman, S[idney]. T[homas]. M[avow]. "The Slow Movement
       of Brahms' First Symphony. A Reconstruction of The Ver-
       sion First Performed Prior to Publication" Music Review 9/1

(2.1948) pp. 4-12. mus., notes. Discusses early performances and subsequent changes, focusing on a version performed in England, Spring 1877, as reconstructed from programme notes and comparison with the published score.

1899   Pascall, Robert. "Brahms's First Symphony Slow Movement. The Initial Performing Version" Musical Times 122/1664 (10.1981) pp. 664-65, 667. mus., fig., notes. Presents a detailed compositional history of this work, examining sections which underwent change.

1900   Paumgartner, Bernhard. "Die erste Symphonie (C moll) von Johannes Brahms unter Artur Nikisch. Versuch einer Analyse der Wiedergabe" Pult und Taktstock 3/3/4 (1926) pp. 79-83. notes. A study in performance technique.

1901   Ravizza, Victor. "Konflikte in Brahms'scher Musik. Zum ersten Satz der c-moll-Sinfonie Op. 68" Schweizer Beiträge zur Musikwissenschaft Bd. 2 (1974) (Schweizerischen Musikforschenden Gesellschaft. Publikationen. Publications de la Société suisse de musicologie. Serie III. vol. 2) pp. 75-90. mus., notes. Describes how Brahms bends the sonata form to achieve his desired end result.

1902   *Salmenhaara, Erkki. "Paatoksen ja uhman symboli. Brahmsin sinfoniat I" Musiikki 28/1 (1975).
       (d)   see: 1827.

1903   Slonimsky, Nicolas. "Musical Oddities" Etude 71/1 (1.1953) pp. 4-5. Brahms: p. 5. Discusses the significance of Bülow's "10th Symphony" label, with reaction to that idea from American critics.

1904   _____. "Musical Oddities" Etude 73/9 (9.1955) pp. 3-4. mus. Brahms: p. 3. Describes the origin of the 4th movement horn solo.

1905   Stäblein, Bruno. "Die motivische Arbeit im Finale der ersten Brahms-Sinfonie" Das Musikleben 2/3 (3.1949) pp. 69-72. facsim., mus., notes. Discusses the form of the movement and use of motivic transformation within it.

1906   *Tretbar, C[harles]. F. Johannes Brahms, Op. 68, Symphony in C minor. (Analytical Reviews of Classical and Modern Compositions) New York: [Author], 1878.

1907   *Warburton, A[nnie]. O. Music Teacher and Piano Student [42-46 (between 1963 and 1967)].
       (a)   reprint: see 1375B. Analysis.

1908   Williams, Michael D. "The "Greatest Hits" of U.S. Symphony

Orchestras" Music Journal 39[36]/[7] (9.1978) pp. 4-7.
Brahms: pp. 5-6. Surveys the top ten works in U.S.
orchestral repertoire, 1973-78, with explanation of the place
of Op. 68 on this list.

1909   Williams, Richard. "How To Enjoy A Symphony. Part V"
House Beautiful 98/6 (6.1956) pp. 36, 152. ill., discog.
Historical background and descriptive analysis of Op. 68;
includes comment on Brahms the composer.

See also 2, 170, 251, 257, 259, 270, 604, 652, 660, 680, 756, 840,
852. 1353A, 1356, 1357,1359, 1372A, 1375B, 1400, 1402, 1776, 1777, 1779-
81,1783,1785-88, 1790, 1792, 1794-1803, 1805-07, 1810, 1813, 1814,
1817, 1820-23, 1825, 1830-32, 1834, 1835, 1837, 1838, 1840, 1842,
1843, 1846, 1847, 1853, 1855, 1943, 2361, 2427, 2469.5, 2470.a.b.,
2509, 2512, 2527, 2554, 2606, 2609, 2899, 3018.

--Op. 73

1910   Musical Times 19/428 (1.10.1878) p. 551. Review.

1911   *Die Tonkunst (Berlin) [5] (21.9.1878) p. 189.

1912   Brahms, Johannes. Symphony Number Number Two [[in D
Major]] Opus 73. For Piano Two Hands. (Analytic Symphony Series. Percy Goetschius, ed. and annotator. no.
6) Philadelphia: Oliver Ditson Company, 1927. [[viii]],
43 pp. Includes biographical and critical notes.

1913   *[Max Schütz] "Brahms' II. D-dur Symphonie. Vorgetragen im
Philharmonischen Konzert. 13.XI.1878" Pester Lloyd
(Budapest) (14.11. and 5.12.;1878).

1914   "Brahms's New Symphony. Opinions of the London Dailies"
Dwight's Journal of Music 38/16 (Whole no. 980) (9.11.1878)
pp. 329-31. Excerpts from reviews from 5 papers, on the
occasion of the first performance of Op. 73 in the Crystal
Palace, London.

1915   *Cherubino. Figaro (London) (12.10.1878).
(c) excerpt: "Brahms's Second Symphony" Dwight's Journal
of Music 38/15 (Whole no. 979) (26.10.1878) p. 325.
Relates background of first performance in England,
reviews opinions to date.

1916   Clifton, Chalmers. "Brahms' Second Symphony. An Interpretation from the Standpoint of the Conductor. Part I-III"
Musical Mercury 1/1-3 (1.-2.;4.-5.;8.-9.;1934) pp. 7-[9],
59-60, 83-84. music, notes. Describes how he brought
out musical effects in this work.

1917 *Conkling, Grace Hazard. "Brahms, No. 2 D Major, Op. 73"
in Conkling. Flying Fish. A Book of Songs and Sonnets.
New York and London: A. A. Knopf, 1926.
(a) reprint: Conkling. The New Republic 46/594 (21.4.
1926) p. 272. Poetic impressions of Op. 73
(a) reprint: Conkling. In Anthology of Magazine
Verse for 1926 and Yearbook of American
Poetry. William Stanley Braithwaite, ed.
Boston: B. J. Brimmer Company, 1926.
Part II, p. 95.

1918 *Dukas, Paul. Chronique des arts et de la curiosité (11.1905).
(a) reprint: Dukas. "La Seconde symphonie de J. Brahms--
La Mer de Debussy" in Dukas. Les Écrits de Paul
Dukas sur la musique. Avant-propos de G. Samazeuilh. (Musique et musiciens) Paris: Société
d'Editions Françaises et Internationales, 1948.
pp. 620-22. Brahms: pp. 620-21. Personal impressions of Op. 73.

1919 Dukas, Paul. "La Symphonie en ré de J. Brahms" La Revue
hebdomadaire 1/6 (11.1892) pp. 459-69. Brahms: pp.
462-69. Personal impressions of Op. 73.
(a) i) reprint: Dukas. in 1918.a. pp. 58-64.
ii) reprint: Dukas. in Dukas. Chroniques musicales
sur deux siècles 1892-1932. Préface de Jean-Vincent
Richard. (Collection "musique") [Paris:] Stock
Musique, 1980. pp. 128-32.

1920 F. K. "La Symphonie en ré majeur de Johannes Brahms"
Le Guide musical (Bruxelles) 24/52 (26.12.1878) pp. [1-2].
descriptive analysis.
(b) English translation: "Brahms's Symphony in D" Musical
Standard 16/755 Third series (18.1.1879) pp. 43-44.

1921 Frost, Henry F. "Analysis of Brahms's New Symphony" London
and Provincial Music Trades Review no. 11 (15.9.1878) pp.
4-5.

1922 Gilman, Lawrence. "Symphony No. 2, in D major, Op. 73.
Johannes Brahms (Orchestral Master Works)" Musical America
49/6 (10.2.1929) pp. 21-22. ill., notes. Descriptive analysis
with comments on the work's original reception.

1923 *Goepp, Philip H. "Brahms" in Goepp. Symphonies and Their
Meaning. [First Series]. Philadelphia & London: J. P.
Lippincott Company, 1897.
*2nd Edition: 1898.
*3rd Edition: 1900.
*5th Edition: 1903.
*6th Edition: 1905.

*7th Edition: 1908.
*8th Edition: 1911.
*9th Edition: [191-?].
   (a) reprint (of ? Edition): Goepp. in 1800.a.i. [title:
     [Volume 1] Great Works of Music [[Symphonies and
     Their Meaning]]] pp. 366-403. mus., ind., notes.
     Descriptive analysis of Op. 73; includes general
     comments on the quality of Brahms's music.

1924 *Hanslick, Eduard. "Die neue Symphonie" Neue freie Presse
     (Wien) (30.12.1877).

1925 Huschke, Konrad. "Brahms' Märchensinfonie" Der Türmer
     32/10 (Bd. 2) (7.1930) pp. 360-63. Descriptive analysis.

1926 *Knorr, Jwan. Johannes Brahms, Zweite Symphonie (D-dur).
     Op. 73. (Der Musikführer. no. 86) Frankfurt a/M.:
     Verlag von H. Bechhold, [1898]. 16 pp.
   *also: Berlin: Schlesinger, n.d.
   *also: Stuttgart: Schmitt, n.d.
   (a) i) reprint: in 1812.
     ii) *reprint: in 1346.

1927 Komma, Karl Michael. "Das "Scherzo" der 2. Symphonie von
     Johannes Brahms. Eine melodisch-rhythmische Analyse"
     in Festschrift für Walter Wiora zum 30. Dezember 1966.
     Ludwig Finscher and Christoph-Hellmut Mahling, eds. Kassel
     [et al.]: Bärenreiter, 1967. pp. 448-57. mus., fig.,
     notes. Presents justification for calling this movement a
     scherzo; also points out influences from music of the Middle
     East.

1928 *Kretzschmar, Hermann. Brahms: Symphonie Nr. 2 (D-dur).
     (Kleiner Konzertführer no. 578) Leipzig: Breitkopf &
     Härtel, 1900. 16 pp.
   (d) *see: 1353A.

1929 *McKeown, Reynold Daniel. "A Harmonic, Melodic and Rhythmic
     Analysis of The First Movement of Brahms's Second Sym-
     phony" M.A. thesis, Music, University of Wisconsin, 1939.

1930 Pleasures of Music. A Reader's Choice of Great Writing About
     Music and Musicians from Cellini to Bernard Shaw. Edited
     [and translated] and With An Introduction by Jacques
     Barzun. New York: Viking Press, 1951.
     i) Hanslick, Eduard. "Brahms' Second Symphony": pp.
        365-67. from 2946 (? Auflage).
     ii) "Johannes Brahms": pp. 566-68. from 954 (1908
        Auflage): 1 letter, 9.1856.
     iii)"Brahms' Song of Triumph ...": pp. 596-97. from
        3048.

*Compass Books Edition: 1960.
[New Edition:] Pleasures of Music. An Anthology of Writing
About Music and Musicians from Cellini to Bernard Shaw.
Edited [and translated] and With a New Preface by Jacques
Barzun. Chicago: University of Chicago Press; London:
Cassell and Co. Ltd., 1977. Omits first section and volume
index.
i) pp. 177-79; ii) pp. 326-28; iii) pp. 351-52.
(d) Pleasures of Music. An Anthology ... Shaw. Edited
[and translated] and With An Introduction by Jacques
Barzun. London: Michael Joseph, 1952. Text
shortened from New York Edition.
i) pp. 319-21; ii) pp. 468-70; iii) pp. 493-94.
[Readers Union Edition:] 1954.

1931 *Salmenhaara, Erkki. "D-duurin valoa ja varjoa. Brahmsin
sinfoniat II" Musiikki 28/2 (1975).
(d) see: 1827.

1932 *Schenk, Erich. "Zur Inhaltsdeutung der Brahmsschen
Wörthersee-Symphonie" Musikverein für Kärnten. Festliche
Jahresschrift (Klagenfurt) (1943) pp. 38-48. mus., notes.
(a) reprint: Schenk. in Schenk. Ausgewählte Aufsätze,
Reden und Vorträge. (Wiener musikwissenschaft-
liche Beiträge Bd. 7) Graz-Wien-Köln: Hermann
Böhlaus Nachf[olger]., 1967. pp. 133-42. Dis-
cusses Op. 73 as an example of a pastoral symphony.

1933 Stringham, Edwin John. "Brahms: The Classical Romanticist"
in Stringham. Listening to Music Creatively. Englewood
Cliffs, N.J.: Prentice-Hall Inc., 1946. pp. 296-306.
ill., mus., ind., notes. Descriptive analysis of Op. 73;
includes biographical information and comment on Brahms
the composer.
*1.-18. Printing: 1946-58.
2nd Edition: 1959. pp. 407-17.

1934 "Symphony in D, No. 2, Op. 73. By Johannes Brahms"
British Musician no. 12 (2/5) (1.1927) pp. 193-99. mus.
Thematic analysis.

See also 94, 251, 259, 270, 619, 660, 1334, 1353A, 1356, 1359, 1372A,
1385, 1400, 1403, 1776, 1777, 1780, 1781, 1783, 1785-88, 1790, 1792,
1794-99, 1801-03, 1805-07, 1810, 1813, 1814, 1817, 1820, 1821, 1825,
1830-32, 1834, 1835, 1837, 1838, 1840, 1842, 1843, 1846, 1847, 1850,
1853, 1855, 1943, 2309.d.ii., 2361, 2372, 2384, 2427, 2469.5, 2470.a.b.,
2509, 2512, 2523, 2596, 2606, 2609, 2899, 2943.c., 3035, 3039.

--Op. 77

1935   Brahms, Johannes. Concerto for Violin, Op. 77. A Facsimile
       of the Holograph Score. With an Introduction by Yehudi
       Menuhin and a Foreword by Jon Newsom. Washington,
       D.C.: Library of Congress, 1979. xix, [3], [[106]] pp.
       mus. Includes historical background and discussion of
       Joachim's involvement with the work, together with per-
       formance practice suggestions.
       (e) i) report: "Brahms' "Violin Concerto" Facsimile Now
                Available" School Musician 50/9 (5.1979) pp. 28-29.
           ii) report: "Library of Congress Publishes Facsimile
                of Brahms' Violin Concerto" Music Clubs Magazine
                58/4 (Spring 1979) p. 18.
          iii) report: Roesner, Linda Correll. Current Musicology
                no. 30 (1980) pp. 60-72. fig., notes.

1936   Cooke, Greville. "Brahms's Violin Concerto (Landmarks in
       Musical History)" Music Teacher 8/5 (M.S. series 21/8)
       (5.1929) pp. 291-92. ill. Comments on Op. 77 and its
       background.

1937   -f. [Heinrich Ehrlich] Neue Berliner Musikzeitung 33/42 (16.
       10.1879) pp. 332-33. Review.

1938   "Fiddler's Incunabula" Musical America 69/1 (1.1.1949) p. 11.
       Notice of Kreisler's manuscript being sold to the Library
       of Congress.

1939   Hartmann, Arthur. "The Brahms Violin Concerto" Musical
       Observer (New York) 13/1 (1.1916) pp. 50-51. ill., mus.
       Discusses the work's inception and Joachim's involvement
       in its creation.

1940   *Heuberger, Richard. Johannes Brahms, Konzert für Violine
       mit Begleitung der Orchesters. Op. 77. (Der Musikführer.
       no. 36) Frankfurt a/M.: Verlag von H. Bechhold, [1895].
       16 pp.
       *also: Berlin: Schlesinger, n.d.
       *also: Stuttgart: Schmitt, n.d.
       (a) *reprint: in 1346.

1941   Krummacher, Friedhelm. "Virtuosität und Komposition im
       Violinkonzert. Probleme der Gattung zwischen Beethoven
       und Brahms" NZ-Neue Zeitschrift für Musik 135/10 (10.1974)
       pp. 604-13. Brahms: pp. 610-12. mus., notes. Discusses
       compositional problems of working within the concerto form.

1942   Lowens, Irving. "[Annual Reports on Acquisitions:] Music"
       Quarterly Journal of the Library of Congress 21/1 (1.1964)
       pp. 15-48. Brahms: pp. 21-22. Describes the purchase

of Op. 77 manuscript, and how this source relates to the concerto's development.

1943 Schnirlin, Ossip. "Erinnerungen an Brahms. Sein Violin-konzert" Berliner Tageblatt 55/70 (11.2.1926) Morgenausgabe 1. Beiblatt p. [3]. Describes the reception of Opp. 77, 68, 73, 90, 98, by the public; includes descriptions of playing under Brahms, Berlin, 1896, and of the Brahms-Fritz Simrock relationship.

1944 Sommers, Lawrence. "Centenary of the Brahms Violin Concerto (1879-1979)" The Strad 89/1066 (2.1979) pp. 905, 907, 909. Describes the history of the work and its slow acceptance.

1945 Spivacke, Harold. "A Recent Gift from Mr. Fritz Kreisler" Library of Congress Quarterly Journal of Current Acqui-sitions 6/3 (5.1949) pp. 57-62. facsim., notes. Brahms: pp. 57-61. Relates the background and description of the manuscript of the score.

1946 Stoeving, Paul. "Two Masterworks for the Violin. "In the Light of Fancy and Facts"" Etude 55/11,12;56/1,2 (11., 12.;1937;1.,2.;1938) pp. 752, 824-25;52-53, 121. Brahms: pp. 52-53. Compares Op. 77 with Mendelssohn's Op. 64.

1947 Swalin, Benjamin F. "The Brahms Violin Concerto. A Stylistic Criticism" in Music Teachers National Association. Pro-ceedings of the Annual Meeting. Chicago, Illinois. 1936. Karl W. Gehrkens, ed. Series 31. pp. 269-81. mus., notes. Discusses the work's background and place in con-certo literature; includes discussion of the work's first performances, and an analysis describing its stylistic features.
(d) reworked: Swalin. "Johannes Brahms" in Swalin. The Violin Concerto. A Study in German Romanti-cism. Chapel Hill: University of North Carolina Press, 1941. pp. 125-40. ind., discog.

1948 Weiss-Aigner, Günter. "Komponist und Geiger. Joseph Joachims Mitarbeit am Violinkonzert von Johannes Brahms" NZ-Neue Zeitschrift für Musik 135/4 (4.1974) pp. 232-36. facsim., mus. Discussion of the Staatsbibliothek Preussischer Kulturbesitz manuscript (solo violin) with its markings by both Brahms and Joachim.
(d) Weiss-Aigner. Johannes Brahms. Violonkonzert D-Dur. (Meisterwerke der Musik. Werkmonographien zur Musikgeschichte. Heft 18) München: Wilhelm Fink Verlag, 1979. 56, [4,1] pp. facsim., mus., notes. Historical background of the work and analysis; includes comments on work's initial reception, together with reprint of 1948.

1949 _____. "Max Reger und die Tradition. Zum Violinkonzert A-Dur opus 101" NZ-Neue Zeitschrift für Musik 135/10 (10.1974) pp. 614-20. mus., notes. Compares Reger's work with Brahms's Op. 77 and Beethoven's Op. 61.

1950 Wendt, Martha. "The Rise and Decline of Virtuosity in the Nineteenth Century as Traced Through the Art of Violin Playing. Part IV." American String Teacher 17/1 (Winter 1967) pp. 14, 16-17. Brahms: pp. 16-17. Traces types of concerti written, with Brahms's work being of the type that are symphonically conceived.

See also 251, 264, 269, 299, 301, 765.d.d., 1359, 1372C, 1384, 1400, 1405, 1408, 1415, 1775, 1782, 1789, 1793-95, 1807, 1816, 1831, 1845, 2553.

See also "Joachim Family" in III.B.2.

--Op. 80

1951 A.R.M. "The query ..." Zeitschrift der Internationalen Musikgesellschaft 3/1 (1901) p. 41. A query as to the identity of work's second subject, as well as the author's identifications of other subjects in the work.
  (d) i) C.A.B. "III. In Answer to A.R.M.'s query ..." Zeitschrift der Internationalen Musikgesellschaft 3/2 (1901) p. 85. Identification of second subject.
      ii) Lichterfelde, A. K. "II. Zur Frage von A.R.M...." Zeitschrift der Internationalen Musikgesellschaft 3/2 (1901) p. 84. Corrects previously given identification for third subject.
     iii) Obrist, Aloys. "I. The query put by A.R.M...." Zeitschrift der Internationalen Musikgesellschaft 3/2 (1901) p. 84. Identification of second subject.

1952 Arvey, Verna. "Christmas with the Composers" Etude 72/12 (12.1954) pp. 16, 50-51. Brahms: p. 16. ill. Describes Op. 80 as a Christmas gift to von Herzogenberg, 1880.

1953 *Eeckhout, Antoon. Muzikale exploraties. Tweede reeks: ouverturen en symfonische gedichten. Michelen-Leuven: Uitgeverij de Monte, 1970. 106 pp.

1954 *Kalbeck, Max. Die Presse (Wien) (2.12.1884). Concerning von Bülow's remarks on Beethoven's Egmont Overture, Op. 84, and Brahms's Op. 80. [from 241]

1955 Mason, Daniel Gregory. "Short Studies of Great Masterpieces. XII. Academic Festival Overture, opus 80 by Johannes Brahms. First Performance in Breslau in 1881." New

Music Review and Church Music Review 16/190 (9.1917)
pp. 718-22. mus., notes. Analysis with information on
the incorporated student songs.
> (a) *reprint: Mason. in Mason. The Appreciation of Music.
>> Vol. III: Short Studies of Great Masterpieces.
>> New York: H. W. Gray, 1918. [includes 1980.a]
>> *issue: 1920.

1956 *Warburton, A[nnie]. O. Music Teacher and Piano Student
[41 or earlier (before 1963)].
> (a) reprint: see 1375A. Analysis.

1957 "Was He Fooling?" Music Journal 9/2 (2.1951) p. 49. Is
the insertion of student tunes in Op. 80 an example of
Brahms's humour?

See also 190, 251, 559.5, 566, 608, 680, 828, 1359, 1372B, 1375A,
1774, 1779, 1794, 1795, 1807, 1810, 1816, 1830-33, 2388, 2622.

--Op. 81

1958 "Analyses and Annotations of Representative Orchestral Works"
British Musician no. 15 (2/8) (4.1927) pp. 294-300. mus.,
notes. Brahms: pp. 294-96. mus., notes. Thematic
analysis.

1959 Korn, Richard. "Brahms" in Korn. Orchestral Accents.
New York: Farrar, Strauss and Cudahy, 1956. pp. 75-87.
Looks at Op. 81 as an example of Brahms's art: analysis
interspersed with general comments on Brahms's style.
> (a) *reprint: (Essay Index Reprint Series) Freeport,
>> N.Y.: Books for Libraries Press, 1971.

1960 *Warburton, A[nnie]. O. Music Teacher and Piano Student
[42-46 (between 1963 and 1967)].
> (a) reprint: see 1375. Analysis.

See also 944.c., 1351, 1372E, 1375B, 1830, 2548, 2899.

See also "Op. 80" in IV.A.3.a. Specific Works.

--Op. 83

1961 Gibson, Michael. "La Figuration de la nature dans la musique.
Deux exemples: Brahms et Mahler" Revue d'esthétique
(Paris) Nouvelle série--no. 4 (1982) pp. 77-91. Brahms:
pp. 79-86. mus. Discusses the horn motif, 1st movement,
as an evocation of nature.

1962 *Kretzschmar, Hermann. Johannes Brahms. Concert für
Pianoforte mit Begleitung des Orchesters. B dur: Op. 83.
(Kleiner Konzertführer no. 59-?) Leipzig: Breitkopf &
Härtel, n.d.

1963 *Pollak, Egmont. "Brahms Klavierkonzert B-dur, op. 83"
Breslauer Zeitung (2.2.1912).

1964 *Söhle, Karl. Johannes Brahms. Klavierkonzert (No. 2) in
B-dur. Op. 83. (Der Musikführer. no. 139) Frankfurt
a/M.: Verlag von H. Bechhold, [1898]. 18 pp.
  *also: Berlin: Schlesinger, n.d.
  *also: Berlin: Seeman Nachf[olger]., n.d.
  (a) *reprint: in 1346.

1965 Stegemann, Michael. "Vor 100 Jahren: "Ein ganz ein kleines
Klavierkonzert ..." Zur Interpretation von Brahms' Opus
83" NZ-Neue Zeitschrift für Musik 143/6/7 (6./7.1982) pp.
11-15. ill., mus., notes. Compares approaches to this
work by six performers and how they deal with tempi,
virtuosic and symphony/concerto elements.

1966 *Tretbar, C[harles]. F. Brahms Op. 83, Concerto for Pianoforte
and Orchestra. (Analytical Reviews of Classical and Modern
Compositions) New York: [Author, 188-?].

1967 Williams, Richard. "A "Tiny, Tiny" Brahms Concerto" House
Beautiful 96/6 (6.1954) pp. 71, 75-77. ill. Presents historical background, a descriptive analysis and comments
on the work's stylistic features.

1968 *Wortham, H. E. Morning Post (London) or The Outlook.
  (a) #reprint: Wortham. "A Note on Brahms" in Wortham.
  A Musical Odyssey. London: Methuen & Co.,
  1924. pp. 40-43. Reflects on this work and its
  musical message.

See also 256, 608, 619, 1351, 1358, 1359, 1372C, 1381, 1384, 1387.d.,
1391-93, 1398-1400, 1404, 1405, 1409, 1410, 1420, 1775, 1778, 1782,
1884, 1791, 1793-95, 1807, 1831, 1844, 1845, 1848, 2547, 2553, 2571.

--Op. 90

1969 *Birmingham Post (9.11.1905). Report on lecture described
in 1975.

1970 *Carnet musical (1954).
  (e) report: "Birthday Symphony" Américas 6/11 (11.1954)
  p. 38. Anecdote on work's conception.

344 / IV. Works

1971   Blom, Eric. "Brahms: Symphony No. 3, F major (Op. 90)"
        Music Teacher 12/3 (M.S. series 26/6) (3.1933) pp. 131-32,
        153. ill., mus., notes. Descriptive analysis.

1972   Brahms, Johannes. Symphony Number Three [[in F major]]
        Opus 90. For Piano Two Hands. (Analytic Symphony
        Series. Percy Goetschius, ed. and annotator. no. 33)
        Philadelphia: Oliver Ditson Company, 1937. [[viii, ii]],
        40 pp. Includes biographical and critical notes.

1973   *Dömpke, Gustav. "Die III. Symphonie" Wiener allgemeine
        Zeitung (5.12.1883).

1974   Dukas, Paul. "Le Vaisseau-Fantôme. La Troisième symphonie
        de J. Brahms" La Revue hebdomadäire 2/10 (3.1893) pp.
        299-308. Brahms: pp. 307-08. Personal impressions of
        Op. 90.
        (a) i) reprint: Dukas. in 1918.a. pp. 95-102.
                Brahms: pp. 102-03.
            ii) reprint: Dukas. in 1919.a.ii.
                Brahms: p. 132.

1975   Elgar, Edward. "Brahms's Symphony No. 3 (November 8,
        1905)" in Elgar. A Future for English Music and Other
        Lectures. Percy Young, ed. Foreword by Anthony Lewis.
        London: Dennis Dobson, 1968. pp. 96-110. ill., mus.,
        ind. Background and descriptive analyses of Op. 90--
        rough notes with editorial comment for lecture given by
        Elgar, 8.11.1905, at the University of Birmingham. In-
        cludes follow-up materials.
        (d) *see: 1969.

1976   *Glinka, [M. J.] "Dopo la "Terza" di Brahms" L'Osservatore
        romano no. 5 (1952) p. 3.

1977   *Kretzschmar, Hermann. Brahms: Symphonie Nr. 3 (F-dur).
        (Kleiner Konzertführer no. 583) Leipzig: Breitkopf &
        Härtel, 1900. 26 pp.
        (d) *see: 1353A.

1978   #Lert, Richard Johannes. "Brahms Symphony No. 3 in F major
        Opus 90. A Measure-by-Measure Interpretation" Phillip
        Spurgeon, ed. Symphony News 23/5 (11.1972) pp. 9-13.
        mus. A conductor's remarks on this work and its interpre-
        tation.
        (d) #comment: Weintraub, Eugene. Symphony News 24/1
                (1.-2.1973) pp. 20-21.

1979   #Lewinski, Wolf-Eberhard von. "Klangfarben bei Johannes
        Brahms. Betrachtungen zu seiner 3. Symphonie" in Lewin-
        ski. Musik wieder gefragt. Gedanken und Gespräche zum

Musikleben von Heute. Hamburg: Claasen Verlag, 1967.
pp. 158-66. Discusses Brahms's use of motivic devices,
rhythm and timbre in Op. 90.

1980   *Mason, Daniel Gregory. "Short Studies of Great Masterpieces
III. Symphony No. 3 in F major Opus 90, by Johannes
Brahms (1882-1883). First Performance at Vienna, 1883"
New Music Review and Church Music Review 16/181 (12.1916)
pp. 390-94. mus., notes. [analysis]
(a) *reprint: in 1955.a.
(d) Mason. "Brahms's Third Symphony" Musical Quarterly
17/3 (7.1931) pp. 374-79. mus., notes. Presents
historical background and descriptive analysis.

1981   *Riemann, Hugo. Johannes Brahms. 3. Symphonie (F-dur),
Op. 90. (Der Musikführer. no. 101) Frankfurt a/M.:
Verlag von H. Bechhold, [1898]. 21 pp.
(a) i) reprint: in 1812.
ii) *reprint: in 1346.

1982   *Salmenhaara, Erkki. "Taistelun turhuus ja tarkoituksettomuus.
Brahmsin sinfoniat III" Musiikki 28/3 (1975).
(d) see: 1827.

1983   #Schaefer, Hans-Jürgen. "Kurt Sanderling dirigiert. Bemerkungen zur Interpretation der III. Sinfonie von Johannes
Brahms" Musik und Gesellschaft 17/[4] (4.1967) pp. 253-57.
mus. Comments on interpreting this work.

1984   *Schütz, Max. "Die dritte Symphonie von Johannes Brahms"
Pester Lloyd(Budapest) (13.4.1884).

1985   *Tretbar, C[harles]. F. Johannes Brahms Op. 90, Symphony
in F no. 3. (Analytical Reviews of Classical and Modern
Compositions) New York: [Author, 1884?].

1986   *Weidemann, Alfred. "Brahms' dritte Symphonie in F-dur"
Skizzen 10/5 (1936) pp. 13-16.

See also 39C.c.iv., 251, 259, 260, 270, 301, 579.d., 660, 680, 756,
1353A, 1356, 1359, 1372A, 1379, 1401, 1586, 1776, 1780, 1781, 1783,
1785-88, 1790, 1792, 1794-1803, 1805-07, 1810, 1813, 1814, 1817,
1820, 1821, 1823, 1825, 1830-32, 1834, 1835, 1837, 1838, 1840, 1842,
1843, 1846, 1847, 1853, 1855, 1943, 2361, 2372, 2391, 2427, 2469.5,
2470.a.b., 2509, 2512, 2606, 2609, 2899, 3048.c.

--Op. 98

1987   Bairstow, Edward. "Brahms's Fourth Symphony, op. 98"
Musical Times 78/1129 (3.1937) pp. 220-24. mus., notes.

Studies what can be learned from this work with respect
To Brahms's compositional methods.

1988   Balmer, Luc. "Interpretation und Texttreue" Schweizerische
        Musikzeitung. Revue musicale suisse 119/6 (1.11.1979)
        pp. 326-28. Brahms: pp. 327-28. mus. Notes on inter-
        pretation.

1989   Bernstein, Leonard. "Brahms: Symphony No. 4 in E minor,
        Opus 98 (Movement I)" in Bernstein. The Infinite Variety
        of Music. New York: Simon and Schuster, 1966. pp.
        229-62. ill. [p. 228], mus. Discusses the use of motifs
        in Brahms's composing.

1990   *Boereboom, Marcel. Symfonie nr. 4 in E klein op. 98 van
        Johannes Brahms. (Leren luisteren, nr. 1) Antwerpen:
        Nederlandsche Boekhandel, 1962. 28, [2] pp. mus.

1991   Brahms, Johannes. Symphony Number Four [[in E minor]]
        Opus 98. For Piano Two Hands. (Analytic Symphony
        Series. Percy Goetschius, ed. and annotator. no. 36)
        Philadelphia: Oliver Ditson Company 1932. [[viii]], 48
        pp. ill., notes. Analysis of form and structural details;
        includes biographical information.

1992   Brahms, Johannes. 4. Symphonie in E-moll Op. 98. Faksimile
        des autographen Manuskripts aus dem Besitz der Allgemeinen
        Musikgesellschaft Zürich. Einleitung von Günter Birkner.
        Adliswil-Zürich: Edition Eulenburg GmbH, 1974. [5,
        102, 36 pp.] Added title page in English. English and
        German text, p. 4 of first paging, gives manuscript pro-
        venance and description.

1993   "Brahms: Symphony in E minor, No. 4; Op. 98" British
        Musician nos. 23, 24, 26, 28 (3/8,9;4/1,3) (12.1927;1.,
        3.,5.;1928) pp. 240-48, 277-82; 25-27, 80. mus. Background,
        together with descriptive analysis of thematic and rhythmic
        materials in each movement; includes impressions of this
        work from the von Herzogenbergs and Clara Schumann.

1994   Cantrell, Byron. "Three B's--Three Chaconnes" Current
        Musicology no. 12 (1971) pp. 63-74. Brahms: pp. 69-74.
        mus., notes. Compares the 4th movement of Op. 98 with
        Bach's BWV 1004, last movement, and Beethoven's WoO 80;
        includes summation.

1995   *Dömpke, Gustav. "Die e-moll Symphonie" Wiener allgemeine
        Zeitung (21.1.1886).

1996   Huschke, Konrad. "Vom Wesen der letzten Brahms-Sinfonie"
        Neue Musikzeitung 47/23 (1.9.1926) pp. 493-96. Discusses

Kalbeck's attempt to attach programmatic elements to Op. 98.

(a) reprint: Huschke. "Vom Wesen der letzten Brahms-Symphonie" Allgemeine Musikzeitung 64/13/14 (26.3.1937) pp. 185-87.

1997 Hutchinson, William R. "Aesthetic and Musical Theory: An Aspect of Their Juncture" Journal of Aesthetics and Art Criticism 24/3 (Spring 1966) pp. 393-400. notes. Op. 98, fourth movement is the example in this discussion, showing that musical analysis can add to the awareness of the significance of aesthetic form.

1998 *Kalbeck, Max. "Die e-moll Symphonie" Die Presse (Wien) (21.1.1886).

1999 Klein, Rudolf. "Die Doppelgerüsttechnik in der Passacaglia der IV. Symphonie von Brahms" Österreichische Musikzeitschrift 27/12 (12.1972) pp. 641-48. fig., notes. Analytical study.

2000 *Kretzschmar, Hermann. Brahms: Symphonie Nr. 4 (e-moll). (Kleiner Konzertführer no. 585) Leipzig: Breitkopf & Härtel, 1900. 24 pp.
(d) *see: 1353A.

2001 *McAree, P. "Brahms's Symphony No. 4: An Analysis" M.Mus. thesis, University of London (Royal Holloway College), 1975.

2002 *Riemann, Hugo. Johannes Brahms. IV. Symphonie in E-moll, op. 98. (Der Musikführer. no. 120) Frankfurt a/M.: Verlag von H. Bechhold, 1898. 19 pp. ill.
*also: Leipzig: Hermann Seemann Nachfolger, n.d.
(a) i) reprint: in 1812.
ii) *reprint: in 1346.

2003 *Salmenhaara, Erkki. "Suuri syksyinen kuva. Brahmsin sinfoniat IV" Musiikki 28/4 (1975).
(d) see: 1827.

2004 Siegmund-Schultze, Walther. "Brahms' vierte Sinfonie" in Festschrift Max Schneider zum achtzigsten Geburtstage. Walther Vetter, ed. Leipzig: Deutscher Verlag für Musik, 1955. pp. 241-54. mus., notes. Discusses Op. 98 in relation to other works of Brahms; includes analysis.

2005 *Speidel, Ludwig. "Brahms' IV. Symphonie e-moll" [Wiener] Fremdenblatt (19.1.1886).

2006 "The Taste for Brahms. The Fourth Symphony" The Times

(London) Royal Edition no. 44,398 (9.10.1926) p. 10.
Comments on the appearance of this work on a concert
programme, as a reflection of the advancement of public
appreciation of Brahms's music.
(a) reprint: "The Taste ... Symphony" British Musician
no. 29 (4/4) (6.1928) pp. 100-01.

2007 #Vetter, Walther. "Der erste Satz von Brahms' e-moll Symphonie. Ein Beitrag zur Erkenntnis moderner Symphonik"
Die Musik (Berlin) 13/13-15 (Bd. 51) (4.-5.1914) pp. 3-15,
83-92, 131-45. mus., notes. Analytical study.

2008 Wallner, Bo. "Brahms fjärde symfoni" Musikrevy 8/2 (1953)
pp. 51-52. Descriptive analysis.

2009 Widmann, Hans-Joachim. "Brahms' vierte Sinfonie" Brahms-
Studien Bd. 4 (1981) pp. 45-54. mus., notes. Historical
background and descriptive analysis.

2010 *Wolf, Hugo. "Brahms' e-moll Symphonie" Münchener Salonblatt
no. 16 (1902).

See also 251, 259, 261, 270, 660, 873, 971, 1285, 1353A, 1359, 1362,
1372A, 1388, 1401, 1586, 1776, 1780, 1781, 1783, 1785-90, 1792, 1794-
1803, 1806, 1807, 1810, 1813, 1814, 1817, 1821, 1822, 1825, 1830-32,
1834, 1835, 1837, 1838, 1840, 1842, 1843, 1846, 1847, 1850, 1853,
1855, 1943, 2010, 2309.d.ii., 2356, 2361, 2368, 2382, 2419, 2427, 2430,
2469.5, 2470.a.b., 2509, 2512, 2514, 2522, 2598, 2606, 2609, 2899,
2944.c.ii.

--Op. 102

2011 *Riemann, Hugo. Hamburgische Musikzeitung 2/1,2,4 (1888).
Review.

2012 *Witte, G[eorg]. H[endrik]. Johannes Brahms. Konzert für
Violine und Violoncell mit Orchester. Op. 102. (Der
Musikführer. no. 136) Frankfurt a/M.: Verlag von H.
Bechhold, [1898]. 14 pp.
*also: Berlin: Schlesinger, n.d.
*also: Berlin: Seemann Nachf[olger]., n.d.
(a) *reprint: in 1346.

See also 2, 262, 1359, 1372C, 1378, 1384, 1400, 1405, 1408, 1775,
1779, 1782, 1791, 1793-95, 1807, 1829, 1831, 1845, 2419, 2899.

b. Cadenzas Composed by Brahms for Other Composers'
Concertos--General

See 1405.

b. Cadenzas Composed by Brahms for Other Composers'
   Concertos--Specific

--Beethoven, Ludwig van

2013   Davis, Richard. "Moscheles Brahms" Musical Times 118/1618
       (12.1977) p. 1006. Hofmann nr. 181, McCorkle Anhang IV,
       nr. 7--discusses the misattribution of this cadenza by
       Moscheles, to Brahms (cadenza is for Beethoven's Op. 37,
       1st movement).
          (d) Bozarth, George S[evers]., [Jr.]. "A Brahms
               Cadenza by Moscheles" Musical Times 121/1643
               (1.1980) p. 14. Relates history of misattribution.

2014   Haase, Rudolf. "Brahms zitiert B-A-C-H" Musica (Kassel)
       17/4 (7.-8.1963) pp. 180-81. mus. Hofmann nr. 135;
       McCorkle WoO posthum 12--examines the altering of the
       1st theme in cadenza (cadenza is for Beethoven's Op. 58,
       1st movement) to read BACH. Speculates on the motive
       behind this action; includes comments on Brahms's links
       to Bach's work.

See also 1405.

--Mozart, Wolfgang Amadeus

2015   *Golovatchoff, Dika. "A Study of Cadenzas to Mozart's Piano
       Concertos K. 466 and K. 491" D.M.A. diss., Piano
       Performance, Indiana University, 1974. 88 pp. mus., notes.
       Analysis and evaluation of Brahms's cadenza for K. 491
       [Hofmann nr. 184; McCorkle WoO posthum 15]. [from
       S202]

See also 1325, 1405.

c. Brahms's Editing and Arranging of Other Composers'
   Orchestral Music

See 793.

B. VOCAL MUSIC--GENERAL

See also "Texts and Text Setting" in V.B.

2016   Averkamp, Ant[on]. "Johannes Brahms en zijn koorwerken"
       Caecilia (Utrecht) 79/11 (10.4.1922) pp. 162-66. notes.

Surveys works for solo and ensemble performance choir.
(d) Averkamp, Anton. "Johannes Brahms als componist
van koorwerken" Symphonia 16/5 (5.1933) pp. 93-95.
Omits notes, adds ill.

2017 #Bobzin, Robert. "Music for Women's Voices by Johannes
Brahms" Musart 24/1 9.-10.1971) pp. 17, 27-29. notes.
A survey of the music for solo and ensemble performance
choir, from the point of view of a conductor wishing to
expand his repertoire.

2018 Colles, H[enry]. C[ope]. "Brahms's Shorter Choral Works"
Musical Times 74/1083 (5.1933) pp. 410-12. A survey of
the literature for solo and ensemble performance choir with
historical background and descriptive analysis.

2019 *Donaldson, Douglas. "Brahms and The Life to Come. A
Brief Consideration of the "Song of Destiny", "German
Requiem", the "Song of the Fates" and the "Serious Songs""
Musical Standard 1/6-8 (1913) pp. 115-16, 140-50.

2020 #e. [Eusebius Mandyczewski] "Neue Werke von Brahms"
Deutsche Kunst- und Musikzeitung (Wien) 18/35 (10.12.
1891) pp. 311-12. Reviews Opp. 112 and 113.

2021 Ed.H. [Eduard Hanslick] "Neue Gesänge von Brahms. (Drei
Liederhefte.-Chöre.-Zigeunerlieder)" Neue freie Presse
(Wien) no. 8728 (11.12.1888). Morgenblatt pp. 1-2 [across
page bottoms]. notes. Reviews Opp. 103-07.
(a) *reprint: Hanslick, Eduard. "2. Neue Gesänge von
Brahms. (Drei Liederhefte.-Chöre.-Zigeunerlieder.)
(1888.)" in 2948.
(a) reprint: in 2948.a. pp. 142-49.

2022 Evans, Edwin. Historical, Descriptive and Analytical Account
of the Entire Works of Johannes Brahms. Treated in The
Order of Their Opus Number, preceded by a Didactic
Section and Followed by Copious Tables of Reference.
Specially designed for the use of Concert-goers, Pianists,
Singers and Students. Vol. I--The Vocal Works... London:
Wm. Reeves, 1912. xviii, [1], 599 pp. fig., ind. Includes
an overview of Brahms's life and an evaluation of the composer, together with comments on Brahms as a composer of
vocal works.
also known as: Handbook to the Vocal Works of Brahms.
(Evans. Historical, Descriptive and Analytical Account of
the Entire Works of Johannes Brahms. Vol. I)
(a) i) *reprint (of Historical title): see 1338.
ii) *reprint (of Handbook title): (Original series)
(Burt Franklin Research and Source Works Series,
1557) New York: B[urt]. Franklin, [1970].

(e) i) report: [Henry T. Finck] Nation (New York)
94/2441 (11.4.1912) p. 373.
ii) report: "Neue Brahms-Literatur" Die Musik (Berlin)
12/1 (Bd. 45) (10.1912) pp. 56-60. Report by
R[ichard]. Hohenemser, who also does report on
48.b.; includes reports on 23.b. by W[ilhelm].
Altmann, and 667 by R. Wanderer.
iii) report: Spanuth, August. "Englische Brahms-
Handbuch" Signale für die musikalische Welt 70/22
(29.5.1912) pp. 726-29.

2023 *Greene, Charles Robert. "Seven of the Small Sacred Choral
Works, including Opus 121, of Brahms" S.M.M. diss., Union
Theological Seminary (New York), 1953. ii, [3], 76 pp.
notes. Descriptive analysis of Opp. 27, 29, 30, 37, 74,
110, 121. [from Library, Union Theological Seminary]

2024 Hernried, Robert. "Brahms und das Christentum" Musica
(Kassel) 3/1 (1.1949) pp. 16-21. facsim., notes. Discusses
Brahms's thoughts towards religion with an overview of
his vocal works that use a religious text.

2025 Kirsch, Winfried. "Religiöse und liturgische Aspeckte bei
Brahms und Bruckner" in Religiöse Musik in nicht-liturgischen
Werken von Beethoven bis Reger. Günther Massenkeil,
Klaus Wolfgang Niemöller, Walter Wiora, eds. (Studien zur
Musikgeschichte des 19. Jahrhunderts. Bd. 51) Regensburg:
Gustav Bosse Verlag, 1978. pp. 143-55. Brahms: pp.
143-53. ind., notes. Surveys works with religious texts.

2026 *Krieger, E. "Brahms und die Kirchenmusik" Die Kirchenmusik
(Berlin) 14 (1933) pp. 81, 97-99.

2027 #Kross, Siegfried. "Brahms und der Kanon" in Festschrift
Joseph Schmidt-Görg zum 60. Geburtstag. Dagmar Weise,
ed. Bonn: Beethovenhaus, 1957. pp. 175-87. mus., fig.
Traces Brahms's use of canons throughout his vocal works,
examines their structure, and describes the intervals he
used.

2028 Mesnard, Léonce. "Brahms et son oeuvre" La Renaissance
musicale 2/34,35 (20.,27.;8.;1882) pp. 265-67, 273-75.
notes. Surveys Brahms's vocal works, both choral (focuses
on Op. 45) and solo, with general analysis.
(d) reworked: see 2403.

2029 S. B. [Selmar Bagge] "Neue Gesangscompositionen von Johannes
Brahms" Allgemeine musikalische Zeitung Neue Folge 2/34
(24.8.1864) cols. 573-77. mus. Reviews Opp. 29-31.

2030 Spitta, Friedrich. "Brahms und Herzogenberg in ihrem

Verhältnis zur Kirchenmusik" Monatsschrift für Gottesdienst und kirchliche Kunst 12/2 (2.1907) pp. 37-45. notes. Compares their views on religion, ties to the music of Bach, and opinions on church music.

2031 #Wiesner, Kurt. "Tod und Auferstehung in der Musik von Johannes Brahms. Zum 60. Todestag des Meisters am 3. April 1957" Glaube und Wissen 3/4 (4.1957) pp. 70-71. Discusses Brahms and music for the church: surveys texts he used in his works.

2032 Wilcox, Lee. "Music for May" House Beautiful 104/5 (5.1962) p. 43. discog. Discusses works by Brahms that evoke the passing of Winter to Spring: Opp. 19, 52, 53.

See also 267, 320.d.iii., 420, 781, 944, 2442, 2523, 2560, 2570, 2579, 2633.5, 2934, 2940.

See also "Texts and Text Setting" in V.B.

1. Works for Solo Voices--General

Includes materials that discuss works for solo ensembles.

2033 Auman, Elizabeth H. and George S[evers]. Bozarth [Jr.]. "New Brahms Acquisitions Led By Gift from Herman Lowin" Impromptu 1/1 (Fall 1982) pp. [1-2]. facsim. Describes acquisition by Library of Congress of manuscript for Op. 3; includes comment on other manuscript purchases: items from Opp. 46, 48, 61, McCorkle Anhang Va, nr. 1, and letters to Simrock and Keller.

2034 Bell, A[rnold]. Craig. The Lieder of Brahms. Darley: Grian-Aig Press, 1979. vi, 137, vii-xx pp. ill., mus., ind., notes. Surveys this genre, integrating the works into the different periods of Brahms's life. Draws attention to many lesser known songs.

2035 *Berry, Corre Ivey Williams. "A Study of the Vocal Chamber Duet Through the Nineteenth Century" Ph.D. diss., North Texas State University, 1974. 363 pp. Examines changing stylistic trends and compositional practices in vocal duet writing from the 16th-19th centuries. [from S202]
    (d) Berry, Corre. "Chamber Duets by Schumann, Cornelius and Brahms" NATS Bulletin 36/5 (5./6.1980) pp. 16-19. Brahms: pp. 18-19. notes. Introduction to Opp. 20, 28, 61, 66, 75; discusses the relation of the texts to their setting, and accompaniments to voice parts.

2036 Bertelin, Alb. "Les "Lieder" de Johannès Brahms" Le Courrier musical 14/19 (1.10.1911) pp. 586-91. notes. A survey with descriptive comments; includes comments on Brahms's historical position, Brahms and Schubert, and Brahms and France.

2037 Bie, Oskar. "Brahms" in Bie. Das deutsche Lied. Drittes Buch. Berlin: S. Fischer Verlag, 1926, pp. 135-88. Presents descriptive analysis of Opp. 3-121 and Deutsche Volkslieder (1894) [Hofmann nr. 133; McCorkle WoO 33], interspersed with comments on practice and solo song.

2038 *Boros, R[ezső]. "Brahms-Petofi megzenésítöje" Muzsika (Budapest) 2 (1959).
(b) German translation: Boros. "Petőfi--in der Vertonung von Brahms" Studia musicologica academiae scientiarum hungaricae 8 (1966) pp. 391-99. mus., notes. Examines settings of Petőfi texts, in German translation by G. Daumer. Focuses on songs from Opp. 46, 52, 92, 96.

2039 *Boyd, Jack Arthur. "Secular Music for the Solo Vocal Ensemble in the Nineteenth Century" Ph.D. diss., Choral Literature, University of Iowa, 1971. 315 pp. Presents a history of the genre, examines representative works and provides an annotated list for this genre. Brahms's works discussed are Opp. 52, 65, 103. [from S202]

2040 Bozarth, George Severs, Jr. "The 'Lieder' of Johannes Brahms--1868-1871: Studies in Chronology and Compositional Process" Ph.D. diss., Musicology, Princeton University, 1978. [16], vi, 245 pp. ill., facsim., mus., notes. Discusses primary poetic and musical manuscript sources for songs published in this time period; focusses on Opp. 57, 58, but also considers songs from other opera, in particular Opp. 43, 46-49, 33.

2041 "Brahms in English. Love-Song Waltzes" The Times (London) Late London Edition no. 49,272 (26.6.1942) p. 6. Reviews new text translation by A. H. Fox-Strangways [Fox-Strangeways] for Opp. 52, 65; includes background of both works.

2042 #Brahms, Johannes. Drei Lieder. "Mainacht", "Sapphische Ode", "Nachtwandler". Nach den Handschriften herausgegeben in Faksimile-Reproduktion vom Besitzer Max Kalbeck. (Musikalische Seltenheiten. Wiener Liebhaberdrucke. Band III) Wien und New York: Universal-Edition A.-G., 1921. x, 9 pp. facsim., notes. Includes: Kalbeck, Max. "Brahms als Lyriker": pp. iii-x. Discusses Brahms as a setter of text, his text sources, together with lyricism in

his instrumental works.
(b) English translation: Brahms. Three Songs. Max
Kalbeck, ed. (Viennese Collection of Musical Rari-
ties. Book Lovers Edition. vol. 3) Vienna and
New York: Universal-Edition A.G., 1921. Includes:
Kalbeck, Max. "Brahms as a Lyrical Composer":
pp. i-x.

2043 *Bunke, Heinrich. "Die Barform im romantischen Kunstlied bei
Franz Schubert, Robert Schumann, Johannes Brahms, Hugo
Wolf und Felix Mendelssohn-Bartholdy" Phil.F. diss., Uni-
versität Bonn, 1955. 136 pp. mus.

2044 Burkhardt, Hans. "Johannes Brahms und das deutsche Volkslied. Ein Beitrag zum Deutschunterricht" Zeitschrift für
deutsche Bildung 9/7/8 (7./8.1933) pp. 364-75. mus.,
notes. Discusses the teaching of folksongs in the schools.

2045 *Citron, Marcia Judith. "Rhythmic-metric Conflicts in the
Brahms Duos" M.A. thesis, Musicology, University of North
Carolina, Chapel Hill, 1968. 120 pp. mus., notes. An
examination with respect to structural and motivic function.
[from S202]

2046 #Conze, Johannes. "Formenstrenge im Brahms-Liede" Signale
für die musikalische Welt 94/44 (28.10.1936) pp. 633-34.
Discusses Brahms as contrapuntalist with examples from the
songs.

2047 [Daniel Gregory Mason] "Critical Summary" in [Mason] "The
Art of Brahms" Masters in Music 5/part 30 (6.1905) pp.
7-9 (Whole pp. 247-49). A general study of Brahms's songs
with respect to style and compositional processes.

2048 *Cursch-Bühren, Franz Theodor. "Zu Johannes Brahms' 70.
Geburtstag. Brahms als Lyriker" Die Sängerhalle 43/19
(1903).

2049 *De Villiers, C.G.S. "Meesters van die kunslied. 3. Johannes
Brahms" Huisgenoot 27/1172 (8.9.1944) pp. 9+. ill.

2050 *Druskin, Mihail. "Vokal'naia lirika Bramsa. K. 125-letiju so
dnja rozhdeniia" Sovetskaia muzyka [22]/5 (5.1958) pp.
56-64. ill., mus., notes.

2051 Finck, Henry T. "Brahms" in Finck. Songs and Song Writers.
(The Music Lover's Library) New York: Charles Scribner's
Sons, 1900. pp. 154-61. notes. A negative evaluation of
Brahms's vocal style.
    issue: 1900.
    *2nd Edition: 1902.

```
*3rd Edition:  1909.
*4th Edition:  1911.
*5th Edition:  1912.
issues:  1914, 1923, 1928.
```

2052 Friedländer, Max. Brahms's Lieder. Einführung in seine
      Gesänge für eine und zwei Stimmen. Berlin und Leipzig:
      N. Simrock G.m.b.H., 1922. xi, 208 pp. mus., ind.,
      notes. Discusses song text origin, historical background,
      and publication information; includes some textual comparison,
      also descriptive analysis in terms of text setting and emotion-
      al tone.
      (b) English translation by C. Leonard Leese: Friedlaender.
      Brahms's Lieder. An Introduction to the Songs for
      One and Two Voices. London: Humphrey Milford,
      Oxford University Press, 1928. xiii, [1], 263 pp.
      (a) *reprint: New York: AMS Press, 1976.

2053 *Giebeler, Konrad. "Die Lieder von Johannes Brahms; ein
      Beitrag zur Musikgeschichte des 19. Jahrhunderts" Phil.F.
      diss., Universität Münster, 1959. 152 pp. mus., notes.
      (a) *reprint: Die Lieder ... Jahrhunderts. Münster/
      Westfalen: M. Kramer, 1959.

2054 Gottfried Keller vertont von Johannes Brahms, Hans Pfitzner,
      Hugo Wolf. Albrecht Dümling, ed. (Lied und Lyrik 3)
      München: Kindler Verlag GmbH, 1981. 143 pp. ill.,
      mus. (pp. 59-63), notes, discog.
      "Johannes Brahms oder: die Bändigung der Leidenschaften":
      pp. 105-15. Relates compositional background for Opp.
      69 no. 8, and 86 no. 1.
      "Die Lieder im Vergleich": pp. 130-37. Brahms: pp.
      130-35. Compares settings: Brahms's Op. 69 no. 8
      with Wolf's Alte Weisen no. 2, and Pfitzner's Op. 33 no. 5;
      and Brahms's Op. 86 no. 1 with Wolf's Alte Weisen no. 3,
      and Pfitzner's Op. 33 no. 3.

2055 #Grimm, Friedrich Karl. "Johannes Brahms als Liedkomponist"
      Bühnen-Genossenschaft 10/2 (1958) pp. 49-50. Describes
      Brahms's style, as well as his vocal works as they fit into
      his musical canon.

2056 H. D. [Hermann Deiters] Allgemeine musikalische Zeitung
      Neue Folge 3/35 (30.8.1865) cols. 572-80. mus., notes.
      Reviews Opp. 32, 33.

2057 H. D. [Hermann Deiters] "Neue Lieder von Johannes Brahms"
      Allgemeine musikalische Zeitung 10/39 (29.9.1875) cols. 613-
      19. mus. reviews Opp. 43, 57-59.

2058 *Hammermann, Walter. "Johannes Brahms als Liedkomponist.

Eine theoretischästhetische Stiluntersuchung" Phil.F. diss.,
Universität Leipzig, 1912. 69 pp.
(a) reprint: Johannes ... Stiluntersuchung. Leipzig:
Spamersche Buchdruckerei, 1912. [4], 69, [1]
pp. mus. Discusses Brahms's position as a composer
of song, with extensive analysis of his works using
Riemann's methods.

2059   Harrison, Max. The Lieder of Brahms. London: Cassell,
1972. [3], 152 pp. mus., ind., notes. Analysis and
historical background; includes comments on Brahms's historical position, as a composer of song, performance practice,
and comparisons with other composers, and other of Brahms's
own works.
*also: New York: Praeger Publishers, 1972.

2060   *Helms, Siegmund. "Die Melodiebildung in den Liedern von
Johannes Brahms und ihr Verhältnis zu Volksliedern und
volkstümlich Weisen" Phil. F. diss., Freie Universität
Berlin, 1967. 270 pp.
(a) #reprint: Die Melodiebildung ... Weisen. [Berlin:]
n.p., 1968. mus., fig., notes. Analytical study;
includes comment on the influence of non-Germanic
songs on the Lied.
(d) #Helms. "Johannes Brahms und das deutsche Kirchen-
lied" Der Kirchenmusiker 2 (3./4.1970) pp. 39-48.
mus., notes. Traces the influence of hymns on
Brahms's vocal compositions; includes comments on
his sources.

2061   Hering, Hans. "Der Klavierpart im Lied des 19. Jahrhunderts"
Melos/NZ für Musik 4/2 (3.1978) pp. 95-101. Brahms:
pp. 98-99. Discusses the relationship between the vocal
line and the piano part, with examples from the songs.

2062   Horton, John. "Three Vignettes" Music Teacher 61/5 (5.1982)
pp. 12-13. "Two Songs in One": p. 12. Background and
analysis of Opp. 49 no. 4 and 91 no. 2.

2063   Huneker, James [Gibbons]. "Johannes Brahms as a Song
Composer" Musician (Boston) 20/10.(10.1915) p. 666. Des-
criptive analysis taken from author's introduction to
Brahms. Forty Songs. (Boston: O. Ditson Company;
New York: C. H. Ditson & Co., [1903]).

2064   *Jacobsen, Christiane. "Das Verhältnis von Sprache und Musik
in ausgewählten Liedern von Johannes Brahms, dargestellt
an Parallelvertonungen" Fachbereich Kulturgeschichte und
Kulturkunde diss., Universität Hamburg, 1976.
(a) reprint: Das Verhältnis ... Parallelvertonungen.
(Hamburger Beiträge zur Musikwissenschaft 16)
Hamburg: Verlag der Musikalienhandlung Karl

Dieter Wagner, 1975. 2 vols. mus., fig., notes.
Describes Brahms's position on the topic with interpretative analysis of poems set by Brahms and also
by other composers. Refers to songs from his Op.
33 and Weber's J.156; his Opp. 43, 46-48, 71 and
Schubert's D.196, 194, 120, 673, 429; his Opp.
47, 71 and Mendelssohn's Op. 86, no. 8; his Op.
3 and Mondnacht and from Schumann's Op. 39;
his Opp. 33, 85, 96 and from Franz's Opp. 1, 11,
18; and his Opp. 96, 6, 59, 69, 86, 19 and from
Wolf's WoO 54, Spanisches Liederbuch, Gedichte
von Eduard Mörike and Alte Weisen.

2065   Kn. Neue Zeitschrift für Musik Bd. 65/52 (24.12.1869) pp.
        451-52. mus. Reviews Opp. 46-49.

2066   Kinsey, Barbara. "Mörike Poems Set by Brahms, Schumann
        and Wolf" Music Review 29/4 (11.1968) pp. 257-67. Brahms:
        pp. 258-63. mus. Analyses Opp. 19 no. 5 and 59 no.
        5 in terms of the rhythmic component of the text setting.

2067   Koelink, J. P. A. "De Heine-Liedern van Joh. Brahms" Mens
        en melodie 9/9 (9.1954) pp. 292-95. ill., notes. Describes
        the background and text settings of songs from Opp. 71,
        85, 96 and "Du bist wie eine Blume".

2068   #Krause, Emil. "Johannes Brahms als Vokal-Komponist" Die
        Sängerhalle 31/1,2 (1.,8.;1891) pp. 3-4, 18+. ill., facsim.,
        notes. Discusses Brahms and the solo song; presents an
        overview of his songs.

2069   Kretzschmar, Hermann. "Neue Werke von J[ohannes]. Brahms.
        II.-III." Musikalisches Wochenblatt 5/2-4 (9.-23.;1.;1874)
        pp. 19-21, 31-32, 43-45. mus., notes. Reviews Opp. 46-
        49, 57-59.

2070   Kross, Siegfried. "Rhythmik und Sprachbehandlung bei
        Brahms" in Bericht über den Internationalen Musikwissen-
        schaftlichen Kongress Kassel 1962. Georg Reichert, Martin
        Just, eds. Kassel [et al.]: Bärenreiter, 1963. pp. 217-19.
        notes. Describes Brahms's use of speech accentuation in
        his melodic lines.

2071   L.Sp. "Vergessene Lieder "Der Strom, der neben mir ver-
        rauschte ..."" Vossische Zeitung (Berlin) Unterhaltungsblatt
        nr. 125 (7.5.1933) p. [3]. Discusses less well-known songs
        from Opp. 32, 86, 94, 106 in an attempt to create a greater
        awareness of their quality.

2072   Landau, Anneliese. "Johannes Brahms (1833-1897)" in Landau.
        The Lied. The Unfolding of Its Style. Washington, D.C.:
        University Press of America, Inc., 1980. pp. 67-75. mus.,

notes., discog. Compares Schumann and Brahms as Lied composers and discusses Lied forms, with Op. 33 and Deutsche Volkslieder (1894) [Hofmann nr. 133; McCorkle WoO 33] as examples. Highlights these composers' sensitivity to text.

2073 Lehmann, Lotte. Eighteen Song Cycles. Studies in Their Interpretation. Foreword by Neville Cardus. New York, Washington, D.C.: Praeger Publishers, 1972. xiii, 185 pp. ind.
"Magelonelieder": pp. 111-20.
"Vier ernste Gesänge": pp. 121-25. Opp. 33, 121: story Opp. 33, 121: story of the texts and suggestions for performance.

2074 Lehmann, Lotte. "Johannes Brahms 1833-1897" in Lehmann. More Than Singing. The Interpretation of Songs. Frances Holden, translator. New York: Boosey & Hawkes Inc., 1945. pp. 43-65. mus. Presents performance suggestions for songs from Opp. 19, 32, 43, 47, 49, 59, 63, 84, 86, 94, 96, 97, 105, 107.
*2nd issue: 1945.
*3rd issue: 1946.
also: London: Boosey & Hawkes, 1946.
(a) *reprint (of New York 1945 Edition): Westport, Conn.: Greenwood Press, 1975.

2075 *Lund, Kirsten Winkler. "En redegørelse for de karakteristuske stiltraek i Johannes Brahms' folkesangsbearbejdelser ("Deutsche Volkslieder" og senere samlinger) samt en undersøgelse af hvorvidt der kan påvises folkesangspraegede elementer i Brahms' større kunstsange" Specialeafhandlinger til skoleembedsekamen i musik, Aarhus Universitet, 1960.

2076 *MacConnel, Wood. "The Songs of Schumann and Brahms" Musical Standard New series 23/591 (1884). (?)

2077 Masters in Music 5/part 30 (6.1905) [3], 48 pp. (volume pp. [3], 241-88). Issue Title: Brahms. Songs. Contains 234, 640, 2047, 2107; also music for songs from Opp. 3, 32, 49, 63, 71, 84, 94, 105 and the Volks-Kinderlieder [Hofmann nr. 125; McCorkle WoO 31].

2078 *"Ein Meister den deutschen Liedes. Vor 45 Jahren starb Brahms" Deutsche Zeitung in Norwegen (Oslo) (2.4.1942).

2079 *Mies, Paul. Stilmomente und Ausdrucksstilformen im Brahms'-schen Lied. [(Breitkopf & Härtels Musikbücher)] Leipzig: Breitkopf & Härtel, 1923. [5], 147 pp. mus., ind., notes.
(a) reprint: Walluf-Nendeln: Sändig-Reprint, 1975.
Analyses the solo vocal works for formal, harmonic and rhythmic considerations.

2080   Misch, Ludwig. "Kontrapunkt und Imitation im Brahmsschen
       Lied" Die Musikforschung 11/2 (4.-6.1958) pp. 155-60.
       mus., notes. Discusses specific types of this compositional
       method, together with Brahms's technique as seen in the
       songs.

2081   *Moser, Hans Joachim. Das deutsche Lied seit Mozart. 2 Bde.
       Berlin und Zürich: Atlantis Verlag, [1937].
        2. wesentlich umgearbeitete und ergänzte Ausgabe: Mit einem
       Geleitwort von Dietrich Fischer-Dieskau und einem Prosa-
       Prolog von Hermann Hesse. Tutzing: Hans Schneider,
       1968. 440 pp. mus., notes.
       "Johannes Brahms und das Lied": pp. 165-78. Discusses
       the general characteristics of Brahms's songwriting, with
       an overview of the individual works.
       "Daumergesänge von Brahms": pp. 372-83. Descriptive
       analysis of songs in Opp. 32, 46, 47, 57, 95, 96.
       "Brahms: Die schöne Magelone op. 33": pp. 384-93.
       Descriptive analysis.

2082   Newman, Ernest. "Brahms and Wolf as Lyrists" Musical Times
       56/871-72 (1.;9.-10.;1915) pp. 523-24, 585-88. mus.,
       notes. Attempts to show that Wolf was superior to Brahms
       as a song composer.

2083   Orselli, Cesare. "Johannes Brahms a il mito del popolare"
       Chigiana 29-30 (Nuova serie no. 9-10) (1975) pp. 121-24.
       Focuses on Op. 52.

2084   Pena, Joaquim. "Les Cançons de J. Brahms" Revista musical
       catalana 30/360 (12.1933) pp. 512-14. Surveys Brahms's
       song output.

2085   Pisk, Paul A. "Dreams of Death and Life: A Study of Two
       Songs by Johannes Brahms" in Festival Essays for Pauline
       Alderman. A Musicological Tribute. Burton L. Karson, ed.
       Provo, Utah: Brigham Young University Press, 1976.
       pp. 227-34. mus., fig., notes. An analysis of Opp. 96
       no. 1 and 105 no. 2 to demonstrate how a text's emotional
       quality is reflected musically.

2086   *Rieger, Erwin. "Die Tonartencharakteristik im einstimmigen
       Klavierlied von Johannes Brahms" Phil.F. diss., Universität
       Wien, 1946. 58, 141, 104 pp.
       (a) reprint: Rieger. Studien zur Musikwissenschaft Bd.
               22 (1955) pp. 142-216. mus., fig., notes. Groups
               Brahms's songs by key type and examines both the
               relationship between key and text, and the combina-
               tion of keys within a song.

2087   Riemann, Hugo. "Die Taktfreiheiten in Brahms' Liedern" Die

Musik (Berlin) 12/1 (Bd. 45) (10.1912) pp. 10-21. mus.
Formal analysis of Op. 105 no. 2 and Op. 107 no. 3 to show
how Brahms used harmony and rhythm to achieve freedom
from the time signature.
(c) excerpt: Riemann. "Brahms' Taktfreiheit im Lied"
Die Musik (Berlin) 25/8 (5.1933) pp. 595-96.
(a) reprint: in 3186.c. pp. 35-36.
(d) see: 2157.

2088 Roberts, Clifford. "Brahms and the Singer" Music Teacher
12/4 (M.S. Series 26/7) (4.1933) p. 185. ill. Describes
the characteristics of Brahms's writings for solo voice.

2089 Salten, Felix. "Brahms-Lieder. Ein Gedankblatt" Neue freie
Presse (Wien) no. 24,658 (7.5.1933) Morgenblatt pp. 1-3
[across page bottoms]. Discusses how Brahms taught and
performed his new songs; includes comments on Brahms in
Wien, and describes a day in his life.

2090 Sams, Eric. Brahms Songs. (BBC Music Guides) London:
BBC, 1972. 68 pp. mus., notes. Presents historical background and analysis.
*also: Seattle: University of Washington Press, 1972.

2091 Sams, Eric. "Zwei Brahms-Rätsel" Osterreichische Musikzeitschrift 27/2 (2.1972) pp. 83-84. Discusses who is the
author of text in Op. 43 no. 1; why Scarlatti motif is cited
in Op. 72 no. 3; includes comment on Brahms's relations
with Schumann.

2092 #Sannemüller, Gerd. "Die Lieder von Johannes Brahms auf
Gedichte von Klaus Groth" Klaus-Groth-Gesellschaft. Jahresgabe 16 (1972) pp. 23-35. notes. Describes their friendship and Brahms's affinity for Groth; examines Brahms's
settings of Groth poetry in Opp. 59, 63, 97, 105, 106
and Regenlied [Hofmann nr. 136; McCorkle WoO posthum
23].

2093 Schmitz, Eugen. "Liebeslieder-Walzer von Brahms in orchestra-
ler Fassung" Deutsche Musikkultur 5/3 (8./9.1940) pp. 64-
68. notes. Hofmann nr. 141--describes the manuscript
and provides historical background; includes a comparison
with Opp. 52 and 65 with respect to the arrangement
of individual numbers.

2094 *Schollum, Robert. "Anmerkungen zur Geschichte des österreichischen Kunstliedes" in Musik und Dichtung. Anton
Dermota zum 70. Geburtstag (4 Juni 1980). Herbert Ze-
man, ed. Wien: Osterreichische Nationalbibliothek, 1980.
pp. 7-19. Traces the evolution of the art song from Haydn
to Wolff. Focuses on the relationship between text and
music. [from S202]

2095 *Stanford, [Sir] Charles V[illiers]. Brahms. (Masterpieces of
Music) London and Edinburgh: T.C. & E.C. Jack; New
York: F. A. Stokes Co., [1912]. 63 pp. ill., facsim.,
mus. "Brahms and His Music"

2096 #Stronck-Kappel, Anna. "Johannes Brahms in zijne liederen"
Symphonia 16/5 (5.1933) pp. 90-92. Surveys the works;
includes comments on Brahms and folkmusic, and on Brahms
as a song composer.

2097 *Sviridenko. Russkaia musykalnaia gazeta 20/34,35 (1913).
On Brahms's songs. [from S201]

2098 Taubert, Ernst Eduard. "Musik" in "Die Kultur der Gegenwart"
Uber Land und Meer Bd. 106/51 (53/26) (1.10.1911) p. 1317.
ill. Discusses Brahms as a song composer: how he is influenced by Schubert, and the quality of Brahms's music.

2099 Van der Elst, Nancy. "Twee Liedcomponisten: Fauré en
Brahms" Mens en melodie 4/10 (10.1949) pp. 308-10. ill.
Compares the two as composers; includes comments on
romanticism in music.

2100 *Vasina-Grossman, Vera Andreevna. Romanticheskaia pesnia
deviatnadtsatogo veka. Moskva: Muzyka, 1966. 404,
[3] pp. ill., mus.

2101 Walker, Ernest. "Brahms and Heine" Monthly Musical Record
63/745 (3.-4.1933) pp. 51-52. mus., notes. Describes
Brahms's settings of Heine poetry in Opp. 71, 85, 96.
(a) reprint: Walker. in Walker. Free Thought and the
Musician and Other Essays. London [et al.]: Oxford University Press, 1946. pp. 162-66.

2102 Walker, Ernest. "Brahms as a Song-Writer" Musical Times
74/1083 (5.1933) pp. 406-10. mus., notes. Divides total
song output into five groups and discusses characteristics
of each group; includes comments on problems faced by
vocal composers.

2103 _____. "The Songs of Schumann and Brahms: Some Contacts and Contrasts" Music and Letters 3/1 (1.1922) pp.
9-19. mus., notes. Discusses the two composers' approach
to song composition in general; includes comparisons of
songs from Brahms's Opp. 58, 59, 96 with songs from
Schumann's Opp. 24, 39, 125.
(a) reprint: Walker. "The Songs of Schumann and
Brahms, Some Contacts and Contrasts" in 2101.a.
pp. 84-96.

2104 *Warburton, A[nnie]. O. Music Teacher and Piano Student

[4] or earlier (before 1963)].
(a) reprint: see 1375A. Analysis of songs from Opp. 7, 19, 43, 49, 86, 91, 96, 106 and Volks-Kinderlieder [Hofmann nr. 125; McCorkle WoO 31].

2105   #Wintzer, Richard. "Die Lieder von Joh. [Johannes in title of second section] Brahms" Neue Musikzeitung 15/13,14 (1894) pp. 148, 160. An introduction to Brahms's songs, with an examination of his text settings.
(d) #reworked: Wintzer. "Johannes Brahms als Lieder-komponist" Allgemeine Musikzeitung 22/22,23 (31.5. and 7.6.;1895) pp. 289-91, 301-03. Refers to more song examples.

2106   Wohlfarth, Paul. "VII.-Brahms' Gypsy Songs and Their Background. A Note by an Amateur" Journal of the Gypsy Lore Society Third series 31/1-2 (1952) pp. 62-64. notes. Discusses the background and texts for Opp. 103 and 112 nos. 3-6; includes comments on folksong influences in Brahms's music.

2107   [Daniel Gregory Mason] "The Works of Brahms" Masters in Music 5/part 30 (6.1905) pp. 9-16 (volume pp. 249-56). Descriptive analysis and performance practice suggestions for songs from Opp. 3, 32, 49, 63, 71, 84, 94, 105, Volks-Kinderlieder [Hofmann nr. 125; McCorkle WoO 31]; includes list of principal works in each genre.

2108   Wüllner, Ludwig. "Brahms und das Lied" Die Musik (Berlin) 25/8 (5.1933) pp. 582-84. Describes the antecedents of Brahms's song style and compares his work to those of Hugo Wolf.
(a) reprint: in 3186.c. pp. 22-24.

See also 170, 251, 271, 320, 420, 944, 1896, 2022, 2153, 2170, 2395, 2443, 2469, 2566, 2579, 2609, 2611, 2612, 2614-17, 2762.3, 2894, 2934.

See also "Texts and Text Setting" in V.B.

1. Works for Solo Voices--Specific

See also 781, 1348, 2022, 2052, 2067, 2343.

See also "Texts and Text Setting" in V.B.

--Op. 3

2109   Caillet, R. and Erhard Göpel. "Ein Brahmsfund in Südfrank-reich" Zeitschrift für Musikwissenschaft 15/8 (5.1933) pp.

371-73. ill., facsim., notes. News of Brahmsiana in Carpentras, France: tells the provenance of manuscript for Op. 3 no. 1, and a picture of Brahms by Jean-Joseph Laurens; includes comments on Laurens's relationship with Brahms and the Schumanns.

2110   Engel, Gustav. "Liederschau" Neue Berliner Musikzeitung 8/28 (12.7.1854) pp. 218-20. Brahms: pp. 218-19. Review.

See also 1060, 1328, 1332, 1345, 1350, 2033, 2064, 2107, 2343.

--Op. 6

See 1327, 1328, 1332, 1345, 1350, 2064, 2343.

--Op. 7

2111   Ker. Signale für die musikalische Welt 13/9 (2.1855) pp. 65-66. Review.

See also 1328, 1332, 1345, 1375A, 2104, 2343.

--Op. 14
2112   Gennrich, Friedrich. "Glossen zu Johannes Brahms' "Sonett" op. 14, Nr. 4 Ach könnt' ich, könnte vergessen Sie! Zum 3. April 1927" Zeitschrift für Musikwissenschaft 10/3 (12.1927) pp. 129-39. mus., notes. Discusses source of text and its possible influence on Brahms's choice of melody.

See also 306, 1332, 2526, 2532.

--Op. 19

2113   Steglich, Rudolf. "Zum Kontrastproblem Johannes Brahms--Hugo Wolf" in Kongress-Bericht. Gesellschaft für Musikforschung. Lüneburg 1950. Hans Albrecht, Helmuth Osthoff and Walter Wiora, eds. Kassel und Basel: Bärenreiter Verlag, [1950]. pp. 140-43. mus., notes. On the question of text determining rhythm: Brahms's setting of Mörike in Op. 19 no. 5 contrasted with Wolf's setting of same text in Gedichte von Eduard Mörike no. 11.

2114   Tausche, Anton. "An eine Aolsharfe.--Cis-mol.--Komp.: 15. April 1888." In Tausche. Hugo Wolf's Mörikelieder in Dichtung, Musik und Vortrag. Wien: Amandus Edition, [1947]. pp. 54-59. Brahms: pp. 55-58. Compares setting of this text by Wolf, in his Gedichte von Eduard Mörike

no. 11, and Brahms's Op. 19 no. 5.
(a) i) reprint: Tausche. ""An eine Aolsharfe". Die
Vertonungen von Eduard Mörikes Gedicht durch
Brahms und Hugo Wolf. Eine vergleichende Studie"
Osterreichische Musikzeitschrift 3/2 (2.1948) pp.
47-48.
ii) reprint: Tausche. ""An eine Aolsharfe". Eine
vergleichende Studie der Vertonungen von Eduard
Mörikes Gedicht durch Johannes Brahms und Hugo
Wolf" Musikerziehung 6/4 (6.1953) pp. 295-96.

See also 2, 156, 1375A, 2032, 2064, 2066, 2074, 2104, 2526, 2530,
2541, 2617, 3031.

--Op. 20

See 1095, 2035.d.

--Op. 28

See 2035.d., 2523.

--Op. 31

See 2029.

--Op. 32

2115 *Zielinski, Shirley McGaugh. "A Biographical and Critical Sketch
of Karl August von Platen-Hallermunde and A Study of the
Settings of His Poems by Schubert, Schumann and Brahms"
Ph.D. diss., Washington University, 1981. 215 pp. Examines musical factors which relate directly to the text and/or
define the individuality of the work; includes discussion
of Brahms's Op. 32 nos. 1,3-6. [from S156]

See also 1377, 2056, 2071, 2074, 2081, 2107, 2530, 2541.

--Op. 33

2116 *Barnard, Monty J. "I. Romanzen aus Magelone, Opus 33
(Brahms); Concertato to Cantata: A Study of Writing for
the Solo Voice in the Early Church Cantatas of Johann
Sebastian Bach; A Comparative Study of the Melodies of
Gabriel Fauré and Claude Debussy. II. Performance"
D.M.A. diss., Performance, Voice, Northwestern University,
1974.

2117 *Boyer, Margaret Gene. "A Study of Brahms' Setting of the
Poems from Tieck's Liebesgeschichte der Schonen Magelone
und des Grafen Peter von Provence" Ph.D. diss., Washington University, 1980. 113 pp. A detailed musical and
literary study including details on the composer and poet
relevant to the evolution of both the poem and song cycle;
includes comments on Op. 33 as an example of a song cycle.
[from S156]

(d) Boyer, Thomas. "Brahms as Count Peter of Provence:
A Psychosexual Interpretation of the Magelone
Poetry" Musical Quarterly 66/2 (4.1980) pp. 262-86.
notes. Examines nature of Brahms's response to
Tieck's poems, both in his personal life and his
setting of them; also discusses the poetry's background and how Brahms came to know it.

2118 Brown, Maurice J. E. "Neapolitan Brahms" Music and Musicians
13/6 (2.1965) p. 31. An introduction to Op. 33: outlines
the story, background of the work and includes a descriptive analysis of the songs.

2119 Ehrlich, H[einrich]. Neue Berliner Musikzeitung 20/3 (17.1.
1866) pp. 18-19. Review.

2120 Fox Strangeways, A. H. "Brahms and Tieck's 'Magelone'"
Music and Letters 21/3 (7.1940) pp. 211-29. Background
and descriptive analysis; includes English translation of
song texts, together with comments on romanticism in music.

2121 *Jack, Dwight Christian. "Two Romantic Songcycles: An Ana-
lytical Description of the Schumann-Eichendorff Liederkreis
II, Op. 39 and the Brahms-Tieck Romanzen aus Magelone,
Op. 33" D.M.A. diss., University of Miami, 1973. 131 pp.
Examines and compares the two works; includes performance
practice suggestions. [from S156]

2122 *Kalbeck, Max. "Die Schöne Magelone" Neues Wiener Tagblatt
(22.11.1902).

2123 Marshall, Russell Joseph. "A Stylistic Study of the Magelone
Lieder of Johannes Brahms" M.A. thesis, Music, University
of Washington, 1955. iii, 67 pp. notes. Analysis of the
cycle and its individual songs; includes comments on poetry's
background, as well as comparison with Beethoven's Op.
98.

2124 *Munk, Jørgen. "Stilistiske og formale karaktertraek i Brahms's
Romanzen aus Ludwig Tiecks "Magelone", op. 33" Specialeaf-
handlinger til skoleembedseksamen i musik, Københavns
Universitet, 1952.

2125 Pulver, Jeffrey. "The "Magelone" Romances of Brahms" Musical
Opinion and Music Trade Review 57/679 (4.1934) pp. 599-
600. Background and descriptive analysis of work; includes history of Magelone story and song cycle's publication.

2126 Ross, George. "A Narration to be Read during Performances
of Die Schöne Magelone" NATS Bulletin 35/5 (5./6.1979) pp.
39-41.

2127 *Tavener, Thomas Theodore. "I. An Acoustical Analysis of
Stressed and Unstressed Consonant-Vowel Syllables Sung
and Spoken in Disyllabic Pairs by Trained Singers. II.
A Recital of Contemporary British Music: Program Notes
for a Doctoral Recital (University of Washington, 1968).
III. "Romanzen aus Tieck's Magelone": Program Notes
for a Doctoral Recital (University of Washington, 1971)"
D.M.A. diss., University of Washington, 1972. 177 pp.
Contains translation of story and the specific poems that
Brahms set. [from S156]

2128 *Turner, Ronald Alan. "A Performer's Guide to Johannes
Brahms' Die Schöne Magelone Opus 33" D.M.A. diss.,
Southern Baptist Theological Seminary, 1976. 315 pp. A
compendium of resources for the performer: includes studies
in musical and literary analysis, interpretation, philosophy/
theology; a parallel German-English translation, history of
the story, and primary documentation on the work's genesis.
[from S156]
(d) Turner, Ronald A[lan]. "Johannes Brahms and Die
Schoene Magelone" NATS Bulletin 35/5 (5.6.1979)
pp. 37-39. notes. Examines Brahms's life to understand climate in which this work was written, and
circumstances which may have drawn Brahms to the
poetry.

See also 48, 297, 1377, 2040, 2056, 2064, 2070, 2072, 2073, 2081,
2541, 2617.

--Op. 43

2129 Barlmeyer, Werner. ""Von ewiger Liebe"--noch einmal zur
Textvorlage von Brahms' Op. 43, 1" Melos/NZ für Musik
4/2 (3.1978) pp. 101-02. notes. Identifies the text author
as Leopold Haupt.

2130 Krauss, Anne McClenny. "Performance Suggestions for "Von
ewiger Liebe", Op. 43, no. 1 by Johannes Brahms" Clavier
17/2 (2.1978) p. 34. mus. [pp. 35-36] Analysis as an
interpretative aid for both singer and pianist.

2131   Peyser, Herbert F. "Chopin's Influence Upon Later Music: Wagner, Schumann, Brahms, and Others" Musical America 69/5 (1.4.1949) pp. 6-7, 34. Brahms: p. 34. An allusion to Chopin's music in Op. 43 no. 2.

2132   Sams, E[ric]. ""Von ewiger Liebe"" Neue Zeitschrift für Musik 133/5 (5.1972) p. 257. States that text author is Hoffmann von Fallersleben.
(d) see: 2129.

2133   Waters, Edward N. "Harvest of the Year. Selected Acquisitions of the Music Division" Quarterly Journal of the Library of Congress 24/1 (1.1967) pp. 47-82. Brahms: p. 48. Provenance of Op. 43 no. 1 manuscript acquired by the Library of Congress.

See also 1357, 1375A, 2040, 2042, 2057, 2064, 2074, 2091, 2104, 2372, 2530, 2541, 2617, 2628.

--Op. 46

See 1342, 2033, 2038, 2040, 2064, 2065, 2069, 2081, 2372.

--Op. 47

See 297, 1342, 2040, 2064, 2065, 2069, 2074, 2081, 3187.

--Op. 48

See 301, 1342, 2033, 2040, 2064, 2065, 2069.

--Op. 49

2134   Gest, Elizabeth. "Brahms and His Famous "Lullaby"" Etude 66/12 (12.1948) pp. 742, 787. ill., mus. Op. 49 no. 4: background to composition (Brahms and Bertha Faber) and discussion of music.

2135   Grasberger, Franz. "Johannes Brahms. Wiegenlied" in Grasberger. Das Lied. Mozart. Beethoven. Schubert. Brahms. Schumann. Wolf. Strauss. (Kostbarkeiten der Musik. Bd. 1) Tutzing: Hans Schneider, 1968. pp. [135-59]. ill., facsim., notes. History of Op. 49 no. 4 as seen in context of Brahms's life: circumstances of composition, source of text, description of autograph manuscripts, publication and performance history.

2136   Möller, Walter. "Das Wiegenlied" Berliner Lokal-Anzeiger.
       Unterhaltungs-Beilage (10.8.1928) pp. [3-4]. Relates
       story of how Op. 49 no. 4 was written; includes comments
       on Brahms's childhood and Brahms and Agathe von Siebold.

See also 306, 1342, 1375A, 2040, 2062, 2065, 2069, 2074, 2104, 2107,
2530, 2617, 3031, 3187.

--Op. 52

2137   A. H. Signale für die musikalische Welt 28/16 (10.3.1870)
       p. 243. Review.

2138   Chr. [Friedrich Chrysander] "Bemerkung" Allgemeine musik-
       alische Zeitung 5/21 (25.5.1870) p. 164. Critical remarks.

2139   Drinker, Henry S[andwith] [Jr.]. "Destiny and a Brahms
       Autograph" Etude 51/7 (7.1933) pp. 441, 486. facsim.
       Background of Albumblatt Drinker bought: his guess as
       to its background compared to the facts [see 1317].

2140   H. D. [Hermann Deiters] Allgemeine musikalische Zeitung 5/21
       (25.5.1870) pp. 163-64. Review.

2141   *Hamburger, Povl. "Omkring Johs. Brahms' "Liebeslieder
       Walzer" Op. 52" in Festskrift Gunnar Heerup. 1903-5.
       April-1973. John Høybe, Frede v. Nielsen and Aksel
       Schiøtz, eds. Egtved: Musikhojskølens Forlag, 1973. pp.
       231-53. ill., mus.

2142   *Neugebauer, Shirley Ann. "Johannes Brahms's Liebeslieder
       Waltzes, Op. 52: A Conductor's Analysis" D.M.A. diss.,
       University of Miami, 1982. 81 pp. fig., notes. Contains
       musical and textual analysis, suggestions for performance,
       and comparison with Opp. 65, 39, and waltzes by Schubert,
       Lanner, and Strauss; includes general comments on Brahms
       the composer. [from S156]

2143   *Schattmann, Alfred. "Geleitwort" in Brahms. Liebeslieder-
       Walzer [arranged for voice and 2-hand piano] (Musik für
       Alle no. 247) Berlin: Verlag Ullstein, 1927.

See also 1317, 1359, 2018, 2032, 2038,2039, 2041, 2083, 2093, 2412,
2548.

--Op. 57

See 2040, 2057, 2069, 2081.

--Op. 58

See 2040, 2057, 2069, 2103, 2548.

--Op. 59

2144   Monthly Musical Record 4/42 (1.6.1874) p. 87.   Review.

2145   Fellinger, Imogen.   "Zur Entstehung der "Regenlieder" von
         Brahms" in Festschrift Walter Gerstenberg zum 60.   Geburt-
         stag.   Georg von Dadelsen und Andreas Holschneider, eds.
         Wolfenbüttel und Zürich: Karl Heinrich Möseler Verlag,
         1964.   pp. 55-58.   notes.   Explains the inter-relationship
         of Opp. 59 nos. 3, 4, together with discussion of the
         manuscripts.

See also 81.d., 957, 959, 960, 1488, 2057, 2064, 2069, 2074, 2092,
2103, 2184, 2561.

--Op. 61

See 2033, 2035.d.

--Op. 63

See 2074, 2092, 2107, 2530, 2548, 2617.

--Op. 65

See 1359, 2018, 2039, 2041, 2042, 2093, 2412, 2548.

--Op. 66

See 957, 959, 960, 2035.d.

--Op. 69

See 2054, 2064, 2523, 2617.

--Op. 71

See 2064, 2067, 2107, 2541.

--Op. 72

See 2091

--Op. 75

2146 Mies, Paul. "Herders Edvard-Ballade bei Joh[annes]. Brahms" Zeitschrift für Musikwissenschaft 2/4 (1.1920) pp. 225-32. mus., fig., notes. Compares Brahms's Op. 10 no. 1 with Op. 75 no. 1 as regards text-music relationships.

See also 2035.d., 2532.

--Op. 84

2147 *Helm, Theodor. "Wiener Musikbrief: Neue Lieder von Brahms" Pester Lloyd (Budapest) (6.3.1883).

See also 1335, 2074, 2107, 2530.

--Op. 85

See 1335, 2064, 2067, 2541, 2609.

--Op. 86

2148 #h. [Heinrich v. Oiste] "(Dichter und Componisten.)" Wiener Abendpost Beilage no. 11 (14.1.1899) p. [1]. Reports Hermann Allmers's comments on Brahms's setting of his poem [Op. 86 no. 2].
(d) see: 2149.
(e) #report: "J. Brahms' herrliches, viel gesungenes Lied ..." Musikalisches Wochenblatt 29 (1898) p. 684.

2149 Protz, Albert. "Die Entstehung von Hermann Allmers' Gedicht "Feldeinsamkeit"" Die Musikforschung 3/[3] (1950) p. 279. Relates how Allmers came to write the poem, as well as his opinion of Brahms's setting of it.

See also 1335, 1375A, 2042, 2054, 2064, 2071, 2074, 2104, 2530.

--Op. 91

2150 *Croan, Robert James. "The Ensemble Song of the Nineteenth Century: A Study of Representative Repertory for Solo Voice and 2 to 5 Instruments" Ph.D. diss., Musicology, Boston University, 1968. 150 pp. mus., notes.

2151 *Hutschenruyter, Wouter. "De aria met een obligaat snaar of
      blaas-instrument" Symphonia 23/4,5 (4.,5.;1940) pp. 59-60,
      68-70.

See also 1344, 1375A, 2062, 2104, 2561.

--Op. 92

See 1325, 2038.

--Op. 94

2152 *Hamburgische Konzert- und Theater-Zeitung [8] (1904).
          (e) report: "Der unsittliche Brahms" Signale für die
              musikalische Welt 62/16/17 (24.2.1904) p. 269.
              Concerning the text for Op. 94 no. 4.

2153 Mason, Daniel Gregory. "Love Songs of the Great Compo-
          sers. "Sapphic Ode" ("Sapphische Ode")" Ladies' Home
          Journal 25/4 (3.1908) p. 31. mus. Analysis and suggestions
          for performance; includes general comments on Brahms's
          songs.

See also 2042, 2071, 2074, 2107, 2547, 2609, 2617.

--Op. 95

See 2081.

--Op. 96

2154 Kielian, Marianne, Marion A. Guck and Charles J. Smith.
          "Analysis Symposium: Brahms, "Der Tod, das ist die kühle
          Nacht", Op. 96/1" In Theory Only 2/6 (9.1976) pp. 16-43.
          fig., notes.
          Kielian: pp. 22-26. Discusses pitch-rhythmic relationships.
          Guck: pp. 27-29. Discusses structural ambiguities between
              the vocal line and the right-hand part of the piano ac-
              companiment.
          Smith: pp. 39-43. Examines the time spans within the
              song.

See also 1040, 1375A, 2038, 2064, 2067, 2074, 2081, 2085, 2103, 2104,
2530, 2541, 2609.

--Op. 97

See 957, 959, 960, 1040, 2074, 2092.

--Op. 103

2155   Linke, Oskar. "Brahms' Zigeunerlieder" Neue Musikzeitung
       13/9 (1892) p. 98. Review.

See also 1359, 2021, 2039, 2106, 2564.

--Op. 105

2156   Clarkson, Austin and Edward Laufer. "Analysis Symposium:
       Brahms Op. 105/1" Journal of Music Theory 15/1-2 (1971)
       pp. 2-32, 34-57. mus., fig., notes.
       Clarkson: pp. 6-32. Studies the setting of the text.
       Laufer: pp. 34-57. Studies the techniques used to bring
          out motivic and musical-poetic relationships above a
          simple harmonic contrapuntal structure.
       (a) i) reprint (of Clarkson section): Clarkson. "[Sym-
                posium IV. Brahms, Song Op. 105 no. 1] 15. A
                Literary-Historical Approach" in Readings in Schenker
                Analysis and Other Approaches. Maury Yeston, ed.
                New Haven and London: Yale University Press,
                1977. pp. 250-53. mus. [pp. 227-29].
            ii) reprint (of Laufer section): Laufer. "[Symposium
                IV. Brahms, Song Op. 105 no. 1] 16. A Schenkerian
                Approach" in 2156.a.i. pp. 254-72.

See also 957, 959, 960, 2021, 2074, 2085, 2087, 2092, 2107, 2609,
2617, 3187.

--Op. 106

See 957, 959, 960, 1375A, 2021, 2071, 2092, 2104, 2530, 3183.

--Op. 107

2157   Federhofer, Hellmut. "Zur Einheit von Wort und Ton im Lied
       von Johannes Brahms" in Bericht über den Internationalen
       Musikwissenschaftlichen Kongress Hamburg 1956. Walter
       Gerstenberg, Heinrich Husmann, Harald Heckmann, eds.
       Kassel, Basel: Bärenreiter-Verlag, 1957. pp. 97-99. fig.,
       notes. Elaborates on 2087, showing how changes in word
       accentuation are related to tonality.

2158 Schenker, Heinrich. Musikalisches Wochenblatt 22/40 (1.10.1891)
pp. 514-17. Review.

See also 2021, 2074, 2087.

--Op. 112

2159 #A. N. [Arnold Niggli] Schweizerische Musikzeitung und Sängerblatt 32 (15.12.1892) p. 31. Review.

See also 2020, 2106, 2564.

--Op. 121

2160 *[Alwin von Beckerath] Neue freie Presse (Wien) (1897).
(e) report: "Sehr allgemein war und ist noch jetzt"
Musikalisches Wochenblatt 28/29 (15.7.1897) p. 396.
Reports on letter from von Beckerath to Hanslick
discussing the false link between Clara Schumann's
death and Op. 121.

2161 Boyd, Malcolm. "Brahms and the Four Serious Songs" Musical
Times 108/1493 (7.1967) pp. 593-95. mus., notes. Discusses the relationship between vocal and piano parts, the
significance of the songs' texts, and how the last song
differs from the other three combined, and the reasons
therefore.

2162 Brahms, Johannes. Vier ernste Gesänge. [Op. 121. München:
Drei Masken Verlag, 1923.] 18 pp. facsim. Manuscript
facsimile (A-Wgm).
(a) reprint: [Brahms. Vier ernste Gesange. Op. 121.
Leipzig-Oetzsch: Sinsel & Co. G.m.b.H., n.d.
16, 1 pp.]
(e) report: Aldrich, Richard. "The Handwriting of the
Masters Reproduced in 'Autograph' Scores" New
York Times 73/24,046 (25.11.1923) Section 8, p. 6.

2163 *_____. Vier ernste Gesänge. Opus 121. Nach eigenhändige
Handschrift von Hermann Zapf gedruckt. Frankfurt a.M.:
Osterrieth, 1939. 26 pp. notes.
(a) *reprint: in Jahresgabe für der Mitglieder der Maximilian-Gesellschaft 9 (1939).

2164 Göhler, Georg. "Johannes Brahms' Vermächtnis" Deutsche
Rundschau 79/5 (5.1953) pp. 217-22. What Op. 121 reveals
about Brahms; includes comments on the Bible and Brahms.

2165 Jones, Earl W. "Brahms' Vier Ernste Gesange ... as a Summation of Style" NATS Bulletin 24/2 (12.1967) pp. 10, 12-13.

ill., mus. Analysis of Op. 121 with overall comments on Brahms's style.

2166 *Kalbeck, Max. "Musikalische Frühlingstage" Neues Wiener Tagblatt (23.6.1897). Corrects background of Op. 121: composed on the occasion of Clara Schumann's birthday, rather than her death. [from 241]

2167 *Okuda, Sue S. "Brahms's Late Song Style: The Vier Ernste Gesange, Op. 121" M.A. thesis, California State University (Fullerton), 1981. 137 pp. An analytical study dealing with music-text relationships and unity within each song as well as within the opus as a whole. [from S155]

2168 Paquin, Marie-Thérèse. "Vier ernste Gesänge. Quatre chants serieux. Four Serious Songs" in Paquin. Dix cycles de lieder. Beethoven, Brahms, Mahler, Schubert, Schumann. Traduction mot à mot accent tonique=Ten Cycles of Lieder. Beethoven, ... Schumann. Translation Word for Word Stress. Montréal: Les Presses de l'Université de Montréal, 1977. pp. 38-45. Original texts plus French and English translation, arranged in parallel columns.

2169 Roltsch, Siegfried. "Klang der Seele" Neue Musikzeitschrift 4/9 (9.1950) pp. 253-55. Fictional account of circumstances behind composition of Op. 121--work as a memorial to Clara Schumann.

2170 *Tramsen, Elisabeth. "Johs. Brahms' sangkompositioner for en enkelt stemme, specielten belysning af de stilistiske ejendommeligheder i "Vier ernste Gesänge", op. 121" Specialeafhandlinger til skoleembedseksamen i musik, Københavns Universitet, 1962.

2171 Vanson, Frederic. "Brahms' Four Serious Songs. A Noble Achievement" The Choir 54/6 (6.1963) p. 104. Discusses Op. 121's compositional background, with comments on the texts.

2172 Wörner, Karl. "Vier ernste Gesänge. Zum 100. Geburtstag Johannes Brahms' am 7. Mai" Die Woche (Berlin) 35/17 (29.4.1933) pp. 522-23. Discusses Op. 121's compositional background and its textual connection to the Bible; includes description of Brahms's last days, May 1896- .

See also 170, 248, 739, 1037, 1344, 1357, 1766, 2019, 2023-25, 2070, 2073, 2285, 2300, 2372, 2493, 2547, 2548, 2637.

--28 Deutsche Volkslieder [Hofmann nr. 138; McCorkle WoO posthum 31]

2173 Wetzel, Justus Hermann. "Eine neue Volksliedersammlung aus Brahms' Jugendzeit. Zu Max Friedlaenders 75. Geburtstag" Zeitschrift für Musikwissenschaft 10/1 (10.1927) pp. 38-44. Compares Brahms's settings published here, with those in the Deutsche Volkslieder (1894) [Hofmann nr. 133; McCorkle WoO 33]; includes discussion of folksong vs. artsong.

See also 2075.

--Dar geiht ein Bek [Hofmann nr. 193]

See 366, 957, 959, 960.

--Deutsche Volkslieder (1894) [Hofmann nr. 133; McCorkle WoO 33]

2174 Musical Times 36/626 (1.4.1895) p. 242. Review.

2175 Becker, Adolf. "Friedrich v. Spe und Johannes Brahms" Musica sacra (Regensburg) 50/8 u. 9 (8.-9.1917) pp. 116-17. mus., notes. Compares no. 42's tune with melody by Spe, together with its antecedents in sacred music.

2176 "Brahms's Volkslieder" The Times (London) no. 34,446 (13.12.1894) p. 10. Reviews edition with Bach's English translation of text.

2177 Cudworth, Charles L. "Ye Olde Spuriousity Shoppe or Put It in the Anhang" Notes Second series 12/1,4 (12.1954; 9.1955) pp. 25-40; 533-53. Brahms: pp. 535-36. Gives source of folktunes used in this collection, as Zuccalmaglio collection.

2178 Döhrn, Gisela. "Die Volksliedbearbeitungen von Johannes Brahms" Phil. F. diss., Universität Wien, 1936. 175, 5 pp. mus., fig., notes. Analytical study; includes general comment on Brahms and folkmusic, as well as comparisons of his folktune settings with those of J. S. Bach and Max Reger.
     (e) report: "Brahms und das Volkslied" Anbruch 19/3 (3.1937) p. 38.

2179 Friedländer, Max. "Brahms' Volkslieder" Jahrbuch der Musikbibliothek Peters 9 (1902) pp. 67-88. mus., notes. Discusses Brahms's sources for melodies and comments on the accompaniments.

2180 Müller, Herman. "Das Volkslied "In stiller Nacht" bei Joh[annes]. Brahms" Cäcilienvereinsorgan 50/9 (9.1915)

pp. 157-61. mus., notes. Gives the text's background
and discusses its settings prior to that of Brahms's; also
comment on source of tune.

See also 1344, 2044, 2072, 2075, 2173, 2450, 2547, 2563, 2572, 2617,
3187.

--Du bist wie eine Blume [McCorkle Anhang IIa, nr. 12*]

See 2067.

--Mondnacht [Hofmann nr. 124; McCorkle WoO 21]

2181   Neue Zeitschrift für Musik Bd. 43/16 (12.10.1855) p. 169.
        Reviews 1st edition.

See also 2064.

--Ophelia Lieder [Hofmann nr. 139; McCorkle WoO posthum 22]

2182   "4 Unknown Songs by Brahms Found" New York Times 84/
        28,062 (23.11.1934) p. 23. Account of their discovery and
        circumstances behind their composition.

--Regenlied [Hofmann nr. 136; McCorkle WoO posthum 23]

2183   "Berlin ..." Allgemeine Musikzeitung 35/51/52 (18./25.12.1908)
        p. 939. Announcement of work's publication.

2184   #Th. "Ein neues Regenlied von Brahms" Rheinische Musik-
        und Theaterzeitung (Köln) 9/50 (1908) pp. 609-10. Back-
        ground and descriptive analysis.

See also 957, 959, 960, 2092.

--Volks-Kinderlieder [Hofmann nr. 125; McCorkle WoO 31]

See 156, 1344, 1375A, 2075, 2104, 2107, 2563, 2617.

2. Works for Chorus--General

2185   *Ar. "Brahms als Schöpfer religiöser Chorwerke" Zeitschrift
        für kirchenmusikalische Beamte (Dresden) 4/1 (1922).

2186 Bellamy, Sister Kathrine Elizabeth. "Motivic Development in
Two Larger Choral Works of Johannes Brahms" Ph.D. diss.,
Musicology, University of Wisconsin, 1973. [1], 181 pp.
mus., ind., notes. Analytical study of Opp. 45 and 54
showing that the basic thematic materials are derived from
motifs; includes summary of all choral works composed by
Brahms.

2187 *Beuerle, Hans Michael. "Untersuchungen zum historischen
Stellenwert der a-cappella-Kompositionen von J[ohannes].
Brahms" Phil.F. diss., Universität Frankfurt a.M., [1976?].
(c) excerpt: Beuerle. "Brahms' Verhältnis zum Chor und
zur Chormusik" Melos/NZ für Musik 2/5 (9.1976)
pp. 357-63. mus. Discusses Brahms's involvement
in choral activities, together with influences on his
choral writing; includes comments on Opp. 45 and
55.

2188 #Bolt, Karl Fritz. "Johannes Brahms in seinem Chorschaffen"
Die Tonkunst (Berlin) 37/9 [(1933)] pp. 99-100. Overview
of the choral ensemble works to encourage their performance.
Works are grouped according to voice type.

2189 *"Brahms in sein Chorschaffen" Neue bayerische Sänger-Zeitung
no. 7 (1941).

2190 *Cooper. "Brahms Part-Music" Church Music (Philadelphia)
2/14 (1906).

2191 *Correll, Linda Ellen. "Contrapuntal Procedures in the Choral
Music of Johannes Brahms. A Study in Structural Development" M.A. thesis, University of Washington, 1964. 132
pp. mus.

2192 *Doll, Alice. "A Study of the Brahms Smaller Choral Compositions for Mixed Voices" M.A. thesis, University of Iowa,
1941. 2 vols. mus. Analysis and appreciation of Opp.
22, 29, 42, 62, 74, 93a, 104, 110. [from Rita Benton Music
Library, University of Iowa]

2193 Drinker, Sophie. Brahms and His Women's Choruses. Merion,
Penn.: Author, 1952. [4], 119, [3] pp. ill., facsim.,
ind., notes. A study of the Hamburg Frauenchor and the
choral works written at that time: 1858-62.
(d) Drinker, Sophie H. "Brahms' Music for Women" Music
Clubs Magazine 19/2,3 (11.-12.1939;1.-2.1940) pp.
9-10;9, 18. Notes only. Surveys the choral works
written 1858-62.
(e) report: Van der Elst, Nancy. "Joh[annes]. Brahms
en het vrouwenkoor" Mens en melodie 15/5 (5.1960)
pp. 148-50. ill. only.

2194 #e. [Eusebius Mandyczewski] "Neue Chorwerke von Brahms"
Deutsche Kunst- und Musikzeitung (Wien) 17/9 (20.3.1890)
p. [1?]. Reviews Opp. 109, 110.

2195 Fellerer, Karl Gustav. "Das deutsche Chorlied im 19. Jahr-
hundert" in Gattungen der Musik in Einzeldarstellungen.
Gedenkschrift Leo Schrade. Erste Folge. Wulf Arlt, Ernst
Lichtenhahn and Hans Oesch, eds. Unter Mitarbeit von
Max Haas. Bern und München: Francke Verlag, 1973.
pp. 785-812. Brahms: pp. 803-06. notes. Discusses
Brahms as a choral composer with a survey of the works.

2196 *Fey, Hermann. "Johannes Brahms und der Frauenchor" Lied
und Chor 50 (1958) p. 80.

2197 *Friedrich, Annette. "Beiträge zur Geschichte des weltlichen
Frauenchores im 19. Jahrhundert in Deutschland" Phil.F.
diss., Universität Köln, 1961. 166 pp. mus.
(a) *reprint: Beiträge ... Deutschland. (Kölner Beiträge
zur Musikforschung Bd. 18) Regensburg: Gustav
Bosse, 1961.

2198 #Graevenitz, Dr., v. [George von]. "Brahms als Chorkomponist" Süddeutsche Sänger-Zeitung (Heidelberg) 27/7 (1933)
pp. 100-01. Overview of the less familiar choral works to
encourage their performance: works for women, sacred
choral works are among music discussed.

2199 H. D. [Hermann Deiters] "Johannes Brahms' geistliche Compositionen" Allgemeine musikalische Zeitung 4/34,35 (25.8
and 1.9.;1869) pp. 266-68, 275-78. Reviews Opp. 12, 13,
22, 27, 29, 30, 37 and 45.

2200 Hancock, Virginia Lee. "Brahms and His Library of Early
Music: The Effects of His Study of Renaissance and Baroque
Music on His Choral Writing" D.M.A. diss., [Music History]
University of Oregon, 1977. vii, 327 pp. mus., ind.,
notes. Also includes an examination of contemporary study
and performance of early music, describes Brahms's holdings
of early music in his library.
(d) Hancock, Virginia L. "Sources of Brahms's Manuscript
Copies of Early Music in the Archiv der Gesellschaft der Musikfreunde in Wien" Fontis artis musicae
24/3 (1977) pp. 113-21. notes. Sources of pre-
Baroque music include early printed editions, autographs, and 19th century editions and manuscript
copies. Also discusses the background of the copies
Brahms made and the markings found in them.

2201 *Hernried, Robert. "Brahms als Chorkomponist" Zeitschrift
für Schulmusik (Wolfenbüttel) 6 (1933) p. 38.

2202 #Herzogenberg, Heinrich von. "Johannes Brahms in seinen
Verhältnis zur evangelischen Kirchenmusik" Monatsschrift
für Gottesdienst und kirchliche Kunst 2/3 (6.1897) pp. 68-
71. Surveys Brahms's music specifically written for the
church; includes assessment of his sacred works.

2203 *Heuberger, Richard. Johannes Brahms, Rhapsodie, Op. 53.
Nänie, Op. 82. (Der Musikführer. no. 44) Frankfurt a/M.:
Verlag von H. Bechhold, [1895]. 14 pp.
*also: Berlin: Schlesinger, n.d.
*also: Stuttgart: Schmitt, n.d.
(a) *reprint: in 1346.

2204 Keller, Hermann. "Die Chorlieder von Brahms" Neue Musikzeitung 43/13 (6.4.1922) pp. 198-200. mus., notes. An
overview òf all choral works written without orchestral
accompaniment: historical background and descriptive remarks.

2205 *Köser, Werner. "Johannes Brahms in seinen geistlichen Chor-
werken a-capella" Phil.F. diss., Universität Hamburg, 1950.
129 or 130 pp.

2206 Krause, Emil. "Johannes Brahms' Vocalwerke mit Orchester"
Neue Zeitschrift für Musik 55/18/19,20,22 (Bd. 84) (8.,16.,
30.;5.;1888) pp. 206-08, 233-34, 251-53. Descriptive analysis
and background for Opp. 12, 13, 45, 50, 53, 54, 82 and
89.
(d) reworked: into 1352.

2207 Kretzschmar, Hermann. "Neue Werke von J. Brahms. III."
Musikalisches Wochenblatt 5/5-9,12 (30.1.;6.-27.2.;20.3.;
1874) pp. 58-60, 70-73, 83-85, 95-97, 107-11, 147-50. mus.,
notes. Reviews Opp. 50, 53-55.
(d) i)*see: 1353C.
ii) *see: 2310, 2319.

2208 *Kross, Siegfried. "Die Chorwerke von Johannes Brahms"
Phil.F. diss., Universität Bonn, 1957. iii, 665 pp. mus.,
ind., notes.
(a) reprint: Die Chorwerke ... Brahms. Berlin-Halensee
und Wunsiedel/fr.: Max Hesses Verlag, 1958.
Presents historical background and musical analysis,
discusses Brahms's style as a choral composer, his
influences, and offers an evaluation.
*2. Auflage: 1963.
*also: Tutzing: Hans Schneider, 1963.

2209 Krummacher, Friedhelm. "Kunstreligion und religiöse Musik.
Zur ästhetischen Problematik geistlicher Musik im 19. Jahrhundert" Die Musikforschung 32/4 ([10.-11.]1979) pp. 365-

93. Brahms: pp. 385-93. mus., notes. Discusses the stylistic influence of the past on the writing of sacred music; compares the Mendelssohn organ works with Brahms's Opp. 109 and 29 no. 1.

2210 #Mies, Paul. "Johannes Brahms und die katholische Kirchenmusik" Gregorius-Blatt. Organ für katholische Kirchenmusik 54/4 (1930) pp. 49-58. mus., notes. Discusses Brahms's position on this topic and his study of older composers' works; includes descriptive analysis of Opp. 12, 37, a look at the Missa canonica [McCorkle WoO posthum 18] , and comments on the compositional techniques Brahms used in this kind of work.

2211 *Ochs, Siegfried. Der deutsche Gesangsverein für gemischten Chor. 4 Bde. Berlin: Hesse 1923-26.
(c) excerpt (in English translation by Tamara Trykar): Ochs. "Encounter with Bruckner and Brahms (Choral Conductors Forum)" American Choral Review 14/4 (10.1972) pp. 12-15. Suggestions for performance for Opp. 45, 54.

2212 Petzoldt, Richard. "Brahms und der Chor" Die Musik (Berlin) 25/8 (5.1933) pp. 578-82. An overview of the choral works, their evolution and style; includes comments on Brahms as a conductor of choirs.
(a) reprint: in 3186.c. pp. 18-22.

2213 *Raben, Anna Lisa. "Arkaiske og moderne stiltraek i Johs. Brahms' a cappellasange for blandet kor" Specialeafhandlinger til skoleembedseksamen i musik, København Universitet, 1957.

2214 *Reuning, D. G. "Lutheran Musical Tradition in the Sacred Choral Works of Brahms" The Springfielder 36 (Summer 1972) pp. 134-37.

2215 #Richard, August. "Die Chorwerke von Johannes Brahms" Süddeutsche Sänger-Zeitung (Heidelberg) 14/8 (1922) pp. 130-32. Overview of choral works with descriptive comments.

2216 Roeder, Michael T. "The Choral Music of Brahms: Historical Models" CAUSM [Canadian Association of University Schools of Music] Journal 5/2 (Autumn 1975) pp. 26-46. mus. [pp. 37-44], notes. Points out characteristics of older composers' works (Bach, Gabrieli, Schütz) that influenced Brahms; discusses Opp. 29, 74, 110, 109, together with analysis and historical antecedents; includes comments on Brahms's links with the music of the past. Includes French summary by Violet Archer: pp. 45-46.

2217 Rose, Michael Paul. "Structural Integration in Selected Mixed

A Cappella Choral Works of Brahms" Ph.D. diss., Musicology,
University of Michigan, 1971. vi, 274 pp. mus., fig.,
notes. An analytical study concerning music-text relationships in Opp. 22, 29, 42, 74, 104, 109-10, and Dem dunkeln
Schoss der Heilgen Erde [Hofmann nr. 178; McCorkle WoO
20].

2217.5 *Schmidt, Leopold. Berliner Tageblatt.
(a) #reprint: in Schmidt. "Brahms" in 3022. pp. 255-67.
"Brahms als Ethiker": pp. 260-62. First impressions
of Opp. 45, 82. 89.

2218 Schönheit, Walter. "Romantik in der Kirche? Johannes Brahms
(1833-1897)" in Credo musicale. Komponistenporträts aus
der Arbeit des Dresdener Kreuzchores. Festgabe zum 80.
Geburtstag des Nationalpreisträgers Kreuzkantor Professor
D. Dr. h.c. Rudolf Mauersberger. Kassel, Basel: Bärenreiter Verlag, [1969]. pp. 73-86. Discusses Brahms as
a sacred choral composer: his influences together with an
overview of the works; includes detailed comments on the
musical structure of Opp. 29, 37, 74, 109-10.
*also: Berlin: Evangelischer Verlag, 1969.

2219 *Sittard, Josef. Johannes Brahms. Schicksalslied, Op. 54.
Gesang der Parzen, Op. 89. (Der Musikführer. no. 37)
Frankfurt a/M.: Verlag von H. Bechhold, [1895]. 18 pp.
*also: Berlin: Schlesinger, n.d.
*also: Stuttgart: Schmitt, n.d.
(a) *reprint: in 1346.

2220 Williams, Alma Stone. "The Motets of Brahms: Their Style
and Heritage" M.M. thesis, [Music History and Literature],
University of Maryland, 1966. [ii, 2], 169 pp. mus. [pp.
118-64], fig., notes. Examines Opp. 29, 74, 110: discusses Brahms's influences, particularly Bach, the use of
texture and form, and the place of the motets in Brahms's
works.

See also 267, 675, 735, 778, 855, 944, 986.d., 1749, 2022, 2335,
2431, 2566.

See also "Texts and Text Setting" in V.B.

2. Works for Chorus--Specific

See also 2022.

See also "Texts and Text Setting" in V.B.

--Op. 12

See 1332, 1344, 1359, 2018, 2024, 2025, 2193, 2199, 2206, 2210.

--Op. 13

See 1332, 1344, 1359, 1376, 2018, 2024, 2025, 2199, 2202, 2206, 2386.

--Op. 17

2221 *Anderson, Julia S. "Music for Women's Chorus and Harp:
       A Study of the Repertory and an Analysis and Performance
       of Selected Compositions" Ed. D. diss., Columbia University
       Teachers College, 1977. 237 pp.

2222 Br., v. Deutsche Musik-Zeitung (Wien) 2/12 (23.3.1861) pp.
       92-93. Brahms: pp. 92-93. Review.

See also 1332, 1359, 1376, 2018, 2193, 2532.

--Op. 22

2223 *Mies, Paul. "Das Marienlied bei Johannes Brahms" Im Dienste
       der Kirche (Essen) (1937) pp. 139-40.

2224 -r- and S. B. [Selmar Bagge]. "Kritische Anzeigen." All-
       gemeine musikalische Zeitung Neue Folge 1/1 (1.1.1863)
       cols. 7-12. S. B. "c) Für gemischten Chor.": cols. 11-12.
       Reviews Op. 22.

See also 1344, 2018, 2024, 2025, 2192, 2199, 2217.

--Op. 27

See 1344, 1353B, 1359, 2023, 2025, 2193, 2199.

--Op. 29

2225 McCray, James. "Observations on Brahms' Two Motets, Opus

29" American Music Teacher 30/3 (1.1981) pp. 12-14. notes.
Presents historical background and general analysis; includes biographical notes.

See also 1344, 1353B, 2023-25, 2029, 2192, 2199, 2202, 2209, 2216-18,
2220, 2386.

--Op. 30

See 1344, 1353B, 1359, 2023-25, 2029, 2199, 2202, 2386.

--Op. 37

2226 *Volkszeitung für Kirchenmusik (1878).

2227 *"Drei geistliche Chöre für Frauenstimme ohne Begleitung von
      Brahms, op. 37" Der Chorwächter [3]/12 (1878).

2228 "Ubersicht neu erschienener Musikwerke. B. Gesangs-Musik.
      2) Mehrstimmige Gesänge ohne Begleitung" Leipziger allge-
      meine musikalische Zeitung 1/22 (30.5.1866) p. 177. Review.

See also 1344, 1377, 2023-25, 2193, 2199, 2210, 2218.

--Op. 42

See 1095, 2018, 2192, 2217, 2532.

--Op. 44

2229 St. Leipziger allgemeine musikalische Zeitung 2/35 (28.8.1867)
      pp. 279-82. mus. Review.

2230 "Uebersicht (sic) neu erschienener Musikwerke. Lieder für
      gemischten Chor" Leipziger allgemeine musikalische Zeitung
      2/22 (29.5.1867) pp. 177-78. Brahms: p. 178. Review.

See also 1095, 1377, 2018, 2193, 2526.

--Op. 45

2231 Illustrirte Zeitung (Leipzig) Bd. 52/1350 (15.5.1869) p. 378.
      Review.

2232 Monthly Musical Record 1/5 (1.5.1871) pp. 63-64. Review.
      (c) *excerpt: in 2915. pp. 272-73.

2233 *Abercrombie, E. Wayne. "A Conductor's Analysis of Johannes
Brahms's Ein Deutsches Requiem, Opus 45" D.M. diss.,
Choral Conducting, Literature and Performance, Indiana
University, 1974. 206 pp. mus., notes. Discusses the
work's background and place in Brahms's musical oeuvre,
and examines the relationship between the music-text elements. [from S202]

2234 *Ambros, A. W. Bunte Blätter (1874) p. 117.

2235 Bellaigue, Camille. "Un Grand musicien conservateur. Le
Requiem allemand de Johannès Brahms" Revue des deux
mondes 68/[part 4] (Bd. 149) ([15.10.] 1898) pp. 933-44.
notes. Discusses Brahms as classicist, using Op. 45 as
the example. Traces his classical influences from the work
of Bach and Beethoven; includes comments on Brahms's
style.

2236 *Beyer, Carl. Johannes Brahms. Ein deutsches Requiem, Op.
45. (Der Musikführer. nos. 40, 41) Frankfurt a/M.:
Verlag von H. Bechhold, [1895 or 1898]. 34 pp.
*also: Berlin: Schlesinger, n.d.
*also: Stuttgart: Schmitt, n.d.
(a) *reprint: see 1346.

2237 Blum, Klaus. Hundert Jahre ein deutsches Requiem von
Johannes Brahms. Entstehung. Uraufführung. Interpretation. Würdigung. Tutzing: Hans Schneider, 1971.
158 pp. ill., mus., fig., ind., notes. Also includes discussion of Op. 45 as a reflection on Brahms's life.

2238 *Börner, Dr. Musik und Depression III. Johannes Brahms Requiem. Depression und Trauerarbeit grosser Komponisten.
Ciba-Geigy: Wehr, 1981. 2 + 3 pp.

2239 Boyd, Malcolm. "Brahms's Requiem. A Note on Thematic Integration" Musical Times 113/1548 (2.1972) pp. 140-41. mus.
Analysis of a germ cell motif and its presence in all six
movements.

2240 *Brahms, Johannes. A German Requiem: After Words of the
Holy Scripture for Soloists, Chorus and Orchestra (Organ
ad libitum). Carol J. Blinn, illustrator. [Easthampton,
Mass.:] Warwick Press, 1975. [8 leaves]. ill. Libretto.

2241 Brahms, Johannes. Ihr habt nun Traurigkeit. 5. Satz aus dem
"Deutschen Requiem". Faksimile der ersten Niederschrift.
Mit Einleitung von Franz Grasberger. Tutzing: Hans
Schneider, 1968. 9, [1, 9] pp. ill., facsim., mus. Historical background on Op. 45 and how the 5th movement contributes to the work as a whole; also provides manuscript
description and provenance.

2242 *Brieger, Georg. "Johannes Brahms' "Deutsches Requiem""
Glaube und Heimat (Jena) 2/16 (1947) p. 3.

2243 DAS. [Adolf Schubring] "Schumanniana Nr. 12" Allgemeine
musikalische Zeitung 4/2,3 (13.,20.;1869) pp. 9-11, 18-20.
mus. Review.

2244 *Deiters, Hermann. Münchener Propyläen (1869) p. 361.

2245 Detel, Adolf. Johannes Brahms. Ein deutsches Requiem.
Eine Einführung und Erläuterung für Konzertbesucher.
Hamburg: n.p., 1973. 20 pp. mus. Discusses the work's
historical background, style, texts; includes descriptive
analysis.

2246 #Dettmer, Hermann. "Ein deutsches Requiem. Johannes
Brahms's Werk 45. Zum Konzert der Musikakademie am
Busstage." Hannoverscher Kurier. [?]beilage (21.11.1917)
p. [?]. Descriptive analysis.

2247 #"Ein deutsches Requiem von Johannes Brahms. (Zur Aufführung durch den Lehrergesangverein am 31. Oktober und
1. November.)" Fränkischer Kurier (Nürnberg) 86/555
(30.10.1918) Abend-Ausgabe p. 3. Descriptive analysis
contrasting this work's purpose with that of a sacred requiem, and discussing instrumentation and voice settings.

2248 *Dieterich, Milton. "An Harmonic Analysis of the German
Requiem of Brahms" M.M. thesis, University of Rochester
(Eastman School of Music), 1941.

2249 *Eppstein, Hans. "Johannes Brahms. Ein deutsches Requiem"
Konsertnytt (Stockholm) Heft 14 (1977/78).

2250 F.G.E. "The Requiem of Brahms. Some Notes on Its Early
Performances" Musical Times 47/755 (1.1.1906) pp. 18-21.
mus., notes. Discusses early performances of the work in
Germany and performances in England.

2251 *Frederichs, Henning. ""Vogel als Prophet." Der Komponist
als Vermittler oder Gestalter von Sprache, dargestellt am
Deutschen Requiem von Johannes Brahms" in "Künstler als
Mittler?" Rudolf Koschnitzke and Ernst-Albrecht Plieg,
eds. (RUB [Schriftenreihe der Ruhr-Universität und der
Stadt Bochum]--Winter (6)) Bochum: Studienverlag Brock-
meyer, 1979. pp. 28-41. mus. Studies the process by
which Brahms musically shaped the text in Op. 45, the
central message of the work, its basic musical motif and
overall form. [from S202]

2251.5#Gallwitz, S[ophie]. D[orothea]. "Ein Brahms-Jubiläum in

Bremen" Weser-Zeitung (Bremen) 75/192 (17.3.1918) 1. Morgen-Ausgabe p. [?]. Discusses Op. 45's development and history, together with its Bremen première.

2252 Gardner, John. "A Note on Brahms's Requiem" Musical Times 95/1342 (12.1954) pp. 649-51. mus., fig. Motivic and thematic unity within this work; includes comment on the use of the chorale from Bach's Cantata no. 21.

2253 *"Gedanken zu "Ein deutsches Requiem" von Johannes Brahms" Glaube und Heimat (Jena) 4/13 (1949) p. 3.

2254 *Gehrenbeck, David M. "A Transcription for Organ and Chorus of Four Movements from A German Requiem of Johannes Brahms" S.M.M. diss., Union Theological Seminary (New York), 1957. v, 95 pp. mus., notes. Transcriptions of movements 1,4,5,7; includes comments on the work's historical background, the religious nature of the text, and the method of transcription. [from Gehrenbeck]

2255 Gerber, Rudolf. "Das "Deutsche Requiem" als Dokument Brahmsscher Frömmigkeit" Das Musikleben 2/7/8,9 (7./8., 9.;1949) pp. 181-85, 237-39. mus., notes. Discusses Brahms and religion.
(d)   continued: "Zu dem Aufsatz über das Brahms-Requiem" Das Musikleben 2/10 (10.1949) pp. 282-83. fig. Corrections; figure indicated in collation is for 2255.

2256 #Guardia, Ernesto de la. "El Requiem alemán y su definición en la personalidad de Brahms" Ars. Revista de arte 17/79 (1957) pp. [56-61]. ill., facsim. Compares Op. 45 to the traditional requiem; relates the circumstances behind the work's evolution and includes descriptive analysis.

2257 *Hernried, Robert. ""Ein deutsches Requiem". Eine Einführung" Der Chorleiter (Hildburghausen) 4/1/2 (1923).

2258 Hollander, Hans. "Gedanken zum strukturellen Aufbau des Brahmsschen "Requiems"" Schweizerische Musikzeitung. Revue musicale suisse 105/6 (11./12.1965) pp. 326-33. mus., notes. Discusses motivic unity in Op. 45, including the use of the chorale tune from Bach's Cantata no. 21.

2259 *Imbert, Hugues. "Le Requiem de Brahms" in Imbert. Portraits et études: César Franck, C.-M. Widor, Edouard Colonne, ... Brahms. Lettres inédites de Georges Bizet. Paris: Fischbacher, 1894.

2260 *Janson, H. "Requiem" Düsseldorfer Heimatblätter 7 (1938) pp. 226-29.

2261 *[Walter Panofsky] Johannes Brahms, Ein deutsches Requiem.
      (Das Christliche Gut in der Musik. 5) München: Schnell
      & Steiner, 1948. 15 pp.

2262 *Johannes Brahms: Ein deutsches Requiem. [Neuhausen bei
      Stuttgart: n.p., 1981] 7 pp. ill., mus.

2263 *Kalbeck, Max. "Ein deutsches Requiem" Neues Wiener Tagblatt
      (7.4.1897).

2264 *_____. "Ein deutsches Requiem" Die Presse (Wien) (21.12.
      1888).

2265 *Kleinert, P. [Paul] [or Hugo W. P. Kleinert] "Ein deutsches
      Requiem von Brahms" Neue evangelische Kirchenzeitung
      11/11,13 (3.1869).

2266 *Klump, George Edward. "An Organ Adaptation of the Orches-
      tral Score of the Brahms Requiem" D.M.A. diss., Perform- /
      ance and Pedagogy, University of Rochester (Eastman School
      of Music), 1962. iii, 25, 206 pp. mus., notes. A trans-
      cription with commentary. [from Klump]

2267 Komorn, Maria. "Zum "Deutschen Requiem" von Brahms" in
      706. pp. 89-95. mus. Discusses Furtwängler's approach
      to this work.
      (d) Komorn. "Brahms und Furtwängler als Chordirigenten
           an gleicher Stelle" Zeitschrift für Musik 100/5
           (5.1933) pp. 441-43. notes. Compares their back-
           ground as choral conductors, together with comments
           on Furtwängler's interpretation of Op. 45.

2268 *Kralik, Heinrich. Johannes Brahms. Ein deutsches Requiem.
      Ein Führer durch die Werk, mit vollständige Text, eine Ein-
      führung, erlauterte Anmerkung und zahlreichnete Noten-
      beispiele. (Tagblatt-Bibliothek nr. 744) Wien: Steyrermühl,
      1929. 29 pp. mus.

2269 Kraus, Gottfried. "...denn sie sollen getröstet werden. Das
      Brahms-Requiem--Oratorium, protestantische Totenmesse
      oder Auseinandersetzung mit dem christlichen Mythos? Eine
      vergleichende Diskografie" fonoforum [15]/4 (4.1970) pp.
      215-17. ill., facsim., discog. Discusses Op. 45's musical
      strengths, as well as its interpreters.

2270 *Kretzschmar, Hermann. Das deutsche Requiem. (Kleiner
      Konzertführer no. 517) Leipzig: Breitkopf & Härtel, 1898.
      18 pp.
      (b) *English translation by A. Eaglefield Hull: ?.
      (d) *see: 1353B.

2271   L., v. "Ein deutsches Requiem von Johannes Brahms" All-
        gemeine Zeitung (München) Beilage nr. 237 (25.8.1875) pp.
        3721-22. Descriptive analysis.

2272   *Lategan, B. C. "Ein deutsches Requiem: Notes on Brahms'
        Selection of Biblical Texts" Scriptura (Stellenbosch) no. 1
        (1980) pp. 29-41.

2273   Leibowitz, René. "Le Malheur d'aimer Brahms" in 1817. pp.
        195-200. mus. In the context of a performance review,
        author puts forward his ideas on the interpretation of Op.
        45.

2274   *Lichtenberg, Emil. Brahms: Requiem. Budapest: Méry,
        [1910]. 37 pp.

2275   *Lissy, Th. "Johannes Brahms' Deutsches Requiem" Kunst-
        garten (Wien) 7 (1929) pp. 112-14.

2276   Loeppert, Theodore W. "What's Going on in The Choir Loft?"
        Romantic Theologizing and Brahms' "How Lovely Is Thy
        Dwelling Place"" Response in Worship, Music and the Arts
        16/3 (1976) pp. 34-38. notes. Analyses the 5th movement
        in light of 19th century theology and metaphysics.

2277   *Lübke, Wilhelm. Schwäbische Chronik (Stuttgart) (28.9.-10.
        10.;1871).
        (c) #excerpted: in 1078.

2278   *Macfarren, George Alexander, Sir. Analytical Remarks on
        a German Requiem. The Music by Johannes Brahms. Lon-
        don: Lucas, Weber & Co., [1873]. 16 pp.

2279   MacKaye, Arvia. Brahms Requiem. Seven Drawings. n.p.,
        n.d. [16 pp.] Each movement inspires a drawing by this
        artist.

2280   Maczweski, A. Musikalisches Wochenblatt 1/1-5 (1.-28.;1.;
        1870) pp. 5, 20-21, 35-36, 52-54, 67-69. mus., notes.
        Review.

2281   *Meinardus, Ludwig. Zeitung für Literatur, Kunst und Wissen-
        schaft. Beilage zum Hamburgischer Correspondent no. 11
        (1882).

2282   *Mies, Paul. "Ein Deutsches Requiem" Halbmonatsschrift für
        Schulmusikpflege 24/18 [=Zeitschrift für Schulmusik (Wolfen-
        büttel) 3] (1930).

2283   Minear, Paul S. "Brahms' German Requiem" Theology Today
        22/2 (7.1965) pp. 236-49. notes. Describes Brahms's life

during the period when the Requiem was developed and first
performed; discusses the significance of the text for movements 1 and 2; includes comments on Brahms and religion.

2284 #Möller, W[alter]. "Ein deutsches Requiem von Brahms. Gesprach" Deutsch-evangelische Blätter 8 (1883) pp. 108-20.
A philosophical discussion of Op. 45, cast in the form of
an interview.

2285 Musgrave, Michael [Graham]. "Historical Influences in the
Growth of Brahms's 'Requiem'" Music and Letters 53/1
(1.1972) pp. 3-17. mus., notes. Describes Brahms's links
to Schütz and Bach; traces thematic unity in Op. 45 through
the use of motif, together with Bach's chorale tune from
Cantata no. 21; includes comments on Robert Schumann,
and allusions to Op. 45 in Brahms's Op. 121.

2286 Newman, Ernest. "Brahms's German Requiem" Musical Times
52/817 (1.3.1911) pp. 157-59. Historical background and
1st performances of this work; also comments on Brahms and
the Bible, as well as his philosophy of life and death.

2287 Newman, William S. "A "Basic Motive" in Brahms' German
Requiem" Music Review 24/3 (8.1963) pp. 190-94. Melodic
relationships as unifying devices in Op. 45.

2288 *Nitsche, H. "Brahms-Requiem mit originaler Klavierfassung"
Der Kirchenmusiker (Kassel) 33/4 (1982) pp. 115-16.

2289 O. R. "Johannes Brahms' deutsche Requiem" Wochenschrift
für Kunst und Musik (Wien) 1/17 (12.4.1903) pp. 153-54.
notes. Presents historical background and descriptive
analysis; includes comments on Brahms's last days in Wien.

2290 Orel, Alfred. "Das deutsche Requiem von Johannes Brahms"
Universitas 7/1 (1.1952) pp. 45-48. Presents historical
background and discusses Brahms's personality as seen in
this work.

2291 *Paumgartner, H. "Das deutsche Requiem" [Wiener] Abendpost
(18.12.1888).

2292 #Regeniter, Artur. "Brahms's "Deutsches Requiem". Zu seiner
Entstehungsgeschichte und stilgeschichtlichen Bedeutung.
Ein Gedenkblatt zur Erstaufführung vor fünfzig Jahren"
Rheinische Musik und- Theaterzeitung (Köln) 18/51/52
(22.12.1917) pp. 395-96. Discusses the work's background,
together with its style as a sacred choral work.

2293 Reinhardt, Klaus. "Motivisch-Thematisches im "Deutschen
Requiem" von Brahms. Zum 100. Jahrestag der ersten

vollständigen Aufführung in Leipzig am 28. Februar 1869"
Musik und Kirche 39/1 (1.1969) pp. 13-17. mus., notes.
Describes the sources for the work's motif; also examines
the use of the motif in unifying the work.

2294   Riemer, Otto. "Zur Kritik am Deutschen Requiem" Der Kirchen-
        musiker (Berlin) 12/5 (9.-10.1961) pp. 177-80. notes.
        Discusses Op. 45's religious connections.

2295   Robertson, Alec. "German Requiems Schütz & Brahms" in
        Robertson. Requiem. Music of Mourning and Consolation.
        London: Cassell, 1967. pp. 171-82. Brahms: pp. 175-82.
        mus., ind., notes. Presents historical background and
        descriptive analysis of Op. 45; includes comments on Brahms
        and religion.

2296   Rudolf, Max. "A Recently Discovered Composer-Annotated
        Score of the Brahms Requiem" With Supporting Authentica-
        tion by Oswald Jonas and "Introductory Remarks" by Elinore
        Barber. BACH 7/4 (10.1976) pp. 2-13. notes. Explains
        the provenance and background of this particular score, and
        presents a discussion/description of its markings.
        (d) continued: Rudolf. BACH 8/3 (7.1977) pp. 32-33.
        Presents a list of Requiem performances in Wien,
        and comments on 1868 Bremen performance.

2297   *Schanzlin, Hans Peter. "Ein unbekannter Brahms-Brief. Zur
        schweizerischen Erstaufführung des "deutschen Requiems"
        in Basel" Neue Zürcher Zeitung (9.5. or 10./11.;5.;1980).

2298   Schmitz, Eugen. "Zur Entstehungsgeschichte des 'Deutschen
        Requiems' von Brahms" Hochland 11/8 (Bd. 2) (5.1914)
        pp. 250-51. Suggests that Op. 45 as a whole is in memory
        of Robert Schumann rather than of Brahms's mother.

2299   Siegmund-Schultze, Walther. "Ein deutsches Requiem von
        Johannes Brahms--Seine historisch-ästhetische Stellung vor
        hundert Jahren und Heute--" in Siegmund-Schultze. "Das
        musikalische Erbe in der sozialistischen Gesellschaft. Aus-
        gewählte Studien zu Problemen der Interpretation und
        Wirkung" [Martin-Luther-Universität Halle-Wittenberg. Wis-
        senschaftliche Zeitschrift. Gesellschafts- und Sprachwissen-
        schaftliche Reihe] 23/6 (1974) pp. 28-33. fig., notes.
        Includes historical background and descriptive analysis;
        also comments on Op. 45 as a work written in the humanistic
        spirit.

2300   Sopeña Ibañez, Federico. "El "Requiem" y la religiosidad de
        Brahms" in Sopeña Ibañez. El "Requiem" en la música
        romantica. (Libros de música 2) Madrid: Ediciones Rialp,
        S.A., 1965. pp. 53-101. Discusses Op. 45 as it reflects

Brahms the man; includes descriptive analysis, as well
as comments on later works having religious connotations.

2301 *Vail, James. "A Study and Performance of A German Requiem
by Johannes Brahms" M.M. thesis, Southern California University, 1956.

2302 #Wessling, Berndt W. ""Ich bin nun getröstet". Vor hundert
Jahren vollendete Brahms sein "Deutsches Requiem"" Weser-
Kurier (Bremen) no. 50 (28.2.1967) p. 20. Discusses the
work's evolution together with its first performance and
reception in Bremen.

2303 Westafer, Walter. "Over-all Unity and Contrast in Brahms's
German Requiem" Ph.D. diss., Music, University of North
Carolina at Chapel Hill, 1973. 3, ii-vii, 319 pp. mus., fig.,
notes. Analyses means by which Brahms achieves unity
and contrast in this work; includes discussion of work's
historical background.

2304 Yvon, Francine. "Requiem de Brahms" Le Monde (Paris) 25/
7183 (16.2.1968) Supplement [Supplement Title=Le Monde des
loisirs] p. V. Discusses historical background of work.

2305 Zeileis, Friedrich G. "Two Manuscript Sources of Brahms's
German Requiem" Music and Letters 60/2 (4.1979) pp. 149-
55. facsim., notes. Presents background and description
of a new manuscript for the piano arrangement, and its relationship to D-brd-Hs manuscript.

See also 39B.e.iv., 55.c., 135, 224, 254, 263, 632, 680, 1078, 1261,
1344, 1353B, 1359, 1372D, 1374, 1375C, 2019, 2025, 2028, 2186, 2187.c.,
2199, 2206, 2211.c., 2217.5, 2309.d.ii., 2388, 2422, 2451, 2539, 2548,
2613, 2618, 2637, 2825.d., 2899.

--Op. 50

2306 *Batka, Johann. Pressburger Zeitung (1.-9.12.1883).

2307 *Grabau, Carl. Johannes Brahms, Rinaldo; Kantate von Goethe
für Tenor-Solo, Männerchor und Orchester, op. 50.
(Schlesinger'sche Musik-Bibliothek. Der Musikführer. no.
299) Berlin: Schlesinger (R. Lienau), [190-?]. 16 pp.

2308 H. D. [Hermann Deiters] Allgemeine musikalische Zeitung
5/13,14 (30.3. and 6.4.;1870) pp. 98-101, 105-07. mus.
Review.

2309 Jullien, Adolphe. "Rinaldo, cantate de Goethe, mise en musique par J. Brahms" Revue et gazette musicale de Paris

41/52 (27.12.1874) pp. 415-16. Comments on Brahms's setting of Goethe's text.
(d) i)*incorporated: Jullien. Goethe et la musique. Ses jugements, son influence, les oeuvres qu'il a inspirées. Paris: G. Fischbacher, 1880. 311 pp.
(c) i) *excerpts (in Spanish translation): España musical (Barcelona).
ii) *excerpts (in Italian translation): Gazzetta musicale di Milano.
ii) Jullien. "Johannes Brahms" in Jullien. Musiciens d'aujourd'hui. Paris: Librairie de l'Art, 1892-94. [1. serie] pp. 246-73. facsim., notes.
"I. Sa musique de chambre. Le Jugement de Schumann": pp. 246-56. Introduction to Brahms and his works, based in part on 2309.
"II. Le Requiem allemand": pp. 256-64. Performance review of Op. 45, from Revue et gazette musicale 42/13 (28.3.1875) pp. 98-100.
"III. Symphonies en ré majeur et mi mineur": pp. 264-73. Performance reviews of Opp. 73,98, source unknown.

2310 *Schwanbeck, Günter. "Die dramatische Chorkantate der Romantik in Deutschland" Phil.F. diss., Friedrich-Wilhelms-Universität Berlin, 1938. 72, [20] pp. mus.
(a) reprint: Die dramatische ... Deutschland. Düsseldorf: Dissertations-Verlag G. H. Nolte, 1938. 72, [1, 19] pp. Brahms: pp. 39-42. notes. Negative comments on the relationship between text and music in Op. 50.

See also 254, 1353C, 1359, 2206-07.

--Op. 53

2311 *Kretzschmar, Hermann. Johannes Brahms. Rhapsodie für eine Altstimme, Männerchor und Orchester. Op. 53. (Kleiner Konzertführer no. 612) Leipzig: Breitkopf & Härtel, n.d.
(d) i) see: 1353C.
ii) see: 2207.

2312 #Liebe, Annelise. "Zur Rhapsodie aus Goethes Harzreise im Winter" in Musa-Mens-Musici. Im Gedenken an Walther Vetter. Leipzig: VEB Deutscher Verlag für Musik, [1969]. pp. 233-42. mus., notes. Discusses the poem, its historical background, and its setting by Brahms.

2313 P. R. Signale für die musikalische Welt 28/22 (1.4.1870) p. 339. Review.

2314   Vulius. "Un Chef-d'oeuvre digne d'être signé par Beethoven"
       Le Courrier musical 14/12 (15.6.1911) pp. 426-29. Des-
       criptive analysis of Op. 53 to show Brahms's importance
       as a composer; points out Beethovenesque features of the
       work.

2315   *Waldrep, Alicia Gail. "Brahms: Rhapsodie Op. 53 (A Study)"
       M.Mus., thesis, University of Wisconsin-Madison, 1968.
       iii, 93 pp. mus., notes. Analysis of the music and text.
       [from Mills Music Library, University of Wisconsin-Madison]

2316   *Weber, Wilh[elm]. Rhapsodie von Brahms. (Kleiner Konzert-
       führer) Leipzig: Breitkopf & Härtel, 1907. 10 pp.

See also 254, 266, 1353C, 1359, 1372D, 2025, 2032, 2203, 2206, 2523,
2534.

--Op. 54

2317   Musical Times 16/376 (1.6.1874) p. 520. Review.

2317.5*Brahms, Johannes. Rhapsody for Contralto, Male Chorus and
       Orchestra, Op. 53. With a History of the Work, a Grapho-
       logical Introduction and a Reprint of the First Edition.
       London: Egret House, 1974. Facsimile edition of US-NYp
       manuscript.

2318   #Döhl, Friedrich. "Zum Problem der Textvertonung. Hölder-
       lins "Schicksalslied" in Vertonungen von Fröhlich, Brahms
       und Fortner" Musik im Unterricht Ausgabe B 55 (1964)
       pp. 43-46. Brahms: pp. 44-45. fig., notes. Compares
       his setting of this poem with those of Friedrich T. Fröhlich,
       and Wolfgang Fortner in his 4 Gesänge (1934).

2319   *Kretzschmar, Hermann. Johannes Brahms. Schicksalslied für
       Chor und Orchester. Op. 54. (Kleiner Konzertführer no.
       613) Leipzig: Breitkopf & Härtel, n.d.
       (d) i) see: 1353C.
          ii) see: 2207.

2320   Miller, Norbert. "Stilreinheit versus Stilvermischung. An-
       merkung zu einer Brahms-Rezension von Hermann Goetz"
       Musica (Kassel) 34/5 (9.-10.1980) pp. 457-62. Comments on
       Goetz's criticism of Op. 54.

2321   *Schuhmacher, Gerhard. "Geschichte und Möglichkeiten der
       Vertonung von Dichtungen Friedrich Hölderlins" Phil.F.
       diss., Universität des Saarlandes, 1966.
       (a) reprint: Geschichte ... Hölderlins. (Forschungs-
          beiträge zur Musikwissenschaft Bd. 18) Regensburg:

Gustav Bosse Verlag, 1967. 456, 27 pp.
"Johannes Brahms: Schicksalslied op. 54 für Chor":
pp. 170-81. facsim., mus., notes. Presents
background of work and analysis of the text's
setting.

2322 Waters, Edward N. "A Brahms Manuscript: The Schicksalslied"
Library of Congress Quarterly Journal of Acquisitions 3/3
(5.1946) pp. 14-18. facsim., notes. Describes manuscript,
discusses work's text and the problems Brahms had with
ending, as seen in the manuscript.

2323 *Weber, Wilh]elm]. Schicksalslied von Brahms. (Kleiner
Konzertführer) Leipzig: Breitkopf & Härtel, 1907. 10 pp.

See also 254, 301, 675, 994, 1344, 1353C, 1359, 1372D, 2019, 2186,
2206, 2211.c., 2219, 2395, 2410, 2450, 2523, 2534.

--Op. 55

2324 Ambros, A. W. "Das "Triumphlied" von Johannes Brahms"
Wiener Zeitung no. 284 (11.12.1872) pp. 2233-34. notes.
Presents historical background and general comments.

2325 *Gehring, Franz. "Triumphlied auf den Sieg der deutschen
Waffen. Von Johannes Brahms" Deutsche Zeitung (Wien) no.
159 (11.6.1872) Morgenblatt pp. 1+.
(d) Gehring. "Triumphlied (auf den Sieg der deutschen
Waffen) von Johannes Brahms" Allgemeine musikalische
Zeitung 7/26 (26.6.1872) cols. 409-14. mus., notes.
Descriptive analysis of Op. 55; includes discussion
of it as an example of the influence Bach and
Händel had on composers of the time.

2326 *Kalbeck, Max. "Das Triumphlied" Die Presse (Wien) (15.1.1887).

2327 *Knorr, Jwan. Johannes Brahms, Triumphlied für achtstimmigen
Chor und Orchester. Op. 55. (Der Musikführer. no. 143)
Frankfurt a.M.: Verlag von H. Bechhold, [1898]. 9 pp.
*also: Berlin: Schlesinger, n.d.
*also: Berlin: Seemann Nachf[olger]., n.d.
(a) *reprint: in 1346.

2328 Schmitz, Eugen. "Das "Triumphlied" von Brahms ..." Hochland
12/8 (Bd. 2) (5.1915) pp. 250-53. Reports on Kalbeck's
comments on this work, in 39.

2329 *Weber, Wilhelm. [Johannes Brahms. Triumphlied für achtstim-
migen Chor und Orchester (Orgel ad libitum). Op. 55.]
(Kleiner Konzertführer no. 614) Leipzig: Breitkopf &
Härtel, 1907.

2330 Weidemann, Alfred. "Unsere grossen Tonmeister als Sänger
      des Vaterlandes; I. Gluck, Mozart, Haydn, Beethoven; II.
      Weber, Loewe, Wagner, Brahms, Reger" Die Musik (Berlin)
      32/5,6 (2.,3.;1940) pp. 148-53, 185-88. Brahms: pp.
      187-88. Op. 55 as an example of a patriotic work.

See also 308, 693, 701, 702, 1097, 1351, 1353C, 1359, 1362, 1930,
2187.c., 2207, 2386, 2388, 2450.

--Op. 62

See 1339, 2018, 2025, 2192.

--Op. 74

2331 Fellinger, Imogen. "Unbekannte Korrekturen in Brahms'
      Motette "Warum ist das Licht gegeben dem Mühseligen"
      (Op. 74,I)" in Logos musicae. Festschrift für Albert Palm.
      Rüdiger Görner, ed. Wiesbaden: Franz Steiner Verlag
      GmbH, 1982. pp. 83-89. facsim., notes. Examines 2
      paste-overs in the A-Wgm manuscript; includes comments
      on the work's evolution.

2332 *Helm, Theodor. "Wiener Musikbrief: Brahms: op. 74.
      Zwei Motetten für gemischten Chor a capella" Pester Lloyd (Buda-
      pest) (12.12.1878).

See also 1344, 1353B, 2018, 2023-25, 2192, 2202, 2216-18, 2220, 2386.

--Op. 82

2333 *Kalbeck, Max. "Schillers Nänie" [Wiener] Allgemeine Zeitung
      (6.1.1882).

2334 *Weber, Wilhelm. [Johannes Brahms. Nänie für Chor und
      Orchester (Harfe ad libitum) Op. 82.] (Kleiner Konzert-
      führer no. 615) Leipzig: Breitkopf & Härtel, 1907.

2335 *Wright, Robert Earl, Jr. "Johannes Brahms's Nänie: A
      Conductor's Analysis" D.M.A. diss., University of Miami,
      1979. 109 pp. Presents historical background and analysis,
      suggestions for performance; includes comments on the re-
      lationship of Op. 82 to other choral works of Brahms with
      a similar text. [from S156]

See also 254, 675, 929, 932, 994, 1353C, 1356, 1359, 2203, 2206,
2217.5, 2410.

--Op. 89

2336   *Kalbeck, Max. "Der Parzengesang" Die Presse (Wien) (20.
       2.1883).

2337   *Ophüls, G[ustav]. Krefelder Zeitung.
       (d) #see: 1101.

2338   _____. (Gustav) "Die fünfte Strophe des "Gesangs der
       Parzen" von Goethe in der gleichnamigen Kantate Opus 89
       von Johannes Brahms" Zeitschrift für Musik 92/1 (1.1925)
       pp. 8-13. mus. Rebuttal to 1101.e.

2339   Steinhauer, C[arl]. "Ueber (sic) Johannes Brahms, mit beson-
       derer Rücksichtnahme auf dessen "Gesang der Parzen".
       Eine musik-ästhetisch-kritische Studie" Neue Musikzeitung
       5/13 2. Beilage (1.7.1884) p. 153. notes. Describes how
       to characterize this work.

See also 254, 675, 1335, 1353C, 1359, 2019, 2206, 2217.5, 2219, 2410.

--Op. 93a

See 2018, 2192.

--Op. 93b

See 1359.

--Op. 104

2340   Schenker, Heinrich. Musikalisches Wochenblatt 23/33/34-36
       (18.,25.;8 and 1.9.;1892) pp. 409-12, 425-26, 437-38. mus.
       Review.

See also 957, 959, 960, 2018, 2021, 2192, 2217.

--Op. 109

2342   #o.r. [Otto Riemer] "Im Zeichen von Reger und Brahms. Ein-
       führung zum geistlichen Konzert am Sonntag in der Peters-
       kirche" Heidelberger Tageblatt (1.7.1966) Feuilleton p. 22.
       Contrasts the choral style of both composers, with Op. 109
       as an example of Brahms's work.

2342   Stockmann, Bernhard. "Die Satztechnik in den Fest- und
       Gedenksprüchen Op. 109 von Johannes Brahms" Brahms-

Studien Bd. 3 (1979) pp. 35-45. mus., notes. An analysis focussing on the exchange between vocal parts.

See also 1344, 1359, 2018, 2025, 2202, 2209, 2216-18, 2548.

--Op. 110

See 1344, 2018, 2023-25, 2192, 2202, 2216-18, 2220, 2548.

--Op. 113

See 1348, 2020, 2193, 2349, 2548.

--Benedictus [Hofmann nr. 144]

See Missa canonica

--Brautgesang [McCorkle Anhang III nr. 12]

See 2193

--Dem Dunkeln Schoss der Heilgen Erde [Hofmann nr. 178; McCorkle WoO posthum 20]

See 2025, 2217, 2349.

--Deutsche Volkslieder für drei- und vierstimmigen Frauenchor [Hofmann nrs. 143, 145, 146, 194; McCorkle WoO posthum 36-38]

2343   Kross, Siegfried. "Brahmsiana. Der Nachlass der Schwestern Völckers" Die Musikforschung 17/2 (4.-6.1964) pp. 110-51. mus., notes. Describes the materials, gives background information on Brahms and the Hamburg Frauenchor; includes transcriptions of correspondence between Brahms and Betty and Marie Völkers (21 items, 1872-96); also includes a list of corrections made by Brahms to first editions of his works in the sisters' possession: Opp. 1-9 and 25.

See also 2193.

--Mir lächelt kein Frühling [Hofmann nr. 176; McCorkle WoO 25]

See 1348, 2217.

--Missa canonica [McCorkle WoO posthum 18]

2344   #Mies, Paul. "Gedanken zu Palestrinas Missa "ad fugam" und
        Zwei Werken von Johannes Brahms und Heinrich Lemacher"
        Musica sacra 78/11/12 (11.-12.1958) pp. 317-22. Brahms:
        pp. 321-22. notes. Comparative study of how each com-
        poser handles use of canon in a representative work:
        Palestrina Reese no. 9, Lemacher Op. 51.

--14 Deutsche Volkslieder für gemischten Chor [Hofmann nr. 127;
    McCorkle WoO 34]

2345   Plüddemann, M. "Neue Bearbeitungen alter Deutscher Volks-
        lieder" Allgemeine deutsche Musikzeitung 6/21,22 (23.,30.;
        5.;1879) pp. 166-67, 175-76. Brahms: p. 167. Review.

See also 1344, 2563.

3. Brahms's Editing and Arranging of Other Composers' Vocal Works--General

2346   Geiringer, Karl. "Zu unserer Notenbeilage" Zeitschrift für
        Musik 100/5 (5.1933) p. 465. Hofmann nr. 172; McCorkle
        Anhang Ib, nr. 1, 7: discusses Brahms's arrangements
        for the chorale "Es ist genug" as set by Bach in Cantata
        BWV 60 and Ahle.

See also 793, 879.c.

3. Brahms's Editing and Arranging of Other Composers' Vocal Works--Specific

--Ahle

See 2346

--Bach

See 793, 2346, 2448.

--Händel

See 879, 2547

--Mozart

2347   Pressel, Gustav. "Brahms' Revision des Mozart'schen Requi-
        ems" Neue Zeitschrift für Musik Bd. 73/32 (3.8.1877) pp.
        337-38. mus. Hofmann nr. 163; McCorkle Anhang VI
        nr. 7: comments on Brahms's editing of this work.

--Schubert

2348   *Jules. "Schubert-Lieder im Nachlass von Brahms. Gespräch
        mit Kammersänger Eduard Erhard" Neues Wiener Journal
        (28.3.1928).

2348.5*Schmidt, Leopold. Berliner Tageblatt.
        (a) #reprint: in Schmidt. "Brahms" in 3022. pp. 255-67.
        "Brahms als Bearbeiter": pp. 256-57. Performance
        review of Brahms's arrangement of Schubert's Op.
        24 nr. 1, D583. [Hofmann nr. 173; McCorkle
        Anhang Ia, nr. 14]

See also 61.e.i., 1365.5, 2193, 2446, 2532.

C. MISCELLANEOUS WORKS

1. Musical Works

Contains materials on music fragments and exercises.

2349   Ellinwood, Leonard. "The Brahms-Joachim Exercises in Counter-
        point" Bulletin of the American Musicological Society nos.
        11-12-13 (9.1948) pp. 50-51. Abstract: discusses the
        background of the exercises and describes Brahms's works
        that show an influence from them: the organ works and
        the vocal canons.

2350   Fischer, Georg. "Vierzehn Operntakte von Joh[annes].
        Brahms" Neue Musikzeitung 18/23 (1897) p. 283. Describes
        Brahms's writing of 14 bars to complete an aria in Schu-
        mann's Genoveva Op. 81 (Act 3, no. 14).
        (a) *reprint: Fischer. In Fischer. Kleine Blätter. Han-
            nover und Leipzig: Hahnsche Buchhandlung, n.d.
            2. vermehrte Auflage: 1916. pp. 65-66.

See also 1348, 1711, 2504.

2. Literary and Theoretical Works--General

See 2641.

2. Literary and Theoretical Works--Specific

--Des jungen Kreislers Schatzkästlein

2351   Brahms, Johannes. Des jungen Kreislers Schatzkästlein.
        Aussprüche von Dichtern, Philosophen und Künstlern.
        Zusammengetragen durch Johannes Brahms. Carl Krebs,
        ed. Berlin: Verlag der Deutschen Brahmsgesellschaft
        m.b.H., 1909. xiii, 201 pp. ind., notes. A collection
        of texts that Brahms transcribed from his favourite authors.
        (c) excerpt: "Aus "Des jungen Kreislers Schatzkästlein".
              Aussprüche ... Künstlern. Gesammelt von Johannes
              Brahms" in 3178. pp. 62-63. ill., notes.
        (e)   i) *report: Daffner, Hugo. "Eine Aphorismensammlung
              von Johannes Brahms" Königsberger allgemeine
              Zeitung no. 567 (1908).
             ii) *report: Scherber, Ferdinand. "Ein Brahms-
              Brevier" Neues Wiener Tagblatt (22.7.1906).
            iii) *report: "Eine Zitatensammlung des jungen Brahms"
              Der Bund (Bern) (9.11.1908).

2352   Geiringer, Karl. "Brahms' zweites "Schatzkästlein des jungen
        Kreisler"" Zeitschrift für Musik 100/5 (5.1933) pp. 443-46.
        Quotes passages that Brahms underlined in books from his
        personal library.

See also 2384, 2619.

--Oktaven und Quinten [McCorkle Anhang Va, nr. 6]

2353   #Brahms, Johannes. Oktaven und Quinten u.A. Aus dem
        Nachlass herausgegeben und erläutert von Heinrich Schenker.
        (Universal Edition no. 10.508) Wien: Universal-Edition,
        1933. 16 pp. facsim., notes. facsimile edition with com-
        mentary.
        (d) *Mast, P[aul]. "Brahms's Study, Octaven und Quinten
              u.A. with Schenker's Commentary Translated" M.A.
              thesis, University of Rochester (Eastman School
              of Music), 1971.
              (d) Mast, Paul. Music Forum 5 (1980) pp. 1-196.
                    facsim., mus., ind., notes. A transcrip-
                    tion of these musical examples, giving
                    sources; includes comments on the dating

of the manuscript, and on Brahms's remarks and markings therein.

See also 793, 2547.

PART V. BRAHMS THE MUSICIAN

A. GENERAL ANALYTICAL STUDIES

Contains materials which attempt to elucidate Brahms's music by studying its components, such as, harmony, rhythm, melody, and form.
General descriptive literature on overall musical style is also included
here. Analyses of individual works can be located either through
this section's cross-references, or through IV's.

Counterpoint: 2393, 2398, 2423, 2433, 2439.
Dynamics: 2370.
Form: 2354.5, 2372, 2380, 2392, 2394, 2399, 2405, 2409, 2412, 2413,
    2415, 2436.
Harmony: 2355, 2360, 2361, 2368, 2374-77, 2394, 2397, 2419, 2420,
    2423, 2440, 2443, 2444.
Melody: 2357, 2372, 2376, 2382, 2384, 2402, 2411, 2423, 2430.
Rhythm: 2356, 2357, 2375, 2376, 2381, 2414, 2423, 2442.
Style: 2354.5, 2357, 2359, 2363-66, 2371, 2373, 2375.5, 2378, 2379,
    2385, 2387, 2389, 2390, 2396, 2400, 2401, 2403, 2404, 2406, 2407,
    2421-23, 2425, 2426, 2429, 2431, 2431.5, 2432, 2435, 2437, 2441,
    2445.

2354 *Caecilia (Utrecht) [54] (15.4.1897).

2354.5*Deutsche Musiker-Zeitung (Berlin) 33 (1903).
        (a) #reprint: Koptjaew, A. "Johannes Brahms in russischer
            Beleuchtung" M. Bessmertny, translator Rheinische
            Musik- und Theaterzeitung (Köln) [4]/45 (6.11.1903)
            pp. 425-27. notes. Describes Brahms as a com-
            poser of absolute music; examines his strengths as
            a vocal composer as well as his use of form; in-
            cludes negative comments on Brahms as instrumental-
            ist.

2355 *Alden, Edgar Hiester. "The Function of Subdominant Harmony
        in the Works of Johannes Brahms" M.A. thesis, University
        of North Carolina at Chapel Hill, 1950. vi, 107 pp. mus.,
        fig., notes. A study of chordal harmony in the instrumental

works, focusing on its role in phrase structure and form.
[from Alden]

2355.5*Bennett, Joseph. Musical Times [16] (1874).

2356   Boretz, Benjamin. "Meta-variations, Part IV.: Analytic
        Fallout (I),(II)" Perspectives of New Music [11/1-2] (Fall-
        Winter 1972; Spring-Summer 1973) pp. 146-223; 156-203.
        "Example 3: The First Eighteen Measures of Brahms's
        Fourth Symphony": (II), pp. 160-66. fig., notes.
        Analytical study showing the importance of rhythm to
        total time structure.

2357   Brusatti, Otto. "Zur thematischen Arbeit bei Johannes Brahms"
        Studien zur Musikwissenschaft Bd. 31 (1980) pp. 191-205.
        mus., notes. Discusses theme as a component of style,
        with examples from Brahms's works showing various rhyth-
        mic elements.

2358   Cardus, Neville. "Brahms 1833-1897" in Cardus. Ten Com-
        posers. London: Jonathan Cape, 1945. pp. 46-62. notes.
        Pictures Brahms as a blend of classicism and romanticism;
        attacks the opinions of Brahms's work that call it austere
        or miniaturistic.
        *2. issue: 1946.
        *3. issue: 1948.
        *4. issue: 1951.
        *[Revised and Enlarged Edition:] Composers Eleven. With
            drawings by Milein Cosman. New York: G. Braziller, 1959.
            "Brahms": pp. 65-85. adds ill.
        also: London: Jonathan Cape, 1958. A Composers Eleven.
            adds ill.
            (b) German translation by Jutta and Theodor Kunst (of
                London 1958 Edition): Cardus. "Brahms 1833-1897"
                in Cardus. Sechs deutsche Romantiker. [Mit
                Nachwort von Walter Abendroth] 1. Auflage München:
                Albert Langen, Georg Müller, 1961. pp. 79-110.
                omits notes.

2359   Chantavoine, Jean. "Brahms. A propos de son centenaire
        (7 Mai 1833--7 Mai 1933)" Le Ménestrel 95/19 (12.5.1933)
        pp. 189-90. Discusses Brahms's work as absolute music:
        its style and the French reaction to it.

2360   Cone, Edward T. "Three Ways of Reading a Detective Story--
        or A Brahms Intermezzo" Georgia Review 31/3 (Fall 1977)
        pp. 554-74. Brahms: pp. 566-70. mus., notes. Describes
        how rehearing musical works results in different levels of
        understanding; analyses, as an example, the opening section
        of Op. 118 no. 1 and the resolution of its harmonic ambi-
        guities.

2361 Cuyler, Louise E. "Progressive Concepts of Pitch Relationships as Observed in the Symphonies of Brahms" in Essays on Music for Charles Warren Fox. Jerald C. Graue, ed. Introduction by Edward G. Evans, Jr. Foreword by Robert S. Freeman. Rochester: Eastman School of Music Press, 1979. pp. 164-80. mus., notes. Overall analysis of tonal and nontonal pitch organization as an aid in interpretation; includes comment on bitonalism in Op. 15 and the symphonies.

2362 Dahlhaus, Carl. "Brahms und die Idee der Kammermusik" Neue Zeitschrift für Musik 134/9 (9.1973) pp. 559-63. Discusses Schoenberg's comment on Brahms and "entwickelnde Variationen" and its use in Brahms's chamber works in general; includes discussion on Schoenberg as a follower of Brahms.
       (a) reprint: Dahlhaus. Brahms-Studien Bd. 1 (1974) pp. 45-57.

2363 Dale, B. J. "Some Aspects of the Technique of Brahms" Music Teacher 5/7 (M.S. series 18/10) (7.1926) pp. 413-15. mus., notes. Considers Brahms's style and his historical position.

2364 Dalton, Sydney. "Johannes Brahms: A Master Builder in Music" Musical America 38/2 (5.5.1923) pp. 3, 31. ill. Describes the general characteristics of Brahms's works.

2365 *Dettelbach, Hans von. "Johannes Brahms" in Dettelbach. Die inneren Mächte. Bekenntnisse und Bekenner. Salzburg: Verlag Anton Pustet, 1940. pp. 56-61. notes.
       [2. Auflage: Graz,] Salzburg, Leipzig: 1940.
       Describes the characteristics of Brahms's style.
       *? Auflage: 1943.

2366 _____. "Reife und Resignation" in Dettelbach. Breviarium musicae. Probleme, Werke, Gestalten. Darmstadt: Hermann Gentner Verlag, 1958. pp. 197-207. notes.
       2. geänderte Auflage: Dettelbach. "Johannes Brahms" in Dettelbach. Breviarium musicae. Werke, Probleme, Gestalten. Graz: Stiasny Verlag, 1967. pp. 174-89. Discusses the character of Brahms's music together with some descriptive analysis; includes comparison of Brahms to Beethoven.

2367 *Dömpke, Gustav. "Die Pflege der Brahms'schen Musik" Wiener allgemeine Zeitung (14.3.1885).

2368 *Dunsby, J[onathan]. M. "Analytical Studies of Brahms" Ph.D. diss., Music, University of Leeds, 1976. 173 pp. mus., notes.
       (d) revised as monograph reprint: Dunsby. Structural Ambiguity in Brahms: Analytical Approaches to Four Works. (Studies in British Musicology [no. 2])

Ann Arbor, Mich.: UMI Research Press, 1981.
130 pp. Examines Opp. 24, 98, 60, 119. Includes
comment about Schoenberg's opinions of Brahms.

2368.5*Engelbrecht, K. "Johannes Brahms, der Deutsche"
Deutsche Adelsblatt (Berlin) 51 (1933) p. 305.
(a) #reprint: Engelbrecht, Kurt. "Brahms der Deutsche.
Zum 100. Geburtstage des Komponisten am 7. Mai"
Schlesische Zeitung (Breslau) no. 227 (6.5.1933)
Unterhaltungsbeilage p. [1]. Discusses the Germanic
qualities of Brahms's music.

2369 *Fässler, Ewald. "Brahms und das Chiavetten-Problem".

2370 *Fellinger, Imogen. "Studien zur Dynamik in Brahms' Musik"
Phil.F. diss., Eberhard-Karls-Universität Tübingen, 1957.
v, 138 pp.
(a) reprint: Uber die Dynamik in der Musik von Johannes
Brahms. Berlin und Wunsiedel: Max Hesses Verlag,
1961. 106 pp. facsim., mus., notes. Discusses
Brahms's use of dynamic markings, and what factor
they play in his creative process as well as in his
work with pre-classical music.

2371 Fiedler, Max and Siegmund v. Hausegger. "Brahms und der
Dirigent" Die Musik (Berlin) 25/8 (5.1933) pp. 587-88.
Comments on the significance of Brahms's music, and what
it represents.
(a) reprint: in 3186.c. pp. 27-28.

2372 Frisch, Walter Miller. "Brahms's Sonata Structures and the
Principle of Developing Variation" Ph.D. diss., Music,
University of California, Berkeley, 1981. iv, [1], 317 pp.
mus., notes. Critical-analytical study of this thematic and
formal procedure in Brahms's works, traces its origins and
development through his works, to Schoenberg's theories
on it, and use of it in his music. Examples from Opp. 1,
2, 5, 8, 25, 26, 34, 43, 46, 51, 73, 78, 90, 99, 120, 121.
(d) Frisch. "Brahms, Developing Variation, and the
Schoenberg Critical Tradition" 19th Century Music
5/3 (Spring 1982) pp. 215-32. Relates Schoenberg's
views and his systematic account of the topic in
his writings; other writer's attempts at relating the
topic to Brahms's sonata forms [see 1461, 1671,
2362, 2405]; also Brahms's thoughts on the topic.

2373 *Furtwängler, Wilhelm. "Brahms Musik hat sich--" in 3123.
p. [37]. Describes the qualities of Brahms's music.

2374 *Gieseler, Walter. "Die Harmonik bei Johannes Brahms" Phil.F.
diss., Universität Göttingen, 1949. iii, 129, [14] pp.
mus., fig.

2375 Grabner, Hermann. "Das Elegische bei Brahms. Ein Beitrag zum Ausdrucksproblem der Harmonik und Rhythmik" Neue Musikzeitung 43/13 (6.4.1922) pp. 195-98. ill., mus. Analyses Brahms's works to show his musical portrayal of suffering and sorrow.

2375.5#Graf, Max. "Johannes Brahms (Geboren am 7. Mai 1833.)" Hamburger Nachrichten no. 212 (7.5.1903) Abend-Ausgabe p. 1. Describes the mixture of old and new in Brahms's music as being a reflection of his Hamburg roots.
(a) #reprint: Graf. "Johannes Brahms. Geboren am 7. Mai 1833" Breslauer Zeitung no. 316 (7.5.1903) p. [?].

2376 *Graziano, John Michael. "A Theory of Accent in Tonal Music of the Classic-Romantic Period" Ph.D. diss., [Music Theory] Yale University, 1975. 283 pp. mus., notes. Studies how accent occurs and is perceived; includes examples of melodic, harmonic and rhythmic accent from Brahms's works. [from S202]

2376.5#Gröhn, Waldemar. "Johannes Brahms. Zu seinem 25. Todestage, 3. April" Schwäbischer Merkur (Stuttgart) (29.3. 1922) p. [1]. Discusses Brahms as a composer, his historical position, and the qualities of his music; includes survey of his works.
(a) *reprint: Gröhn. Badische Landeszeitung (Karlsruhe) (3.4.1922).

2377 *Guseva, A. "Garmoniia kak faktor stilia I. Bramsa" in Problemy vysotnoi i ritmičeskoi organizacii muzyki. (Trudii Gosudarstvennyi muzykal'-pedagogičeskii institut Gresinyh [Gnessiny?]) Moskva: Gosudarstvennyi muzykal'-pedagogiceskii institut Gresinyh [Gnessiny?], 1980. mus.

2378 *Haics, Géza. "Brahms" Magyarság (Budapest) (7.5.1933). Comments on Brahms's music, its ties with Hungarian folkmusic; also discusses his Hungarian friends: Reményi, Joachim, Liszt, Hubay, and Dohnányi. [from 241]

2379 Hathaway, Thomas. "Off the Record. Chamber Music-- Part 1" The Chelsea Journal 6/1 (1.-2.1980) pp. 39-43. Brahms: pp. 41-42. ill., notes. Makes negative comments on his style.

2380 Henderson, W. J. "Music" New York Times Sunday Magazine Supplement (11.4.1897) pp. 12-13. Refutes the argument that Brahms's use of form in his music implies lack of creativity.

2381 *Hirsch, Hans. "Rhythmisch-metrische Untersuchungen zur

Variationstechnik bei Johannes Brahms" Phil.F. diss., Universität Hamburg, 1963. vi, 177 pp.
(a) *reprint: Rhythmisch-metrische ... Brahms. Hamburg: 1963 [or Freiburg i.Br.: Krause, 1963]. ill., notes.

2382   Hollander, Hans. "Die Terzformel als musikalisches Bauelement bei Brahms" NZ-Neue Zeitschrift für Musik 133/8 (8.1972) pp. 439-41. mus. Examines the use of the interval of a third as foundation for thematic development: examples presented are from Opp. 98 and 119 no. 1.

2383   *Huschke, Konrad. "Johannes Brahms und der Tanz" Pforzheimer Musik- und Sänger-Zeitung no. 7-8 (1937) pp. 5-6.

2384   "Inner Betrachtung gewidmet" Zeitschrift für Musik 89/7 (4.1922) pp. 164-65. mus. Links Des jungen Kreislers Schatzkästlein to musical processes: unity through the use of motif correlated to a Lessing quotation, Op. 73, 1st movement as example.

2385   Jacobson, Bernard. The Music of Johannes Brahms. London: Tantivy Press; Rutherford, N.J.: Fairleigh Dickinson University Press, 1977. [1-13], 14-222 pp. ill., mus., fig., ind., notes, discog. Discusses for the nonspecialist, Brahms's style, with reference to recordings that author feels best illustrate Brahms's wishes for performance.

2386   Jordahl, Robert Arnold. "A Study of the Use of the Chorale in the Works of Mendelssohn, Brahms and Reger" Ph.D. diss., Theory, University of Rochester (Eastman School of Music), 1965. iii, [4], iv, 441 pp. "Brahms": pp. 122-252. mus., fig., ind., notes. Descriptively analyses instrumental and vocal works of these 3 composers, which utilize choral melodies, with particular attention to formal treatment. Brahms's works discussed: Opp. 13, 29, 30, 55, 74, 122, Choral-Vorspiel und Fugue über 'O Traurigkeit o Herzeleid' [Hofmann nr. 131; McCorkle WoO 7]. Includes comparative harmonic tabulation for Mendelssohn's Op. 65 no. 6, Brahms's Op. 74 no. 2, and Reger's Op. 52 no. 3.

2387   Joubert, M. "The Problem of Johannes Brahms" Contemporary Review 143 (5.1933) pp. 592-98. notes. Discusses the style of Brahms's music in order to encourage appreciation of his work; includes comments on Brahms, Bruckner and Wagner.

2388   Kalbeck, Max. "Johannes Brahms, ein deutscher Musiker" Deutsches Volkstum [21]/1 (1.1919) pp. 15-18. notes. Describes the nationalistic quality of Brahms's music, as seen in Opp. 45, 55, 80.

2389   Kerper, Willem. "Brahms als componist in't algemeen" Symphonia
        16/5 (5.1933) pp. 81-82. Comments on Brahms's style;
        includes contemporary [1800's] opinions.

2390   Klein, Maria. "Die Ostermusik des Johannes Brahms (Johannes
        Brahms in meinem Leben)" Die Christliche Welt 51/6 (20.3.
        1937) cols. 243-44. Describes the qualities of Brahms's
        music, in an account of the author's regard for Brahms's
        works.

2391   Klein, Rudolf. "Rudolph Retis Erkenntnisse der thematischen
        Prozesse in der Musik" Osterreichische Musikzeitschrift
        36/9 (9.1981) pp. 465-69. fig. Uses examples from Brahms's
        Op. 90 to illustrate Reti's ideas of analysis.

2392   Korte, Werner F. Bruckner und Brahms. Die Spätromantische
        Lösung der autonomen Konzeption. Tutzing: Verlegt bei
        Hans Schneider, 1963. 136 pp. mus., notes. Examines
        how both composers treat formal music structures without
        being constrained thereby in their works.

2393   *Kratzer, Rudolf. "Die Kontrapunktik bei Johannes Brahms,
        mit besonderer Berücksichtigung der grosskontrapunktischen
        Formen" Phil.F. diss., Universität Wien, 1939. 197 pp.

2394   *Kurzweil, Fritz. "Die Harmonik als formbildendes Element
        bei Johannes Brahms. Unter besonderer Berücksichtigung
        der Sonatenform" Phil.F. diss., Universität Wien, 1938.
        135 pp.

2395   Lach, Robert. "Das Ethos in der Musik von Johannes Brahms"
        N. Simrock Jahrbuch 3 (1930-34) pp. 48-84. mus., notes.
        Defines ethos, and shows how it is achieved in Brahms's
        music; most examples taken from solo songs.

2396   Leinburg, Mathilde, Frenn v. "Brahms und sein Deutschtum
        (Zu seinen 20. Todestag am 3. April)" Münchner neueste
        Nachrichten 70/169 (3.4.1917) Abendausgabe p. 2. Describes
        the nationalistic qualities of his music.

2397   Lester, Joel. "Simultaneity Structures and Harmonic Functions
        in Tonal Music" In Theory Only 5/5 (6.1981) pp. 3-28.
        Brahms: pp. 18-25. mus. Op. 116 no. 6 used as an ex-
        ample of how analyzing music necessitates examination of
        all aspects, not merely harmony.

2397.5#Lionello, Levi. "Johannes Brahms e Bologna" Comune di
        Bologna 20 (5.1933) pp. 29-32. ill. Discusses qualities
        of his music, both in general and in terms of various musical
        works, and the musical genres; contrasts Brahms and Wag-
        ner as composers; includes comment on the Bolognese

reception of his music, local Brahms advocates, and the Brahms cult in general.

2398 *Linke, Norbert. "Die Orchesterfuge in Spätromantik und Moderne" Phil.F. diss., Universität Hamburg, 1960. 194 pp. mus.

2399 *Luithlen, Victor J. "J. Brahms' Werke in Variationenform" [Phil.F.] diss., Universität Wien, 1926.
    (a) reprint: Luithlen, Victor. "Studie zu Johannes Brahms' Werken in Variationenform" Studien zur Musikwissenschaft (Wien) Bd. 14 (1927) pp. 286-320. mus., fig., notes. Studies Brahms's use of variation format and his historical position in relation to it.
    also known as Festschrift zur Beethoven-Zentenarfeier.

2400 Mason, Daniel Gregory. "Yankee Doodle as It might have been treated by Grieg, Tschaikowsky, Brahms and Liszt. Object Studies in Musical Expression" The Outlook 100/[4] (27.1. 1912) pp. 219-28. "Second Study. Brahms and Liszt": pp. [224-28]. Brahms: pp. [224-26, 228] mus. An attempt to understand Brahms's style through this hypothetical setting.

2401 Matter, Jean. "Brahms et Fauré" Schweizersiche Musikzeitung. Revue musicale suisse 99/2 (1.2.1959) pp. 58-59. mus., notes. Compares the musical styles of these two composers.

2402 "Melody and Motif. Brahms's Practice" The Times (London) Late London Edition no. 52,266 (21.3.1952) p. 2. Brahms as a composer of melodic lines and his use of motif.

2403 *Mesnard, Léonce. "Johannes Brahms" in Mesnard. Essais de critique musicale. Hector Berlioz, Johannes Brahms. Paris: Librairie Fischbacher, 1888. iii, 83 pp.
    (a) #reprint: Mesnard. In Mesnard. Essais de critique musicale. R. Schumann.--R. Wagner. Hector Berlioz.--Johannes Brahms. Affinités musicales chez Beethoven. Sur la musique, etc., etc. (Mesnard. [Oeuvres.] III) Paris: Librairie Fischbacher, 1892. pp. 313-91. notes. Stylistic analysis.
    (d) see: 2028.

2404 *Michael, George Albert. "The Style of Brahms as Based Upon An Analysis of His Violin Sonatas" M.M. thesis, Theory, University of Rochester (Eastman School of Music), 1942. 328 pp. mus., fig. Studies Brahms's use of harmony, counterpoint, rhythm and form, as a basis for arriving at the characteristics of Brahms's compositional style. [from Sibley Music Library, Eastman School of Music]

2405 *Mitschka, Arno. "Der Sonatensatz in den Werken von Johannes
Brahms" Phil.F. diss., Johannes-Gutenberg-Universität
Mainz, 1959. 386 pp.
(a) #reprint: Der Sonatensatz ... Brahms. Gütersloh:
n.p., 1961. [2], 386, [1] pp. mus., fig., notes.
A study of all movements in sonata form within
Brahms's chamber music, symphonies and solo piano
works; includes systematic analysis. Also contains
discussion of Brahms's development of sonata form.

2405.5#Moser, Hans Joachim. "Und Johannes Brahms? Eine musikalische
Kriegsbetrachtung" Der Tag (Berlin) Ausgabe B no. 9
(12.1.1916) Illustrierter Teil pp. [1-3] [across page bottoms].
Describes Brahms as a Germanic composer and how this is
reflected in his music; includes comments on Brahms's links
with Germany.

2406 *Mrevlov, Aleksandr. "Certy pozdnego stilia Bramsa" in Tradicii
muzykal'nogo iskusstva i muzykal'naia praktica sovremennosti.
Anna Porfir'eva ed. and compiler. Leningrad: Leningrad-
skaia Gosudarstvennyi Institut teatra, muzyki i kinomato-
grafii, 1981. mus.

2407 #Müller, Konrad. "Johannes Brahms. Zu seinem 40. Todestage
am 3. April 1937" Signale für die musikalische Welt 95/12/13
(24.3.1937) pp. 185-86. Describes the qualities of Brahms's
music.

2408 #Müller-Hartmann, Robert. "Brahms" Die Musikwelt (Hamburg)
2/9 (1.6.1922) pp. 231-33 [Heft pp. 11-13]. facsim. Discusses Brahms the musician and compares him with Wagner.

2409 *Nemirovskaia, Iza. "Val's v instrumental'nyh ciklah Bramsa"
in Problemy muzykal'nogo zanra. Tat'iana Leie, ed. (Trudii
Gosudarstvennyi muzykalpedagogičeskii institut Gnesinyh
[Gnessiny?] 54) Moskva: Gosudarstvennyi muzykal-peda-
gogičeskii institut Gnesinyh [Gnessiny?], 1981. mus.

2410 Newman, Ernest. "Brahms & The Greek Spirit" Sunday Times
London Late Edition no. 6093 (21.1.1940) p. 3. Suggests
that any evoking of Grecian ideals in Opp. 54, 82, 89 is
owing to Brahms's compositional technique, rather than to
his musical score.
(a) reprint: Newman. "Brahms and The Greek Spirit"
in Newman. From The World of Music. Essays from
the 'Sunday Times'. Selected by Felix Aprahamian.
London: John Calder, 1956. pp. 142-44.
(a) *reprint: (Da Capo Press Music Reprint Series)
New York: Da Capo Press, 1978.
(d) continued: Newman. "More About Brahms" Sunday

Times London Late Edition no. 6094 (28.1.1940)
p. 4. Points out Germanic qualities in Op. 54.
(a) reprint: Newman. in 2410.a. pp. 145-47.

2411 _____. "Brahms & The Serpent - I, II" Sunday Times
London Late Edition nos. 6169,6170 (6.,13.;7.;1941) pp. 2,
2. Examines Brahms's method of continually developing
thematic material, as seen in the late piano pieces, Opp.
76, 79, 116-19.
(a) reprint: Newman. "Brahms and the Serpent I. II."
in Newman. More Essays from The World of Music.
Essays from The 'Sunday Times'. Selected by Felix
Aprahamian. London: John Calder, 1958. pp.
50-53.
(a) *reprint: New York: Da Capo Press, 1968.

2412 _____. "Brahms and The Waltz" Musical Times 57/882
(1.8.1916) pp. 359-60. mus., notes. Describes Brahms's
handling of the waltz form, through examination of Opp.
39, 52 and 65.
(a) reprint: Newman. in 2484.a. pp. 254-62. omits
mus., notes.
(a) reprint: see 2484.a.a. pp. 216-23.

2413 #Null, Edwin v. der. "Strukturelle Grundbedingungen der
Brahmsschen Sonatenexposition im Vergleich zur Klassik"
Die Musik (Berlin) 22/1 (10.1929) pp. 32-37. notes.
Brahms compared to Mozart and Beethoven.

2414 *Partridge, Eleanor. "A Study of Rhythmic Devices in Brahms"
M.A. thesis, University of Rochester (Eastman School of
Music), 1940.

2415 *Pascall, Robert. "Formal Principles in the Music of Brahms"
Ph.D. diss., Musicology, Oxford University, 1973. vi, 258
pp. mus., ind., notes. Examines 4 different principles
in relation to the musical forms in Brahms's work. [from
S202]
(d) i) Pascall. "Rumination on Brahms's Chamber Music"
Musical Times 116/1590 (8.1975) pp. 697-99. notes.
Discusses stylistic points and how Brahms's work
was influenced by models taken from Beethoven and
Schubert (Opp. 34 and 18, respectively); includes
comments on Brahms's use of melody.
(d) comment: Newbould, Brian. "Brahms and
Schubert" Musical Times 116/1592
(10.1975) p. 877. mus. Points out
links between last movement of Brahms's
Op. 34 and Schubert's D.812.
ii) Pascall. "Some Special Uses of Sonata Form by
Brahms" Soundings no. 4 (1974) pp. 58-63. notes.

Examines sonata form movements in solo instrumental, chamber and symphonic works which show interesting modifications in their development and recapitulation sections.

2416 *Pečman, R[udolf]. Brahms a Reger--predchudci novodobe hudby. Brno: Koncertni oddeleni PKO, 1974. 56 pp.

2417 *Reissmann, August. Was wird aus unserer deutschen Musik? Ein Mahnwort an der Wande des Jahrhunderts für Alle, die es angeht. Berlin: Driesner, 1897. 164 pp.

2418 *Riemann, H[ugo]. "Brahms und die Theorie der Musik. Ein Paar kleine Erinnerungen" in 2745.

2419 _____. (Hugo) "Uber einige seltsame Noten bei Brahms und anderen" Musikalisches Wochenblatt 20/27-29/30 (27.6. and 4.,18.;7.;1889) pp. 317-18, 329-31, 345-47. mus., fig. Analyzes sections from Opp. 98, 102 with their corresponding harmonic patterns.
(a) *reprint: Riemann. "Einige seltsame ... anderen" in 3019.a. pp. 109-23. omits fig., adds notes.
(a) reprint: see 3019.a.a.

2420 _____. (Hugo) "Von verdeckten Octaven und Quinten. Ein Beitrag zur Lehre vom strengen vierstimmigen Satze" Musikalisches Wochenblatt21/40-43 (25.9. and 2.,9.,16.; 10.;1890) pp. 481-83, 497-500, 513-16, 525-26. Brahms: pp. 498-500. mus. These examples are from Op. 109.
(a) reprint: Riemann. in 3019.a. pp. 220-39. Brahms: pp. 225-30.
(a) reprint: see 3019.a.a.

2421 Ronga, Luigi. "Nuovo tempo Brahmsiano" Revista musicale italiana 57/2 (4.-6.1955) pp. 99-108. notes. Discusses the qualities of Brahms's music as they relate to his time and his fellow composers.

2422 Rubinstein, Joseph. "Einige Betrachtungen über den musikalischen Styl der Gegenwart in Deutschland" Bayreuther Blätter 3/3 (3.1880) pp. 61-84. Brahms: pp. 69-78. mus., notes. Describes his musical links to Beethoven, especially as seen in Opp. 15 and 26; includes comment on Op. 45.

2423 #Saenz, Pedro. "Brahms, estilo y aspectos de su técnica" Ars. Revista de arte 17/79 (1957) pp. [62-69]. ill., mus. General remarks on Brahms's style and on his use of melodic materials, harmony, counterpoint, and rhythm.

2424 *Salmenhaara, Erkki. "Hitaan osan arvoitus" Musiikki 26/3-4 (1973).

2425   Schenker, Heinrich. "Johannes Brahms" Die Zukunft (Berlin)
       Bd. 19/[6] [(5/19)] (8.5.1897) pp. 261-65. Discusses
       Brahms the composer and the qualities of his music.

2426   #Schrenk, Walter. "Johannes Brahms. Zum 25. Todestage am
       3. April" Deutsche allgemeine Zeitung (Berlin) 61/156
       (1.4.1922) Abend-Ausgabe p. [1]. Describes the qualities
       of Brahms's music.
       (a) *reprint: Hamburger Fremdenblatt (4.1.1922).

2427   Schulze, Werne. Temporelationen im symphonischen Werk von
       Beethoven, Schubert und Brahms. (Schriften über Har-
       monik nr. 6) Bern: Kreis der Freunde um Hans Kayser,
       1981. 44 pp. Brahms: pp. 7, 12-16, 20-24. fig. Compares
       absolute and relative tempi in works of Beethoven and
       Brahms.

2428   *Stanford, Charles Villiers, Sir. Interludes. Records and
       Reflections. London: J. Murray, 1922. xi, 212 pp.
       [contains a study of Brahms's music?]
       *also: New York: E. P. Dutton and Co., 1922. 212 pp.

2429   Stefan, Paul. "Brahms" Der Merker (Wien) 3/2 (1.1912) p.
       58. A poem on the qualities of his music.

2430   Stein, Erwin. "Bemerkungen zu Brahms' Formgestaltung"
       Anbruch 15/4/5 (4./5.1933) pp. 59-61. Discusses Brahms's
       use of thematic and motivic materials using Op. 98, 1st
       movement as example.
       (b) English translation by Hans Keller: Stein. "Some
           Observations on Brahms's Shaping of Form" in Stein.
           Orpheus in New Guises. London: Rockliff, [1953].
           pp. 96-98.

2431   *Sturke, [Roland] August. "Der Stil in Johannes Brahms'
       Werken. Eine stilkritische Untersuchung seiner Klavier-,
       Kammermusik-, Chor- und Orchesterwerke" Phil.F. diss.,
       Universität Hamburg, 1932.
       (a) #reprint: Der Stil ... Orchesterwerke. Würzburg:
           Buchdruckerei Konrad Triltsch, 1932. [5], 90, 8,
           [1] pp. mus., notes. Detailed systematic analysis
           by time period; includes comment on Brahms's musi-
           cal antecedents, and his use of form.

2432   #Thoms-Paetow, Johanna. "Johannes Brahms geb[oren]. 7.
       Mai 1833 in Hamburg, gest[orben]. 3. April 1897, in Wien"
       Deutscher Glaube 4/2 (1937) pp. 182-88. Describes the
       qualities of Brahms's music and how his works reflect his
       character.

2433   *Trapp, Klaus. "Die Fuge in der deutschen Romantik von

Schubert bis Reger. Studien zu ihrer Entwicklung und
Bedeutung" Phil.F. diss., Johann Wolfgang Goethe-Universität,
1958. 334, [1] pp. mus., fig., notes.
(a) reprint: Die Fuge ... Bedeutung. [Frankfurt:
n.p., 1958]. "Johannes Brahms. 1833-1897": pp.
136-52. Detailed systematic analysis of the A flat
minor Fugue for Organ [Hofmann nr. 126; McCorkle
WoO 8] and sections of Opp. 45 and 24; includes
comments on Op. 29 and the other organ fugues.

2434   #Trautwein, S. "Brahms und der Walzer" Deutsche Zeitung
(Berlin) (2.4.1922) [2 pages]. Presents the history of
the waltz together with descriptive analysis of Brahms's
works that contain waltzes.

2435   #Tsareva, E[katerina]. "K probleme smulia(?) I. Bramsa" in
Iz istorii zarubezhnai muzyki. Sof'ia Pitina, ed. 2 vols.
Moskva: Muzyka, 1971. vol. 1, pp. 19-34. mus., notes.
Discusses Brahms's musical style.

2436   *Urbantschitsch, Viktor. "Die Sonatenform bei Brahms. Ein
Beitrag zur Geschichte der Instrumentalmusik" Universität
Wien, 1925.
(a) #reprint?: Urbantschitsch. "Die Entwicklung der
Sonatenform bei Brahms" Studien zur Musikwissenschaft (Wien) 14 (1927) pp. 265-85, XV-XVI. mus.,
notes. Traces Brahms's use of sonata form throughout his life, focusing on exposition sections.

2437   Walker, Ernest. "Brahms" Proceedings of the Musical Association. 25th Session, 1898-99. pp. 115-38. mus. Presents a critical analysis of Brahms's style; includes an overview of Brahms literature.

2438   Welti, Heinrich. "Johannes Brahms" Die Nation (Berlin) 14/28
(10.4.1897) pp. 426-27. Discusses Brahms as a composer
and how the music reflects the man; includes comments on
his historical position.

2439   *Wetschky, Jürgen. "Die Kanontechnik in der Instrumental-
musik von Johannes Brahms" Phil.F. diss., Universität
Köln, 1967.
(a) reprint: Die Kanontechnik ... Brahms. (Kölner
Beiträge zur Musikforschung Bd. 35) Regensburg:
Gustav Bosse Verlag, 1967. 298 pp. mus., notes.
A systematic analysis by canon type, by time period,
and by medium.

2440   Wetzel, [Justus] Hermann. "Zur Harmonik bei Brahms" Die
Musik (Berlin) 12/1 (Bd. 45) (10.1912) pp. 22-31. mus.
Examines his techniques, especially the use of major/minor
key, and modulation.

(c) excerpt: Wetzel, Justus Hermann. "Die Harmonik bei Brahms" Die Musik (Berlin) 25/8 (5.1933) pp. 597-99.
(a) reprint: in 3186.c. pp. 37-39.

2441 #_____. (Justus Hermann) "Johannes Brahms Werke" Musik-pädagogische Blätter 50/3 (2./3.1928) pp. 25-26. Describes the qualities of Brahms's music.

2442 Wilson, Charles. "Brahms and the Triplet" Monthly Musical Record 83/946 (5.1953) pp. 92-95. Discusses the ways that Brahms uses the triplet, with examples from the instrumental and vocal works.

2443 *Wunsiedler, Friedrich. "Liederschlüsse bei Johannes Brahms" Erlangen Universität, 1922. 157 pp.

2444 Zingerle, Hans. "Chromatische Harmonik bei Brahms und Reger. Ein Vergleich" Studien zur Musikwissenschaft Bd. 27 (1966) pp. 151-85. fig., notes. Compares harmonic technique used in the instrumental works.

2445 [Arthur Smolian] "Zur Verständigung über Johannes Brahms" Musikalisches Wochenblatt 32/34,35 (15.,22.;8.;1901) pp. 443-44, 455-56. Describes the character and quality of Brahms's music.

See also 20.d., 22, 42, 50, 58, 67, 95, 97, 115, 119, 128, 138, 145, 147, 149, 150, 154.d., 165.d.c., 166, 170, 171, 178, 189, 202, 203, 218, 219, 250, 254, 318, 404, 417, 420, 434, 435, 445.5, 488, 493, 496, 507, 514, 518, 520, 521, 528, 641, 643, 646, 660, 665, 694, 695, 746, 808, 809, 822, 967, 971, 995, 1072, 1137, 1193, 1265, 1277, 1322, 1332, 1333, 1336, 1338, 1364, 1366, 1367, 1375, 1380, 1383, 1385-87, 1390, 1391, 1393-95, 1403, 1405-07, 1411, 1414, 1416, 1418, 1423, 1425-28, 1440, 1442, 1442.5, 1444, 1445, 1447, 1452-54, 1468, 1472, 1477, 1483, 1488, 1498, 1508, 1510, 1513, 1514, 1517, 1523, 1527, 1530, 1531, 1534, 1540, 1541, 1548, 1555, 1556, 1558-60, 1565, 1567, 1571-74, 1578-80, 1584, 1585, 1588-91, 1594, 1595, 1599, 1600, 1606, 1608, 1609, 1620-23, 1629, 1630, 1635, 1636, 1639, 1640, 1642-44, 1654, 1656-59, 1662-65, 1667, 1669, 1671, 1672, 1676, 1677, 1679, 1680, 1683, 1684, 1688, 1689-95, 1698-1701, 1703, 1704, 1709, 1743, 1744, 1749, 1757, 1758, 1767, 1772, 1776, 1783, 1785, 1786, 1788, 1791, 1796, 1799, 1803, 1805, 1806, 1809, 1813, 1818, 1819, 1821, 1822, 1824-28, 1834-36, 1839, 1840, 1843, 1846, 1850, 1862, 1879, 1881, 1887, 1890.d., 1897, 1901, 1905, 1906, 1912, 1921, 1923, 1927, 1929, 1932, 1934, 1947, 1948.d., 1955, 1958, 1959, 1966, 1967, 1972, 1979, 1980, 1985, 1987, 1989, 1991, 1994, 1997, 1999, 2001, 2004, 2007, 2015, 2022, 2027, 2043, 2045-47, 2051, 2055, 2058-60, 2064, 2066, 2079, 2080, 2085-88, 2096, 2108, 2113, 2117, 2121, 2123, 2124, 2128, 2130, 2142, 2153, 2154, 2156, 2157, 2165, 2167, 2170, 2178, 2186, 2191, 2192, 2208, 2212, 2213, 2216-18, 2220, 2221, 2225, 2233,

2235, 2239, 2245, 2248, 2251, 2252, 2258, 2269, 2285, 2287, 2292,
2293, 2303, 2315, 2335, 2341, 2343, 2349, 2401, 2429, 2550, 2568,
2608, 2623, 2629, 2636, 2643, 2652, 2654, 2760, 2799, 2808, 2853,
2871, 2872, 2878, 2880, 2898, 2906, 2916, 3002, 3015, 3019.5, 3028,
3031, 3033, 3044, 3050, 3139.

See also "Composing", "Instrumentation", "Musical Mottos and Motifs",
"Texts and Text Setting" in V.B.

B. THE TECHNIQUES

Contains materials which examine Brahms's own thoughts on composing
and his application of various compositional methods; his compositional
background, use of the techniques in his own music, and in that of
other composers.

1. Arranging

2446   Einstein, Alfred. "Brahms und Wagner auf gleichen Pfaden.
        Zum 7. und 22. Mai 1933" Berliner Tageblatt 62/177 Ausgabe
        A (16.4.1933) p. [1]. mus. Compares the two composers
        as arrangers: Wagner's orchestration of Rossini's "I Mari-
        nari" [Les Soirées musicales no. 12], and Brahms's orches-
        tration of three Schubert songs. [Hofmann nr. 171; Mc-
        Corkle Anhang Ia nrs. 12, 13, 15].
        (a) reprint: Einstein. "Brahms und Wagner auf gleichen
            Pfaden" in Einstein. Von Schütz bis Hindemith.
            Essays über Musik und Musiker. Zürich/Stuttgart:
            Pan-Verlag, 1957. pp. 99-104.

2447   Feder, Georg. "Geschichte der Bearbeitungen von Bachs
        Chaconne" in Bach-Interpretationen. Martin Geck, ed.
        (Kleine Vandenhoeck-Reihe 291S) Göttingen: Vandenhoeck
        und Ruprecht, 1969. pp. 168-89. Brahms: pp. 180-81.
        Describes Brahms's arrangement for Funf Studien für
        Pianoforte nr. 5 [Hofmann nr. 130; McCorkle Anhang Ia,
        nr. 1].

2448   Jacobi, Erwin R. ""Vortrag und Besetzung Bach'scher Cantaten-
        und Oratorienmusik" Ein unbekannter Brief von Moritz
        Hauptmann an Johannes Brahms (15. February 1859)"
        Bach-Jahrbuch 55 (1969) pp. 78-86. notes. Presents
        background and provenance of letter; includes comments
        on Brahms's thoughts concerning arranging.

2449   Janetschek, Edwin. "Brahms' Bearbeitung der D-moll-Chaconne

von Joh[ann]. Seb[astian]. Bach" Zeitschrift für Musik
89/2 (21.1.1922) pp. 33-34. notes. Describes the style
and character of Brahms's setting in Funf Studien für Pianoforte nr. 5 [Hofmann nr. 130; McCorkle Anhang Ia, nr.
1].

2450 Jonas, Oswald. "Eine private Brahms-Sammlung und ihre
Bedeutung für die Brahms-Werkstatt-Erkenntnis" in Gesellschaft der Musikforschung. Bericht über den Internationalen
Musikwissenschaftlichen Kongress Kassel 1962. Georg
Reichert, Martin Just, eds. Kassel [et al.]· Bärenreiter,
1963. pp. 212-15. notes. Discusses Brahms as an arranger
of his own works: examines the manuscripts for piano
scores of Opp. 54 and 55, Opp. 52a, 65a, the viola arrangement of Op. 120, and alterations in the Deutsche Volkslieder
(1894) [Hofmann nr. 133; McCorkle WoO 33].

2451 Komaiko, Robert. "The Four-Hand Piano Arrangements of
Brahms and Their Role in the Nineteenth Century" Ph.D.
diss., Music History & Literature, Northwestern University,
1975. 2 vols. mus. [vol. 2], notes. Genre-by-genre analysis and comparison of original and 4-hand piano versions
of specific sections from Brahms's works to show changes
that Brahms made; includes a compilation of techniques
Brahms used in his arrangements, together with a survey
of his life and times.

See also 793, 794, 848, 1075.d., 1081, 1082, 1408, 1484, 1486, 1491,
1493, 1504, 1586, 1658, 1708, 1718, 1721, 1723, 1724, 1726, 1727,
1731, 1894, 2093, 2173, 2178, 2179, 2305, 2346, 2348, 2348.5, 2400.

See also "Works Catalogues and Indexes" in I.C.

2. Composing

Brahms the Progressive: 2459, 2461, 2461.5, 2463.5, 2467, 2468.5,
2469, 2469.5, 2474, 2477, 2482, 2490.5, 2491, 2493, 2501.

2452 *Berliner Tageblatt (1897).
    (e) report: "Wie Johannes Brahms seine Melodien erfand
    ..." Neue Zeitschrift für Musik 64/18 (Bd. 93)
    (5.5.1897) p. 214. Relates how Brahms said melodies
    came to him for his works.

2453 Abell, Arthur M[aynard]. "Johannes Brahms" in Abell. Talks
With Great Composers. New York: Philosophical Library,
1955. pp. 1-81. ill. Reports on a conversation with Brahms
and Joachim in the late Fall, 1896, concerning their mental
state while composing and how the creative process manifested
itself.

also: London: Spiritualist Press, [1956].
*3. Auflage: Talks ... Composers. Strauss-Brahms-Puccine-
Humperdinck-Bruch-Grieg. Garmisch-Partenkirchen: G.
E. Schroeder, [1964].
(b) German translation by Christian Dehm (of New York
Edition): Abell. "Johannes Brahms" in Abell.
Gespräche mit berühmten Komponisten. So entstan-
den ihre unsterblichen Meisterwerke. Garmisch-
Partenkirchen: G. E. Schroeder, 1962. pp. 55-
152.
*3. Auflage: Gespräche ... Komponisten. Richard
Strauss-Johannes Brahms-Puccini-Humperdinck-Max
Bruch-Edvard Grieg. Uber die Entstehung ihrer
unsterblichen Meisterwerke. Inspiration und Genius.
Jörl: G. Ewald Schroeder, 1977.
*4. Auflage: 1981.

2454 #Albrecht, Norbert. "Johannes Brahms Heute. Zum 75.
Todestag des Komponisten" Musik und Gesellschaft 22 (1972)
pp. 214-17. ill., notes. Describes influences on Brahms
the composer: folk music, Schumann, and the study of
Bach and other pre-Classical composers.

2455 Altmann, Wilhelm. "Johannes Brahms" Allgemeine Musikzeitung
60/18 (5.5.1933) pp. 249-51. Traces development of Brahms
as a composer.

2456 Antcliffe, Herbert. "The Poetic Basis of Brahms's Pianoforte
Music" Monthly Musical Record 38/449 (1.5.1908) p. 100.
Describes the sources of inspiration for these works.

2457 *Boros, Rezső. "Brahms és a többiek. (A mester művészegyéniséges viszonya a kortársakhoz és utódokhoz.)" A Zene
[15]/13-16 (1934) pp. 206-08, 229-32, 247-51. Discusses
Brahms the composer: his relationship with his contemporaries and the musical influence he has had on successive
generations of composers. [from 241]

2458 Borowski, Felix. "A Lecture on Liszt and Brahms" Musical
Courier 53/6 (8.8.1906) p. 28. A review of a lecture by
the author--compares their artistic idiosyncracies and compositional methods.

2459 Brent-Smith, A. "Johannes Brahms, 1833-1897" Musical Times
74/1080 (2.1933) pp. 113-16. Discusses Brahms's qualities
as a composer; includes comment on his historical position.

2460 Budde, Elmar. "Schönberg und Brahms" in Bericht über den
1. Kongress der Internationalen Schönberg-Gesellschaft.
Wien, 4. bis 9. Juni 1974. Rudolf Stephan, ed. (Publikationen der Internationalen Schönberg-Gesellschaft Bd. 1)

Wien: Verlag Elisabeth Lafite, 1978. pp. 20-24. notes.
Schoenberg's comments on Brahms, and what he learned
from Brahms; includes a summary of 2493.

2461   Bücken, Ernst. "Die historische Mission von Johannes Brahms"
Melos 12/8/9 (8./9.1933) pp. 281-85. mus. Examines
Brahms's musical background, affinities with his contempor-
aries, and his polarity to Wagner.

2461.5#Bürck, Alfons. "Bekenntnis zum avantgardisten Brahms"
Badisches Tagblatt (Baden-Baden) no. 134 (12.6.1968) p.
[?]. Discusses how Brahms contributed to the development
of musical language; includes comments on the Brahmshaus
in Baden-Baden.

2462   Colles, H[enry]. C[ope]. "Some English Musicians" in Colles.
Essays and Lectures. With a Memoir of the Author by
H. J. C. London, New York: Geoffrey Cumberlege, Oxford
University Press, 1945. "Brahms and Elgar": pp. 80-82.
Compares compositional methods for symphonic works.
*issue: 1947.
*also: London, New York: H. Milford, Oxford University
Press, 1945.
(a) *reprint: (of ? Edition): (Essay Index Reprint Series)
Freeport, N.Y.: Books for Libraries Press, [1970].

2463   *Eppstein, Hans. "Brahms och hans forebilder" Musikvärlden
3 (1947) pp. 200-05.

2463.5#es. [Heinrich Ehrlich] "Johannes Brahms in seinem Verhältnis
zur musikalischen Moderne" Leipziger Volkszeitung no. 211
(13.9.1909) p. [?]. Examines the qualities of Brahms's
work and his compositional techniques to understand his
link to music of the 20th century.

2464   Fellinger, Imogen. "Grundzüge Brahmsscher Musikauffassung"
in Beiträge zur Geschichte der Musikanschauung im 19.
Jahrhundert. Walter Salmen, ed. (Studien zur Musikgeschichte des 19. Jahrhunderts 1) Regensburg: Gustav
Bosse Verlag, 1965. pp. 113-26. mus., notes. Examines
Brahms's correspondence and contemporaries' comments to
discover his thoughts on what music is, and what it should
be; includes comments on his interest in older music.
*2. Auflage: 1974.

2465   Friedland, Martin. Zeitstil und Persönlichkeitsstil in den
Variationwerken der musikalischen Romantik. Zur Geistes-
geschichte und Schaffenpsychologie der Romantik. (Sammlung musikwissenschaftlicher Einzeldarstellungen. 14) Leipzig: Breitkopf & Härtel, 1930. 87, x pp. Brahms: pp.
36-40, 45-55, 73-77. mus., notes. Comparative analysis

of Op. 24, Schumann's Op. 13 and Schubert's D. 810,
2nd movement. Includes comments on Brahms and types of
variation technique he used in composing.

2466 Fry, J. "Brahms's Conception of the Scherzo in Chamber
Music" Musical Times 84/1202 (4.1943) pp. 105-07. mus.
Discusses how Brahms composed this type of movement.

2467 Furtwängler, Wilhelm. "Johannes Brahms. Ein Zeitgemässe
und notwendige Betrachtung" Allgemeine Musikzeitung
64/13/14 (26.3.1937) pp. 177-78. Discusses Brahms the
musician and composer, and his contribution to the evolution
of music.
(a) i) reprint: Furtwängler. Münchner neueste Nachrichten 90/91 (3.4.1937) p. 5.
ii) #reprint: Furtwängler. Geist der Zeit 18/5 (5.1940)
pp. 257-59.
iii) reprint: Furtwängler. "Brahms und die Krise
unserer Zeit" in 2931.a.ii. pp. 17-21.
iv) reprint: Furtwängler. "Brahms und die Krise unserer Zeit. 1934" in 2931.a.iii. pp. 86-90.

2468 [R. P. Downes] "A Great Composer. Brahms" Great Thoughts
From Master Minds 2/5th series (38) (1903) pp. 396-98.
ill. Discusses Brahms as a romantic composer as well as
the qualities of his music; includes look at his life up to
1855, together with comment on Brahms the man.

2468.5#Grebe, Karl. "Musik an der Swelle des 20. Jahrhunderts.
Vergangenheit und Zukunft in einem: Vor 125 Jahren wurde
Johannes Brahms geboren" Die Welt (Hamburg) no. 105
Feuilleton (?,7.;5.;1958) p. 9. Explains why Brahms is
a composer relevant to the current times; includes comments
and explanation on the Brahms-Wagner polarization.

2469 #Groeg, Ernst. "Die Kunst Johannes Brahms" Sozialistische
Monatshefte 7/4-8/1 (1903-04) pp. 59-69. notes. Discusses
Brahms's affinity for older music principles, Brahms as a
song composer; includes an overview of his works.

2469.5*Gui, Vittorio. Corriere d'Italia (1914).
(d) *expanded: Gui. "Brahms primo dei moderni" Il
Pianoforte [3] (1922).
(a) reprint: Gui, V. in Gui. Battute d'Aspetto.
Meditazioni di un musicista militante. Firenze:
Case editrice Monsalvato, 1944. pp. 110-22.
Discusses Brahms's links to Schumann, Wagner
and Bach; describes 20th century elements
that are found in Brahms's works, with examples mainly drawn from the symphonies.

2470 *Hanslick, Eduard. "Joh[annes]. Brahms" Neue freie Presse
      (Wien) (1862).
      (a) *reprint: Hanslick. In 2950.dB. pp. 255-58. [from
          2950.dB.a.] Describes Brahms the composer and
          pianist. [from 2950.dB.a.]
      (b) English translation by Henry Pleasants III: Hanslick.
          "Brahms[[1862]]" in Hanslick. Vienna's Golden
          Years of Music. Pleasants, ed. New York: Simon
          and Schuster, 1950. pp. 81-86. ill., notes. In-
          cludes English translation of reviews of the sym-
          phonies from 2944, 2946.
          *also: London: Victor Gollancz Ltd., 1951.
          *reissue (of New York Edition): Hanslick. Music
          Criticisms, 1846-99. Baltimore: Penguin Books,
          [1950].
          [Revised Edition (of Baltimore Edition):] (Peregrine
          Books Y32) 1963. pp. 82-87.
          (a) *reprint (of New York Edition): (Essay In-
              dex Reprint Series) Freeport, N.Y.: Books
              for Libraries Press, [1969].

2471 Hathaway, Thomas. "The Greatness of Brahms" Queen's
      Quarterly 88/4 (Winter 1981) pp. 620-31. discog. Discusses
      Brahms's success and failure as a composer.

2472 Helm, Theodor. "Johannes Brahms. Versuch einer Charakter-
      istik des Meisters aus seinem Schöpfungen" Der Klavier-
      Lehrer 2/18,19 (15.9.;1.10.;1879) pp. 209-12, 220-23.
      notes. Examines Brahms as a composer in light of 3013;
      includes comments on the qualities of his music.

2473 Hernried, Robert. "Musikertypen. (Mit einer unbekannten
      Brahms-Anekdote)" Signale für die musikalische Welt 81/36
      (5.9.1923) pp. 1285-90. Brahms: p. 1287. Relates a re-
      mark made to Heuberger on the importance of study for a
      composer, and how it is also important to put what one
      learns to practice.

2474 Heuss, Alfred. "Johannes Brahms als Hüter und Mehrer musik-
      alischen Kulturgutes" Zeitschrift für Musik 100/5 (5.1933)
      pp. 427-30. mus., notes. Discusses how Brahms used
      principles of classical music as a foundation upon which to
      build.

2475 Hill, Ralph. "Brahms and the Symphony" Hallé no. 2 (10.1946)
      pp. 15-16. Discusses Brahms's characteristics as a sym-
      phonic composer; includes comment on his classical music
      foundation.

2476 #J. F. R. [John F. Runciman] "A Note on Brahms" Saturday
      Review 83 (1.5.1897) pp. 468-70. Disparaging remarks on
      Brahms as a composer and the qualities of his music.

2477 J. G. H. [James Gibbons Huneker] "A Brahmsody" M'lle (New
      York) 1/6 (10.1895) p. [12]. ill. Describes Brahms and
      what he was attempting musically; includes comments on his
      historical position.
      (a) i) *reprint: Huneker, James Gibbons. "Brahmsody"
              in Huneker. Unicorns. New York: Charles Scrib-
              ner's Sons, 1917. pp. 106-10.
              *issues: 1921, 1924.
              *also: London: T. W. Laurie, [1918].
              (a) reprint (of New York 1917 Edition): New
                  York: AMS Press, 1976.
          ii) *reprint: Huneker, James Gibbons. "Brahmsody"
              in Backgrounds of Book Reviewing. Herbert S.
              Mallory, ed. Ann Arbor, Mich.: George Wahr, 1923.
              pp. 352-55. notes.
              Revised Edition: 1931.

2478 Joseph, Charles M. "Origins of Brahms's Structural Control"
      College Music Symposium 21/ 1 (Spring 1981) pp. 7-23.
      facsim., mus., fig., notes. Examines Brahms's use of
      formal coherence in composition, as influenced by his compo-
      sition studies; includes study of Op. 4, comment on Marxsen,
      and examination of music from all periods of Brahms's life
      to see if he applied these compositional principles.
      (d) Nisula, Eric. College Music Symposium 22/ 1 (Spring
           1982) pp. 194-95. mus. Brings forward further
           examples from Op. 4.
           (d) Joseph, Charles M. College Music Symposium
                22/1 (Spring 1982) pp. 195-96. Acknow-
                ledges Nisula's work.

2479 Kelley, Edgar Stillman. "Why Brahms Fails to Inspire Us.
      An Apology" Looker-On 3/2 (8.1896) pp. 89-101. mus.
      Comments and elaborates on 220: describes Brahms's com-
      positional faults.

2480 Mason, Daniel Gregory. "Two Tendencies in Modern Music.
      Tschaikovsky and Brahms" Atlantic Monthly 89/532 (2.1902)
      pp. 175-84. Brahms the craftsman versus Tschaikovsky
      the user of affect; compares how both composers show these
      qualities in their music.
      (e) report: Komorzynski, Egon von. "Atlantic Monthly:
           ..." Die Musik (Berlin) 1/13 (Bd. 3) (4.1902)
           pp. 1205-07.

2481 *Mencken, H[enry]. L[ouis]. Baltimore Evening Sun (2.8.1926).
      (a) i) *reprint: Mencken. "Brahms" Vossische Zeitung
              (Berlin) (21.8.1926?).
          ii) reprint: Mencken. "[Five Little Excursions.]
              1. Brahms" in Mencken. Prejudices [:] Sixth
              Series. New York: Alfred A. Knopf, 1927. pp.

163-69. mus. Discusses the superiority of Brahms
as a composer.
*also: London: J. Cape, [1928].
iii)*reprint: in Mencken. A Mencken Chrestomathy.
Edited and annotated by the Author. New York:
A. A. Knopf, 1949. pp. 532-35. mus.
*issues: 1953, [1956]. [1956 in series (Borzoi Books)]
iv) reprint: Mencken. "Brahms (1833-97)" in Mencken.
Mencken on Music. A Selection of His Writings on
Music Together with an Account of H. L. Mencken's
Musical Life and a History of The Saturday Night
Club. Louis Chedlock, ed. New York: Schirmer
Books, 1961. pp. 45-50. mus.
*First Paperback Printing: 1975.

2482   Mendl, R. W. S. "Was Brahms a Conservative?" The Chesterian 29/180 (10.1954) pp. 39-43. Gives examples of how
Brahms's work contains departures from compositional norms,
but concludes he is no revolutionary.

2483   Mersmann, Hans. "Johannes Brahms. On the 125th Anniversary
of the German Composer--1833/1897" Canon 11/11 (6.1958)
pp. 333-36. ill. Discusses Brahms the musician, his
place in the Romantic period, and thereafter; includes comments on his links to music of the past.
(d) i) #Mersmann. "Johannes Brahms" Arte musical
(Lisbon) 28/8 (1959) pp. 213-15.
ii) Mersmann. "Johannes Brahms und sein Werk" Universitas 13/9 (9.1958) pp. 947-54.
(a) *reprint: in Mersmann. Lebensraum der Musik.
Aufsätze--Ansprachen. (Kontrapunkte:
Schriften zur deutschen Musik der Gegenwart.
Bd. 7) Rodenkirchen/Rhein: P. J. Tonger,
[1964]. pp. 83-89.

2484   *Newman, Ernest. Birmingham Post.
(a) reprint: Newman. ""Professionalism" in Composition"
in Newman. A Musical Motley. London: John
Lane, The Bodley Head Limited, [1919]. pp. 248-
53. Discusses Brahms as a composer who uses
craftsmanship for skills' sake, and not for expressiveness.
*issues: 1920, 1923.
*also: London: John Lane, The Bodley Head Limited;
New York: John Lane Company, 1919.
*issues: 1920, 1923.
[American Edition:] New York: Alfred A. Knopf,
1925. Includes text changes and revision. [from
2484.a.]
(a) reprint (of American Edition): (Da Capo Press
Music Reprint Series) New York: Da
Capo Press, 1976. pp. 210-15.

2485   Orel, Alfred. "Johannes Brahms. Das Leben im Werk" in
        Orel. Aufsätze und Vorträge. Wien-Berlin: Verlag für
        Wirtschaft und Kultur, Payer & Co., [1939]. pp. 126-35.
        Surveys Brahms's life as seen through his composing acti-
        vities.

2486   Parry, C[harles]. Hubert H[astings]., Sir. "Johannes
        Brahms, 1897" in Parry. College Addresses. Edited with
        a Recollection of the Author by H[enry]. C[ope]. Colles.
        London: Macmillan & Co., Ltd., 1920. pp. 44-48. Dis-
        cusses Brahms as an example of what to strive for as a
        composer.
        (c) *excerpt: in 2915. pp. 280-82.

2487   #Pfohl, Ferdinand. "Johannes Brahms" Die Musikwelt (Hamburg)
        2/9 (1.6.1922) pp. 221-26 [Heft pp. [1]-6]. ill. Describes
        Brahms's artistic destiny as evidence in his youth; includes
        comments on his style, Wagner's comments on him, and views
        of his historical position.

2488   Piguet, J[ean].-Claude. "Brahms et Fauré" Schweiz[erische].
        Musikzeitung. Revue musicale suisse 91/4 (1.4.1951) pp.
        143-47. mus. Compares how both composers approach com-
        position.

2489   Piovesan, Alessandro. "Ritratto di Brahms" La Rassegna
        musicale 13/5 (21 di Il Pianoforte) (5.1940) pp. 227-36.
        Compares Brahms as a composer, to other romantic compo-
        sers.

2490   *Popdimitrov, Karen and Slavčo Božinov. Solfeži iz tvorčestvoto
        na kompozitorite romantici. Subert, Suman, Mendelson,
        Brams. sus. 2 izd. Sofija: Nauka i izkustvo, 1962. 158
        pp. mus.

2490.5*Reich, Willi. "Grenzgebiete des neuen Tons" Die Musik (Ber-
        lin) 25/2 (1932). Discusses Brahms as a precursor to the
        new music of the 20th century. [from 2783.d.]
        (d) see: 2783.

2491   Rosenberg, Wolf. "Die Theorien im Lichte der Praxis" in
        Herausforderung Schönberg. Was die Musik des Jahrhun-
        derts veränderte. Ulrich Dibelius, ed. (Reihe Hanser 166)
        München: Carl Hanser Verlag, 1974. pp. 47-61. Brahms:
        pp. 53-56. notes. Expresses reservations on how Schoen-
        berg really viewed Brahms as a composer.

2492   Schlang, Wilhelm. "Johannes Brahms" Neue Musikzeitung
        18/9 (1897) Beilage p. 117. notes. Traces Brahms's compo-
        sitional development as prophesized by Schumann in 3013.

2493 Schoenberg, Arnold. "Brahms the Progressive" in Schoenberg.
Style and Idea. [Dika Newlin, ed.] New York: Philosophical Library, 1950. pp. 52-101. mus., notes. Discusses
how Brahms contributed to the development of musical
language: examines Op. 51 no. 2, 2nd movement, and Op.
121 no. 3, focusing on motivic elaboration, internal organization, and harmonic structure.
*also: London: Williams and Norgate, [1951].
(a) reprint (of ? Edition): Schoenberg. In Schoenberg.
Style and Idea. Selected Writings of Arnold
Schoenberg. Leonard Stein, ed. Leo Black, translator. London: Faber & Faber, 1975. pp. 398-441.
*also: New York: St. Martins Press, 1975.
(b) i)*Czech translation (of ? Edition): Schönberg,
Arnold. "Pokrokový Brahms" Hudebnî rozhledy
23/10-11 (1970) pp. 474-90.
ii) German translation (of ? Edition): Schönberg,
Arnold. "Brahms, der Fortschrittliche" in Schönberg. Stil und Gedanke. Aufsätze zur Musik. Ivan
Vojtěch, ed. (Arnold Schönberg. Gesammelte
Schriften 1) [Frankfurt a.M.:] S. Fischer Verlag,
1976. pp. 35-71.
iii) *Italian translation by Maria Giovanni Moretti and
Luigi Pestalozza (of ? Edition): in Schoenberg.
Stile e idea. Con un saggio introduttivo e a cura
di Luigi Pestalozza. Preface di Luigi Rognoni.
(Le Poetiche) Milano: Rusconi e Paolazzi, [1960].
iv)*Spanish translation by Juan J. Esteve (of ? Edition):
in Schoenberg. El estilo y la idea. Introducción
de Ramon Barce. (Ser y tiempo, 33) Madrid:
Taurus, [1963].

2494 #Siegmund-Schultze, Walther. "Grosse Musik vor hundert
Jahren. (Wagner-Verdi-Brahms-Tschaikowski.) Funktion,
Aussage, Weiterwirkung" Musik in der Schule 25/7/8
(7./8.1974) pp. 298, 311-17. Brahms: pp. 313-17. mus.
Juxtaposes the compositional style of these four composers
against their time, focuses on Wagner and Brahms.

2495 Slonimsky, Nicolas. "Musical Oddities" Etude 71/6 (6.1953)
pp. 4-5. Brahms: p. 5. Describes time of day when inspiration for a composition strikes.

2496 Sollertinskii, I[van]. I[vanovich]. "Brahms" [Ilse Filter,
translator] Aufbau. Kulturpolitische Monatsschrift mit
literarischen Beiträgen (Berlin) 4/1 (1.1948) pp. 12-17.
notes. Analyzes Brahms the composer, focusing on the
symphonic works; includes comment on his historical position.

2497 *Spark, Frederick Robert and Joseph Bennett. History of the
Leeds Musical Festivals, 1858-1889. Leeds: F. R. Spark

& Son, 1892. viii, 407 pp. ill., facsim., mus.
*2nd Edition: 1892.
    (e) report (on 2nd Edition): ""If, however, the charm of
        novelty be an absolute necessity ... distinction."
        ... " Musical Times 33/[594] (1.8.1892) pp. 467-
        68. Brahms declining an invitation to write a new
        work for the Festival, together with his reasons.

2498   Steinhard, Erich. "Brahms. Zum 40. Todestag" Der Auftakt
        17 (1938) pp. 197-98. Discusses Brahms the musician and
        his historical position.

2499   *Suzuki, Kenneth Hisao. "Brahms' Use of Pre-Existent Material"
        Ph.D. diss., Yale University, in progress.

2500   Terenzio, Vincenzo. "J[ohannes]. Brahms poeta intimista"
        in Terenzio. Da Bach a Debussy. Studi critici. Bari:
        Gius. Laterza & Figli, 1947. pp. 178-92. notes. Discusses
        Brahms the musician and his style; includes an overview of
        his works.

2501   #Truding, Lona. ""Der Einsame im Herbst"" Das Goetheanum
        36 (1957) pp. 364-66. Discusses the significance of Brahms
        for music of the 20th century.

2502   Turner, W. J. "The Difficulty of Being Great" New Statesman
        30/761 (26.11.1927) pp. 205-06. Brahms: p. 206. Des-
        cribes Brahms as a craftsman with no intellectual power.

2503   Van Cleve, John S. "The Influence of Brahms" in "Johannes
        Brahms (The New Education--The Mastery of Teaching
        Material)" Musician (Philadelphia) 3/5 (5.1898) pp. 127-28.
        Examines Brahms's influence as seen in his skills as a com-
        poser.

2504   *Vetter, Isolde. "Der Austausch von Kompositionsstudien
        zwischen Johannes Brahms und Joseph Joachim" Phil.F.
        diss., Universität Berlin, in progress.

2505   Vogel, Bernhard. "Johannes Brahms" Illustrirte Zeitung
        (Leipzig) Bd. 80/2080 (12.5.1883) pp. 403-04. ill. Looks
        at the kind of composer Brahms is from the point of view
        of 3013; includes a survey of his works to date.

2506   _____. "Zu Johannes Brahms' 60. Geburtstage" Illustrirte
        Zeitung (Leipzig) Bd. 100/2601 (6.5.1893) p. 478. ill.
        [on issue cover] Evaluates Brahms as a composer.

2507   W. S. B. M[athews]. "Johannes Brahms" Music (Chicago)
        7/6 (4.1895) pp. 594-604. Examines Brahms as a composer
        from a historical point of view.

2508 *[H. Lamberg] "Die Zeit der künstlerischen Entscheidung bei
Johannes Brahms" Schweizerische Instrumentalmusik. L'Instrumental suisse. Istrumentale svizzero (Luzern) 26/7,9
(1937) pp. 150-51, 197.

See also 1, 5.d., 18, 20, 25, 26, 27.d., 33, 39, 40, 44, 45, 50, 55,
58, 70, 73, 76.d., 81, 85-87, 95-97, 102, 107, 107.5, 108, 111, 117,
121, 136, 149.d., 153, 165, 174, 213, 254, 313, 380, 413, 433, 436,
437, 445.5, 457, 471, 488, 493, 494, 497, 515, 518, 638, 645, 654,
670, 675, 680, 694, 696, 744, 755, 764, 768, 791, 793, 794, 805, 807,
808, 813, 848, 854, 855, 860, 862, 863, 866, 878, 902, 979, 986.d.,
995, 1024, 1063, 1071, 1093, 1118, 1119, 1147, 1150, 1199, 1253-55,
1258, 1260, 1278, 1310, 1311, 1320, 1322, 1337, 1338, 1341, 1348,
1369, 1380, 1386, 1387, 1404, 1405, 1410, 1419, 1422, 1426-28, 1435,
1442, 1446, 1447, 1465, 1467, 1478, 1479, 1482, 1483, 1485, 1534,
1547, 1550, 1586, 1590, 1593, 1601, 1635, 1683, 1688, 1698, 1748.d.,
1750, 1767, 1767.5, 1788, 1789, 1798, 1803, 1807, 1809, 1811, 1814,
1829, 1836, 1841, 1845, 1847, 1850, 1852, 1890, 1898, 1909, 1933,
1941, 1950, 1970, 1987, 1989, 2022, 2040, 2042, 2047, 2048, 2061,
2063, 2064, 2066, 2068, 2080, 2082, 2096, 2098, 2102, 2103, 2128,
2135, 2142, 2187, 2195, 2200, 2209, 2210, 2216, 2247, 2342, 2372,
2376.5, 2392, 2404, 2405.5, 2410, 2423, 2438, 2440, 2575, 2576, 2578,
2579, 2581, 2607, 2633.5, 2634, 2636, 2642, 2647, 2654, 2658, 2663,
2804, 2810.5, 2812, 2821, 2825, 2832, 2833, 2839, 2845, 2849, 2854,
2860, 2880, 2884, 2902, 2913, 2931, 2934, 2937, 2968, 2977, 2998,
3032, 3041, 3126.

See also II.B.; "Musical Mottos and Motifs" and "Texts and Text
Setting" in V.B.; and "Creative Process" in V.C.

3. Editing

See 793, 879, 1122.e.iv., 1674.

See "Brahms's Editing and Arranging ..." sections in IV.; and "Music
Previous to the Classical Period" in VI.A.

4. Instrumentation

2509 Anderson, John D[rummond]. "Brass Scoring Techniques in
the Symphonies of Mozart, Beethoven and Brahms" Ph.D.
diss., Music, George Peabody College for Teachers, 1960.
ix, 376 pp. "Brass Writing in Brahms's Symphonies": pp.
172-286. mus., fig., notes. A systematic analysis to trace
the development of a compositional style for brass instruments.

2510 *Feiertag, Hans. "Das orchestrale Klangbild in Brahms' Or-
chester-Werken" diss., Universität Wien, 1938. iii, 125 pp.
facsim.

2511 H. C. C. [Henry Cope Colles] "The Colour in Brahms" Academy
[71]/1798 (20.10.1906) pp. 401-02. General comments on
scoring in orchestral and chamber works.

2512 Holle, Hugo. "Max Regers Einzeichnungen in den Symphonien
von Johannes Brahms" Almanach der deutschen Musikbücherei
(Regensburg) (1924/25) pp. 145-58. mus., notes. Compares changes Reger made in his own scores for these
works with Brahms's original scoring; includes comments
on Reger's changes to Brahms's expressive markings.

2513 *Mies, Paul. In [Beethovensche Materiale und Untersuchungen.
Moskau: 1971.]
(a) reprint: Mies. "Die Bedeutung der Pauke in den Werken Ludwig van Beethovens" Beethoven-Jahrbuch
(1971/72) pp. 49-71. Brahms: p. 68. How Brahms
viewed Beethoven's use of drums, and how Brahms
used them in his own works.

2514 "The Mind's Ear" Etude 62/8 (8.1944) pp. 435, 478. Brahms:
p. 435. ill., mus. Discusses listening to music in one's
mind, with Op. 98, 2nd movement as an example.

2515 *Scutiero, Amedeo. "Su alcuni aspetti dell'uso del corno dal
'700 fino a Debussy" Tesi di laurei in storia della musica,
Facoltà di lettere, Università degli studi di Roma, 1978-79.
152 pp. "L'Uso del corno in alcune coposizioni di Brahms":
pp. 96-105. [from Biblioteca universitaria Alessandrina-
Roma]
(d) Scutiero. "Sull'uso del corno dal '700 a Debussy"
Nuova rivista musicale italiana (Roma) 14/3 (9.1980)
pp. 350-67. Brahms: p. 363. Discusses Brahms's
use of the horn, focusing on Op. 40.

2516 *Seiffert, Stephen Lyons. "Johannes Brahms and the French
Horn" D.M.A. thesis, Performance and Pedagogy, University
of Rochester (Eastman School of Music), 1969. 227
pp. ill., mus., notes. Analyzes Brahms's horn parts;
includes comments on contemporary horns and their usage.
[from S202]

2517 "Den Spielern von Brahms' Horntrio Op. 40 zur Nachachtung
..." Neue Zeitschrift für Musik 73/29/30 (Bd. 102) (25.7.
1906) p. 626. From 887: Brahms commenting to Max Brode
on how the sound of a natural horn compares to a valved
horn.

2518 Tenschert, Roland. "Zur Frage der Brahmsschen Instrumentation" Allgemeine Musikzeitung 64/13/14 (26.3.1937) pp. 182-
83. Examines Brahms's preference for individual instrument
color, rather than total orchestral color; also its parallel

in his appreciation for the visual arts, especially the work of Klinger.
(d) Tenschert. "Die Klangwelt von Johannes Brahms" Osterreichische Musikzeitschrift 6/11/12 (11.-12.1951) pp. 307-10.
(e) report: Babel. "Brahms and Max Klinger" Musical Times 93/1310 (4.1952) pp. 176-77.

2519 #Weingartner, Felix. "Brahms, ein Meister der Instrumentationskunst" Allgemeine Musikzeitung 32/1 (6.1.1905) pp. 5-8.
Refutes the argument that Brahms is poor at instrumentation.
(b) i)*English translation: Weingartner. "Brahms, a Master of Instrumentation" New Music and Church Music Review 4/40 (3.1905) pp. 137-40.
ii) *Russian translation: Weingartner. Russkaia muzykal'naia gazeta 12 (1905).
(d) *reworked: Weingartner. In Weingartner. Akkorde. Gesammelte Aufsätze. (Breitkopf & Härtels Musikbücher) Leipzig: Breitkopf & Härtel, 1912. pp. 145-54.
(a) reprint: Walluf-Nendeln: Sändig, 1977. Series omitted.
(e) report: R. S. "M. Felix Weingartner et Johannès Brahms" Le Guide musical (Bruxelles) 51/18 (30. 4.1905) pp. 353-54.

2520 *Wetz, R. "Instrumentation Brahms" Das Orchester (Berlin) 10 (1933) p. 33.

See also 254, 534.c., 1094, 1504, 1543, 1749, 1788, 1803, 1807, 1821, 1822, 1836, 1848, 1869, 1885, 1894, 1979, 2247, 2455, 2647.

See also "Op. 40" in IV.A.1.a. Specific Works.

5. Musical Mottos and Motifs

2521 *Fellinger, Richard. "Zu Mozarts "Lieblingsmotiv"" Mitteilungen für die Mozart-Gemeinde in Berlin no. 39/3 (2.1921) pp. 18-19.
(d) *Malsch, K. "Zu Mozarts Lieblingsmotiv" Mitteilungen für die Mozart-Gemeinde in Berlin no. 39/4 (4.1921) pp. 30-31.

2522 Heuss, Alfred. "Eine Händel-Beethoven-Brahms-Parallele" Die Musik (Berlin) 7/21 (Bd. 28) (8.1908) pp. 147-51. mus., notes. Points out a common motif while comparing compositional technique in Händel's Messiah, Beethoven's Op. 106, and Brahms's Op. 98.

2523   King, A. H. "A Favourite Theme of Mozart and Brahms"
       Musical Opinion 63/753 (6.1940) pp. 389-90. The theme
       discussed is first 4 notes of last movement, Symphony no.
       41, Mozart K. 551. Traces occurrences of motto prior to
       Mozart, other occurrences in Mozart's music, and uses by
       Brahms in his vocal and instrumental works.

2524   Musgrave, Michael [Graham]. "Frei aber Froh: A Reconsidera-
       tion" 19th Century Music 3/3 (3.1980) pp. 251-58. mus.,
       notes. Discusses the circumstances behind Kalbeck's linking
       of the F-A-F motto to Brahms.

2525   Sams, Eric. "Brahms and his Clara Themes" Musical Times
       112/1539 (5.1971) pp. 432-34. ill., mus., notes. Describes
       how Brahms borrowed the idea of alluding musically to Clara
       Schumann from Robert Schumann and used C-(L)-A-(R)-A
       motif in his Opp. 8 and 60; includes comment on the rela-
       tionship between Brahms and Clara Schumann.

2526   Sams, Eric. "Brahms and his Musical Love Letters" Musical
       Times 112/1538 (4.1971) pp. 329-30. mus., notes. Traces
       the use of the motif A-G-A-D-H-E in Opp. 14, 19, 36, 44
       as a message to Agathe von Siebold.

2527   "Schumann and the Cipher. Letters and Comments." Musical
       Times 106/1472 (10.1965) pp. 767-71. In relation to Eric
       Sams. "Did Schumann Use Ciphers?" Musical Times 106/
       1470 (8.1965) pp. 584-91.
       Boyd, Malcolm. "Schumann and Brahms": pp. 770-71.
       Speculates on how Brahms learned about cipher technique
       from Schumann, and examines Op. 68 showing how use of
       technique reveals Brahms's feelings toward Clara Schumann.

See also 1886, 1891, 1904, 1961.

See also "Allusions" in V.D.

6. Texts and Text Settings

Includes materials that discuss the texts Brahms used in his vocal
works.

2528   B. R. "Das malerische Element in den Liedern von Johannes
       Brahms" Neue Musikzeitung 20/3-5 (1899) pp. 31-32, 44-45,
       57-58. Discusses word painting in Brahms's solo songs.

2529   Bernet Kempers, Karel Philippus. "Die "Emanzipation des
       Fleisches" in den Liedern von Johannes Brahms" Studien

zur Musikwissenschaft 25 (1962) pp. 28-30. notes.
also known as Festschrift für Erich Schenk.
Describes how Brahms picked song texts that portray Love
in a realistic manner, in contrast to the Romantic period's
ideal of Love.

2530 Brody, Elaine and Robert A. Fowkes. "Minor Poems and Major
Lieder" in Brody and Fowkes. The German Lied and Its
Poetry. New York: New York University Press, 1971.
pp. 225-50. Reviews the synthesis of music and poem in
Brahms's songs: arrangement is by poet, with literary
and musical comment on the setting, together with note of
any textual changes in Brahms's settings. Includes comments on songs from Opp. 19 (Uhland); 32 (Daumer); 43
(Folk text, Hölty); 49 (Folk text); 63 (Groth); 84 (Folk
text); 86 (Storm, von Schenkendorf); 96 (Heine); 106
(Kugler).

2531 Eaglefield Hull, A. "Brahms and His Poets" Musical Opinion
and Music Trade Review 49/578 (11.1925) pp. 153-54. A
list of poets and Brahms's settings of their texts; includes
comments on the poetic influence on Brahms's instrumental
music, and on Brahms's use of Biblical and folk texts.

2532 Fiske, Roger. "Brahms and Scotland" Musical Times 109/1510
(12.1968) pp. 1106-07, 1109-11. ill., mus. Discusses
Brahms and Scottish poetry: his acquaintance with it, how
it inspired him in Opp. 1, 10, 117, his settings in Opp. 14,
17, 42, 75 and his arrangement of Schubert's D.838 [Hof-
mann nr. 170; McCorkle Anhang Ia nr. 17].

2533 Gerber, Rudolf. "Formprobleme im Brahmsschen Lied" Jahrbuch
der Musikbibliothek Peters 39 (1932) pp. 23-42. mus.,
fig., notes. Presents examples of poem's form determining
a song's setting.

2534 Hayes, Deborah. "Brahms on Destiny" Choral Journal 14/3
(11.1973) pp. 23-25. notes. An investigation of the text
sources for Opp. 53 and 54, together with circumstances
behind their composition.

2535 Hirshowitz, Betty. "Ha tanach biyitzirot Johannes Brahms"
[The Old Testament in the Works of Johannes Brahms
(Hamburg 1933-Vienna 1897)] Tatzlil no. 18 (1978) pp. 70-
72. Notes references to Biblical texts in Brahms's works.
Hebrew and English text.

2536 Ivey, Donald. "Johannes Brahms" in Ivey. Song. Anatomy,
Imagery and Styles. New York: The Free Press; London:
Collier-Macmillan Limited, 1970. pp. 204-09. ind. Examines
text setting and the relationship between vocal line and
accompaniment as a component of song style.

2537 *Mies, Paul. "Chortexte bei Schubert, Cornelius und Brahms.
      Eine statistischstilistische Betrachtung" Jahrbuch des deut-
      schen Sängerbundes (1928) pp. 98-102.

2538 _____. "Die Tonmalerei in den Brahmsschen Werken. Ein
      Beitrag zum Persönlichkeitsstil" Die Musik (Berlin) 16/3
      (12.1923) pp. 184-88. notes. Describes word painting in
      Brahms's songs.

2539 Motte, Diether de la. "Sondern der Geist selbst. Anmerkungen
      zu Bachs Motette "Der Geist hilft unser Schwachheit auf""
      Musica (Kassel) 28/3 (5.-6.1974) pp. 235-38. mus. Ex-
      amines musical portrayals of the Holy Spirit: compares
      Bach's BWV 226, Haydn's HXXI:2, and Brahms's Op. 45.

2540 *Ophüls, G[ustav], ed. Brahms-Texte. Vollständige Sammlung
      der von Johannes Brahms componirten und musikalisch
      bearbeiteten Dichtungen. Berlin: N. Simrock, 1898.
      viii, 527 pp.
      2., durchgesehene Auflage: Berlin: Verlag der Deutschen
      Brahms-Gesellschaft m.b.H., 1908. viii, 406 pp. ind.,
      notes. Includes background information on poets and poems.
      *3., durchgesehene Auflage: 1923.
      (e) report (on 1898 Auflage): see 618.a.e.ii.

2541 Stein, Jack M. "Johannes Brahms" in Stein. Poem and Music
      in the German Lied from Gluck to Hugo Wolf. Cambridge:
      Harvard University Press, 1971. pp. 129-54, 157-60. mus.,
      notes. Analyzes Brahms's settings of various poets' works;
      includes a comparison of Wolf's and Brahms's setting of "An
      eine Aolsharfe" [Wolf. Gedichte von Eduard Mörike. no.
      11; Brahms Op. 19 no. 5]

2542 Stohrer, Sister Mary Baptist, O. P. "The Selection and Setting
      of Poetry in the Solo Songs of Johannes Brahms" Ph.D.
      diss., Music, University of Wisconsin, 1974. v, 241 pp.
      mus., notes. Investigates how Brahms effected a synthesis
      of music and poetry through choice of text and through
      musical interpretation. Includes comparisons of settings
      of poems similar in nature.

2543 Thiessen, Karl. "Johannes Brahms und Hugo Wolf als Lieder-
      komponisten. Eine vergleichende Studie" Neue Musikzeitung
      27/7 (4.1.1906) pp. 145-49. mus., notes. Compares how
      the two composers set texts to music.

2544 Thomas-San-Galli, Wolfgang A[lexander]. "Brahms als Lyriker"
      in Thomas-San-Galli. Musikalische Essays. [(Bibliothek
      der Gesamt-Litteratur des Ins- und Auslandes 2113-2116)]
      Halle a.S.: Verlag von Otto Hendel, [1909?]. pp. 13-22.
      Discusses Brahms's setting of texts and Brahms as a com-
      poser of vocal line. Includes 1416.

See also 570, 652, 1686, 2035.d., 2038, 2040, 2042, 2052, 2054, 2064,
2066, 2067, 2070, 2072, 2073, 2085, 2086, 2091, 2092, 2094, 2101,
2103, 2105, 2112-15, 2117, 2129, 2132, 2135, 2142, 2146, 2148, 2152,
2156, 2157, 2167, 2171, 2180, 2217, 2245, 2251, 2309, 2310, 2312,
2318, 2321, 2335, 2354.5, 2541, 2543, 2560, 2561, 2563, 2633.5.
See also individual poets in III.B.2.; "Des Jungen Kreislers Schatzkästlein" in IV.C.2.; "Text Translations" in VI.A.; and "Brahms
and Literature" and "Religion" in VI.B.

C. MUSICAL EVOLUTION

Contains materials which examine the various stages of the compositional process.

1. Creative Process

2545   Altmann, Wilhelm. "Originalhandschrift oder Erstdruck?" All-
       gemeine Musikzeitung 56/11 (15.3.1929) p. 254. On the
       merits of these two types of sources in reflecting a com-
       poser's intentions, Brahms's Op. 5 mentioned as an example.
       (d) Altmann. "Ist die Originalhandschrift oder der Erst-
              druck massgebend? Mit Bezug auf Brahms" All-
              gemeine Musikzeitung 67/30/31 (26.7.1940) pp. 243-
              44. notes.

2546   Jonas, Oswald. "Adventures with Manuscripts" Notes 2nd
       series 3/2 (3.1946) pp. 135-45. Brahms: pp. 135,139,144.
       mus., notes. Why one should study manuscripts to discover
       a composer's intent: comments on Opp. 24, 51 and 117.

2547   _____. "Brahmsiana" Die Musikforschung 11/3 (7.-9.1958)
       pp. 286-93. facsim., mus., notes. Examines Brahms's
       corrections on his manuscripts, with examples from Opp.
       26, 79, 83, 94, 121, Händel Vocal Duets [Hofmann nrs.
       165, 197, 198; McCorkle Anhang Ia nrs. 10, 11], Oktaven
       und Quinten u.A., Deutsche Volkslieder (1894) [Hofmann
       nr. 133; McCorkle WoO 33].

2548   Mies, Paul. "Aus Brahms' Werkstatt. Vom Entstehen und
       Werden der Werke bei Brahms" N. Simrock Jahrbuch 1
       (1928) pp. 42-63. facsim., mus., notes. Describes a
       collection of Brahms's sketches at A-Wgm which includes
       materials for Opp. 45, 52, 56, 58, 63, 65, 81, 113, 109-10,
       117, 120-21.

2549   _____. "Der kritische Rat der Freunde und die Veröffent-
       lichung der Werke bei Brahms. Eine Untersuchung aus

dem Briefwechsel" N. Simrock Jahrbuch 2 (1929) pp. 64-83.
ill., mus., notes. Describes how Brahms asked his friends
for comments on work in progress, and how he altered
works upon receiving their advice; with examples from correspondence [848, 892, 920, 954, 983, 1009, 1062, 1122,
1179, 1203, 1204, 1215, 1297, 1314].

2550   Van der Elst, Nancy. "Melodische merkwaardigheden bij
        Brahms" Mens en melodie 4/12 (12.1949) pp. 384-85.
        Remarks on Brahms's friends who offered him opinions on
        his music; includes comments on his melodic style.

See also 24, 276, 304, 765.d.e., 984, 1092, 1093, 1380, 1397, 1415,
1442, 1465, 1467, 1482, 1484, 1485, 1496, 1586, 1634, 1639, 1683,
1727, 1773, 1791, 1829, 1866, 1867, 1890, 1898, 1899, 1935, 1939,
1942, 1945, 1948, 2040, 2128, 2135, 2145, 2200, 2237, 2305, 2322,
2331, 2343, 2349, 2370, 2372, 2450, 2451, 2595, 3050.

See also "Textual Criticism" in I.C.4.; and "Composing" in V.B.

D. MUSICAL INFLUENCES

1. Allusions

Contains materials which point out similarities in musical text between
Brahms's works and those of his predecessors, contemporaries or
successors.

2551   Chapman, Louis. "The Brahms Horn Motif" New York Times
        80/26,643 (4.1.1931) Section 8, p. 9. Points out further
        allusions in Brahms's music to material from Beethoven,
        Cherubini and Grieg.

2552   Liebling, Leonard. "The Origin of Melody or The Descent
        of Music. No. IX" Musical Courier 52/24 (Whole no. 1368)
        (13.6.1906) pp. 25-26. mus. Points out similarities to
        Wagner's Der Meistersinger in Op. 108, also Wagnerian in-
        fluences in Op. 5.

2553   Rosen, Charles. "Influence: Plagiarism and Inspiration"
        19th Century Music 4/2 (Fall 1980) pp. 87-100. Brahms:
        pp. 91-100. mus., notes. Points out allusions to Beethoven
        in Op. 15 and 83; to Chopin in Op. 77; and the use of
        quotations in Op. 4 (from Chopin) and Op. 1 (from Bee-
        thoven).

2554 Taylor, Deems. "Finders, Keepers" in Taylor. The Well
Tempered Listener. New York: Simon and Schuster,
1940. pp. 92-101. Describes the resemblance of theme
from Op. 68, 4th movement, to one from Beethoven's Op.
125, 4th movement; includes comment on the sources for
the Ungarische Tänze [Hofmann nr. 128; McCorkle WoO 1].
*issues: 1943, 1945.
(a) *reprint (of 1940 Edition): Westport, Conn.: Greenwood Press, [1972].

See also 680, 808, 878, 972, 1250, 1251, 1276, 1281, 1356, 1402, 1474,
1475, 1610, 1616, 1674, 1718, 1823, 1895, 1896, 2014, 2091, 2131,
2175, 2499.

See also "Musical Mottos and Motifs" in V.B.

2. Ethnic and Folksong Influences

Hungarian folkmusic: 2555, 2559, 2563, 2564, 2567, 2568.

2555 *A. S. [Albert Siklós] "A magyar zene tükrözése külföldi
mesterek műveiben" A Zene [13]/5-6,7 (1931-32).

2556 Aronson, Maurice. "Brahms and the National and Folksong
Element in His Music" Musical Courier 76/17 (Whole no.
1987) (25.4.1918) pp. 35-36. ill., mus.

2557 Capri, Antonio. "Brahms e la melodia popolare" La Scala
(Milan) no. 135 (2.1961) pp. 11-15. ill., facsim. Describes
Brahms's use of folkmusic in his works and compares his
treatments with those of other composers; includes Brahms's
own views on folkmusic.

2558 *Eppstein, Hans. "Brahms och folkmusiken" Röster i radio 22/35
(1955) p. 18.

2559 #Franze, Johannes. "Brahms y la música magiar" Ars. Revista
de arte 17/79 (1957) pp. [104-07, 109-10]. ill., facsim.
Discusses Brahms's affinity to Hungarian folkmusic, his
connection with Reményi, also examples of how he utilizes
such material in his works.

2560 Friedländer, Max. "Brahms' Deutsche Volkslieder" Deutsche
Rundschau 49/2 (Bd. 193) (11.1922) pp. 177-82. notes.
Discusses folksong sources used by Brahms, his settings
of them, and their place in his music.

2561 Gerber, Rudolf. "Brahms und das Volkslied" Die Sammlung
3 (1948) pp. 652-62. Discusses Brahms's thoughts on and

exposure to folkmusic, the sources he used and his settings;
includes a comparison of the settings of Brahms and Wolf
for Brahms's Op. 59 no. 5 and Op. 91 no. 2 and Wolf's
Gedichte von Eduard Möricke no. 14 and Spanisches Liederbuch No. 4, respectively.

2562   Graevenitz, Dr., [George] von. "Brahms und das Volkslied"
Deutsche Rundschau 33/2 (Bd. 129) (11.1906) pp. 229-45.
notes. Discusses Brahms's sources as well as his thoughts
on folkmusic, and surveys his settings; includes comment
on the history of folkmusic and the Romantic period's general
interest in folkmusic.
(d) *Graevenitz, G[eorge]. v. "Brahms und das deutsche
Volkslied" Süddeutsche Sänger-Zeitung (Heidelberg)
31 (1936/37) pp. 136-37.

2563   Hohenemser, M. [Richard Hohenemser] "Johannes Brahms und
die Volksmusik" Die Musik (Berlin) 2/15,18 (Bd. 7) (5.,
6.;1903) pp. 199-215, 422-26. notes. Compares Brahms's
Deutsche Volkslieder collections with their sources, discusses whether Brahms originally composed some of his
folk melodies, also his use of chorale tunes and other sacred
works; includes an examination of the use of non-Germanic
materials, especially Hungarian, in all his works, and analysis of settings in the songs.
(c) excerpt: Hohenemser, Richard. "Brahms und die
Volksmusik" Die Musik (Berlin) 25/8 (5.1933) pp.
599-601.
(a) reprint: in 3186.c. pp. 39-41.

2564   *Hubay, Károlyi. "Zeneviszonyaínk" Magyar szalon (1890) pp.
507-15. Discusses the influence of Hungarian folkmusic on
Opp. 103, 112 and the Ungarische Tänze [Hofmann nr. 128;
McCorkle WoO 1]. [from 241]

2565   #Jöde, Fritz. "Brahms und das deutsche Volkslied" Die Laute
3/7/8 (1920) pp. 42-45. mus. [in Heft Beilagen] Discusses
Brahms as a setter of folksong, together with the origin
of the melodies that he used.

2566   Kross, Siegfried. "Zur Frage der Brahmsschen Volksliedbearbeitungen" Die Musikforschung 11/1 (1.-3.1958) pp. 15-21.
notes. An index showing the sources for the folktunes
Brahms used in his songs.

2567   *Lakatos, István. "Magyaros részek Brahms muzsikájában"
A Zene 20 (1938-39) pp. 167-70.

2568   Lesznai, Lajos. "Egy magyaros intonáció nyomában Johannes
Brahms műveiben" Magyar zene 10/2 (6.1969) pp. 183-88.
mus., notes. Describes occurrences in Brahms's works of

a particular rhythmic pattern used a great deal in Hungarian folkmusic.
(b) #German translation: Lesznai. "Auf den Spuren einer ungarischen Intonation in den Werken von Johannes Brahms" Musik und Gesellschaft 21/7 (7.1971) pp. 455-58.

2569   Mila, Massimo. "L'Ispirazione popolare nell'arte di Brahms" La Rassegna musicale 17/4 (10.1947) pp. 277-84. mus., notes. Discusses the influence of folkmusic on Brahms's art.

2570   *Morik, Werner. "Johannes Brahms und sein Verhältnis zum deutschen Volkslied" Phil.F. diss., Universität Göttingen, 1953. 301 pp. mus., notes.
        (a) reprint: Johannes Brahms ... Volkslied. Tutzing: Verlegt bei Hans Schneider, 1965. [5], xii, 301 pp. Discusses Brahms's folktune sources, and his use of folktune in mixed ensemble and solo vocal works; includes comments on the relationship between artsong and folksong.

2571   Sackett, S. J. "Johannes Brahms's Body" Journal of American Folklore 79/[314] ([10.] 1966) pp. 609-11. mus., notes. Points out similarity of a melody and rhythm in Op. 83, 1st movement to "John Brown's Body" ["Battle Hymn of the Republic"], notes Brahms's affinity to folkmusic, and speculates on a connection.

2572   #Wehle, Gerhard F. "Brahms und das Volkslied" Die neue Schule 2/15 (1947) pp. 553-54. ill., mus. Discusses how Brahms gave folksong new impetus, citing no. 5 of Deutsche Volkslieder (1894) [Hofmann nr. 133; McCorkle WoO 33] as example; includes overview of his life and general influence of folksong on his work.

2573   *Wiora, Walter. "Die Herkunft der Melodien in Kretzschmers und Zuccalmaglios Sammlung" Habilitationsschrift, Universität Freiburg i. Br., 1941.
        (a) reprint: Die rheinisch-bergischen Melodien bei Zuccalmaglio und Brahms: Alte Liedweissen in romantischer Färbung. (Quellen und Studien zur Volkskunde 1) (Beiträge zur rheinischen Musikgeschichte 7) Bad Godesberg: Voggenreiter Verlag, 1953. 205 pp. mus., ind., notes. Discusses whether songs in the Kretzschmar/Zuccalmaglio collection are real folksongs, or originally composed by Zuccalmaglio.
            (e) report: Veldhuyzen, Marie. "Brahms, Zuccalmaglio en het duitse volkslied" Mens en melodie 9/3 (3.1954) pp. 72-74.

PART VI. MISCELLANEOUS SUBJECTS

A. DIRECTLY RELATED TO MUSICAL WORKS

1. Music Prior to the Classical Period

Contains materials on Brahms's exposure to, study of, and involvement with early music.

2574 *Adler, Guido. "Johannes Brahms und die Denkmäler der Tonkunst in Osterreich" in Festschrift Max Friedländer zum 70. Geburtstag. [Leipzig: C. F. Peters, 1922].

2575 *Dadelsen, Georg von. "Alter Stil und alte Techniken in der Musik des 19. Jahrhunderts" Phil.F. diss., Freie Universität Berlin, 1951. 138 pp. Brahms: pp. 92-188.

2576 Fellinger, Imogen. "Brahms und die Musik vergangener Epochen" in Die Ausbreitung des Historismus über die Musik. Aufsätze und Diskussionen. Walter Wiora, ed. (Studien zur Musikgeschichte des 19. Jahrhunderts. Bd. 14) Regensburg: Gustav Bosse Verlag, 1969. pp. 147-67. mus., notes. Focuses on music of the 16th-18th centuries: Discusses Brahms's study, ownership, editing, and performances of this music.

2577 Geiringer, Karl. "Brahms als Musikhistoriker" Die Musik (Berlin) 25/8 (5.1933) pp. 571-78. notes. Discusses Brahms's interest in music of the past: his collection of books and manuscripts, his editing and performing it, his friends who shared this interest with him.
(a) reprint: in 3186.c. pp. 11-18.

2578 Grasberger, Franz. "Tradition in schöpferischer Sicht. Zur Arbeitsweise von Johannes Brahms" Osterreichische Musikzeitschrift 22/6 (6.1967) pp. 319-24. notes. Discusses Brahms's study of earlier music and theoretical works; his involvement with it as an editor, and its influence in his own work.

2579 Hohenemser, Richard. Welche Einflüsse hatte die Wiederbele-
bung der älteren Musik im 19. Jahrhundert auf die deutschen
Komponisten? I. II. (Breitkopf & Härtels Sammlung musik-
wissenschaftlicher Arbeiten von deutschen Hochschulen.
Bd. 4) Leipzig: Breitkopf & Härtel, 1900. vi, 135 pp.
Brahms: pp. 70-78, 84-85, 90-93, 116-19, 122-26. notes.
How earlier music influences the vocal music of the Romantic
period.

2580 *Horusitzky, Zoltán. "Brahms nagy szenvedélye" A Zene 20
(1938-39) pp. 171-72. Discusses Brahms's interest in earlier
music, as seen in his library and in his choice of choral
works for performances. [from 241]

2581 Kern, Edith. "Brahms et la musique ancienne" Revue de
musicologie 24/2 (7.1942) pp. 13-20. Discusses Brahms's
involvement with earlier music as an editor and performer;
comments on his copying of it and on its influence in his
own work; includes remarks concerning Brahms's associates
who shared this interest with him.

2582 *Sholund, Edgar Roy. "Johannes Brahms, The Music Scholar"
M.A. thesis, Columbia University, 1939.

See also 95, 179, 413, 554, 1419, 1573, 1760.5, 1848, 1994, 2187.c.,
2200, 2208, 2209, 2213, 2216, 2218, 2220, 2252, 2257, 2285, 2370,
2375.5, 2386, 2454, 2464, 2469, 2483, 2647.

See also individual composers in III.B.2.; "Arranging" and "Editing"
in V.B.

2. Opera

Contains materials on Brahms's attempts to write opera.

2583 Antcliffe, Herbert. "Composers' Limitations" The Chesterian
32/191 (Summer 1957) pp. 15-19. Brahms: pp. 16-17.
Explains how Brahms's personality contains no qualities that
would help him create a theatrical work.

2584 Baser, Friedrich. "Brahms und die Oper" Die Musik (Berlin)
25/8 (5.1933) pp. 584-87. Chronicles Brahms's search for
the right libretto for an opera, and compares him with
Wagner.
(a) reprint: in 3186.c. pp. 24-27.

2585 Berges, Ruth. "No Wife, No Opera" Opera News 33/9 (28.12.
1968) pp. 8-12. ill. Links these two deficiencies in
Brahms's life, and asks if there is a common denominator;

includes comments on his relationship with Clara Schumann and on his consideration of an opera project, as well as his thoughts on opera in general.

2586 Hernried, Robert. "Did Brahms Plan an Opera?" Musical Courier 135/6 (Whole no. 3148) (15.3.1947) p. 5. ill. Describes how the only poet Brahms trusted was J. V. Widmann, who was too much influenced by the Wagnerian dramatic style.

2587 _____. "Die Stimme einer Brahms-Sängerin. Aus ungedruckten Briefen von Hermine Spies" Anbruch 19/3 (3.1937) pp. 39-40. notes. 1 letter, Spies to Richard Heuberger, 6.1887, inquiring about Brahms writing an opera.

2588 *Kühn, Alfred. "Weshalb Brahms keine Oper geschrieben hat?" Strassburger Post no. 296 (13.4.1897).

2589 #Otto, Eberhard. "Brahms und die Oper" Oberpfälzer Nachrichten (Weiden/Opf) (10.9.1976) p. [?]. Traces Brahms's attempts with both Heyse and Widmann to decide on an opera libretto.

2590 Siedentopf, Henning. "Der Nachlass des musikgelehrten Josef Sittard" Die Musikforschung 26/3 (7.-9.1973) pp. 350-52. Brahms: pp. 350-51. Sittard in correspondence with Brahms in 1887, on the subject of opera.
(d) Siedentopf. "Brahms und die Oper oder: Ein lautes Geheimnis" in Siedentopf. Musiker der Spätromantik. Unbekannte Briefe aus dem Nachlass von Josef und Alfred Sittard. Tübingen: Verlag Studio 74, 1979. pp. 13-23. notes, ind. Describes Sittard's correspondence to Brahms, 4 letters in 1887.

2591 #Waddington, Patrick. "Turgenev's Scenario for Brahms" New Zealand Slavonic Journal [6] (1982) pp. 1-16. notes. Presents background description with transcription of a scenario for an opera libretto prepared in the late 1860's; includes comments on Brahms's relationship with Turgenev, and on Brahms and opera in general.

2592 *Willmann, H. "Brahms und die komische Oper" Deutsche Musikdirektoren-Zeitung 10/22 (1908).

See also 695, 726, 729, 755, 788, 868, 928, 947, 958, 1256, 1302, 1759, 2350.

3. Performance Practice

Contains materials which suggest how to conduct or perform Brahms's music.

2593 "Brahms's Chamber Music. The Piano's Place" The Times
      (London) Late London Edition no. 50,888 (10.10.1947) p.
      7. Comments on the balance between parts.

2594 Deas, Steward. "Reflections on Brahms" Country Life 152/
      3936 (30.11.1972). pp. 1512, 1514. ill., facsim. To gain
      insight into the performance of Brahms's music, author
      looks for links through contemporaries, with Brahms:
      Tovey's comments on Joachim, remarks by Fanny Davies,
      Felix Weingartner and Leopold Premyslav.

2595 Fellinger, Imogen. "Zum Problem der Zeitmasse in Brahms's
      Musik" in Gesellschaft für Musikforschung. Bericht über
      den Internationalen Musikwissenschaftlichen Kongress, Kassel
      1962. Georg Reichert and Martin Just, eds. Kassel [et
      al.]: Bärenreiter, 1963. pp. 219-22. mus., notes. Dis-
      cusses Brahms's concerns with tempi and metronome mark-
      ings.

2596 #Jäckel, Hildegard and Gottfried Schmiedel. Bildnis des
      schaffenden Künstlers. Ein Dirigent bei der Arbeit.
      Leipzig: VEB Breitkopf & Härtel, Musikverlag, 1954.
      [97] pp. ill., mus. Rudolf Kempe rehearsing the Staats-
      kapelle Dresden in Brahms's Op. 73: juxtaposes music score
      and photographs of conductor to show his approach to in-
      terpreting the symphony and how he communicates his wishes
      to the orchestra.

2597 *Lévy, Lazare. "Johannes Brahms. Cours d'interprétation et
      de technique" Le Monde musicale (Paris) 47 (1916) pp. 235-
      36.

2598 Mather, Betty Bang. "Expressing Appoggiaturas, From Bach
      to Brahms" Woodwind World--Brass & Percussion 14/2 (Spring
      [4.] 1975) pp. 12-14. mus. Brahms: p. 14. Performance
      suggestions for flute solo in Op. 98, 4th movement.

2599 Mies, Paul. "Uber ein besonderes Akzentzeichen bei Johannes
      Brahms" Beiträge zur Musikwissenschaft 5/3 (1963) pp.
      213-22. mus., notes. Studies a particular type of accent
      as used by Brahms: its use throughout his works and the
      criteria for its use.
      (d) Mies. "Uber ... Joh[annes]. Brahms" in 2595. pp.
          215-17. Omits notes.

2600 *Mueller, Erwin Carl. "A Timpani Method based on the Per-
      formance Practices of Edward M. Metzenger with an Appli-
      cation of these Practices to the Symphonies of Beethoven
      and Brahms" D.A. diss., Ball State University, 1976. 439
      pp. discog.

2601 Robinson, Edith. "The Interpretation of Brahms's Chamber
      Music. A Few Pitfalls Discussed" The Strad 64[44]/524
      (12.1933) pp. 305-07. Deals with performance indications,
      with examples drawn mainly from the violin sonatas.

2602 *Schibli, Sigfried or Johannes. "Ein Johannes Brahms für
      Jedermann. Des Komponisten Kammermusik und die Willkür
      der Interpreten" Musik + Medizin (Neu-Isenburg) 8/15
      (1982) pp. 65-67, 70, 72, 74.

2603 #Schmidt, Leopold. "Johannes Brahms und seine Interpreten"
      Berliner Tageblatt no. 484 (23.9.1909) pp. [1-2] [across
      page bottoms]. Discusses Fritz Steinbach as a Brahms
      interpreter, based on Steinbach's activities at the München
      Deutsche Brahms-Gesellschaft Festival.

2604 Szigeti, Joseph. "A Note About Brahms Sonatas" The Strad
      72/856 (8.1961) pp. 121, 123. Discusses expressive mark-
      ings and dynamics together with their significance; uses
      Op. 108 as example.

2605 Temianka, Henri. "The Interpretation of Dynamic Markings"
      Instrumentalist 24/10 (5.1970) pp. 37-39. mus. Observa-
      tions on the usage and development of dynamic markings:
      Brahms's comments on the matter of markings, with examples
      drawn from Opp. 34 and 78.

2606 Weingartner, Felix. "Brahms oder Wagner? Wie soll der
      Dirigent Brahms nahen? (Aus einem Gespräch)" Neue freie
      Presse (Wien) no. 24,658 (7.5.1933) Morgenblatt. Beilage
      p. 22. Discusses how to conduct Brahms's symphonies;
      includes comment on author's relationship with Brahms,
      1896- .

2607 Weiss, Josef. "Johannes Brahms. The Interpretation of His
      Music" in The Century Library of Music. Ignace Jan Pader-
      ewski, ed. Vol. 8. New York: Century Co., 1901. pp.
      233-53. ill., notes. Describes Brahms's personality,
      together with contemporary interpretations of his music;
      includes comments on Brahms as a composer.
      (a) reprint: Weiss. In The International Library of
          Music for Home and Studio. Music Literature.
          Volume I. The History of Music. New York: The
          University Society, 1925. pp. 261-78.

See also 256, 269, 793, 1376, 1431, 1477, 1478, 1490, 1497, 1503,
1504, 1538, 1560-62, 1568, 1576, 1579, 1588, 1589, 1596, 1602, 1605,
1612-14, 1624, 1633, 1635, 1637, 1642, 1645, 1651-53, 1666, 1670,
1673, 1675, 1682, 1684-87, 1689-91, 1694, 1696, 1699, 1700, 1710,
1717, 1743, 1749, 1752, 1754, 1756, 1768, 1777, 1780, 1781, 1784,
1788, 1797, 1842, 1866, 1868, 1880, 1900, 1916, 1935, 1965, 1978,

1983, 1988, 2037, 2059, 2073, 2074, 2107, 2121, 2128, 2130, 2142, 2153, 2211.c., 2233, 2237, 2267, 2273, 2296, 2301, 2335, 2442, 2512, 2601, 2698, 2762.9.

See also II.C. for materials on Brahms's own interpretations of his own works.

4. Program Music

Contains reference to materials that attempt to trace symbolic or programmatic elements in Brahms's music.

See 48, 1627, 1686, 1792, 1890.d., 1996.

5. Settings of Brahms's Music

Contains materials that discuss other composers' settings of Brahms's works.

2608 *Houston, Robert Ewing, Jr. "A Comparative Analysis of Selected Keyboard Compositions of Chopin, Brahms, and Franck as Transcribed for the Marimba by Clair Omar Musser, Earl Hatch and Frank Maccallum Together with Three Recitals of Works by Bartok, Crumb, Miyoshi, Kraft, and Others" D.M.A. diss., North Texas State University, 1980.

2609 "Max Reger über seine Bearbeitungen Brahms'scher Werke. Aus Briefen an den Verlag N. Simrock G.m.b.H." N. Simrock Jahrbuch 1 (1928) pp. 64-71. notes. Excerpts from 20 letters, 12.1913-4.1916, concerning Reger's instrumental arrangement of 5 songs from Opp. 85, 94, 96, 105 for orchestra, his arrangements for solo piano of the slow movements of Brahms's symphonies, and his arrangements for solo piano of songs from Opp. 3, 19, 49, 71, 105, 121.

2610 Mies, Paul. "Brahms-Bearbeitungen bei Max Reger" Mitteilungen des Max-Reger-Instituts no. 11 (8.1960) pp. 7-17. mus. Summarizes the techniques used by Reger in his arrangements for orchestra and solo piano, and solo piano, respectively, of Brahms songs and Brahms symphony movements, together with some short historical background.

See also 1457, 1459, 1461, 2254, 2266.

See also "Works Catalogues and Indexes" in I.C.

6. Text Translations

Contains materials which contain translations of texts from Brahms's vocal works, or materials that discuss text translations of Brahms's vocal works.

2611 Brahms, Johannes. Texts of the Vocal Works of Johannes Brahms in English Translation. By Henry S[andwith]. Drinker [Jr.]. New York: Association of American Colleges Arts Program, [1945]. xi, 210 pp. Includes texts for the solo songs in a "free" translation, showing syllabification. Includes: Drinker, Henry S. "On Translating Brahms Texts": pp. i-xi.

2612 *Brahms dalok. 38 dalszöveg. Boros Dezső [or Rezső] műfordítása. Szabados Béla előszavával. Budapest: Magyar Goethe Társaság, 1934. 31 pp.

2613 "Brahms's Requiem: A New Text" Musical Times 88/1253 (7.1947) pp. 232-33. mus. Reports on a new English translation by Sir Ivor Atkins which, while adhering more closely to the Biblical text than W. G. Rothery's 1910 translation, needs musical adaptation.

2614 Closson, Ernest. "Schubert, Schumann, Brahms und Hugo Wolf in Frankreich und Belgien" Neue Musikzeitung 49/12 (1928) pp. 369-71. Brahms: p. 370. Discusses the reception of his songs in France, author prefers that the works be sung in their original language rather than in French translation.

2615 *Ingold, John G. Translations of Brahms Mastersongs in Singable Modern English. Portland, Me.: Fred L. Tower, 1923.

2616 Kuhe, Ernest. "Brahms's Songs Translated" Monthly Musical Record 61/728 (1.8.1931) pp. 235-36. Review of Robert Whistler's English translation for the Alfred Lengnick & Co. edition of Brahms's songs [London, ?].

2617 [Walter Ford] "Song-Translations" Music and Letters 3/1 (1.1922) pp. 1-8. English translations of selected songs from Opp. 19, 33, 43, 49, 63, 69 and 94, by Duminster Castle (from Op. 19); F.S. (from Opp. 43, 69); E. M. Lockwood (from Op. 49): E.B.R.S. (from Op. 63); Una A. Taylor (from Op. 94); E. M. Mott (from Op. 94); F. W. (from Deutsche Volkslieder (1894) and Volks-Kinderlieder); and 3 unknown or anonymous translations (from Opp. 43, 69, 105).

2618 Tallack, Gerard. "Queen of Which Night? A Mistranslated

Article" Music Review 40/2 (5.1979) pp. 141-42. Brahms:
p. 142. mus. Describes the problem of adding definite
and indefinite articles in English translations, with Op. 45,
2nd movement as one example.

See also 2041, 2120, 2127, 2128, 2168.

B. INDIRECTLY RELATED TO MUSICAL WORKS

1. Brahms and Literature

Contains materials that discuss the relationship between Brahms and
the literary movements of his time.

2619   Bernet Kempers, Karel Philippus. "Die Komponisten und die
        Dichtkunst" in Festschrift für Walter Wiora zum 30. Dezem-
        ber 1966. Ludwig Finscher and Christoph-Hellmut Mahling,
        eds. Kassel: Bärenreiter, 1967. pp. 95-104. Brahms:
        pp. 102-03. notes. Discusses Brahms and E. T. A. Hoff-
        man, the extent of Brahms's reading as seen in 2351,
        and literary allusions in Brahms's early works.

2620   #Graevenitz, G[eorge]. von. "Zur literarischen Bedeutung von
        Johannes Brahms" Die Brücke. Heimatblätter für Geist und
        Gemüt. [Konstanzer Zeitung. Freitagsbeilage] no. 17
        (5.5.1933) pp. 66-67. ill., notes. Discusses the background
        to 2351; includes comments on 2540.

2621   Smith, Fanny Morris. "Brahms's Relation to the Literature
        of the Nineteenth Century" Century Library of Music. Ig-
        nace Jan Paderewski, ed. Vol. 8. New York: Century Co.,
        1901. pp. 254-59. ill. Discusses Brahms's similarities with
        Browning; includes comments on Brahms's classical-romantic
        duality and on his philosophy.

See also 364, 672, 673, 689, 690, 995, 1628.

See also "Des Jungen Kreislers Schatzkästlein" in IV.C.2.; "Texts
and Text Setting" in V.B.; and "Romanticism" in VI.B.

2. Brahms in Fiction

2622   Brophy, Brigid. "Variations on Themes of Elgar and Brahms"
        in Brophy. The Adventures of God in His Search for the
        Black Girl. London and Basingstoke: Macmillan London

Limited, 1973. pp. 39-44. mus. Tells of Brahms discussing a theme from Elgar's Op. 85 with "Polyhymnia" and comparing it to his own Op. 80.

2623 *Clark, Frederic Horace. Brahms Noblesse. Berlin: n.p., 1912. also: (Eudämonie-Legende. V) Zürich: Pianisten-harmonie-Presse, 1914. 439 pp. Brahms: pp. 20-237. ill. Contains author's reminiscences of Brahms and his two keyboard piano from 1890's; includes discussion of the ethics of music and its links with God. German and English text.

2624 Findeisen, Kurt Arnold. Lied des Schicksals. Roman um Johannes Brahms. Leipzig: Koehler & Amelang, 1933. 331, [1] pp. A fictional treatment of Brahms's life, 1856-97.
  *2. Auflage: 1933.
  *Neue Bearbeitung: Leipzig: v. Hase & Koehler, [1940]. 326 pp.
  *Ausgabe: [1944].
  *also: (Auswahlreihe des Volksverband der Bücherfreunde) Berlin: Volksverband der Bücherfreunde; Wegweiser-Verlag, [1936].
  (c) excerpt (of ? Auflage): Findeisen. "Capriccio auf dem Kontrabass" Zeitschrift für Musik 100/5 (5.1933) pp. 454-57.
  (e) report (on ? Auflage): see 66.e.i.

2625 *Hohlbaum, Robert. "Die Stunde der Sterne" in Hohlbaum. Himmlisches Orchester. Der Unsterblichen. Neue Folge. Novellen. Leipzig: L. Staackmann, 1924.
  *9. und 10. Tausend: 1927.
  (a) i) *reprint (of ? Tausend): Hohlbaum. Die Stunde der Sterne. Eine Bruckner-Novelle. Eingeleitet und herausgegeben von Karl Plenzat. (Eichblatts deutsche Heimatbücher 41) Leipzig: Hermann Eichblatt, [193-?]. 23 pp.
      *2. Auflage: [194-?]. ill.
    ii) *reprint (of ? Tausend): in Hohlbaum. Die Stunde der Sterne. Künstlernovellen. [Einführung schreib Dr. Josef Marschall] (Wiesbadener Volksbücher 254) Stuttgart: Deutsche Volksbücher, [1942].
      *6. - 25. Tausend: [1942]. 86 pp.
      *26. - 35. Tausend: [1942].
      *36. - 65. Tausend: Deutsche Volksbücher G.m.b.H., [1943].
  (b) English translation by Marie Busch (of ? Tausend): Hohlbaum. "At The Hour of The Stars" in Selected Austrian Short Stories. Busch, translator. (The World's Classics. no. 337) London: Humphrey Milford, Oxford University Press, 1928. pp. 192-212. Historical fiction using the Brahms and

Bruckner meeting for dinner in the Rote Igel as
its central event. Detailed characterizations for
both composers; they begin the story at opposite
extremes, but come to understand each other
through their music.

2626   Kanin, Garson. "The Brahms Kick" Cosmopolitan 145/2 (8.
1958) pp. 80-89. Brahms: pp. 87-88. Brahms's music
as a rekindler of romance.

2627   *Nothingham, Ethel. Die Stunde (?)
(a) #reprint: "Der Besuch bei Brahms. Ein Brief von
Ethel Nothingham" Die Musik (Berlin) 13/10 (Bd.
50) (2.1914) pp. 218-19. An imaginary meeting
with Brahms in Bad Ischl, 1890.

2628   *Richter, Hermann. "Von ewiger Liebe". Ein Schumann-
Brahms-Roman. Leipzig: Verlegt bei Koehler & Amelang,
1929. 222, [1] pp.
2. Auflage: 1938. Brahms and Clara Schumann, their relationship from the time of Robert Schumann's first being admitted
to the asylum, to his death (3.1854-7.1856). Uses Op. 43
no. 1 as a symbol of Brahms's unrequited feelings for
Clara.
*Sonderausgabe: [1933].
*Auflage: 1938.

See also 28, 145, 228, 337, 360, 814, 842, 1155-58, 1162, 1169, 1174,
1194, 2136, 2169.

3. Brahms in Poetry

Contains reference to poems on Brahms and his music.

2629   La Claustra, Vera. "Brahms" in La Claustra. Gongs of Light.
1st ed. Los Angeles: The Swordsman Publishing Co., 1971.
p. 40. Praises Brahms as a musician.

2630   *Matthes, Alfons. Berühmte Tondichter. Bach, Händel, Gluck,
Haydn, Mozart, Beethoven, Schubert, Weber, Schumann,
Mendelssohn, Löwe, Wagner, Gounod, Brahms, Wolf, Humper-
dinck. 16 Seelengemälde in Versen. Berlin: Buchverlag
Humanitas, 1927. 32 pp.

2631   Widmann, Josef Victor. Gedichte. Frauenfeld: Huber & Co.,
1912. viii, 192 pp. These 2 poems first appeared in 618.a.
"Thunersonate von Johannes Brahms. Violin- und Klavier-
sonate Opus 100": pp. 41-43. mus. Poet dreams about
the life and times of courtly love.

"Die Mehlspeis'": pp. 122-23. Brahms works on a score
for the price of a Mehlspeis' [a dessert dish] and a kiss
from the waitress.

See also 39D, 188, 222, 447, 522, 529, 571, 1257, 1343, 1587, 1917,
2429, 2904, 3018, 3126, 3168.

4. Classicism

Contains materials that discuss Brahms as a proponent of the classical
ethic.

2632 *Feldman, Evelyn A. "Brahms the Classicist" M.A. thesis,
University of Wisconsin, 1933.

2633 #Furtwängler, Wilhelm. "Brahms" Allgemeine Musikzeitung
49/1 (6.1.1922) p. 241. Discusses Brahms as a classical
artist.

2633.5#Glock, W. F. "Brahms and the Devil" Cambridge Review [51]
(7.2.1930) pp. 238-39. Negative discussion of Brahms as
a classical composer; includes comment on his reception,
and skills as a vocal composer.

2634 Hadow, W[illiam]. H[enry].,[Sir]. "Brahms and the Classical
Tradition" Contemporary Review 71 (5.1897) pp. 653-61.
Examines Brahms as a proponent of classicism: his compositional training and his works.
  (a) i) reprint: Hadow. Eclectic Magazine New series
      65/6 (6.1897) pp. 800-06.
    ii) reprint: Hadow. Living Age 213/2763 (Sixth series
      vol. 14) (19.6.1897) pp. 829-35.
   iii) reprint: Hadow. Music (Chicago) 12/[5] (9.1897)
      pp. 538-48.
   iv) reprint: Hadow. In Hadow. Collected Essays.
      London: Oxford University Press, Humphrey Mil-
      ford, 1928. pp. 135-47.

2635 #Otto, Eberhard. "Der "letzte Klassiker". Am 7. Mai vor hun-
dertvierzig Jahren wurde Johannes Brahms geboren."
Oberpfälzer Nachrichten (Weiden/Opf) (4.5.1973). Discusses
Brahms as a proponent of classicism and how its qualities
are reflected in his music.
  (a) i) *reprint: in Tagespost (Rendsburg) (5.5.1973).
    ii) *reprint: in Fränkische Presse (Bayreuth) (5./6.5.
      1933).
  (d) #abridged: Otto. "Der letzte Klassiker. Vor 140
      Jahren wurde Johannes Brahms geboren" Mindener
      Tageblatt (5.5.1973) p. [?]. adds ill.

(a) #reprint: Otto. "Der letzte "Klassiker". Dem Komponisten Johannes Brahms zum 140. Geburtstag am 7. Mai 1973" Passauer neue Presse (5.1973) p. [?]. omits ill.

2636   Slonimsky, Nicolas. "Brahms: Third B of Music" Christian Science Monitor 47/42 (15.1.1955) p. [8]. ill. Describes Brahms as the bearer of the classical tradition; includes comments on Brahms the man, and his musical style.

See also 157, 493, 668, 902, 1403.d., 1422, 1851, 2235, 2375.5, 2474, 2475, 2663, 3003, 3033.

See also "Romanticism" in VI.B.

5. Religion

Contains materials that discuss Brahms's attitudes towards religious tenets and texts.

2637   #Curtius, Friedrich. "Johannes Brahms. † 3. April" Die Christliche Welt 11/15 (15.4.1897) cols. 348-49. Discusses Brahms as a Christian artist, using Opp. 45 and 121 as examples.

2638   *Heise, P. "Johannes Brahms in seinem Verhältnis zur Religion" Christliche Freiheit 37 (1925) pp. 245-53.

2639   #Reimann, Wolfgang. "Zum 50. Todestag von Johannes Brahms" Die Kirche (Berlin) 2/19 (6.4.1947) p. 3. facsim. Discusses Brahms's position on church music, his interest in organized religion, and the use of Biblical texts in his works.

See also 356, 574, 617.d., 638, 715, 725, 793, 862, 986, 1202, 1757, 2019, 2024, 2025, 2030, 2031, 2060.d., 2128, 2164, 2172, 2185, 2202, 2209, 2210, 2214, 2218, 2254, 2255, 2272, 2276, 2283, 2286, 2294, 2295, 2299, 2453, 2531, 2535, 2540, 2563, 2623, 2646, 2805, 2845, 2854.

6. Romanticism

Contains materials that discuss Brahms as a proponent of the 19th-Century romantic ethic.

2640   *Blessinger, K[arl]. "Brahms, der Romantiker" Neue Mannheimer Zeitung (6.5.1933).

2641   "Brahms at the Proms.   Classic or Romantic?"   The Times
       (London) Late London Edition no. 52,082 (17.8.1951) p. 6.
       Presents evidence from Brahms's music and writings to show
       that Brahms is a romantic compsoer.

2642   "Brahms the Romantic" The Times (London) Late London Edition
       no. 56,792 (18.11.1966) p. 18.   Refutes notion of Brahms
       being a classical composer by pointing out the characteris-
       tics of romanticism in his music.

2643   #Franze, Juan Pedro.   "Brahms y el romanticismo" Ars. Revista
       de arte 17/79 (1957) pp. [70-73, 75-77, 79-81].   ill., facsim.
       Discusses Brahms's position in the romantic period, how
       his musical style contrasted with that of the Wagnerian
       school, as well as how his music reflects the romantic
       spirit.

2644   Graf, Max.   "Brahms-Probleme" Wiener Rundschau Bd. 3/7
       ([7.2.] 1899) pp. 173-75.   Discusses Brahms's position in
       the romantic period.
       (a)   reprint: Graf.   "Brahms-Studie" in Graf.   Wagner-
             Probleme und andere Studien.   [Wien:]   Wiener
             Verlag, [1900].   pp. 100-08.

2645   Grebe, Karl, see 2468.5.

2646   Hamel, Fred.   "Seele und Geist des Brahms-Werkes" Nordwest-
       deutsche Hefte 2/4 (4.1947) pp. 48-51.   ill.   Discusses
       Brahms as a romantic composer; includes comments on
       Brahms and religion, Brahms and Beethoven, and on
       Brahms's classical-romantic duality.

2647   Hill, Ralph.   "Concerning Brahms" The Chesterian 14/106
       (11.-12.1932) pp. 33-39.   Discusses Brahms as a true ro-
       manticist; includes comment on Brahms as symphonist and
       orchestrator, as well as his links to the music of the past.

2648   Högler, Fritz.   "Johannes Brahms--Ein moderner Musiker?"
       Osterreichische Musikzeitschrift 8/5 (5.1953) pp. 147-50.
       Examines the problem of labeling Brahms, by showing how
       Brahms embraces both romantic and classical tendencies
       in his music.

2649   Koussevitzky, Serge.   "The Emotional Essence of Brahms"
       Atlantic Monthly 169/5 (5.1942) pp. 553-56.   mus.   Describes
       how Brahms's music reflects its times; includes comments
       on his historical position.

2650   Kühn, Hellmut.   "Zur deutschen Musik der Gründerzeit und
       Jahrhundertwende" NZ-Neue Zeitschrift für Musik 135/11
       (11.1974) pp. 667-73.

"Johannes Brahms und die Akademiker in Berlin":   pp. 670-
72. mus., notes. Sees Brahms as building on classical
foundations, paving the way for the new romanticism.

2651   *Lüthje, Hans. "Johannes Brahms und das Ende der klassisch-
romantischen Musikepoche" Christengemeinschaft 34(1962)
pp. 338-40.

2652   Mackay, L. A. "The Romantic Listener's Brahms" Canadian
Forum 13/148 (1.1933) pp. 141-42. Describes the emotions
aroused by a performance of Brahms's music; includes comments on the general characteristics of his music.

2653   Mila, Massimo. "L'Età brahmsiana" in Arte e storia. Studi in
onore di Leonello Vincenti. Università di Torino. Facoltà
di lettere e filosofia. Torino: Giappichelli Editore, 1965.
pp. 363-74. Examines, from a socio-cultural perspective,
the times in which Brahms lived.

2654   *Niemöller, Klaus Wolfgang. "Brahms als romantischer Klassiker"
Philharmonische Blätter no. 6 (1971/72) pp. 4-7. Examines
Brahms's music as a fusion of classicism and romanticism.

2655   Raynor, Henry B. "Brahms and The Romantic Crisis" Musical
Opinion and Music Trade Review 80/954 (3.1957) pp. 339,
341. Relates the background of differences between the
Brahms and Wagner/Bruckner schools.

2656   *Schering, Arnold. "Johannes Brahms und seine Zeit" Deutsche
Tonkünstler-Zeitung 31 (1933) p. 81.

2657   #Schünemann, Georg. "Johannes Brahms, der deutsche Romantiker. Zu seinem 100. Geburtstag am 7. Mai" Die Brücke.
Heimatblätter für Geist und Gemüt. [Konstanzer Zeitung.
Freitagsbeilage] no. 17 (5.5.1933) p. 65-66. ill. Describes
qualities that make Brahms a romantic composer, and discusses both Wagner and Brahms as proponents of romanticism; includes remarks on Brahms the man as well as his
links to the Hochschule für Musik in Berlin.

2658   Watson, Sara Ruth. "The Romantic Brahms" American Scholar
17/1 (Winter 1947-1948) pp. 69-78. Examines Brahms's
music as a fusion of classicism and romanticism.

See also 96, 752, 862, 1556, 1668, 1786, 1790, 1851, 2099, 2120, 2358,
2375.5, 2468, 2483, 2494, 2621, 2849, 2900, 2934.

See also "E. T. A. Hoffmann" in III.B.2.; and "Classicism" in VI.B.

PART VII. BRAHMS'S PERPETUATION

A. BRAHMS FESTIVALS

Contains materials that report on commemorative festivals with Brahms
as their theme: includes proposed, as well as actually held events.

1. Unidentified Locations and General Remarks

2659 *"Brahms-Fest" Neue freie Presse (Wien) (20.4.1933).

2660 "Deutsches Brahms-Fest 1939", see 2668.

2661 #Ehrmann, Alfred von. "Brahmsfeste" Die Musik (Berlin) 30/1
(10.1937) pp. 13-17. ill. Relates the history of the
Deutsche Brahms-Gesellschaft Brahms-Fests, 1909-37.

2662 *Ott, Alfons. "Zur Geschichte der Tönkunstlerfeste" Musik im
Unterricht [Ausgabe A] 58/9 (9.1967) p. 289.

2663 #Vancsa, Max. "Nachklänge zur Brahms-Feier" Die Wage 10/15
(13.4.1907) pp. 350-51. Questions the small number of
Brahms commemorative activities in this year; includes comments on Brahms the classicist and composer.

See also 2673, 2759, 2767, 2798, 3079.

2. Particular Locations

This section is arranged alphabetically by city.

--Baden-Baden

2664 Hausswald, Günter. "Brahms-Tage. Baden-Baden" Musica
(Kassel) 26/4 (7.-8.1972) pp. 367-68. Describes works
performed; includes comments on Brahms and the city.

2664.5#"Lucretia West singt Brahmslieder. Bekannte Solisten gastieren
während der Brahmsfesttage in Baden-Baden" Badisches
Tageblatt (Baden-Baden) no. 134 (12.6.1968) p. [?]. ill.
Reviews festival programmes.

2665   Stolz, E. O. "Die Brahms-Festtage in Baden-Baden. 19.-22.
Mai 1910" Allgemeine Musikzeitung 37/23 (3.6.1910) p. 560.
Reports on activities.

--Berlin

1913: 2675.
1917 (Deutsche Brahms-Gesellschaft Brahms-Fest): 2667, 2673, 2674.
1939: 2668-70, 2672, 2676, 2677.
1947: 2666, 2671.

2666   *Berner, Alfred. "Das Berliner Brahms-Fest 1947" Berliner
Musikbericht 1/[3] (1947) pp. 3-5.

2667   Deutsche Brahms-Gesellschaft. Drei Brahms-Abende, veranstaltet von der Deutschen Brahms-Gesellschaft und der
Vereinigung der Brahms-Freunde. Philharmonie 5.,6.,7.
Mai, 1917. Vortragsfolgen nebst Beiträgen von Max Kalbeck
und Wilhelm Altmann. Berlin: Author, [1917?]. 63 pp.
ill., facsim. Includes 345, 576, 760, 1323.

2668   "Deutsches Brahms-Fest 1939" Die Musik (Berlin) 31/8 (5.1939)
p. 523. Reports on festival's opening.

2669   Diestering, Adolf, Richard Petzoldt and Ernst Boucke.
"Deutsches Brahms-Fest der Berliner Kunstwochen" Allgemeine Musikzeitung 66/21 (26.5.1939) pp. 341-43. notes.

2670   Gerigk, Herbert, Hermann Killer, and Gerhard Schultze. "Das
Berliner Brahms-Fest" Die Musik (Berlin) 31/9 (6.1939)
pp. 632-34. Reports on works performed.

2671   *Harth, Walther. "Berliner Brahms-Fest" Berliner Musikbericht
1/3 (1947) p. 6.

2672   *Krienitz, Ernst. "Berlin--Deutsche Brahms-Fest (in den
Berliner Kunstwochen)" Die Musik-Woche 7 (1939) pp. 314-
15.

2673   Schmidt, Leopold. "Vom Brahms-Fest in der Philharmonie"
Berliner Tageblatt 46/233 (8.5.1917) Abendausgabe p. [2].
Reports on works performed; includes comment on Brahms's
music as well as on the idea of holding Brahms-Festivals.

2674   Schünemann, Georg. "Die "Drei Brahms-Abende" in Berlin"
       Frankfurter Zeitung 61/127 (9.5.1917) Abendblatt p. 1.
       Reports on works performed.

2675   Schwers, Paul. "Die Berliner Bach-Beethoven-Brahms-Woche"
       Allgemeine-Musikzeitung 40/18 (2.5.1913) pp. 650-52. Re-
       ports on activities.

2676   Stege, Fritz. "Berliner Musik" Zeitschrift für Musik 106/6
       (6.1939) pp. 613-21. Brahms: pp. 613-15. Reports on
       works performed.

2677   *Westphal, Kurt. "Berlin--Deutsche Brahms-Fest (in der Ber-
       liner Kunstwochen)" Deutsche Adelsblatt (Berlin)   57
       (1939) pp. 949-50.

See also 576, 3150.

--Bonn

2678   #G. T. [Gerhard Tischer] "Vom Schumann-Brahmsfest in Bonn"
       Rheinische Musik- und Theaterzeitung (Köln) 11/19 (1910)
       pp. 341-42. Brahms: p. 342. Discusses works performed.

2679   Kross, Siegfried. "Von "roten" und anderen Brahms-Festen"
       in Ars musica, musica scientia. Festschrift Heinrich Hüschen
       zum funfundsechzigsten Geburtstag am 2. März 1980.
       Detlev Altenburg, ed. (Beiträge zur rheinischen Musikge-
       schichte Bd. 126) Köln: Gitarre und Laute Verlagsgesell-
       schaft, 1980. pp. 305-18. notes. Traces attempts by
       Deutsche Brahms-Gesellschaft to hold a Brahms-Fest in
       Bonn, and explains its failure.
       (a) *reprint: Kross. Bonner Geschichtsblätter 34 (1982)
           pp. 297-311.

2680   Neitzel, Otto. "Vom Schumann-Brahmsfest in Bonn" Allgemeine
       Musikzeitung 37/20 (13.5.1910) pp. 470-71. Reports on
       works performed.

2681   *Tischer, Gerhard. "Betrachtungen über die Frage, Warum
       das nächste Brahms-Fest nicht in Bonn stattfindet" Rheinische
       Musik- und Theaterzeitung (Köln) 29/33/34 (1928).

2682   Wolff, Karl. "Das Schumann-Brahms-Fest in Bonn" Signale
       für die musikalische Welt 68/20 (18.5.1910) pp. 757-58.
       Reports on works performed.

--Boston

2683   M. S. "Elaborate Brahms Festival Held in Back Bay City"

Musical Courier 106/18 (Whole no. 2769) (6.5.1933) p. 7.
Reports on works performed.

--Bremen

1918: 2685.
1922: 2684, 2687.
1933: 2686.

2684   Blume, R. "Das Brahmsfest in Bremen. (22. bis 26. April
        1922)" Allgemeine Musikzeitung 49/19 (12.5.1922) p. 398.
        Reports on works performed.

2685   Gallwitz, Sophie Dorothea, See 2251.5.

2686   Kratzi, Dr. "Brahmsfest in Bremen" Zeitschrift für Musik
        100/7 (7.1933) p. 751. Reports on works performed.

2687   #Seiffert, Karl. "Das Brahmsfest in Bremen" Die Musikwelt
        (Hamburg) 2/9 (1.6.1922) p. 239 [Heft p. 19].

--Detmold

2688   E. K-r. [Erwin Kerschbaumer] "Johannes Brahms-Jahrhundert-
        Gedächtnisfeier der Stadt Detmold" Zeitschrift für Musik
        100/6 (6.1933) p. 628. Reports on works performed.

--Detroit

2689   "Detroit is [[or was]] renowned ..." 19th Century Music 4/2
        (Fall 1980) p. 185. Reports on Detroit Brahms-Festival
        and Brahms-Congress.

2690   Grzelka, Connie. "The Detroit Symphony Orchestra's Inter-
        national Brahms Festival" Symphony Magazine 31/3 (6./7.
        1980) pp. 15-19. ill. Reports on works performed; in-
        cludes comments on city.

See also 3109, 3120.

--Essen

1922: 2693.
1933: 2691, 2692.

2691   Beckmann, Gustav. "Das Essener Brahmsfest" Allgemeine
        Musikzeitung 60/27 (7.7.1933) p. 369. Reports on activities.

2692 Grimmelt, Otto. "Brahmsfest zu Essen. 12.-19. Juni 1933"
      Zeitschrift für Musik 100/8 (8.1933) p. 850. Reports on
      works performed.

2693 Müllner, Hans. "Brahmsfest der Stadt Essen" Signale für die
      musikalische Welt 80/22 (31.5.1922) pp. 712, 714-15.
      Reports on works performed.

--Freiburg

2694 Lange, Ernst. "Freiburger Brahms-Fest 1937" Allgemeine
      Musikzeitung 64/25 (18.6.1937) p. 396. Reports on activi-
      ties.

--Gmunden

See 3094.

--Griefswald

2695 Altman, Wilh[elm]. "Das Greifswalder Brahms-Reger-Fest"
      Allgemeine Musikzeitung 50/32/33 (17.8.1923) pp. 532-33.
      Reports on activities.

--Güstrow

2696 -er. "Brahmsfest in Güstrow am 12., 18. und 19. Juni 1922"
      Neue Zeitschrift für Musik 89/13/14 (7.1922) p. 319.
      Reports on works performed.

--Halle a.S.

2697 Klanert, Paul. "Ein Brahmsfest in Halle a.S." Allgemeine
      Musikzeitung 55/19 (11.5.1928) p. 557. Reports on activities.

--Hamburg

1922 (Deutsche Brahms-Gesellschaft Brahms-Fest): 2698, 2704, 2710,
      2714.
1933: 2703, 2713, 2715.
1937 (Deutsche Brahms-Gesellschaft Brahms-Fest): 2702, 2705, 2708,
      2709, 2711, 2712.
1958: 2699, 2707, 2716.
1973: 2700, 2706.

2698 #Aber, Adolf. "Fünftes Brahms-Fest der Deutschen Brahms-
Gesellschaft" Leipziger neueste Nachrichten no. 151 (2.6.
1922) p. 2. General comments on the soloists and works
performed, as well as on how the 2 Festival conductors,
Spengel and Furtwängler, represent the approaches of two
generations towards Brahms's music.

2699 *Bachmann, Claus-Henning. "Die Hamburger Brahms-Woche"
Musikblätter 12 (1958-59) pp. 85-86.

2700 *[Hamburg. Behörde für Wissenschaft und Kunst. Kulturamt.]
Brahms Wochen Hamburg 1973. 7.-26. Mai. Veranstaltet
von der Freien und Hansestadt Hamburg zum 140. Geburtstag von Johannes Brahms am 7. Mai 1973. Programm.
[56] pp. ill., facsim.

2701 *Brahmsfest. Festfolge. [Hamburg, etc. 19-].

2702 Broesike-Schoen, Max. "Deutsches Brahms-Fest in Hamburg"
Kölnische Zeitung no. 533 (21.10.1937) Morgenblatt p. 2.
Reports on works performed.

2703 _____. "Das Reichs-Brahmsfest in Hamburg" Die Musik
(Berlin) 25/10 (7.1933) pp. 761-62. Reports on works
performed.

2704 Chevalley, Heinrich. "V. Brahms-Fest der Deutschen Brahms-
Gesellschaft. Erster Tag" Hamburger Fremdenblatt 94/245
(28.5.1922) Morgenausgabe p. 1. Reports on programming;
includes comment on Brahms's music.
(d) H.Ch. "V. Brahms-Fest ... -Gesellschaft. Zweiter-
Vierter Tag" Hamburger Fremdenblatt 94/246, 248,
250 (29.-31.5.1922) Abendausgabe pp. 1;2;2.
Reports on works performed.

2705 Fuhrmann, Heinz. "9. Deutsches Brahmsfest der "Deutschen
Brahms-Gesellschaft" in Hamburg. 11.-17. Oktober 1937"
• Zeitschrift für Musik 104/11 (11.1937) pp. 1270-71. Reports
on works performed.

2706 Herbort, Heinz Josef. "Nicht aus dem Herzen" Die Zeit (Hamburg) U.S. Edition 28/21 (25.5.1973) p. 12. ill. Reports
on activities for 104th anniversary of Brahms's birth; includes comments on Brahms and Hamburg and describes
work written by Kegel, which is based on Brahms's Op. 24.

2707 *Johannes Brahms Festwoche. Hamburg 1958. Programm.
[Hamburg: Author?, 1958]. [42 pp.] ill., facsim.

2708 Krüger, Walther. "Neuntes Brahms-Fest in Hamburg" Allgemeine Musikzeitung 64/45 (5.11.1937) pp. 659-60. Reports
on activities.

2709 Kulenkampff, Hans-Wilhelm. "9. Deutsches Brahmsfest in
      Hamburg" Die Musik (Berlin) 30/2 (11.1937) p. 107. Re-
      ports on works performed.

2710 Leitzmann, Albert. "Brahms-Fest" Vossische Zeitung (Berlin)
      no. 260 (3.6.1922) 1. Beilage p. [1]. Reports on works
      performed.

2711 *9. Brahmsfest der Deutschen Brahms-Gesellschaft Hamburg
      1937. [Festfolge.] Herausgegeben von General-Intendanten
      der Hamburgischen Staatsoper und die Philharmonischen
      Staatsorchesters. Hamburg: Christian, 1937. 36 pp.

2712 Ohlekopf, Richard. "9. Brahmsfest in Hamburg" Signale für
      die musikalische Welt 95/43 (20.10.1937) pp. 563-64. Re-
      ports on works performed.

2713 Peyser, Herbert F. "Germany's Nationalistic Revival" New
      York Times 82/27,539 (18.6.1933) Section 10, p. 4. Re-
      ports on centenary celebrations in Hamburg.

2714 Schaub, Hans F. "Das V. Deutsche Brahmsfest in Hamburg"
      Allgemeine Musikzeitung 49/24 (16.6.1922) pp. 550-51. Re-
      ports on activities.

2715 _____. "Die Reichs-Brahmsfeier in Hamburg" Allgemeine
      Musikzeitung 60/22 (2.6.1933) p. 301. Reports on activities.

2716 Wagner, Klaus. "Um einen Brahms für Heute bittend ..."
      Musica (Kassel) 12/7/8 (7./8.1958) pp. 461-62. Reports
      on works performed; includes comments on Brahms and
      Hamburg.

See also 4, 49, 69, 243, 3100, 3121.

--Heidelberg

1926 (Deutsche Brahms-Gesellschaft Brahms-Fest): 2717-22, 2724.
1966: 2723.

2717 *Aber, A[dolf]. "Deutsches Brahms-Fest in Heidelberg" Die
      Musikwelt (Hamburg) 6/8 (1926).

2718 *Aber, Adolf. "Das Heidelberger Brahmsfest" Leipziger neueste
      Nachrichten (5.6.1926).

2719 Hunek, Rudolf. "Das Sechste Deutsche Brahms-Fest in Heidel-
      berg" Signale für die musikalische Welt 84/25 (23.6.1926)
      pp. 1000-04. Reports on works performed.

2720   Kraemer, Jul. "6. Deutsches Brahmsfest in Heidelberg"
        Zeitschrift für Musik 93/7/8 (7./8.1926) p. 454. Reports
        on works performed.

2721   Krauss, Karl Aug[ust]. "Heidelberg: ..." Die Musik (Berlin)
        18/10 (7.1926) p. 782. Reports on works performed.

2722 #_____. "6. Deutsches Brahmsfest der Deutschen Brahms-
        gesellschaft in Heidelberg vom 29. Mai bis 2. Juni 1926"
        Süddeutsche Sänger-Zeitung (Heidelberg) 18/10 (1926)
        pp. 233-35. ill. Reports on works performed.

2723   Riemer, Otto. "Brahms-Reger-Tage in Heidelberg" Musik
        und Kirche 36/6 (11./12.1966) pp. 284-85. Reports on
        works performed.

2724   Sonnemann, Kurt. "Sechstes Deutsches Brahms-Fest in Heidel-
        berg" Allgemeine Musikzeitung 53/25 (18.6.1926) pp. 548-49.
        Reports on activities.

--Jena

1929   (Deutsche Brahms-Gesellschaft Brahms-Fest): 2725, 2728-30.
1933:   2726, 2727.

2725   Abendroth, Walter. "Siebentes deutsches Brahmsfest der
        Deutschen Brahmsgesellschaft in Jena" Allgemeine Musik-
        zeitung 56/26/27 (5.7.1929) pp. 698-99. Reports on works
        performed.
        (d) Abendroth. Die Musikwelt (Hamburg) 9/7 (1.7.1929)
            p. 48.

2726   Eickemeyer, Willy. "Das Jenaer Brahmsfest" Allgemeine Musik-
        zeitung 60/23 (9.6.1933) p. 313. Reports on activities.

2727   Funk, Heinrich. "Brahmsfest in Jena" Zeitschrift für Musik
        100/6 (6.1933) p. 632. Reports on works performed.

2728   *M. U. "Das Jenaer Brahms-Fest" Deutsche Musikerzeitung
        (Berlin) 60/24 (1930).

2729   #Reuter, Otto. "Das Siebente deutsche Brahmsfest in Jena"
        Signale für die musikalische Welt 87/25 (19.6.1929) pp. 755-
        57. Reports on works performed.

2730   Wensel, Viktor. "Jena: Das 7. deutsche Brahms-Fest ..."
        Die Musik (Berlin) 21/12 (9.1929) p. 932. Reports on works
        performed.

--Koblenz

2731 *Berten, W. M. "Brahms-Woche am Niederrhein" Rheinischer
      Merkur 2/19 (1947) p. 6.

--Königsberg

2732 [Brahms-Fest Königsberg 1933.] Brahms-Fest zum 100. Ge-
      burtstag des Meisters (1833-7.Mai-1933). Veranstaltet vom
      Ostmarken-Rundfunk und der Stadt Königsberg Pr. am 6.
      und 7. Mai 1933. Programm-Buch. [Königsberg Pr.:
      Ostmarken-Rundfunk G.m.b.H., 1933.] 47 pp. ill.,
      facsim., mus. Contains 55.d.ii.a., 585, 982, 1351, 1412,
      1779.

2733 Fedtke, Traugott. "Brahmsfest in Königsberg am 6. und 7.
      Mai 1933" Zeitschrift für Musik 100/6 (6.1933) pp. 632-33.
      Reports on works performed.

--Leipzig

2734 Heuss, Alfred. "Musik in Leipzig" Zeitschrift für Musik 100/6
      (6.1933) pp. 601-03. Brahms: pp. 601-02. Reports on
      works performed.

--London

See 3162.

--Meiningen

2735 *Joachim, Joseph. Zum Gedächtnis des Meisters Joh[annes].
      Brahms. Rede zur Weihe der Brahms-Denkmals in Meiningen
      am 7. Okt. 1899. [Leipzig: n.p., 1899.] 7 pp.
      (d) "Festrede Prof. Dr. Joachims zur Enthüllung des
            Brahms-Denkmals in Meiningen" Allgemeine Musik-
            zeitung 26/42 (20.10.1899) pp. 622-23. Trans-
            cription of speech.

2736 Lessmann, Otto. "Das II. sächs.-meiningensche Musikfest
      7.-10. Oktober 1899. [I], II, III" Allgemeine Musikzeitung
      26/41-43 (13.,20.,27.;10.;1899) pp. 606-07, 621-22, 639-40.
      Reports on Festival activities and the dedication of Brahms
      memorial.

2736.5 *Schmidt, Leopold. Berliner Tageblatt (1899).
      (a) #reprint: in Schmidt. "Brahms" in 3022. pp. 255-67.

"Brahms in Meiningen":   pp. 255-56.   Reports on
activities.

2737   W-r.   "Das II. s.-meiningische Landesmusikfest vom 7. bis
einschliesslich 10. October 1899" Neue Zeitschrift für Musik
66/43,44 (Bd. 95) (25.10. and 1.11.;1899) pp. 467-69,
479-82.   Reports on activities and dedication of Brahms
memorial.

2738   *Widmann, J[osef]. V[iktor].   Der Bund (Bern) (3.1891).

See also 3086, 3087, 3143, 3168.

--München

1909 (Deutsche Brahms-Gesellschaft Brahms-Fest):   2739-51, 2753-69.
1931:   2752.

2739   *Adler, Felix.   "Das Erste Deutsche Brahmsfest" Neues Wiener
Tagblatt (16.9.1909).

2740   *_____.   "Das Erste deutsche Brahmsfest" Pester Lloyd
(Budapest) (17.9.1909).

2741   *Bertha, Alexandre.   "Au 1er Festival Brahms, Munich 10-14
Septembre 1909" La Vie musicale 3/2 (1909/10).

2742   Binzer, E. von.   "Erstes Deutsches Brahms-Fest zu München.
10. bis 14. September 1909. I.-II." Musikalisches Wochenblatt. Neue Zeitschrift für Musik 40 or 76/26-27 (23.9.
and 1.10.;1909) pp. 358, 374-75.   Reports on works performed.

2743   "Brahms Festival at Munich" The Times (London) no. 38,961
(17.5.1909) p. 11.   Announces that festival is to be held.

2744   *"Brahms Tage in München" Tägliche Rundschau (Berlin) (11.
9.1909(?)).

2745   *Brahmsfest.   Erstes Deutsches Brahms-Fest, München.   10.
-14. September 1909 im Königl. Odeon. Programmbuch.
Konzertbureau Emil Gutmann München, ed. [München:
F. Bruckmann, 1909.] 97 pp. ill. Contains 398, 578,
741, 2418.
(e) #report: "Erstes Deutsches Brahmsfest" Müncher neueste
Nachrichten (1.9.1909) p. [?].

2746   #Brandes, Friedrich.   "Vom ersten deutschen Brahmsfest" Der
Kunstwart 23/2 (10.1909) pp. 128-29.   Justifies the festival's
location, and comments on the works performed.

2747 *Daffner, Hugo. "Das Erste Deutsche Brahmsfest in München"
Dresdener neueste Nachrichten nos. 257-58, 263 (1909).

2748 Ehlers, Paul. "Erstes deutsches Brahmsfest. I. II." Allgemeine Musikzeitung 36/38,39 (17.,24.;9.;1909) pp. 696-97,
715-16. Provides the festival's circumstances and reports
on the works performed.

2748.5#"Erstes Deutsches Brahmsfest" Münchner neueste Nachrichten
(11.9.1909) p. 2. Gives various concert programmes.

2749 *Glöckner, Willy. "Beethoven-Brahms-Bruckner-Zyklus und
das erste deutsche Brahmsfest in München" Blätter für
Haus- und Kirchenmusik 13 (10.1909).

2750 #Humbert, Georges. "Au 1er Festival Brahms, Munich 10-14
Septembre 1909" La Vie musicale 3/2 (1.10.1909) pp. 21-27.
Criticism and comments on all aspects of the Festival.

2751 *Korngold, Julius. "Das Münchner Brahms-Fest" Neue freie
Presse (Wien) (15.9.1909).

2752 Krienitz, Willy. "Münchner Brahms-Woche" Allgemeine Musikzeitung 58/45 (6.11.1931) pp. 772, 774. Reports on works
performed.

2753 #"Montag Vormittag 11 Uhr findet das zweite Morgenkonzert
statt...." Münchner neueste Nachrichten (13.9.1909) p.
[?]. Gives a concert programme.

2753.5#"Morgen Dienstag findet ..." Münchner neueste Nachrichten
(14.9.1909) [2 pp.] [across page bottoms]. Gives concert
programmes.

2754 "München ..." Allgemeine Musikzeitung 36/20 (14.5.1909) pp.
420-21. Announces proposal for a Brahms Festival.

2755 "München ..." Allgemeine Musikzeitung 36/24 (11.6.1909) p.
504. Reports that Brahms Festival will take place.

2756 "München ..." Allgemeine Musikzeitung 36/26 (25.6.1909) p.
543. Brahms Festival programme announced.

2757 "München. Das für September geplante Brahmsfest ..." Allgemeine Musikzeitung 36/22/23 (28.5./4.6.;1909) p. 471.
Brahms Festival may not be held owing to withdrawal of
some of the participants.

2758 "München. Der Münchener Lehrergesangverein hat, ..."
Allgemeine Musikzeitung 36/21 (21.5.1909) p. 439. Reports
on this group's withdrawal from Brahms Festival.

2759   Paetow, Walter. "Erstes deutsches Brahmsfest" Die Musik
       (Berlin) 9/2 (Bd. 33) (10.1909) pp. 129-31. Comments on
       the idea of this festival and the works performed.
       (d) *Paetow, W. Tägliche Rundschau (Berlin) (11.9.1909).

2760   Riezler, Walter. "München und Johannes Brahms. Ein Epilog
       zum ersten deutschen-Brahms-Fest" Frankfurter Zeitung
       54/269 (28.9.1909) Abendblatt p. 1. Reports on works
       performed; includes comment on the qualities of Brahms's
       music.

2761   Riller, William. [William Ritter] "Brahms et les fêtes de Munich"
       Bulletin français de la S.I.M. Société Internationale de
       Musique (Section de Paris) 5/11 (15.11.1909) pp. 950-52.
       notes. Discusses Brahms and his supporters; includes
       report on festival activities.

2762   *Ritter, William. "Les Fêtes de Brahms à Munich" Journal de
       Genève (21.9.1909).
       (d) *Ritter. La Suisse liberale (9.1909).

2762.3#R. L-s. [Rudolf Louis] "Erstes Deutsches Brahms-Fest"
       Münchner neueste Nachrichten (13.9.1909) p. [?]. Reviews
       a Brahms lieder programme.

2762.6#_____. "Erstes Deutsches Brahms-Fest" Münchner neueste
       Nachrichten (14.9.1909) p. [?]. Concert reviews.

2762.9#_____. "Erstes Deutsches Brahms-Fest" Münchner neueste
       Nachrichten (16.9.1909) p. [?]. Concert report with com-
       ments on the interpretation of the works performed.

2763   Schmidt, Leopold. "Ein Deutsches Brahmsfest" Signale für
       die musikalische Welt 67/36 (8.9.1909) pp. 1255-57. notes.
       Relates the background to the festival; includes comment
       on Brahms's worth.

2764   #_____. "Das erste deutsche Brahms-fest" Berliner Tageblatt
       no. 466 (14.9.1909) p. [1]. Comments mainly on the choice
       of site, since München is a city that favors Wagner.

2765   #Schmitz, Eugen. "Das Erste deutsche Brahmsfest in München.
       (10.-14. September 1909)" Die Orgel 10/10 (1910) pp.
       212-14. Describes the works performed.

2766   _____. "Münchener Brahms-Feste" Allgemeine Zeitung
       (München) 112/39 (25.9.1909) pp. 879-80. Reports on
       works performed.

2767   Spanuth, August. "Das "Erste deutsche Brahms-Fest." I."
       Signale für die musikalische Welt 67/37 (15.9.1909) pp.

1287-93. Comments on the premise of the festival and its programming.
(d) continued: Istel, Edgar. "Das "Erste deutsche Brahms-Fest." II." Signale für die musikalische Welt 67/38 (22.9.1909) pp. 1325-27. Reports on works performed.

2768 Tarub. "Das Brahms-Fest in Krähwinkel" März 3/12 (Bd. 2 of 1909) (6.1909) pp. 493-94. A humorous look at the festival.

2769 #Thomas-San-Galli, Wolfgang A[lexander]. "Erstes deutsches Brahmsfest" Rheinische Musik- und Theaterzeitung (Köln) 10/38/39 (1909) pp. 484-86. Surveys the Festival, describing concert programmes and including personal criticisms of the performances. Includes comments on the public's reception of Brahms's music.

See also 2603, 2899.

--New York

2770 *"Brahms Festival" New Music and Church Music Review 12/125 (5.1912) pp. 248-50.

2771 "A Brahms Festival in New York" The Times (London) no. 39,872 (13.4.1912) p. 11. Reports on works performed.

--Paris

2772 *Bruyr, José. "Le Cas Brahms" La Revue musicale belge 9/5 (1933).

2773 Jarosy, Albert. "Brahms-Feier in Paris" Allgemeine Musikzeitung 59/47 (25.11.1932) p. 593. Reports on activities, as well as the French attitude toward Brahms and his music.

2774 Marcel, Gabriel. "Le Cas Brahms" La Revue musicale (Paris) 14/137 (6.1933) pp. 46-49. Reports on works performed, together with comments on Brahms's music.

--Pörtschach

See 3123.

--Remscheid

2775 *Brahms-Feier der Stadt Remscheid zum Gedenken des 100.
      Geburtstages von Johannes Brahms (geb[oren]. am 7. Mai
      1833 in Hamburg). März bis Mai 1933. Remscheid: Magis-
      trat, 1933. 40 pp.

--Tutzing

2776 Krienitz, Willy. "Brahmsfest in Tutzing" Allgemeine Musik-
      zeitung 60/36 (8.9.1933) pp. 429-30. Reports on activities;
      includes comments on Brahms and Tutzing.

--Wien

1908: 2780.
1933 (Deutsche Brahms-Gesellschaft Brahms-Fest): 2777-79, 2781-88.
1937: 2789.

2777 "Brahms Centenary. A Vienna Festival" The Times (London)
      Royal Edition no. 46,410 (4.4.1933) p. 14. Announces the
      holding of a Brahms Festival.

2778 "The Brahms Centenary. Celebrations at Vienna in May" The
      Times (London) no. 46,392 (14.3.1933) p. 17. Announces
      holding of Brahms Festival and its programming.

2779 "Brahms Centenary, Vienna" New York Times 82/27,525 (4.6.
      1933) Section 9, p. 4. Notes performances during the week
      of celebration.

2780 *Hirschfeld, Robert. "Ein Festtag in Wien" Berliner Tageblatt
      (5.1908).

2781 Hoffmann, R[udolph]. St[ephan]. "Brahmsfest in Wien" All-
      gemeine Musikzeitung 60/22 (2.6.1933) pp. 301-02. Reports
      on activities.

2782 *Johannes Brahms-Fest (100 Jahr-Feier) in Wien vom 16. bis 21.
      Mai 1933. Veranstaltet von der Deutschen Brahms-Gesell-
      schaft, Berlin, gemeinsam mit der Gesellschaft der Musik-
      freunde in Wien. Wien: Karner, 1933. 32 pp.

2783 *Jonas, Oswald. "Ein Auftakt zur Brahms-Feier" Allgemeine
      Musikzeitung 60/1 (1933). Attacks 2490.5, saying that
      Brahms is not a major figure with respect to modern music;
      it is only his centennial that encourages such speculation.
      [from 2783.d.]
      (d) Reich, Willi. "Brahmsschänder" 23. Eine Wiener Musik-
          zeitschrift no. 10 (15.5.1933) pp. 1-5. notes.

Rebuts 2783 with details on Brahms's links to specific 20th century composers.

2784   Junk, Victor. "Wiener Musik" Zeitschrift für Musik 100/7 (7.1933) pp. 723-27. Brahms: pp. 725-26. reports on works performed.

2785   Korngold, Julius. "Festliche Brahms-Abende" Neue freie Presse (Wien) no. 24,671 (20.5.1933) Morgenblatt pp. 1-3 [across page bottoms]. Reports on works performed; includes author's comments.

2786   _____. "Johannes-Brahms-Fest. (Feier zur hundertsten Wiederkehr des Geburtstages.)" Neue freie Presse (Wien) no. 24,642 (20.4.1933) Morgenblatt pp. 1-3 [across page bottoms]. Reports on activities; includes comments on Brahms's music, Brahms and Wagner, and the worth of Brahms.

2787   _____. "Musik vom Sonntag. Brahms-Fest.-Gäste in der Staatsoper" Neue freie Presse (Wien) no. 24,675 (24.5.1933) pp. 1-3 [across page bottoms]. Brahms: p. [1-2]. Reports on works performed; includes author's comments.

2788   r. "Das Wiener Brahms-Fest. Zweites Kammermusikkonzert" Neue freie Presse (Wien) no. 24,673 (22.5.1933) Abendblatt p. 4. Reports on works performed.

2789   "Tribute to Brahms is paid by Vienna" New York Times 86/ 28,926 (5.4.1937) p. 17. Reports on observances of 40th anniversary of Brahms's death.

See also 31, 2930, 2931, 3093, 3130, 3152, 3177.

--Washington, D.C.

2790   Stander, Paula Forrest. "Brahms Year" Impromptu 1/1 (Fall 1982) p. [2-3]. ill. Announces 1983 Brahms Congress and other festivities.

--Wiesbaden

1911: 2800.
1912 (Deutsche Brahms-Gesellschaft Brahms-Fest): 2791, 2793-98, 2802-04.
1921 (Deutsche Brahms-Gesellschaft Brahms-Fest): 2792, 2799, 2801.

2791   *Deutsche Brahms-Gesellschaft, ed. Programmbuch des zweiten deutschen Brahms-Festes in Wiesbaden 1912. Berlin: Author, 1912.

468 / VII. Brahms's Perpetuation

2792 *_____. Viertes Brahms-Fest zu Wiesbaden. 6. bis 9. Juni
      1921. Programmbuch. 64 pp. ill., facsim.

2793 "The Deutsches Brahms-Verein ..." The Times (London) no.
      39,675 (28.8.1911) p. 9. Announces holding of festival in
      1912.

2794 Dorn, Otto. "Wiesbaden: ..." Die Musik (Berlin) 11/20 (Bd.
      44) (7.1912) p. 127. Reports on works performed.

2795 _____. "2. Deutsches Brahms-Fest in Wiesbaden" Neue
      Zeitschrift für Musik 79/24 (13.6.1912) p. 344. Reports
      on works performed.

2796 #Louis, Rudolf. "Das Zweite deutsche Brahmsfest zu Wiesbaden
      (2.-5. Juni 1912)" Münchner neueste Nachrichten (8.6.1912)
      [2 pages] [across page bottoms]. notes. Reviews festival;
      includes comments on Brahms's links to Wiesbaden.

2797 *Schmidt, Leopold. "Das II. deutsche Brahms-Fest in Wies-
      baden" Berliner Tageblatt (6.1912).

2798 Spanuth, August. "Das Zweite deutsche Brahms-Fest" Signale
      für die musikalische Welt 70/24 (12.6.1912) pp. 828-31.
      Presents justification for the demand for the event, com-
      ments on Fritz Steinbach being the only conductor and re-
      ports on works performed.

2799 Tessmer, Hans. "Zum Brahmsfest in Wiesbaden" Signale für
      die musikalische Welt 79/22 (1.6.1921) pp. 566, 568. De-
      scribes the qualities of Brahms's music.

2800 Uhl, Edm[und]. "Das Brahms-Kammermusikfest zu Wiesbaden
      (29.,30. März, 1.,3.,5. und 7. April)" Allgemeine Musik-
      zeitung 38/16 (21.4.1911) pp. 457-58. Reports on works
      performed.

2801 _____. (Edmund) "Viertes Brahmsfest in Wiesbaden. (6.-9.
      Juni 1921)" Allgemeine Musikzeitung 48/26 (24.6.1921) pp.
      488-89. Reports on activities.

2802 _____. (Edmund) "Das Zweite deutsche Brahmsfest" Frank-
      furter Zeitung 56/155 (6.6.1912) 2. Morgenblatt p. 1.
      notes. Reports on works performed.

2803 _____. (Edmund) "Zweites Deutsches Brahmsfest (Wiesbaden,
      2.-5. Juni 1912)" Allgemeine Musikzeitung 39/24 (14.6.1912)
      pp. 658-59. Reports on works performed.

2804   Weingartner, Felix. "Zum Brahms-Fest in Wiesbaden" Signale
       für die musikalische Welt 70/22 (29.5.1912) pp. 721-23.
       Discusses Brahms's attributes as a composer, and his his-
       torical position.
       (d) see: 2910.

B. COMMEMORATIVE PIECES

Contains materials written to observe either the anniversary of
   Brahms's birth or of his death. The comments are very general,
   invariably celebratory in nature, sometimes overwhelming in their
   adulation.

1907 (10th anniversary of death): 2821.
1922 (25th anniversary of death): 2805, 2816, 2833, 2842, 2866, 2874,
   2878, 2880.
1933 (100th anniversary of his birth): 2806, 2809, 2811, 2814, 2815,
   2822, 2823, 2825-29, 2831, 2832, 2835, 2839, 2840, 2843-45, 2849,
   2851, 2855, 2858, 2859, 2862, 2863, 2865, 2867-71, 2873, 2876,
   2879, 2881-83.
1937 (40th anniversary of death): 2830, 2872, 2875.
1943 (110th anniversary of birth): 2846-48, 2861.
1947 (50th anniversary of death): 2819, 2856, 2857, 2860, 2877.

2805   Andriessen, Willem. "3 April 1922" Caecilia (Utrecht) 79/11
       (10.4.1922) pp. 174-75. Comments on Brahms's spiritual
       qualities.

2806   *Baser, Friedrich. "Johannes Brahms. Zu seinem hundertsten
       Geburtstag am 7. Mai" Neue Mannheimer Zeitung Sonntags-
       Ausgabe nr. 208 (6./7.5.1933) p. 3.
       (a) reprint: Baser. "Johannes Brahms. (Zu seinem 100.
           Geburtstag am 7. Mai 1933)" Der Türmer 35/8
           (5.1933) pp. 161-63. Describes Brahms the man;
           includes comments on Brahms's relations with the
           Schumanns, and Wagner.

2807   *Berten, Walter. "Brahms' 30. Todestag" Musik im Leben 3/5
       (1927).

2808   Bie, Oscar. "Brahms. Zu seinem 100. Geburtstage" Die Neue
       Rundschau 44/5 (5.1933) pp. 684-88. Compares Brahms
       and Wagner; includes comments on the quality of Brahms's
       music.

2809   *Brachtel, K. "Zum 100. Geburtstag von Brahms" Bundes-

Kalender 8 (1934) p. 112.
(a) *reprint: Brachtel. Bundes-Zeitweiser. Bund der
deutsche Nordmährens 8 (1934) p. 112.

2810 *"Brahms" Lantern 6 (6.1957) pp. 328-35. ill., notes.

2810.5#Buenzod, Emmanuel. "Notes sur Brahms" Schweizerische
musikpädagogische Blätter [41]/17 (1953) pp. 17-23. notes.
A philosophical discussion on the importance of Brahms's
music; includes comments on Brahms the composer and the
French attitude towards Brahms's music.

2811 *Dettelbach, Hans von. "Brahms. Zum 100. Geburtstag"
Deutscher Volkskalender (1933) p. 67.

2812 *Diepenbrock, Alphons. "De Brahms-Herdenking te Amsterdam"
1898.
(d) Diepenbrock. "[De Brahms-Herdenking te Amsterdam]"
in Diepenbrock. Verzamelde Geschriften van Alphons
Diepenbrock. Eduard Reeser and Thea Diepenbrock,
eds. Utrecht, Brussels: Uitgeverij het Spectrum,
1950. pp. 314-18, 414. ind. Discusses Brahms's
historical position; includes comment on Brahms the
composer and on performances of his music in Amsterdam.

2813 Ehrmann, Alfred von. "Rückblick auf das Brahms-Jahr 1933"
Die Musik (Berlin) 26/5 (2.1934) pp. 339-42. Reviews
Brahms festivals, new recordings, and books.

2814 *"Der 100. Geburtstag" Mitteilungen des Verlags Breitkopf &
Härtel [=Mitteilungen der Musikalien-handlung] no. 166
(1933).

2815 Fleischmann, H. R. "Il Centenario di Johannes Brahms" Musica
d'oggi 15/3 (3.1933) pp. 101-04. Describes Brahms the
man; includes comments on Brahms in Wien and Italy,
together with an overview of his musical works.

2816 *Friedländer, E. "Zum 25. Wiederkehr des Todestages von
Brahms" Vaterländische Blätter (1921) p. 34.

2817 *Furtwängler, Wilhelm. "Johannes Brahms" Der Musiker.
Mitteilungsblatt des deutschen Musikerverbandes in der
Gewerkschaft Kunst des DGB (Düsseldorf) [=Der Berufs-
musiker] 11/5 (1958) p. 4.

2818 Geissler, H. "Brahms in Potsdam. Gedanken am Rande des
Krieges" Münchner neueste Nachrichten 97/348 (29.12.1944)
p. 3. Discusses Brahms's Germanic qualities.

2819 *Gervais, O. R. "Johannes Brahms. Zu seinen 50. Todestag am 3.4.1947" Zeit im Bild 2/7 (1947).

2820 *Goldschmidt, Harry. "Das Vermächtnis von Johannes Brahms. Zu seinem 120. Geburtstag am 7. Mai" Musik und Gesellschaft 3/5 (5.1953) pp. 2-7.
(a) *reprint: Goldschmidt. Hudebnî rozhledy 6 (1953) pp. 446-48.

2821 #Gusinde, A[lois]. "Johannes Brahms. Ein Gedenkblatt zur Wiederkehr seines zehnjährigen Todestages." Die Stimme 1/8 (1.5.1907) pp. 244-46. notes. Contains a brief survey of life and an account of works; includes comments on Brahms the composer.

2822 *Hell, H. "Brahms zum 100. Geburtstag" Die Propyläen (München) 30 (1933) p. 126.

2823 *Henschel, A. K. "100 Jahre Brahms" Die Sendung (1933) p. 397.

2824 *Holmqvist, Bengt. "Dialog om Brahms" Röster i radio [24 or 25]/24 (1957) pp. 10, 36.

2825 "Johannes Brahms. Born May 7, 1833" The Times (London) Royal Edition no. 46,437 (6.5.1933) p. 10. facsim., ill. [p. 16]. Discusses Brahms's music and his character.
(d) Terry, C. Sanford. The Times (London) Royal Edition no. 46,440 (10.5.1933) p. 15. "Centenary of Brahms" recalls performing Op. 45 earlier than the date mentioned in previous article.
(d) Mountain, Thomas. The Times (London) Royal Edition no. 46,443 (13.5.1933) p. 8. States an earlier performance of Op. 45 than Terry.

2826 *"Die Jubiläumsjahr zweier Meistersinger" Prager Presse (5.1.1933).

2827 *K. S. [Karl Stromenger] "Jan Brahms w setną rocznicę urodzin" Tygodnik ilustrowany 74/18 (1933) p. 355. ill.

2828 *Köhler, W. "Brahms. Zu seinem 100. Geburtstag am 7.5. 1933" Die Völkische Schule 1 (1933) p. 42.

2829 *Koppel, Hermann D. "Brahms" Dansk musiktidsskrift 8/2 (1933).

2830 *Kraus, Hedwig. "Johannes Brahms zum Gedächtnis! Anlässlich des 40. Todestages am 3. April 1937." Musica (Wien) 8/9 (1936/37) pp. 9-12.

2831   Kuznitzky, Hans.   "Zum 100.   Geburtstage Brahms" Signale
       für die musikalische Welt 91/18 (3.5.1933) pp. 325-26.
       notes.   Describes the moderns' interest in Brahms; includes
       comments on Brahms the man.

2832   Levi, Lionello.   "Johannes Brahms nel centenario della nascita"
       Ateneo veneto 111/3 (Annata 24) (9.6.1933) pp. 182-86.
       Discusses Brahms and the Wagnerian school, Brahms as a
       composer; includes an appreciation of his work and comments
       on Brahms and Italy.

2833   Liebleitner, Karl.   "Johannes Brahms" Deutsche Volkslied
       24/5,6 (5./6.1922) pp. 31-32.   Discusses Brahms the mu-
       sician with comment on the works based on folksong.

2834   *Limbert, K. E.   Parents Review 42 (1.1932) pp. 20-26.

2835   *M. Kl.   "Johannes Brahms.   Z okazji stulecia urodzin" Swiat
       28/20 (1933) p. 15.   ill.

2836   M. Oszi, Kató.   "Brahms emlékezete.   A nagy zeneköltő hal-
       álának 33.   évfordulója alkalmából" Budapesti hirlap 50/79
       (6.4.1930) p. 41.   ill.   Reviews Brahms's life and the people
       and places in it, especially Wien; includes comments on
       honors he received, as well as on his historical position.

2837   Maine, Basil.   "For My Part" Musical Opinion and Music Trade
       Review 56/668 (5.1933) p. 687.   Cautions that lessons are
       to be learned from the Beethoven and Schubert celebrations
       previously held, with respect to Brahms festivities.

2838   Marschalk, Max.   "Brahms' 30. Todestag" Vossische Zeitung
       (Berlin) Unterhaltungsblatt no. 78 (2.4.1927) p. [1].
       Describes the strengths of Brahms's music; includes comments
       on Brahms, Wagner, Liszt; on Brahms's character; and on
       lifting of copyright limitations on his music.

2839   _____.   "Johannes Brahms.   Zum 100. Geburtstag am 7.
       Mai" Vossische Zeitung (Berlin) Unterhaltungsblatt nr. 125
       (7.5.1933) p. [1].   Describes Brahms's strengths as a
       musician; includes comment on his historical position.

2840   *Merbach, Paul Alfred.   "Brahms.   Welt und Wesen, Werk und
       Wirkung zu seinem 100. Geburtstag" Deutsche Wille (1933)
       pp. 221-38.

2841   *Mětšk, Juro.   "Mysle k 80. posmjertninam J. Brahmsa" Rozhlad
       27/4 (4. 1977) pp. 159-60.

2842   Misch, Ludwig.   "Zum Brahms-Gedenktag" Allgemeine Musik-
       zeitung 49/13 (31.3.1922) pp. 241-44.   notes.   Discusses

Brahms's position in music history and the necessity for commemorative activities.

2843   Montés, John. "Johannes Brahms. Zum hundertsten Geburts-
       tag des Komponisten (am 7. Mai 1933)" Phoenix. Zeitschrift
       für deutsche Geistesarbeit in Südamerika 19/4/5 (1933) pp.
       105-07. ill. Surveys life and works; includes comment on
       his historical position as well as on Brahms and Wagner.

2844   *Morold, M. "Brahms zum 100. Geburtstag" Der Getreue Eckard
       10 (1933) pp. 593-96.

2845   *Moser, Hans Joachim. "Brahms" Leipziger neueste Nachrichten
       (5.5.1933).
       (a) reprint: Moser. "Johannes Brahms" Zeitwende 9 [(8.
       1933)] pp. 117-23. Discusses Brahms's position as
       a composer, his Germanic qualities, and his links
       to religion.

2846   *_____. (H. J.) "Brahms--Die ewige Deutsche" Deutsche
       Zeitung in Norwegen (Oslo) (8.5.1943).

2847   *_____. (Hans J.) "Johannes Brahms--ein Stück deutschen
       Wesens. Zum 110. Geburtstag" Dresdner Zeitung (8.,
       9.;5.;1943).

2848   *_____. "Musiker deutschen Wesens. Brahms zum Gedenken"
       Deutsche Zeitung in Ostland (Riga) (7.5.1943).

2849   Nadkarni, D. "Johannes Brahms: Last of the Musical Roman-
       tists. May 7, 1833--April 3, 1897" The Modern Review
       53/5 (Whole no. 317) (5.1933) pp. 537-42. Discusses Brahms
       as a musician and romantic and reviews the music; includes
       comments on Brahms the man and an overview of his life.

2850   #Niggli, Arnold. "Johannes Brahms. Zur 60. Wiederkehr
       seines Geburtstages (7. Mai 1893)" Schweizerische Musik-
       zeitung und Sängerblatt [32] (4.1893) pp. 74-75. Dis-
       cusses Brahms the musicians and looks at his works; in-
       cludes comment on Brahms's connections to Switzerland.

2851   *Nowowiejski, F[eliks]. M[aria]. "Jan Brahms 1833-1877
       [1833-1897]" Tecza 7/12 (1933) p. 40. ill.

2852   #Otto, Eberhard. "Musik, die einzig aus sich selbst wirkt.
       Unserer Zeit tief wesensverwandt: Johannes Brahms" Der
       Neue Tag (Weiden/Opf) (1.4.1967) p. [?]. Discusses
       Brahms as a composer and his relevance to music of the
       20th century; includes comments on Brahms and Wagner.

2853   Perger, H. von. "Johannes Brahms. (Zur zwanzigsten

Wiederkehr seines Todestages am 3.   April 1897.)"   Der
Merker (Wien) 8/7 (4.1917) pp. 256-58.   Describes the
strengths of Brahms's music.

2854   Petzoldt, Richard.   "Johannes Brahms.   1833-1897" Musik in
der Schule 9/5 ([5.] 1958) pp. 196-211.   facsim., mus.,
fig.   Discusses Brahms the man and the composer; includes
comments on his interest in folksong and religion.

2855   *Pischel, M[aria].   "Brahms" Monatsschrift für katholische
Lehrerinnen 46 (1933) p. 159.

2856   *Pylkkänen, Tauno.   "Johannes Brahms in kuoleman 50-vuotis-
muisto" Musiikki 1/3-4 (1947).

2857   *Radio Audizioni Italia.   Celebrazione del cinquantesimo anniver-
sario della morte di Johannes Brahms [Aprile-Maggio, 1947].
[Torino:] Radio Italiana, [1947].   31 pp.   ill., facsim.
Cover title: "Celebrazione Brahmsiane, dirette da Vittorio
Gui."

2858   *Reiff, A.   "Brahms zum 100.   Geburtstag" Schwaben-Spiegel
(Stuttgart) 27 (1933) p. 139.

2859   *Sänger, E.   "Brahms" Astrologische Rundschau 25 (1933)
pp. 13-17.

2860   Schilling, Otto-Erich.   "Johannes Brahms.   Zu seinem 50.
Todestag am 3.   April 1947" Die Wochenpost 2/14 (6.4.1947)
p. 3.   Discusses Brahms's historical position; includes
comment on Brahms the composer.

2861   *Schoenewolf, K[arl].   "Vorbild und Vermächtnis Brahms.   Zu
seinem 110.   Geburtstag" Schlesische Zeitung (Breslau)
(1.5.1943).

2862   Schumann, Georg.   "Johannes Brahms 1833-1933" The Choir
and Musical Journal 24/281 (5.1933) pp. 95-96.   Discusses
Brahms and Wagner, also Brahms's childhood; includes
comments on Brahms the man and a postcard sent by Brahms
to the author.

2863   *Schwarz, Gerhard.   "Johannes Brahms" Hamburger Kirchenkalender (1933) pp. 59-65.

2864   *Schweich, B.   "Johannes Brahms.   Ein Gedenkblatt" Kompass
no. 416 (1908).

2865   *Sebestyén, Ede.   "Brahms Johannes élete.   Születésének 100.
évfordulójára" A Zene 14 (1932/33) pp. 214-18.

B. Commemorative Pieces / 475

2866 *Segnitz, E[ugen]. "Brahms" Leipziger Tageblatt (2.4.1922).

2867 *Simon, James. "Brahms" Nationaltheater 5/3+ (1933).

2868 *Sonkoly, István. "Apróságok a százéves Brahmsról" Nemzeti
újság (Budapest) (7.5.1933). Describes Peterffy's opinion
of Brahms, discusses Brahms and Hungarian folkmusic, focusing on the Ungarische Tänze [Hofmann nr. 128; McCorkle
WoO 1]; also includes Brahms anecdotes. [from 241]

2869 *Speckhahn, W. "Brahms, zum Gedenken in Haus und Schule"
Die Mittelschule 47 (1933) p. 180.

2870 *Springer, Max. "Johannes Brahms" Reichspost (Wien) (7.5.
1933).

2871 #Stahl, Heinrich. "Johannes Brahms" Deutsche Erde 4 (1933)
pp. 203-06. Discusses Brahms versus the Wagner-Wolf-
Bruckner schools; includes comment on his character and
on the qualities of his music.

2872 Steinhard, Erich. "Brahms. Zum 40. Todestag" Der Auftakt
17/12 ([12.] 1937) pp. 197-98. Discusses Brahms as a
musician; includes comments on Brahms and Wagner, Brahms
and the Schumanns.

2873 *Steinhauer, W. "Brahms" Die Sendung 10 (1933) p. 845.

2874 *Tessmer, H[ans]. "Zu Brahms' 25. Todestag" Tägliche
Rundschau (Berlin) (3.4.1922).

2875 "Tribute to Brahms is paid by Vienna" New York Times 86/
28,926 (5.4.1937) p. 17. Describes activities to observe the
40th anniversary of Brahms's death.

2876 *Unger, Hermann. "Brahms" Skizzen 7/4 (1933).

2877 *_____. (H.) "Gebändigte Romantik. Zum 50. Todestag
von Johannes Brahms" Melodie 2/4 (1947).

2878 v.W. [P. A. van Westrheene] "Belangrijke data. 3. April†
Johannes Brahms 1833-1897" Caecilia (Utrecht) 79/11 (10.
4.1922) pp. 175-76. Discusses Brahms's historical position
and the qualities of his music.

2879 *Vogel, R. "Brahms" Deutsche Monatshefte für Chile 14 (1933)
pp. 331-33.

2880 Werner, Th. W. "Johannes Brahms" Die Unterhaltung. Literarische Beilage zum Hannoverscher Kurier (31.3.1922) p.
[1]. Discusses Brahms the composer, his place in music

history and the qualities of his music; includes comparisons
with Bach and Beethoven with regard to both compositional
style and personal qualities.

2881 *Weyl-Nissen, A. "Zum 100. Geburtstag Brahms" Bayrische
Staatszeitung (München) (6.5.1933).

2882 *Zimmermann, R. "Brahms" Die Sonne 10 (1933) pp. 225-31.

2883 *"Zum 100. Geburtstag von Johannes Brahms" Zentral-Verein-
Zeitung 12 (1933) p. 161.

See also 4, 31, 49, 2899.

See also "Serial and Section Materials" in I.A.

C. EVALUATION

Contains materials that assess Brahms's position in music history,
discuss the reception accorded him by other composers and the
general public, or describe the honors he received during his
lifetime.

Stature in 1850's: 2957, 2972, 3013, 3019.5, 3026.
Stature in 1860's: 2919, 2925, 2926, 2950, 2960, 3026, 3030.
Stature in 1870's: 2925, 2946, 2950, 3011, 3012, 3018, 3026, 3027,
3030, 3038, 3039.
Stature in 1880's: 2924, 2925, 2935, 2944, 2946, 2948, 2979, 2985,
3026, 3027, 3030, 3048.
Stature in 1890's: 2904, 2909, 2913, 2935, 2939, 2943-47, 2955, 2956,
2961-63, 2966, 2967, 2992, 2997, 3010, 3019, 3025-27, 3030, 3037,
3048.
Stature in 1900's: 2886, 2911, 2920, 2933, 2951, 2965, 2973, 2976,
2980, 2994, 2996, 3026, 3027, 3033, 3044-46.
Stature in 1910's: 2910, 3004, 3026-28, 3041.
Stature in 1920's: 2884, 2885, 2889, 2890, 2900, 2903, 2908, 2929,
2936, 2940, 2953, 2958, 2959, 2981, 2986, 2988, 2998, 3021, 3024,
3027, 3040, 3049.
Stature in 1930's: 2888, 2896, 2898, 2901, 2902, 2906, 2912, 2916,
2921, 2922, 2927, 2930, 2931, 2937, 2942, 2968, 2978, 2987, 2989,
2999, 3000, 3001, 3005, 3006, 3008, 3014, 3016, 3020, 3023.
Stature in 1940's: 2938, 2982, 2984, 3003, 3015, 3017, 3031, 3034.
Stature in 1950's: 2895, 2905, 2917, 2918, 2971, 2977, 2991, 3007.
Stature in 1960's: 2928, 2941.
Stature in 1970's: 2914, 3029, 3042.

2884 "[Verschillende bijdragen]" Caecilia (Utrecht) 79/11 (10.4.

1922) pp. 172-74.
Kes, W. "De 25ste terugkeer van Brahms sterfdag ...":
pp. 172-73. Describes Brahms in Amsterdam; includes
comment on Brahms the composer.
Messchaert, Joh. "Waarom wordt Brahms nog niet voldoende
...": p. 173. exhorts the need for proper Brahms
research; includes an assessment of Brahms as composer.
Röntgen, Julius. "In de troebele zee ...": p. 173.
Discusses Brahms's links to 20th century music.
Wagenaar, Joh. "Voor mij behoort Brahms tot ...": pp.
173-74. Assesses Brahms's stature as a composer.
Verhey, A. B. H. "Laat ik volstaan met u te zeggen dat
ik Brahms zeer hoog stel en wat nog meer zegt, heel
veel Brahms houd": p. 174. Offers a personal opinion
on Brahms's worth.
Swaap, Sam. "Als kamermuziekspeler zend ik u hierby
mijn meening over Brahms ..."; p. 174. Offers an
assessment of Brahms's music, focusing on the chamber
works.
Spanjaard, Martin. "Het feit, dat men maar al te dikwijls
...": p. 174. Assesses Brahms's artistic worth.

2885 *Illinois Staats-Zeitung (1927).
(d) see: 3051.

2886 A. E. Neue Musikzeitung 28/13 (4.4.1907) p. 293. Describes
the French opinion of Brahms.

2887 A. F. S. "Brahms und die Wiener" Frankfurter Zeitung
77/338 (7.5.1933) 2. Morgenblatt Dreimalige Ausgabe p. 7.
Describes the success of Brahms's music in Wien, and the
public's understanding of his work.

2888 Abendroth, Walter. "Brahms' Bedeutung für seine und unsere
Zeit" Allgemeine Musikzeitung 64/13/14 (26.3.1937) pp. 178-
81. ill. Discusses Brahms's historical position.
(d) #incorporated: Johannes Brahms. Sein Wesen und
seine musikgeschichtliche Bedeutung. Berlin:
Ed. Bote & G. Bock, 1939. 47 pp. ill. Background and descriptive analysis of Brahms's works;
Includes critical assessment and evaluation.
*also in series (Berliner Kunstwochen).
(c) *excerpt (of ? Auflage): Abendroth. "Orches-
tersatz und -stil bei Brahms" Die Musikwoche
7 (1939) p. 242.

2889 *Aber, Adolf. "Brahms und die Gegenwart" Leipziger neueste
Nachrichten (2.4.1922).

2890 *Alioth, Marguerite. "Zum Streit über Brahms" Schweizerische
musikpädagogische Blätter 9/9 (1920).

2891 Altmann, Wilhelm. "Brahms als Mensch" Die Musik (Berlin)
25/8 (5.1933) pp. 588-92. Describes how Brahms's greatness helped him overcome the trials and tribulations of his
life; also lists some of his interests.
(a) reprint: in 3186.c. pp. 28-32.

2892 Araiz, Andres. "Brahms memorias de un viejo estudiante de
musica" Heterofonia 10/2 (no. 53) (3.-4.1977) pp. 15-18.
Records his change in attitude towards Brahms as he grew
older.
(d) summarized in English translation: Araiz. "Souvenirs
of An Old Music Student" Heterofonia 10/2 (no.
53) (3.-4.1977) pp. 47-48.

2893 [Daniel Gregory Mason] "The Art of Brahms" Masters in Music
5/part 29 (5.1905) pp. 7-12. (volume pp. 199-204). notes.
Includes 1556 and excerpts in both original language and
English translation of Brahms criticism from 138, 871, 1392,
1548.d.

2894 [Daniel Gregory Mason] "The Art of Brahms" Masters in Music
5/part 30 (6.1905) pp. 6-9 (volume pp. 246-49). Criticism
of Brahms in general and, in particular, as a songwriter:
includes 2047 and excerpts in both original language and
English translation of Brahms criticism from 117.b.i., 461.e.,
1336, 1392.

2895 #Bachmann, Claus-Henning. "Brahms in unserer Zeit" Musikblätter 12 (1958/59) pp. 61-62. Sees Brahms not as the
end of an era, but pointing towards the future.

2896 *Baser, Friedrich. "Brahms in unserer Heimat" Neue Mannheimer
Zeitung (6.5.1933).

2897 Bekker, Paul. "Brahms" Anbruch 15/4/5 (4./5.1933) pp.
56-58. Analyses why Brahms's advocates are so intolerant
of any criticism of the Master; includes comment on the rewards to be gained in understanding Brahms's music.

2898 Bernhard, Paul. "Johannes Brahms. Geboren am 7. Mai
1833" Deutsche Rundschau 59/8 (Bd. 235) (5.1933) pp. 116-
19. Examines Brahms's position in music history and the
qualities of his music.

2899 *Berrsche, Alexander. "Brahms" in Berrsche. Trösterin
Musika. Gesammelte Aufsätze und Kritiken. Hermann Rinn
and Hans Rupé, eds. München: Verlag Hermann Rinn, 1942.
2. Auflage: 1949. pp. 273-94. ind. Contains author's
writings on Brahms from Münchener Zeitung and other
sources, 1912-40: discusses specific works, as well as
Brahms and Wagner, Brahms the man, etc.

3., von Horst Leuchtmann bearbeitete Auflage der von Hermann
Rinn und Hans Rupé herausgegebenen Trösterin Musika.:
Kritik und Betrachtung. Hamburg und München: Verlag
Heinrich Ellermann, 1964. pp. 238-60. Adds notes.

2900 Binns, Richard. "Brahms: Some Thoughts Towards a Re-
valuation" Musical Times 65/977 (1.7.1924) pp. 599-601.
Examines the new interest in Brahms and how standards
change: takes a new look at Brahms as a romantic and as
a philosopher.

2901 *Blom, Eric. Birmingham Post (8.5.1933).
(a) reprint: Blom. "Johannes Brahms To-day" in Blom.
A Musical Postbag. London: J. M. Dent & Sons
Ltd., 1941. pp. 20-23. Discusses why there is
still interest in Brahms.
*issues: 1943, 1945, 1949.

2902 _____. "The Status of Brahms" The Listener 9/225 (3.5.
1933) pp. 685-87. ill., notes. Describes Brahms as a
compositional master and discusses his overall achievement.

2903 Böttcher, Georg. "Johannes Brahms. Skizze" Neue Musikzeitung 43/13 (6.4.1922) p. 205. An appreciation of Brahms's
greatness.

2904 "Brahms" Musical Times 32/578 (1.4.1891) p. 210. A sonnet
on Brahms as a master musician.

2905 *"Brahms in unserer Zeit" Musikalische Jugend. Jeunesses
musicales 7/2 (7.1958) p. 4.

2906 Bücken, Ernst. "Der Meister der Spätwirkung. Zum Brahms-
Jubiläum" Melos 12/5/6 (5./6.1933) pp. 178-81. mus. Discusses Brahms's historical position and musical style.

2907 *Buhlmann, E. "Als Johannes Brahms im Gewandhaus durchfiel"
Leipziger neueste Nachrichten (15.3.1937).

2908 *Bundi, G. Schweizerische musikpädogogische Blätter 9/5
(1920) p. 68.

2909 C. S. "Nochmals Berliner Musik-"Kritik"" Musikalisches Wochenblatt 27/6 (30.1.1896) p. 77. Comments on the Berlin music
critics' anti-Brahms posture.

2910 Cahn-Speyer, Rudolf. "Eine Erwiderung an Felix Weingartner"
Die Musik (Berlin) 11/18 (Bd. 43) (6.1912) pp. 361-64.
notes. Response to 2804: positive comments on Brahms
and the Brahms-Wagner controversy.

2911 *Carraud, Gaston. La Liberté.
(d) report: "Brahms" Revue musicale de Lyon 1/25 (6.4.
1904) p. 299. Comments on Brahms and his music.

2912 *Connor, Herbert. "Was bedeutet uns Brahms?" Kunstgemeinde
7/2 (1933).

2913 Cowie, Francis S. "Two Views of Brahms" New Quarterly
Musical Review 2/6 (8.1894) pp. 113-18. notes. Discusses
the pros and cons of Brahms the composer.

2914 Craft, Robert. "Brahms (Part 2): A "Reproach to the Haste
of a Superficial Generation"" World 1/12 (5.12.1972) pp.
74-75. ill. Discusses Brahms's greatness but points out
his weaknesses as a symphonist.
(a) reprint (in slightly revised form): Craft. "Brahms -
A ... Generation"" in Craft. Prejudices in Dis-
guise. Articles, Essays, Reviews. New York:
Alfred A. Knopf, 1974. pp. 175-81. omits ill.

2915 *Demuth, Norman. "On Brahms (1833-1897)" in Demuth, comp.
An Anthology of Musical Criticism. London: Eyre &
Spottiswoode, 1947. pp. 271-85.
(a) reprint: Westport, Conn.: Greenwood Press Publishers, 1971. Excerpts from performance reviews, and
23, 152.d., 469, 1421, 1572, 2232, 2486, 2963.
*issue: 1977.

2916 #Dent, Edward J. "Johannes Brahms 1833-1933" Cambridge
Review 54 (17.2.1933) pp. 247-48. Describes attitudes
towards Brahms and comments on Brahms's music.

2917 *Dobel, Richard. "Der heitere Brahms" Allgemeine Volksmusikzeitung 8 (1958) pp. 145-47.

2918 #D'Urbano, Jorge. "Brahms, el músico" Ars. Revista de arte
17/79 (1957) pp. [10-12, 14-15]. ill., facsim. Discusses
Brahms's importance to music history; includes comment
on Brahms and Wagner and on the influence of Bach on
Brahms's music.

2919 E. R. "Die moderne 'grosse' Oper und die Musik im Concert.
Meyerbeer, Wagner und--Brahms" Leipziger allgemeine musikalische Zeitung 1/8 (21.2.1866) pp. 62-65. Brahms: pp.
64-65. Assesses Brahms as having potential, based on the
music that has appeared.

2920 Ehrlich, Heinrich, see 2463.5.

2921 Einstein, Alfred. "Johannes Brahms--100 Jahre. Der in
sich beruhende Brahms" Berliner Tageblatt 62/211 (7.5.1933)

Ausgabe A p. [27]. Discusses the significance of Brahms in relation to Wagner.

(a) reprint: Einstein. In Einstein. Von Schütz bis Hindemith. Essays über Musik und Musiker. Zürich/Stuttgart: Pan Verlag, 1957. pp. 96-98. *also: Kassel: Bärenreiter, 1957.

2922 Elsenaar, E. "De veel-omstreden figuur onder de componisten der oudere generatie" Symphonia 16/5 (5.1933) p. 86. Reviews critics' and composers' opinions of Brahms.

2923 #Engelke, Bernhard Johannes. "Brahms im Lichte der französische Kritik" Kieler neueste Nachrichten (22. or 23.(?); 7.;1939) p. [?]. Examines Paris music critics' writings for comments on Brahms.

2924 Ernst. "Eine moderne Fabel" Musikalisches Wochenblatt 11/41 (1.10.1880) pp. 481-83. notes. Takes exception to the view that Brahms is in the Schumann school of composers.

2925 Fellinger, Imogen. "Das Brahms-Bild der Allgemeinen Musikalischen Zeitung (1863 bis 1882)" in Beiträge zur Geschichte der Musikkritik. Heinz Becker, ed. (Studien zur Musikgeschichte des 19. Jahrhunderts Bd. 5) Regensburg: Gustav Bosse Verlag, 1965. pp. 27-54. notes. Studies how writers and correspondents for this journal viewed Brahms as a composer, conductor and performer; focuses on Selmar Bagge, Adolf Schubring and Hermann Deiters.

2926 Fétis père. [François-Joseph Fétis] "Effets des circonstances sur la situation actuelle de la musique, au point de vue de la composition. Ce qu'il faudrait faire pour améliorer cette situation" Revue et gazette musicale de Paris 30/32, 35, 38, 41, 44 (9. and 30.;8. and 20.9.; 11.10.;1.11.;1863) pp. 251-52, 275-77, 297-99, 321-32, 345-47. Brahms: p. 276. Describes Brahms as a pupil of Schumann.

2927 *Frerichs, E. "Das Werk Brahms und die Musik unserer Zeit" Monatshefte für Literatur, Kunst und Wissenschaft. Zeitschrift der Buchgemeinde 9 (1933) pp. 686-91.

2928 Fuller, Roy. "Brahms" The Listener 82/2123 (4.12.1969) p. 801. ill. Describes the genius of Brahms.

2929 Furtwängler, Wilhelm. "Brahms" Allgemeine Musikzeitung 49/13 (31.3.1922) p. 241. Assesses Brahms's historical position.

2930 *_____. "Johannes Brahms" Neue freie Presse (Wien) (28.5. 1933).
(d) see: 2931.

2931 _____. "Johannes Brahms. Vortrag, gehalten anlässlich
des Brahms-Festes in Wien am 16. Mai 1933" Deutsche
allgemeine Zeitung (Berlin) 72/224-225 (28.5.1933) Reichsausgabe Beiblatt [p. 3]. Discusses the history of Brahms's
reception, his artistic development, and his Germanic qualities.
  (a) i) reprint: Furtwängler. Neue freie Presse (Wien)
        no. 24,682 (31.5.1933) Morgenblatt p. 10.
     ii) *reprint: in Furtwängler. Johannes Brahms. Anton
        Bruckner. Mit einem Nachwort von W[alter].
        Riezler. [(Reclams Universal-Bibliothek, 7515)]
        Leipzig: P. Reclam jun., [1942]. 72 pp.
        Nachwort: Riezler, W[alter]. "Wilhelm Furtwängler":
        pp. 47-72.
        *[Neu Auflage:] Stuttgart: Reclam, 1952. 63 pp.
        *[Neuauflage Nachdruck:] [1963].
        issue: 1971.
        "Johannes Brahms": pp. 3-16.
        Riezler, W[alter]: pp. 43-63. Includes 2467.a.iii.
    iii) reprint: Furtwängler. "Johannes Brahms. 1931"
        in Furtwängler. Ton und Wort. Aufsätze und
        Vorträge 1918 bis 1954. Wiesbaden: F. A. Brock-
        haus, 1954. pp. 40-52. Includes 2467.a.iv.
        *7. Auflage: 1956.
        *8. Auflage: 1958.
        *9. Auflage: 1966.
     (b) *French translation by Jacques and Jacqueline
        Feschotte (of ? Auflage): Musique et
        verbe. Paris: A. Michel, [1963].
  (d) i) Furtwängler. "Aus der Gedenkrede beim Wiener
        Brahms-Fest 1933. Gekürzt nach der Niederschrift
        in der Neue freie Presse (28.5.1933)" Anbruch
        19/3 (3.1937) pp. 33-37.
     ii) comment: "Zur Brahms-Rede Furtwänglers" 23.
        Eine Wiener Musikzeitschrift no. 11/12 (30.6.1933)
        pp. 30-36. notes.
  (e) i) report: "Auftakt zur Brahms Feier. Wilhelm
        Furtwängler als Festredner" Neue freie Presse
        (Wien) no. 24,668 (17.5.1933) Morgenblatt p. 8.
        Includes report on opening ceremony of Brahms-
        Fest in Wien.
     ii) report: Kralik, Heinrich. "Das Brahms-Fest in
        Wien" Die Musik (Berlin) 25/9 (6.1933) pp. 676-77.

2932 Gay, Peter. "Aimez-vouz Brahms? Reflections on Modernism"
Salmagundi no. 36 (Winter 1977) pp. 16-35. notes. A
history of Brahms's reputation, showing how evaluation and
categorization is far from being absolute.
  (a) reprint (in revised form): Gay. "Aimez-vous Brahms?
     On Polarities in Modernism" in Freud, Jews and
     Other Germans. Masters and Victims in Modernist

Culture. Gay, ed. New York: Oxford University
Press, 1978. pp. 231-56.

2933 Göhler, Georg. "Johannes Brahms" Der Kunstwart 13/14
(4.1900) pp. 52-58. Brahms's artistic position with a survey
of the works.
(b) French translation: Göhler, Georges. "Johannes
Brahms" [end of Part II signed Georg Göhler] La
Musique en Suisse 2/24,25 (15.10. and 1.11.; 1902)
pp. 42-46, 56-57.

2934 Gray, Cecil. "Johannes Brahms (1833-1897)" in The Heritage
of Music. [Volume1] Hubert J. Foss, ed. London: Humphrey
Milford, Oxford University Press, 1927. pp. 177-98. Discusses Brahms's classic/romantic duality and how he has
suffered from the critics; includes comment on Brahms as
a composer and songwriter, and Brahms and Wordworth.
*issues: 1934, 1940, 1944.
(a) i) reprint: Gray. "Johannes Brahms" in Gray.
Contingencies and Other Essays. London [et al.]:
Oxford University Press, Geoffrey Cumberlege,
1947. pp. 58-76. notes.
(a) *reprint: (Essay Index Reprint Series) Freeport, N.Y.: Books for Libraries Press,
[1971].
ii) *reprint: London, New York: Oxford University
Press, G[eoffrey]. Cumberlege, [1948].
iii) *reprint: (Essay Index Reprint Series) Freeport,
N.Y.: Books for Libraries Press, [1969].

2935 [George Bernard Shaw] The Great Composers. Reviews and
Bombardments by Bernard Shaw. Edited with an Intro-
duction by Louis Crompton. Berkeley, Los Angeles,
London: University of California Press, 1978. "Brahms":
pp. 62-63, 143-50. Concert reviews and comments on
Brahms's music, gathered together from Bernard Shaw.
Music in London 1890-94. 3 vols. Standard Edition (Lon-
don: Constable and Company Limited, 1932); [George
Bernard Shaw] London Music in 1888-89 as Heard By Corno
di Bassetto (Later Known as Bernard Shaw) With Some
Further Autobiographical Particulars. (London: Constable
and Company Limited, 1937); and Bernard Shaw. How to
Become a Musical Critic. Edited with an Introduction by
Dan H. Laurence. (New York: Hill and Wang, 1961).

2936 *Grimstedt. "Johannes Brahms" Aftonbladet (Stockholm)
(27.3.1928).

2937 *"The Growing Brahms" Musical Courier 106/18 (Whole no. 2769)
(6.5.1933) p. 16. Discusses Brahms's strengths as a composer.

2938 Gui, Vittorio, see 2469.5.

2939 *H. Sch. [Heinrich Schenker] "Johannes Brahms hat das
Ehrenkreuz für Kunst und Wissenschaft erhalten ..." Die
Zeit [Wochenschrift] (Wien) [2]/85 (16.5.1896) p. 110.
(d) see: 2970.

2940 Haelssig, Artur. "Brahms und die junge Generation" Neue
Musikzeitung 49/11 (1928) pp. 346-47. Author gives his
opinion of the quality of the vocal works.

2941 *Hallenberg, A. "Tycker ni om Brahms?" Musikern 60/4
(4.1967) p. 5.
(a) *reprint: Hallenberg. Slöjd och ton 38/1 (1968) pp.
6-7.

2942 *Hammerschlag, János. "Johannes Brahms" A Zene 14 (1932/33)
pp. 207-09.

2943 *Hanslick, Eduard. Am Ende des Jahrhunderts [[1895-1899]].
Musikalische Kritiken und Schilderungen. (Der "Modernen
Oper" VIII. Teil) Berlin: Allgemeiner Verein für deutsche
Litteratur, 1899.
*2. Auflage: 1899. vi, 452 pp.
*3. Auflage: 1899 or 1911.
(a) reprint (of 2. Auflage): (The Collected Musical Criticism of Eduard Hanslick VIII) Westmead: Gregg
International Publishers Limited, 1971. Includes
reprints of performance reviews of Brahms' works
from Neue freie Presse (Wien), also 443.a., 969.a.,
1153.a., 3102.a.
(c) excerpt (of 2. Auflage): Hanslick. "Brahms and
Dvorak" in 969.a.c. pp. 165-70. Brahms: pp.
165-68. Performance review of Op. 73.

2944 *Hanslick, Eduard. Aus dem Tagebuche eines Musikers. Kritiken und Schilderungen. (Der "Modernen Oper" VI. Theil)
Berlin: Allgemeiner Verein für deutsche Litteratur, 1892.
v, [1], 360 pp.
*3. Auflage: 1892 or 1911.
(a) reprint (of 1. Auflage?): (The Collected Musical
Criticism of Eduard Hanslick VI) Westmead: Gregg
International Publishers Limited, 1971. Includes
reprints of performance reviews of Brahms's works
from Neue freie Presse (Wien).
(c) i) excerpt (of ? Auflage in English translation by
Henry Pleasants III): in 2470.a.b.
ii) excerpt (of 3. Auflage): Hanslick. "Vierte Symphonie in e-moll von Brahms" in 969.a.c. pp. 162-
65. Performance review of Op. 98.

2945 *_____. Aus neuer und neuester Zeit. Musikalische Kritiken
und Schilderungen. (Der Modernen Oper IX. Teil) Berlin:
Allgemeiner Verein für deutsche Litteratur, 1900. [ii],
377 pp.
  *2. Auflage: 1900.
  *3. Auflage: 1900 or 1911.
    (a) reprint (of 3. Auflage): (The Collected Musical Cri-
        ticism of Eduard Hanslick IX) Westmead: Gregg
        International Publishers Limited, 1971. Includes
        reprints of performance reviews of Brahms's works
        from Neue freie Presse (Wien).

2946 *Hanslick, Eduard. Concerte, Componisten und Virtuosen der
letzten fünfzehn Jahre. 1870-1885. Kritiken. Berlin:
Allgemeiner Verein für deutsche Litteratur, 1886.
  *2. Auflage: 1886. [2], viii, 447 pp.
  *4. Auflage: 1896.
    (a) reprint (of 2. Auflage): Westmead: Gregg International
        Publishers Limited, 1971. Includes reprints of per-
        formance reviews of Brahms's works from Neue freie
        Presse (Wien).
    (c) i) excerpt (of 4. Auflage in English translation by
            Margit L. McCorkle): see 1380.
        ii) excerpt (of ? Auflage in English translation by
            Henry Pleasants III): see 2470.a.b.
       iii) excerpt (of ? Auflage in English translation by
            Jacques Barzun): see 1930.

2947 *Hanslick, Eduard. Fünf Jahre Musik [[1891-1895]]. Kritiken.
(Der "Modernen Oper" VII. Teil) Berlin: Allgemeiner
Verein für deutsche Litteratur, 1896. vii, [3], 402 pp.
  *2. Auflage: 1896.
  *3. Auflage: 1896 or 1911.
    (a) reprint (of 3. Auflage): (The Collected Musical Criti-
        cism of Eduard Hanslick VII) Westmead: Gregg
        International Publishers Limited, 1971. Includes re-
        prints of performance reviews of Brahms's works
        from Neue freie Presse (Wien).

2948 *_____. "IV. Johannes Brahms" in Hanslick. Musikalisches
und Litterarisches. Kritiken und Schilderungen. (Der
"Modernen Oper" V. Theil) Berlin: Allgemeiner Verein für
deutsche Litteratur, 1889.
  *2. Auflage: 1889. iv, 359 pp.
  *3. Auflage: 1890 or 1911.
    (a) reprint (of 2. Auflage): (The Collected Musical Criti-
        cism of Eduard Hanslick V) Westmead: Gregg In-
        ternational Publishers Limited, 1971. pp. 129-56.
        notes. Contains 320.e.a., 1378.a., 2021.a.

2949 *Hanslick, Eduard. Musikkritiken. [Lothar Fahlbusch. ed.]

(Reclams Universal-Bibliothek, Bd. 465. Musik und Musik-
theater) Leipzig: P. Reclam, 1972.

2950 *_____. Zur Geschichte des Concertwesens in Wien. [Wien:
n.p., 1864]. [141 pp.].
   (c) *excerpt: Hanslick. Osterreichische Revue 2/Bd.
      4-6,8 (1864).
   (d) elaborated and revised: Hanslick. Geschichte des
      Concertwesens in Wien. Wien: W. Braumüller,
      1869-70. 2 volumes.
      A. 1. Theil.
      Contains only scattered references to Brahms.
      B. 2. Theil.
      *Hanslick. Aus dem Concertsaal. Kritiken und Schil-
      derungen aus den letzten 20 Jahren des Wiener
      Musiklebens nebst einem Anhang: Musikalische
      Reisebriefe aus England, Frankreich und der Schweiz.
      (Hanslick. Geschichte des Concertwesens in Wien.
      2. Theil) Wien: Wilhelm Braumüller k.k. Hof-
      und Universitätsbuchhändler, 1870. x, 534 pp.
      *2. Auflage: München und Berlin: Bruckmann, 1886
      or 1896.
      *2. Auflage [revised and enlarged]: Wien: W[ilhelm].
      Braumüller, 1897. xvi, 604 pp. omits series.
      (a) reprint (of 1870 Auflage): Westmead: Gregg
         International Publishers Limited, 1971.
         Includes reprints of performance reviews
         of Brahms's works from Neue freie Presse
         (Wien), also 1655.a.ii., 2470.a.

2951 Harding, H. A. "Some Thoughts Upon The Position of Johannes
Brahms Among The Great Masters of Music" Proceedings of
the Musical Association 33rd Session, 1906-07. pp. 159-74.
notes. Discusses why Brahms is not more readily and
generally placed among the great composers; includes comment on the piano works up to Op. 10.
   (d) summary: Harding. "Johannes Brahms and His Peers"
      Musical Opinion and Music Trade Review 30/359
      (1.8.1907) p. 813. Omits notes, adds ill.

2952 Henderson, W. J. "Fifty Years of Brahms" Musical Courier
106/18 (Whole no. 2769) (6.5.1933) pp. 6, 23. ill. Discusses American response to Brahms's music.

2953 Heuss, Alfred. "Was kann Brahms uns Heute bedeuten? Zum
25. Todestage des Meisters" Zeitschrift für Musik 89/7
(4.1922) pp. 153-56. ill. Discusses Brahms's historical
position.

2954 #Hill, Ralph. "Fact and Fiction About Brahms" in Hill.

Challenges. A Series of Controversial Essays on Music.
With an Introduction by John Ireland and an Envoi by C.
B. Rees. London: J. Williams Limited, 1943. pp. 90-96.
notes. Comments on the weaknesses of some arguments
that present a negative evaluation of Brahms.

2955 *Hirschfeld, Robert. Neue musikalische Presse [=Internationale
Musik- und Instrumenten-Zeitung] 5 (5.1896).
(e) report: "Ueber (sic) die Bedeutung der auch von
uns ..." Musikalisches Wochenblatt 27/28 (2.7.1896)
p. 375. On the significance of the Ehrenzeichens
für Kunst und Wissenschaft awarded to Brahms.

2956 *"Hogy támadták Brahms zenei gondolatait?" Egyetértés (Budapest) (9.4.1897).

2957 Hoplit. [Richard Pohl] "Johannes Brahms. I.II." Neue Zeitschrift für Musik Bd. 43/2,24,25 (6.7.;and 7.,14.;12.;1855)
pp. 13-15, 253-55, 261-64. notes. Examines Brahms in
light of Schumann's claims in 3013; includes comments on
Schumann's influence on Brahms's music.

2958 *Humbert, G[eorges]. Schweizerische musikpädagogische
Blätter 9/5 (1920) p. 69.

2959 Hutschenruyter, Wouter. "Wat is Brahms voor ons, ouderen?"
Caecilia (Utrecht) 79/11 (10.4.1922) pp. 166-67. Discusses
what the present generation can learn from Brahms.

2960 *J. C. E.
(e) report: "Urtheil eines schweizerischen Musikers über
Johannes Brahms" Leipziger allgemeine musikalische
Zeitung 1/26 (27.6.1866) pp. 208-09. notes. Relates comments from a Zürich concert review.
(a) #reprint: in 3167.e.

2961 J. F. R. [John F. Runciman] "A Note on Brahms" Saturday
Review 83/2166 (1.5.1897) pp. 468-70. A negative evaluation:
on the difficulty of assessing Brahms.
(a) reprint: Runciman, John F. in Runciman. Old Scores
and New Readings: Discussions on Musical Subjects.
London: At The Sign of The Unicorn [Unicorn
Press], 1899 [1898]. pp. 239-47.
*[2nd Edition Revised and Enlarged:] 1901.

2962 J. S. S. [J. S. Shedlock] "Johannes Brahms" Academy
[51]/1301 New series (10.4.1897) pp. 407-08. Discusses Brahms's position as a composer and his
music.

2963 _____. "Johannes Brahms" Monthly Musical Record 27/317

(1.5.1897) pp. 97-99. Discusses the qualities of Brahms's works that make him a great composer.
(c) *excerpt: in 2915. pp. 282-83.

2964 Jacobi, Frederick. "Brahms und Amerika" Frankfurter Zeitung 77/338 (7.5.1933) 2. Morgenblatt Dreimalige Ausgabe p. 7. Examines concert programming as an indicator of the reception of Brahms's music.

2965 *Járosi, Dezső. Brahms János zeneesztétikai méltatása. Temesvár: Csanád egyházmegyei kvny, 1908. 15 pp.

2966 "Johannes Brahms" The Outlook 50/9 (1.9.1894) pp. 337-38. Discusses why Brahms is a great composer; includes comment on the appreciation of Brahms.

2967 [W. S. B. Mathews] "Johannes Brahms: His Individuality and Place in Art. A Symposium" Music (Chicago) 12/1 (5.1897) pp. 59-66. ill. Opinions of Brahms from Theodore Thomas, Eugene Grünberg, Calvin Brainard Cady, Otto Lohse and Henry Eames.
(c) excerpt: in 2894. p. 7 (volume p. 247).

2968 "Johannes Brahms. Zur Erinnerung an seinen 100. Geburtstag am 7. Mai" Deutsche Welt 10/5 (5.1933) pp. 320-21. mus. Describes the significance and place of Brahms both in his own time, and since; includes comments on Brahms as a composer and on Brahms compared with Wagner.

2969 Jullien, Adolphe. "Brahms jugé par Schumann" Le Guide musical (Bruxelles) 26/7 (12.2.1880) pp. [1-2]. notes. Relates Schumann's opinion of Brahms from letters between Schumann and Maurice Strakergan and from 3013.
(b) English translation by Stella: "Schumann's Opinion of Brahms" Musical Standard 18/814 Third series (6.3.1880) p. 151.

2970 "Der junge Schenker über Brahms" Der Dreiklang. Monatsschrift für Musik no. 2 [(1937)] p. 61. Provides Schenker's opinion of Brahms, and quotes from 2939.

2971 #Kahl, Willi. "Aus den Kämpfen um Brahms" [Niederrheinisches Musikfest. Jahrbuch. (Düsseldorf)] 106 (1951) pp. 57-63. notes. Studies contemporary critics Carl von Noorden and Hermann Deiters and what they said about Brahms's works; includes comments on Hermann Deiters and Selmar Bagge.

2972 Keyzer, Wm. [William Keyzer] "Brahms, The Young Composer" Dwight's Journal of Music 8/14 (Whole no. 196) (5.1.1856) p. 110. Asserts Brahms's potential as a musician.

2973   Koptjaew, A., see 2354.5.

2974   Kraemer, Uwe. "Johannes Brahms" in Kraemer. Komponisten
       über Komponisten. Ein Quellenlesebuch. (Taschenbücher
       zur Musikwissenschaft 16) Wilhelmshaven: Heinrichshofen's
       Verlag, 1972. pp. 71-79. notes. Includes opinions of
       Brahms from nine 19th and 20th century individuals.

2975   Kralik, Heinrich. "Johannes Brahms. Zur 50. Wiederkehr
       des Todestages" Osterreichische Musikzeitschrift 2/4/5
       (4./5.1947) pp. 85-88. Surveys opinions of Brahms from
       his times and the present; includes comments on Brahms
       and Wagner, and on Brahms and Wien.

2976   Krause, Emil. "Zu Johannes Brahms' 70. Geburtstag. 7. Mai
       1903. Würdigung seiner Schöpfungen.--Die Brahms-Liter-
       atur.--Eigene Erlebnisse" Musikalisches Wochenblatt 34/19
       (7.5.1903) pp. 257-62. ill., facsim., notes. Discusses
       Brahms's worth as a composer and reviews the published
       literature on Brahms to date; includes accounts of personal
       meetings with Brahms in the 1850's and 1880's, together
       with a letter from Brahms, 12.1884.
       (d) *see: 1055.

2977   Kross, Siegfried. "Brahms in heutiger Sicht. Zum 125.
       Geburtstag am 7. Mai" Neue Zeitschrift für Musik 119/5
       (5.1958) pp. 271-75. ill., notes. Addresses the current
       view of Brahms; includes comment on Brahms as a composer.
       (a) reprint: Kross. Das Orchester (Berlin) 6/5 (5.1958)
       pp. 129-34.

2978   Krug, Walther. "Brahms unter den Jungen" Zeitschrift für
       Musik 100/5 (5.1933) pp. 425-27. Describes the ease with
       which youth of the day can relate to Brahms.

2979   *L. H-i. [Ludwig Hevesi] "Wiener Brief: Brahmsiana" Pester
       Lloyd (Budapest) (14.2.1886). Describes how Anton Rubin-
       stein ignores Brahms's works in his recitals; includes an
       overview of Brahms's life. [from 241]

2980   *Lalo, Pierre. Le Temps (Paris) (?. 1907).
       (e) report: in 2886. Comments on Lalo's negative criti-
       cism of Brahms's Op. 56.

2981   *Lemacher, H. "Brahms im Urteil dieser Zeit" Hellweg 2 (1924)
       p. 784.

2982   Liess, Andreas. "Johannes Brahms im Lichte der Moderne"
       Osterreichische Musikzeitschrift 2/4/5 (4./5.1947) pp. 91-93.
       Describes Brahms's position in his own time and since.

2983 Lindner, Dolf. "Der Kritiker Hugo Wolf. Einblick in sein Verhältnis zu Komponisten, Musikern und Sängern" Oster- reichische Musikzeitschrift 15/2 (2.1960) pp. 70-75. Brahms: pp. 71-72. notes. Describes Wolf's criticism of Brahms's works.

2984 Litterscheid, Richard. "Der "bürgerliche" Brahms. Eine not- wendige Korrektur" Musik im Kriege 1/3/4 (6./7.1943) pp. 50-52. A reevaluation of Brahms, showing his links to tradition, as well as how his North German background is reflected in his music.

2985 *Lomagne, R. de. [A. Soubies] Le Soir (Paris) [(1888?)]. (e) report: Simon, Paul. "Eine Pariser Stimme über die Werthsschätzung fremder Componisten, besonders Brahms" Neue Zeitschriftt für Musik 55/47 (Bd. 84) (21.11.1888) pp. 507-09.

2986 *Markees, E. Th. "Brahms in der Beurteilung eines franzö- sischen Musikers" Schweizerische musikpädagogische Blätter 9/4/5 (1920) pp. 50-53.

2987 *Marle, Friedrich. "Brahms und die Franzosen" Das Orchester (Berlin) 8/6 (1931).

2988 *Mason, Daniel Gregory. "Postscript: After Twenty-five Years" in Mason. From Grieg to Brahms. Studies of Some Modern Composers and Their Art. New and Enlarged Edition. New York: The Macmillan Company, 1927. pp. 229-55. issue: 1936. Brahms: pp. 252-55. Reevaluates Brahms's historical position.

2989 Mayer-Mahr, M. "Bürger Brahms" Vossische Zeitung (Berlin) Unterhaltungsblatt no. 147 (28.5.1932) pp. [1-2]. Reply to 659: comments on the significance of Brahms as seen in his music and on Brahms's character. (c) #excerpt: Mayer-Mahr. ""Bürger" Brahms" Die Musik (Berlin) 25/8 (5.1933) p. 610.

2990 #Michelmann, Emil. Johannes Brahms und die Kritik. Eine lustige Erinnerung, [Göttingen:] n.p., 1938. 7, [1] pp. Comments on the reception of Brahms's music, and relates an anecdote showing Brahms's own reaction to his work.

2991 #Mies, Paul. "Johannes Brahms zum 125. Geburtstage" Musik- handel 9/5-6 (1958) pp. 115-16. ill. Draws parallels be- tween Brahms and Bartok, Hindemith and Schoenberg.

2992 Moszkowski, Alexander. "Modern Composers in The Light of Contemporary Criticism" Forum 22 (1.1897) pp. 547-62. Brahms: pp. 560-62. Evaluates his position.

2993　Mueller, Kate Hevner. Twenty-Seven Major Symphony Orchestras. A History and Analysis of Their Repertoires, Seasons 1842-43 Through 1969-70. Bloomington: Indiana University Studies, 1973. 398 pp.
"Brahms, Johannes": pp. 62-71. Data on when Brahms's music was programmed by the orchestras studied.
"Group VI, Chart VI, The Most Played Composers, The Eminent Group: Bach, Beethoven, Brahms, Tschaikovsky, Wagner": pp. xliv-xlix. fig., notes. Traces and compares the quantity of works programmed for each of these composers.

2994　"The Musical Courier has been taken to task ..." Musical Courier 52/12 (Whole no. 1356) (21.3.1906) p. 20. Discusses the differing opinions of Brahms's works.

2995　Newman, Ernest. "Brahms and Wolf" Sunday Times London Late Edition no. 6123 (18.8.1940) p. 3. Describes Wolf as a critic of Brahms's work and why he was so harsh.
(a)　reprint: Newman. In Newman. More Essays From The World of Music. Essays from the 'Sunday Times'. Selected by Felix Aprahamian. London: John Calder, 1958. pp. 54-56.
(a)　reprint: (Da Capo Press Music Reprint Series) New York: Da Capo Press, 1978.

2996　Niemann, Walter. "Brahms und die Gegenwart. Zum zehnjährigen Todestage des Meisters am 3. April" Neue Musikzeitung 28/13 (4.4.1907) pp. 273-77. ill., notes. Describes the Bruckner/Brahms camps and the need for a reassessment of the two composers' positions.

2997　#Nodnagel, Ernst Otto. "Johannes Brahms. Ein Gedächtniswort" Das Magazin für Litteratur [66]/16 (1897) cols. 469-72. Evaluates Brahms's historical position and compares him to Wagner; includes an overview of the works.

2998　Nolthenius, Hugo. "Wat Brahms voor mij is geweesten nog is" Caecilia (Utrecht) 79/12 (10.5.1922) pp. 179-82. Author describes his own opinion of Brahms's music; includes comments on Brahms and Schumann as composers.

2999　Nowell, J. Langley. "Brahms and His Critics" The Choir and Musical Journal 24/281 (5.1933) pp. 100-01. mus. Relates the history of Brahms's reception, as well as how the current standing is the true assessment of his value.

3000　Nülls, Edwin von der. "Wie stehen wir zu Brahms?" Vossische Zeitung (Berlin) Unterhaltungsblatt no. 120 (30.4.1932) pp. [1-2]. Compares Brahms to the Wagner school and finds him wanting.
(d)　see: 659.

3001 Oboussier, Robert. "Brahms und Frankreich" Frankfurter
Zeitung 77/338 (7.5.1933) 2. Morgenblatt Dreimalige Ausgabe
p. 7. Explains the French indifference to Brahms's music.

3002 #Osthoff, Helmuth. Johannes Brahms und seine Sendung.
(Kriegsvorträge der rheinischen Friedrich-Wilhelms-Universität Bonn a. Rh. Heft 81. Aus der Vortragsreihe: "Kunst
und Wissenschaft") Bonn: Bonner Universitäts-Buchdruck-
erei Gebr[uder]. Scheur, G.m.b.H., Abteilung Verlag,
1942. 16 pp. notes. Discusses Brahms's historical position;
includes comment on his character and the qualities of his
music.

3003 Otto, Eberhard. "Johannes Brahms und unsere Zeit. Gedanken
zum 3. April 1947" Fränkische Presse (Bayreuth) 3/26
(1.4.1947) Stadtausgabe Bayreuth p. [4]. Discusses
Brahms's historical position as a classicist and compares
him with Wagner.

3004 *Parker, [D. C.]. "Word on Brahms" Musical Standard [Series
4] 3 (1914) p. 75.
(d) Parker, D. C. "Brahms and The Brahmsians" Musical
Opinion and Musical Trade Review 39/461 (2.1916)
pp. 313-15. Claims Brahms is just an ordinary
musician, not a great master composer.

3005 #Pasche, Hans. "Johannes Brahms. Zum 100. Geburtstag am
7. Mai" Rundfunk 11/19 (1933) pp. 3-4. ill., facsim.
Describes how Brahms's music fares in modern times.

3006 *Paul, E. "Sind Brahms Werke schwer verständlich" Orchester-
Magazin 5/2 (1933) p. 3.

3007 *Petersen, U. "Hamburgs Honoratioren contra Brahms" Musik
und Gesellschaft 8 (1858) pp. 398-400.

3008 #Pfohl, Ferdinand. "Wie wir Brahms erlebten. Zum hundertsten
Geburtstag des Meisters am 7. Mai" Velhagen und Klasings
Monatshefte 47/Bd. 2 (1933) pp. 284-87. Discusses the
greatness of Brahms, together with contemporary and modern
reactions and opinions.

3009 #Pilcz, Alexander. "Musiker über Brahms, Brahms über Musiker" Monatsschrift für Kultur und Politik 1 (1936) pp. 726-
36. Six composers on Brahms, Brahms on six composers;
all taken from their respective writings.

3010 Pirani, Eugenio v. [Eugenio di] "Brahmscultus in Berlin" Neue
Zeitschrift für Musik 63/5 (Bd. 92) (29.1.1896) pp. 49-50.
Negative comments on Brahms's supporters' schemes for
perpetuating him and his music.

3011 *Pohl, Richard. (?) Musikalische Wochenblatt [3] (1872) (?).

3012 *_____. "Brahms" Bade-Blatt (Baden-Baden) (8.1872).
Discusses Brahms's standing as a composer. [from 241]

3013 R. S. [Robert Schumann] "Neue Bahnen" Neue Zeitschrift
für Musik Bd. 39/18 (28.10.1853) pp. 185-86. notes. A
tribute to the young Brahms, vividly describing him as a
person and a pianist.
(a) i) reprint: R. S. in Robert Schumann. Gesammelte
Schriften über Musik und Musiker. 4. Auflage mit
Nachträgen und Erläuterungen von F. Gustav Jensen. 2 vols. in 1 Leipzig: Breitkopf & Härtel,
1891. vol. 2, pp. 184-85.
*5. Auflage: Mit den durchgesehenen Nachträgen
und Erläutern ungen zur 4. Auflage und weiteren
herausgegebenen von Martin Kreisig. 2 vols, 1914.
vol. 2, pp. 301-02.
(a) reprint (of 1914 Auflage): Westmead: Gregg
International Limited, 1969.
(b) English translation by Paul Rosenfeld (of 1914
Auflage): Schumann, Robert "New Roads
[[1853]]" in Schumann. On Music and
Musicians. Konrad Wolff, ed. New York:
Pantheon Books Inc., 1946. pp. 252-54.
*issue: 1952.
*also: London: Dennis Dobson, 1947.
(c) excerpt: in "Robert Schumann 1810-
1856" in 1179.d.c.iii. pp. 147-60.
"Brahms": pp. 159-60.
ii) reprint: in 1171.
iii) reprint: in 3035.
iv) *reprint: in 61.
(d) English translation by Catherine Alison Phillips
[from 61.b.], edited by Phoebe Rogoff
Cave: Schumann, Robert "New Paths" in
758. pp. 331-33.
v) *reprint?: in Robert Schumann. Gesammelte Schrift-
en über Musik und Musiker. In Auswahl
herausgegeben und eingeleitet von Paul
Bekker. (Bd. 8 der 7. Sonderreihe des
Volksverbandes der Bücherfreunde) Berlin:
Volksverband der Bücherfreunde, Wegweiser-
Verlag, 1922.
vi) *reprint: in 82.
vii) *reprint: "Neue Bahnen" Leipziger neueste Nachrichten (5.5.1933).
viii) *reprint?: "Neue Bahnen. Der berühmte Aufsatz
Robert Schumanns über den jungen Brahms"
Lied und Heimat (Sollingen) 12 (1936) p.
31.

ix) *reprint?: in Schumann. Gesammelte Schriften
über Musik und Musiker. Eine Auswahl.
Herbert Schulze, ed. (Reclams Universal-
Bibliothek) Leipzig: Reclam, 1956.
*2. Auflage: 1965
x) reprint: R. S. in 38.
(b)i) English translation by Henry Pleasants [III]: R. S.
"New Paths (1853)" in Robert Schumann.
The Musical World of Robert Schumann.
A Selection From His Own Writings. Trans-
lated, Edited, and Annotated by Henry
Pleasants [III]. London: Victor Gollancz
Ltd., 1965. pp. 199-200.
ii) French translation by Adolphe Jullien?: in 2969.
(c)i) excerpt (in English translation by Daniel Gregory
Mason): in 2893 p. 7 (volume p. 199).
ii) excerpt (in English translation): Schumann, Robert.
"On Brahms" in 1179.d.c.i. pp. 143-44.

3014 Raabe, Peter. "Johannes Brahms. Rede, gehalten beim
Brahms-Fest in Freiburg" Zeitschrift für Musik 104/6
(6.1937) pp. 605-09. Discusses Brahms's position in his
time and currently.
(a) *reprint: Raabe. "Johannes Brahms. Rede, gehalten
am. 25. Mai 1937 beim Brahms-Fest in Freiburg/Br."
in Raabe. Deutsche Meister. Reden. [(Von deutsche
Musik. 58)] Regensburg: Gustav Bosse Verlag,
1937. pp. 72-82.
6. bis 9. Auflage: 1937. ill., notes.

3015 Radcliffe, Philip. "Some Reflections on Brahms" Cambridge
Journal 2/2 (11.1948) pp. 106-10. Judges Brahms's music
on its own merits; includes comments on Brahms's style.

3016 Rawsthorne, Alan. "The Greater and the Lesser Brahms"
Sackbut 12/[2] (1.1932) pp. 90-92. Describes Brahms as
occupying a position between first and second rank composers.

3017 #Reitler, Joseph. "Brahms' Place in Music" New Friends of
Music 10/1 (1945) pp. 34-40. Discusses Brahms's contemporary reception and historical position.

3018 Rhenanus Beatus. "Auf Johannes Brahms" Deutsche Rundschau
23/10 (Bd. 92) (7.1897) pp. 86-88. 2 poems.
"I. Dem Genius. (1874)": pp. 86-87.
on Brahms's genius as a composer, and its enduring
quality.
"II. Brahms's erste Sinfonie. Prometheus. (1876)": pp.
87-88. Uses the Prometheus myth to create a descriptive
programme in poetry for Op. 68.

3019 Riemann, Hugo. "Johannes Brahms (geb[oren]. 7. Mai 1833
zu Hamburg, gest[orben]. 3. April 1897 zu Wien)" Blätter
für Haus- und Kirchenmusik 1/5 (5.1897) pp. 73-77. notes.
Rebuts 3025 on Brahms's worth.
(a) *reprint: Riemann. in Riemann. Praeludien und Studien.
Gesammelte Aufsätze zur Asthetik, Theorie und
Geschichte der Musik. [Bd. 3] [(Musikalische
Studien no. 7)] Leipzig: H. Seemann Nachfolger,
[1901]. pp. 215-23. Includes 2419, 2420.
(a) i) reprint: Riemann. in Riemann. Praeludien
und Studien I-III. Gesammelte ... der
Musik. 3 vols. in 1. Hildesheim: Georg
Olms Verlagsbuchhandlung, 1967. III,
215-23.
ii) *reprint: 3 vols. in 2. Nendeln: Kraus
Reprint, 1976.

3019.5 Rummenhöller, Peter. "Die Musik der Zukunft" in Rummenhöller. Der Dichter Spricht. Robert Schumann als Musik-
schriftsteller. Köln: G + L [Gitarre + Laute Verlagsgesellschaft m.b.H], 1980. pp. 85-97. notes. Discusses Schumann's relationship to the two movements in music which
developed around Wagner and Brahms: how he contributed
to the polarization, and reacted to it in his writings.

3020 Schering, Arnold. "Johannes Brahms und seine Stellung in
der Musikgeschichte des 19. Jahrhunderts" Jahrbuch der
Musikbibliothek Peters 39 (1932) pp. 9-22. mus., notes.
Describes the state of Brahms research and Brahms's his-
torical position.
(a) i) *reprint: Schering. In Schering. Von grossen
Meistern der Musik. Leipzig: Koehler & Amelang,
1940. pp. 153-84. Omits notes.
2. Auflage: 1940. omits notes.
*?. Auflage: 1941.
ii) reprint: Schering. In Schering. Vom Wesen der
Musik. Ausgewählte Aufsätze von Arnold Schering.
Karl Michael Komma, ed. Stuttgart: K. F. Koehler
Verlag, 1974. pp. 284-303.

3021 *Schliepe, Ernst. "Brahms und die Gegenwart" Das Schwalbennest (Erfurt) 9/7 (1927).
(a) i) *reprint: Schliepe. "Brahms" Die Tonkunst (Berlin)
31/15 (1927).
ii) *reprint: Schliepe. "Johannes Brahms und die
Gegenwart" Deutsche Militärmusikerzeitung 50/12
(1928).

3022 *Schmidt, Leopold. "Brahms" in Schmidt. Aus dem Musikleben
der Gegenwart. Beiträge zur zeitgenössischen Kunstkritik.
Mit einem Geleitwort von Richard Strauss. Berlin: A.

Hofmann & Comp., 1909. pp. 265-67. Consists of 910.a.,
983.e.ix.a., 1009.e.x.a., 1365.5.a, 2217.5.a., 2348.5.a.,
2736.5.a.

3023　*Schorlich, P.　"Ist Brahms volkstümlich?" Deutsche Zeitung
(Berlin) (7.5.1933).

3024　*Schultz, H.　"Brahms und die heutige Musik" Königsberger
allgemeine Zeitung (21.12.1928).

3025　#Seidl, Arthur.　"Johannes Brahms †" Deutsche Wacht (Dresden)
(7.4.1897) pp. 1-2 [across page bottoms].　Discusses the
placement of Brahms and his music in music history.
(a)　reprint:　Seidl.　"Zur Brahms Frage (1897)" in Seidl.
Von Palestrina zu Wagner.　Bekenntnisse eines
musikalischen "Wagnerianers".　(Seidl.　Wagneriana.
Bd. 2) Berlin und Leipzig:　Verlag von Schuster
& Loeffler, 1901.　pp. 363-75.
(c)　excerpt:　Sdl.　[Arthur Seidl] "Münchner Rundschau"
Die Gesellschaft (München) 18 (Bd. 1/1) (1902)
pp. 45-50.　Compares Bruckner and Brahms.
(d)　see:　3019.

3026　*Siegmund-Schultze, Ute.　"Zur Geschichte der Brahms-Rezeption
im deutschsprachigen Raum von 1853-1914" Phil.F. diss.,
Martin Luther-Universität Halle, 1982.

3027　Slonimsky, Nicolas.　"Brahms" in Slonimsky.　Lexicon of Musical
Invective.　Critical Assaults on Composers since Beethoven's
Time.　New York:　Coleman-Ross Company, Inc., 1953.
pp. 68-79.　ind.　Includes comment on Brahms's works from
American daily newspapers and in translation from French
and German music periodicals:　1878-1922.
2nd Edition:　1965.

3028　Specht, Richard.　"Zum Brahms-Problem" Der Merker (Wien)
3/2 (1.1912) pp. 41-46.　Uses the qualities of Brahms's
music as a basis for his historical position.

3029　*Stahmer, Klaus.　"Jak vidĕt Brahnse.　Studie o chybných
interpretacích:　Opus musicum 3/3 (1971) pp. 75-83.　notes.
(b)　German translation:　Stahmer.　"Korrekturen am
Brahmsbild.　Eine Studie zur musikalischen Fehlin-
terpretation" Die Musikforschung 25/2 (4.-6.1972)
pp. 152-67.　fig., notes.　Analyses Op. 115 to
show Brahms's originality in composition, and to
correct misconceptions about his worth.

3030　*Stange, Eberhard.　"Die Musikanschauung Eduard Hanslicks
in seinen Kritiken und Aufsätzen.　Eine Studie zur musikalisch-geistigen Situation des 19. Jahrhunderts" Phil.F.
diss., Universität Münster, 1954.　257 pp.

3031   Steglich, Rudolf.   "Johannes Brahms. Vermächtnis und Auf-
       gabe" Neue Musikzeitschrift 1/5 (4.1947) pp. 135-44. notes.
       Discusses Brahms's historical position; includes comment on
       the qualities of his music, with examples from Opp. 19 and
       49.

3032   Stephenson, Kurt. "Der Komponist Brahms im eigenen Urteil"
       Brahms-Studien Bd. 1 (1974) pp. 7-24. notes. Examines
       Brahms's writings to find out what he thought of his own
       works, and discusses his skills as a composer.

3032.5*Sullivan, J. W. N.   The Listener [(1927?)].

3033   #Thomas-San-Galli, Wolfgang A[lexander]. "Brahms Heute"
       Rheinische Musik- und Theaterzeitung (Köln) 9/50 (12.12.1908)
       pp. 607-08. Discusses Brahms's historical position; includes
       comment on Brahms the classicist.

3034   *Thomson, Virgil. "The "Brahms Line"" New York Herald-
       Tribune (26.4.1942).
       (a) reprint: Thomson. in Thomson. Music Reviewed
            1940-1954. New York: Vintage Books, 1967. pp.
            70-73. Describes the public's reaction to Brahms's
            music.

3035   Vogel, Bernhard. "Zum Heimgang von Johannes Brahms"
       Neue Zeitschrift für Musik 64/15 (Bd. 93) (14.4.1897) pp.
       169-71. Examines Brahms in light of Schumann's "Neue
       Bahnen" article; includes reprint of 3013.

3036   "Von Brahms und über Brahms" Musik in der Schule 9/5
       ([5.] 1958) pp. 212-15, 218-19. ill. Excerpt from the
       literature, of contemporaries' opinions on Brahms.

3037   W. S. B. M[athews]. "There are curious differences ..."
       Music (Chicago) 13/[6] (4.1898) pp. 723-24. Opinions
       on Brahms of Siloti, Marteuz and Godowsky.

3038   Wagner, Manfred. "Johannes Brahms (1833-1897). Haydn-
       Variationen op. 56a. Wien, 2. November 1873 (Uraufführung)"
       in Wagner. Geschichte der österreichischen Musikkritik
       in Beispielen. Mit einem einleitenden Essay von Norbert
       Tschulik. (Publikationen des Instituts für österreichische
       Musikdokumentation 5) Tutzing: Hans Schneider, 1979.
       pp. 132-43. Contains excerpts from 8 Viennese daily and
       weekly serial publications.

3039   Wagner, Manfred. "Johannes Brahms (1833-1897). 2. Sinfonie
       D-Dur op. 73. Wien, 30. Dezember 1877 (Uraufführung)"
       in 3038. pp. 218-34. Contains excerpts from 7 Viennese
       daily and weekly serial publications.

3040 *Weber, F. W. "Johannes Brahms und seine Stellung in der
Musikgeschichte" Merseburger Korrespondent (24.10.1925).

3041 Wessem, Constant van. "Over Johannes Brahms" Caecilia
(Utrecht) 70/10 (15.10.1913) pp. 286-89. Discusses Brahms's
historical position; includes comments on Brahms the composer.

3042 *Westphal, Kurt. "Brahms--Heute" Philharmonische Blätter
[10]/6 (1972/73) pp. 3, 5-6.

3043 While, Felix. "Brahms' Music in England--I, II" Sackbut
11/[7,8] (2.,3.;1931) pp. 176-81, 220-23. Describes
Brahms's advocates in England (performers) and the
English reception of his works.

3044 Wild, Irene. "Etwas von Johannes Brahms. Geb[oren]. 7.
Mai 1833--gest[orben]. 3. April 1897" Allgemeine Musikzeitung
33/18 (4.5.1906) pp. 308-09. Describes why Brahms is
great; includes comment on the qualities of the works,
and Brahms's childhood.

3045 #Wild, Irene. "Was ist uns Johannes Brahms? Ein Gedenkblatt
zum 10. Todestage des Meisters. (Geb[oren]. 7. Mai
1833, gest[orben]. 3. April 1897)" Allgemeine Musikzeitung
34/13 (29.3.1907) pp. 229-32. Discusses the reasons for
Brahms's greatness and genius.

3046 Wilfferodt, Felix. "Zum zehnjährigen Todestage von Johannes
Brahms" Musikalisches Wochenblatt. Neue Zeitschrift für
Musik 38,74 [respectively]/13/14 (28.3.1907) pp. 313-14.
Assesses Brahms's worth and influence.
(c) excerpt (in English translation): "An Estimate of
Brahms' Work" Etude 25/6 (6.1907) p. 362.

3047 *Wilson, Colin. "The Romantic Half-Century" in Wilson. Brandy
of the Damned. Discoveries of a Musical Eclectic. London:
John Baker Publishers Ltd., 1964.
also titled: Chords and Discords. Purely Personal Opinions
on Music. New York: Crown Publishers, Inc., 1966. pp.
21-48. Brahms: pp. 32-38. Discusses Brahms, Wagner and
Hanslick, and how Brahms was shoved into the spotlight.
[Revised Edition:] Colin Wilson on Music. (Brandy of the
Damned). London: Pan Books Ltd., 1967. pp. 23-53.
Brahms: pp. 35-42.

3048 Wolf, Hugo. Hugo Wolfs musikalische Kritiken. Richard
Batka und Heinrich Werner, ed. Leipzig: Breitkopf & Här-
tel, 1911. vi, [2], 378 pp. ind. Includes criticisms on
Brahms from Wiener Salonblatt (1884-87).

(c) i) excerpt: in 858.
   ii) excerpt (in English translation): in 1930.
   iii) excerpt: Wolf. "Brahms' 'Dritte Sinfonie'" in 969.
       a.c. pp. 200-02.
(d) English translation by Henry Pleasants [III]: Wolf.
    The Music Criticism of Hugo Wolf. Pleasants [III],
    editor and annotator. New York, London: Holmes
    and Meier Publishers, Inc., 1979. xvii, 291 pp.
    ind., notes. Source for this material is only Wiener
    Salonblatt.
(e) i) report: Hirschberg, Walter. "Wolf und Brahms"
       Signale für die musikalische Welt 70/22 (29.5.1912)
       pp. 729-31.
   ii) report: Jong, J. de. "Hugo Wolf en Brahms"
       Onze eeuw 13/3 (2.1913) pp. 238-64. notes. In-
       cludes comment on Wolf's criticism of composers
       other than Brahms, and Wolf's relation to Wagner.
   iii)*report: Kaiser, Georg. "Hugo Wolf über Brahms
       als Kritiker" Dresdner Nachrichten (14.4.1912).
   iv) report: Kanth, Gustav. "Hugo Wolf als Kritiker
       Brahms'" Die Musik (Berlin) 11/3 (Bd. 41) (11.1911)
       pp. 148-60. notes. Includes comment on Brahms's
       reaction to Wolf's writings.

3049 #Wulsten, Friedrich. "Deutsches Wesen und Wirken. Zum 90.
      Geburtstage von Johannes Brahms am 7. Mai 1923" Bur-
      schenschaftliche Blätter [37] (1923) pp. 72-74. Describes
      Brahms's greatness and his Germanic character.

3050 Zàccaro, Gianfranco. "Dialogo su Brahms" Il Convegno musicale
      2/1-2 (1965) pp. 123-29. A philosophical discussion of
      Brahms's historical position; includes comment on Brahms's
      style and creative processes.

3051 #Ziehn, Bernhard. "Der "edle neidlose" Brahms" Deutsch-
      Amerikanische Geschichtsblätter Bd. 26/27 (1927) pp. 49-51.
      Describes how Brahms's association with Hanslick propelled
      him to fame.

See also 5.d., 14, 16, 23.e.ii., 23.e.iii., 27.d., 37, 40.e.i., 41-43,
48.e.ii., 50, 57, 58, 62, 67, 75, 76, 78, 83, 90, 115, 117, 124, 125,
128, 135, 138, 150, 152, 202, 204, 220-22, 225-226.5, 229, 280, 419,
436, 457, 469, 470, 476, 487, 488, 492, 492.5, 507, 509, 518, 521,
532, 554, 612, 613, 620, 659, 683, 695, 705, 746, 749, 791, 813, 817,
819.c.ii.e.ii, 824, 831, 848, 881, 918, 1015, 1116, 1142, 1146, 1171,
1175, 1183.e., 1277, 1322, 1329, 1332, 1336, 1365, 1371, 1373, 1380,
1381, 1392, 1400, 1402, 1435, 1440, 1441, 1563, 1609, 1778, 1808,
1817, 1845, 1853, 1914, 1915, 1922, 1930, 1943, 1944, 1948.d., 2006,
2022, 2036, 2051, 2202, 2208, 2302, 2314, 2320, 2359, 2363, 2376.5,
2379, 2380, 2389, 2397.5, 2438, 2459, 2460, 2471, 2472, 2476, 2477,
2479, 2481-83, 2491-93, 2496, 2502, 2505, 2506, 2519, 2633.5, 2644,

2649, 2761, 2763, 2769, 2773, 2810.5, 2812, 2839, 2845, 2860, 2878, 2880, 3083, 3108, 3121.

See also "Bruckner," "Bülow," Tchaikovsky," "Wagner" and "Wolf" in III.B.2.

D. MEMORIAL ACTIVITIES

Contains materials which report on the commemoration of Brahms and his music by the building of memorials, founding of Brahms societies, assembling exhibits, etc.

Exhibits: 3054, 3066, 3093, 3094, 3100, 3109, 3121, 3123, 3130, 3131, 3143, 3150, 3162.
Houses and Museums: 3059, 3061, 3063, 3070, 3071, 3073, 3076, 3088, 3090,3091, 3095, 3099, 3107, 3111-13, 3124, 3125, 3127, 3128, 3135, 3136, 3140, 3154, 3156, 3159, 3161, 3165, 3166, 3170.
Memorials and Monuments (Other than Hamburg or Wien): 3082, 3086, 3087, 3098, 3116, 3133, 3168.
Memorials and Monuments (Hamburg): 3056, 3062, 3065, 3072, 3081, 3084, 3106, 3115, 3138, 3142, 3149, 3158, 3174.
Memorials and Monuments (Wien): 3052, 3053, 3057, 3060, 3067-69, 3075, 3084, 3085, 3096, 3097, 3102, 3119, 3122, 3126, 3129, 3131, 3137, 3140, 3145-48, 3152, 3153, 3155, 3160, 3169, 3172, 3173, 3177.
Plaques: 3058, 3092, 3101, 3114.
Societies: 3053, 3055, 3064, 3078-80, 3105, 3110, 3117, 3124, 3163, 3164.

3052   *Neue freie Presse (Wien) (1902).
        (e) report: "In Wien soll bekanntlich Johannes Brahms
             ein Denkmal gesetzt werden ..." Allgemeine Musik-
             zeitung 29/43 (24.10.1902) p. 718. On the judging
             of the sketches for the memorial.

3053   *Neue freie Presse (Wien) (1905).
        (e) report: "Aus Wien berichtet die 'N.fr.Pr.' ..." All-
             gemeine Musikzeitung 32/13 (31.3.1905) p. 250.
             Reports on founding of Wiener Brahms-Gesellschaft.

3054   Albrecht, Otto E. "The Brahms Centenary Exhibition" Uni-
        versity of Pennsylvania Library Chronicle 1/2 (6.1933) pp.
        28-30. Describes the exhibit's contents.

3055   "Als bedeutsames Ereignis für die musikalische Welt ..." All-
        gemeine Musikzeitung 33/14 (6.4.1906) p. 251. Reports
        on the founding of the Deutsche Brahms-Gesellschaft in
        Berlin, and its plans.

3056   "An dem ausgeschriebenen Wettbewerb um das in Hamburg ..."
        Musikalisches Wochenblatt 32/27/28 (4.7.1901) p. 368. An-
        nounces the winners of the design contest for the Hamburg
        memorial.

3057   "Auf dem im Wiener Zentralfriedhofes befindlichen ..." Musik-
        alisches Wochenblatt 34/17 (23.4.1903) p. 237. Announces
        date for memorial unveiling.

3058   "Aus dem in Göttingen ..." Musikalisches Wochenblatt 30/46
        (9.11.1899) p. 626. Reports on the putting of a plaque on
        the house where Joachim and Brahms stayed in 1853.

3059   "Aus Wien wird berichtet ... Haus in der Karlsgasse ..."
        Allgemeine Musikzeitung 33/28/29 (13./20.7.1906) p. 476.
        Reports on destruction of Brahms's Karlsgasse residence,
        and the moving or removal of original details for safekeeping.

3060   "Aus Wien wird geschrieben ..." Allgemeine Musikzeitung 29/7
        (14.2.1902) p. 140. Reports that the local Memorial Com-
        mittee will hold a competition for the memorial's design.

3061   "Aus Wien wird geschrieben: ..." Allgemeine Musikzeitung
        33/12 (23.4.1906) pp. 214-15. Reports on the Memorial
        Committee looking for a building site for a Brahms Memorial
        House, as Karlsgasse residence is to be torn down.

3061.5*Azzonni, Giulio. "Johannes Brahms" 1903. (?)
        (d) *Azzonni. Giovanni Brahms. Un Elogio. Dal tedesco,
            con aggiunte e nuove illustrazioni biografiche.
            Cremona: [Frisi e Marenghi], 1905. 11 pp.

3062   *Bahr, Hermann. "Brahms von Klinger" Neue freie Presse
        (Wien) (21. or 25.;2.;1908).
        (a) reprint: Bahr. "Brahms" in Bahr. Essays. Leip-
             zig: Insel-Verlag, 1912. pp. 40-46. A description
             and critique of Klinger's Brahms Memorial; includes
             comments on Wolf's criticisms of Brahms.
          *2. Auflage: 1921.

3063   Baser, Friedrich. "Brahms-Gedenkstätte in Gefahr" Musica
        (Kassel) 20/4 (7.-8.1966) p. 181. Reports on attempts to
        procure house in Baden-Baden-Lichtental where Brahms
        stayed, for a memorial site.

3064   "Berlin. Eine Vereinigung der Brahms-Freunde ..." Allgemeine
        Musikzeitung 35/24 (12.6.1908) p. 484. On the forming of
        a Verein to work with the Deutsche Brahms-Gesellschaft.

3065   "A Brahms Monument.-..." The Times (London) no. 35,390
        (18.12.1897) p. 12. Announces Hamburg's decision to erect

a monument, includes an invitation for Times' readers to make contributions.

3066   "Brahms-Ausstellung in Charlottenburg" Die Musik (Berlin) 31/9 (6.1939) p. 634. Describes the exhibit and its contents.

3067   "[[Brahms-Denkmal]]" Neue freie Presse (Wien) no. 12,372 (31.1.1899) Morgenblatt p. 5. Reports on total monies in Memorial fund.

3068   *"Brahms-Denkmal in Wien" Illustrierte Zeitung (14.5.1908).

3069   *"Brahms-Denkmal in Wien" Musikwoche no. 28 (1903).

3070   "Ein Brahms-Gedenkraum im Wiener Haydn-Haus" Osterreichische Musikzeitschrift 35/11 (11.1980) p. 608. ill. On the establishment of this memorial room, with a description of its collection.

3071   *"Eine Brahms-Gedenkstätte in Gmunden" Heimatblätter [previously Salzkammergutzeitung] no. 34 (26.8.1939).

3072   *Brahms-Gedenkstätte in Hamburg. Errichtet von der Körber-Stiftung und der Freien und Hansestadt Hamburg 17. Oktober 1981. Hamburg: n.p., 1981. 47 pp. ill. Includes: Mayer, Hans "Brahms und die Nachwelt": pp. 14-28.

3073   *Brahmsgesellschaft Baden-Baden e.V. Brahmshaus Baden-Baden. Baden-Baden: Author, 1974.

3074   *Brahms-Gesellschaft in Wien. Mitteilungen. [Gmunden:] n.p., 1907. 46 pp. Includes 3134.

3075   Coster, Johann H. "Brieven uit weenen" Weekblad voor muziek 10/21 (23.5.1903) pp. 203-04. Reports on Brahms Memorial Ceremony in Wien.

3076   dpa. "Brahms-Haus soll Gedenkstätte werden" Musica (Kassel) 21/2 (3.-4.1967) pp. 83-84. Announces that Lichtenthal house is to become a Brahms Memorial House.

3077   "Denen Veranstaltern von "Brahms-Abenden" zur Nachachtung ..." Neue Zeitschrift für Musik 73/29/30 (Bd. 102) (25.7. 1906) p. 626. Quotes from 894 on Brahms's thoughts about the holding of a "Brahms-Abend".

3078   "Die Deutsche Brahms-Gesellschaft" Die Musik (Berlin) 25/8 (5.1933) pp. 602-05. A history of the group and its activities.
       (a) reprint: in 3186.c. pp. 42-45.

3079 #"Die Deutsche Brahms-Gesellschaft" Die Musikwelt (Hamburg)
2/9 (1.6.1922) pp. 233-35 [across page bottoms] (Heft pp.
3-5). Reports on its founding members and its activities.

3080 "Die Deutsche Brahms-Gesellschaft ..." Allgemeine Musikzeitung
33/27 (6.7.1906) p. 461. Announces the Gesellschaft's
publication programme.

3081 *Dresdner, Dr. "Klingers Brahms-Denkmal" Die Propyläen
(München) [6] (24.2.1909).
(a) *reprint: Dresdner, A. "Klinger's Brahms-Denkmal"
Fränkischer Kurier (Nürnberg) (2.9.1909).

3082 *Droste, C. "Die erste deutsche Brahms-Denkmal in Meiningen"
Illustrierte Zeitung 112 or 113/2938 (1899) ill.
(a) *reprint: Droste. Die Sängerhalle 39/48 (1899).

3083 *"Ehrenbürgerrecht für Brahms in Hamburg" Deutsche Kunst-
und Musikzeitung (Wien) [16] (10.11.1889).

3084 "Die Enthüllung des Grabdenkmals für Johannes Brahms" Neue
freie Presse (Wien) no. 13,899 (7.5.1903) Morgenblatt p.
7. Describes the Memorial in Wien.

3085 "Die Entwürfe der H. H. Max Klinger und Carl Kundmann ..."
Musikalisches Wochenblatt 33/42 (9.10.1902) p. 599. Kling-
er's designs for Wien Memorial rejected by the Committee,
Prof. Meyer's slated for their acceptance.

3086 "Das erste Brahms-Denkmal, ..." Musikalisches Wochenblatt
30/26 (22.6.1899) p. 362. Announces erection of Monument
at Meiningen.

3087 "Das erste Denkmal für Johannes Brahms ..." Neue freie Presse
(Wien) no. 12,498 (10.6.1899) Morgenblatt p. 7. Outlines
plans for Meiningen Memorial festivities.

3088 F. B. [Friedrich Baser] "Eine Brahmsgedenkstätte" Musica
(Kassel) 11/6 (6.1957) p. 353. Proposes that Lichtenthal
house where Brahms stayed, become a memorial.

3089 *Fellinger, Richard. "Klänge um Brahms. Erinnerungen" Die
Heimat (Krefeld) 12/3/4 (1933) p. 183. Concerns a bust
of Brahms donated to the Krefeld Museum by Fellinger.
[from the Serial and Government Publications Division,
Library of Congress]

3090 Fisenne, Otto von. "Abschied vom Brahms-Keller" Musica
(Kassel) 14/9 (9.1960) pp. 604-05. Reports on an attempt
to set up a Hamburg museum in the place where Brahms
and his father were known to have worked.

3091 "Gedenkstätte für Johannes Brahms" Die Bühne (Wien) no. 266
(11.1980) p. 12. On establishment of Brahms room in Wiener
Haydn-Haus, with items from Brahms's Karlsgasse residence.

3092 "[[Gedenktafel für Johannes Brahms]]" Neue freie Presse
(Wien) no. 12,679 (8.12.1899) Morgenblatt p. 8. On putting
plaque on Viennese residence.

3093 Gesellschaft der Musikfreunde in Wien. Museum. J. Brahms
Zentenar-Ausstellung der Gesellschaft der Musikfreunde in
Wien. Beschreibendes Verzeichnis zusammengestellt von
Dr. H[edwig]. Kraus, Dr. K[arl] Geiringer, Dr. V[ictor
J.] Luithlen. [Wien: Gesellschaft der Musikfreunde, 1934].
121 pp. Describes items on display; includes items from
Brahms's circle of friends.
(e) report: Deutsch, Otto Erich. "The Brahms Exhibition
in Vienna" E. van der Straeten, translator and
editor Musical Opinion and Music Trade Review
57/673 (10.1933) pp. 24-25.

3094 *Gmunden. Kammerhofmuseum. Johannes Brahms Ausstellung
[22.6.-15.10.1972] Kammerhofmuseum der Stadt Gmunden.
Seine Beziehung zur Traunseestadt--Zum Gedächtnis des
75. Todestages. 1972. [Gmunden: Author?, 1972?]

3095 *Gottgetreu, Johannes Oskar. "Das Brahms-Museum in Gmunden"
Rheinische Musik- und Theaterzeitung (Köln) 8/41 (1907)
pp. 488-90.

3096 "Das Grabdenkmal Brahms' an dem Wiener Zentralfriedhof"
Illustrirte Zeitung (Leipzig) Bd. 120/3124 (14.5.1903) p.
731. ill. Reports on dedication ceremony and describes
the memorial.

3097 "Das Grabdenkmal für Johannes Brahms" Neue freie Presse
(Wien) no. 13,899 (7.5.1903) Abendblatt p. 3. Describes
the dedication ceremony.
(e) report: see 526.e.

3098 "Graz ..." Allgemeine Musikzeitung 36/27 (2.7.1909) p. 561.
Reports on Brahms memorial to be placed in Mürzzuschlag.

3099 H. P. "Bei Johannes Brahms auf dem Lande. Im Gmundner
Gartenhäuschen der Familie Miller-Aichholz" Neue freie
Presse (Wien) no. 24,658 (7.5.1933) Morgenblatt Beilage
pp. 21-22 [across page bottoms]. Describes Brahms's con-
nections to Bad Ischl and Gmunden and the collection of the
Gmunden Museum.

3100 Hamburg. Staats- und Universitätsbibliothek. Johannes
Brahms Ausstellung anlaesslich (sic) der 125. Wiederkehr

seines Geburtstages am 7. Mai 1833. Dokumente seines
Lebens und Schaffens. Zusammengestellt von Gustav Fock
und Kurt [W.] Richter. Hamburg: Staats- und Universitätsbibliothek Hamburg, [1958]. 21 pp. Exhibit catalogue;
includes identification of exhibit items' owners.

3101   "Die Hamburger Bürgervereine ..." Allgemeine Musikzeitung
31/46 (11.11.1904) p. 761. On the placing of a plaque
on Brahms's birthplace.

3102   *Hanslick, Eduard. "Ein Monument für Brahms" Neue freie
Presse (Wien) (4.4.1898).
(a) *reprint: Hanslick. "Alice Barbi für das Brahms-
Monument" in 2943.
(a) reprint: see 2943.a. pp. 296-301. Reports
on her Brahms memorial fundraiser concert
and on 85 and 958.

3103   #Heilbut, Emil. "Klingers Brahms-Denkmal. Ausstellung der
Berliner Sezession" Der Tag (Berlin) Ausgabe B no. 36
(12.2.1909) Illustrierter Teil pp. [1-3] [across page bottoms].
Discusses what this exhibit shows of Klinger the artist,
focuses on Brahms memorial which is on display here.

3104   "Hr. Max Klinger in Leipzig ist von dem Comité ..." Musikalisches Wochenblatt 32/39 (19.9.1901) p. 518. On Klinger's
appointment to execute the Hamburg Brahms Memorial.

3105   "Der Herzog von Meiningen hat das Protektorat über die
Deutsche Brahms-Gesellschaft übernommen" Allgemeine Musikzeitung 34/12 (22.3.1907) p. 219. Announces the Herzog's
patronage.

3106   Hevesi, Ludwig. "Max Klinger's Entwurf zu einem Brahms-
denkmal" Zeitscheift für bildende Kunst N.F. 14/9 ([9.]
1903) pp. 236-38. ill. Discusses Klinger's plans for Hamburg Memorial and how its classic lines will be a reflection
of the composer and his music.

3107   Hofmann, Kurt. "Das "Brahms-Haus" in Baden-Baden" Mitteilungen der Brahms-Gesellschaft Hamburg e.V. no. 1
(10.1970) p. 5. Describes the establishment of the "Haus"
and its facilities; includes comment on Brahms in Baden-
Baden.

3108   Hofman, Kurt. "Zur Brahms-Medaille" Mitteilungen der Brahms-
Gesellschaft Hamburg e.V. no. 2 (4.1971) pp. 8-9. Discusses medallion presented by the Gesellschaft der Musikfreunde to Brahms on the occasion of his 60th birthday.

3109   Hofmann, Kurt and Jutta Fürst. Johannes Brahms. The Man

and His Work. Catalogue of an Exhibition of Rare and
Unique Items drawn from the Life and Times of a Great
Composer. Detroit Public Library Biography Room. April
1980. Revised and Amended Translation by Ellwood Derr.
Detroit: Detroit Symphony Orchestra, 1980. 64 pp. ill.,
facsim. Descriptive exhibition catalogue; exhibit includes
items from his contemporaries.
(e) report: "Johannes Brahms: The Man and His Work,
is the title ..." Notes 37/1 (9.1980) p. 39.

3110   "In Berlin ..." Allgemeine Musikzeitung 33/20 (18.5.1906)
        p. 346. On the founding of the Deutsche Brahms-Gesell-
        schaft.

3111   "In Gmunden ist das in der Villa von Miller ..." Allgemeine
        Musikzeitung 29/36 (5.9.1902) p. 585. Announces museum's
        opening, with a general overview of its collection.

3112   "In Gmunden ist in der Villa von Millner (sic) [Miller] ..."
        Musikalisches Wochenblatt 33/38 (11.9.1902) p. 547. An-
        nounces Brahms museum's opening, in replica of Bad Ischl
        house where Brahms stayed.

3113   "In Gmunden sind von dem Kunstmäcen Hrn. v. Aichholz ..."
        Musikalisches Wochenblatt 31/39 (20.9.1900) p. 512.
        Announces founding of Brahms Haus and Brahms Museum.

3114   "In Hamburg ..." Allgemeine Musikzeitung 33/18 (4.5.1906)
        p. 313. On city's plans to put a plaque on Brahms's birth-
        place.

3115   "In Hamburg wird ..." Allgemeine Musikzeitung 31/44 (28.10.
        1904) p. 721. Reports that city will be getting a Brahms
        Memorial.

3116   "In Pressbaum bei Wien ..." Allgemeine Musikzeitung 32/25
        (23.6.1905) p. 448. On placing of Brahms Memorial in this
        city.

3117   "In Wien hat sich am 23. April eine Brahms-Gesellschaft
        gebildet" Allgemeine Musikzeitung 31/20 (13.5.1904) p. 361.
        On founding of Wiener Brahms-Gesellschaft.

3118   "In Wien soll das Haus in der Karlsgasse, ..." Allgemeine
        Musikzeitung 32/20 (19.5.1905) p. 371. Reports on plans
        to tear down house where Brahms had his residence.

3119   "In Wien wird das Brahms-Denkmal ..." Allgemeine Musikzeitung
        34/12 (22.3.1907) p. 220. Reports on location of Brahms
        Memorial.

3120   "The International Brahms Congress" <u>Symphony Magazine</u> 31/3
       (6./7.1980) p. 19. Reports on this meeting in Detroit,
       April 1980, and how discussion casts Brahms in a new light,
       and the resultant effect on Brahms research.

3121   *Johannes Brahms: <u>geboren 7. Mai zu Hamburg, gestorben 3.</u>
       <u>April 1897 zu Wien. Eine Ausstellung der Deutsche Bank</u>
       <u>Hamburg in Verbindung mit der Einweihung des von der</u>
       <u>Körber Stiftung errichteten Brahms-Denkmals, vom 19.</u>
       <u>Oktober 1981-6. November 1981 im Hause Deutsche Bank</u>
       <u>Hamburg.</u> [Deutsche Bank-AG in Hamburg und Constantin
       Floros, eds.] Hamburg: Deutsche Bank, Abteilung Privat-
       kunden, 1981. 72 pp. ill., notes. Includes: Floros,
       Constantin. "Brahms' Popularität": pp. 7-17.
       (e) report: "Frühstart für Brahms und andere Hamburgen-
              sien" <u>HiFi Stereophonie</u> 21/1 (1.1982) pp. 74-75.
              Includes comments on Brahms and Hamburg.

3122   "[[Johannes Brahms-Denkmal in Wien]]" <u>Neue freie Presse</u>
       (Wien) no. 12,362 (21.1.1899) Morgenblatt p. 7. Progress
       report on total of Memorial Fund.

3123   Johannes-Brahms Wochen. Pörtschach am Wörthersee. (Aus-
       <u>stellungskatalog.) (1.Juli-2. August 1964).</u> [Pörtschach:
       n.p., 1964?]. [50 pp.] ill., facsim. Contains concert pro-
       grammes [pp. 39, 41] and exhibition catalogue [pp. 43-50]
       and 542 and 2373.

3124   Jong, W. C. de. "Het Brahms-Museum te Hamburg" <u>Mens en</u>
       <u>melodie</u> 30/[5] (5.1975) pp. 135-37. ill., notes. Reports
       on establishment of the Brahms-Gesellschaft Hamburg e.V.
       and its mandate; includes comments on earlier memorial
       activities in Hamburg.

3125   K. R. [Kurt W. Richter] "Die Johannes Brahms-Gedenkräume
       in der Peterstrasse" <u>Mitteilungen der Brahms-Gesellschaft</u>
       <u>Hamburg e.V.</u> no. 4 (4.1973) pp. 13-15. ill. Reports on
       background of this Hamburg project, and its intended users.

3126   #Kalbeck, Max. "Jamben" <u>Rheinische Musik- und Theaterzeitung</u>
       (Köln) 4/20 (15.5.1903) pp. 179-80. Poem written for oc-
       casion, describes Brahms in the hereafter, and his strengths
       as a composer. A description of the Wien memorial ceremony
       is also included.
       (c) excerpt: Kalbeck. <u>Jamben. Gesprochen vom k.u.k.</u>
       <u>Hofburgschauspieler Herrn Georg Reimers zur Feier der</u>
       <u>Enthüllung des Grabdenkmales von Johannes Brahms am 7.</u>
       <u>Mai 1903.</u> Wien: Author, 1903. 6, [1] pp. Poem only.

3127   *_____ . "Das Brahms-Museum in Gmunden" <u>Mitteilungen der</u>
       <u>Brahms-Gesellschaft in Wien</u> (6.1907).

3128 *_____. "Das Brahms-Museum in Gmunden" Neues Wiener
        Tagblatt (20.10.1902).

3129 Karpath, Ludwig. "Die Enthüllung des Brahms-Denkmals"
        Signale für die musikalische Welt 66/20 (13.5.1908) pp.
        621-24. Describes the memorial installation ceremony in
        Wien, and the background of the project.

3130 #Keller, Otto. "Die Brahms-Ausstellung in Wien. Unbekannte
        Briefe und Dokumente des Meisters" Augsburger Postzeitung
        222/124 (27.5.1908) pp. 3-4 [across page bottoms]. An
        overview of exhibit's contents and what they reveal of
        Brahms the man.

3131 *_____. "Die Enthüllung des Brahms-Denkmales in Wien und
        die Brahms-Ausstellung" Neue musikalische Rundschau 1/1
        (1908).

3132 Klengel, Julius. "Zu der neuen Brahms-Büste von Albrecht
        Leistner" Zeitschrift für Musik 92/7/8 (7./8.1925) p. 418.
        ill. [after p. 416], notes. Describes how the bust reflects
        Brahms's qualities.

3133 "Das Komitee für ein Brahms-Denkmal in Thun" Die Musik
        (Berlin) 26/1 (10.1933) pp. 44-45. Reports on the estab-
        lishment of committee and its purpose.

3134 *Korngold, Julius. In 3074.

3135 *_____. "Ein Brahms-Haus in Wien" Neue freie Presse (Wien)
        (6.5.1904).

3136 _____. "Ein Brahms-Haus in Wien" Neue freie Presse (Wien)
        no. 14,619 (6.5.1905) Morgenblatt pp. 1-3 [across page
        bottoms]. Discusses why such a house is needed, and what
        it will contain.

3137 *_____. "Zur Enthüllung des Brahms-Monuments" Neue freie
        Presse (Wien) (6.5.1908).

3138 *Krause, Emil. "Die Enthüllungsfeier des Max Klingerschen
        Brahms-Denkmales" Blätter für Haus- und Kirchenmusik
        13/9 (1909).

3139 Lederer, Victor. "Das Brahms-Denkmal in Wien" Neue Musik-
        zeitung 29/16 (21.5.1908) pp. 346-47. ill. Reflects on
        memorial's qualities, its location, and how Brahms's art is
        reflected in it.

3140 Lissauer, Ernst. "Im Brahms Museum ..." Münchner neueste
        Nachrichten 79/77 (18.3.1926) p. 3. Describes content of
        Gmunden museum; includes comment on its conception.

3141 "Marmorbusten von Beethoven und Brahms ..." Allgemeine
Musikzeitung 36/2 (8.1.1909) p. 36. On busts of these two
composers, presented to Meiningen Hoftheater by Princess
Marie von Sachsen-Meiningen.

3142 "Max Klingers Brahms-Denkmal ..." Allgemeine Musikzeitung
36/3 (15.1.1909) p. 56. Progress report on the memorial.

3143 *Meiningen. Brahms-Ausstellung. Katalog einer kleinen Brahms-
Ausstellung aus Anlass der Enthüllung des Brahms-Denkmals
... Meiningen 7.-11. October 1899. [Eusebius Mandyczewski,
ed.] Meiningen: n.p., 1899. 16 pp.

3144 Mohr, Wilhelm. "Hommage à Johannes Brahms" Mitteilungen der
Brahms-Gesellschaft Hamburg e.V. no. 4 (4.1973) pp. 11-12.
ill. Reports on commemorative items issued for the 75th
anniversary of Brahms's death.

3145 "Monument to Johannes Brahms" The Times (London) no. 38,628
(23.4.1908) p. 5. Announces date for Wien Monument unveiling and the ceremony's plans.

3146 "The Monument to Johannes Brahms" The Times (London) no.
38,636 (2.5.1908) p. 12. An invitation to all English sub-
scribers of the Brahms Memorial to attend dedication ceremony in Wien.

3147 "A Monument to Johannes Brahms" The Times (London) no.
38,641 (8.5.1908) p. 14. Reports on Memorial dedication
ceremony in Wien.

3148 n. "Das Johannes-Brahms-Denkmal in Wien" Illustrirte Zeitung
(Leipzig) Bd. 130/3385 (14.5.1908) p. 953. ill. Provides
a complete description of the monument.

3149 "Die neuliche Blättermeldung das man Hr. Prof. Max Klinger
..." Musikalisches Wochenblatt 32/40 (26.9.1901) p. 533.
It was incorrectly reported previously that Klinger is to
do the Hamburg monument, Committee's decision had not
been made.

3150 Petzoldt, Richard. "Brahms-Ausstellung der preussischen
Staatsbibliothek" Allgemeine Musikzeitung 64/16 (16.4.1937)
pp. 234-35. Describes exhibit.

3151 *"Pomnik Jana Brahmsa w wiednui, dłuta Rudolfa Meyra" Tygodnik ilustrowany no. 21 (1908) p. 423. ill.

3152 Püringer, Aug[ust]. "Ein Brahmsdenkmal in Wien" Allgemeine
Musikzeitung 35/21/22 (29.5.1908) p. 422. ill. Describes
Monument and the festivities surrounding its unveiling.

3153 -r. [August Püringer] "Brahms' Denkmal auf dem Wiener
Zentralfriedhof" Neue Musikzeitung 24/14 (28.5.1903) p.
176. ill. [p. 177] Describes the ceremony and the monument.

3154 R. "Das Brahms-Heim in Gmunden" Neue freie Presse (Wien)
no. 12,966 (28.9.1900) Abendblatt p. 3. Presents the
museum's history and describes its collection; article includes letters from Brahms to Miller v. Aichholtz and to
an unidentified person.

3155 *R. Hr. [Richard Heuberger] "Johannes Brahms und sein Denkmal" Neues Wiener Tagblatt (2.4.1898).

3156 Reisenbichler, A. "Brahms and Gmunden" Hallé no. 43 (12.
1951) pp. 8-10. Relates the history of the Brahms Museum
and describes its collection; also describes Brahms the man
and times that he spent with the Miller von Aichholzes.

3157 Richter, Kurt [W.]. "Das Johannes Brahms-Archiv in der
Staats- und Universitätsbibliothek Hamburg" Mitteilungen
der B ahms-Gesellschaft Hamburg e.V. no. 1 (10.1970) pp.
3-4. ill. Provides historical background to the Archiv,
and describes its holdings and publications.

3158 Sack, Manfred. "Brahms für die Provinz" Die Zeit (Hamburg)
36/44 (23.10.1981) p. 42. ill. Describes how little Hamburg
has done to commemorate a native son; includes comments
on a recently erected sculpture in Brahms's memory.

3159 Schweizer, Gottfried. "Das Brahms-Haus in Lichtenthal.
Jugend musiziert in diesem Sommeridyll" Musica (Kassel)
23/4 (7.-8.1969) p. 383. Describes the opening of Memorial
House; includes account of Brahms's stays in Lichtenthal,
1865-74.

3160 "Seit dem 7. Mai 1903 ..." Bühne und Welt 6/13 (1904) p. 550.
notes. On erection of Brahms memorial in Wien.

3161 *"70 Jahre Museum" Festschrift des Museal- und Heimatvereins
Gmunden. Gmunden: n.p., 1978. pp. 6+.

3162 "Souvenirs of Brahms. Coda to the Centenary" The Times
(London) Royal Edition no. 46,491 (8.7.1933) p. 10. Describes London exhibit at the Royal College of Music.

3163 Stephenson, Kurt. "Rückblick und Ausblick" Mitteilungen der
Brahms-Gesellschaft Hamburg e.V. no. 1 (10.1970) p. 2.
Discusses founding of Brahms-Gesellschaft Hamburg e.V.,
and its expectations.

3164 "Die Veröffentlichung von Johannes Brahms' Nachlass ..." Neue Zeitschrift für Musik 73/29/30 (Bd. 102) (25.7.1906) pp. 625-26. Presents details of Deutsche Brahms-Gesellschaft's publishing programme.
  (e) report: "Der Nachlass von Johannes Brahms ..." Allgemeine Musikzeitung 33/34/35 (24./31.8.1906) p. 524.

3165 "Wertvolle Brahms-Reliquien ..." Allgemeine Musikzeitung 34/25 (21.6.1907) p. 446. Describes the acquisitions that the Wiener Brahms-Gesellschaft is making.

3166 *Widmann, J[osef]. V[iktor]. Der Bund (Bern) (1902).
  (e) report: "In Gmunden ist ..." Allgemeine Musikzeitung 29/46 (14.11.1902) p. 776. Comments that a composer is best remembered by his work, rather than by gathering his personal effects in a museum.

3167 *_____. Neue Zürcher Zeitung (1897 or 1899?). Comments on derogatory remarks on Brahms in 466, and presents background on Brahms and Nietzsche, 1887, to explain latter's thoughts on Brahms. [from 3167.e]
  (e) #report: "Polemiken über Brahms" Harmonie (Hannover) [12]/28 (12.7.1899) pp. 2-3. Includes reprint of 2960.

3168 Widmann, J[osef]. V[iktor]. "Prolog zur Enthüllung des Brahms-Denkmals in Meiningen am 7. Oktober 1899" Allgemeine Musikzeitung 26/41 (13.10.1899) pp. 607-08. Poem.

3169 "Wien ..." Allgemeine Musikzeitung 35/20 (15.5.1908) p. 404. Reports on Memorial Ceremony in Wien.

3170 "Wien. Brahms-Haus ..." Zeitschrift der Internationalen Musikgesellschaft 7/1 (1905) p. 28. Reports on Wiener Brahms-Gesellschaft's plans for a Brahms-Haus, and how Wien's Mayor made a decree that permits them to carry out this objective.

3171 "Wien. Das Haus Karlsgasse no. 4, ..." Allgemeine Musikzeitung 32/37 (15.9.1905) p. 590. Announces destruction of house that Brahms lived in.

3172 "Wien. Die feierliche Enthüllung ..." Allgemeine Musikzeitung 35/15 (10.4.1908) p. 318. Announces date of Memorial Ceremony.

3173 *Wiener Brahms-Gesellschaft. [Broschure.] Wien: n.p., 1907.
  (e) report: "Wien. Die Wiener Brahms-Gesellschaft ..." Allgemeine Musikzeitung 34/30/31 (26.7.;2.8.;1907) p. 534. Describes contents of Brochure: reports on Gesellschaft's activities and calls for donations for Brahms-Haus.

3174   Wild, Irene. "Das Brahms-Denkmal von Max Klinger" Signale
       für die musikalische Welt 67/1 (6.1.1909) pp. 9-12. Author
       describes her reaction to the memorial.

3175   *"Der 10. Todestag. Gedenkfeier am Wiener Zentralfriedhof"
       Neues Wiener Journal (5.4.1907).

3176   *"Zur Enthüllung des Brahms-Denkmals" Die Zeit [Tageszeitung]
       (Wien) (7.5.1908) Morgenblatt p. 2.
       (d) Specht, Richard. "Zur Enthüllung des Wiener Brahms-
       denkmals" Die Musik (Berlin) 7/18 (Bd. 27) (6.1908) pp.
       353-56. ill., notes. Describes the monument; includes
       author's memories of Brahms from 1894.

3177   [Das Johannes-Brahms-Denkmal-Komitee in Wien] Zur Enthüllung
       des Brahms-Denkmals in Wien. 7. Mai 1908. Wien: [Author],
       1908. 67 pp. ill. Includes indexes of cities that contri-
       buted to the Memorial, concert programmes in honour of the
       occasion, exhibit notices, and the gift's deed.
       includes: Kalbeck, Max. "Brahms und Wien": pp. 3-18.
       Describes Brahms's residences, his friends, and performances
       of his works in the city.
       includes: Mandyczewski, Eusebius. "Chronik des Denkmals":
       pp. 19-33. Surveys the memorial's history and provides
       a list of Committee members.

See also 39D, 243, 331, 350, 370, 443.c.iii., 580, 594, 673, 684, 721,
732, 755.d., 781, 925, 930, 1028, 1220, 1308, 1314, 2461.5, 2661,
2735-37.

See also II.A.4 and VII.A.

E. PUBLICATIONS

1. Brahms Festschriften

a. Monographs

3178   #Brahms-Kalender auf das Jahr 1909. Herausgegeben von der
       "Musik" Berlin: und Leipzig: Verlegt bei Schuster & Loeff-
       ler, [1908]. 89 pp. ill., facsim., mus. Calender: pp.
       6-29. Includes 39A.c.iii., 983.c.ix., 990.a., 1067.a.c.,
       2351.c.

See also 3186.c.

b. Periodical Issues

3179 #Ars. Revista de arte 17/79 (1957) [135 pp.] ill., facsim.
"Número extraordinario dedicado a Brahms" contains 203.d.,
293, 764.b.iii., 908, 1329.c., 1389, 1439, 1798, 2256, 2423,
2559, 2643, 2918.

3180 Caecilia (Utrecht) 79/11 (10.4.1922) pp. 162-76. Contains 639,
1193, 1753, 2016, 2805, 2878, 2884, 2959.
(d) continued: Caecilia (Utrecht) 79/12 (10.5.1922) pp.
177-92. Brahms: pp. 179-89. Includes 660, 619,
1435, 2998.
(e) report: "On Johannes Brahms" Musical Times 63/953
(1.7.1922) p. 490. Also includes reports on 933,
1320, 3180.d., 3188, 3190, 3192.

3181 Der Merker (Wien) 3/2 (1.1912) pp. 41-80. Brahms: pp. 41-
71. ill., facsim., mus. Contains 39C.c.iv., 392, 970,
1299, 2429, 3028.

3182 Musical Quarterly 19/2 (4.1933) pp. 113-232. Brahms: pp.
113-68. Contains 672, 706.d., 1224, 1322.b.

3183 Die Musik (Berlin) 2/15 (Bd. 7) (5.1903) pp. [170]-248, [17].
ill., facsim., mus. [music for Op. 106 no. 4] Contains 482,
694, 899, 1760, 2563.

3184 Die Musik (Berlin) 12/1 (Bd. 45) (10.1912) pp. [2]-64, [14].
ill., facsim.
"Brahms-Heft No. 2" Contains 792, 1591.d., 1839, 1867, 2022.
e.ii., 2087, 2440.
includes: "Anmerkungen zu unseren Beilagen": p. 64.

3185 Die Musik (Berlin) 12/2 (Bd. 45) (10.1912) pp. [66]-128,
[18].
"Brahms-Heft No. 3": Brahms: pp. [66]-101, 128. ill.,
facsim. Contains 23.b.c., 240, 1084, 1474.
includes: "Anmerkungen zu unseren Beilagen": p. 128.

3186 #Die Musik (Berlin) 25/8 (5.1933) pp. 561-615. Contains
61.e.i., 397, 608.d., 665, 899.c.i., 900.a., 944.c., 957.
a.c., 1074.c., 1306.d., 1364.c., 1839.c., 2087.c., 2108,
2212, 2371, 2440.c., 2563.c., 2577, 2584, 2891, 2989.c.,
3078.
(c) excerpt: Johannes Brahms Festschrift. Deutsche
Brahms-Gesellschaft, ed. Berlin: Max Hesses
Verlag, [1933]. 47, [1] pp. ill., facsim. Contains
61.e.i.a., 397.a., 665.a., 899.c.i.a., 1364.c.a.,
2087.c.a., 2108.a., 2212.a., 2371.a., 2440.c.a.,
2563.c.a., 2577.a., 2584.a., 2891.a., 3078.a.

514 / VII. Brahms's Perpetuation

3187   Musik für Alle 7/3 (No. 75) [(1911)] pp. 37-56. facsim.,
        mus. [pp. 41-56]
        "Brahms-Heft" Contains 95; music is for items from Opp. 47,
        49, 76, 105, Deutsche Volkslieder (1894) [Hofmann nr. 133;
        McCorkle WoO 33] and Ungarische Tänze [Hofmann nr. 128;
        McCorkle WoO 1].

3188   #Die Musikwelt (Hamburg) 2/9 (1.6.1922) pp. 221-39 (Heft pp.
        1-19). Contains 363, 394, 1465, 2408, 2487, 2687, 3078.
        (e) report: see 3180.e.

3189   Neue Musik-Zeitung 28/13 (4.4.1907) pp. 273-96, [6]. "Brahms-
        Nummer" Brahms: pp. 273-93. ill. Contains 226, 589,
        948, 1453, 2886, 2996.
        includes: "Unsere Bilder": pp. 287-88.

3190   Neue Musikzeitung 43/13 (6.4.1922) pp. [2], 193-212. "Jo-
        hannes Brahms Gedächtnisheft zur fünfundzwanzigsten
        Wiederkehr seines Todestages (3. April 1897)" Brahms:
        pp. 193-207. ill., facsim. Contains 58.d., 712, 1281,
        2204, 2375, 2903.
        (e) report: see 3180.e.

3191   #Symphonia 16/5 (5.1933) pp. 81-106.
        "Brahms-Heft" [title p. 81: "1833 Johannes Brahms 1933"]
        Brahms: pp. 81-102. Contains 981, 1175, 1434, 1810, 2016.d.,
        2096, 2389, 2923.

3192   Zeitschrift für Musik 89/7 (4.1922) pp. 153-76. Brahms: pp.
        153-65. Contains 1101.e., 1447, 2384, 2953.
        (e) report: see 3180.e.

3193   Zeitschrift für Musik 100/5 (5.1933) pp. [1], 425-528. Brahms:
        pp. 425-28, 454-57, 465, 476. ill., facsim. Contains
        618.a.c.i., 848.d.ii., 929.d.i., 1117, 2267.d., 2346, 2352,
        2474, 2624.c., 2978.

                        2. Brahms Serials

3194   *The Brahms Song Society. Notes. 1 [(12.1936)].

3195   Brahms-Gesellschaft Hamburg e.V. Mitteilungen. no. 1-
        (1970-).

3196   *Brahms-Gesellschaft in Wien. Jahresbericht. 1-10 (1904-13).

3197   Brahms-Studien. Bd. 1- (1974-).

PERSONAL NAME INDEX

The Personal Name Index contains references to persons or
bodies who are responsible for the content of the citations included
in this work--not only including authors, but also editors, translators
and illustrators. Persons who are the subject of commemorative
volumes, or festschriften, are also indexed here.

Alphabetization follows the general principles used in the body
of the work, except that acronyms and initialisms file at the beginning
of each letter. A reference to a citation number includes appearances
in all applicable sections within that number.

Friedrich, Annette 2197
Friedrich, Julius 22
Friedrich, Paul 1037
Friedrich, W. 954.e.iii
Fries, Hildegaard 1221
Frisch, Walter Miller 2372
Frost, Henry F. 1921
Fry, J. 2466
Fuchs, Anton 536
Fürst, Jutta 3109
Fuhrmann, Heinz 2705
Fuller, Roy 1257, 2928
Fuller-Maitland, John Alexander
  23, 117.b.i, 128, 1013.c.i,
  1014.b, 1795
Funk, Heinrich 129, 2727
Furtwängler, Wilhelm 130, 131,
  2373, 2467, 2633, 2817, 2929-
  31

G. 1505.d
G.E.B. 447
G.T. 2678; See also Tischer,
  Gerhard
Gablentz, Otto Heinz v.d. 1340
Gae, Gianni 25.b.i.b.ii
Gärtner, Gustav 1887
Gal, Hans 24, 272, 819.c.vi,
  1009.c.x, 1179.c.i
Gale, Harlow 132
Gallois, Jean 257
Gallwitz, Sophie Dorothea 1159,
  1258, 2251.5
Galston, Gottfried 1562
Gamer, Carlton 1683
Ganghofer, Ludwig 937
Ganz, Rudolph 1393
Garbett, A.S. 894.b.c.iv, 979.
  c.iii, 1126.a.c.ii, 1180.b.c
Gardner, John 2252
Garrison, Fielding H. 821
Gartenberg, Egon 385
Gast, Peter 1098.d.i
Gauer, Oscar 671
Gaukstad, Øystein 155
Gavrilă, Silviu 109
Gay, Harry W. 1748
Gay, Peter 2932
Gebhardt, Peter von 344
Geck, Martin 2447

Geeraert, Nicole 1863
Gehrenbeck, David M. 2254
Gehring, Franz 2325
Gehrkens, Karl W. 1947
Geiringer, Irene 25.a, 25.b.i,
  673
Geiringer, Karl 25, 386, 448,
  672, 673, 841, 871.c.iv, 879,
  892.c.iii, 907, 954.c.v, 962,
  977, 983.c.v, 1009.c.vii, 1079,
  1110, 1160, 1203.c.iv, 1204.
  c.iv, 1252, 1259, 1297.c.iii,
  1314.c.iii, 1617, 1618, 2346,
  2352, 2577, 3093
Geiser, Samuel 618.a
Geisler-Schubert, Carola 674
Geissler, H. 2818
General-Intendanten der Hambur-
  gischen Staatsoper und die
  Philharmonischen Staatsorches-
  ters 2711
Gennrich, Friedrich 2112
George, Graham 1796
Georgii, Walter 1563
Gerber, Rudolf 26, 2255, 2533,
  2561
Gerber, Walther 346
Gerdes, Karl 675
Gerigk, Herbert 2670
Gerlach, Reinhard 1145
Gerstenberg, H. 996
Gerstenberg, Walter 2145, 2157
Gertrude Clarke Whittall Founda-
  tion 295
Gervais, O.R. 2819
Gesellschaft der Musikforschung
  2450
Gesellschaft der Musikfreunde
  449, 450, 2782
Gesellschaft der Musikfreunde.
  Museum 3093
Gest, Elizabeth 2134
Gibson, Michael 1961
Giebeler, Konrad 2053
Gieseler, Walter 2374
Gilbert, Richard 258
Gil'bukh, Ia 1717
Gildemeister, Anna 374
Gilman, Lawrence 1797, 1922
Ginastera, Alberto 1798
Ginder, C. Richard 1161

Glahn, Henrik 1799
Glinka, M.J. 1976
Glinski, M. 1240
Glock, W.F. 2633.5
Glöckner, Willy 2749
Gloger, Bruno 1133.a.ii.a
Glover, Cedric Howard 133
Glowacki, John 1574
Gmunden. Kammerhofmuseum 3094
Godwin, Edward 337
Godwin, Stephani 337
Goebels, Franzpeter 800
Göhler, Georg 872, 2164, 2993
Göhler, Georges; See Göhler, Georg
Göpel, Erhard 2109
Goepp, Philip H. 1800, 1923
Görner, Rüdiger 2331
Goetschius, Percy 1801, 1882, 1912, 1972, 1991
Goldhammer, O. 1718
Goldmark, Carl 949, 950
Goldmark, Karl; See Goldmark, Carl
Goldron, Roman 27, 819.c.ii.e.ii; See also Burkhalter, A. Louis
Goldschmidt, Harry 2820
Goldstein, Max 1126.e
Golovatchoff, Dika 2015
Good, Margaret 1653
Goodfriend, James 1341
Goodwin, Amina 677
Goss, Madeleine 28
Gottgetreu, Johannes Oskar 3095
Gottlieb-Billroth, Otto 819
Gotwals, Vernon 1749
Gould, Murray J. 1380
Grabau, Carl 1059, 2307
Grabner, Hermann 2375
Grace, Michael D. 1683
Graener, Paul 387, 952
Graevenitz, George von 941, 2198, 2562, 2620
Graf, Harry 908
Graf, Max 953, 1260, 2644
Grasberger, Franz 29, 30, 285, 388, 537, 857, 1261, 1311, 2135, 2241, 2578
Graue, Jerald C. 2361

Graves, Charles L. 23.e.ii, 48.e.ii; See also C.L.G.
Gray, Cecil 2934
Graziano, John Michael 2376
Grebe, Karl 2645
Greenberg, Beth 1669
Greene, Charles Robert 2023
Greenspan, Bertram 1514
Greither, Aloys 819.c.i
Gren, Donald Allen 1864
Gresky, W. 572
Grew, Eva M. 339
Grey, Robin 1168.e.ii.a
Grimm, Friedrich Karl 2055
Grimmelt, Otto 2692
Grimsted 2936
Grindel, Gerhard 573
Grippe, Kerry Joseph 1684
Groathouse, Daniel Lynn 1445
Groeg, Ernst 2469
Gröhn, Waldemar 2376.5
Grolman, Adolf von 819.e.i, 1262
Grosser, F. 679
Groth, Klaus 958, 1214
Grove, George 1888
Groves, Cecil T. 135
Gruber, Albion 1654
Grun, Bernard 680
Grzelka, Connie 2690
Guardia, Ernesto de la 2256
Guck, Marion A. 2154
Gülke, Peter 1457
Gui, Vittorio 1564, 2469.5, 2857
Guinzburg, Juana 627.5
Gumprecht, Otto 136
Gund, Robert 966
Gunn, Glen Dillard 221
Gunther, Hannah 764.b.i.a
Guseva, A. 2377
Gusinde, Alois 2821
Gutmann, Albert 389
Guttmann, Alfred 137

h.; See Oiste, Heinrich v.
H., Dr. 452; See also Hanslick, Eduard
H.B. 25.b.i.e, 1068.b; See also Weiner, H.B.
H.C.C. 1608, 2511; See also Colles, Henry Cope

H.Ch.; See Chevalley, Heinrich
H.D. 1342, 1458, 1469, 1515,
1525, 2056, 2057, 2140, 2199,
2308; See also Deiters,
Hermann
H.E. 1646 ; See also Ehrlich,
Heinrich
H.Fr., Mme. 117.b.ii
H.J.C. 2462
H.M. 778
H.P. 3099
H. Sch. 2939; See also
Schenker, Heinrich
H.-W., Susanne 763
H-Abrahall, Clare 888
Haas, Max 2195
Haas, Rudolf 453
Haase, Rudolf 1565, 2014
Hack, Gwendolyn; See Kelley,
Gwendolyn Dunlevy
Hadden, James Cuthbert 681
Hadow, Grace 1170.d.i
Hadow, Sir William Henry 138,
1170.d.i, 1263, 2634
Häfner, Roland 1540
Haelssig, Artur 2940
Hagen, Hans Wilhelm 1162
Haggin, Bernhard H. 1802
Hahn, A. 1566
Haics, Géza 2378
Halbreich, Harry 259
Hallenberg, A. 2941
Hallis, Adolphe 1700
Hamand, L.A. 652.d
Hambourg, Mark 1624
Hamburg 3072
Hamburg. Behörde für Wissen-
schaft und Kunst. Kulturamt
2700
Hamburg. Philharmonische
Staatsorchester 2711
Hamburg. Staats- und Univer-
sitätsbibliothek 3100
Hamburg. Staatsoper 2711
Hamburger, Povl 2141
Hamel, Fred 332, 2646
Hammermann, Walter 2058
Hammerschlag, János 2942
Hampe, Johann Christoph
139
Hancock, Virginia Lee 2200

Hannover, Dorothea 1012
Hansen, W. 682
Hanslick, Eduard 117.e.ii, 320.e,
443, 968, 969, 1153, 1378.a,
1655, 1924, 1930 i), 2021,
2470, 2943-50, 3102; See also
Ed.H.; H., Dr.
Haraszti, Emil 1000
Harden-Rauch, Philipp 649
Harding, H.A. 2951
Harrison, Julius 1803
Harrison, Max 2059
Harth, Walther 2671
Hartmann, Arthur 1939
Hartmann, Hans 806
Hary, Judit 19.b
Hase, Oskar von 849
Hasse, Karl 140
Hathaway, Thomas 2379, 2471
Hauptman, Hans 1804
Hausegger, Friedrich von 971
Hausegger, Siegmund von 971,
2371
Hauser, Carry 953.b.i
Hausswald, Günter 2664
Hautz, Hilar 1567
Havemann, Hans 1163
Hawn, Margaret Elizabeth 1428
Hayes, Deborah 2534
Hecht, Dora 618.a, 894.b
Heckmann, Harald 2157
Heermann, Hugo 974
Heger, Theodore E. 1821
Heilbut, E. 3103
Heimann, Wilhelm 683
Heise, P. 2638
Held, Ernst 1133.a.i
Hell, H. 2822
Helm, Theodor 31, 154, 390,
440, 454, 455, 685, 1470,
1487, 1865, 1889, 2147, 2332,
2472
Helms, Siegmund 793, 2060
Henckell, Karl 1343
Henderson, W.J. 2380, 2952
Hendrickson, Hugh R. 1805
Henle, Günter 296, 972, 1454
Henning, Laura; See Schmidt-
Delbrück, Lore
Henschel, A.K. 2823
Henschel, George 978, 979

Henschel, Helen 979.d.iii
Henschel, Maria 686
Herbort, Heinz Josef 2706
Hering, Hans 2061
Hermann, László 347
Hermenau, Dr. 982
Hernried, Robert 32, 391, 538,
687, 989, 1158.e.iii, 2024,
2201, 2257, 2473, 2586, 2587
Herrmann, Felix 376
Herrmann, Kurt 1568
Herrmann, Marcelle 1060
Herrup, Gunnar 2141
Herttrich, Ernst 1454
Herwig, Hans 1264
Herzfeld, Viktor 456
Herzogenberg, Heinrich von
2202
Hess, Viktor 141
Hesse, Hermann 2081
Hessen, Alexander Friedrich
von 987
Heuberger, Richard 39B.e.iii,
149, 392, 457, 688, 887, 990,
991, 1299, 1429, 1940, 2203,
3155; See also R., R.H.
Heulhard, M. 458
Heusinkveld, Frances 1762
Heuss, Alfred 150.a, 2474,
2522, 2734, 2953
Hevesi, Ludwig 1073, 2979, 3106;
See also L.H.-i.
Hewitt, Helen Margaret 1344
Heyer, Wilhelm 291
Heyer, Frau Wilhelm 291
Heyne, Hildegard 1038
Hicks, David 1691
Hiebert, Elfrieda Franz 574
Higgins, Thomas 1734
Highet, Gilbert 1242
Hill, Ralph 33, 48, 1793, 1855,
2475, 2647, 2954
Hill, William G. 1527
Hiller, Ferdinand 992
Hillmann, Adolf 34
Hinson, Maurice 1681.d.i
Hirsch, Hans 2381
Hirschberg, Walter 3048.e.i
Hirschfeld, Georg 993
Hirschfeld, Robert 689, 1009.e.iv,
1569, 2780, 2955

Hirschowitz, Betty 2535
Hirtschmann, Eduardo; See Hit-
schmann, Eduard
Hitschmann, Eduard 764
Hitschmann, Edward; See Hit-
schmann, Eduard
Hodzava, R. 1611
Höcker or Hoecker, Karla 393,
842
Högler, Fritz 2648
Hofer, H. 1719
Hoffmann, E. 142
Hoffmann, Rudolph Stephan 394,
2781
Hoffmann von Fallersleben, August
Heinrich 996
Hofmann, Kurt 277, 575, 690,
799, 843, 1031, 1107, 1246,
3107-09
Hohenemser, M.; See Hohenemser,
Richard
Hohenemser, Richard 2022.e.ii,
2563, 2579
Hohlbaum, Robert 143, 2625
Holde, Artur 955, 1009.d
Holden, Frances 2074
Holl, Karl 144
Hollander, Hans 1488, 2258,
2382
Holle, Hugo 2512
Holley, Joan 898
Holmqvist, Bengt 2824
Holschneider, Andreas 2145
Holst, Gustav 1841
Holstad, Albert John 1625
Holstein, Hedwig von 997.a
Hoplit; See Pohl, Richard
Horney, Anna Louise 1806
Horovitz-Barnay, Ilka 926, 998,
999, 1248; See also Ilias
Horton, Charles T. 1663
Horton, John 1807, 2062
Horusitzky, Zoltán 2580
Houston, Robert Ewing, Jr. 2608
Howard-Jones, Evlyn 33, 1391
Howes, Frank 1265
Høybe, John 2141
Hrabussay, Zoltán 35, 547, 548
Hubay, Andor von 1001
Hubay, Eugen v.; See Hubay,
Jenő von

Hubay, Eugène de 1002;
See also Hubay, Jenő von
Hubay, Jenő von 1002-04;
See also Hubay, Eugène de
Hubay, Károlyi 2564
Hubbard, Elbert 1165
Hübbe, Thomas 844, 1711
Hübbe, Walter 348
Hürlimann, Martin 627
Hüschen, Heinrich 1103, 1160, 1733, 2679
Huettner, Dr. 145
Hughes, Edwin 1685
Hughes, Gervase 1208.c
Humbert, Georges 2750, 2958
Hume, Paul 1808
Humphries, Rolfe 1587.a
Hunek, Rudolph 2719
Huneker, James Gibbons 146, 635.a.i.a, 1381, 1392, 1809, 2063, 2477; See also J.G.H.
Hunnius, Monika 1006
Hunziker, Rudolf 945, 1128
Huschka, Konrad; See Huschke, Konrad
Huschke, Conrad; See Huschke, Konrad
Huschke, Konrad 691-93, 765, 796, 858, 881, 929, 984, 1039, 1088, 1116, 1219, 1225, 1241, 1266, 1293, 1890, 1925, 1996, 2383
Husmann, Heinrich 879.c, 2157
Hutcheson, Ernest 1393
Hutchinson, William R. 1997
Hutschenruyter, Wouter 36, 1810, 2151, 2959
Hutton, Winfield 539

Ignatius-Metsola, Eeva 1570
Ilias 999; See also Horovitz-Barnay, Ilka
Imbert, Hugues 37, 147, 461, 1853.b.iv.d, 2259
Ingold, John G. 2615
Ingster, Eugenio 18.b.ii
Ireland, John 2954
Isler, Ernst 628, 1764
Ismer, Ursula 1394
Isóz, Kálmán 923

Istel, Edgar 1267, 2767.d
Ivey, Donald 2536
Ivichich, Max v. 540

J.B.K. 443.c.ii, 969.c, 1168.e.i
J.F.R. 2476, 2961; See also Runcimann, John F.
J.G.H. 2477; See also Huneker, James Gibbons
J.S.S. 2962, 2963; See also Shedlock, J.S.
J.V.W.; See Widmann, Josef Viktor
JWSch. 1891; See also Schott-länder, Johann-Wolfgang
Jack, Dwight Christian 2121
Jacob, Gorden 1459
Jacobi, Erwin R. 2448
Jacobi, Frederick 2964
Jacobs, Robert L. 1199.e.ii, 1811
Jacobsen, Christiane 2064
Jacobson, Bernard 2385
Jäckel, Hildegard 2596
Jagic, Nikolaus von 822
James, Burnett 38
James, Roberta Aileen 1866
Janetschek, Edwin 2449
Jansen, F. Gustav 1183
Jansen, Ferdinand 1179.e.iii
Janson, H. 2260
Janssen, Georg 349
Járosi, Dezső 2965
Jarosy, Albert 2773
Jemnitz, Sándor 766
Jenner, Gustav 694, 1084, 1867
Jensen, F. Gustav 3013.a.i
Jensen, Gunver Hasseriis 1571
Jervis-Read, Harold Vincent 1572
Jirásek, Arnold 823
Joachim, Johannes 1013
Joachim, Joseph 1013, 2735
Jöde, Fritz 2565
Johannes Brahms Festwoche (1958) 2707
Johannes-Brahms-Denkmal-Komitee in Wien, Das 3177
Johansen, David Monrad 155
John, Hanna 1394
Johnson, Martin 1516
Jonas, Oswald 1639, 1735, 1736,

2548, 2549, 2599, 2610, 2991
Miesner, Heinrich 959
Mila, Massimo 47, 178, 2569, 2653
Miller, Max B. 1768
Miller, Norbert 2320
Miller zu Aichholz, Viktor von 721
Minear, Paul S. 2283
Minotti, Giovanni 1701
Mirsky, Reba Paeff 51
Misch, Ludwig 52, 756.d.i, 2080, 2842
Mitchell, William J. 1659
Mitringer, Hedwig 399
Mitropoulos, Dimitri 251
Mitscherlich-Claus, Luise 1702
Mitschka, Arno 2405
Möller, Walter 2136, 2284
Mohr, Ernst 633.a
Mohr, Wilhelm 1406, 3144
Moldavskiĭ, A. 1717
Moldenhauer, Hans 1586
Molnár, Antal 53
Monma, Naomi 54
Montefal, Heriberto 1439
Montés, John 2843
Moore, Earl V. 1821
Moretti, Maria Giovanni 2494.b.iii
Morgan, Bayard Quincy 1895
Morgenstern, Sam 1179.d.ii.c.iii
Morik, Werner 2570
Morin, A. 1812
Morold, M. 2844
Morris, Herbert 1587
Morse, Peter 267
Moser, Andreas 1009, 1013, 1014
Moser, Dietz-Rüdiger 1160
Moser, Hans Joachim 179, 1588, 1896, 2081, 2405.5, 2845-48
Moser, Karl 1306
Moszkowski, Alexander 2992
Mott, E.M. 2617
Motte, Diether de la 2539
Mountain, Thomas 2825.d.d
Mrevlov, Aleksandr 2406
Mühlhäuser, Siegfried 300
Müller, Erich H. 934, 1286
Mueller, Erwin Carl 2600
Müller, Hans 542

Müller, Herman 2180
Müller, Herta 939
Mueller, Kate Hevner 2993
Müller, Konrad 2407
Müller von Asow, Erich H. 1292
Mueller von Asow, Hedwig 1179. c.xi
Müller-Blattau, Joseph 55
Müller-Dombois, Richard 378
Müller-Hartmann, Robert 2408
Müller-Marein, Josef 722
Mueller-Reuter, Theodor 1359
Müllner, Hans 2693
Münkel, Wolfgang 453
Münster, Robert 594
Münz, Sigmund 617, 1096
Muir, Percy H. 275
Mulach, G.A. 826
Muller, H.J.M. 56
Mumford, L. Quincy 301
Munk, Jørgen 2124
Munte, Frank 1173
Murdoch, William David 57
Murdoch, William J. 359
Museum Villa Stuck 1047
Musgrave, Michael Graham 1146, 2285, 2524
Musik, Die 3178
Musikantiquariat Hans Schneider 239
Muzzi, Nino 60.b
Myrdal, Jan 1772

-n. 497, 969.e.ii
n. 498, 3148
N. 1522, 1857 ; See also Noorden, Carl von
Naaff, A. 181
Nadeau, Roland 360
Nadkarni, D. 2849
Nägele, H. 723
Nagel, Wilibald; See Nagel, Willibald
Nagel, Willibald 40.e.ii, 58, 808, 1589, 1590
Nasatyr', G. 25.b.iii
Nattiez, Jean-Jacques 1703
Naylor, E.W. 1548.d
Neider, Charles 1897
Neitzel, Otto 101, 476, 2680

Paladi, Marta 66
Palm, Albert 2331
Panofsky, Walter 2261
Paquin, Marie-Thérèse 2168
Parker, D.C. 1853.b.i, 3004
Parry, Charles Hubert Hastings,
 Sir 2486
Partridge, Eleanor 2414
Pascall, Robert 1476, 1592,
 1593, 1899, 2415
Pasche, Hans 3005
Passuth, László 9.b
Pastor, Willy 1048
Patrick, Lynus 1694
Patrick, Susan Bess 875
Patterson, Grace Dickinson 223
Pauer, F.X. 1447
Paul, E. 3006
Pauli, Walter 67
Pauls, Volquart 956
Paumgartner, Bernhard 402,
 1104, 1900
Paumgartner, H. 1362, 1502,
 1537, 1542, 2291
Pečman, Rudolf 905, 1145,
 2416
Pelusi, Mario Joseph 1667
Pena, Joaquim 2084
Pennequin, Louis 211.b
Perger, H. von 2853
Perger, Richard von 68, 506,
 859, 1106
Peschnig, Emil 730
Pessenlehner, R. 988
Pestalozza, Luigi 2494.b.iii
Peters, C.F. 318
Petersen, Toni 1107
Petersen, U. 3007
Petri, Norbert 622
Petzold-Angermünde, Max 1108
Petzoldt, Richard 2212, 2669,
 2854, 3150
Peyser, Herbert F. 694.e,
 989.e, 1823, 2131, 2713
Pfannenstiel, Alexander 272.e
Pfannkuch, Wilhelm 1053
Pfister, Kurt 837.e, 1028.5
Pfisterer, Manfred 1147
Pfohl, Ferdinand 69, 445.5,
 507, 2487, 3008
Pfordten, Hermann von der 731,
 860

Phillips, Catherine Alison 61.b,
 3013.a.iv.d
Pieper, Carl 597, 598
Pierce, Esther Mayo 1448
Pierpont Morgan Library 303
Piguet, Jean-Claude 2488
Pilcz, Alexander 1229, 1274,
 3009
Piovesan, Alessandro 2489
Pirani, Eugenio di 185, 509,
 3010
Pischel, Mari 733, 2855
Pisk, P.A. 861
Pisk, Paul A. 1574, 2085
Pitina, Sof'ia 2435
Pleasants, Henry, III 2470.a.b,
 2944.c.i, 3013.b.i, 3048.d
Plenzat, Karl 2625.a.i
Plessing, Generalkonsul 1109
Plieg, Ernst-Albrecht 2251
Plüddemann, M. 2345
Poetter, Joachim 1047
Pohl, Louise; See Pohl, Luise
Pohl, Luise 1111, 1112
Pohl, Richard 2957, 3011, 3012
Pohlig, Carl 1113, 1114
Poliński, Aleksander 510
Pollak, Egmont 1963
Popdimitrov, Karen 2490
Porfir'eva, Anna 2406
Portnoy, Bernard 1093
Potts, Joseph E. 599
Pousseur, Henri 809
Prahm, Adolf 1115
Preising 954.5, 1363
Prelinger, Fritz 983.e.viii,
 1009.e.viii, 1009.e.ix, 1122.e.vi
Pressel, Gustav 2347
Pretzsch, Paul 1275
Prilipp, E. 768
Prillinger, Elfriede 973
Prime-Stevenson, Irenaeus 511
Prochaska, Heinrich 543
Prohaska, Carl 1449, 1499
Prohaska, Karl 1473
Promintzer 403
Protz, Albert 2149
Puchelt, Gerhard 1594
Püringer, August 3152; See also
 -r.
Pulver, Jeffrey 70, 186, 554,
 555, 735, 884, 976, 1015,

Riis-Vestergaard, H. 84.b.i
Riis-Vestergaard, K. 84.b.i
Riller, William; See Ritter,
  William
Rilling, Helmuth 1023
Rinn, Hermann 2899
Rittenhouse, Robert John 1825
Ritter, William 224, 2761, 2762
Ritz, Erika 846
Ritzer, Walter 301
Robert, Walter 1595
Roberts, Clifford 2088
Roberts, W. Wright 1751
Robertson, Alec 75, 2295
Robertson, Alex 12
Robinson, Edith 2601
Robinson, Edward 739
Robjohns, Sydney 1497
Roeder, Michael T. 2216
Röntgen, Julius 65, 621, 920,
  2884
Rösch, Friedrich 876
Roesner, Linda Correll 1935.e.iii
Rössler, Oskar 601
Röttgers, B. 39A.e.vi
Röttges, Willy 1169
Roftmann, L. 1018
Rognoni, Luigi 2494.b.iii
Roltsch, Siegfried 2169
Ronde, H.W. de 1175
Roner, Anna 740, 1179.e.v
Ronga, Luigi 2421
Roores, Groker 152.d
Roquebrune, Fernand-Georges
  40.e.iii
Rose, Michael Paul 2217
Rosegger, Peter 1030.d., 1133
Rosen, Charles 2553
Rosenberg, Julius 514
Rosenberg, Wolf 2491
Rosenfeld, Paul 3013.a.i.b
Rosenthal, Moritz 1076
Ross, George 2126
Rost, G.W. 1876
Rostand, Claude 76, 88
Roubakine, Boris 194
Roy, Otto 1364
Rubarth, Hermann 1826
Rubinstein, Joseph 2422
Rudolf, Max 2296
Rudorff, Ernst 1137

Rüdiger, Theo 195
Rütten, Erich 595
Rufener, R. 247
Ruiz Tarazona, Andrés 77
Rummenhöller, Peter 3019.5
Runcimann, John F. 2476, 2961
Rupé, Hans 2899

S.- 515
S.B. 196, 1451, 1641, 1660, 1741,
  1873, 2029, 2224; See also
  Bagge, Selmar
Sdl.; See Seidl, Arthur
Sp. 1057
Sp-r. 544; See also Spitzer,
  Daniel
S.T. 1365
St. 2229
Sachau, Eduard 1138
Sack, Manfred 3158
Sackett, S.J. 2571
Sänger, E. 2859
Saenz, Pedro 2423
Saerchinger, Cesar 1254; See
  also C.S.
Salmen, Walter 2464
Salmenhaara, Erkki 1827, 1902,
  1931, 1982, 2003, 2424
Salocks, Madeline Katherine
  Bacon 1596
Salten, Felix 2089
Samazeuilh, G. 1918.a
Sampson, George 23.e.iii
Sams, Eric 2090, 2091, 2132,
  2525-27
Samsour, Roberta Finlayson 913
Sandvik, Ole Mørk 155
Sanford, Ralph S. 1127
Sannemüller, Gerd 960, 2092
Santner, Inge 304
Sartori, Claudio 40.b
Sauer, Emil von 1139
Savill, Mervyn 1179.c.xiv.b
Sbornik, Trudov 1611
Schabacher-Bleichröder, Anna
  197
Schaefer, Hans-Jürgen 1983
Schäfer, Rudolf 996
Schanzlin, Hans Peter 1129, 1130,
  2297

Weingartner, Felix 1288, 1853,
2519, 2606, 2804
Weinhold, Liesbeth 606
Weinrich, Otto 369
Weinstock, Herbert 1237
Weintraub, Eugene 1978.d
Weir, Neil F. 830
Weise, Dagmar 1496, 2027
Weismann, W. 1283
Weiss, Ferdinand 1494
Weiss, Josef 754, 2607
Weiss, Joseph 1289
Weiss, Piero 39B.c.i, 39C.c,
73.c, 913, 1013.c.c, 1069.b.ii,
1179.c.xvi, 1183.c
Weiss-Aigner, Günter 1948, 1949
Welti, Heinrich 2438
Wendt, Gustav 1290
Wendt, Martha 1950
Wensel, Viktor 2730
Werba, E. 248
Werner, Heinrich 3048
Werner, Hildegard 431.c.e
Werner, Th.W. 2880
Wessem, Constant van 1419,
3041
Wessling, Berndt W. 1123, 2302
Westafer, Walter 2303
Westermeyer, Karl 20.e.ii
Westphal, Kurt 2677, 3042
Westrheene, P.A. van 2878;
See also v.W.
Wetschky, Jürgen 2439
Wetz, R. 2520
Wetzel, Justus Hermann 1179.
e.vii, 1179.e.viii, 1180.e.iii,
2173, 2440, 2441
Weyl-Nissen, A. 2881
White, Felix 3043
Whittal, Gertrude Clarke; See
Gertrude Clarke Whittall
Foundation
Whitwell, David 1376
Wichmann, Hermann 1294, 1295
Widmann, Hans-Joachim 2009
Widmann, Josef Viktor 215,
532, 618, 755, 940, 1062.e,
1098, 1302, 1303, 2631, 2738,
3166-68
Widmann, Max 532, 618.a
Widmark, Ulrika 112.b

Wiedemann, E. 831
Wiener Brahms-Gesellschaft 3173
Wiener Stadtbibliothek 310
Wienke, Gerhard 249
Wiens, Erich 607
Wiepking, Henny 358.e.ii
Wiesengrund-Adorno, Theodor
282
Wiesner, Kurt 2031
Wilbrandt, Adolf 1304
Wilcox, Lee 2032
Wild, Irene 370, 3044, 3045, 3174
Wilfferodt, Felix 983.e.xi, 1192.e,
3046
Wilke, Rainer 1518
Willers, Anni 765.d.e
Williams, Alma Stone 2220
Williams, Michael D. 1908
Williams, Richard 1909, 1967
Willige, Jochen 785
Willmann, H. 2592
Willner, A.M. 924
Wilson, Charles 2442
Wilson, Colin 3047
Wincenty 164
Winkel, Fritz 1305
Winston, Edmund W. 1094
Winterfeld, A.V. 1171; See also
M.H.
Wintzer, Richard 608, 2105
Wiora, Walter 1406, 1927, 2025,
2113, 2573, 2576, 2619
Wirth, Helmut 972, 1119
Wirth-Stockhausen, Julia 1223
Wiseman, Herbert 1855
Wisoko-Meytsky, Karl 409
Witt, Kl. 371
Witte, C.; See Witte, Georg Hendrik
Witte, Georg Hendrik 1307, 1632,
2012
Wittmann, Karl Friedrich 1309
Wöhler, Willi 216
Wörner, Karl 2172
Wohlfahrt, Frank 756
Wohlfarth, Paul 2106
Wolf, Hugo 2010, 3048
Wolf, Werner 1313
Wolff, Ernst 1314
Wolff, Felix 847
Wolff, Karl 2682
Wolff, Konrad 3013.a.i.b

TITLES, MONOGRAPHIC SERIES and DEGREE-GRANTING INSTITUTIONS INDEX

Information in this index is interfiled in one alphabetical sequence, word by word. A reference to a citation number includes appearances in all applicable sections within that number.

Alphabetization follows the general principles used in the body of the work, with the following refinements:

a) A title in quotation marks files before the same title underlined.

b) The only points of punctuation that affect filing are closing punctuation, e.g., periods, question marks.

c) Symbols file before letters, except when they have a word equivalent. In that case, they file by their spelled-out form.

d) Initials in a title file according to their full word spelling.

e) Acronyms and initialisms file as words.

f) Cardinal numbers in a title file as if they were a cardinal number spelled-out in English. 3 files as three, 1833 as one thousand eight hundred and thirty-three. Ordinal numbers file according to their spelling in the respective language. If the ordinal number is the first element in the title, the user will need to check for all possible language options; for example, first, erste, première. Numbers used as chapter or section designations are ignored in filing.

g) Initial articles as the first word in a title are disregarded in filing.

h) Uniform titles have been derived in order to standardize the collocation of information. For example, all titles that begin with Brahms's name in the possessive file as [Brahms's], regardless of their original spellings; all entries that consist of "Brahms" and his dates are filed as [Brahms 1833-1897].

"†Johannes Brahms" 412.5

A Magyar Nemzeti Múzeum könyvtárának. Cimjegyzéke 923

"A magyar zene tükrözése külföldi mesterek műveiben" 2555

"A Művészet rabszolgája" 766

A Világ urai. Visszaemlékezések és intimitások világnirai művézek életéböl 900.d

Aarhus universitet 2075

Abhandlungen zur Kunst- , Musik- und Literaturwissenschaft 1405

"About Brahms' Seven Fantasien Op. 116" 1677

"Abschied von Brahms-Keller" 3090

"I. Acoustical Analysis of Stressed and Unstressed Consonant-Vowel Syllables Sung and Spoken in Disyllabic Pairs by Trained Singers, An. II. A Recital of Contemporary British Music: Program Notes for A Doctoral Recital (University of Washington, 1968). III. "Romanzen aus Tieck's Magelone": Program Notes for A Doctoral Recital (University of Washington, 1971)" 2127

Acta musicologica fennica 1827

"Ad vocem Dreigestirn Wagner-Brahms-Mahler in der Beziehung zur tschechischen Musik" 905

"Adventures and Discoveries of a Manuscript Hunter" 284

Adventures of God in His Search for the Black Girl, The 2622

"Adventures with Manuscripts" 2546

"Adventurous Concertos. A Note on Brahms" 1775

"Aesthetic and Musical Theory: An Aspect of Their Juncture" 1997

Agathe von Siebold 1200.a

"Agathe von Siebold. Johannes Brahms' Jugendliebe" 1199.c

Agathe von Siebold. Johannes Brahms' Jugendliebe 1199

"Agathe von Siebold. Rede bei der Gedenkfeier am hunderstengeburtstag der Jugendliebe von Johannes Brahms im Geburtshause am Geismartor 5. Juli 1935" 1200

"Ahnenreihe von Johannes Brahms, Die" 334

"Aimez-vous Brahms?" 726, 1817

"Aimez-vous Brahms? On Polarities in Modernism" 2932.a

"Aimez-vous Brahms? Reflections on Modernism" 2932

Akkorde. Gesammelte Aufsätze 2519.d

Album von Handschriften berühmter Persönlichkeiten von Mittelalter bis zur Neuzeit 653

"Als bedeutsames Ereignis für die musikalische Welt" 3055

"Als Johannes Brahms im Gewandhaus durchfiel" 2907

"Als Johannes Brahms Musikdirektor in Düsseldorf werden sollte. Briefdokumente aus der Zeit um 1876" 558

"Als kamermuziekspeler zend ik u hierby mijn meening over Brahms" 2884

""Also blus das Alphorn Heut"" 1891

"Alte Typen im neuen Rom" 1294

"Alte Wiener Wirtshäuser: der Rote Igel" 406

"Alter Stil und alte Techniken in der Musik des 19. Jahrhunderts" 2575

"Auftakt zur Brahms-Feier, Ein" 2783
Aus allen Tonarten. Studien über Musik 121
"Aus Brahms' Jugendzeit" 39A.d.i
"Aus Brahms Jugendzeit" 327
"Aus Brahms' Jugendzeit" 368
"Aus Brahms' Werkstatt. Vom Entstehen und Werden der Werke bei
    Brahms" 2548
"Aus dem Briefwechsel von Brahms mit B. und L. Scholz" 1122.e.i
"Aus dem Briefwechsel von Johannes Brahms mit Karl Reinthaler"
    1122.e.ii
"Aus dem Briefwechsel von Johannes Brahms mit Max Bruch und
    Ernst Rudorff" 1122.e.iii
"Aus dem Briefwechsel zwischen Johannes Brahms mit Heinrich und
    Elisabet von Herzogenberg" 983.c.ix
"Aus dem Briefwechsel zwischen Johannes Brahms und Joseph Joachim"
    1009.c.ii
Aus dem Concertsaal. Kritiken und Schilderungen aus den letzten
    20 Jahren des Wiener Musiklebens nebst einem Anhang: musikal-
    ische Reisebriefe aus England, Frankreich und der Schweiz
    2950.dB
"Aus dem Haus in Göttingen" 3058
"Aus dem Johannes Brahms-Archiv der Staats- und Universitätsbiblio-
    thek Hamburg veröffentlichen wir den nachstehenden Bericht von
    Anastasia Tettinek, der Hausgehilfin von Frau Truxa, über seinen
    Sterbetag" 414
"Aus dem Leben von Johannes Brahms" 637, 776
Aus dem Musikleben der Gegenwart. Beiträge zur zeitgenössischen
    Kunstkritik 3022
Aus dem Tagebuche eines Musikers. Kritiken und Schilderungen 2944
Aus dem Weltleben des Waldbauernbuben. Erinnerungen und Bekennt-
    nisse 1133.a.ii.a
Aus dem Wiener Musikleben. Künstler-Erinnerungen 1873-1908 389
Aus den Erinnerungen eines Musikers 901
"Aus den Kämpfen um Brahms" 2971
"Aus den Zeitungen" 412.5.c, 734, 755.c
"Aus der ersten Zeit meiner Bekanntschaft mit Brahms" 990
"Aus der Gedenkrede beim Wiener Brahms-Fest 1933. Gekürzt nach
    der Niederschrift in der Neue Freie Presse (28.5.1933)" 2931.d.i
"Aus der Jugendzeit von Johannes Brahms" 324
Aus der Tonwelt. Essays 1336.a
"Aus der Zeit des Jungen Brahms. Nach Erinnerungen von Elisabeth
    Proffen, geb. Rösing. Zu unserer Bilderbeilage" 1132
"Aus "Des jungen Kreislers Schatzkästlein". Aussprüche ... Künstlern.
    Gesammelt von Johannes Brahms" 2351.c
Aus Ferdinand Hillers Briefwechsel. Beiträge zu einer Biographie
    Ferdinand Hillers 992
"Aus Johannes Brahms' Jugendtagen" 1089, 1090
"Aus Johannes Brahms Jugendzeit" 327.d
"Aus Johannes Brahms' Schulzeit" 325
"Aus Johannes Brahms' Schulzeit. Zur Kritik der Darstellung von
    Max Kalbeck.--Der Schullehrer Johann Friedrich Hoffmann" 358

Backgrounds of Book Reviewing 2477.a.ii
"Bad Ischl" 539
"Bad Neuenahr hundert Jahre Heilbad" 595
Ball State University 2600
""Ballade, Op. 10, no. 1" of Brahms, The. A Master Lesson by the
    Renowned Piano Virtuoso" 1624
"I. Ballades of Chopin, Liszt, Brahms and Grieg, The; A Study of
    The Major Variations of Beethoven's Second Creative Period; The
    Piano Sonatas of Charles T. Griffes and Ernest Bloch. II. Perform-
    ance" 1625
"Barform im romantischen Kunstlied bei Franz Schubert, Robert
    Schumann, Johannes Brahms, Hugo Wolf und Felix Mendelssohn-
    Bartholdy, Die" 2043
Barnbiblioteket saga 112.b
"Basels private Musikpflege im 19. Jahrhundert" 1129
Basic Formal Structures in Music 1388
""Basic Motive" in Brahms' German Requiem, A" 2287
Battute d'aspetto. Meditazioni di un musicista militante 2469.5.d.a
BBC Music Guides 1404.d.ii, 1432, 1807, 2090
"Bedeutender Brahms-Fund in Bonn. Uber ein ungedrucktes Klavier-
    trio des Meisters" 1510
"Bedeutung der Pauke in den Werken Ludwig van Beethovens, Die"
    2513.a
"Beerdigung von Johannes Brahms, Die. Persönliche Erinnerungen"
    491
"Beethoven and Brahms" 671, 970.e
"Beethoven im Rücken und überflüssige Noten under dem Tisch.
    Der 'unbekannte, kammermusikalische' Johannes Brahms" 1434
"Beethoven, Schubert and Brahms" 1404.d.i
"Beethoven und Brahms" 806, 811
"Beethoven, Wagner und Brahms" 1277
"Beethoven-Brahms-Bruckner-Zyklus und das erste deutsche Brahms-
    fest in München" 2749
Beethovens flyttlass och andra essäer: kring musiker och deras
    boningar i österrike 738
"Beethovens frühe Kantaten" 969.a.c
"Beethovens Nachwirkung bei bedeutenden Komponisten des 19.
    Jahrhunderts" 810
"Beethoven's Signature in the "Tenth Symphony"" 1895
Beethovensche Materiale und Untersuchungen 2513
"Begegnung mit Brahms" 1288.a.d.i
Begegnung mit dem Genius. Denkwürdige Erlebnisse mit Johannes
    Brahms--Gustav Mahler--Hans Richter--Max Reger--Puccini--
    Mascagni Leoncavallo--Fürstin Marie Hohenlohe Fürstin Pauline
    Metternich--Franz Léhar und vielen anderen bedeutenden Menschen
    1028
"Begegnung mit Johannes Brahms" 815
"Begegnung von Brahms und Tschaikowsky in Hamburg 1889" 1237
Begegnungen mit Anton Bruckner, Johannes Brahms, Cosima Wagner.
    Aus den Lebenserinnerungen von Dr. Felix von Kraus (1870-1937)
    1054

and A Study of the Settings of his Poems by Schubert, Schumann and Brahms" 2115
Biographies of Great Musicians 75
"Birthday Symphony" 1970.e
"Birthplace of Johannes Brahms" 328
"Birthplaces of Mendelssohn and Brahms" 336
Bol'shaia sovetskaia entsiklopediia 93
Bol'shaia sovetskaia entsiklopediia. Reihe Kunst und Literatur 93
Book of the First International Congress Devoted to the Works of Frederick Chopin, The. Warszawa 16th-22nd February 1960 1599
Book of the Symphony, A 1802
Borzoi Books 2481.a.iii
Boston University 1551, 1742, 2150
""Bottom" Brahms" 1894
"Bowing to Brahms" 1838
"Brahms" or "Brahms, The":
 no date: 108
 1872: 3012
 1879: 94
 1880: 1336
 1891: 2904
 1897: 433, 1923
 1898: 2437
 1900: 101, 2051
 1903: 983.e.ix.a
 1904: 2911.d
 1906: 839
 1909: 681, 910.a, 1365.5.a, 2217.5.a, 2348.5.a, 2736.5.a, 3022
 1910: 1562
 1912: 205, 2429.5, 3062.a
 1915: 1155
 1919: 1208
 1922: 1564, 2408, 2633, 2866, 2929
 1923: 189
 1925: 1180
 1926: 344, 2037, 2481.a.i
 1927: 172, 195, 1180.b, 2481.a.ii, 3021.a.i
 1929: 102, 129
 1930: 82.b.e.ii
 1931: 108.d, 1816.d
 1933: 23.c.ii, 2378, 2829, 2845, 2855, 2859, 2867, 2873, 2876, 2879, 2882, 2897
 1935: 142, 1372A, 1372B
 1936: 1372C
 1937: 1372D
 1940: 1400
 1941: 1401, 1402
 1942: 2899
 1944: 98, 1372F
 1948: 2496
 1950: 1586.a

560 / Titles, Series and Institutions Index

"Brahms és a nők" 765.b
"Brahms és a többiek. (A mester művészegyéniséges viszonya a kortársakhoz és utódokhoz.)" 2457
"Brahms és Joachim erdélyi hangversenykörútja" 625
"Brahms és Joachim kolozsvári hangversenyének elözetes jelentése" 624
"Brahms és Joachim 1879 IX. 19-én Brassóban, 21-én Szebenben, 23-én Kolozsvárott hangversenyezett" 623
"Brahms, estilo y aspectos de su técnica" 2423
"Brahms et Fauré" 2401, 2488
"Brahms et la musique ancienne" 2581
"Brahms et le goût français" 40.e.iii
"Brahms et les fêtes de Munich" 2761
"Brahms et son oeuvre" 2028
"Brahms Exhibition in Vienna, The" 3093.e
"Brahms Family, The. With Hitherto Unpublished Letters" 841.d.ii
"Brahms Festival" 2770
"Brahms Festival at Munich" 2743
"Brahms Festival in New York, A" 2771
"Brahms--Feuerbach und Menzel" 929.d.ii
"Brahms fjärde symfoni" 2008
"Brahms for Piano--Study" 1577
"Brahms für die Provinz" 3158
"Brahms, Grove and Pohl. Two Unpublished Letters" 962
"Brahms--Hans Rott" 1135
"Brahms hat seinen letzten Willen" 422
"Brahms Heute" 3033
"Brahms--Heute" 3042
"Brahms Himself" 718
"Brahms--His Music for Winds" 1376
"Brahms Horn Motif, The" 2551
"Brahms Horn Trio and Hand Horn Idiom, The" 1478
"Brahms i Billroth" 817
"Brahms ifjúkora" 347
"Brahms im Briefwechsel mit dem Ehepaar Herzogenberg" 983.e.ii
"Brahms im Briefwechsel mit Hermann Levi und andern Zeitgenossen" 1062.e
"Brahms im Urteil dieser Zeit" 2981
"Brahms in Berlin" 576
"Brahms in Berlin. Zu seinem 50. Todestag am 3. April" 573
"Brahms in Bern" 633.d.i
"Brahms in Breslau" 560
"Brahms in Briefen" 983.e.ix.a
"Brahms in D minor and B flat" 1784
"Brahms in der Beurteilung eines französischen Musikers" 2986
Brahms in der Meininger Tradition. Seine Sinfonien und Haydn-Variationen in der Bezeichung von Fritz Steinbach 1781
"Brahms in der Schule" 1360
"Brahms in der Schulmusik" 1364
"Brahms in der Schweiz. (Zum 100. Geburtstag des Komponisten am 7. Mai 1933)" 633

"Brahms Klavierkonzert B-dur, op. 83" 1963
"Brahms, Levi, und Stockhausen" 39B.c.iii
"Brahms Library in the "Gesellschaft der Musikfreunde" Wien, The"
   673.d
Brahms Lieder 271
"Brahms: Light and Sombre" 641
""Brahms Line", The" 3034
"Brahms, Liszt und Schumann" 1070
"Brahms Magyarországon. Brahms in Ungarn" 611
Brahms Magyarországon. Brahms in Ungarn 611.a
"Brahms Manuscript, A: The Schicksalslied" 2322
"Brahms meghalt" 424
"Brahms memorias de un viejo estudiante de musica" 2892
"Brahms Monument, A" 3065
"Brahms Musik hat sich--" 2373
"Brahms Musik im Gewandhaus" 564
"Brahms nagy szenvedélye" 2580
"Brahms Night. Tschaikovsky as Critic" 1238
Brahms Noblesse 2623
"Brahms, No. 2 D Major, Op. 73" 1917
"Brahms och folkmusiken" 2558
"Brahms och hans förebilder" 2463
"Brahms oder Wagner? Wie soll der Dirigent Brahms nahen? (Aus
   einem Gespräch)" 2606
"Brahms on British Music" 552
"Brahms on Destiny" 2534
"Brahms on Handel" 1633
Brahms on Records 251
"Brahms on the Baltic: A Romance and a Dedication" 1140.d
"Brahms on the Gramophone" 252
"Brahms[[1862]]" 2470.a.b
"Brahms 1833-1897" 168
"Brahms, 1833-1897" 170
"Brahms (1833-1897)" 291, 1404.d.i
"Brahms 1833-1897" 2358
"Brahms (1833-97)" 2481.a.iv
Brahms Op. 83, Concerto for Pianoforte and Orchestra 1966
"Brahms, op. 51.1" 1518.a
"Brahms, op. 51.2" 1518.a
"Brahms: Opus 1" 1608
"Brahms, op. 67" 1518.a
"Brahms, Op. 38; Piracy, Pillage, Plagiarism or Parody?" 1475
Brahms Orchestral Music 1807
"Brahms: Output, Resources and Chronology" 1407
"Brahms (Part 2): A "Reproach to the Haste of a Superficial Gen-
   eration"" 2914
"Brahms Part-Music" 2190
"Brahms Peruses the Score of 'Siegfried'" 1257.a.a
"Brahms Peruses the score of Siegfried. The Photograph by von
   Eichholz" 1257
"Brahms: Piano Concerto, D minor (Op. 15)" 1859

Brahms-Bibliográfia. Brahms-Bibliographie 241.a

"Brahms-Bild der Allgemeinen Musikalischen Zeitung (1863 bis 1882), Das" 2925

Brahms-Bilder 667

Brahms-Bilderbuch, Ein 721

"Brahms-Biographie, Eine" 39B.e.iii

"Brahms-Brevier, Ein" 2351.e.ii

"Brahms-Briefe" 926

"Brahms-Briefe aus Basler Privatbesitz" 1130

Brahms-Briefwechsel 848.a, 920.a, 954.a, 983.a, 1009.a, 1062.a, 1122.a, 1203.a, 1204.a, 1215.a.a., 1297.a, 1314.a

"Brahms-Bruckner" 862

"Brahms-Ciaikovski-Sibelius" 1240

"Brahmscultus in Berlin" 3010

"[[Brahms-Denkmal]]" 3067

"Brahms-Denkmal in Wien" 3068, 3069

"Brahms-Denkmal in Wien, Das" 3139

"Brahmsdenkmal in Wien, Ein" 3152

"Brahms-Denkmal von Max Klinger, Das" 3174

"Brahms-Dvořák, eine Musikerfreundschaft" 912

"Brahms-Einflüsse bei Max Reger" 1638

"Brahmsens Klavierspiel und Klaviersatz" 1588

"Brahms-Erinnerung, Eine" 774

"Brahms-Erinnerung, Eine" 1025

"Brahms-Erinnerungen" 1111, 1120, 1205

"Brahms-Erinnerungen. Aus dem Tagebuch von Frau Wasserbaudirektor Lentz, geb. Meier" 1061

"Brahms-Erinnerungen. Nach eigenen Erlebnissen erzählt von Gustav Manz" 1080

"Brahms-Erinnerungen an Breslau. Bei der Kegelpartie-Begeisterung im ersten Sinfonie-Konzert unter seiner Leitung Ehrendoktor der Friedrich-Wilhelms-Universität" 566

"Brahms-Erinnerungen eines alten Esseners" 559

"Brahms-Erinnerungen eines Wiener Musikfreundes" 1189

"Brahms-Erlebnisse" 1179.e.iii

Brahms-Feier der Stadt Remscheid zum Gedenken des 100. Geburtstages von Johannes Brahms (geb. am 7. Mai 1833 in Hamburg). März bis Mai 1933 2775

"Brahms-Feier in Paris" 2773

"Brahms-Fest" 2659

"Brahms-Fest" 2710

"Brahmsfest der Stadt Essen" 2693

"Brahmsfest in Bremen" 2686

"Brahmsfest in Bremen, Das" 2687

"Brahmsfest in Bremen. (22. bis 26. April 1922)" 2684

"Brahmsfest in Güstrow am 12., 18. und 19. Juni 1922" 2696

"Brahmsfest in Halle a.S., Ein" 2697

"Brahmsfest in Jena" 2727

"Brahmsfest in Königsberg am 6. und 7. Mai 1933" 2733

"Brahms-Fest in Krähwinkel, Das" 2768

"Brahmsfest in Tutzing" 2776

"Brahmsfest in Wien" 2781
"Brahms-Fest in Wien, Das" 2931.e.ii
"Brahmsfest zu Essen. 12.-19. Juni 1933" 2692
Brahms-Fest zum 100. Geburtstag des Meisters (1833-7. Mai-1933).
Veranstaltet vom Ostmarken-Rundfunk und der Stadt Königsberg
Pr. am 6. und 7. Mai 1933. Programm-Buch 2732
"Brahmsfeste" 2661
"Brahms-Festtage in Baden-Baden. 19.-22. Mai 1910" 2665
"Brahms-Freund C.F. Pohl., Der. Unbekannte Briefe des Haydn-
Biographen an Johannes Brahms" 1110
Brahmsfreundin Ottilie Ebner und ihr Kreis, Die 914
"Brahmsfund in Südfrankreich, Ein" 2109
"Brahms-Gedenkraum im Wiener Haydn-Haus, Ein" 3070
"Brahmsgedenkstätte, Eine" 3088
"Brahms-Gedenkstätte in Gefahr" 3063
"Brahms-Gedenkstätte in Gmunden, Eine" 3071
"Brahms-Gedenkstätte in Hamburg" 3072
"Brahms-Häuser" 350
Brahmshaus Baden-Baden 3073
""Brahms-Haus" in Baden-Baden, Das" 3107
"Brahms-Haus in Lichtenthal. Jugend musiziert in diesem Sommeridyll,
Das" 3159
"Brahms-Haus in Wien, Ein" 3135
"Brahms-Haus in Wien" 3136
"Brahms-Haus soll Gedenkstätte werden 3076
"Brahms-Heft" 3187
Brahms-Heft 3191
Brahms-Heft No. 3 3185
Brahms-Heft No. 2 3184
"Brahms-Heim in Gmunden, Das" 3154
"Brahms-herdenking" 1193
"Brahms-herdenking te Amsterdam, De" 2812
"Brahmsiana" 431, 443.c.ii, 618.a.e.iii, 969.c, 2547
"Brahmsiana. Der Nachlass der Schwestern Völckers" 2343
"Brahmsiana. Erlebtes, Erhörtes, Erlesenes" 225.5
"Brahmsiana der Familie Petersen. Erinnerungen und Briefe" 1107
"Brahmsin suhteesta wagneriin" 1270
"Brahms-Joachim Exercises in Counterpoint, The" 2349
"Brahms-Joachim-Hausmann-Erinnerung, Eine" 1112
"Brahms-Jubiläum in Bremen, Ein" 2251.5
"Brahms-Kadenz zu Mozarts d-moll Konzert KV 466 und andere un-
bekannte Musikerhandschriften aus der Leipziger Universitätsbib-
liothek, Eine" 1325
Brahms-Kalender aus das Jahr 1909 3178
"Brahms-Kammermusikfest zu Wiesbaden (29., 30. März, 1., 3., 5.
und 7. April), Das" 2800
"Brahmskenner von Fiesole, Der" 756.d.i
"Brahms-Lieder. Ein Gedankblatt" 2089
"Brahms-Museum in Gmunden, Das" 3095
"Brahms-Museum in Gmunden, Das" 3127
"Brahms-Museum in Gmunden" 3128

""Bürger Brahms"" 659
"Bürger Brahms" 2989
""Bürger" Brahms" 2989.c
""Bürgerliche" Brahms, Der. Eine notwendige Korrektur" 2984
Buff 1257
Buffets and Rewards. A Musician's Reminiscences 1288.a.d.ii
Burt Franklin Research and Source Works Series 1386.a.ii, 1387.
    d.a.ii, 2022.a.ii
"Busnois, Brahms, and the Syntax of Temporal Proportions" 1683
Byways of Europe 539

"C Sharp Minor Version of Brahms's Op. 60, The" 1482
California State College (Fullerton) 1644
California State University (Fullerton) 2167
"Cançons de J. Brahms, Les" 2084
"Capriccio auf dem Kontrabass" 2624.c
Carl Retter's Six Performances of Pianoforte Music in Strictly Chrono-
    logical Order 209
Carl Theodor Billroth 815, 826
"Cas Brahms, Le" 218, 2772, 2774
"Cas de "Brahms", Le" 219
"Catching the Temperament of a Brahms "Caprice"" 1675
Catholic University of America 1503
Celebrazione Brahmsiane, dirette da Vittorio Gui 2857
Celebrazione del cinquantesmino anniversario della morte di Johannes
    Brahms [[Aprile-Maggio, 1947]] 2857
Census of Autograph Music Manuscripts of European Composers in
    American Libraries 286
Cent'anni di musica moderna 178.a
"Centenario di Johannes Brahms, Il" 2815
"Centenary of Brahms" 1087, 2825.d
"Centenary of the Brahms Violin Concerto (1879-1979)" 1944
Century Library of Music 754, 2621
Century Library of Music, The 2607
"Certo suonatore d'organetto, Un" 605
"Certy pozdnego stilia Bramsa" 2406
Challenges. A Series of Controversial Essays on Music 2954
"Chamber Duets by Schumann, Cornelius and Brahms" 2035.d
"Chamber Music of Brahms, The" 1422
Chamber Music of Brahms, The 1424, 1436
"Chamber Music of Brahms on Records, The" 250
Chamber Music of Johannes Brahms, The 1425
Charakterbilder grosser Tonmeister. Persönliches und Intimes aus
    ihrem Leben und Schaffen. Für junge und alte Musikfreunde.
    Vierter Band. Chopin/Brahms/Bruckner/Reger. Zerstreute Blätter
    177
"Charakteristisches in Brahms' Kunstschaffen" 23.b.c, 3185
"Chef-d'oeuvre digne d'être signé par Beethoven, Un" 2314
Chicago Musical College 1586
Child Brahms, The 335
Child's Book of Famous Composers, A 106

"Clara Schumann und Brahms" 1159
"Clara Schumann und Johannes Brahms" 1170C.e.i, 1179.e.viii
"Clara Schumann und Johannes Brahms. Eine chronologische Darstellung" 1177
"Clara Schumann und Johannes Brahms als Opfer einer Hintertreppenphantasie" 1158.e.i
"Clara Schumann und Johannes Brahms in ihren Briefen" 1179.e.v
"Clara Schumanns Weihnachtsgeschenk vor 100 Jahren: Erinnerung an Brahms" 297
"Clara Wieck Schumann as Pianist and Composer: A Study of Her Life and Works" 1187
"Clarinet and Its Use in the String Trios and String Quintets by Mozart and Brahms" 1543
"Clarinet Music of Johannes Brahms, The" 1431
Clásicos de la música 74
"Claviermusik" 1646
Clerk of Oxenford, A. Essays on Literature and Life 1242
"C-minor Symphony by Brahms, The" 1884
Cobbett's Cyclopedic Survey of Chamber Music 657, 1443
Colección músicos 77
Colin Wilson on Music. (Brandy of the Damned) 3047
Colleccão cultura musical 58.b
Collección el mástil 98
Collected Essays 2634.a.iv
Collected Musical Criticism of Eduard Hanslick, The 2943.a, 2944.a, 2945.a, 2947.a, 2948.a
Collection alternance 42
Collection amour de la musique 76
Collection esthétique 1703.a
Collection musicale 1179.c.xiv
"Collection musique" [monographic series] 1919.a.ii
Collections microcosme. Solfèges 6
College Addresses 2486
Collezione il pensiero 178.a
Colloquia on the History and Theory of Music at the International Music Festival in Brno 905, 1145
Colloquium amicorum. Joseph Schmidt-Görg zum 70. Geburtstag 1383.d
Colloquium musica bohemica et europaea Brno 1970 905
Colloquium musica cameralis Brno 1971 1145
"Colour in Brahms, The" 2511
Columbia University 1560, 1806, 2582
Columbia University Teachers College 2221
"Comparative Analysis of Selected Keyboard Compositions of Chopin, Brahms, and Franck as Transcribed for the Marimba by Clair Omar Musser, Earl Hatch and Frank Maccallum together with Three Recitals of Works by Bartok, Crumb, Miyoshi, Kraft and Others, A" 2608
"Comparative Analysis of the Quartets, Opus 51 by Johannes Brahms" 1530
"Comparative Aspects of Variation Technique as Applied to the

578 / Titles, Series and Institutions Index

"Den Spielern von Brahms' Horntrio op. 40 zur Nachachtung" 2517
"Denen Veranstaltern von "Brahms-Abenden" zur Nachachtung" 3077
"Denkmal der Freundschaft, Ein" 1179.e.iv
" ... Denn Sie sollen getröstet werden. Das Brahms-Requiem--
  Oratorium, protestantische Totenmesse oder auseinandersetzung
  mit dem christlichen Mythos? Eine vergleichende Diskografie" 2269
Des einigen deutschen Reiches Musikzustände. 12 Briefe 780
Des jungen Kreislers Schatzkästlein 2384, 2619
Des jungen Kreislers Schatzkästlein. Aussprüche von Dichtern,
  Philosophen und Künstlern 2351
"Destiny and a Brahms Autograph" 2139
"Detroit is [[or was]] renowned" 2689
"Detroit Symphony Orchestra's International Brahms Festival" 2690
Deutsche Angesicht, Das 1155.a.ii
"Deutsche Brahms-Gesellschaft, Die" 3078
"Deutsche Brahms-Gesellschaft, Die" 3079
"Deutsche Brahms-Gesellschaft, Die" 3080
"Deutsche Chorlied im 19. Jahrhundert, Das" 2195
Deutsche Gesangsverein für gemischten Chor, Der 2211
Deutsche Jugendbücherei 143
Deutsche Lied, Das. Drittes Buch 2037
Deutsche Lied seit Mozart, Das 2081
Deutsche Meister. Reden 3014.a
"Deutsche Requiem, Das" 2291
Deutsche Requiem, Das 2270
"Deutsche Requiem von Johannes Brahms, Das" 55.c, 2290
"Deutscher Meister der Tonkunst, Ein. Zum 20. Jahrestage von
  Brahms' Tode" 702
"Deutsches Brahmsfest, Ein" 2763
"Deutsches Brahms-Fest der Berliner Kunstwochen" 2669
"Deutsches Brahms-Fest in Hamburg" 2702
"Deutsches Brahms-Fest in Heidelberg" 2717
"Deutsches Brahms-Fest 1939" 2668
"Deutsches Brahms-Verein, The" 2793
"Deutsches Requiem, Ein" 2263, 2264, 2282
""Deutsches Requiem, Ein." Eine Einführung" 2257
"Deutsches Requiem, Ein. Johannes Brahms' Werk 45. Zum Konzert
  der Musikakademie am Busstage" 2246
""Deutsches Requiem" als Dokument Brahmsscher Frömmigkeit, Das"
  2255
"Deutsches Requiem, Ein: Notes on Brahms' Selection of Biblical
  Texts" 2272
"Deutsches Requiem von Brahms, Ein" 2265
"Deutsches Requiem von Brahms, Ein. Gesprach" 2284
"Deutsches Requiem von Johannes Brahms, Ein" 2271
"Deutsches Requiem von Johannes Brahms, Ein--seine historisch-
  ästhetische Stellung vor hundert Jahren und Heute--" 2299
"Deutsches Requiem von Johannes Brahms, Ein. (Zur Aufführung
  durch den Lehrergesangverein am 31. Oktober und 1. November)"
  2247
"Deutsches Wesen und Wirken. Zum 90. Geburtstage von Johannes
  Brahms am 7. Mai 1923" 3049

Wiedergabe von 209 Titelblättern   277
"Erste Begegnungen"   1302
"Erste Brahms-Abend in Wien, Der"   1286
"Erste Brahms-Denkmal, Das"   3086
"Erste Denkmal für Johannes Brahms, Das"   3087
"Erste deutsche Brahms-Denkmal in Meiningen"   3082
"Erste deutsche Brahmsfest, Das"   2739, 2740
"Erste deutsche Brahms-fest, Das"   2764
""Erste deutsche Brahms-Fest.", Das. I"   2767
""Erste deutsche Brahms-Fest.", Das. II"   2767.d
"Erste deutsche Brahmsfest in München, Das"   2747
"Erste deutsche Brahmsfest in München, Das. (10.-14.   September
   1909)"   2765
"Erste Geigerin, die das Brahmssche Violinkonzert meisterte, Die.
   Zum 75.   Geburtstag von Marie Röger-Soldat am 25. Marz"   765.d.d
"Erste Satz von Brahms' e-moll Symphonie, Der.   Ein Beitrag zur
   Bekenntnis moderner Symphonik"   2007
"Erste Symphonie (c moll) von Johannes Brahms unter Artur Nikisch.
   Versuch einer Analyse der Wiedergabe"   1900
"Ersten Schritte des jungen Brahms in die Offentlichkeit, Das.   Das
   zweite Kapitel der grossen Brahmsbiographie von Max Kalbeck"
   39A.c.iii
"Erstes Deutsches Brahms-Fest"   2762.3-2762.9
"Erstes deutsches Brahmsfest"   2745.e, 2748.5, 2759, 2769
"Erstes deutsches Brahmsfest. I. II"   2748
Erstes deutsches Brahms-Fest, München. 10.-14.   September 1909
   im Königl. Odeon. Programmbuch   2745
"Erstes deutsches Brahms-Fest zu München. 10. bis 14.   September
   1909. I.-II."   2742
"Erwiderung an Felix Weingartner, Eine"   2910
"Es hat wenige grosse Künstler gegeben"   695
"Es war einmal"   834
"Es wird unsere Leser interessiren, dass Max Klinger"   1041.e
"Esquisse pour une rhapsodie pathétique"   809
Essais de critique musicale. Hector Berlioz, Johannes Brahms   2403
Essais de critique musicale. R. Schumann.--R. Wagner. Hector
   Berlioz.--Johannes Brahms. Affinités musicales chez Beethoven.
   Sur la musique, etc., etc.   2403.a
Essay Index Reprint Series   119.a, 124.a, 206.a, 1403.d.a, 1561.a,
   1959.a, 2462.a, 2470.a.b.a, 2934.a.
Essays   3062.a
Essays and Lectures   2462
Essays and Lectures on Music   1443.a
Essays by James Huneker   1392.a.i
Essays in Musical Analysis   1372
Essays in Musical Analysis. Volume V. Vocal Music   1372D
Essays in Musical Analysis. Volume I. Symphonies   1372A
Essays in Musical Analysis. Vol. 1: Symphonies and Other Orchestral
   Works   1372
Essays in Musical Analysis. [[Volume VIII]] Chamber Music   1372F
Essays in Musical Analysis. Volume VI. Miscellaneous Notes. Glos-
   sary and Index   1372E

"Form in den Instrumentalwerken Johannes Brahms" 1395
"Formal Coherence in Nineteenth-Century Variations: A Study of
Selected Works of Beethoven, Schumann and Brahms" 1367
"Formal Principles in the Music of Brahms" 2415
"Formenstrenge im Brahms-Liede" 2046
"Formprobleme im Brahmsschen Lied" 2533
Forschungsbeiträge zur Musikwissenschaft 2321.a
"Fortepiannaia sonata Bramsa fa-minor" 1611
"Fortepiannoe tvorchestvo Bramsa" 1554
Forty Songs 146, 2063
"42 millionen Deutsche auf der Strecke" 1303
Forumbücher 1179.c.vi
"Four Brahms Relatives Hear Composer's Work First Time" 840
4. Gesänge (1934) 2318
4. Symphonie in e-moll op. 98. Faksimile des autographen Manu-
skripts aus dem Besitz der Allgemeinen Musikgesellschaft Zürich
1992
"Four Unknown Songs by Brahms Found" 2182
"Four-Hand Piano Arrangements of Brahms and Their Role in the
Nineteenth Century, The" 2451
Fragmente--Gelerntes und Gelebtes 921
Frankfurter Lebensbilder 1223
"Frau Cosima Wagner hat folgendes seltsame, fast komische schreiben"
1279.e
"Frauen im Leben von Johannes Brahms, Die. Zu seinem 100. Ge-
burtstag am 7. Mai" 763
"Frauen um Brahms" 762
Frauen um Brahms 765.d
Free Thought and the Musician and Other Essays 2101.a
"Frei aber froh: A Reconsideration" 2524
"Freiburger Brahms-Fest 1937" 2694
Freie Satz, Der 1380
Freie Universität Berlin 2060, 2575
Freie Universität West Berlin 1411
"Fremder Herr (1886), Ein" 1133.a.ii
"French View of Brahms, A" 40.e.i
Freud, Jews and Other Germans. Masters and Victims in Modernist
Culture 2932.a
"Freund von Brahms, Ein" 893
"Freunde, Die. Theodor Billroth's Leistung und Brahms' Musik" 833
Freundschaft Clara Schumanns mit Johannes Brahms, Die. Aus Briefen
und Tagebuchblättern 1164
"Freundschaft zwischen Brahms und Antonín Dvořák" 911
"Freundschaft zwischen Johannes Brahms und Klaus Groth" 960
"Friedrich v. Spe und Johannes Brahms" 2175
Friedrich-Wilhelms-Universität Berlin 2310
"Fritz Steinbach und Joh. Brahms. Erstgenannten zum Gedenken in
seinen 20. Todesjahr" 1219
Frohes und Ernstes aus meinem Leben 1295
"From Analysis to Performance: The Musical Landscape of Johannes
Brahms's Opus 118. no. 6" 1694

"Geburtshaus von Johannes Brahms, Das" 345, 369
"Gedächtnissfeier für Brahms. [[Wiesbaden, 8. Mai]]" 442
Gedanken eines Schauenden. Gesammelte Aufsätze 971
"Gedanken zu "Ein Deutsches Requiem" von Johannes Brahms" 2253
"Gedanken zu Palestrinas Missa "Ad fugam" und zwei Werken von
   Johannes Brahms und Heinrich Lemacher" 2344
"Gedanken zum strukturellen Aufbau des Brahmsschen "Requiems""
   2258
"Gedenkstätte für Johannes Brahms" 3091
"[[Gedenktafel für Johannes Brahms]]" 3092
Gedichte 2631
Geen huis, geen vaderland. Het leven van Johannes Brahms (1833–
   1897) 89
Geheimdokumente der Davidsbündler, Die. Grosse Entdeckungen
   über Bach, Mozart, Beethoven, Schumann, Liszt und Brahms
   1701
"Geleitwort" 2143
"Generalprobe unter Brahms, Eine. Das letzte Konzert des Meisters
   in Berlin" 608.a
"Generalprobe unter Brahms, Eine. Zum letzten Konzert des Meisters
   in Berlin" 608
"Georg Friedrich Daumer und Johannes Brahms--ein Fränkischer
   Dichter und sein Komponist" 885
Georg Friedrich Händel. Thema mit 20 Variationen 1643
George Peabody College for Teachers 2509
German Lied and Its Poetry, The 2530
"German Lieder" 1375A
German Requiem. After Words of the Holy Scripture for Soloists,
   Chorus and Orchestra (Organ ad libitum), A 2240
"German Requiems Schuetz and Brahms" 2295
"Germany's Nationalistic Revival" 2713
"Gerüchte um den "späten" Schumann" 1186
Gesammelte Aufsätze über Musik und Anderes aus den Grenzboten
   150.a
Gesammelte Schriften 2493.b.ii
Gesammelte Schriften über Musik und Musiker 3013.a
Gesammelte Schriften über Musik und Musiker. Eine Auswahl
   3013.a.ix
Gesammelte Werke 1133.a.ii.d, 1343
"Geschäftsbriefe von grossen Musikern, persönlich und historisch
   betrachtet. Ungedruckte Briefe von Schumann, Brahms und Reger
   an das Leipziger Konservatorium und Gewandhaus" 606
Geschehenes, Gesehenes 1100
"Geschichte der Bearbeitungen von Bachs Chaconne" 2447
"Geschichte der Familie Brahms" 343
Geschichte der österreichischen Musikkritik in Beispielen 3038
Geschichte des Badeortes Ischl 543
Geschichte des Concertwesens in Wien 2950.d
"Geschichte und Möglichkeiten der Vertonung von Dichtungen Fried-
   rich Hölderlins" 2321
Geschichte und Möglichkeiten der Vertonung von Dichtungen Friedrich
   Hölderlins 2321.a

Great Lives 33.d

Great Men. Psychoanalytic Studies 764.b.i.a

Great Modern Composers 1403.d

"Great Modern Composers. No. 12. Brahms" 1403

"Great Musical Women of Yesterday" 1161

Great Musicians 33.d, 337

Great Symphonies. How to Recognize and Remember Them 1838

Great Works of Music [[Symphonies and Their Meaning]] 1800.a.i, 1923.a

"Greater and the Lesser Brahms, The" 3016

""Greatest Hits" of U.S. Symphony Orchestras, The" 1908

"Greatness of Brahms, The" 2471

"Greifswalder Brahms-Reger-Fest, Das" 2695

"Grenzgebiete des neuen Tons" 2490.5

"Grösste Komponist, Der" 678

"Grosse Brahms, Der" 130

"Grosse Erinnerungen einer "kleinen Stadt". Erinnerungen an Friedrich Hebbel und Johannes Brahms" 973

"Grosse Musik vor hundert Jahren. (Wagner-Verdi-Brahms-Tschaikowski.) Funktion, Aussage, Weiterwirkung" 2494

Grosse Musiker in Baden-Baden 561

"Grosse Musikergestalten der Romantik: Franz Schubert, Johannes Brahms, Frédéric Chopin, Robert Schumann" 200

Grosse Sinfonie, Die. Roman einer Künstler-Freundschaft 1174

Grossen Komponisten gesehen von ihren Zeitgenossen 758.b

Grossen Meister deutscher Musik in ihren Briefen und Schriften, Die 198

"Groths Musikbibliothek" 959.d

"Group VI, Chart VI, The Most Played Composers, The Eminent Group: Bach, Beethoven, Brahms, Tschaikovsky, Wagner" 2993

"Growing Brahms, The" 2937

"Grundzüge Brahmsscher Musikauffassung" 2464

"Guide Musicale Gives the Following Anecdote About Brahms, Le" 495.e.ii

"Gustav Jenner 1865-1920. Ein Beitrag zur Brahmsnachfolge" 1007

Gustav Jenner 1865-1920. Ein Beitrag zur Brahmsnachfolge 1007.a

"Gute Freund, Der. Erinnerungen" 1024

"Ha tanach biyitzirot Johannes Brahms" 2535

"Händel-Beethoven-Brahms-Parallele, Eine" 2522

Hamburger Beiträge zur Musikwissenschaft 2064.a

"Hamburger Brahms-Woche, Die" 2699

"Hamburger Bürgervereine, Die" 3101

"Hamburger Frauenchor des jungen Johannes Brahms, Der" 375

Hamburgische Hausbibliothek 847

Hamburgische Liebhaberbibliothek 348, 744

Hamburgisches Welt-Wirtschafts-Archiv 243

"Hamburgs Honoratioren contra Brahms" 3007

Handbook to The Chamber and Orchestral Music of Johannes Brahms. Historical and Descriptive Account of Each Work with Exhaustive

"Herinnerungen aan Johannes Brahms" 39A.d.i.e.ii
Heritage of Music, The 2934
"Herkunft der Melodien in Kretzschmers und Zuccalmaglios Sammlung"
2573
"H. Deiters über Johannes Brahms" 117.e.i
"Hermann Goetz und Johannes Brahms" 945
Hermann Goetz und Johannes Brahms 945.a
"Hermann Goetz und J. Brahms. Zu Goetz' 100. Geburtstag" 946
Hermine Spies. Ein Gedenkbuch für ihre Freunde von ihrer Schwes-
ter 1214
"Hermine Spies und Johannes Brahms" 1213
"Herr H. Wichmann, ein intimer Freund" 1294.c.e
"Herr Max Klinger in Leipzig ist von dem Comité" 3104
"Herzog von Meiningen hat das Protektorat über die Deutsche Brahms-
Gesellschaft übernommen, Der" 3105
Herzogenberg Correspondence, The 983.b
"Heuberger's Diary of Brahms" 989.e.d
"Hey Day of Brahms and Schumann, The" 1185
Hi Fidelity Discography 254
High Fidelity Discography 250
Himmel voller Geigen, Der. Das Leben der grosser Symphoniker 749
Himmlisches Orchester. Der Unsterblichen. Neue Folge. Novellen
2625
Hinrichsen's Miniature Surveys 12
Historical, Descriptive and Analytical Account of the Entire Works
of Johannes Brahms 1338, 2022
Historical, Descriptive and Analytical Account of the Entire Works of
Johannes Brahms 1386, 1387.d
Historical, Descriptive and Analytical Account of the Entire Works of
Johannes Brahms. Treated in the Order of Their Opus Number,
Preceded by a Didactic Section and Followed by Copious Tables of
Reference. Specially Designed for the Use of Concert-goers,
Pianists, Singers and Students. Vol. I--The Vocal Works 2022
"Historical Influences in the Growth of Brahms's 'Requiem'" 2285
"Historische Mission von Johannes Brahms, Die" 2461
History of the Leeds Musical Festivals, 1858-1889 2497
History of the Pianoforte and Pianoforte Players, A 1548.d
History of the Sonata Idea, A 1407
"History of This Concerto ..., The" 1871
"Hitaan osan arvoitus" 2424
"h-moll Quintett, Op. 115, Das" 1542
"Höchst interessante Beiträge zu dem Charakterbild von Johannes
Brahms" 617.e.ii
"Hölderlin und Feuerbach--durch Chorgesänge Brahms geehrt" 994
"Hofrat Hanslick veröffentlicht" 969.e.ii
"Holograph of Johannes Brahms's Fugue in A-flat Minor for Organ,
A" 1773
"Hommage à Johannes Brahms" 3144
Hommes et faits de l'histoire 27.d
"Hos Johannes Brahms. Et rejseminde" 813
"How Brahms Worked" 39A.c.iv

How to Become a Musical Critic 2935
"How to Enjoy a Symphony." Part V" 1909
"How to Play ... Brahms's Waltzes, Op. 39, nos. 15 and 2" 1653
"How to Study and Play Two Brahms Waltzes, Op. 39, nos. 13 and 3" 1651
Hubay Jeno. Egy élet szimfóniája 1005
Hubay Jenő élete és munkái 1000
Hudobné profily 35
"Hugo Wolf als Kritiker Brahms" 3048.e.iv
"Hugo Wolf en Brahms" 3048.e.ii
"Hugo Wolf über Brahms als Kritiker" 3048.e.iii
Hugo Wolf's Mörikelieder in Dichtung, Musik und Vortrag 2114
Hugo Wolfs musikalische Kritiken 3048
Humboldt-Universität, Berlin 942
Hundert Jahre Ein Deutsches Requiem von Johannes Brahms. Entstehung. Uraufführung. Interpretation. Würdigung 2237
"Hundertste Geburtstag von Johannes Brahms, Der. Letzte Begegnung" 1190
"Hungarian Dance Composers" 1723
"Hungarian Dance, No. 6 by Johannes Brahms. A Master Lesson" 1716
Hymne zur Verherrlichung des grossen Joachim. Walzer für zwei Violin und Kontrabass oder Violoncello 1544.d

"I Have a Friend" 1849
""Ich bin nun getröstet". Vor hundert Jahren vollendete Brahms sein "Deutsches Requiem"" 2302
"Ideals of Brahms, The" 550
"If a Little Brahms is Good, then a Lot is Better" 1808
""If, However, The Charm of Novelty be an Absolute Necessity ... Distinction." ..." 2497.e
"Igel, Der" 401
Ignaz Brüll und sein Freundeskreis. Erinnerungen an Brüll, Goldmark und Brahms 868.a
Ihr habt nun Traurigkeit. 5. Satz aus dem "Deutschen Requiem". Faksimile der ersten Niederschrift 2241
"Illness of Herr Brahms, The" 459
"Im Brahms Museum" 3140
Im Konzertsaal gehört 1863
"Im Nachlass Johannes Brahms'" 460
"Im Verlage von N. Simrock" 1763
"Im Zeichen von Reger und Brahms. Einführung zum geistlichen Konzert am Sonntag in der Peterskirche" 2341
Image and Structure in Chamber Music 1427
"Immer wieder versuchen es gewisse Biedermänner" 1124.e
"Important Brahms Correspondance Issued" 819.e.iii
"Impressions of Brahms" 1208.c
Impressions That Remained. Memoirs 1208
Imprimatur 837.c.ii
"In Answer to A.R.M.'s Query ..." 1951.d.i

"In Berlin" 3110
"In dem Process um die Erbschaft Johannes Brahms" 462
"In den tröbele zee" 2884
"In der Brahms-Wohnung" 407
"In der "Frankfurter Zeitung"" 795.e
"In der "N. fr. Pr." veröffentlichte kürzlich" 1096.e
In Dur und Moll. Briefe grosser Komponisten von Orlando di Lasso
    bis Arnold Schönberg" 1009.c.x
"In einem Briefe, den Johannes Brahms seiner Zeit" 463
"In Frankfurt a.M." 1220.e
"In Gmunden ist" 3166.e
"In Gmunden ist das in der Villa von Miller" 3111
"In Gmunden ist in der Villa von Millner" 3112
"In Gmunden sind von dem Kunstmäcen Hrn. v. Aichholz" 3113
"In Hamburg" 3114
"In Hamburg starb kürzlich die Stiefmutter" 845.e
"In Hamburg wird" 3115
"In Pressbaum bei Wien" 3116
"In The Shadow of Beethoven" 805
"In Wien hat kürzlich ... gerichtliche Verhandlung ..." 464
"In Wien hat sich am 23. April eine Brahms-Gesellschaft gebildet"
    3117
"In Wien soll bekanntlich Johannes Brahms ein Denkmal gesetzt werden"
    3052.e
"In Wien soll das Haus in der Karlsgasse" 3118
"In Wien wird das Brahms-Denkmal" 3119
"In Wien wurde am 7. d. M." 526.e
"Index of Brahms Autographs Prepared for the Library of Congress,
    An" 294
Indiana University 1428, 1514, 1558, 1600, 1623, 1645, 1676, 1684,
    1709, 1822, 1880, 2015, 2233
Infinite Variety of Music, The 1989
"Influence of Brahms, The" 2503
"Influence of Paganini, The" 1649
"Influence: Plagiarism and Inspiration" 2553
"Inner Betrachtung gewidmet" 2384
Inneren Mächte, Die. Bekenntnisse und Bekenner 2365
"Innowacje Chopinowskie w miniaturach fortepianowych Brahmsa"
    1557
Instrumentalkonzert, Das 1384
"Instrumentation Brahms'" 2520
"Interesting Book About Brahms, An" 73.e.iii
Interludes. Records and Reflections 2429
Intermezzi Opus 119 nr. 2 und 3. Faksimile des Autographs 1697
"--Intermezzo Op. 119 no. 3 de Brahms, L'" 1703.a
"International Brahms Congress, The" 3120
International Library of Music for Home and Studio, The. Music
    Literature. Volume I. The History of Music 2607.a
International Library of Music for Home and Studio, The. Music
    Literature. Volume III. The Pianist's Guide 1602
"Interpretation of Brahms's Chamber Music, The. A Few Pitfalls Dis-
    cussed" 2601

Johann Strauss schreibt Briefe 1230
"Johann Strauss und Brahms" 1230
"Johann Strauss und Johannes Brahms" 1229
Johann Wolfgang Goethe-Universität 2433
"Johannes Brahms" or "J. Brahms":
  no date--113, 133, 1165.a.ii, 1336.a.b
  1854-1609
  1860-1345
  1862-2470
  1863-196
  1864-152
  1874-165
  1876-97, 209
  1880-117, 121
  1881-187
  1882-162
  1883-2505
  1886-199
  1887-136, 147
  1888-117.b.i.e, 147.a, 2403
  1889-181, 2948
  1891-159
  1892-1369, 2309.d.ii
  1893-149, 224
  1894-128, 138, 2966
  1895-204, 2507
  1897-151, 161, 413, 419, 420, 434, 435, 445.5, 456, 457, 461, 467-
    72, 483, 484, 487, 493, 494, 496, 516-18, 520.d, 524, 528, 531,
    695, 2425, 2438, 2492, 2962, 2963
  1898-124, 193, 245, 696, 1358, 1577, 2503
  1899-123
  1900-617, 1121.d, 2933
  1901-132, 210
  1902-174.a, 2933.b
  1903-899.c.ii, 971, 1260, 3061.5
  1904-39A.e.ii, 166
  1905-48.e.ii, 115, 153
  1906-211
  1907-215, 983.e
  1909-1009.e.x.a
  1910-211.b, 1056
  1911-95, 103, 207
  1913-532.a.i
  1914-389
  1915-146, 1398
  1916-1403.d
  1917-183
  1918-111
  1919-849
  1920-114, 177
  1921-185, 1144, 1343, 1359

"Johannes Brahms. †3. April" 2637
"Johannes Brahms. (†3. April 1897.)" 457.a
Johannes Brahms. A Biographical Sketch 117.b.i
"Johannes Brahms. A Character Study in Miniature" 3.d
Johannes Brahms. A Short Biography 111.d
Johannes Brahms. Akademische Fest-Ouvertüre, Op. 80. Die
Tragische Ouvertüre, Op. 81 1833
Johannes Brahms. Anton Bruckner 2931.a.ii
"Johannes Brahms. Auf seinen Spuren in Kärnten" 536
"Johannes Brahms. Aus H. Imberts Brahmsbiographie" 37.c
Johannes Brahms. Biographische Skizze 64
"Johannes Brahms. Birth Centenary. Born 1833. Died 1897" 104
"Johannes Brahms. Born May 7, 1833" 2825
"Johannes Brahms. Born 1833: Died 1897" 174.a.d
Johannes Brahms. Briefwechsel 848, 892, 920, 954, 983, 1009, 1062,
1122, 1203, 1204, 1215, 1297, 1314
"Johannes Brahms. Briefwechsel, Band III und IV" 1122.e.vi
"Johannes Brahms. Cenni biografici" 312
Johannes Brahms. Charakterstudie 744
Johannes Brahms. Concert für das Pianoforte mit Begleitung des
Orchesters. D moll, Op. 15 1870.d
Johannes Brahms. Concert für Pianoforte mit Begleitung des Or-
chesters. B dur: Op. 83 1962
"Johannes Brahms. Cours d'interprétation et de technique" 2597
"Johannes Brahms. Das Leben im Werk" 2485
Johannes Brahms. Der Mensch und Künstler 69
"Johannes Brahms. Die letzten Tage" 969.a
"Johannes Brahms. Die letzten Tage. (Wien, 3. April 1897)" 443.a
"Johannes Brahms. Ein Denkblatt" 507
Johannes Brahms. Ein Deutscher Künstler 80
"Johannes Brahms. Ein Deutsches Requiem" 2249
Johannes Brahms. Ein Deutsches Requiem. Ein Führer durch die
Werk, mit vollständige Text, eine Einführung, erlauterte Anmerkung
und zahlreichnete Notenbeispiele 2268
Johannes Brahms. Ein Deutsches Requiem. Eine Einführung und
Erläuterung für Konzertbesucher 2245
Johannes Brahms. Ein Deutsches Requiem, Op. 45 2236
Johannes Brahms. Ein Festvortrag zur Feier des 50. Geburtstages
des Meisters 31
Johannes Brahms. Ein Führer durch seine Werke mit einer einleitenden
Biographie, zahlreichen Notenbeispielen sowie einer anzahl Illustra-
tionen u. einem Uberblick über die Brahmsliteratur 1329
"Johannes Brahms. Ein Gedächtniswort" 2997
"Johannes Brahms. Ein Gedenkblatt" 2864
"Johannes Brahms. Ein Gedenkblatt zur Wiederkehr seines zehnjährigen
Todestages" 2821
Johannes Brahms. Ein Meister und sein Weg 62
"Johannes Brahms. Ein Nachruf" 418
"Johannes Brahms. Ein zeitgemässe und notwendige Betrachtung"
2467
Johannes Brahms. Eine Biographie 81.d

"Johannes Brahms. (1833-1897). L'Avènement d'une renommée musicale" 147.d.iii

Johannes Brahms. 1833-1897. Sein Leben in Bildern 63

"Johannes Brahms. 1931" 2931.a.iii

"Johannes Brahms. 1.-4." 150

Johannes Brahms. Persönlichkeit, Leben und Schaffen 20

"Johannes Brahms. Rede, gehalten am 25. Mai 1937 beim Brahms-Fest in Freiburg/Br." 3014.a

"Johannes Brahms. Rede, gehalten beim Brahms-Fest in Freiburg" 3014

Johannes Brahms. Rhapsodie für eine Altstimme, Männerchor und Orchester. Op. 53 2311

Johannès Brahms. Sa vie et son oeuvre 37, 147.d.ii

Johannes Brahms. Schicksalslied für Chor und Orchester. Op. 54 2319

Johannes Brahms. Schicksalslied, Op. 54. Gesang der Parzen, Op. 89 2219

Johannes Brahms. Sein Leben in Bildern 9

Johannes Brahms. Sein Leben und Schaffen 25

Johannes Brahms. Sein Lebensgang und eine Würdigung seiner Werke 90

Johannes Brahms. Sein Lebensgang vom Jahre 1833-1862 39A

Johannes Brahms. Sein Wesen und seine musikgeschichtliche Bedeutung 2888.d

Johannes Brahms. Serenade für grosses Orchester (D-dur, Op. 11) 1856

Johannes Brahms. Serenade für kleines Orchester, Op. 16 1872

"Johannes Brahms. 7. Mai 1833 geb. in Hamburg--in Wien gest. 3. April 1897" 96

"Johannes Brahms. 7. Mai 1833--3. April 1897" 321

Johannes Brahms. Sextett in B-dur. Op. 18 1520

"Johannes Brahms. Skizze" 2903

Johannes Brahms. Symphonien und andere Orchesterwerke. Erläutert von I. Knorr, H. Riemann und J. Sittard nebst einer Einleitung: Johannes Brahms' Leben und Schaffen von A. Morin 1812

"Johannes Brahms. Teil 1, 2" 85

"Johannes Brahms. The Interpretation of His Music" 2607

Johannes Brahms. The Man and His Work. Catalogue of an Exhibition of Rare and Unique Items drawn from the Life and Times of a Great Composer. Detroit Public Library Biography Room. April 1980 3109

"Johannes Brahms. The Master as Teacher" 694.e

"Johannes Brahms. The Musician. Born 1833. Died 1897" 104.d

Johannes Brahms. Thematisches Verzeichnis seiner Werke 313

"Johannes Brahms. Thinker in Music. Born 1833-Died 1897" 106

Johannes Brahms. III. Erster Halbband. 1874-1881 39C

Johannes Brahms. III. Zweiter Halbband. 1881-1885 39C

Johannes Brahms. 3. Symphonie (F-dur, Op. 90) 1981

"Johannes Brahms. To the Editor of the London Musical World" 152.d.a

"[[Johannes Brahms und Julius Stockhausen.]]", 1220
"Johannes Brahms und Karlsruhe. Uraufführungen im Hoftheater und im Museum" 603
"Johannes Brahms und Kiel. Ein Beitrag zur Musikgeschichte Kiels" 575
"Johannes Brahms und Mannheim" 609
Johannes Brahms und Mathilde Wesendonck. Ein Briefwechsel 1292
"Johannes Brahms und Max Reger" 1119
"Johannes Brahms und Osterreich. Zum hundertsten Geburtstage des Meisters am 7. Mai 1933" 545
"Johannes Brahms und Philipp Spitta" 1216.e
"Johannes Brahms und Philipp Spitta. Aus einem Briefwechsel" 1216
"Johannes Brahms und Richard Mühlfeld" 1092
"Johannes Brahms und sein Denkmal" 3155
"Johannes Brahms und sein Freundeskreis. Nach einem Briefe von Gustav Ophüls von 6. Oktober 1892" 597
"Johannes Brahms und sein Verhältnis zum deutschen Volkslied" 2570
Johannes Brahms und sein Verhältnis zum deutschen Volkslied 2570.a
"Johannes Brahms und sein Violinkonzert. Nach seinem Briefwechsel mit Jos. Joachim" 1009.e.ix
"Johannes Brahms und sein Werk" 2483.d.ii
"Johannes Brahms und seine Beziehungen zu Krefelder Mennoniten" 1066
"Johannes Brahms und seine Interpreten" 2603
"Johannes Brahms und seine Künstlerfreundschaften. Zum 3. April, der 25. Wiederkehr seines Todestages" 930
Johannes Brahms und seine Musik 1326
"Johannes Brahms und seine neuesten Werke" 1335
"Johannes Brahms und seine niederdeutsche Heimat" 366
"Johannes Brahms und seine schwäbischen Freunde" 591
"Johannes Brahms und seine sechs ersten Werke" 1350
Johannes Brahms und seine Sendung 3002
"Johannes Brahms und seine Stellung in der Musikgeschichte" 3040
Johannes Brahms und seine Stellung in der Musikgeschichte 705
"Johannes Brahms und seine Stellung in der Musikgeschichte des 19. Jahrhunderts" 3020
"Johannes Brahms und seine Verleger" 239
"Johannes Brahms und seine Zeit" 2656
"Johannes Brahms und Theodor Billroth" 819.c.ii.e.i
"Johannes Brahms und Theodor Kirchner. Mit ungedruckten Briefen Th. Kirchners" 1032
"Johannes Brahms und Ungarn. Liebesroman der Agathe von Siebold" 1199.e.iii
"Johannes Brahms und unsere Zeit. Gedanken zum 3. April 1947" 3003
"Johannes Brahms und Wilhelm Raabe" 1115
Johannes Brahms und Zürich. Ein Beitrag zur Kulturgeschichte von Zürich 627.d
"Johannes Brahms und Zürich. Zum hundertsten Geburtstage des Meisters" 626
"Johannes Brahms: Variationen über ein Thema von Schumann (Op. 9) fis-moll" 1621

Magyar zenetudomány 1724.a

"Magyaros részek Brahms muzsikájában" 2567

"Mahler und Brahms: Gedanken zu "Reminiszenzen" in Mahlers Sinfonien" 1356

Main Stream of Music and Other Essays, The 1443.a

Mainzer Studien zur Musikwissenschaft 1287

Maîtres de la musique, Les 40

Makers of Music. Biographical Sketches of the Great Composers with Chronological Summaries of Their Works, Portraits, Facsimiles of Their Compositions and a General Chronological Table 206

"Mal qui a emporté Brahms, Le" 495

"Malerische Element in den Liedern von Johannes Brahms" 2528

"Malheur d'aimer Brahms, Le" 2273

"Man, The" 696

Manesse Bibliothek der Weltliteratur 72

"Mannheim und Brahms" 602

Manuskripte, Briefe, Dokumente, von Scarlatti bis Stravinsky. Katalog der Musikautographen Sammlung Louis Koch 292

"Marginalien zu Fragen des Stils und der Interpretation (I)" 1842

"Marie Luise Meyer-Dustmann und Johannes Brahms" 1088

"Marienlied bei Johannes Brahms, Das" 2223

"Marmorbusten von Beethoven und Brahms" 3141

Martin Luther-Universität Halle 3026

Martin-Luther Universität, Halle 1394

Mary Flagler Cary Music Collection, The. Printed Books and Music. Manuscripts. Autograph Letters. Documents. Portraits 303

"Master Builder, The" 1809.a

"Master Class: A Brahms Jewel" 1696

"Master Lesson: Brahms's Intermezzo Op. 117, no. 3" 1682

"Master Lesson by Guy Maier, A. Brahms' Intermezzo in E-flat Major, Op. 117, no. 1" 1686

"Master Lesson on the Brahms' Rhapsody Op. 79, no. 2" 1673

Master Musicians 18, 41

Master Musicians. A Book for Players, Singers & Listeners 681

Master Musicians, The. New Series 41

Masterpieces of Music 2095

Masters of Contemporary Music 128

Masters of German Music 128

Masters of Music 70

"Masters of Music" 175

Masters of The Symphony. Fifth Year of A Study Course in Music Understanding, Adopted by the National Federation of Music Clubs 1801

"Max Bruch und Johannes Brahms. Zu Max Bruchs 70. Geburtstag" 1122.e.v

"Max Kalbeck's Brahms-Biographie" 39C.e

Max Klinger 1036, 1048

Max Klinger. Die Graphischen Zyklen. 28 November 1979 bis 17 Februar 1980 1047

Max Klinger als Poet 1034

"Max Klinger und die Musik. 3. Klinger und Brahms" 1039.a.i

"Musikalische Frühlingstage" 2166

"Musikalische Griffelkunst. Zu Max Klingers "Brahms-Phantasie""
1037

"Musikalische Nachlass von Brahms, Der" 1766.a

"Musikalische Nachlass von Johannes Brahms (Original-Mittheilung der
"Signale"), Der" 1766

Musikalische Schriftenreihe der NS Kulturgemeinde 22

Musikalische Selbstporträt von Komponisten, Dirigenten, Instrumental-
isten, Sängerinnen und Sängern unsurer Zeit, Das 722

Musikalische Seltenheiten. Wiener Liebhaberdruckte 2042

Musikalische Skizzen 149.a

Musikalische Studien 149.a.a

Musikalische Studien 149.a, 3019.a

Musikalische Studienköpfe. Dritter Band: Jüngstvergangenheit und
Gegenwart 165.a.d

Musikalische Studienköpfe aus der Jüngstvergangenheit und Gegenwart.
Charakterzeichnungen von Moscheles, David, ... Brahms, Tausig,
nebst den Verzeichnissen ihrer Werke 165.a

Musikalische Volksbücher 58, 658, 1180

Musikalisches Opfer. Ein Altar in Worten mit vier Seitentafeln um
den Mittelschrein 1162

Musikalisches und Litterarisches. Kritiken und Schilderungen 2948

"Musikalsk spøg, En" 1544

"Musikanschauung Eduard Hanslicks in seinen Kritiken und Aufsätzen,
Die. Eine Studie zur musikalisch-geistigen Situation des 19.
Jahrhunderts" 3030

Musikbibliographische Arbeiten 277

Musiken i det nittende aarhundrede 5.d

Musiken under det nittonde arhundradet 5.d.b

Musikens mästare 84

Musikens trollmakt. (Samlung 3: Chopin, Schumann, Brahms.)
112.b

Musiker der Spätromantik. Unbekannte Briefe aus dem Nachlass von
Josef und Alfred Sittard 2590.d

"Musiker deutschen Wesens. Brahms zum Gedenken" 2848

Musiker, Maler und Dichter als Freunde und Gegner 858.d.i

"Musiker über Brahms, Brahms über Musiker" 3009

Musiker und ihre Werke 1346

"Musiker untereinander. Schumann, Brahms, Wagner" 1252

Musiker-Biographien 32, 68

Musikerbriefe 954.c.iv

Musikerbriefe aus fünf Jahrhunderten 1069

Musiker-Handschriften. Zeugnisse des Zürcher Musiklebens 627

Musikerreihe 62

"Musikertypen. (Mit Einer unbekannten Brahms-Anekdote)" 2473

"Musikerzieher von einst: Wie gab Brahms der Tochter Schumanns
Klavier-Unterricht?" 1180.c.i

Musikführer, Der 1429, 1449, 1473, 1499, 1520, 1526, 1833, 1856,
1858, 1872, 1874, 1892, 1926, 1940, 1964, 1981, 2002, 2012, 2203,
2219, 2236, 2307, 2327

Musikgeschichte und Genealogie 330

Musikhandschriften in Basel aus verschiedenen Sammlungen. Ausstellung im Kunstmuseum Basel vom 31. Mai bis zum 13. Juli 1975
306
Musikherön der Neuzeit 90
Musikhistorisches Museum von Wilhelm Mayer in Cöln. Katalog. Bd. 4. Musik-Autographen 291
Musikkens store B'er. Bach, Beethoven, Brahms 113
Musik-Konzepte 1457.a
Musikkritiken 2949
Musikstadt Königsberg. Geschichte und Erinnerung 585.d
Musikwissenschaftliche Kolloquien der Internationalen Musikfestspiele 905
Musings & Memories of A Musician 979.d.ii
Musique et musiciens 1918.a
Musique et musiciens modernes 211.b
Musique et verbe 2931.a.iii.b
Muzikale exploraties. Tweede reeks: Ouverturen en symfonische gedichten 1953
"Musikale memoires van Ilka Horovitz-Barnay (I), De" 999.a.e
Muzyka fortepianowa IV 1557
Muzykal'naia literatura zarubezhnykh stran 169
Muzykal'no-istoricheskie etiudy 1738
Muzykal'no-kharakteristischekie etiudy 165.a.d.b
"My Early Acquaintance with Brahms" 990.b
My Life and Friends 1212
"My Memories of Brahms, Liszt and Massanet" 1002
"My Recollections of Brahms" 890
"Mysle k 80. posmjertninam J. Brahmsa" 2841

"Nach München" 1288.a
"Nachklänge zur Brahms-Feier" 2663
"Nachlass des musikgelehrten Josef Sittard, Der" 2590
"Nachlass von Johannes Brahms, Der" 498, 3164.e
"Nachruf an Brahms" 522
"Nachtrag (bis Ende Oktober 1912) zu Otto Kellers "Johnnes Brahms-Bibliographie"" 240.d.ii
"Nachwirkungen der Musik Joseph Haydns auf Johannes Brahms" 972
"Nachwort" 239
"Nad symfonickou tvorbou J. Brahmse. K. 125. výročí narozeni skladatelů" 1847
"Narration to be Read during Performances of Die Schoene Magelone, A" 2126
Nationale und universale Musik. Neue Essays 1255.a
"Neapolitan Brahms" 2118
Nedderdüütsche Welt 21
"Nekrolog" 532.a.ii
"Neo-Classicism in the Later Piano Works of Brahms" 1559
"Neuaufgefundener Brief von Johannes Brahms an seine Stiefmutter, Ein" 843

"Neuestes über Brahms" 117.e.ii
"Neuliche Blättermeldung das Man Hr. Prof. Max Klinger, Die" 3149
"Neuntes Brahms-Fest in Hamburg" 2708
"New Analysis of Brahms's Intermezzo in B Minor Op. 119, no. 1" 1704
New and Collected Poems 1934-84 1257.a
"New Brahms Acquisitions Led by Gift from Herman Lowin" 2033
"New Brahms Letters" 1179.c.iv.b
New Education, The--The Mastery of Teaching Material 245, 696, 1358, 1577, 2503
"New Etude Gallery of Musical Celebrities, The" 182
"New in Review, The" 1869
New Library of Music, The 23
"New Light on Schumann's Last Years" 1618
"New Light on Signor Crescendo and Onkel Bähmsen" 78.e.ii
"New Paths" 3013.a.iv.d
"New Paths (1853)" 3013.b.i
New Poems by American Poets #2 1587.a
"New Roads [[1853]]" 3013.a.i.b
"New York on Brahms, A" 78.e.i
New York University 1642, 1848
"Nicht aus dem Herzen" 2706
N. Simrock Thematic Catalog of the Works of Johannes Brahms, The. [[Thematisches Verzeichniss sämmtlicher im Druck erschienenen Werke von Johannes Brahms]] 320.a
"Niedersachsens Seele in der Musik. Ein Erinnerungsblatt an den 25. Todestag von Johannes Brahms (3. April 1897)" 145
"Nietzsche and Brahms: A Forgotten Relationship" 1097
"Nietzsche und Brahms" 1098.d.i
"Nietzsches Totengericht über Brahms" 1097.d
"9. Brahmsfest in Hamburg" 2712
9. Brahmsfest Programmbuch 355.a
"9. Deutsches Brahmsfest der "Deutschen Brahms-Gesellschaft" in Hamburg. 11.-17. Oktober 1937" 2705
"9. Deutsches Brahmsfest in Hamburg" 2709
Nineteenth-Century Autograph Music Manuscripts in the Pierpont Morgan Library. A Check List 303.d.d
"Nineteenth-Century Autograph Music Manuscripts in the Pierpont Morgan Library: A Checklist" 303.d
Nittende aarhundrede, Det 5.d
"No Wife, No Opera" 2585
"Noch ein Beitrag zur Charakteristik von Brahms" 1294.c
"Noch einmal Brahms" 235
"Noch waren die irdischen Überreste des ebebso Grossen" 509.e
"Nochmal "Chorale Sancti antonii"" 1878
"Nochmals Berliner Musik-"Kritik"" 2909
"Nochmals der Nachlass von Johannes Brahms" 502
"Noordwyk und Brahms. Ein Reisebrief" 646
North Texas State University 1606, 2035, 2608
Northwestern University 1625, 1761, 2116, 2451
Norton Critical Scores 1380

"Notation und Herausgabe bei einigen Werken von W. A. Mozart,
Franz Schubert und Johannes Brahms" 1496
"Note About Brahms Sonatas" 2604
"Note on Brahms, A" 725, 1968.a, 2476, 2961
"Note on Brahms's Requiem, A" 2252
Notes From the Life of A Viennese Composer. Karl Goldmark 949.b
"Notes on Playing Brahms. With Special Reference to Rhapsody in
E Flat, Op. 119" 1700
"Notes sur Brahms" 2810.5
Novello's Biographies of Great Musicians 75
"Novye issledovaniia o roli funktsional'noĭ muzyki" 1717
"No. 1: The Six Sonatas for Unaccompanied Violin and Musical
Legacy of Eugene Ysayë. No. 2: The Sextets by Brahms: An
Analysis" 1514
Número extraordinario dedicado a Brahms 3179
"Numerous Brahms Anecdotes Have, of Course, Been Current" 431.
c.e.e
"Nuovo tempo Brahmsiano" 2421
"Ny-Klassicismen. Johannes Brahms" 5.d

"Observations on Brahms' Two Motets, Opus 29" 2225
Occasional Parallels 850
"Ode To A Nightingale" 1897
Oeuvres 2403.a
Of German Music. A Symposium 863
Of Men and Music 1278
"Off The Record. Chamber Music--Part I" 2379
"Offener Brief" 184
""Oh No!"" 1127
Oktaven und Quinten u.A. 2353
Old Fogy. His Musical Opinions and Grotesques 635.a.i.a
Old Scores and New Readings: Discussions on Musical Subjects
2961.a
Om mennesket Johannes Brahms 4.d.b
"Omkring Johs. Brahms' "Liebeslieder Walzer" Op. 52" 2141
"On Brahms" 1239.b.d, 3013.c.ii
"On Brahms (1833-1897)" 2915
"On Harmony and Meter in Brahms's Op. 76, no. 8" 1665
"On Johannes Brahms" 3180.e
On Music and Musicians 3013.a.i.b
"On The Study of Chopin's Manuscripts" 1735
"On Translating Brahms Texts" 2611
"100. Geburtstag, Der" 2814
"100 Jahre Brahms" 2823
"100 Jahre Musikvereinsgebäude" 388
125 Jahre Philharmonie. Philharmonische Staatsorchester 1237
"100jährige Brahms-Haus, Das" 338
"1833 Johannes Brahms 1897. The Classical Spirit in Modern Music"
125
"1833 Johannes Brahms 1933" 3191

"Second Study. Brahms and Liszt" 2400
"Seconde symphonie de J. Brahms, La--La Mer de Debussy" 1918.a
Secrets of Success of Great Musicians 185
"Sectionalized Variations" 1388
"Secular Music for the Solo Vocal Ensemble in the Nineteenth Century"
    2039
"Seele und Geist des Brahms-Werkes" 2646
"Sehr allgemein war und ist noch jetzt" 2160.e
"Seit dem 7. Mai 1903" 3160
Select Bibliographies. Reprint Series 1436.a.ii
Select Bibliographies. Reprint Series. Facsimile Editions 1180.b.a.i
Selected Austrian Short Stories 2625.b
Selected Piano Compositions 146, 1392.d
"Selection and Setting of Poetry in the Solo Songs of Johannes
    Brahms" 2542
Ser y tiempo 2493.b.iv
Set Works for 'O' Level" 1476
"Seven Capriccios of Johannes Brahms. Op. 76, nos. 1,2,5,8 and
    Op. 116, nos. 1,3,7" 1560
"Seven of the Small Sacred Choral Works, including Opus 121, of
    Brahms" 2033
"70. Jahre Museum" 3161
"75. Todestag des deutschen Komponisten. Johannes Brahms geb.
    am 7.5.1833 in Hamburg gest. am 3.4.1897 in Wien. Nachtrag zu
    dem Bibliographischen Kalenderblatt über Johannes Brahms anlässl.
    seines 70. Todestages am 3.4.1967 (Jg. 1967, Folge 4, s. 13-27)"
    237.d
"Short Studies of Great Masterpieces. III. Symphony no. 3 in F
    Major Opus 90 by Johannes Brahms (1882-1883). First Performance
    at Vienna, 1883" 1980
"Short Studies of Great Masterpieces. XII. Academic Festival Over-
    ture, Opus 80 by Johannes Brahms. First Performance in Breslau
    in 1881" 1955
"Sieben unbekannte Briefe von Brahms. Aus der Handschrift erst-
    malig veröffentlicht" 1233
"Siebente Deutsche Brahmsfest in Jena, Das" 2729
"Siebentes Deutsches Brahmsfest der Deutschen Brahmsgesellschaft
    in Jena" 2725
"Simfonii Bramsa" 1837
"Simultaneity Structures and Harmonic Functions in Tonal Music"
    2397
"Sind Brahms Werke schwer verständlich" 3006
"Sinfonías de Brahms, Las" 1798
"6. Deutsches Brahmsfest in Heidelberg" 2720
"16. Band des Brahmsschen Briefwechsels, Der" 1215.a.e
Sizilien und andere gegenden Italiens. Reiseerinnerungen 618.d
Sizilien und andere gegenden Italiens. Reisen mit Johannes Brahms
    618.d
"Sketches for Analyses of Opp. 35, 39, 76, 79, 116-19" 1597
"Skizzen zu Joh. Brahms' Haydn-Variationen" 1662
"Slow Movement of Brahms' First Symphony, The. A Reconstruction

"Two Views of Brahms" 2913
"Two Waltzes by Brahms. How to Study, How to Teach no. 2 and
    no. 9 from Opus. 39" 1652
"Tycker ni om Brahms?" 2941
"Tyylikehitys Johannes Brahmsin duosonaateissa" 1570

"Uber Brahms' Geigensonaten" 1447
"Ueber den Demnächst in der Offentlichkeit erschienenden Briefwechsels
    Johannes Brahms" 983.e.i.e
"Ueber die Angelegenheit Brahms-Remenyi theilt Albert in Oldenburg"
    1730
"Uber die aus tondern stammenden Ahnen des Komponisten Johannes
    Brahms" 333
"Ueber die Bedeutung der auch von uns" 2955.e
Uber die Dynamik in der Musik von Johannes Brahms 2370.a
"Uber ein besonderes Akzentzeichen bei Johannes Brahms" 2599
"Uber ein besonderes Akzentzeichen bei Joh. Brahms" 2599.d
"Uber einige seltsame Noten bei Brahms und Anderen" 2419
"Ueber Johannes Brahms, mit besonderer Rücksichtnahme auf dessen
    "Gesang der Parzen". Eine musik-ästhetisch-kritische Studie"
    2339
"Uber Schönbergs Brahms-Bearbeitung" 1457
"Uebersicht neu erschienener Musikwerke. A. Instrumental-Musik"
    1417
"Ubersicht neu erschienener Musikwerke. B. Gesangs-Musik. 2)
    Mehrstimmige Gesänge ohne Begleitung" 2228
"Ubersicht neu erschienener Musikwerke. Claviermusik zu vier
    Händen" 1661
"Ubersicht neu erschienener Musikwerke. Kammermusik" 1430
"Uebersicht neu erschienener Musikwerke. Lieder für gemischten
    Chor" 2230
Uit het leven van Johannes Brahms 65
"Ultima composizione di Brahms, L': i "Preludi corali" opera 122"
    1759
"Um einen Brahms für Heute bittend" 2716
"Umgang mit Brahms" 749
"Unbekannte Aufzeichnungen über Johannes Brahms" 989.c
Unbekannte Brahms, Der 78.b
"Unbekannte Brahms-Briefe" 877
"Unbekannte Briefe von Brahms" 900
"Unbekannte Korrekturen in Brahms' Motette "Warum ist das Licht
    gegeben dem Hühseligen (Op. 74, I)" 2331
"Unbekannter Brahms-Brief, Ein. Zur schweizerischen Erstaufführung
    des "Deutschen Requiems" in Basel" 2297
"Unbekanntes Blatt aus Schumanns Endenicher Zeit, Ein" 1617
"Unbekanntes Brahms-Studienblatt aus dem Briefwechsel mit F. Wüllner,
    Ein" 1348
"Unbekanntes von Johannes Brahms. Relikvien und Briefe aus seinem
    Nachlass" 519
"Unbekanntes Werk von Brahms?" 1505

University of London 1146
University of London (Royal Holloway College) 2001
University of Maryland 2220
University of Massachusetts 1584
University of Miami 2121, 2142, 2335
University of Michigan 1679, 1694, 2217
University of Michigan Official Publication 1552
University of North Carolina 1448
University of North Carolina at Chapel Hill 875, 2303, 2355
University of North Carolina, Chapel Hill 2045
University of Oregon 2200
University of Rochester (Eastman School of Music) 2, 1479, 1767,
    2248, 2266, 2353.d, 2386, 2404, 2414, 2516
University of Southern California 1628
University of Washington 1592, 2123, 2127, 2191
University of Wisconsin 1426, 1445, 1541, 1929, 2542, 2632
University of Wisconsin-Madison 2315
Unknown Brahms, The. His Life, Character and Works; Based on
    New Material 78
"Unknown Gavottes by Brahms" 1593
"Unmaid Bed, The" 767
"Unpublished Letters by Beethoven, Liszt and Brahms" 955
"Unsere Bilder" 3189
"Unsere grossen Tonmeister als Sänger des Vaterlandes; I. Gluck,
    Mozart, Haydn, Beethoven; II. Weber, Loewe, Wagner, Brahms,
    Reger" 2330
Unsere Tonmeister unter Einander 984.a, 1225.d, 1266
Unsere Tonmeister unter Einander. Johannes Brahms, Anton Bruckner
    und Hugo Wolf 858
"Unsittliche Brahms, Der" 2152.e
Unsterbliche Tonkunst. Lebens- und Schaffensbilder grosser Musiker
    26
Unsterlichen, Der. Neue Folge. Novellen 2625
"Untersuchungen zum Brahmsstil und Brahmsbild" 81
"Untersuchungen zum historischen Stellenwert der a-cappella-Kompo-
    sitionen von J. Brahms" 2187
"Unüberbrückbar?" 856
"Unveröffentlicher Brahms-Brief, Ein" 1052
"Unveröffentlicher Brief von Brahms aus den Zeiten der Stuttgarter
    Erstaufführung seines Requiems" 1078
"Ursprung und Geschichte der Sammlung Wittgenstein im 19. Jahr-
    hundert" 1308
"Urtheil eines schweizerischen Musikers über Johannes Brahms"
    2960.e
"Uso del corno in alcune composizioni di Brahms, L'" 2515

"Vaisseau-Fantôme, Le. La Troisième symphonie de J. Brahms" 1974
"Val's v instrumental'nyh ciklah Bramsa" 2409
""Variationen für eine liebe Freundin" von Johannes Brahms, Die"
    1639

"Von Sinfoniker Brahms" 1890.d
"Von verdeckten Octaven und Quinten. Ein Beitrag zur Lehre vom
    strengen vierstimmigen Satze" 2420
"Voor mij behoort Brahms tot" 2884
"Vor 95 Jahren ... Johannes Brahms konzertierte in Bad Neuenahr"
    593
"Vor 100 Jahren: "Ein ganz ein kleines Klavierkonzert ..." Zur In-
    terpretation von Brahms' Opus 83" 1965
"Vor Zehn Jahren. Brahms und Bruckner--Erinnerungen und Bekennt-
    nisse" 1106
"Vorbild und Vermächtnis Brahms. Zu seinem 110. Geburtstag"
    2861
"Vortrag der Brahmschen Orchesterwerke, Der" 1830
"Vortrag über Brahms im Brahms-Abende des Musikpädagogischen
    Vereins zu Dresden" 208
""Vortrag und Besetzung Bach'scher Cantaten- und Oratorienmusik"
    Ein unbekannter Brief von Moritz Hauptmann an Johannes Brahms
    (15. Februar 1859)" 2448
Vypusk III 1611

"Waarom wordt Brahms nog niet voldönde" 2884
"Waffenruhe am Clavier" 1655
"Waffenruhe am Clavier. (Wien, im August 1866.)" 1655.a.ii
"Wagner and Brahms" 1255.d
"Wagner and Brahms On Each Other" 1250.a
"Wagner and Brahms, with Unpublished Letters" 1259
"Wagner, Brahms and Their Contemporaries" 1263
"Wagner Brahms und Wir. Eine Neujahrs-Betrachtung" 1255.a
"Wagner und Brahms" 1264, 1266.d.ii, 1267
"Wagner und Brahms. Ein beinahe tragikomischer Briefwechsel"
    1283
"Wagner und Brahms in persönlichem Verkehr und Briefwechsel"
    1272
"Wagner-Brahms Year, The" 1254
Wagneriana 3025.a
"Wagnerianer und Brahmsianer" 1273
Wagner-Probleme und andere Studien 2644.a
"Waltz and Brahms' Opus 39, The" 1659
"War Marxsen der rechte Lehrer für Brahms?" 1084
"War Schönberg von Dvorak beeinflusst?" 1145
"Warum ist Brahms berühmt? Provokation eines unzeitgemässen
    Themas" 229
"Was bedeutet uns Brahms?" 2912
"Was Brahms A Conservative" 2482
"Was He Fooling?" 1957
"Was ist uns Johai. .es Brahms? Ein Gedenkblatt zum 10. Todestage
    des Meisters. (geb. 7. Mai 1833, gest. 3. April 1897)" 3045
"Was kann Brahms uns Heute bedeuten? Zum 25. Todestage des
    Meisters" 2953
Was weist du von Brahms? 11

NEWSPAPER AND MAGAZINE INDEX

Information in this index is interfiled in one alphabetical sequence, word by word. A reference to a citation number includes appearances in all applicable sections within that number.

Alphabetization follows the principles used in the Title, Monographic Series and Degree-Granting Institutions Index. Breakdown of years is indicated by chronological sequence within individual newspaper or magazine entries.

A Fővárosi könyvtár évkönyve
    1932:   611
    1942:   241
A Zene
    1910:   347
    1912:   1139.d.d
    1931:   2555
    1932:   765.b, 1004, 1814, 2865, 2942
    1933:   613
    1934:   2457
    1935:   766
    1938:   2567, 2580
Abendpost, see Wiener Abendpost
Academy
    1897:   2962
    1906:   1608, 2511
Acta musicologica
    1963:   1736
    1976:   230
Aftonbladet (Stockholm)
    1928:   2936
Allgemeine deutsche Musikzeitung
    See also Allgemeine Musikzeitung
    1877:   1481
    1879:   2345
    1880:   1729
    1882:   874
Allgemeine musikalische Zeitung
    See also Leipziger allgemeine Musikzeitung

1863: 196, 1462, 1631, 2224
1864: 2029
1865: 1458, 2056
1868: 1152, 1741
1869: 1342, 2199, 2243
1870: 2138, 2140, 2308
1872: 2325.d
1874: 1731
1875: 2057
1878: 1515
1881: 117.e.i
Allgemeine Musikgesellschaft in Zürich. Neujahrsblatt, see Neujahrs-
    blatt der Allgemeinen Musikgesellschaft in Zürich
Allgemeine Musikzeitung
    See also Allgemeine deutsche Musikzeitung
    no date: 1111.a
1893: 1041.e
1895: 2105.d
1897: 431, 492, 1294.c
1898: 503, 999.e, 1096.e
1899: 2735.d, 2736, 3168
1900: 889
1901: 280, 1027.e
1902: 39A.d.i.e.i, 416, 464, 617.e.ii, 845.e, 1763, 3052.e,
    3060, 3111, 3166.e
1903: 526.e
1904: 3101, 3115, 3117
1905: 2519, 3053.e, 3116, 3118, 3171
1906: 795.e, 940.e, 950.e.ii, 983.e, 1220.e, 1363.e, 3044,
    3055, 3059, 3061, 3080, 3110, 3114, 3164.e
1907: 1122.e.iv, 3045, 3105, 3119, 3165, 3173.e
1908: 68.e, 1192, 2183, 3064, 3152, 3169, 3172
1909: 1112, 2748, 2754-59, 3098, 3141, 3142
1910: 2665, 2680
1911: 2800
1912: 1170C.e.i, 2803
1913: 308, 2675
1917: 559, 1204.e.i
1918: 920.e
1920. 1203.e.i
1921: 848.d.i, 2801
1922: 812.d.ii, 1251, 2633, 2684, 2714, 2842, 2929
1923: 1215.a.e, 1314.e, 2695
1925: 670, 756.d.i
1926: 1158.e.i, 1890, 2724
1927: 1179.e.ii, 1996.a
1928: 2697
1929: 1199.e.i, 2545, 2725
1930: 1890.d
1931: 2752
1932: 659, 1088, 2773

1933: 16.e, 1819, 2455, 2691, 2715, 2726, 2776, 2781, 2783
1934: 1079.e
1935: 1266.d.i
1936: 1219
1937: 811, 812.d.ii.a, 881, 2467, 2518, 2694, 2708, 2888, 3150
1938: 1118, 1508
1939: 765.d.d, 1315, 2669, 2676
1940: 1241, 2545.d
Allgemeine Volksmusikzeitung
  1958: 2917
Allgemeine Zeitung, see Wiener allgemeine Zeitung
Allgemeine Zeitung (München)
  1875: 2271
  1897: 518
  1899: 887
  1907: 654
  1909: 39B.e.iv, 2766
Almanach der Deutschen Musikbücherei (Regensburg)
  1924: 2512
  1926: 862
Almanach für Arbeitersänger (Wien)
  1930: 861
Alpenländische Monatshefte (Graz)
  1927: 118
Amerbach Bote: Almanach (Basel)
  1947: 618.a.c.ii
American Choral Review
  1972: 2211.c
American Imago
  1949: 764.b.i
American Medical Association. Journal see Journal of the American
  Medical Association
American Music Lover
  1938: 253
American Music Teacher
  1972: 1762
  1976: 556
  1981: 2225
American Musicological Society. Bulletin see Bulletin of the American
  Musicological Society
American Musicological Society. Journal see Journal of the American
  Musicological Society
American Musicological Society. Papers see Papers of the American
  Musicological Society
American Organist (New York)
  1970: 1758
  1979: 1768
American Scholar
  1947: 2658
American String Teacher
  1967: 1950

American String Teacher (cont'd)
    1970:   828
    1980:   1504
American-German Review, The
    1939:   1895
Américas
    1954:   1970.e
Amerikanische Rundschau, Die
    1946:   955.b
Anbruch
    See also Musikblätter des Anbruch
    1932:   282
    1933:   2430, 2897
    1934:   25.c
    1935:   1617
    1936:   989.c
    1937:   448, 841.d.ii.c, 2178.e, 2587, 2931.d.i
Appenzellische Jahrbücher
    no date: 577
Arc, L'
    1970:   809
Archiv für Musikwissenschaft
    1955:   1639
    1974:   1534
Archivio generale di neurologia psichiatria, e psicoanalisi (Naples)
    1934:   764.b.ii
Ars. Revista de arte
    1957:   203.d, 293, 764.b.iii, 908, 1329.c, 1389, 1439, 1798,
            2256, 2423, 2559, 2643, 2918, 3179
Ars organi
    1963:   1745
ARSC Journal   see   Association for Recorded Sound Collections.
    Journal
Arte Musical (Lisbon)
    1959:   2483.d.i
Arts Magazine
    1979:   655
Association for Recorded Sound Collections.   Journal
    1979:   266
Astrologische Rundschau
    1933:   2859
Ateneo veneto
    1933:   2832
Athenaeum, The
    1897:   467
Athenaion-Blätter
    1934:   55.c
Atlantic Monthly
    1902:   2480
    1942:   2649
Atlantis Almanach (Zürich)
    1946:   1104

Atlant[isches]. Tageblatt
    1911: 588.a
Audio and Record Review
    1968: 268
Aufbau. Kulturpolitische Monatsschrift mit literarischen Beiträgen
    (Berlin)
    1948: 2496
Auftakt, Der
    1922: 582
    1933: 1272, 1819.d
    1935: 25.e.d
    1937: 907, 2872
    1938: 2498
Augsburger Abendzeitung
    1911: 802
Augsburger Postzeitung
    1908: 3130

BACH
    1975: 1023
    1976: 2296
    1977: 2296.d
Bach-Jahrbuch
    1969: 2448
    1971: 793
Bade-Blatt (Baden-Baden)
    1872: 3012
Badener Buch
    1923: 1026
Badische Landeszeitung (Karlsruhe)
    1922: 2376.5.a
Badische neueste Nachrichten (Karlsruhe)
    1976: 603
Badische Presse (Karlsruhe)
    1911: 103
Badisches Tagblatt (Baden-Baden)
    1968: 600, 2461.5, 2664.5
Baltimore Evening Sun
    1926: 2481
Basler Nachrichten
    1916: 1077
    1924: 629
    1933: 633.d.ii
Basler Stadtbuch. Jahrbuch für Kultur und Geschichte
    1966: 1130
Bass World. International Society of Bassists Annual Journal
    1977: 1894
Bau und die Bauindustrie (Düsseldorf), Der
    1954: 698
Baukasten (Düsseldorf), Der
    1954: 698

Bayerische Staatszeitung (München)
    1975: 596
Bayreuther Blätter
    1880: 2422
Bayrische Staatszeitung (München)
    1933: 1070, 2881
Beethoven-Jahrbuch
    1971: 2513.a
Beiträge zur Musikwissenschaft
    1963: 2599
    1975: 1457
    1978: 939
Beobachter deutsche Brenzlande (Potsdam)
    1934: 837.e
Bergland
    1933: 545
Bergstadt
    1925: 715
Berliner Börsen-Courier
    1897: 1218
Berliner Börsen-Courir
    1908: 1122.e.v
Berliner Börsen-Zeitung or Berliner Börsenzeitung
    1924: 941.a
    1931: 929.e, 1028.5
    1940: 736
    1942: 833
Berliner Lokal-Anzeiger
    1928: 2136
Berliner Musikbericht
    1947: 2666, 2671
Berliner Musikzeitung
    1876: 1712
Berliner neueste Nachrichten
    1908: 226.5
Berliner Tageblatt
    See also Zeitgeist, Der
    no date: 1365.5, 2217.5, 2348.5
    1897: 1065, 1235, 2452
    1898: 910, 935
    1899: 2736.5
    1900: 525
    1907: 39B.c.v, 983.e.ix
    1908: 39B.c.iv, 39A.e.v, 2780
    1909: 1009.e.x, 2603, 2764
    1912: 2797
    1913: 701
    1917: 2673
    1926: 1943
    1927: 1158.e.ii
    1930: 568

British Musician and Musical News
  1933: 339
Brücke (Klagenfurt), Die
  1976: 536
Brücke, Die. Heimatblätter für Geist und Gemüt
  1933: 2620
Brücke, Die. Heimatblatt für Geist und Gemüt
  1933: 2657
Budapester Rundschau
  1968: 610
Budapesti hirlap
  1930: 2836
Bühne (Wien), Die
  1980: 3091
Bühne und Welt
  1899: 1239.b.c.ii
  1903: 1260
  1904: 880.a, 3160
Bühnen-Blättern von Landestheater (Braunschweig)
  1920: 1113
Bühnen-Genossenschaft
  1958: 2055
Bündner Haushaltungs- und Familienbuch
  1934: 107.5.a
Buenos Aires musical
  1973: 627.5
Bulletin der diplomatischen Mission der Tschechoslowskischen Republik (Berlin)
  1955: 911
Bulletin français de la S.I.M. Société Internationale de Musique
  (Section de Paris)
  1909: 2761
Bulletin of the American Musicological Society
  1948: 1595, 2349
Bulletin of the Medical Library Association
  1937: 829
Bulletin of the Society of Medical History of Chicago
  1920: 821
Bund (Bern), Der
  1888: 1303
  1891: 2738
  1897: 532, 1098
  1902: 3166
  1908: 2351.e.iii
  1909: 1009.e.v.
  1910: 39C.e, 1062.e
  1927: 1298
  1932: 1296
  1974: 1301
Bundes-Kalender
  1934: 2809

Dansk musiktidsskrift
    1933: 2829
    1959: 1001
Deichwanderer, Der
    1960: 357
Deutsch-Amerikanische Geschichtsblätter
    1927: 3051
Deutsche Adelsblatt (Berlin)
    1933: 2368.5
    1939: 2677
Deutsche allgemeine Zeitung (Berlin)
    1922: 1138, 1832, 2426
    1930: 1126.5
    1933: 2931
    1939: 842
Deutsche Arbeiter-Sängerzeitung (Berlin)
    1927: 137
Deutsche Dichtung
    1899: 999.a.c
Deutsche Erde
    1933: 2871
Deutsche Kunst- und Musikzeitung (Wien)
    1889: 3083
    1890: 2194
    1891: 1536, 2020
    1893: 149
    1897: 484
Deutsche Militärmusikerzeitung
    1909: 924.a
    1910: 1290
    1911: 642
    1928: 3021.a.ii
    1932: 858.d.ii
Deutsche Monatshefte für Chile
    1933: 2879
Deutsche Monatsschrift für das gesamte Leben der Gegenwart
    1907: 986
Deutsche Musikbücherei. Almanach (Regensburg)   see   Almanach
    der Deutschen Musikbücherei (Regensburg)
Deutsche Musikdirektoren-Zeitung
    1907: 871.e.i
    1908: 2592
Deutsche Musiker-Zeitung (Berlin) or Deutsche Musikerzeitung (Berlin)
    1903: 2354.5
    1906: 772
    1922: 197
    1925: 376
    1927: 96, 666
    1930: 2728
Deutsche Musikkultur
    1937: 1068.c, 1891
    1940: 2093

Deutsche Musikzeitung (Berlin)
  1919: 1203.e.ii
Deutsche Musikzeitung (Köln)
  1933: 1264
  1937: 1211
  1938: 1211
Deutsche Musikzeitung (Wien) or Deutsche Musik-Zeitung (Wien)
  1860: 1327, 1345, 1615
  1861: 1857, 1860, 1873, 2222
  1862: 1332.d, 1519, 1522, 1641
Deutsche Revue (Stuttgart)
  1898: 999
  1902: 782
  1918: 868
  1922: 860
Deutsche Rundschau
  1880: 1336
  1897: 487, 618, 968, 1302, 3018
  1898: 618.a.e.ii
  1902: 39A.d.ii
  1903: 39A.c.v.
  1906: 2562
  1908: 1009.c.ii
  1909: 1216
  1910: 915
  1922: 2560
  1928: 227
  1933: 2898
  1953: 2164
  1963: 1285
Deutsche Sängerbundes. Jahrbuch see Jahrbuch der Deutschen
  Sängerbundes
Deutsche Sängerbundeszeitung (Berlin)
  1936: 693.a
Deutsche Tonkünstler-Zeitung or Deutsche Tonkünstlerzeitung (Berlin)
  1911: 812
  1919: 1095
  1927: 806
  1928: 934.a.ii
  1931: 691
  1933: 2656
Deutsche Volksbildung
  1927: 731
Deutsche Volkslied
  1922: 2833
  1930: 1291.e
Deutsche Wacht (Dresden)
  1897: 3025
  1898: 1124
Deutsche Welt
  1933: 2968

Deutsche Wille
    1933: 2840
Deutsche Zeitschrift
    1898: 618.a.e.iii
    1933: 1142
Deutsche Zeitung (Berlin)
    1922: 746, 2434
    1925: 756.d.ii
    1933: 3023
Deutsche Zeitung (Wien)
    1872: 2325
    1897: 440
Deutsche Zeitung in Norwegen (Oslo)
    1942: 2078
    1943: 699, 2846
Deutsche Zeitung in Ostland (Riga)
    1943: 2848
Deutscher Glaube
    1937: 2432
Deutscher Volkskalender
    1933: 2811
Deutscher Volkskalender (Wien)
    1937: 535
Deutsches Arzteblatt
    1965: 819.c.i.c
Deutsches Volkstum
    1919: 2388
    1921: 39.e.ii
    1925: 1340
Deutsch-evangelische Blätter
    1883: 2284
Diapason, The
    1958: 1743
    1959: 1748.d
Diapason (Paris)
    1976: 257
Disques (Philadelphia)
    1933: 1521
Dithmarschen
    1932: 343, 959.d
Dreiklang, Der. Monatsschrift für Musik
    1937: 2970
Dresdener neueste Nachrichten
    1909: 2747
Dresdner Anzeiger
    1909: 1009.e.vi
    1917: 1204.e.iii
    1936: 371
Dresdner Nachrichten
    1911: 207, 743
    1912: 208, 3048.e.iii

Dresdner Zeitung
    1943: 2847
Düsseldorfer Heimatblätter
    1938: 2260
Dur und Moll
    1897: 323, 413, 1121
Dwight's Journal of Music
    1856: 2972
    1864: 152.d.a
    1866: 1655.b
    1876: 209
    1877: 1884
    1878: 1914, 1915.c

Echo
    1876: 1712
Echo de Paris, L'
    no date: 1085
Echo musical (Bruxelles), L'
    1897: 410
Eclectic Magazine
    1897: 2634.a.i
Education musicale, L'
    1977: 1668
Egyetértés (Budapest)
    1897: 421, 429, 430, 2956
Ekkhart. Jahrbuch für das Badener Land
    1972: 994
Energetiker, Der. Blätter für musikalische Hand- und Willenskultur
    (Berlin)
    1922: 1289
Er
    1974: 1486
Ergebnisse der Immunitatsforschung
    1916: 1155.a.i
España musical (Barcelona)
    no date: 2309.d.i.c.i
Etude
    no date: 635.a.i
    1906: 1126.a.c.i
    1907: 125, 950.b, 979.c.vi, 3046.c
    1921: 185
    1923: 894.b.c.iv, 1126.a.c.ii
    1924: 979.c.iii
    1929: 102, 182
    1930: 1180.b.c
    1931: 638
    1932: 326
    1933: 188, 1064, 1317, 1673, 2139
    1935: 814.a

Etude (cont'd)
            1937:   78.c.ii, 1946
            1938:   1624, 1946
            1939:   1613, 1716, 1750
            1940:   384
            1941:   386, 1161
            1942:   1185, 1579
            1944:   2514
            1945:   1685
            1948:   2134
            1950:   359, 1686
            1953:   1903, 2495
            1954:   895, 1952
            1955:   755.d, 1904
            1956:   1659
Evangelischen Kirchengesangvereins für Deutschland. Korrespondenz-
    blatt see Korrespondenzblatt des Evangelischen Kirchengesang-
    vereins für Deutschland

Familiengeschichtliche Blätter
            1933:   349
Familiengeschichtliches Such- und Anzeigenblatt
            1926:   344
Feuilles musicales (Lausanne)
            1955:   27.c.i
Figaro (London)
            1878:   1915
Figaro (Paris), Le
            1897:   433
Finsk tidskrift
            1897:   435
fono forum
            1964:   260
            1965:   261
            1968:   265
            1970:   263
            1971:   264
            1973:   262
fonoforum
            1970:   2269
Fontis artis musicae
            1977:   2200.d
Fortnightly, The
            1936:   1208.d.d.iii
Forum
            1897:   161, 2992
Fővárosi lapok (Budapest)
            1879:   94, 623
Fränkische Heimat (Nürnberg)
            1936:   932.d.i

Fränkische Presse (Bayreuth)
    1947: 3003
    1973: 2635.a.ii
Fränkischer Kurier (Nürnberg)
    1909: 3081.a
    1918: 2247
Frankfurter allgemeine Zeitung
    1958: 953.d.i
    1979: 1148
Frankfurter Zeitung
    See also Frankfurter Zeitung und Handelsblatt
    1903: 899.c.ii
    1906: 795, 950.e.iii, 1220
    1907: 1111
    1909: 646, 2760
    1910: 601
    1912: 2802
    1915: 1182.c.i
    1917: 2674
    1922: 1410.d
    1926: 1163
    1927: 1179.c.iv
    1933: 144, 987, 2887, 2964, 3001
Frankfurter Zeitung und Handelsblatt
    See also Frankfurter Zeitung
    1900: 513
    1902: 584
    1903: 689
    1908: 979.e.c
    1909: 1216.e
Frau unserer Zeit, Die
    1922: 763
Freiburger Tagblatt
    1904: 86.d
Freiburger Theaterblätter
    1935: 142
Fremdenblatt see Wiener Fremdenblatt
Fugue
    1980: 767
Fuldaer Geschichtsblätter
    1958: 988
Funk (Berlin), Der
    1933: 989.d.i

Garbe, Die. Schweizerisches Familienblatt (Basel)
    1933: 141
Gartenlaube, Die
    1880: 709
    1897: 418
Gaulois (Paris), Le
    1897: 445

Gazzetta musicale di Milano
    no date: 2309.d.i.c.ii
Gegenwart
    1883: 1335
    1897: 413.d.i, 496, 958
Geist der Zeit
    1940: 2467.a.ii
Gelbe Hefte
    1939: 1178
Genealogie. Deutsche Zeitschrift für Familienkunde
    1975: 330
General-Anzeiger (Bonn)
    1974: 1484
Georgia Review
    1977: 2360
Germania (Berlin)
    1922: 716
    1927: 276
Gesellschaft (München), Die
    1902: 3025.a.c
Gesellschaft Hamburgischer Kunstfreunde. Jahrbuch see Jahrbuch
    des Gesellschaft Hamburgischer Kunstfreunde
Gesellschaft zu Beförderung des Guten und Gemeinnützigen (Basel).
    Neujahrsblatt see Neujahrsblatt der Gesellschaft zur Beförderung
    des Guten und Gemeinnützigen (Basel)
Gesnerus (Aarau)
    1960: 486
Getreue Eckard, Der
    1933: 2844
Glasgow Herald
    1926: 1841
Glaube und Heimat (Jena)
    1947: 2242
    1949: 2253
Glaube und Wissen
    1957: 2031
Goetheanum, Das
    1957: 2501
Gramaphone, The
    1946: 1467.d
Gramophone
    1940: 1400
    1941: 1357, 1401, 1402
Grazer Tagespost
    1899: 546
    1900: 853
Great Thoughts From Master Minds
    1903: 2468
Gregorius-Blatt. Organ für katholische Kirchenmusik
    1930: 2210
Grenzboten, Die
    1884: 150

Guardian (London)
    1964: 1583
Guide du concert
    1963: 1490
Guide musical (Bruxelles), Le
    1878: 1920
    1880: 2969
    1897: 461, 495, 523
    1900: 1853.b.iv.d
    1905: 2519.e
Gut Ton (Dresden)
    1939: 382.d.i, 1226
    1941: 338
Gypsy Lore Society. Journal see Journal of the Gypsy Lore Society

Hagener Zeitung
    1905: 1183
Halbmonatshefte der Deutschen Rundschau
    1908: 1009.c.ii.a
    1909: 916.a.i
Halbmonatsschrift für Schulmusikpflege
    1923: 1108
    1930: 2282
Hallé
    1946: 2475
    1951: 3156
Hallische Nachrichten
    1929: 1231
Hamburger Abendblatt
    1954: 297
    1958: 375, 1365
    1966: 304
Hamburger Anzeiger
    1956: 1188
Hamburger Correspondant or Hamburger Correspondent
    1900: 617.c
    1904: 39A.e.i
Hamburger Fremdenblatt
    1903: 1055
    1911: 48.b.e.ii
    1915: 327.d
    1922: 617.d, 2426.a, 2704
    1927: 723
    1928: 499
    1933: 837.d.ii
Hamburger Hafennachrichten
    1958: 297.d.ii
Hamburger Kirchenkalender
    1933: 2863

Hamburger Nachrichten
    1882: 870
    1897: 445.5
    1902: 479
    1903: 2375.5
    1904: 370
    1905: 324
    1907: 48.c
    1908: 1192.a
    1915: 325
    1918: 868.c
    1921: 883
    1922: 714.a, 1224.5
    1925: 715.e
    1932: 608, 944
Hamburgerischer Correspondent
    1907: 954.e.iii
Hamburgische Konzert- und Theater-Zeitung
    1904: 2152
Hamburgische Musikzeitung
    1888: 2011
Hamburgischer Correspondent
    1882: 2281
    1901: 502
    1911: 812.d.iii
Hamburgischer Korrespondent
    no date: 362
Hannoverscher Kurier
    1917: 2246
    1922: 716.a.i, 2880
    1942: 826
Harmonie
    1968: 259
    1978: 269
    1980: 270
Harmonie (Hannover)
    1897: 492.5
    1899: 3167.e
    1901: 776
Harvard Musical Review
    1915: 820
Haydn-Studien
    1978: 288
Heidelberger Tageblatt
    1966: 2341
Heimat (Düsseldorf), Die
    1958: 379, 558
Heimat (Kiel), Der
    1898: 364
    1929: 333

Heimat (Krefeld), Die
   1922: 598
   1925: 964
   1931: 963
   1933: 1311.5, 3089
   1938: 597
   1958: 562
   1973: 873
Heimatblätter
   1939: 3071
Heimatjahrbuch für den Landkreis Ahrweiler (Rheinberg)
   1958: 595
   1964: 593
Heimgarten, Der
   1894: 1133
Hellweg
   1924: 1307.d, 2981
Heterofonia
   1977: 1151, 2892
Hi Fidelity
   See also High Fidelity
   1956: 254
HiFi Stereophonie
   1982: 3121.e
High Fidelity
   See also Hi Fidelity
   1954: 250
High Fidelity and Musical America
   See also Hi Fidelity
   1974: 1082
Hilfe, Die
   1912: 39A.e.vii
   1933: 1258
Hirlap (Budapest) see Pesti hirlap (Budapest)
History of Medicine
   1975: 830
Hochland
   1912: 1276
   1913: 1877
   1914: 2298
   1915: 2328
Horn Call
   1979: 1478
House Beautiful
   1954: 1967
   1956: 1909
   1962: 2032
Hudebni revue
   1911: 909
Hudebni rozhledy
   1953: 2820.a

Hudebnî rozhledy (cont'd)
   1958:   1847
   1970:   2493.b.i
Hudebnî věda
   1973:   906.b
Hudobný život
   1972:   548
Huis en haard
   1964:   100
Huisgenoot
   1944:   2049

Illinois Staatszeitung or Illinois Staats-Zeitung
   1879:   1714
   1927:   2885
Illustrierte Zeitung
   See also Illustrirte Zeitung
   1899:   3082
   1908:   3068
   1933:   171, 1038
Illustrirte Zeitung (Leipzig)
   See also Illustrierte Zeitung
   1869:   2231
   1872:   213
   1876:   97
   1883:   2505
   1893:   2506
   1897:   528
   1903:   3096
   1908:   3148
Im Dienste der Kirche
   1937:   2223
Impromptu
   1932:   2033, 2790
In Theory Only
   1975:   1669
   1976:   635.a.ii, 1695, 1805.c, 2154
   1981:   2397
   1982:   1663
Indépendance musicale et dramatique, L'
   1887:   147
Independent (New York), The
   1901:   511
Inselschiff, Das
   1934:   1131
Instrumental suisse, L'   see   Schweizerische Instrumentalmusik.
   L'Instrumental suisse.   Instrumentale svizzero (Luzern)
Instrumentale svizzero   see   Schweizerische Instrumentalmusik.
   L'Instrumental suisse.   Instrumentale svizzero (Luzern)

Instrumentalist
    1966: 1376
    1970: 2605
International Society of Bassists. Journal   see   Bass World
Internationale Musik- und Instrumenten-Zeitung
    1896: 2955
Internationalen Musikgesellschaft. Zeitschrift   see   Zeitschrift der
    Internationalen Musikgesellschaft

Jahrbuch der Gesellschaft Hamburgischer Kunstfreunde
    1902: 1061
Jahrbuch der Musikbibliothek Peters
    1902: 2179
    1932: 2533, 3020
Jahrbuch des Deutschen Sängerbundes
    1928: 2537
Jahrbuch des Staatlichen Instituts für Musikforschung. Preussischer
    Kulturbesitz
    1969: 1657
Jahresbericht
    1904: 3196
Jahresgabe für der Klaus-Groth-Gesellschaft   see   Klaus-Groth-
    Gesellschaft. Jahresgabe
Jahresgabe für der Mitgleider der Maximilian-Gesellschaft
    1939: 2163.a
Jeunesses musicales   see   Musikalische Jugend. Jeunesses musicales
Journal de Genève
    1909: 2762
Journal of Aesthetics and Art Criticism
    1966: 1997
Journal of American Folklore
    1966: 2571
Journal of Church Music
    1960: 1754
Journal of Music Theory
    1960: 1822.c
    1971: 2156
Journal of the American Medical Association
    1934: 814
Journal of the American Musicological Society
    1951: 1586.d
Journal of the Gypsy Lore Society
    1952: 1726, 2106
Journal of the National Association of College Wind and Percussion
    Instructors   see   NACWPI Journal
Junge Musik
    1955: 184
Junge Musikfreund, Der
    1964: 297.d.i
Junges Leben. Zeitschrift für die Jugend (Berlin)
    1947: 753

Kasseler Volksblatt
    1927: 807
Kelet (Kolozsvár)
    1879: 624
Keyboard
    1982: 1666, 1670
    1983: 1670
Keyboard Classics
    1982: 1696
Kieler neueste Nachrichten
    1939: 2923
Kirche (Berlin), Die
    1947: 2639
Kirchenmusik (Berlin), Die
    1933: 2026
Kirchenmusik (Düsseldorf), Die
    1942: 1876, 1878
Kirchenmusiker, Der
    1970: 2060.d
Kirchenmusiker (Berlin), Der
    1961: 2294
Kirchenmusiker (Kassel), Der
    1982: 2288
Klaus-Groth-Gesellschaft. Jahresgabe
    1969: 960
    1972: 2092
Klavier-Lehrer, Der or Klavierlehrer, Der
    1879: 1730, 2472
    1898: 422
Klavierspiel, Das
    1964: 1588
Kleine Bund (Bern), Der
    1933: 633.d.i
Kölner Stadt-Anzeiger
    1942: 571
Kölnische Zeitung
    1897: 476
    1900: 101
    1908: 771
    1909: 607
    1925: 768
    1927: 938
    1935: 819.e.i
    1936: 765.d.e
    1937: 334, 2702
Königsberger allgemeine Zeitung
    1908: 1009.e.ii, 2351.e.i
    1928: 3024
Königsberger hartungsche Zeitung
    1922: 896, 1141
    1931: 1018

Kompass
    1908: 2864
Konsertnytt (Stockholm)
    1977: 2249
Konstanzer Zeitung
    1933: 2620, 2657
Kontakte
    1964: 297.d.i
Korrespondenzblatt des Evangelischen Kirchengesangvereins für
    Deutschland
    1907: 986.d
Krakauer Zeitung
    1944: 1262
Krefelder Zeitung
    no date: 2337
Kultur, Die
    1910: 1274
Kunst (München), Die
    1931: 929
    1933: 1037.a, 1039.a.i
Kunst für Alle (München)
    1916: 1051
    1933: 1037, 1039
Kunst und das schöne Heim
    1931: 929
    1933: 1037.a, 1039.a.i
Kunstgarten (Wien)
    1927: 172
    1929: 2275
Kunstgemeinde
    1933: 2912
Kunstwart, Der
    1896: 520.d
    1898: 618.a.e.iii
    1900: 2933
    1907: 688, 1441
    1909: 2746
    1914: 39D.e
    1933: 1142
Kurier Tägeblatt see Hannoverscher Kurier

Ladies' Home Journal
    1908: 2153
Lantern
    1957: 2810
Laute, Die
    1920: 2565
Leipziger allgemeine musikalische Zeitung
    See also Allgemeine musikalische Zeitung
    1866: 1417, 1430, 1469, 1655.a.i, 1660, 1661, 2228, 2919, 2960.e
    1867: 1451, 1525, 2229, 2230

Leipziger Jahrbuch
    1940: 606
Leipziger neueste Nachrichten
    1908: 1196
    1911: 937.e
    1922: 2698, 2889
    1926: 934.a.i, 2718
    1931: 796
    1933: 563, 2845, 3013.a.vii
    1937: 2907
Leipziger Tagblatt
    1904: 866
Leipziger Tageblatt
    1908: 1192.e
    1911: 893
    1922: 2866
Leipziger Volkszeitung
    1908: 1009.e.iii
    1909: 2463.5
Leipziger Zeitung
    1897: 488
    1906: 694.a.e.i
Leisure Hour
    1903: 1217.a.i
Lesestunde, Die
    1938: 784
Leuchtfeuer. Heimatblatt für die Jugend zwischen Niederelbe und Ems
    1974: 329, 361
Liberté
    1965: 643
Liberté, La
    no date: 2911
    1897: 478
Library of Congress. Quarterly Journal see Quarterly Journal of the Library of Congress
Library of Congress Quarterly Journal of Acquisitions
    1946: 2322
Library of Congress Quarterly Journal of Current Acquisitions
    1949: 1945
Lied und Chor
    1958: 299, 2196
Lied und Heimat (Sollingen)
    1936: 834, 3013.a.viii
Listener, The
    1927: 3032.5
    1933: 2902
    1936: 1208.d.d.i
    1939: 1618
    1952: 1811
    1965: 1265
    1969: 2928

Masters in Music
1905: 174.a.d, 234, 640, 871.c.ii, 880.d.c, 894.b.c.i, 978.d.c,
1336.a.b.c, 1392.c, 1545, 1548.d.c, 1556, 1605, 2047, 2077,
2107, 2893, 2894
Max Hesse's Deutscher Musiker-Kalender
1898: 193
Maximilian-Gesellschaft. Jahresgabe see Jahresgabe für die
Mitglieder der Maximilian-Gesellschaft
Max-Reger-Instituts. Mitteilungen see Mitteilungen der Max-Reger-
Instituts
Medecin du Quebec, Le
1974: 1815
Medical Library Association. Bulletin see Bulletin of the Medical
Library Association
Medizinische Welt
1931: 20.d
Melodie
1947: 2877
Melos
See also Weihergarten, Der
1933: 1120, 2461, 2906
Melos/NZ für Musik
See also Neue Zeitschrift für Musik, NZ-Neue Zeitschrift für
Musik, Zeitschrift für Musik, Musikalisches Wochenblatt.
Neue Zeitschrift für Musik
1976: 2187.c
1977: 1356
1978: 2061, 2129
Ménestrel, Le
1897: 420
1933: 2359
1938: 1787
Mennonite Life
1958: 574
Mens en melodie
1949: 2099, 2550
1954: 2067, 2573.a.e
1960: 2193.e
1965: 999.a.e
1975: 277.e.ii, 3124
Mercure musical (Paris), Le
1905: 173
Merker (Berlin), Der
1937: 382.d.ii
Merker (Wien), Der
1910: 1234
1912: 39C.c.iv, 87.c, 392, 970, 979.c.ii, 1299, 2429, 3028, 3181
1913: 750
1917: 1638, 2853
Merseburger Korrespondent
1925: 3040

Music Journal
    1951: 1957
    1978: 1908
    1981: 1091
Music Library Association see Notes
Music Lover's Guide
    1933: 255
Music Magazine/Musical Courier
    1962: 590
Music Review
    1940: 275
    1943: 1649
    1944: 1582
    1948: 1898
    1952: 1527
    1957: 1390
    1959: 1869
    1963: 2287
    1964: 1523
    1968: 2066
    1973: 1475, 1634
    1975: 1835
    1977: 1704
    1979: 2618
Music Student
    1914: 212
Music Teacher
    no date: 656
    1926: 2363
    1928: 1700
    1929: 1936
    1933: 252, 1333, 1635, 1859, 1971, 2088
    1973: 1614
    1975: 1472
    1976: 1672
    1981: 1476
    1982: 2062
Music Teacher and Piano Student
    no date: 1604, 1956, 2104
    1952: 1081
    196-: 1705, 1907, 1960
    1966: 1881
    1969: 1374
Music: The A.G.O. and R.C.C.O Magazine
    1970: 648, 1749
    1972: 1752
Musica (Chaix)
    1960: 726
Musica (Kassel)
    1947: 231
    1948: 284.b

```
1949:  2024
1957:  3088
1958:  647, 819.c.ii.e.iii, 2716
1960:  3090
1963:  2014
1966:  3063
1967:  3076
1969:  3159
1972:  2664
1974:  985, 2539
1980:  2320
```
Musica (Wien)
```
1936:  402, 2830
```
Musica d'oggi
```
1928:  1179.e.vi
1933:  2815
```
Musica sacra
```
1958:  2344
```
Musica sacra (Regensburg)
```
1917:  2175
```
Musica Schallplatte. Zeitschrift für Schallplattenfreunde
```
1958:  647
```
Musical America
```
1923:  2364
1928:  788.e, 1243
1929:  1922
1933:  1489
1934:  78.e.ii
1935:  819.e.iii, 840
1944:  1823
1947:  694.e
1949:  1938, 2131
1956:  320.d.iv.e
1960:  953.d.ii
```
Musical Association. Proceedings see Proceedings of the Musical Association
Musical Courier
    See also Music Magazine/Musical Courier
```
1893:  635
1897:  328, 1381
1901:  1550
1906:  331, 710, 2458, 2552, 2994
1917:  1072
1918:  1547, 2556
1927:  732
1932:  1254
1933:  258, 1456.c, 2683, 2937, 2952
1935:  651
1947:  2586
1950:  1140.d
```
Musical Gazette
```
1902:  1086
```

Musical Herald (London)
    1897:   411
    1911:   92
    1920:   114
Musical Magazine
    1902:   1086
Musical Mercury
    1934:   1916
Musical Mirror
    1930:   3.d
Musical Mirror and Fanfare
    1931:   1816.d
Musical News (London)
    1897:   431.c.e.e, 434, 495.e.ii
    1911:   878
Musical Observer (New York)
    1915:   1637
    1916:   1939
Musical Opinion
    See also Musical Opinion and Music Trade Review
    1940:   2523
    1971:   747, 1650
    1975:   1746
Musical Opinion and Music Trade Review
    See also Musical Opinion
    1897:   436.a, 443.c.ii, 447
    1898:   443.c.ii, 1549
    1900:   894.b.e.i
    1904:   967
    1907:   671, 2951.d
    1916:   3004.d
    1920:   1885
    1925:   2531
    1929:   759.b
    1933:   104, 2837, 3093.e
    1934:   2125
    1935:   735, 1068.b
    1936:   25.b.i.e, 841.d.ii
    1937:   841.d.ii
    1953:   641
    1955:   1851
    1957:   2655
    1958:   1850
Musical Quarterly
    1916:   1182.c.ii
    1921:   821.a.i
    1927:   791
    1931:   1980.d
    1932:   78.c.i
    1933:   672, 706.d, 1224, 1322.b, 3182
    1936:   1259

```
        1937:   662
        1943:   1102, 1310
        1945:   284
        1946:   955
        1959:   1009.d
        1971:   906
        1980:   2117.d
Musical Standard
        1879:   1920.b
        1880:   2969.b
        1884:   2076
        1905:   115
        1909:   1387
        1913:   2019
        1914:   3004
Musical Times
        1872:   1739
        1874:   2317, 2355.5
        1878:   1910
        1881:   1774
        1883:   1495, 1533
        1891:   2904
        1892:   2497.e
        1894:   1546
        1895:   2174
        1897:   469
        1904:   39A.e.ii
        1905:   1888
        1906:   839, 2250
        1911:   2286
        1915:   2082
        1916:   1297.e, 2412
        1920:   40.e.i
        1922:   3180.e
        1924:   886, 2900
        1925:   1015
        1926:   890
        1929:   1790
        1930:   1002
        1931:   1468, 1747
        1932:   1460, 1463, 1528
        1933:   186, 1288.a.c, 1471, 1480, 1529, 1532, 1795, 2018, 2102,
           2459
        1935:   1539
        1937:   1987
        1938:   977
        1943:   2466
        1947:   2613
        1952:   2518.d.iii
        1954:   2252
        1965:   2527
        1967:   2161
        1968:   2532
```

Musikalische Jugend. Jeunesses musicales
    1958: 2905
Musikalisches Wochenblatt
    See also Musikalisches Wochenblatt. Neue Zeitschrift für Musik
    no date: 1875
    1870: 154, 2280
    1871: 1632
    1872: 3011
    1874: 1870, 2069, 2207
    1876: 1883
    1880: 1732, 2924
    1889: 2419
    1890: 2420
    1891: 2158
    1892: 2340
    1894: 1678
    1896: 2909, 2955.e
    1897: 415, 455, 509.e, 520, 2160
    1898: 1124.e, 2148.e
    1899: 475, 3058, 3086
    1900: 462, 3113
    1901: 512, 2445, 3056, 3104, 3149
    1902: 460, 3085, 3112
    1903: 390, 2976, 3057
    1907: 3046
    1909: 2742
Musikalisches Wochenblatt. Neue Zeitschrift für Musik
    1907: 3046
    1909: 2742
Musikbibliothek Peters. Jahrbuch see Jahrbuch der Musikbibliothek
    Peters
Musikblätter
    1953: 781
    1958: 2699, 2895
Musikblätter der Wiener Philharmoniker
    1951: 857
    1979: 903
    1980: 277.e.i
    1981: 405
Musikblätter des Anbruch
    See also Anbruch
    1922: 1320
Musikbote
    1925: 966
Musikbuch aus Osterreich
    no date: 506.a
    1904: 719
Musiker (München), Der
    1966: 304
Musiker, Der. Mitteilungsblatt des Deutschen Musikerverbandes in
    der Gewerkschaft Kunst des DGB (Düsseldorf)
    1957: 1804

Musikwoche, Die (cont'd)
    1937: 334.a
    1939: 2672, 2888.d.c
Musique de tous les temps
    1970: 809.a
Musique en Suisse, La
    1902: 2933.b
Muzsika (Budapest)
    1959: 2038
Muzyka (Warszawa)
    1955: 817

NACWPI Journal
    1976: 1094
Nation (Berlin), Die
    1897: 755, 2438
Nation (New York)
    1894: 128.e
    1897: 969.e.i
    1911: 23.e.i
    1912: 2022.e.i
National Association of College Wind and Percussion Instructors.
    Journal see NACWPI Journal
National Association of Teachers of Singing. Bulletin see NATS
    Bulletin
National Review
    1982: 1845
National Zeitung (Berlin)
    See also National-Zeitung (Berlin) or Nationalzeitung (Berlin)
    1907: 954.e.ii
Nationaltheater
    1933: 2867
National-Zeitung (Basel)
    1960: 1292.d, 1708
National-Zeitung (Berlin) or Nationalzeitung (Berlin)
    See also National Zeitung (Berlin)
    1904: 369
    1907: 1122.e.iii
NATS Bulletin
    1967: 2165
    1979: 2126, 2128.d
    1980: 2035.d
Nemzeti újság (Budapest)
    1933: 2868
Neue Badische Landes-Zeitung
    1933: 609
Neue Bayerische Sänger-Zeitung
    1941: 2189
Neue Berliner Musikzeitung
    1854: 2110

Neue freie Presse (Wien) (cont'd)
    1908:   724, 1009.e.vii, 1189, 1309, 3062, 3137
    1909:   1232, 2751
    1917:   540
    1922:   949.c
    1933:   408, 570, 1190, 2089, 2606, 2659, 2785-88, 2930, 2931,
            3099
    1936:   382
Neue Leipziger Zeitung
    1935:   1036.5, 1042
Neue Mannheimer Zeitung
    1933:   2640, 2806, 2896
Neue Militärmusikzeitschrift (Hannover)
    1904:   904
Neue Militärmusikzeitung
    1907:   983.e.xi
    1908:   1195
Neue musikalische Presse
    1896:   2955
    1897:   456
    1899:   546.a
Neue musikalische Rundschau
    1908:   3131
Neue Musikzeitschrift
    1947:   3031
    1950:   2169
Neue Musikzeitung or Neue Musik-Zeitung
    1881:   187
    1884:   2339
    189-:   1133.a.i
    1890:   1834.e
    1891:   1352.e, 1399
    1892:   1171, 2155
    1894:   996, 2105
    1897:   368, 431.c.e.e.e, 441, 463, 515, 557, 618.e, 637, 695,
            1235.a.ii, 1295.c.e, 1302.e, 2350, 2492
    1898:   85.e.i, 618.d.e, 894.e.i, 1025
    1899:   85.e.iv, 2528
    1903:   816.e.ii, 880, 3153
    1904:   39A.e.vi
    1905:   588
    1906:   2543
    1907:   226, 589, 948, 983.e.iii, 1453, 2886, 2996, 3189
    1908:   3139
    1910:   1687
    1911:   1191, 1687
    1912:   1063, 1505
    1913:   1590
    1914:   1590
    1916:   567
    1919:   947

Orchester-Magazin
    1933: 3006
Orgel, Die
    1910: 2765
Osservatore romano, L'
    1952: 1240, 1976
Outlook, The
    no date: 1968
    1894: 2966
    1902: 174
    1903: 1217
    1912: 2400

Papers of the American Musicological Society
    1941: 794
Parents Review
    no date: 133
    1932: 2834
    1938: 170
    1946: 170.d
Passauer neue Presse
    1973: 2635.d.a
Pasztortuz
    1942: 625
Pauliner-Zeitung (Leipzig)
    1931: 176, 1059
    1933: 564, 932
Perspectives of New Music
    1972: 2356
    1973: 2356
Pester Lloyd (Budapest)
    1878: 1889, 1913
    1879: 1470, 1865
    1880: 1147.5
    1882: 1073
    1883: 2147
    1884: 1984
    1886: 1487, 2979
    1897: 412, 419, 426, 454, 473, 474, 490, 775, 951, 1080
    1898: 2332
    1908: 979.e, 1009.e.iv
    1909: 2740
    1931: 1199.e.iii
    1933: 818, 1004.d.i
Pesti hirlap (Budapest) or [Pesti] Hirlap (Budapest)
    1897: 424
    1932: 612
Pfälzische Heimatblätter (Neustadt, Aisch)
    1964: 586
Pforzheimer Musik- und Sänger-Zeitung
    1937: 2383

Philharmonische Blätter
    1971: 2654
    1972: 912, 3042
    1973: 1021
    1975: 1147
    1976: 1355
Phoenix (Wien)
    1897: 452
Phönix. Zeitschrift für deutsche Geistesarbeit in Südamerika
    1933: 2843
Phono
    1950: 249
    1958: 247
    1959: 248
Piano Quarterly
    1958: 1677
    1966: 1559
    1969: 1610
    1981: 1552.d.d
Pianoforte, Il
    1922: 1564, 2469.5
    1940: 2489
Pianoforte di Schubert e di Brahms, Il
    1970: 1581
Poetry
    1956: 1587
Prager Presse
    1933: 2826
Pressburger Zeitung
    1883: 2306
Presse (Wien), Die
    1883: 2336
    1884: 1954
    1886: 1998
    1887: 2326
    1888: 2264
    1894: 1569
Preussische Lehrerzeitung (Magdeburg)
    1933: 341, 1149
Preussische Volksschullehrerinnenzeitung
    1933: 1184
Proceedings of the Musical Association
    1910: 1391
Propyläen (München), Die
    1909: 3081
    1921: 1252
    1922: 941
    1933: 2822
    1937: 713.a
Przeglad tygodniowy zycia spoľecznego, literatury i sztuk pieknych
    (Warszawa)
    1869: 164

Psychoanalytische Bewegung
    1933: 764
Pult und Taktstock
    1926: 1900

Quarterly Journal of the Library of Congress
    1964: 1942
    1967: 2133
Queen's Quarterly
    1981: 2471

Raabe-Gesellschaft. Mitteilungen see Mitteilungen des Raabe-
    Gesellschaft
Radio Bremen Hausbuch
    1967: 1123
Radio Times
    no date: 108
    1933: 1208.d.d.ii
Rassegna musicale, La
    1940: 2489
    1947: 2569
Reichspost (Wien)
    1933: 2870
Reichswehr (Wien)
    1897: 517
Renaissance musicale, La
    1882: 2028
Residenz-Anzeiger (Karlsruhe)
    1933: 565
Response in Worship, Music and the Arts
    1976: 2276
Review of Reviews (London)
    1933: 718
Revista musical catalana
    1933: 116, 1576, 1818, 2084
Revista musicale italiana
    1955: 2421
Revue bleue
    1894: 968.c
    1903: 147.d.iii
Revue critique des idées et des livres
    1920: 40.e.iii
Revue d'esthéthique (Paris)
    1982: 1961
Revue de musicologie
    1942: 2581
Revue des deux mondes
    1898: 2235

Revue du temps présent
   1910: 211.b.d
Revue et gazette musicale
   See also Revue et gazette musicale de Paris
   1875: 2309.d.ii
Revue et gazette musicale de Paris
   See also Revue et gazette musicale
   1863: 2926
   1874: 2309
Revue générale (Bruxelles), La
   1893: 224
Revue hebdomadáire, La
   1892: 1919
   1893: 1974
Revue internationale de musique
   1898: 158
Revue musicale (Paris), La
   1904: 505, 880.d
   1933: 2774
   1936: 1620
Revue musicale belge, La
   1933: 218, 2772
Revue musicale de Lyon
   1904: 2911.d
Revue musicale de Suisse Romande
   1967: 682
   1969: 634
Rheinische Heimatblätter
   1936: 1510
Rheinische Musik- und Theaterzeitung (Köln)
   1902: 1767.5
   1903: 1040, 2394.5.a, 3126
   1905: 350.a, 954.5, 1213
   1906: 1363
   1907: 236, 3095
   1908: 2184, 3033
   1909: 2769
   1910: 225.5, 1442.5, 2678
   1912: 48.b.c, 205
   1915: 628
   1916: 1277
   1917: 2292
Rheinische Musik- und Theaterzeitung (Köln) (cont'd)
   1920: 1095.a.ii
   1928: 2681
Rheinische Musikzeitung
   1854: 1607
Rheinischer Merkur
   1947: 2731
Rheinisch-Westfälische Zeitung (Essen)
   1917: 961

Rheinisch-Westfälische Zeitung (Essen) (cont'd)
    1921: 883
    1922: 272.e, 1307
    1926: 1158.e.iii.d, 1158.e.iv.d
Rhein-Mainische Volkszeitung (Frankfurt a.M.)
    1931: 916
Ringeren
    1899: 123
Röster i radio
    1955: 2558
    1957: 2824
Rondo
    1953: 1896
Royal Institution of Great Britain. Proceedings
    1905: 978.d.d
Rozhlad
    1977: 2841
Ruiter
    1948: 99
Rundfunk
    1933: 3005
Russkaia musykalnaia gazeta
    See also Russkaia muzykal'naia gazeta or Russkaia muzykalnaia
        gazeta
    1913: 2097
Russkaia muzykal'naia gazeta or Russkaia muzykalnaia gazeta
    See also Russkaia musykalnaia gazeta
    1905: 2519.b.ii
    1913: 694.c

Sackbut
    1926: 884
    1931: 3043
    1932: 3016
    1933: 555
Sächsische Sängerbundes-Zeitung (Leipzig)
    1933: 1347
Sängerhalle, Die
    1891: 2068
    1899: 3082.a
    1903: 2048
Salmagundi
    1977: 2932
Salve hospes
    1958: 216
    1960: 1114
Salzkammergutzeitung
    1939: 3071
Salzspeicher (Lübeck), Die
    1929: 1109

Schweizerische Instrumentalmusik. L'Instrumental suisse. Instrumen-
tale svizzero (Luzern)
    1937: 2508
Schweizerische musikpädagogische Blätter
    1920: 1095.a.i, 2890, 2908, 2958, 2986
    1923: 1029
    1933: 107.5
    1937: 687
    1938: 194
    1953: 2810.5
    1958: 819.c.ii.e.ii
Schweizerische Musikzeitung. Revue musicale Suisse
    See also Schweizerische Musikzeitung und Sängerblatt,
        Schweizerische Musikzeitung und Sängerblatt. Gazette
        musicale Suisse
    1946: 340
    1951: 2488
    1957: 1137
    1958: 975
    1959: 2401
    1965: 1060, 2258
    1979: 1988
Schweizerische Musikzeitung und Sängerblatt
    See also Schweizerische Musikzeitung. Revue musicale Suisse,
        Schweizerische Musikzeitung und Sängerblatt. Gazette
        musicale Suisse
    1881: 214
    1892: 808, 2159
    1893: 2850
    1902: 1764
    1906: 1106.a
    1907: 859
    1910: 1009.e.ix
    1926: 934
    1927: 1179.e
Schweizerische Musikzeitung und Sängerblatt. Gazette musicale Suisse
    See also Schweizerische Musikzeitung. Revue musicale Suisse,
        Schweizerische Musikzeitung und Sängerblatt
    1933: 633
    1935: 25.e
    1936: 841
Schweizerische Zeitung für Gesang (St.-Gallen)
    1915: 327
Schweizerisches Jahrbuch für Musikwissenschaft
    1927: 1128
Score, The
    1957: 1789
    1958: 1789
Scriptura (Stellenbosch)
    1980: 2272
Sendung, Die
    1933: 2823, 2873

Sie. Die führende Zeitung für die Frau
    1947: 573
Signale für die musikalische Welt
    1854: 1350
    1855: 1455, 1619, 2111
    1856: 1626
    1869: 1706, 1722
    1870: 2137, 2313
    1877: 1884
    1879: 1707
    1897: 412.5.e, 471, 521.a, 734, 755.c
    1902: 1766, 1771
    1904: 369.c, 2152.e
    1907: 39B.e.v, 983.e.viii
    1908: 39B.c.iv, 1122.e.vi, 3129
    1909: 1009.e.viii, 2763, 2767, 3174
    1910: 2682
    1912: 2022.e.iii, 2798, 2804, 3048.e.i
    1918: 228
    1921: 579.d, 2799
    1922: 2693
    1923: 2473
    1924: 730
    1925: 1181
    1926: 2719
    1927: 683
    1929: 2729
    1930: 675
    1933: 2831
    1936: 1233, 2046
    1937: 2407, 2712
    1938: 353, 1008
Simrock Jahrbuch see N. Simrock Jahrbuch
Skizzen
    1931: 742
    1933: 1230.d, 1282, 2876
    1936: 1986
    1938: 1719
Slöjd och ton
    1968: 2941.a
Slovenská hudba
    1958: 547
Social Monitor, The
    1968: 1846
Société Internationale de Musique. Bulletin see Bulletin français de
    la S.I.M. Société Internationale de Musique (Section de Paris)
Society of Medical History of Chicago. Bulletin see Bulletin of the
    Society of Medical History of Chicago
Soir (Paris), Le
    1888: 2985

Sonne, Die
    1933: 2882
Sonntagsblatt. Unabhängige Wochenzeitung für Politik, Wirtschaft
    und Kultur(Hamburg)
    1958: 139
Sotsiashstileskiĭ trud
    1968: 1717
Soundings
    1974: 2415.d.ii
Southwestern Musician
    1954: 898
Sovetskaia muzyka
    1954: 898
    1958: 2050
    1972: 1179.c.x
Sozialistische Monatshefte
    1903: 2469
Spectator
    1888: 117.b.i.e
    1905: 48.e.ii
    1911: 23.e.ii
Springfielder, The
    1972: 2214
Staatlichen Instituts für Musikforschung. Jahrbuch see Jahrbuch
    des Staatlichen Instituts für Musikforschung
Stereo Review
    1970: 504
    1972: 1341
Stimme, Die
    1907: 2821
Strad, The
    1910: 1440, 1531
    1933: 1016, 1408, 2601
    1941: 1446
    1944: 1477
    1961: 2604
    1968: 599
    1979: 1944
Strassburger Post
    1897: 2588
Studia musicologica academiae scientiarum hungaricae
    1963: 1718
    1966: 2038.b
    1969: 1648
Studia musicologica norvegica
    1976: 1176
Studien zur Musikwissenschaft
    1955: 2086.a
    1962: 1727, 2529
    1966: 2444
    1980: 2357

Tag (Berlin), Der (cont'd)
    1914: 708
    1916: 2405.5
    1917: 1204.e.ii
    1922: 714
Tagespost (Rendsburg)
    1973: 2635.a.i
Tatzlil
    1978: 2535
Tęcza
    1933: 2851
Temesi lapok (Temesvar)
    1879: 1721
Temple Bar
    1905: 153
Temps (Paris), Le
    1897: 476.b, 493
    1907: 2980
Theology Today
    1965: 2283
Therapeutische Berichte
    1957: 819.c.ii.e.i
Thüringer Heimatkalender
    1964: 572
Tilskueren
    1897: 813
    1911: 954.e.i
Time
    1974: 1493
Times (London), The
    1894: 2176
    1897: 438, 446, 3065
    1908: 3145-47
    1909: 2743
    1911: 1438, 2793
    1912: 2771
    1915: 552
    1917: 550
    1926: 2006
    1928: 1179.d.ii.e
    1929: 1775
    1931: 677, 1238
    1933: 1087, 2777, 2778, 2825, 3162
    1936: 962
    1941: 650, 674
    1942: 2041
    1947: 2593
    1948: 752
    1949: 298.5, 305
    1950: 305.d.i, 652
    1951: 2641

1952: 1843, 2402
1961: 1854
1964: 852
1966: 2642
Times Literary Supplement
  1902: 1769
Tonkunst (Berlin), Die
  1876: 1723.c
  1878: 1911
  1927: 3021.a.i
  1933: 2188
Tonwille, Der
  1924: 1636
Tor, Das. Düsseldorfer Heimatblätter
  1965: 373, 377
Tribüne (Berlin)
  1880: 1728
Türmer, Der
  1910: 1273
  1922: 491, 872
  1930: 1925
  1931: 1283
  1933: 2806.a
  1940: 131
23. Eine Wiener Musikzeitschrift
  1933: 2783.d, 2931.d.ii
Tygodnik ilustrowany
  1893: 148
  1897: 510
  1908: 3151
  1933: 2827

Uber Land und Meer
  1911: 2098
  1917: 702
Uj idök
  1933: 1004.d.ii
Umschau (Frankfurt), Die
  1897: 417, 472
Ungarn (Budapest)
  1942: 625.b
Universitätsbundes Göttingen. Mitteilungen see Mitteilungen des
  Universitätsbundes Göttingen
Universitas
  1952: 2290
  1958: 2483.d.ii
  1966: 179
University of Pennsylvania General Magazine and Historical Chronicle
  1932: 163
University of Pennsylvania Library Chronicle
  1933: 869, 3054

716 / Newspaper and Magazine Index

Universum
    1894: 149.d
Unser Bayern
    1975: 596
Unterhaltung, Die   see Hannoverscher Kurier
Uusi musiikkilehti
    1956: 1760.5
    1970: 1270

Vasárnapi Ujság (Budapest)
    1897: 465
Vaterländische Blätter
    1921: 2816
Velhagen und Klasings Monatshefte
    1907: 1227
    1922: 592
    1928: 1179.e.iv
    1933: 3008
    1939: 393
Vereins für Hamburgische Geschichte. Mitteilungen   see Mitteilungen
    des Vereins für Hamburgische Geschichte
Vesmir
    1966: 823
Vie musicale, La
    1909: 2741, 2750
Violins and Violinists
    1949: 1477.a
Völkische Musikerziehung
    1940: 864
Völkische Schule, Die
    1933: 2828
Völkischer Beobachter (Berlin)
    1935: 693
    1940: 615
Volk und Heimat
    1953: 403
Volksbühne (Hamburg), Die
    1958: 367
Volksgesundheitskalender (Zürich)
    1933: 679
Volkszeitung für Kirchenmusik
    1878: 2226
Vom Jungfernstieg zur Reeperbahn
    1962: 358.e.ii
Vossische Zeitung (Berlin)
    1897: 497, 1256
    1913: 39D.d
    1922: 2710
    1926: 279, 2481.a.i
    1927: 993, 1179.c.iii, 2838

1932: 2989, 3000
1933: 394, 400, 668, 704.c, 717, 1024, 1313, 2071, 2839

Wage, Die
    1907: 2663
Warschauer Zeitung
    1940: 946
Washington Post
    1977: 1808
Wedrowiec (Warszawa)
    1897: 439.d, 748
Weekblad voor muziek
    1903: 3075
    1904: 39A.d.i.e.ii
Weihergarten, Der
    1933: 1120
Welt (Hamburg), Die
    1958: 2645
    1970: 659.5
Welt-Stimmen (Stuttgart)
    1957: 200
Weltwacht der Deutschen (Hellerau)
    1943: 815
Weser-Kurier (Bremen)
    1967: 2302
Weser-Zeitung (Bremen)
    1918: 2251.5
    1919: 1159
    1922: 145
Westermanns illustrierte deutsche Monatshefte
    See also Westermanns illustrierte deutsche Monatshefte für das
        gesamte geistige Leben der Gegenwart, Westermann's illustrirte
        deutsche Monatshefte
    1933: 765
Westermanns illustrierte deutsche Monatshefte für das gesamte geistige
    Leben der Gegenwart
    See also Westermanns illustrierte deutsche Monatshefte, Wester-
        mann's illustrirte deutsche Monatshefte
    1887: 136
Westermanns illustrirte deutsche Monatshefte
    See also Westermanns illustrierte deutsche Monatshefte, Wester-
        manns illustrierte deutsche Monatshefte für das gesamte
        geistige Leben der Gegenwart
    1874: 165
Wiener Abendpost or [Wiener] Abendpost
    1875: 1466
    1887: 1362
    1888: 2291
    1890: 1537
    1891: 1502

Wiener Abendpost or [Wiener] Abendpost (cont'd)
    1892: 1542
    1899: 2148
    1905: 401, 406
    1907: 39B.e.iii
Wiener allgemeine Zeitung or [Wiener] Allgemeine Zeitung
    1882: 2333
    1883: 1973
    1885: 1334, 2367
    1886: 1995
Wiener Almanach
    1911: 786
Wiener Bühne
    1937: 917
Wiener Fremdenblatt or [Wiener] Fremdenblatt
    1886: 2005
    1897: 521, 524
    1906: 950
    1907: 983.e.v
Wiener Goethe-Vereins. Chronik see Chronik des Wiener Goethe-
    Vereins
Wiener Konzertschau
    1911: 778
    1912: 1139.d
Wiener Mode
    no date: 167
    1907: 770
Wiener Montagszeitung
    1884: 1820
Wiener Philharmoniker. Musikblätter see Musikblätter der Wiener
    Philharmoniker
Wiener Rundschau
    1898: 813.b
    1899: 2644
Wiener Salonblatt
    no date: 3048.d
    1884: 3048
    1885: 3048
    1886: 3048
    1887: 3048
Wiener Tagblatt see Neues Wiener Tagblatt
Wiener Zeitung
    1857: 1328
    1872: 2324
Winterthurer Stadtanzeiger
    1974: 630
Winterthurer Tagblatt
    1974: 630
Wissenschaftliche Beilage see Leipziger Zeitung
Wissenschaftliche Zeitschrift see Martin-Luther-Universität Halle-
    Wittenberg. Wissenschaftliche Zeitschrift. Gesellschafts- und
    sprachwissenschaftliche Reihe

Woche (Berlin), Die
   1933: 2172
Wochenpost, Die
   1947: 2860
Wochenpost, Die. Zeitfragen, Kultur, Kunst, Unterhaltung
   1948: 1293
Wochenschrift für katholische Lehrerinnen (Paderborn)
   1933: 733
Wochenschrift für Kunst und Musik (Wien)
   1903: 2289
Woodwind Magazine
   1949: 1093
Woodwind World
   See also Woodwind World--Brass & Percussion
   1961: 1431
   1963: 1093.a
Woodwind World--Brass & Percussion
   See also Woodwind World
   1975: 2598
World
   1972: 38.e, 2914

Zeit (Hamburg), Die
   1958: 332
   1973: 2706
   1981: 3158
Zeit (Wien), Die
   1897: 506
   1903: 1209
   1904: 39A.e.iv
Zeit [Tageszeitung] (Wien), Die
   1902: 381
   1906: 1106
   1908: 3176
   1911: 1085.b
Zeit [Wochenschrift] (Wien), Die
   1896: 2939
   1897: 531
   1898: 1284
Zeit im Bild
   1947: 2819
Zeitgeist, Der
   1907: 39B.c.v
   1908: 39B.c.iii
Zeitschrift der Internationalen Musikgesellschaft
   1901: 525, 1951
   1902: 533
   1903: 1236
   1905: 3170